What Is Hinduism?

को हिन्दुधम

A MANIVEL

MANIVEL

First Edition

Published by
Himalayan Academy
India • USA

PRINTED IN USA

Library of Congress Control Number: 2006937562
ISBN 978-1-934145-00-5 (Paperback)
ISBN 978-1-934145-01-2 (Hardcover)

DAVE TROFF

What Is Hinduism?

Modern Adventures Into a Profound Global Faith

को हिन्दुधर्मः

भूमण्डलीक उत्कृष्टतर श्रद्धायां
नवीन साहसिक कृत्यानि

From the Editors of
Hinduism Today
Magazine

TABLE OF CONTENTS

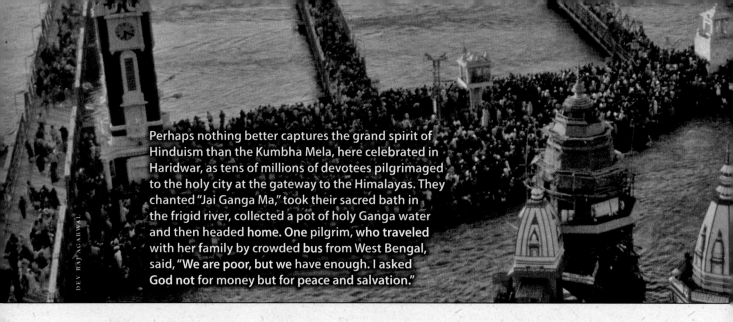

Perhaps nothing better captures the grand spirit of Hinduism than the Kumbha Mela, here celebrated in Haridwar, as tens of millions of devotees pilgrimaged to the holy city at the gateway to the Himalayas. They chanted "Jai Ganga Ma," took their sacred bath in the frigid river, collected a pot of holy Ganga water and then headed home. One pilgrim, who traveled with her family by crowded bus from West Bengal, said, "We are poor, but we have enough. I asked God not for money but for peace and salvation."

DEV RAJ AGARWAL

At the height of puja, a priest lights the sacred lamp which he will slowly wave before the Deity as an act of veneration, carrying out liturgy that is thousands of years old. Such ceremonies facilitate communion between this physical world and the realms of the Gods and angels.

PREFACE

BY SATGURU BODHINATHA VEYLANSWAMI

All faiths are grappling with their self-definition as we rev up to the breathtaking speed of the information age—a period more intense and kinetic than any other in the history of the world. Teachings and practices that were once accepted without question are often now rejected unless evidence and logic are marshalled to give them plausibility. To survive, customs and traditions must bear up under intellectual scrutiny, must prove themselves helpful and immediately usable.

Hinduism is no exception. Hindu education for youth is languishing, and communities around the world are struggling to compose clear, concise presentations of the dharma. It would be possible to spend an entire lifetime, indeed, many lifetimes, absorbing and practicing the teachings of just one sect or of the Hindu faith. Yet, there is also a need to understand this complex conglomerate as a whole as well. There is a preeminent need, the world over, for cogent, comprehensive explanations of the various facets of Hinduism—and the shared features of its various sects—from a mountaintop perspective—to answer the sincere questions of children, coworkers, neighbors, critics and colleagues, and to provide a nonacademic presentation for those of other religions seeking insight into this ancient path.

Producing quality educational materials on Hinduism is inherently difficult precisely because it is one of the world's most paradoxical and easily misunderstood religious traditions. It can be equally confounding to the outsider and to those born in dharma's embrace. This is because it is actually a family of many different faiths that share essential practices and characteristics.

Most Hindus have an intuitive sense of, but can't articulate, the "whys and wherefores" of their philosophy and practices. The boldness to ask questions about such matters has only recently developed. Just confer with Hindu parents who have stumbled when confronted with the direct and innocent questions posed by their own children, questions they never voiced and therefore never learned satisfying answers to.

This book seeks to be a bridge between generations of past centuries that grew up immersed in a pristine Hindu culture—with vast communal knowledge available to them—and current generations that have little or no access to such knowledge. In those olden times, living in a homogenous society with the faith's culture and traditions interwoven in every aspect of daily life, one didn't need to ask the whys of everything. He only needed to participate, enjoy and absorb the nuances and meanings from the inside out. In today's fragmented societies, we no longer have such cocoon-like training for children, so teachings must be rearticulated and presented in ways that will make intellectually clear their purpose, relevance and value in competition with the compelling flood of media that youths and adults are subjected to day after day. Hinduism must also compete in the arena of ideas with its aggressively evangelical counterparts.

The idea of creating a book called "What Is Hinduism?" came to me from the "inner sky" one day while I was meditating on our faith's educational needs. It was as if the inner-plane masters, among them our dear Gurudeva, Satguru Sivaya Subramuniyaswami, were sending the thought form that such a work would be just what is needed at this time. Approached from scratch, the book in your hands would take years to produce, especially with the amount of patience and care that you will find here in each chapter. Thus, the serendipitous beauty of the project was that the necessary thousands of hours of loving attention had already gone into researching and designing its chapters, as Educational

THOMAS KELLY

Insight sections over the last ten years by the talented team of editiors, writers and photographers of our international magazine, HINDUISM TODAY. All that was needed now, in 2007, was to choose the best features and put them together in a way that offers a thorough yet highly readable introduction to Hinduism. Voilà!

As a small group of renunciate Hindu monks at Kauai's Hindu Monastery in Hawaii, we have produced HINDUISM TODAY for more than a quarter century, tracking, monitoring and encouraging the current renaissance of the grandfather faith of the human race. One of the main reasons Gurudeva founded the magazine was to help Hindus become more aware of the activities of their Hindu brothers and sisters in other parts of the world and thus draw strength and courage from that knowledge. Another was to dispel myths and misinformation promulgated by invaders and missionaries of alien religions. A third was to present the beliefs and practices common to all Hindus, as well as the teachings and traditions of the individual sects, traditions and lineages that together form this quilt of dharma. *What Is Hinduism?* is an insider's view, honoring the beauties of culture, tradition, celebration, worship, belief and discipline.

In addition to the reams of scripture available to readers, there are many books on Hinduism by writers and scholars of both East and Wests But few offer much relief to the parent looking for simple answers, or the social studies teacher looking for an authentic overview of the faith. Texts by Westerners, often academic in nature, tend to paint Hinduism into the past and distort it by wrong emphasis, dwelling on peripheral, controversial issues such as caste and the "Aryan Invasion." Those by Easterners generally focus on just one *sampradaya* or lineage—such as Sankaran Vedanta, Madhva Vaishnavism or Saiva Siddhanta—often presenting its philosophy and tradition as if it were the whole of Hinduism, which, of course, it is not. When each sect and lineage is presented in this way, it is no small wonder readers get confused.

Rare is the book that presents Hinduism in a comprehensive, contemporary, complementary way—as a family of faiths and philosophies—that a modern, English-speaking audience can relate to, understand and appreciate. *What Is Hinduism?* is just such a rare gem. Exploring it, readers now and then spontaneously stop and sigh, "Ahh, now I get it. I now understand this basic concept of Hinduism." It is an authoritative and inspired work, an inclusive, sophisticated, user-friendly explanation of Sanatana Dharma. Far from the arcane, sea-of-text descriptions of Hinduism, this book is rich with potent images, traditional symbols and photographs depicting each aspect of the culture and faith. If one were to simply study the photos and art and their captions, that would itself serve as a meaningful glimpse into the Hindu heart.

This book is inspired by and draws heavily from the remarkable spiritual legacy of Gurudeva, without doubt one of the most significant Hindu saints and leaders of the twentieth century. An American by birth, Gurudeva showed the world by his pure and dedicated life that Hinduism is a vibrant, relevant and living force. He renewed the pride of Hindus in their faith and gave them guidelines for following Hindu Dharma. He boldly spoke of Hinduism as the greatest religion in the world and showed millions that Hinduism is destined to teach our newly emerging global civilization that harmonious coexistence—in peace, mutual respect, and with a deep sense of spiritual values—is not merely a dream, but a living reality. We know that Gurudeva is smiling approvingly at the creation of *What Is Hinduism?* We believe it will be hailed as a classic, and hopefully a best seller, so that uncounted souls may enjoy its heartfelt messages.

Bodhinatha Veylanswami

PUBLISHER OF HINDUISM TODAY

In mystical Bali, where Hindus are intensely sensitive to the inner worlds, devas and demons are known to walk beside men and women. Nature sees, hears, feels and responds. On a remote beach in that sacred land, devotees perform Kechak, the spectacular monkey dance.

INTRODUCTION

A SIMPLE OVERVIEW OF A COMPLEX FAITH

A Google search on the title of this book yields some 15,000 answers. Many are from outsiders offering their best take; many are from antagonists taking their best shot. Too few are knowledgeable; fewer still are authentic. Rare is the answer that goes beyond parochial sectarian understandings; scarcely any encompasses the huge gamut implied in the question. For these reasons alone, this book was inevitable. Written by devout Hindus and drawn from the deepest wells of spiritual experience and cultural insight, it is a 416-page definition coming from deep inside the inner sanctum and depicting in words and amazing images the living, breathing entity that is Hinduism.

The forty-six chapters of this book have been drawn from HINDUISM TODAY magazine, whose founder, Satguru Sivaya Subramuniyaswami (1927–2001), well understood the challenges that all religions face in today's world, whether from outside or within. He wrote that every religion consists of the spiritual precepts, practices and customs of a people or society, transmitted from generation to generation, that maintain the connection with higher realms of consciousness, thus connecting man to God and keeping alive the highest ideals of culture and tradition. Gurudeva, as he was affectionately known, observed that if this transmission misses even one generation, a religion can be lost for all time, left to decay in the dusty libraries of history, anthropology and archeology. He strove to protect the religion he loved so dearly. He would ask rhetorically, "Where are the once

prominent religions of the Babylonians, Egyptians, Aztecs, Mayans, American Indians or Hawaiians?" Little remains of them. Not long ago it was feared by some and hoped by many that Hinduism—the religion of a billion people, one sixth of the human race living mostly in India—would meet the same fate. That it survived a history of religious conquest and extermination that wiped out virtually every other ancient religion is exceptional.

Ironically, this noble faith, having withstood the ravages of invasion, plunder and brutal domination by foreign invaders for over a thousand years, stumbled into the 20th century to meet the subtler forces of secularism and the temptations of materialism. Christian propaganda, fabricated by 16th-century Jesuit missionaries, empowered by the 19th-century British Raj and carried forth today by the Western and Indian media, had dealt heavy blows over the centuries to the subjugated, prideless Hindu identity. A typical Christian tactic was to demean the indigenous faith, impeaching it as rife with superstition, idolatry, antiquated values, archaic customs and umpteen false Gods. India's Communist/secular media stressed caste abuse and wretched social ills, branding as radical, communal and fundamentalist all efforts to stand strong for anything Hindu.

Most recently, safeguarding the anti-Hindu mind-set, Western professors of Asian studies brandished the tarnished term *Hindutva* to suppress pleadings by Indian parents to improve the pitiful portrayal of their faith in the textbooks their children

must study in American schools—a portrayal that makes them ashamed of their heritage.

More than a few Hindus, succumbing to the avalanche of ridicule, gave up their faith, changed their names to Western ones and stopped calling themselves Hindu, giving more credence to the notion that this is a faith of the past, not the future. Even those who were Hindus in their hearts would demur, "No, I'm not really a Hindu. I'm nonsectarian, universal, a friend and follower of all religions. Please don't classify me in any particular way." In a further dilution, many swamis and other leaders promulgated the false claim that Hinduism is not a religion at all, but a universalistic amalgam of Vedic, yogic wisdom and lifestyle that anyone of any religion can adopt and practice without conflict. Tens of thousands who love and follow Hindu Dharma avoid the H word at all costs. Rare it is to find a spiritual leader or an institution who stands courageously before the world as a Hindu, unabashed and unequivocal.

Despite these erosive influences, an unexpected resurgence has burst forth across the globe in the last twenty years, driven in part by the Hindu diaspora and in part by India's newfound pride and influence. Hinduism entered the 21st century with fervent force as recent generations discovered its treasures and its relevance to their times. Temples are coming up across the Earth by the thousands. Communities are celebrating Hindu festivals, parading their Deities in the streets of Paris, Berlin, Toronto and Sydney in grand style without worrying that people might think them odd or "pagan." Eloquent spokesmen are now representing Hinduism's billion followers at international peace conferences, interfaith gatherings and discussions about Hindu

rights. Hindu students in high schools and universities are going back to their traditions, turning to the Gods in the temples, not because their parents say they should, but to satisfy their own inner need, to improve their daily life, to fulfill their souls' call.

Hinduism is going digital, working on its faults and bolstering its strengths. Leaders are stepping forth, parents are striving for ways to convey to their children the best of their faith to help them do better in school and live a fruitful life. Swamis and lay missionaries are campaigning to counteract Christian conversion tactics. Hindus of all denominations are banding together to protect, preserve and promote their diverse spiritual heritage.

Articulating Our Faith

A major reason why Hinduism seems difficult to understand is its diversity. Hinduism is not a monolithic tradition. There isn't a one Hindu opinion on things. And there is no single spiritual authority to define matters for the faith. There are several different denominations, the four largest being Vaishnavism, Saivism, Shaktism and Smartism. Further, there are numberless schools of thought, or *sampradayas*, expressed in tens of thousands of guru lineages, or *paramparas*. Each is typically independent and self-contained in its authority. In a very real sense, this grand tradition can be defined and understood as ten thousand faiths gathered in harmony under a single umbrella called Hinduism, or Sanatana Dharma. The tendency to overlook this diversity is the common first step to a faulty perception of the religion. Most spiritual traditions are simpler, more unified and unambiguous.

All too often, despite its antiquity, its profound systems of

thought, the beauty of its art and architecture and the grace of its people, Hinduism remains a mystery. Twisted stereotypes abound that would relegate this richly complex, sophisticated and spiritually rewarding tradition to little more than crude caricatures of snake-charmers, cow-worshipers and yogis lying on beds of nails.

While Hindus do not share these coarse stereotypes, they are often aware of just one small corner of the religion—their village or family lineage—and oblivious to the vastness that lies outside it. Many Hindus are only aware of the Northern traditions, such as that of Adi Shankara, and remain unaware of the equally vigorous and ancient Southern traditions, such as Saiva Siddhanta.

Unfamiliarity with the greater body of Sanatana Dharma may have been unavoidable in earlier centuries, but no longer. Those who are sufficiently determined can track down excellent resources on every facet of the faith. It has, after all, possibly the largest body of scriptural literature of any living religion on Earth. Mountains of scriptures exist in dozens of languages; but they are not all packaged conveniently in a single book or cohesive collection. To ferret out the full breadth of Sanatana Dharma, a seeker would need to read and analyze myriad scriptures and ancillary writings of the diverse philosophies of this pluralistic path. These days, few have the time or determination to face such a daunting task.

Fortunately, there is an easier, more natural way to approach the vastness of Hinduism. From the countless living gurus, teachers and pandits who offer clear guidance, most seekers choose a preceptor, study his teachings, embrace the *sampradaya* he propounds and adopt the precepts and disciplines of his tradition.

That is how the faith is followed in actual practice. Holy men and women, counted in the hundreds of thousands, are the ministers, the defenders of the faith and the inspirers of the faithful.

Back to Basics

For Hindus and non-Hindus alike, one way to gain a simple (though admittedly simplistic) overview is to understand the four essential beliefs shared by the vast majority of Hindus: karma, reincarnation, all-pervasive Divinity and dharma. Gurudeva stated that living by these four concepts is what makes a person a Hindu.

Karma: Karma literally means "deed" or "act" and more broadly names the universal principle of cause and effect, action and reaction which governs all life. Karma is a natural law of the mind, just as gravity is a law of matter. Karma is not fate, for man acts with free will, creating his own destiny. The *Vedas* tell us, if we sow goodness, we will reap goodness; if we sow evil, we will reap evil. Karma refers to the totality of our actions and their concomitant reactions in this and previous lives, all of which determines our future. It is the interplay between our experience and how we respond to it that makes karma devastating or helpfully invigorating. The conquest of karma lies in intelligent action and dispassionate reaction. Not all karmas rebound immediately. Some accumulate and return unexpectedly in this or other births. The *Vedas* explain, "According as one acts, so does he become. One becomes virtuous by virtuous action, bad by bad action" (*Yajur Veda, Brihadaranyaka Upanishad* 4.4.5).

The snow-capped peak of Mount Kailas, mystical crown of the universe and home of Lord Siva, towers majestically among the Himalayan peaks, symbolizing the ultimate truths of Sanatana Dharma.

THOMAS KELLY

Reincarnation: Reincarnation, *punarjanma*, is the natural process of birth, death and rebirth. At death we drop off the physical body and continue evolving in the inner worlds in our subtle bodies, until we again enter into birth. Through the ages, reincarnation has been the great consoling element within Hinduism, eliminating the fear of death. We are not the body in which we live but the immortal soul which inhabits many bodies in its evolutionary journey through samsara. After death, we continue to exist in unseen worlds, enjoying or suffering the harvest of earthly deeds until it comes time for yet another physical birth. The actions set in motion in previous lives form the tendencies and conditions of the next. Reincarnation ceases when karma is resolved, God is realized and moksha, liberation, is attained. The *Vedas* state, "After death, the soul goes to the next world, bearing in mind the subtle impressions of its deeds, and after reaping their harvest returns again to this world of action. Thus, he who has desires continues subject to rebirth" (*Yajur Veda, Brihadaranyaka Upanishad* 4.4.6).

All-Pervasive Divinity: As a family of faiths, Hinduism upholds a wide array of perspectives on the Divine, yet all worship the one, all-pervasive Supreme Being hailed in the Upanishads. As Absolute Reality, God is unmanifest, unchanging and transcendent, the Self God, timeless, formless and spaceless. As Pure Consciousness, God is the manifest primal substance, pure love and light flowing through all form, existing everywhere in time and space as infinite intelligence and power. As Primal Soul, God is our personal Lord, source of all three worlds, our Father-Mother God who protects, nurtures and guides us. We beseech God's grace in our lives while also knowing that He/She is the essence of our soul, the life of our life. Each denomination also venerates its own pantheon of Divinities, Mahadevas, or "great angels," known as Gods, who were created by the Supreme Lord and who serve and adore Him. The *Vedas* proclaim, "He is the God of forms infinite in whose glory all things are—smaller than the smallest atom, and yet the Creator of all, ever living in the mystery of His creation. In the vision of this God of love there is everlasting peace. He is the Lord of all who, hidden in the heart of things, watches over the world of time" (*Krishna Yajur Veda, Shvetashvatara Upanishad* 4.14-15).

Dharma: When God created the universe, He endowed it with order, with the laws to govern creation. Dharma is God's divine law prevailing on every level of existence, from the sustaining cosmic order to religious and moral laws which bind us in harmony with that order. In relation to the soul, dharma is the mode of conduct most conducive to spiritual advancement, the right and righteous path. It is piety and ethical practice, duty and obligation. When we follow dharma, we are in conformity with the Truth that inheres and instructs the universe, and we naturally abide in closeness to God. Adharma is opposition to divine law. Dharma is to the individual what its normal development is to a seed—the orderly fulfillment of an inherent nature and destiny. The *Tirukural* (verses 31-32) reminds us, "Dharma yields Heaven's honor and Earth's wealth. What is there then that is more fruitful for a man? There is nothing more rewarding than dharma, nor anything more ruinous than its neglect."

Lifesize images of Lord Venkateshvara, wearing the distinctive tilaka, or forehead mark, of the Vaishnava denomination.

Hinduism's Unique Value Today

There are good reasons for today's readers, Hindu and non-Hindu alike, to study and understand the nature of Hinduism. The vast geographical and cultural expanses that separate continents, peoples and religions are becoming increasingly bridged as our world grows closer together. Revolutions in communications, the Internet, business, travel and global migration are making formerly distant peoples neighbors, sometimes reluctantly.

It is crucial, if we are to get along in an increasingly pluralistic world, that Earth's peoples learn about and appreciate the religions, cultures, viewpoints and concerns of their planetary neighbors. The Sanatana Dharma, with its sublime tolerance and belief in the all-pervasiveness of Divinity, has much to contribute in this regard. Nowhere on Earth have religions lived and thrived in such close and harmonious proximity as in India. For thousands of years India has been a home to followers of virtually every major world religion, the exemplar of tolerance toward all paths. It has offered a refuge to Jews, Zoroastrians, Sufis, Buddhists, Christians and nonbelievers. Today over one hundred million Indians are Muslim, magnanimously accepted by their majority Hindu neighbors. Such religious amity has occurred out of an abiding respect for all genuine religious pursuits. The oft-quoted axiom that conveys this attitude is *Ekam sat anekah panthah,* "Truth is one, paths are many." What can be learned from the Hindu land that has given birth to Buddhism, Sikhism and Jainism and has been a generous protector of all other religions?

India's original faith offers a rare look at a peaceful, rational and practical path for making sense of our world, for gaining personal spiritual insight, and as a potential blueprint for grounding our society in a more spiritually rewarding worldview.

Hinduism boasts teachings and practices reaching back 8,000 years and more, its history dwarfing most other religions. In fact, there is no specific time in history when it began. It is said to have started with time itself. To emphasize the relative ages of the major religions, and the antiquity of Hinduism, Raimon Panikkar, author of *The Vedic Experience,* cleverly reduced them to proportionate human years, with each 100 years of history representing one year of human life. Viewed this way, Sikhism, the youngest faith, is five years old. Islam, the only teenager, is fourteen. Christianity just turned twenty. Buddhism, Taoism, Jainism and Confucianism are twenty-five. Zoroastrianism is twenty-six. Shintoism is in its late twenties. Judaism is a mature thirty-seven. Hinduism, whose birthday remains unknown, is at least eighty years old—the white-bearded grandfather of living spirituality on this planet.

The followers of this extraordinary tradition often refer to it as Sanatana Dharma, the "Eternal Faith" or "Eternal Way of Conduct." Rejoicing in adding on to itself the contributions of every one of its millions of adherents down through the ages, it brings to the world an extraordinarily rich cultural heritage that embraces religion, society, economy, literature, art and architecture. Unsurprisingly, it is seen by its followers as not merely another religious tradition, but as a way of life and the quintessential foundation of human culture and spirituality. It is, to Hindus, the

most accurate possible description of the way things are—eternal truths, natural principles, inherent in the universe that form the basis of culture and prosperity. Understanding this venerable religion allows all people to fathom the source and essence of human religiosity—to marvel at the oldest example of the Eternal Path that is reflected in all faiths.

While 860 million Hindus live in India, forming 85 percent of the population, tens of millions reside across the globe and include followers from nearly every nationality, race and ethnic group in the world. The US alone is home to three million Hindus, roughly two-thirds of South Asian descent and one-third of other backgrounds.

Hindu Scriptures

All major religions are based upon a specific set of teachings encoded in sacred scripture. Christianity has the *Bible*, for example, and Islam has the *Koran*. Hinduism proudly embraces an incredibly rich collection of scripture; in fact, the largest body of sacred texts known to man. The holiest and most revered are the *Vedas* and *Agamas*, two massive compendia of *shruti* (that which is "heard"), revealed by God to illumined sages centuries and millennia ago. It is said the *Vedas* are general and the Agamas specific, as the *Agamas* speak directly to the details of worship, the yogas, mantra, tantra, temple building and such. The most widely known part of the *Vedas* are the *Upanishads*, which form the more general philosophical foundations of the faith.

The array of secondary scripture, known as *smriti* (that which is "remembered"), is equally vast, the most prominent and widely celebrated of which are the *Itihasas* (epic dramas and history—specifically the *Ramayana* and *Mahabharata*) and the *Puranas* (sacred history and mythology). The ever-popular *Bhagavad Gita* is a small portion of the *Mahabharata*. The Vedic arts and sciences, including ayurveda, astrology, music, dance, architecture, statecraft, domestic duty and law, are reflected in an assembly of texts known as *Vedangas* and *Upavedas*. Moreover, through the ages God Realized souls, sharing their experience, have poured forth volume upon volume that reveal the wonders of yoga and offer passionate hymns of devotion and illumination. The creation of Hindu scripture continues to this day, as contemporary masters reiterate the timeless truths to guide souls on the path to Divinity.

A clear sign that a person is a Hindu is that he embraces Hindu scripture as his guide and solace through life. While the *Vedas* are accepted by all denominations, each lineage defines which other scriptures are regarded as central and authoritative for its followers. Further, each devotee freely chooses and follows one or more favorite scriptures within his tradition, be it a selection of *Upanishads*, the *Bhagavad Gita*, the *Tirumantiram* or the writings of his own guru. This free-flowing, diversified approach to scripture is unique to the Hindu faith. Scripture here, however, does not have the same place as it does in many other faiths. For genuine spiritual progress to take place, its wisdom must not be merely studied and preached, but lived and experienced as one's own.

The Nature of God

What is the nature of God in Hinduism is a question that defies a facile answer, for in the Hindu family of faiths each has its own perspective on the Supreme Being, and its own Deity or Deities. For this reason, Hinduism may, to an outsider, appear polytheistic—a term avidly employed as a criticism of choice, as if the idea of many Gods were primitive and false. For the Hindu the many Gods in no way impair the principle of the oneness of Reality. Further complexity and confusion have been introduced with the diaspora, that phenomenon of recent history that has, for the first time, spread Hindus throughout the globe. Outside their native soil, groups of mixed Hindu backgrounds have tended to bring the Deities of all traditions together under one roof in order to create a place of worship acceptable, and affordable, to all. This is something that does not happen in India. This all-Gods-under-one-roof phenomenon is confusing, even to many Hindus, and it tends to lend credence to the polytheistic indictment. Nevertheless, ask any Hindu, and he will tell you that he worships the One Supreme Being, just as do Christians, Jews, Muslims and those of nearly all major faiths. The Hindu will also tell you that, indeed, there is only one Supreme God. If he is a Saivite, he calls that God Siva. If a Shakta Hindu, he will adore Devi, the Goddess, as the ultimate Divinity. If a Vaishnava Hindu, he will revere Vishnu. If he is a Smarta Hindu, he will worship as supreme one chosen from a specific pantheon of Gods. Thus, contrary to prevailing misconceptions, Hindus all worship a one

Supreme Being, though by different names. This is because the diverse peoples of India, with different languages and cultures, have, through the longest existing religious history, understood the one God in their own distinct ways. Analogously, India is the only nation with fourteen official languages on its paper currency. All those names don't change the value of the note!

A crucial point that is often overlooked is that having one Supreme God does not repudiate the existence of lesser Divinities. Just as Christianity acknowledges great spiritual beings who dwell near God, such as the cherubim and seraphim, who have both human and animal features, so Hindus revere Mahadevas, or "great angels," who were created by the Supreme Lord and who serve and adore Him. Each denomination worships the Supreme God and its own pantheon of divine beings. The elephant-faced Lord Ganesha is among the most popular, and is perhaps the only Deity worshiped by Hindus of all denominations. Other Deities include Gods and Goddesses of strength, yoga, learning, art, music, wealth and culture. There are also minor divinities, village Gods and Goddesses, who are invoked for protection, health and such mundane matters as a fruitful harvest.

Each denomination identifies its primary Deity as synonymous with Brahman, the One Supreme Reality exalted in the lofty *Upanishads*. There, in the cream of Hinduism's revealed scripture, the matter is crystal clear. God is unimaginably transcendent yet ubiquitously immanent in all things. He is creator and He is the creation. He is not a remote God who rules from above, as in Abrahamic faiths, but an intimate Lord who abides within all as the essence of everything. There is no corner of

During the early morning hours of July 24, 2004, at the Stafford Performing Arts Centre in Houston, a peacock wanders near His Divine Holiness Pramukh Swami Maharaj, spiritual head of the Bochasanwasi Shri Akshar Purushottam Swaminarayan Sanstha (BAPS), as he performs a rite of worship to bless his saffron-clad monks and thousands of devotees from around the world who came to witness the ten-day consecration of Houston's new Swaminarayan Temple. The growth of this large institution is representative of Hinduism's benevolent strength and global presence.

creation in which God is not present. He is farther away than the farthest star and closer than our breath. Hinduism calls God "the Life of life." If His presence were to be removed from any one thing, that thing would cease to exist.

If terms be required, we could characterize this family of faiths as both monotheistic and henotheistic. Hindus were never polytheistic in the sense of believing in many equal Gods. Henotheism (literally, "one God") better defines the Hindu view. It means the worship of one Supreme God without denying the existence of other Gods. Another set of philosophical terms describes God's relationship to the universe: panentheism, pantheism and theism. Hindus believe that God is an all-pervasive reality that animates the universe. We can see Him in the life shining out of the eyes of humans and all creatures. This view of God as existing in and giving life to all things is called panentheism. It differs from the similar sounding view, pantheism, in which God is the natural universe and nothing more, immanent but not transcendent. It also differs from traditional theism in which God is above the world, apart and transcendent but not immanent. Panentheism is an all-encompassing concept. It says that God is both in the world and beyond it, both immanent and transcendent. That is the highest Hindu view.

Unlike purely monotheistic religions, however, Hinduism tends to be tolerant and welcoming of religious diversity, embracing a multiplicity of paths, not asking for conformity to just one. So, it's impossible to say all Hindus believe this or that. Some Hindus give credence only to the formless Absolute Reality as God; others accept God as personal Lord and Creator. Some venerate God as male, others as female, while still others hold that God is not limited by gender, which is an aspect of physical bodies. This freedom, we could say, makes for the richest understanding and perception of God in all of Earth's existing faiths. Hindus accept all genuine spiritual paths—from pure monism, which concludes that "God alone exists," to theistic dualism, which asks, "When shall I know His Grace?" Each soul is free to find his own way, whether by devotion, austerity, meditation, yoga or selfless service.

The Nature of Self

The driving imperative to know oneself—to answer the questions "Who am I?" "Where did I come from?" and "Where am I going?"—has been the core of all great religions and schools of philosophy throughout human history. Hindu teachings on the nature of self are as philosophically profound as they are pragmatic. We are more than our physical body, our mind, emotions and intellect, with which we so intimately identify every moment of our life, but which are temporary, imperfect and limiting. Our true self is our immortal soul, or atma, the eternal, perfect and unlimited inner essence, unseen by the human eye—undetectable by any of the human senses, which are its tools for living in this physical world.

The *Vedas* teach that the Divine resides in all beings. Our true, spiritual essence is, like God, eternal, blissful, good, wise and beautiful by nature. The joining of Brahman, or God, and the atman, or soul, is known as yoga, a Sanskrit word that shares the same root as the English word *yoke*. We spend so much of

Dressed up for a festival, these girls exemplify the traditional Hindu way of life, rich in pageantry, graceful ways, modesty, joy and refinement.

our time pursuing beauty, knowledge and bliss in the world, not knowing that these objects of our desire are already within us as attributes of our own soul. If we turn our focus within through worship and meditation, identifying with our true spiritual self, we can discover an infinite inner treasure that easily rivals the greatest wealth of this world.

Personal spiritual development is enhanced through understanding the closely related processes of karma and reincarnation. The individual soul undergoes repeated cycles of birth, death and rebirth. This is known as the wheel of samsara. During each earthly manifestation, an individual's karma (literally "work" or "actions") determines his future psycho-physical state. Every ethically good act results, sooner or later, in happiness and spiritual development; whereas ethically wrong actions end in loss and sorrow. Thus, the principle of karma is an idea that celebrates freedom, since at every moment we are free to create our future states of existence through our present actions and states of consciousness. This philosophical worldview encourages followers of Hinduism to live happily, morally, consciously and humbly, following the Eternal Way.

Hinduism is a mystical religion, leading the devotee to personally experience the Truth within, finally reaching the pinnacle of consciousness where the realization is attained that man and God are one. As divine souls, we are evolving into union with God through the process of reincarnation. We are immortal souls living and growing in the great school of earthly experience in which we have lived many lives. Knowing this gives followers a great security, eliminating the fear and dread of death. The Hindu does not take death to be the end of existence, as does

the atheist. Nor does he, like Western religionists, look upon life as a singular opportunity, to be followed by eternal heavenly existence for those souls who do well, and by unending hell for those who do not. Death for the Hindu is merely a moment of transition from this world to the next, simultaneously an end and a new beginning. The actions and reactions we set in motion in our last life form our tendencies in the next.

Despite the heartening glory of our true nature spoken of in scripture, most souls are unaware of their spiritual self. This ignorance or "veiling grace" is seen in Hinduism as God's purposeful limiting of awareness, which allows us to evolve. It is this narrowing of our awareness, coupled with a sense of individualized ego, that allows us to look upon the world and our part in it from a practical, human point of view. Without the world, known as maya, the soul could not evolve through experience. The ultimate goal of life, in the Hindu view, is called moksha, liberation from rebirth. This comes when earthly karma has been resolved, dharma has been well performed and God is fully realized. All souls are destined to achieve the highest states of enlightenment, perfect spiritual maturity and liberation, but not necessarily in this life. Hindus understand this and do not delude themselves that this life is the last. While seeking and attaining profound realizations, they know there is much to be done in fulfilling life's other three goals: dharma, righteousness; artha, wealth; and kama, pleasure.

In some Hindu traditions, the destiny of the soul after liberation is perceived as eternal and blissful enjoyment of God's presence in the heavenly realms, a form of salvation given by God through grace, similar to most Abrahamic faiths. In others, the

soul's destiny is perfect union in God, a state of undifferentiated oneness likened to a river returning to its source, the sea, and becoming one with it—either immediately upon death, or following further evolution of the soul in the inner worlds. For still others, the ultimate state has no relationship with a Godhead, but is understood as undifferentiated oneness without form or being, a return or merger in the infinite All, somewhat akin to the Buddhist's nirvana.

Hinduism in Practice

Hinduism's three pillars are temple worship, scripture and the guru-disciple tradition, around which all spiritual disciplines revolve. These include prayer, meditation and ritual worship in the home and temple, study of scripture, recitation of mantras, pilgrimage to holy places, austerity, selfless service, generous giving, the various yogas, and following good conduct. Festivals and singing of holy hymns are dynamic activities.

Hindu temples, whether they be small village sanctuaries or towering citadels, are esteemed as God's consecrated abode. In the temple Hindus draw close to the Divine and find a refuge from the world. God's grace, permeating everywhere, is most easily known within these holy precincts. It is in this purified milieu that the three worlds—physical, astral and causal—commune most perfectly, that devotees can establish harmony with inner-plane spiritual beings. Traditional temples are specially sanctified, possessing a ray of spiritual energy connecting them to the celestial worlds.

Temple rituals, performed by Hindu priests, take the form of puja, a ceremony in which the ringing of bells, passing of flames, presenting of offerings and intoning of chants invoke the devas and Gods, who then come to bless and help the devotees. Personal worship during puja may be an expression of festive celebration of important events in life, of adoration and thanksgiving, penance and confession, prayerful supplication and requests, or contemplation and the deepest levels of superconsciousness. The stone or metal Deity images enshrined in the temple are not mere symbols of the Gods; they are the form through which their love, power and blessings flood forth into this world. Devout Hindus adore the image as the Deity's physical body, knowing that the God or Goddess is actually present and conscious in it during puja, aware of devotee's thoughts and feelings and even sensing the priest's gentle touch on the metal or stone.

Hindus consider it most important to live near a temple, as it is the center of spiritual life. It is here, in God's home, that the devotee nurtures his relationship with the Divine. Not wanting to stay away too long, he visits weekly and strives to attend each major festival, and to pilgrimage to a far-off temple annually for special blessings and a break from his daily concerns.

For the Hindu, the underlying emphasis of life is on making spiritual progress, while also pursuing one's family and professional duties and goals. He is conscious that life is a precious, fleeting opportunity to advance, to bring about inner transformation, and he strives to remain ever conscious of this fact. For him work is worship, and his faith relates to every department of life.

Hinduism's spiritual core is its holy men and women—millions of sadhus, yogis, swamis, *vairagis*, saints and *satgurus* who have dedicated their lives to full-time service, devotion and God

As a modern young Hindu family enjoy breakfast together in Delhi, the daughter asks Mom a pressing question about their faith.

DINODIA

Realization, and to proclaiming the eternal truths of Sanatana Dharma. In day-to-day life, perhaps no facet of dharma is as crucial as the spiritual teacher, or *satguru*. These holy men and women are a living spiritual force for the faithful. They are the inspirers and interpreters, the personal guides who, knowing God themselves, can bring devotees into God consciousness. In all Hindu communities there are gurus who personally look after the spiritual practices and progress of devotees. Such preceptors are equally revered whether they are men or women. In few other religions are women allowed such access to the highest seats of reverence and respect.

Within the Hindu way is a deeply rooted desire to lead a productive, ethical life. Among the many virtues instilled in followers are truthfulness, fidelity, contentment and avoidance of greed, lust and anger. A cornerstone of dharma is ahimsa, noninjury toward all beings. Vedic rishis who revealed dharma proclaimed ahimsa as the way to achieve harmony with our environment, peace between people and compassion within ourselves. Devout followers tend to be vegetarians and seek to protect the environment. Selfless service, *seva*, to God and humanity is widely pursued as a way of softening the ego and drawing close to the Divine. Charity, *dana*, is expressed though myriad philanthropic activities.

Hindus wear sectarian marks, called *tilaka*, on their foreheads as sacred symbols, distinctive insignia of their heritage. They prefer cremation of the body upon death, rather than burial, knowing that the soul lives on and will inhabit a new body on Earth.

Perhaps one of this faith's most refreshing characteristics is that it encourages free and open thought. Scriptures and gurus encourage followers to inquire and investigate into the nature of Truth, to explore worshipful, inner and meditative regimens to directly experience the Divine. This openness is at the root of Hinduism's famed tolerance of other cultures, religions and points of view, capsulated in the adage, *Ekam sat viprah bahuda vadanti*, meaning "Truth is one, the wise describe it in different ways." The Hindu is free to choose his path, his way of approaching the Divine, and he can change it in the course of his lifetime. There is no heresy or apostasy in Hinduism. This, coupled with Hinduism's natural inclusiveness, gives little room for fanaticism, fundamentalism or closed-mindedness anywhere within the framework of Hinduism. It has been aptly called a threshold, not an enclosure.

There is a false concept, commonly found in academic texts, that Hinduism is world-negating. This depiction was foisted upon the world by 19th-century Western missionary Orientalists traveling in India for the first time and reporting back about its starkest and strangest aspects, not unlike what Western journalists tend to do today. The wild-looking, world-renouncing yogis, taking refuge in caves, denying the senses and thus the world, were of sensational interest, and their world-abandonment became, through the scholars' eyes, characteristic of the entire religion. While Sanatana Dharma proudly upholds such severe ways of life for the few, it is very much a family oriented faith. The vast majority of followers are engaged in family life, firmly grounded in responsibilities in the world. Hinduism's essential, time-tested monastic tradition makes it no more world-negating than Christianity or Buddhism, which likewise have traditions

of renunciate men and women living apart from the world in spiritual pursuits. Young Hindu adults are encouraged to marry; marriages are encouraged to yield an abundance of children; children are guided to live in virtue, fulfill duty and contribute to the community. The emphasis is not on self-fulfillment and freedom but on the welfare of the community, as expressed in the phrase, *Bahujan hitaya, bahujan sukhaya*, meaning "the welfare of the many and the happiness of the many."

Definitions from Prominent Hindus

In our magazine and books we have offered this dictionary-style definition of our faith: India's indigenous religious and cultural system, followed today by nearly one billion adherents, mostly in India, but with large populations in many other countries. Also called Sanatana Dharma, "eternal religion" and Vaidika Dharma, "religion of the *Vedas*." Hinduism is the world's most ancient religion and encompasses a broad spectrum of philosophies ranging from pluralistic theism to absolute monism. It is a family of myriad faiths with four primary denominations: Saivism, Vaishnavism, Shaktism and Smartism. These four hold such divergent beliefs that each is a complete and independent religion. Yet, they share a vast heritage of culture and belief— karma, dharma, reincarnation, all-pervasive Divinity, temple worship, sacraments, manifold Deities, the guru-shishya tradition and a reliance on the *Vedas* as scriptural authority. Great minds have tackled the thorny challenge of defining Sanatana Dharma, and we would like to share a few of their efforts here.

Dr. S. Radhakrishnan, renowned philosopher and president of India from 1962 to 1967, states in *The Hindu View of Life*: "The Hindu recognizes one Supreme Spirit, though different names are given to it. God is in the world, though not as the world. He does not merely intervene to create life or consciousness, but is working continuously. There is no dualism of the natural and the supernatural. Evil, error and ugliness are not ultimate. No view is so utterly erroneous, no man is so absolutely evil as to deserve complete castigation. There is no Hell, for that means there is a place where God is not, and there are sins which exceed His love. The law of karma tells us that the individual life is not a term, but a series. Heaven and Hell are higher and lower stages in one continuous movement. Every type has its own nature which should be followed. We should do our duty in that state of life to which we happen to be called. Hinduism affirms that the theological expressions of religious experience are bound to be varied, accepts all forms of belief and guides each along his path to the common goal. These are some of the central principles of Hinduism. If Hinduism lives today, it is due to them."

Bal Ghangadhar Tilak, scholar, mathematician, philosopher and Indian nationalist, named "the father of the Indian Revolution" by Jawaharlal Nehru, summarized Hindu beliefs in his *Gitarahasya*. This oft-quoted statement, so compelling concise, is considered authoritative by Bharat's courts of law: "Acceptance of the *Vedas* with reverence; recognition of the fact that the means or ways to salvation are diverse; and realization of the truth that the number of Gods to be worshiped is large, that indeed is the distinguishing feature of the Hindu religion."

Traditional priests, 121 in all, pose at Sringeri Sadhana Center of Stroudsburg, Pennsylvania, during a break in the biggest Vedic worship ceremony ever performed on American soil.

MIKE BRYCIDER

Sri K. Navaratnam, esteemed Sri Lankan religious scholar, enumerated a more extensive set of basic beliefs in his book, *Studies in Hinduism,* reflecting the Southern Saiva Agamic tradition. 1) A belief in the existence of God. 2) A belief in the existence of a soul separate from the body. 3) A belief in the existence of the finitizing principle known as *avidya* or *mala.* 4) A belief in the principle of matter—prakriti or maya. 5) A belief in the theory of karma and reincarnation. 6) A belief in the indispensable guidance of a guru to guide the spiritual aspirant towards God Realization. 7) A belief in moksha, or liberation, as the goal of human existence. 8) A belief in the indispensable necessity of temple worship in religious life. 9) A belief in graded forms of religious practices, both internal and external, until one realizes God. 10) A belief in ahimsa as the greatest dharma or virtue. 11) A belief in mental and physical purity as indispensable factors for spiritual progress.

Mahatma Mohandas K. Gandhi: "I call myself a Sanatani Hindu because I believe in the *Vedas,* the *Upanishads,* the *Puranas* and all that goes by the name of Hindu scriptures, and therefore in avatars and rebirth. In a concrete manner he is a Hindu who believes in God, immortality of the soul, transmigration, the law of karma and moksha, and who tries to practice truth and ahimsa in daily life, and therefore practices cow protection in its widest sense and understands and tries to act according to the law of *varnashrama.*"

Sri Pramukh Swami Maharaj of the Bochasanwasi Shri Akshar Purushottam Sanstha (Swaminarayan Faith) propounds: 1) Para-brahman, one, supreme, all-powerful God: He is the Creator, has a divine form, is immanent, transcendent and the giver of moksha. 2) *Avatarvad,* manifestation of God on Earth: God Himself incarnates on Earth in various forms to revive dharma and grant liberation. 3) *Karmavad,* law of action: the soul reaps fruits, good or bad, according to its past and present actions, which are experienced either in this life or future lives. 4) *Punarjanma,* re-incarnation: the mortal soul is continuously born and reborn in one of the 8,400,000 species until it attains liberation. 5) Moksha, ultimate liberation: the goal of human life. It is the liberation of the soul from the cycle of births and deaths to remain eternally in the service of God. 6) *Guru-shishya sambandha,* master-disciple relationship: guidance and grace of a spiritually perfect master, revered as the embodiment of God, is essential for an aspirant seeking liberation. 7) *Dharma,* that which sustains the universe: an all-encompassing term representing divine law, law of being, path of righteousness, religion, duty, responsibility, virtue, justice, goodness and truth. 8) *Vedapramana,* scriptural authority of the *Vedas:* all Hindu faiths are based on the teachings of the *Vedas.* 9) *Murti-puja,* sacred image worship: consecrated images represent the presence of God which is worshiped. The sacred image is a medium to help devotees offer their devotion to God.

Sri Swami Vivekananda, speaking in America, proclaimed: "All Vedantists believe in God. Vedantists also believe the *Vedas* to be the revealed word of God—an expression of the knowledge of God—and as God is eternal, so are the *Vedas* eternal. Another

common ground of belief is that of creation in cycles, that the whole of creation appears and disappears. They postulate the existence of a material, which they call akasha, which is something like the ether of the scientists, and a power which they call prana."

Sri Jayendra Saraswati, 69th Shankaracharya of the Kamakoti Peetham, Kanchipuram, defines in his writings the basic features of Hinduism as follows. 1) The concept of idol worship and the worship of God in His *nirguna* as well as *saguna* form. 2) The wearing of sacred marks on the forehead. 3) Belief in the theory of past and future births in accordance with the theory of karma. 4) Cremation of ordinary men and burial of great men.

The Vishva Hindu Parishad declared its definition in a Memorandum of Association, Rules and Regulations in 1966: "Hindu means a person believing in, following or respecting the eternal values of life, ethical and spiritual, which have sprung up in Bharatkhand [India] and includes any person calling himself a Hindu."

The Indian Supreme Court, in 1966, formalized a judicial definition of Hindu beliefs to legally distinguish Hindu denominations from other religions in India. This list was affirmed by the Court as recently as 1995 in judging cases regarding religious identity. 1) Acceptance of the *Vedas* with reverence as the highest authority in religious and philosophic matters and acceptance with reverence of *Vedas* by Hindu thinkers and philosophers as the sole foundation of Hindu philosophy. 2) Spirit of tolerance and willingness to understand and appreciate the opponent's point of view based on the realization that truth is many-sided. 3) Acceptance of great world rhythm—vast periods of creation, maintenance and dissolution follow each other in endless succession—by all six systems of Hindu philosophy. 4) Acceptance by all systems of Hindu philosophy of the belief in rebirth and pre-existence. 5) Recognition of the fact that the means or ways to salvation are many. 6) Realization of the truth that numbers of Gods to be worshiped may be large, yet there being Hindus who do not believe in the worshiping of idols. 7) Unlike other religions, or religious creeds, Hindu religion's not being tied down to any definite set of philosophic concepts, as such.

Swami Shankarananda of Melbourne, Australia, offers this definition: "In the late sixties when spirituality arose within me for the first time, I could have said (had I enough awareness), 'I'd like a path that is as spacious as the universe. A path that includes everyone and every possible belief system. A path that is as tolerant and forgiving as a mother, yet as precise and on-purpose as a brain surgeon. A path whose mode of thinking is so broad that no thought or idea is left outside of it. A path of inner transformation and self-development. A path of truth that is also a path of kindness. A path whose love is so deep and all-embracing that no sinner is excluded from its mercy. A path whose source is Universal Consciousness.' Had I been able to formulate those thoughts that were in me in an inchoate way, perhaps the sky would have parted and a voice from on high might have said, 'Your path is Hinduism.'"

The Nature

Hinduism's special treasures, its four main
denominations, its precepts and practices,
scriptures and two paths of dharma

# of Hinduism

Hinduism is a joyous, reverent, mystical faith, as evidenced in its fabulous festivals, such as the Kumbha Mela, pictured here being celebrated in Haridwar in 1998 on Mahasivaratri, Siva's great night, where 25 million devotees gathered to honor and seek blessing of the Divine.

CHAPTER 1

Hinduism, the Greatest

A Satguru's Penetrating Insights on the Earth's Oldest Living Faith

MIKE PPYCIDEP

Religion in the World

BY SATGURU SIVAYA SUBRAMUNIYASWAMI,
FOUNDER OF HINDUISM TODAY

Religion is man's association with the Divine, and the ultimate objective of religion is realization of Truth. Forms which symbolize Truth are only indications; they are not Truth itself, which transcends all conceptualization. The mind in its efforts to understand Truth through reasoning must always fail, for Truth transcends the very mind which seeks to embrace it. Hinduism is unique among the world's religions. I boldly proclaim it the g reatest religion in the world. To begin with, it is mankind's oldest spiritual declaration, the very fountainhead of faith on the planet. Hinduism's venerable age has seasoned it to maturity. It is the only religion, to my knowledge, which is not founded in a single historic event or prophet, but which itself precedes recorded history. Hinduism has been called the "cradle of spirituality" and the "mother of all religions," partially because it has influenced virtually every major religion and partly because it can absorb all other religions, honor and embrace their scriptures, their saints, their philosophy. This is possible because Hinduism looks compassionately on all genuine spiritual effort and knows unmistakably that all souls are evolving toward union with the Divine, and all are destined, without exception, to achieve spiritual enlightenment and liberation in this or a future life. ¶Of course, any religion in the world is a mind stratum within people, isn't it? It is a group of people who think consciously, subconsciously and subsuperconsciously alike and who are guided by their own superconsciousness and the superconsciousness of their leaders which make up the force field which we call a religion. It does not exist outside the mind. People of a certain religion have all been impressed with the same experiences. They have all accepted the same or similar beliefs and attitudes, and their mutual concurrence creates the bonds of fellowship and purpose, of doctrine and communion.

Rites of Communion: *(Photo, left) for eleven days in 1997, one-hundred-twenty-one priests surrounded 11 fire altars in a huge worship hall at the Sringeri Sadhana Center in Pennsylvania for the grandest of all fire ceremonies. The Ati Rudra Maha Yajna, witnessed by 6,000 devotees and following liturgy set thousands of years ago, was performed for the first time on American soil, a demonstration of Hinduism's strength and geographical breadth in our modern age.*

The people who are Hinduism share a mind structure. They can understand, acknowledge, accept and love the peoples of all religions, encompass them within their mind as being fine religious people. The Hindu truly believes that there is a single Eternal Path, but he does not believe that any one religion is the only valid religion or the only religion that will lead the soul to salvation. Rather, the Eternal Path is seen reflected in all religions.

To put it another way, the will of God or the Gods is at work in all genuine worship and service. It is said in Hindu scripture that "Truth is one. Paths are many." The search for Truth, for God, is called the Sanatana Dharma, or the Eternal Path, because it is inherent in the soul itself, where religion begins. This path, this return to the Source, is ever existent in man, and is at work whether he is aware of the processes or not. There is not this man's search and that man's search. Where does the impetus come from? It comes from the inside of man himself. Thus, Hinduism is ever vibrant and alive, for it depends on this original source of inspiration, this first impulse of the spirit within, giving it an energy and a vibrancy that is renewable eternally in the now.

Naturally, the Hindu feels that his faith is the broadest, the most practical and effective instrument of spiritual unfoldment, but he includes in his Hindu mind all the religions of the world as expressions of the one Eternal Path and understands each proportionately in accordance with its doctrines and dogma. He knows that certain beliefs and inner attitudes are more conducive to spiritual growth than others, and that all religions are, therefore, not the same. They differ in important ways. Yet, there is no sense whatsoever in Hinduism of an "only path." A devout Hindu is supportive of all efforts that lead to a pure and virtuous life and would consider it unthinkable to dissuade a sincere devotee from his chosen faith. This is the Hindu mind, and this is what we teach, what we practice and what

. . . .

Profundity: *(Clockwise) Prof. E. Chamuramoki reviews precious scriptures at the Oriental Research Institute, Tirupati; the Porram Festival in Thrissur, Kerala, led by 15 gold-caparisoned elephants; a woman rings the bell as she enters the Gadhikalika temple in sacred Ujjain city, signalling her presence to the angelic hosts*

THOMAS KELLY

THOMAST KELLY

The Joys of Hinduism

Tonight we want to speak on the joys and happiness found in Hinduism, our ancient religion which brings forth the wonderful feelings of a belief in the cosmic processes of reincarnation coupled with knowledge of the laws of karma and the wisdom of dharma in which everyone has his rightful place and purpose in life. It brings the broadmindedness of total acceptance of all other religions as expressions of the One God's creation, the blessing of a complete devotional path revolving around powerful temples, the fulfillment of a profound mystical teaching founded on yoga and brought forth by the seers and saints and gurus, and so much more. Our religion is so strong, so rich and varied that very few can claim to under-stand it in its completeness. It is immense, an immense religion, so immense that we have difficulty sometimes explaining it to those who hold to a simpler doctrine, especially if they have been subjected to erroneous concepts about our religion promulgated by invaders and missionaries of a score of alien religions. It is time that the world knew of the greatness of Hinduism, knew it as it is. Of course, we cannot explain it in an evening. My satguru, the great Siva Yogaswami of Columbuthurai, would say, "The time is short and the subject is vast." But we can have a look at some of the aspects of Hinduism that bring such joys and happiness to over a billion devotees around the world. ¶Each Hindu's belief in reincarnation is so strong that it totally eliminates

we offer aspirants on the path.

We often send people back to their own religion, for Hindu doctrine would consider it an unseemly karma to draw someone away simply because he believed differently. To the Hindu, conduct and the inner processes of the soul's maturation are more essential than the particular religion one may be by the accidents of birth, culture or geography. The Hindu knows that he might unknowingly disturb the dharma of the individual if he pulls him away from his religious roots, and that would cause an unsavory karma for them both. He knows, too, that it is not necessary that all people believe exactly the same way or call God by the same name.

A Religion of Experience

Still, Hinduism is also extremely sectarian, altogether adamant in its beliefs. Its doctrines of karma and reincarnation, its philosophy of nonviolence and compassion, its certainty of mystical realities and experience and its universality are held with unshakable conviction. Perhaps this is due to the fact that Hinduism is a religion more of experience than of doctrine. It prefers to say to its followers, "This is the nature of Truth, and these are the means by which that Truth may be realized. Here are the traditions which have withstood time and proved most effective. Now you may test them in your own life, prove them to yourself. And we will help as we can." Hinduism will never say, "You must do or believe thusly or be condemned." In Hinduism it is believed that none is eternally condemned. That loving acceptance and unremitting faith in the goodness of life is another reason I boldly say that Hinduism is the greatest religion in the world.

Within Hinduism, as within every religious system, are the practical means of attaining the purity, the knowledge and the serenity of life. Each Hindu is enjoined to attend a puja every day, preferably at a certain and consistent time. He must observe the laws of virtue and the codes of ethics. He must serve others, support religion within his community. He should occasionally pilgrimage to sacred shrines and temples and partake in the sacraments. If he is more advanced, an older soul, then he is expected, expects of himself, to undertake certain forms of *sadhana* and tapas, of

the fear and dread of death. No true Hindu really fears death; nor does he look forward to it. The word death in the vocabulary of the Hindu holds a different meaning. He does not take death to be the end of existence; nor does he look upon life as a singular opportunity to be followed by eternal heavenly existence for those souls who do well, and by unending hell for those who do not. Death for the Hindu is merely transition, simultaneously an end and a new beginning. Over two thousand years ago, Saint Tiruvalluvar wrote, "Death is like falling asleep, and birth is like awakening from that sleep" (Tirukural 339). In one of the ancient languages of our religion, the physical body had a name which literally meant "that which is always drop-

ping off." ¶The Hindu's knowledge of reincarnation gives him the hope of attaining a future birth and in that birth making further prog-

ress toward the perfection that he intuitively knows is his atman, his soul. He is working in this life to gain enough good merit, enough

discipline and asceticism.

Though it is broad and open in the freedom of the mind to inquire, Hinduism is narrowly strict in its expectations of devotees—the more awakened the soul, the higher the demands and responsibilities placed upon him. And though other systems of belief are fully acceptable mind structures within the structure of the higher mind, there is no way out of Hinduism. There is no excommunication. There is no means of severance. There's no leaving Hinduism once you have formally accepted and been accepted. Why is that? That is because Hinduism contains the whole of religion within itself. There is no "other religion" which one can adopt by leaving Hinduism, only other aspects of the one religion which is the sum of them all, the Eternal Path, the Sanatana Dharma.

I would say that, if it lacked all the qualities of open-mindedness and compassion and tolerance just mentioned, Hinduism would be the greatest religion on the basis of its profound mysticism alone. No other faith boasts such a deep and enduring comprehension of the mysteries of existence, or possesses so vast a metaphysical system. The storehouse of religious revelations in Hinduism cannot be reckoned. I know of its equal nowhere. It contains the entire system of yoga, of meditation and contemplation and Self Realization. Nowhere else is there such insightful revelation of the inner bodies of man, the subtle pranas and the chakras, or psychic centers within the nerve system. Inner states of superconsciousness are explored and mapped fully in Hinduism, from the clear white light to the sights and sounds which flood the awakened inner consciousness of man. In the West it is the mystically awakened soul who is drawn to Hinduism for understanding of inner states of consciousness, discovering after ardent seeking that Hinduism possesses answers which do not exist elsewhere and is capable of guiding awareness into ever-deepening mind strata.

· ·

Dedication: *(Clockwise) Shaven-headed aspirants await the auspicious moment of brahmachari initiation and entry into an order of world-renouncing sadhus; pilgrims touch the sculpted stone feet of Vishnu in Tirumala Temple's Srivari Padalu shrine; a traditional Kathak dancer in outrageous, colorful costume*

THOMAS KELLY

punya, to deserve welcome into a fine religious family as a good soul that will not upset the family but add to its love and harmony and productivity. That is one aim ever on the mind of the devout Hindu, to live well that he may live even more perfectly in a future life on this planet. That is our aim; and our other beliefs, our accumulated knowledge and the many facets of our religion, give us the strength and the wisdom to believe in such a far-reaching way, to look beyond the immediate day-to-day concerns into our ultimate objective, which is realization and liberation, moksha. ¶Nor is this belief in the cycles of earthly existence, in reincarnation, merely a belief. It is a certain knowledge for those who have had even a tiny glimpse into their origins to the point of remembering another life or just intuiting that the soul did not come

DAVID TROPP

into existence just before one's birth. The Hindu believes that the soul undertakes many sojourns on the planet. We see the wisdom in this cycle of birth, death and rebirth.

Karma Is Always Just: We see reincarnation as an explanation for many of the apparent inequalities observed in life. Thus we understand the fairness even in a bad birth, say a birth as a cripple or a child who dies in infancy. To the Hindu this is not an accident, but is a natural event brought forth by the soul itself through the karma of unseemly acts and desires in a previous life. To the Hindu there is not one force in the universe at work to make all things good and an opposing force trying to destroy the soul. No. All is God's work. All karma is natural and worthy of the soul to which it comes. ¶The Hindu knows that it is the younger souls who lack understanding, who cannot live in harmony with others and who shun the higher forms of culture

Hinduism's Unbounded Tolerance

In apparent conflict, the scriptures written thousands of years ago explain how we should live, and saints and rishis and seers throughout the ages have told us that it is impossible to live that way. So, Hinduism has a great tolerance for those who strive and a great forgiveness for those who fail. It looks in awe at those who succeed in living a life according to its own strict ethics. In Hinduism, we have many, many saints. You don't have to die to be acknowledged a saint in our religion, you have to live. The Hindus, perhaps beyond all other people on the earth, realize the difficulties of living in a human body and look in awe at those who achieve true spirituality.

The Hindu believes in reincarnation. He believes that he is not the body in which he lives, but the soul or awareness which takes on a body for a definite purpose. He believes he is going to get a better body in a better birth, that the process does not begin and end in a single life, that the process is continuous, reaching beyond the limits that one life may impose on inner progress. Of course, his belief in karma assures him that a better birth, that progress inwardly will come only if he behaves in a certain way. He knows that if he does not behave according to the natural laws, to the Hindu ethics, that he will suffer for his transgressions in a future life, or future lives, that he may by his own actions earn the necessity of a so-called inferior birth, earn the right to start over where he left off in the birth in which he failed.

The belief in karma and reincarnation is exclusively Hindu, and yet many people in the world today, whether they call themselves religious or not, are coming to the same conclusions, not from being told to believe but in a natural way, from the inside out. This belief in more than a single life brings to the Hindu a great sense of peace. He knows that the maturity of the soul takes many lives, perhaps hundreds of lives. If he is not perfect right now, then at least he knows that he is progressing, that there will be many opportunities for learning and growing. This eliminates anxiety, gives the serene perception that everything is all right as it is. There is no sense of a time limit, of an impending end or an ultimate judgment of his actions and attitudes. This understanding that the soul evolves

and faith. Rather than inheriting eternal suffering for their acts, they earn instead another opportunity for experience, for learning, for evolving. The ideas of sin and evil are different in Hinduism from the concepts held by Abrahamic religions. If there is such a thing as sin to the Hindu, it is the breaking of the natural laws, a lapse in the patterns of karma and dharma, and that transgression brings its own punishment in the form of an additional karma created to then be worked out. Thus the Hindu does not live in fear of sin or under the notion of original sin. We do not look upon humanity as inherently sinful, but inherently perfect and striving to unfold that perfection from within. The Hindu knows that

we will have as many opportunities as needed to refine and evolve our nature—a thousand lives or more if needed. We don't have to think

that we only have a single chance, a one life in which everything must be accomplished and all desires must be fulfilled. Therefore, we are not in a hurry. We are patient. We exhibit more patience with circumstances than do those who believe in a one life, and we are more forgiving of ourselves when we fall short. Thus it is that Hinduism offers a great joy to its followers—a blessing of fearlessness in the face of death, an assurance of the continuation of consciousness after physical death, another assurance that each soul creates its own karma and that such karma is just and right, even when it seems that some people are less fortunate than others and that

THOMAST KEELY

gives the Hindu remarkable insight into the human condition and appreciation for all men in all stages of spiritual development.

Hinduism is so broad. Within it there is a place for the insane and a place for the saint. There is a place for the beggar and for those who support beggars. There is a place for the intelligent person and plenty of room for the fool. The beauty of Hinduism is that it does not demand of every soul perfection in this life, a necessary conclusion for those who believe in a single lifetime during which human perfection or grace must be achieved. Belief in reincarnation gives the Hindu an acceptance of every level of humanity. Some souls are simply older souls than others, but all are inherently the same, inherently immortal and of the nature of the Divine.

Hindu Views of the Divine

In Hinduism it is believed that the Gods are living, thinking, dynamic beings who live in a different world, in an inner world in the microcosm within this world in which there exists a greater macrocosm than this visible macrocosm. For the Hindu, surrender to the Divine Will that created and pervades and guides the universe is essential. The Hindu believes that these beings guide our experiences on Earth, actually consciously guide the evolutionary processes. Therefore, he worships these beings as greater beings than himself, and he maintains a subjective attitude toward them, wondering if he is attuned with these grand forces of the universe, if his personal will is in phase with what these great beings would have him do. This gives birth to a great culture, a great attitude, a great tolerance and kindness one to another. It gives rise to humility in the approach to life—not a weak or false humility, but a

Intensity: *(Clockwise) Devotees in North York, Ontario, pull the chariot of Goddess Durga around their temple on July 21, 2004; a sadhu sits in a circle of embers for three hours, part of a 12-year, daily penance, using fire in summer, standing in cold water in winter and in the rain during the rainy season; the elegant face of a Deity icon of Lord Siva Nataraja at Kauai's Hindu Monastery, site of the editorial offices of Hinduism Today*

BASIL SAGE

fate has unfairly given all the advantages to a few. All these things are bestowed on Hindus simply because they understand the doctrine of reincarnation. ¶Hinduism is a hopeful and comforting religion. Hope for a future life makes this life worthwhile, joyous, contented and happy, because the Hindu can live and deal with current problems, knowing that they are transitory problems, that they will not last forever; nor will they affect us forever. They are problems; we cannot deny that. But they are problems to be worked out with a positive attitude and a high energy and a helping hand from our Gods.

The World As Our Teacher: The Hindu also wants to improve conditions in the world, in the physical world. We do not look upon all that

happens to us as unreal. That is a misconception. It is real. Life is real. It is through life that we progress. Life is the means provided by the Primordial God for finding Reality. True,

HIMALAYAN ACADEMY

it is maya. But it is maya in the form of mind, in the form of form. Maya, or form, or mind, is created for a purpose, to help man evolve, not to bind him in illusion. The Hindu understands this. We want to help humanity, and simultaneously we know that we may well return in another physical body. So we are working not only for ourselves, but for our loved ones, not only now, but in the future as well. We are improving the world for future generations in which we will play a part. ¶Through our knowledge of reincarnation, we have a great love and understanding for every human being, for they have been our mothers, our fathers, our sons and daughters, our grandparents and companions in many past lives, or perhaps will be in a future incarnation. This expanded knowledge of the interrelatedness of humanity brings

strong and mature sense of the grand presence and purpose of life before which the head naturally bows.

There are said to be millions of Gods in the Hindu pantheon, though only a few major Deities are actually worshiped in the temples. That God may be worshiped as the Divine Father or a Sainted Mother or the King of kings is one of the blessings of Hinduism. It offers to each a personal and significant contact, and each Hindu will choose that aspect of the Deity which most appeals to his inner needs and sensibilities. That can be confusing to some, but not to the Hindu. Within his religion is monism and dualism, monotheism and polytheism, and a rich array of other theological views.

God in Hinduism is accepted as both transcendent and immanent, both beyond the mind and the very substratum of the mind. The ideal of the Hindu is to think of God always, every moment, and to be ever conscious of God's presence. This does not mean the transcendent God, the Absolute Lord. That is for the yogi to ponder in his contemplative discipline. That is for the well-perfected Hindu who has worshiped faithfully in the temples, studied deeply the scriptures and found his *satguru*.

For most Hindus, God means the Gods, one of the many personal devas and Mahadevas which prevail in our religion. This means a personal great soul which may never have known physical birth, a being which pervades the planet, pervades form with His mind and Being, and which guides evolution. Such a God is capable of offering protection and direction to the followers of Hinduism. The Hindu is supposed to think of God every minute of every day, to see God everywhere. Of course, most of us don't think of God even one minute a day. That's the reason that each Hindu is obliged to conduct or attend at least one religious service, one puja or ceremony, every day in his temple or home shrine. This turns his mind inward to God and the Gods.

Hinduism, Sanatana Dharma, is an Eastern religion, and the Eastern religions are very different from those of the West. For one thing, they are more introspective. Hinduism gave birth to Buddhism, for Buddha was born and died a good Hindu. And it gave birth to other religions of the East, to Taoism, to Jainism, to Sikhism and others.

with it a deepened appreciation, helping us to understand why it is that some people seem so close to us though we hardly know them and others are strangers or even enemies after years of close association. To the Hindu, everyone younger is his brother or sister. Everyone older is his mother or father, and he maintains a deep respect for others. We have this knowledge by having lived through many hundreds of lives on this planet and having been associated with many thousands of people. We know that in our current pattern in this life we often attract those to us whom we have been with in past lives. So we have a great joy and happiness in meeting them again and a deep knowledge of our relationships, our psychic relationships, with them in past lives. ¶The Hindu believes in the law of karma, the ability to earn one's rewards

as well as punishments. All this we can do ourselves with the help of our Gods and our personal relationship with our Ishta Devata, the individual God that we have chosen, or rather

that God who has chosen to love, guide and protect us through an incarnation. ¶In Hinduism there is no priest standing between the devotee and God. The priest is a servant of the God, just as is every other devotee. Even the satguru, the spiritual teacher, does not stand between the disciple and God, but seeks instead to strengthen the devotee's direct experiential relationship with the Divine. The Hindu thus finds a great joy in his relationship with God and the Gods. It is his relationship, and he alone is able to perpetuate it. No one can do this work for him or on his behalf. There is a great happiness there between the devotee and the God resident in the Hindu temple, which is the communication point with the God, as is the sacred home shrine.

Three Pillars: Temples, Philosophy, Preceptors

There are three distinct aspects of Hinduism: the temples, the philosophy and the *satguru*. It is very fortunate that in the last two decades Hindu temples have nearly circumferenced the world. There are temples in Europe, in North America, in South America, Australia, in Africa and throughout Southeast Asia. The Hindu temple and stone images in it work as a channel for the Deity, for the Gods, who hover over the stone image and, in their subtle etheric forms, change people's lives through changing the nerve currents within them through their darshana. People come to a sanctified temple and go away, and in that process they are slowly changed from the inside out. They have changed because their very life force has changed, their mind has been changed and their emotions have undergone a subtle transformation. The temples of Hinduism are magnificent in their immensity and in their ability to canalize the three worlds, the First World of physical, outer existence and the inner Second and Third Worlds.

Hindu temples are not centered around a priest or minister, though there may be a holy man associated with a temple whose advice is cautiously and quietly sought. There is no sermon, no mediator, no director to guide the worship of pilgrims. The temple is the home of the Deities, and each devotee goes according to his own timing and for his own particular needs. Some may go to weep and seek consolation in times of sorrow, while simultaneously others will be there to rejoice in their good fortune and to sing God's name in thanksgiving. Naturally, the sacraments of name-giving and marriage and so forth are closely associated with the temple. One has only to attend a Hindu temple during festival days to capture the great energy and vitality of this ancient religion.

In its second section, philosophy, Hinduism has influenced the

DINODIA

Joyousness: *(Clockwise) In Jejuri, as the palanquin carrying the images of Khandoba and Malshabai circumvent the temple, an exuberant crowd showers turmeric powder, coloring everyone in the yellow kinship of devotion. Modern, well-to-do Hindus on pilgrimage in Tirupati; women at the marketplace in Nepal*

The Joy of Pilgrimage: In our religious life, one of the most fulfilling aspects is pilgrimage. We have a joy in looking forward to a spiritual journey, and we experience a contentment while on our pilgrimage and later bask in the glowing aftermath of the pujas. It is like going to see a great friend, a devotee's most loved friend—the Ishta Devata. We travel to the far-off temple where this great friend is eminently present. At that particular temple, this personal God performs a certain function, offers a specific type of blessing to pilgrims who make the pilgrimage to that home. In this way, different temples become famous for answering certain types of prayers, such as requests for financial help, or prayers for the right mate in mar-

THOMAS KELLY

riage, prayers to be entrusted with the raising of high-souled children, or help in matters of yoga, or help in inspiring bhakti and love. ¶The Hindu does not have the feeling of having to take a vacation to "get away from it all." We don't lead a life of mental confusions, religious contradictions and the frustrations that result from modern hurried living. We lead a moderate life, a religious life. In living a moderate life, we then look at our pilgrimage as a special moment, a cherished time of setting ordinary concerns aside and giving full stage to our religious longings. It is a time to take problems and prayers to our personal God. ¶Unlike the proud "free thinkers" who deem themselves emancipated, above the religious life, we Hindus feel that receiving the darshana from the Gods and the help that comes therein invigorates our being and inspires us to be even more diligent in our spiritual life. Unlike the rationalists who feel

deep religious thinkers of all cultures through known history. There is not a single philosophy which can be labeled "Hinduism." Rather, it is a network of many philosophies, some seeming to impertinently contradict the validity of others, yet on deeper reflection are seen as integral aspects of a single, radiant mind flow. In the area of philosophy must be included the enormous array of scripture, hymns, mantras, devotional bhajana and philosophical texts which are certainly unequaled in the world.

In the natural order of things, temple worship precedes philosophy. It all starts with the temple, with this sacred house of the Deities, this sanctified site where the three worlds communicate, where the inner and outer mesh and merge. It is there that devotees change. They become more like the perfect beings that live in the temple, become the voice of the Deity, writing down what is taught them from the inside, and their writings, if they are faithful to the superconscious message of the God, become scripture and make up the philosophies of Hinduism. The philosophies then stand alone as the voice of the religion. They are taught in the universities, discussed among scholars, meditated upon by yogis and devout seekers. It is possible to be a good Hindu by only learning the philosophy and never going to the temple, or by simply going to the temple and never hearing of the deeper philosophies.

Hinduism has still another section within it, and that is the guru—the teacher, the illuminator, the spiritual preceptor. The guru is the remover of darkness. He is one who knows the philosophy, who knows the inner workings of the temple, and who in himself is the philosopher and the temple. The guru is he who can enliven the spirit within people. Like the temple and the philosophy, he stands alone, apart from the institutions of learning, apart from sites of pilgrimage. He is himself the source of knowledge, and he is himself the pilgrim's destination.

Should all the temples be destroyed, they would spring up again from the seeds of philosophy, or from the presence of a realized man. And if all the scriptures and philosophical treatises were burned, they would be written again from the same source. So Hinduism cannot be destroyed. It can never be destroyed. It exists as the spirit of religion within each being. Its three aspects, the temple, the philosophy and the *satguru*, individually proficient, taken together make Hinduism the most vital and abundant religion in the world.

confident that within themselves lie all the resources to meet all needs, and that praying to Gods for help is a pathetic exercise in futility, the Hindu wisely submits to the Divine and thus avoids the abyss of disbelief. ¶All in life that one would want to "get away from" the Hindu takes with him on a pilgrimage to the temple, to the feet of his personal God, to the inner-plane being or Mahadeva, who needs no physical body with which to communicate with people—to the God who has a nerve system so sensitive and well developed that as it hovers over the stone image, which looks similar to how the Deity would look on the inner planes, this being of light can communicate with the pilgrims who visit the temple. This being of light, this Mahadeva, can and does absorb all of the dross the devotees have to offer, and

gives back blessings which bring happiness and release to them. Thus, the pilgrimage is not travel in the ordinary sense of travel, but rather going to see a personal friend, one who is nearest and dearest, but does not live in a physical body. ¶The Hindu has another great joy—the certainty of liberation. Even in difficult times, we are solaced in the knowledge of our religion which tells us that no soul that ever existed or ever will exist in future extrapolations of time and space will ever fail to attain liberation. The Hindu knows that all souls will one day merge into God; and he knows that God, who created all souls, slowly guides our maturing into His likeness, brings us back to Himself, which is not separate from ourselves. The Hindu, through striving and personal development in this life on this planet, knows that liberation into God is the final goal. This knowing and this belief release us from any ego, from any superiority by which one person

Hinduism's Fathomless Diversity

Hinduism has a grand diversity among its many sects. That diversity is itself a strength, showing how broad and encompassing Hinduism is. It does not seek to have all devotees believe exactly alike. In fact, it has no central authority, no single organized institution which could ever proclaim or enforce such sameness. There is an immense inner unity, but the real strength and wisdom of Hinduism is its diversity, its variety. There are so many sects within Hinduism that you could spend a lifetime studying them and never begin to assess them all. More is there than any single human being could assimilate in a single lifetime. Hinduism, therefore, has the magnetism to draw us back into its immensity life after life. Each sect may be said to be a full religion in its own right, with all the increments of faith, with no necessary part missing. Therefore, each sect works for the individuals within it completely, and each tolerates all the other sects. It does not totally divorce itself from the other sects, denying their beliefs, but simply separates to stress or expound a limited area of the vast philosophy, apart from all others, to be understood by the limited faculties of man.

These various sects and divisions within Hinduism all spring from a one source. Most Hindus believe in the transcendental God as well as the personal Lord or God, and yet there is within the boundaries of the faith room for the non-believer, for the atheist or for the agnostic who is assessing and developing his beliefs. This brings another unique asset to our religion—the absence of heresy. There is no such thing as a heretic in Hinduism, for there is no single right perspective or belief. Doctrine and *sadhana* are not considered absolutes, but the means to an absolute end, and they can be tailored to individual needs and natures. My *satguru* would say that different prescriptions are required for different ailments.

● ●
Devotion: (*Clockwise*) *Devotees observe evening fire offerings to the Ganga River at the Kumbha Mela in Haridwar,* 1998; *the Kandaswamy Temple in Kuala Lumpur; a boy, representing Lord Ganesha, is ceremoniously bathed during the Holy Waters Festival at Toronto's Varasiththi Vinaayagar Temple*

DEV RAJ AGARWAL.

considers himself or herself as especially meriting God's grace while others are lost. For the Hindu, there is an assurance that all souls will eventually enjoy liberation, and that includes ourselves and all of our friends and family. We need never fear otherwise.

The Joy of Mystisicm: Then there is the joy of the mysticism of Hinduism. It is the world's most magical religion, offering worlds within worlds of esoteric discovery and perception. The inner worlds are what Hindu mystics tell of in the greatest richness and freedom of expression that exists on the planet. Mysticism in Hinduism is more out-front than in all the other religions of the world. As a result, it is enjoyed by more of the people in our religion. Mysticism is discussed more broadly and not limited to a few great

souls or a handful of pandits. The mysticism of Hinduism is for all the people; yet, too, in its esoteric aspect it is protected at its core and kept sacred by being kept secret. How grand is the Hindu mystical tradition, with its *sadhanas* and yogas, with its wealth of understanding of the etheric bodies, of the nadis and the chakras, of the aura and the pranas, of the various states of consciousness and levels of existence, and so much more. No other religion on the Earth can ever begin to equal Hinduism's mystical teachings; all that wealth is the rightful inheritance of each Hindu. ¶The Hindu enjoys all the facets of life as transmuted into a religious expression in art. The Hindu's art is a religious art—drawing, painting and sculpture of the Gods, the devas, and the saints of our religion. The music is devotional and depicts the tones of the higher chakras, echoes the voices of the Gods; and the dance emulates the movements of the Gods. We are

ZUMA PRESS, CHARLA JONES

In Hinduism there is no person or spiritual authority who stands between man and God. In fact, Hinduism teaches just the opposite. The priests in the temples are the servants of the Deity, the helper, the keeper of the Gods' house. He prepares and purifies the atmosphere of the temple, but he does not intervene between the devotee and his God—whichever of the many Gods within our religion that he may be worshiping. Without a mediator, responsibility is placed fully upon the individual. There is no one to intercede on his behalf. He is responsible for his actions, for his thoughts, for his emotions, for his relationship with his God. He must work out his beliefs from the inside, without undue dependence upon external influences. Of course, there is much help, as much as may be needed, from those who have previously gone through what he is now going through. It is not enough that he adopts an authorized dogma. He must study and bring the teachings to life from within himself.

Within the philosophy, each philosopher proclaims that God can be found within man if man practices the proper precepts of yoga and delves within himself through his kundalini force. The guru himself teaches the awakening of that force and how God can be realized in His transcendental as well as His personal aspect within the sphere of one's own personal experience in this very lifetime if he but pursues the path and is obedient.

Hinduism is unique because God and man, mind and God, instinctive mind, intellectual mind and superconscious mind, can merge as one, according to the evolution of the individual. Each one, according to his own self-created karma, has his own fulfillment. Those in the first stages of evolution, whose interests and experiences are basically instinctive, who possess little intellect or mental prowess, are guided by their emotions and impulses, are generally fearful. They have a personal experience of the Deity in the temple, but it is generally a fearful experience. They are afraid of God. Alongside of them during a puja is a great rishi who has had many hundreds of lives on this planet. He has his own personal experience of God, but it is an experience of love, of oneness and of union. There they are, side by side. Each experience of God is as real to one as to the other. There is no one in-between, no arbitrator of the experience to compel the one to see God exactly as the other one does.

never far away from sights, sounds and symbols of our religion. A mountaintop represents Lord Siva; a hill represents Lord Murugan, Karttikeya; and sugar cane fields represent Lord Ganesha. Everything that one sees on the planet represents something religious. Art is not merely for egotistical and existential self-expression, but for spiritual expression, done consciously in service to the Divine. That is why one seldom sees or even knows the name of the artist of the great Hindu artistic creations. The artist is not creating in order to become famous or rich. He is surrendering his talents, serving his Gods and his religion through his art, and his art takes on a certain sacredness. ¶One great joy that the Hindu has is the appreciation for all other religions. Hinduism is theocentric, that means God-centric, whereas most other religions are prophet-centric, revolving around the personality of some living person

or some person who once lived in history and interpreted religion to his culture in his time. Hinduism has no founder. It was never found-

DAVID TROPF

ed. It has neither a beginning nor an end. It is coexistent with man himself. That is why it is called the Sanatana Dharma, the Eternal Path. It is not one man's teaching or interpretation. It is not limited to a single facet of religion, but consists of the entire spectrum, seen in its various components as if through a prism. It does not say that this religion is wrong and this one right. It sees God everywhere, manifesting all the great religions. The Hindu can appreciate Buddha without becoming a Buddhist. He can understand Jesus without becoming a Christian. Therefore, the joys of all the religions of the world become the joys of the Hindu. ¶But as Hindus, we must first think of the joys and happiness within our own religion. Consider our blessings. Come closer to the Gods of our religion. The many Gods are in the Western world now and have circumferenced the planet with their shakti of radiant rays that

Within Hinduism Is a Place for Everyone

Hinduism is as broad as humanity is, as diverse as people are diverse. It is for the rich and the poor, for the mystic and the materialist. It is for the sage and the fool. None is excluded. In a Hindu temple you can find every variety of humanity. The man of accumulated wealth is there, supporting the institutions that have grown up around the temple, seeking to spend his abundance wisely and for its best purpose so that good merit may be earned for his next life. The pauper is there, begging in hopes that perhaps he will eat tomorrow and the God will inspire some devotee to give him a coin or two. So, a Hindu temple is a reflection of life, set in the midst of the life of the community. It is not making an effort to be better than the life of the village, only to serve that life and direct it to its next stage of evolution. The same Hindu mind which can consume within it all the religions of the world can and does consume within it all of the peoples of the world who are drawn to the temple by the shakti, the power, of the temple. Such is the great, embracing compassion of our religion.

The greatness of Hinduism cannot be compared with other religions. There is no basis for comparison. Hinduism, the Eternal Way or Sanatana Dharma, has no beginning, therefore will certainly have no end. It was never created, and therefore it cannot be destroyed. It is a God-centric religion. The center of it is God. All of the other religions are prophet-centric. The center of those religions is a great saint or sage, a prophet, a messenger or messiah, some God-Realized person who has lived on Earth and died. Perhaps he was born to create that particular sect, that particular religion,

People: *(Clockwise) Holy men at the Allahabad Kumbha Mela in 2001 parade to the bathing ghats, carrying elaborate dandas, symbols of spiritual authority; flower vendors in Kalikut, ready at dawn with garlands of marigolds, prepared as offerings to the Gods. During Raksha Bhandan a girl ties a bracelet on her brother's wrist, betokening her love and prayers for his welfare, and his commitment to protect her. Pilgrims arrive at Tirupati Temple wearing yellow as a sign of austerity and sacrifice.*

PRADIP GUPTA/DINODIA

penetrate with spiritual power, bringing harmony and culture, balancing out the dharma of the planet. ¶Hinduism is such a great religion. All practicing Hindus are very proud of their religion. Unfortunately, these days too many born into the religion are not all that proud to be Hindus, but this is slowly changing. Hindus are now welcoming into their religion others who are, of their own volition, adopting or converting into the Sanatana Dharma. They are proud enough of their faith to want others to share its wisdom, its mysticism, its scriptures, its broadmindedness, its magnificent temples and its final conclusions for all mankind. To all Hindus, who today are found in every country on the Earth, I say: Courage! Courage! Courage! Have the courage to know beyond a doubt that Hinduism is the greatest religion in the world. We must be proud of this.

Hinduism Cannot Be Destroyed: It is false to think that one has to be born a Hindu in order to be a Hindu. That is a concept postulated by certain caste-based Hindu lineages and reinforced by the Christians in their effort to hinder the growth of our religion, to deprive it of new life, to hold it down while they in turn try to convert Hindus en masse to their religion. Swami Vivekananda (1863–1902), a Hindu monk and missionary who wrote extensively on the Hindu Dharma, when confronted by this same issue in the West would explain how Hindus who have been converted by force should not be denied an opportunity of returning to their ancestral religion. As for the case of those not born into Hinduism who might be interested to join it, he simply said, "Why, born aliens have been converted in the past by crowds, and the process is still going on." Dr. S. Radhakrishnan (1888–1975), the distinguished Hindu philosopher who became

THOMAS KELLY

needed by the people of a certain part of the world at a certain time in history. The Hindus acknowledge this and recognize all of the world's religious leaders as great prophets, as great souls, as great incarnations, perhaps, of the Gods, or as great beings who have through their realization and inward practices incarnated themselves into, or transformed themselves into, eminent religious leaders and attracted devotees to them to give forth the precepts of life all over again and thus guide a tribe or a nation or a race into a better way of life.

The Hindu mind can encompass this, appreciate it, for it is firmly settled in a God-centric religion. The center of Hinduism is the Absolute, the timeless, formless, spaceless God who manifests as Pure Consciousness and as the most perfect form conceivable, the Primal Soul. He radiates out from that form as a myriad of Gods and Goddesses who inhabit the temples and bless the people, inspire the scriptures, inspire the spiritual leaders and uplift humanity in general. It is a one God in many forms. We recently heard a sannyasini at the Ganesha Temple in New York describe this in a most wonderful and profound way, "Siva is the fire. Shakti is the heat of that fire. Ganesha is the red color of that fire. Murugan is the light of that fire."

There are nearly a billion Hindus in the world today. That's roughly four times the population of the entire United States. Every sixth person on the planet is a Hindu. Hinduism attends to the needs of each one. It is the only religion that has such breadth and depth. Hinduism contains the Deities and the sanctified temples, the esoteric knowledge of inner states of consciousness, yoga and the disciplines of meditation. It possesses a gentle compassion and a genuine tolerance and appreciation for other religions. It remains undogmatic and open to inquiry. It believes in a just world in which every soul is guided by karma to the ultimate goal of Self Realization, leading to moksha, freedom from rebirth. It rests content in the knowledge of the divine origin of the soul, its passage through one life and another until maturity has been reached. It offers guidance to all who take refuge in it, from the nonbeliever to the most evolved maharishi. It cherishes the largest storehouse of scripture and philosophy on the earth, and the oldest. It is endowed with a tradition of saints and sages, of realized men and women, unrivaled on the earth. It is the sum of these, and more, which makes me boldly declare that Hinduism is the greatest religion in the world.

the second president of India, confirms this view in writing, "In a sense, Hinduism may be regarded as the first example in the world of a missionary religion. Only its missionary spirit is different from that associated with the proselytizing creeds. It did not regard as its mission to convert humanity to one opinion. For what counts is conduct and not belief. The ancient practice of *vratyastoma*, described fully in the *Tandya Brahmana*, shows that not only individuals but whole tribes were absorbed into Hinduism." ¶During the era of India's domination by alien religions, when Hinduism was scheduled to be destroyed, the attack was to be carried out in three ways. The first strategy was to convince the women to abandon their age-old *stri* dharma—of maintaining the home, its purity and ways of worship—thus draw-

ing them away from the household in order to receive a so-called "higher education" or to teach in alien religious schools, thus denying future generations the mother's religious coun-

sel and grounding in the dharma. The second strategy was to overtly break down the various castes of temple priests by enticing them to accept other, often higher paying, occupations, thus leaving the temples unattended. ¶The third strategy was to convince Hindus that they had inherited a crude and outdated religion. This last attack was accomplished mainly through ridicule, by ridiculing every aspect of the religion that could possibly be ridiculed. For example, those who slandered Hinduism claimed it has no sacraments. Why, Hinduism has more sacraments, more sacred rites and ceremonies for its members, than perhaps any other religion in the world. These sacraments include the *namakarana samskara*, name-

Where Hindus Live

While India is home to 94 percent of the world's nearly one billion Hindus, nearly 57 million are scattered widely across the globe. This map shows larger communities, with smaller ones listed to the right, and world populations below.

WORLD POPULATION 2002

Hindus	1 billion
Catholics	1.4 billion
Muslims	1.3 billion
Nonbelievers	900 million
Protestants	600 million
Confucian	400 million
Buddhists	360 million
Tribals	100 million
Taoists	50 million
Shintoists	30 million
Jews	18 million
Sikhs	16 million
Jains	6 million
Zoroastrians	125,000
Other Faiths	77 million
Total	**6.25 billion**

Neth 18
England: 1,300,0
Canada: 470,000
Germany: 100,000
France: 150,000
Belgium: 6,000
Austria: 6,100
Spain: 12,500
United States: 2,000,000
Portugal: 8,000
Italy: 25,000
Bahrain: 24,000
Kauai Aadheenam: 30
Martinique and Guadaloupe 50,000
Egypt: 6,000
Gulf States: 310,000
Ethiopia: 3,000
Hawaii: 700
Jamaica 25,000
Trinidad: 320,000
Guyana: 450,000
Suriname: 200,000
French Guyana: 5,000
Nigeria: 30,000
Brazil: 25,000
Uganda: 20,000
Zambia: 25,00
Malavi: 3,00
Botswana: 7,00
Zimbabwe: 6,
Argentina 4,000

---

giving sacrament; *annaprashana*, first feeding; *karnavedha*, ear-piercing; *vidyarambha*, commencement of learning; *vivaha*, marriage; and many others. ¶Though India was politically dominated for generations by adherents of alien faiths, and though every attempt was made to discourage, weaken and crush the native religion, the carefully calculated, systematic assault failed to destroy Hinduism. Hinduism cannot be destroyed. It is the venerable eternal religion, the Sanatana Dharma. But it was an effective campaign that has left in its wake deep *samskaric* patterns, deep subconscious impressions, which still persist in the minds of the Indian people. It is going to be difficult to completely eradicate these impressions, but with the help of all the millions of Hindus throughout the world, in adhering to and extolling the benefits and joys of Hinduism and the gifts which it

holds for mankind, this is possible and feasible, within the range of accomplishment, perhaps within this very generation.

Bringing in Ardent Seekers: Hindus should freely welcome sincere devotees into

their religion, not those who already have a firm religion and are content, but those who are seeking, who believe, as millions in the West already believe, in the laws of karma and reincarnation and the existence of the ever-present God that permeates this planet and the universe. Hindus should freely embrace those who believe in the Gods and all we have been speaking about earlier, for whom other religious avenues have proved empty and fruitless. There are certain matured souls for whom the Sanatana Dharma can be the only true religion, who have no other religion and who will seek and seek until they come upon its profound truths, perhaps in an old scrip-

Youth: *(Left) Hindu school girls in Bangalore; right, boys attending Rameshbhai Oza's Hindu school at Sandipani Vidyaniketan near Porbandar, Gujarat*

SUNDER RAJ

Norway: 11,000
~~eden~~: 8,000
Denmark: 15,000
Switzerland: 60,000
Serbia & Montenegro: 8,000
Russia: 15,000
Nepal: 21,000,000
Japan: 6,000
Bhutan: 300,000
Bangladesh: 12,100,000
Myanmar: 291,000
China: 93,000
Pakistan 1,200,000
India 895,000,000
Vietnam: 5,500
Thailand: 7,000
Philippines: 1,100
Indonesia: 5,900,000
Afghanistan 130,000
Sri Lanka 2,200,000
S. Yemen: 7,000
Somalia: 6,000
Kenya: 75,000
Tanzania: 70,000
Malaysia 1,290,000
Singapore 171,000
Fiji: 600,000
Mauritius: 700,000
Reunion: 290,000
Madagascar: 1,100
South Africa: 1,430,000
Australia: 75,000
New Zealand 47,000

Algeria	600	Jordan	1,000
Barbados	100	Lebanon	100
Brunei	500	Liberia	500
Cameroon	60	Laos	600
C. African Rep.	20	Libya	500
Czech Republic and Slovakia	150	Mexico	50
Chad	20	Morocco	60
Chile	20	Mozambique	600
China	170	Panama	600
Congo	100	Poland	100
Colombia	60	Qatar	500
Cuba	100	Senegal	100
Ecuador	600	Seychelles	600
Finland	100	Sierra Leone	500
Gabon	100	South Korea	60
Ghana	600	Sudan	500
Guinea	50	Syria	100
Hungary	50	Tunisia	100
Iceland	7	Turkey	100
Ireland	20	Upper Volta	100
Israel	200	Yemen, North	100
Ivory Coast	1,000	Zaire (Congo)	500
Zambia	600		

ture, or in a temple sanctum during puja or in the eyes of an awakened siddha yogi. These souls we must help. We must teach them of our religion and allow them to fully accept or reject it, to accept it because they know it, or to reject it because they know it and are not ready to meet Maha Ganapati and humbly sit at the feet of this most profound Lord. ¶There are many lost souls on the planet today who die in the physical world—lose their physical body—wander on the astral plane a short time and are caught up immediately in another womb. They have no knowledge of other states of existence or of the workings of reincarnation. They have no time for the bliss of these in-between, astral states. They have no time for assessing their last life and preparing for the next, which they could then enter with new knowledge, no time for inner attunement

with the Gods in the inner worlds between death and birth. Instead, they are caught in a constant cycle of flesh, making flesh and living in flesh, with the soul being immersed in ignorance and the darkness of the conscious-

ness of flesh. Hinduism eradicates this cycle by offering knowledge of the states between life and death and then life again. It creates deep impressions within the mind of these individuals, which then bring them out of this syndrome so that they can enjoy months, years, in fact, of education and knowledge in the inner planes of consciousness between births, so that they can come back into a physical body a more awakened soul than when they left their last physical sheath at death. ¶We must not be reluctant to welcome these sincere Hindu souls and to assist them in finding the answers they seek and do not find elsewhere. It is our dharma to help them. Hinduism has always welcomed adoptives and converts. Bring in new people to the religion. Teach them. Help them. Counsel them. Proceed with confidence. Have courage, courage, courage.

SAT SAHITYA PRAKASHAN TRUST

CHAPTER 2

Hinduism's Four Denominations

Hinduism Is A Splendrous Lotus with Four Superb Petals

Saivism

Saivite Hindus worship the Supreme God as Siva, the Compassionate One. Saivites esteem self discipline and philosophy and follow a *satguru*. They worship in the temple and practice yoga, striving to be one with Siva within.

Shaktism

Shaktas worship the Supreme as the Divine Mother, Shakti or Devi. She has many forms. Some are gentle, some are fierce. Shaktas use chants, real magic, holy diagrams, yoga and rituals to call forth cosmic forces and awaken the great kundalini power within the spine.

Vaishnavism

Vaishnavites worship the Supreme as Lord Vishnu and His incarnations, especially Krishna and Rama. Vaishnavites are mainly dualistic. They are deeply devotional. Their religion is rich in saints, temples and scriptures.

Smartism

Smartas worship the Supreme in one of six forms: Ganesha, Siva, Sakti, Vishnu, Surya and Skanda. Because they accept all the major Hindu Gods, they are known as liberal or nonsectarian. They follow a philosophical, meditative path, emphasizing man's oneness with God through understanding.

or over 200 years, Western scholars have struggled to understand Hinduism, a faith whose followers seemed (to outsiders) to arbitrarily worship any one of a dozen Gods as the Supreme, a religion vastly diverse in its beliefs, practices and ways of worship. Some Indologists labeled the Hinduism they encountered polytheistic; others even coined new terms, like *henotheism,* to describe this baffling array of spiritual traditions. Few, however, have realized, and fewer still have written, that India's Sanatana Dharma, or "eternal faith," known today as Hinduism and comprising nearly a billion followers, is a family of religions with four principal denominations—Saivism, Shaktism, Vaishnavism and Smartism. This single perception is essential for understanding Hinduisim and explaining it accurately to others. Contrary to prevailing misconceptions, Hindus all worship a one Supreme Being, though by different names. For Vaishnavites, Lord Vishnu is God. For Saivites, God is Siva. For Shaktas, Goddess Shakti is supreme. For Smartas, liberal Hindus, the choice of Deity is left to the devotee. Each has a multitude of **guru** lineages, religious leaders, priesthoods, sacred literature, monastic communities, schools, pilgrimage centers and tens of thousands of temples. They possess a wealth of art and architecture, philosophy and scholarship. These four sects hold such divergent beliefs that each is a complete and independent religion. Yet, they share a vast heritage of culture and belief—karma, dharma, reincarnation, all-pervasive Divinity, temple worship, sacraments, manifold Deities, the guru-disciple tradition and the *Vedas* as scriptural authority. In this eight-page Insight, drawn from Satguru Sivaya Subramuniyaswami's *Dancing with Siva,* we offer a synopsis of these four denominations, followed by a point-by-point comparison.

Each of Hinduism's philosophies, schools and lineages shares a common purpose: to further the soul's unfoldment to its divine destiny. Nowhere is this process better represented than in the growth of the renowned lotus, which, seeking the sun, arises from the mud to become a magnificent flower. Its blossom is a promise of purity and perfection.

What Is the Deeply Mystical Saiva Sect?

Saivism is the world's oldest religion. Worshiping God Siva, the compassionate One, it stresses potent disciplines, high philosophy, the guru's centrality and bhakti-raja-siddha yoga leading to oneness with Siva within. Aum.

ART BY S. RAJAM

Seated on Nandi, his bull mount, the perfect devotee, Lord Siva holds japa beads and the trident, symbol of love-wisdom-action, and offers blessings of protection and fearlessness. Mount Kailas, His sacred Himalayan abode, represents the pinnacle of consciousness.

AIVISM IS ANCIENT, TRULY AGELESS, FOR it has no beginning. It is the precursor of the many-faceted religion now termed Hinduism. Scholars trace the roots of Siva worship back more than 8,000 years to the advanced Indus Valley civilization. But sacred writings tell us there never was a time when Saivism did not exist. Modern history records six main schools: Saiva Siddhanta, Pashupatism, Kashmir Saivism, Vira Saivism, Siddha Siddhanta and Siva Advaita. Saivism's grandeur and beauty are found in a practical culture, an enlightened view of man's place in the universe and a profound system of temple mysticism and siddha yoga. It provides knowledge of man's evolution from God and back to God, of the soul's unfoldment and awakening guided by enlightened sages. Like all the sects, its majority are devout families, headed by hundreds of orders of swamis and sadhus who follow the fiery, world-renouncing path to *moksha*. The *Vedas* state, "By knowing Siva, the Auspicious One who is hidden in all things, exceedingly fine, like film arising from clarified butter, the One embracer of the universe—by realizing God, one is released from all fetters." Aum Namah Sivaya.

What Is the Magic and Power Of Shaktism?

Shaktism reveres the Supreme as the Divine Mother, Shakti or Devi, in Her many forms, both gentle and fierce. Shaktas use mantra, tantra, yantra, yoga and puja to invoke cosmic forces and awaken the kundalini power. Aum.

Shakti, depicted in Her green form, radiates beauty, energy, compassion and protection for followers. Wearing the *tilaka* of the Shakta sect on Her forehead, She blesses devotees, who shower rosewater, hold an umbrella and prostrate at Her feet.

WHILE WORSHIP OF THE DIVINE MOTHER extends beyond the pale of history, Shakta Hinduism arose as an organized sect in India around the fifth century. Today it has four expressions—devotional, folk-shamanic, yogic and universalist—all invoking the fierce power of Kali or Durga, or the benign grace of Parvati or Ambika. Shakta devotionalists use puja rites, especially to the Shri Chakra yantra, to establish intimacy with the Goddess. Shamanic Shaktism employs magic, trance mediumship, firewalking and animal sacrifice for healing, fertility, prophecy and power. Shakta yogis seek to awaken the sleeping Goddess Kundalini and unite her with Siva in the *sahasrara* chakra. Shakta universalists follow the reformed Vedantic tradition exemplified by Sri Ramakrishna. "Left-hand" tantric rites transcend traditional ethical codes. Shaktism is chiefly advaitic, defining the soul's destiny as complete identity with the Unmanifest, Siva. Central scriptures are the *Vedas, Shakta Agamas* and *Puranas*. The *Devi Gita* extols, "We bow down to the universal soul of all. Above and below and in all four directions, Mother of the universe, we bow." Aum Chandikayai Namah.

What Is the Devotional Vaishnava Sect?

Vaishnavism is an ancient Hindu sect centering on the worship of Lord Vishnu and His incarnations, especially Krishna and Rama. Largely dualistic, profoundly devotional, it is rich in saints, temples and scriptures. Aum.

Vishnu is the infinite ocean from which the world emerges. He stands on waves, surrounded by the many-headed Seshanaga, who represents agelessness and is regarded as an extension of divine energy and an incarnation of Balarama, Lord Krishna's brother.

THE WORSHIP OF VISHNU, MEANING "PERvader," dates back to Vedic times. The Pancharatra and Bhagavata sects were popular prior to 300 bce. Today's five Vaishnava schools emerged in the middle ages, founded by Ramanuja, Madhva, Nimbarka, Vallabha and Chaitanya. Vaishnavism stresses *prapatti,* single-pointed surrender to Vishnu, or His ten or more incarnations, called avataras. Japa is a key devotional sannyasin, as is ecstatic chanting and dancing, called *kirtana.* Temple worship and festivals are elaborately observed. Philosophically, Vaishnavism ranges from Madhva's pure dualism to Ramanuja's qualified nondualism to Vallabha's nearly monistic vision. God and soul are everlastingly distinct. The soul's destiny, through God's grace, is to eternally worship and enjoy Him. While generally nonascetic, advocating bhakti as the highest path, Vaishnavism has a strong monastic community. Central scriptures are the *Vedas, Vaishnava Agamas, Itihasas and Puranas.* The *Bhagavad Gita* states, "On those who meditate on Me and worship with undivided heart, I confer attainment of what they have not, and preserve what they have." Aum Namo Narayanaya.

What Is the Universalistic Smarta Sect?

Smartism is an ancient brahminical tradition reformed by Shankara in the ninth century. Worshiping six forms of God, this liberal Hindu path is monistic, nonsectarian, meditative and philosophical. Aum.

Adi Shankara lived from 788 to 820 CE, a mere 32 years, yet he gave Hinduism a new liberal denomination—Smartism. Here, wearing sacred marks, he holds his writings and is flanked by the six Deities of the Smarta altar: Surya the Sun, Siva, Shakti, Vishnu, Kumaran and Ganesha.

MARTA MEANS A FOLLOWER OF CLASSICAL smriti, particularly the *Dharma Shastras, Puranas and Itihasas*. Smartas revere the *Vedas* and honor the *Agamas*. Today this faith is synonymous with the teachings of Adi Shankara, the monk-philosopher known as Shanmata Sthapanacharya, "founder of the six-sect system." He campaigned India-wide to consolidate the Hindu faiths of his time under the banner of Advaita Vedanta. To unify the worship, he popularized the ancient Smarta five-Deity altar—Ganapati, Surya, Vishnu, Siva and Shakti—and added Kumara. From these,

devotees may choose their "preferred Deity," or Ishta Devata. Each God is but a reflection of the one Saguna Brahman. Shankara organized hundreds of monasteries into a ten-order, *dashanami* system, which now has five pontifical centers. He wrote profuse commentaries on the *Upanishads, Brahma Sutras* and *Bhagavad Gita*. Shankara proclaimed, "It is the one Reality which appears to our ignorance as a manifold universe of names and forms and changes. Like the gold of which many ornaments are made, it remains in itself unchanged. Such is Brahman, and That art Thou." Aum Namah Sivaya.

Comparing the Four Major Denominations

S JUST SEEN, THE SPECTRUM of Hindu religiousness is found within four major sects or denominations: Saivism, Shaktism, Vaishnavism and Smartism. Among these four streams, there are certainly more similarities than differences. All four believe in karma and reincarnation and in a Supreme Being who both is form and pervades form, who creates, sustains and destroys the universe only to create it again in unending cycles. They strongly declare the validity and importance of temple worship, the three worlds of existence and the myriad Gods and *devas* residing in them. They concur that there is no intrinsic evil, that the cosmos is created out of God and is permeated by Him. They each believe in maya (though their definitions differ somewhat), and in the liberation of the soul from rebirth, called moksha, as the goal of human existence. They believe in dharma and in ahimsa, non-injury, and in the need for a *satguru* to lead the soul toward Self Realization. They wear the sacred marks, *tilaka*, on their foreheads as sacred symbols, though each wears a distinct mark. Finally, they prefer cremation of the body upon death, believing that the soul will inhabit another body in the next life. While Hinduism has many sacred scriptures, all sects ascribe the highest authority to the *Vedas* and *Agamas,* though their *Agamas* differ somewhat. Here, now, is a brief comparison of these four denominations.

On the Personal God/Goddess

SAIVISM: Personal God and temple Deity is Siva, neither male nor female. Lords Ganesha and Karttikeya are also worshiped.

SHAKTISM: Personal Goddess and temple Deity is Shri Devi or Shakti, female, worshiped as Rajarajeshvari, Parvati, Lakshmi, Sarasvati, Kali, Amman, etc. —the Divine Mother.

VAISHNAVISM: Personal God and temple Deity is Vishnu, male. His incarnations as Rama and Krishna are also worshiped, as well as His divine consort, Radharani.

SMARTISM: Personal God and temple Deity is Ishvara, male or female, worshiped as Vishnu, Siva, Shakti, Ganesha and Surya or another Deity of devotee's choice, e.g., Kumara or Krishna.

On the Nature of Shakti

SAIVISM: Shakti is God Siva's inseparable power and manifest will, energy or mind.

SHAKTISM: Shakti is an active, immanent Being, separate from a quiescent and remote Siva.

VAISHNAVISM: No special importance is given to Shakti. However, there are parallels wherein the divine consorts are conceived as the inseparable powers of Vishnu and His incarnations: e.g., Krishna's Radharani and Rama's Sita.

SMARTISM: Shakti is a divine form of Ishvara. It is God's manifesting power.

On the Nature of Personal God

SAIVISM: God Siva is pure love and compassion, immanent and transcendent, pleased by our purity and *sadhana*.

S RAJAM

SHAKTISM: The Goddess Shakti is both compassionate and terrifying, pleasing and wrathful, assuaged by sacrifice and submission.

VAISHNAVISM: God Vishnu is loving and beautiful, the object of man's devotion, pleased by our service and surrender.

SMARTISM: Ishvara appears as a human-like Deity according to devotees' loving worship, which is sometimes considered a rudimentary, self-purifying practice.

On the Doctrine of Avatara

SAIVISM: There are no divine earthly incarnations of the Supreme Being.

SHAKTISM: The Divine Mother does incarnate in this world.

VAISHNAVISM: Vishnu has ten or more incarnations.

SMARTISM: All Deities may assume earthly incarnations.

On the Soul and God

SAIVISM: God Siva is one with the soul. The soul must realize this advaitic (monistic) Truth by God Siva's grace.

SHAKTISM: The Divine Mother, Shakti, is mediatrix, bestowing advaitic moksha on those who worship Her.

VAISHNAVISM: God and soul are eternally distinct. Through Lord Vishnu's grace, the soul's destiny is to worship and enjoy God.

SMARTISM: Ishvara and man are in reality Absolute Brahman. Within maya, the soul and Ishvara appear as two. *Jnana* (wisdom) dispels the illusion.

Spiritual Practice

SAIVISM: With bhakti as a base, emphasis is placed on *tapas* (austerity) and yoga. Ascetic.

SHAKTISM: Emphasis is on bhakti and tantra, sometimes occult, practices. Ascetic-occult.

VAISHNAVISM: Emphasis is on supreme bhakti or surrender, called *prapatti*. Generally devotional and nonascetic.

SMARTISM: Preparatory *sadhanas* are bhakti, karma, raja yoga. The highest path is through knowledge, leading to *jnana*.

Major Scriptures

SAIVISM: *Vedas*, *Saiva Agamas* and *Saiva Puranas*.

SHAKTISM: *Vedas, Shakta Agamas (Tantras)* and *Puranas*.

VAISHNAVISM: *Vedas, Vaishnava Agamas, Puranas* and the *Itihasas (Ramayana and Mahabharata,* especially the *Bhagavad Gita)*.

SMARTISM: *Vedas, Agamas* and classical *smriti—Puranas, Itihasas,* especially the *Bhagavad Gita,* etc.

Regions of Influence

SAIVISM: Strongest in South and North India, Nepal and Sri Lanka.

SHAKTISM: Most prominent in Northeast India, especially Bengal and Assam.

VAISHNAVISM: Strong throughout India, North and South.

SMARTISM: Most prominent in North and South India.

Paths of Attainment

SAIVISM: The path for Saivites is divided into four progressive stages of belief and practice called *charya, kriya, yoga* and *jnana*. The soul evolves through karma and reincarnation from the instinctive-intellectual sphere into virtuous and moral living, then into temple worship and devotion, followed by internalized worship, or yoga, and its meditative disciplines. Union with God Siva comes through the grace of the *satguru* and culminates in the soul's maturity in the state of *jnana,* or wisdom. Saivism values both bhakti and yoga, devotional and contemplative *sadhanas,* or disciplines.

SHAKTISM: The spiritual practices in Shaktism are similar to those in Saivism, though there is more emphasis in Saktism on God's Power as opposed to Being, on mantras and yantras, and on embracing apparent opposites: male-female, absolute-relative, pleasure-pain, cause-effect, mind-body. Certain sects within Shaktism undertake "left-hand" tantric rites, consciously using the world of form to transmute and eventually transcend that world. The "left-hand" approach is somewhat occult in nature; it is considered a path for the few, not the many. The "right-hand" path is more conservative in nature.

VAISHNAVISM: Most Vaishnavites believe that religion is the performance of bhakti *sadhanas,* devotional disciplines, and that man can communicate with and receive the grace of the Gods and Goddesses through the darshan (sight) of their icons. The paths of karma yoga and *jnana* yoga lead to bhakti yoga. Among the foremost practices of Vaishnavites is chanting the holy names of the Avataras, Vishnu's incarnations, especially Rama and Krishna. Through total self-surrender, *prapatti,* to Vishnu, to Krishna or to His beloved consort Radharani, liberation from samsara (the cycle of reincarnation) is attained.

SMARTISM: Smartas, the most eclectic of Hindus, believe that moksha is achieved through jnana yoga alone—defined as an intellectual and meditative but non-kundalini-yoga path. *Jnana* yoga's progressive stages are scriptural study (*shravana*), reflection (*manana*) and sustained meditation (dhyana). Guided by a realized guru and avowed to the unreality of the world, the initiate meditates on himself as Brahman, Absolute Reality, to break through the illusion of maya. Devotees may also choose from three other non-successive paths to cultivate devotion, accrue good karma and purify the mind. These are bhakti yoga, karma yoga and raja yoga, which certain Smartas teach can also bring enlightenment.

Artwork: *The Divine is reflected in four pots, representing Hinduism's four main denominations, their common source being the radiant Aum, the sacred mystic syllable and symbol of Sanatana Dharma.*

THOMAS KELLY

COURTESY SHARANYA MUKHOPADHYAY

DAVE TROPF

CHAPTER 3

God, Soul & the World

Hindu Views on the Nature of Existence

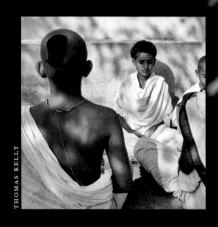

THOMAS KELLY

THOMAS KELLY

JANGAMAWADIMATH

CORBIS

HINDUISM TODAY

THOMAS KELLY

MARC HAVELI

THOMAS KELLY

JASON AND ZAC TROPF

The images here, capturing moments of wonder, introspection, bliss and communion, are windows on the eternal human quest to know the Self, realize God and understand our purpose in the world

DAVE TROPF

ANANDAMAYI ASHRAM ARCHIVES

THOMAS KELLY

THOMAS KELLY

THOMAS KELLY

THOMAS KELLY

In a very real sense, we are like the spaceman in the photo above, totally dependent on our body, mind, emotions and personal identity to persist in life, just as he depends on his space suit and its supply of oxygen to enable him to exist in space. Take away our body, remove our emotions, erase our identity and what is left? Do we cease to exist? What are we really? Rishis assure us that we are immortal souls on a journey of spiritual evolution. We will take on many bodies, many lives, many different identities through the repetitive cycle of birth, death and rebirth. Each advent into a new birth is like an astronaut's voyage into the great unknown. The soul's underlying joy throughout this adventure is to commune with and realize God, learning of its true nature in the great classroom of experience, known as the world, or maya. The three realities of existence, God, soul and world, constitute the fundamentals of Hindu theology, known as *tattva-trayi* in Sanskrit, describing a view in which Divinity, self and cosmos are a profound, integrated unity. Each and every soul is on the same journey, spanning many lifetimes. The path has been made clear by those who have gone before. The answers to life's ultimate questions have been given time and time again, but still must be asked and answered by each soul in its own time: "Who am I?" "Where did I come from?" "Where am I going?"

Subtlest of the subtle, greatest of the great, the atman is hidden in the cave of the heart of all beings. He who, free from all urges, beholds Him overcomes sorrow, seeing by grace of the Creator, the Lord and His glory.
Krishna Yajur Veda, Shvetashvatara Upanishad 3.20

ever have there been so many people living on the planet wondering, "What is the real goal, the final purpose, of life?" However, man is blinded by his ignorance and his concern with the externalities of the world. He is caught, enthralled, bound by karma. The ultimate realizations available are beyond his understanding and remain to him obscure, even intellectually. Man's ultimate quest, the final evolutionary frontier, is within man himself. It is the Truth spoken by Vedic rishis as the Self within man, attainable through devotion, purification and control of the mind. On the following pages, we explore the nature of the soul, God and the world. Offered here is a broad perspective that Hindus of most lineages would find agreement with, though in such matters there naturally arise myriad differences of perspective. To highlight the most important of these we offer a comparison of Hinduism's four major denominations. Next we explore the views of these four denominations on liberation from the cycle of birth, death and rebirth. Finally, we present a chart of Hindu cosmology that seeks to connect the microcosm and the macrocosm and is a lifetime meditation in itself.

JASON AND ZAC TROTF

Who Am I? Where Did I Come From?

Rishis proclaim that we are not our body, mind or emotions. We are divine souls on a wondrous journey. We came from God, live in God and are evolving into oneness with God. We are, in truth, the Truth we seek. ¶We are immortal souls living and growing in the great school of earthly experience in which we have lived many lives. Vedic rishis have given us courage by uttering the simple truth, "God is the Life of our life." A great sage carried it further by saying there is one thing God cannot do: God cannot separate Himself from us. This is because God is our life. God is the life in the birds. God is the life in the fish. God is the life in the animals. Becoming aware of this Life energy in all that lives is becoming aware of God's loving presence within us. We are the undying consciousness and energy flowing through all things. Deep inside we are perfect this very moment, and we have only to discover and live up to this perfection to be whole. Our energy and God's energy are the same, ever coming out of the void. We are all beautiful children of God. Each day we should try to see the life energy in trees, birds, animals and people. When we do, we are seeing God in action. The *Vedas* affirm, "He who knows God as the Life of life, the Eye of the eye, the Ear of the ear, the Mind of the mind—he indeed comprehends fully the Cause of all causes."

Above: Seated by a lotus pond, symbol of his quieted mind, a seeker performs japa and contemplates his destiny, which blooms as naturally as the flower he holds. Behind are depicted the past lives that brought him to his maturity.

Different Views of God, Soul & World...

As explained in Chapter Two, there is a wide spectrum of religious belief within Hinduism's four major sects or denominations: Saivism, Shaktism, Vaishnavism and Smartism. While they share far more similarities than differences, they naturally hold unique perspectives on God, soul and the world. In Saivism the personal God and primary temple Deity is Siva. He is pure love and compassion, both immanent and transcendent, pleased by devotees' purity and striving. Philosophically, God Siva is one with the soul, a mystic truth that is ultimately realized through His grace. ¶In Saktism the personal Goddess is Shri Devi or Shakti, the Divine Mother, worshiped as Kali, Durga, Rajarajeshvari and Her other aspects. Both compassionate and terrifying, pleasing and wrathful, She is assuaged by sacrifice and submission. Emphasis is on bhakti and tantra to achieve advaitic union. ¶For Vaishnavas the personal God and temple Deity is Vishnu, or Ven-

Where Am I Going? What Is My Path?

Above, an aspirant climbs the highest peak of all, the summit of consciousness. Though the higher reaches of this path are arduous, solitary, even severe, he remains undaunted, impervious to distraction, his eyes fixed firmly on the goal—Self Realization.

We are all growing toward God, and experience is the path. Through experience we mature out of fear into fearlessness, out of anger into love, out of conflict into peace, out of darkness into light and union in God. ¶We have taken birth in a physical body to grow and evolve into our divine potential. We are inwardly already one with God. Our religion contains the knowledge of how to realize this oneness and not create unwanted experiences along the way. The peerless path is following the way of our spiritual forefathers, discovering the mystical meaning of the scriptures. The peerless path is commitment, study, discipline, practice and the maturing of yoga into wisdom. In the beginning stages, we suffer until we learn. Learning leads us to service; and selfless service is the beginning of spiritual striving. Service leads us to understanding. Understanding leads us to meditate deeply and without distractions. Finally, meditation leads us to surrender in God. This is the straight and certain path, the San Marga, leading to Self Realization—the inmost purpose of life—and subsequently to moksha, freedom from rebirth. The *Vedas* wisely affirm, "By austerity, goodness is obtained. From goodness, understanding is reached. From understanding, the Self is obtained, and he who obtains the Self is freed from the cycle of birth and death."

from Hinduism's Four Denominations

kateshwara, and His incarnations, especially Rama and Krishna, a loving and beautiful Lord, pleased by service and surrender. Among the foremost means of communion is chanting His holy names. In most schools of Vaishnavism, God and soul are eternally distinct, with the soul's destiny being to revel in God's loving presence. ¶In Smartism, the Deity is Ishvara. Devotees choose their Deity from among six Gods, yet worship the other five as well: Vishnu, Siva, Shakti, Ganesha, Surya and Skanda. Ishvara appears as a human-like Deity according to devotees' loving worship. Both God and man are, in reality, the Absolute, Brahman; though under the spell of maya, they appear as two. *Jnana*, enlightened wisdom, dispels the illusion. ¶Here now (along the lower section of the next four pages), are verses from the writings of seers of these four denominations that offer a glimpse of their perspectives on the nature of things ultimate.

What Is the Nature of God?

THOMAS KELLY

God is all and in all, One without a second, the Supreme Being and only Absolute Reality. God, the great Lord hailed in the *Upanishads* and adored by all denominations of Hinduism, is a one being, worshiped in many forms and understood in three perfections, with each denomination having its unique perspectives: Absolute Reality, Pure Consciousness and Primal Soul. As Absolute Reality, God is unmanifest, unchanging and transcendent, the Self God, timeless, formless and spaceless. As Pure Consciousness, God is the manifest primal substance, pure love and light flowing through all form, existing everywhere in time and space as infinite intelligence and power. As Primal Soul, God is our personal Lord, source of all three worlds. Extolling God's first Perfection, the *Vedas* explain, "Self-resplendent, formless, unoriginated and pure, that all-pervading being is both within and without. He transcends even the transcendent, unmanifest, causal state of the universe" (*Manduka Upanishad* 2.1.2). Describing the second Perfection, the *Vedas* reveal, "He is God, hidden in all beings, their inmost soul who is in all. He watches the works of creation, lives in all things, watches all things. He is pure consciousness, beyond the three conditions of nature" (*Shvetashvatara Upanishad* 6.11). Praising the third Perfection, the *Vedas* recount, "He is the one God, the Creator. He enters into all wombs. The One Absolute, impersonal Existence, together with His inscrutable maya, appears as the Divine Lord, endowed with manifold glories. With His Divine Power He holds dominion over all the worlds" (*Shvetashvatara Upanishad* 3.1). In summary, we know God in His three perfections, two of form and one formless. We worship His manifest form as Pure Love and Consciousness. We worship Him as our Personal Lord, the Primal Soul who tenderly loves and cares for His devotees—a being whose resplendent body may be seen in mystic vision. And we worship and ultimately realize Him as the formless Absolute, which is beyond qualities and description.

Verses from Sages of Diverse Traditions

Smarta Hinduism

I bow to Govinda, whose nature is bliss supreme, who is the *satguru*, who can be known only from the import of all Vedanta, and who is beyond the reach of speech and mind. ¶Let people quote the scriptures and sacrifice to the Gods, let them perform rituals and worship the Deities, but there is no liberation without the realization of one's identity with the atman; no, not even in the lifetime of a hundred Brahmas put together. ¶It is verily through the touch of ignorance that thou who art the Supreme Self findest thyself under the bondage of the non-Self, whence alone proceeds the round of births and deaths. The fire of knowledge, kindled by the discrimination between these two, burns up the effects of ignorance together with their root. ¶As a treasure hidden underground requires [for its extraction] competent instruction, excavation, the removal of stones and other such things lying above it and [finally] grasping, but never comes out by being [merely] called out by name, so the transparent Truth of the Self, which is hidden by maya and its effects, is to be attained through the instructions of a knower of Brahman, followed by reflection, meditation and so forth, but not through perverted arguments.

Adi Shankaracharya, Vivekachudamani, verses 1.1, 6, 47 & 65, translated by Swami Madhavananda

How Do We Worship the Supreme Being?

As a family of faiths, Hinduism upholds a wide array of perspectives on the Divine, yet all worship the one Supreme Being, adoring that Divinity as our Father-Mother God who protects, nurtures and guides us. We beseech God's grace in our lives while also knowing that He/She is the essence of our soul, the life of our life, closer to us than our breath, nearer than hands and feet. We commune with the Divine through silent prayer, meditation, exaltation through singing and chanting, traditional music and dance. We invoke blessings and grace through puja—ritual offering of lights, water and flowers to a sacred image of the Lord—and through *homa*, or fire ceremony. At least once a year we make a pilgrimage to a distant temple or holy site, devoting heart and mind fully to God. Annual festivals are joyous observances. ¶The four major denominations worship God in their own way. To the Saivite, God is Siva. To the Shakta, Devi, the Goddess, is the Supreme One. The Vaishnava Hindu adores God as Vishnu and His incarnations, and the Smarta worships his chosen Deity as the Supreme. Each denomination also venerates its own pantheon of Divinities, Mahadevas, or "great angels," who were created by the Supreme Lord and who serve and adore Him. The elephant-faced Lord Ganesha, worshiped by Hindus of all denominations, is the most popular Mahadeva. Other Deities include Gods and Goddesses of strength, yoga, learning, art, music, wealth and culture.

Left, the face of Lord Siva, worshiped as the Supreme God by millions of Hindus around the world. Right, a priest offers ghee into the sacred fire during a homa *ritual prescribed in the Vedas that has been performed for thousands of years.*

Vaishnava Hinduism

The intrinsic form of the individual soul consists of intuitive knowledge; it is dependent on God, capable of union with and separation from the body; it is subtle and infinitesimal; it is different and distinct in each body. ¶There are various types of individual souls, such as liberated, devoted and bound. The intrinsic form of the individual self is covered by the mirific power of Krishna. This covering can only be removed by Krishna's grace. ¶Krishna is the Absolute, the Brahman, whose nature excludes all imperfection and is one mass of all noble qualities. He embodies the Theophanies and is identical with Vishnu himself. Radha, Krishna's consort, is all radiant with joy, and is endowed with a loveliness that reflects His nature. She is always surrounded by thousands of attendant maids, symbolizing finite souls. She also grants every desire. Krishna is to be worshiped by all who seek salvation, so that the influx of the darkness of ignorance may cease. This is the teachings of the Four Youths to Narada, witness to all truth.

Sri Nimbarka, Dashashloki, 2, 4, 5, 8, translated by Geeta Khurana, Ph.D.

Is the World Also Divine?

es, the world is divine. God created the world and all things in it. He creates and sustains from moment to moment every atom of the seen physical and unseen spiritual universe. Everything is within Him. He is within everything. God created us. He created the Earth and all things upon it, animate and inanimate. He created time and gravity, the vast spaces and the uncounted stars. He created night and day, joy and sorrow, love and hate, birth and death. He created the gross and the subtle, this world and the other worlds. There are three worlds of existence: the physical, subtle and causal, termed Bhuloka, Antarloka and Brahmaloka. The Creator of all, God Himself, is uncreated. He wills into manifestation all souls and all form, issuing them from Himself like light from a fire or waves from an ocean. Rishis describe this perpetual process as the unfoldment of thirty-six *tattvas,* stages of manifestation, from the Siva tattva—Parashakti and *nada*—to the five elements. Creation is not the making of a separate thing, but an emanation of Himself. God creates, constantly sustains the form of His creations and absorbs them back into Himself. The *Vedas* elucidate, "As a spider spins and withdraws its web, as herbs grow on the earth, as hair grows on the head and body of a person, so also from the Imperishable arises this universe."

Right, the sleek towers of Singapore's famous Raffles Place exemplify our contemporary high-tech world. Above, an ancient stone carving of Lord Ganesha in Tirupati, is worshiped each day by hundreds of devotees for help and guidance.

THOMAS KELLY

COREL

Shakta Hinduism

Siva, having freely taken limitations of body upon Himself, is the soul. As He frees Himself from these, He is Paramasiva (supreme consciousness). Self realization is the aim of human life. Through the realization of unity of guru, mantra, Goddess, the Self and powers of kundalini, inwardly manifested as faculties of consciousness and outwardly as women, the knowledge of the subjective Self is acquired. Bliss is the form of the absolute consciousness manifested in body. The five *makaras* reveal that Bliss. By the power of *bhavana* [intention, resolve] everything is achieved.

Parashurama-kalpasutra, Prathama-khanda, 5-6, 11-13

The real nature is realized by dwelling in the great spontaneity. A firm stay in the universal consciousness is brought about by the absorption of duality. The great union arises from the unification of male and female [principles], and the perceiver with the perceived. Upon the enjoyment of the triple bliss, the unfettered supreme consciousness involuntarily and suddenly [reveals itself]. With the immersion into the great wisdom comes freedom from merit and demerit.

Vatulanatha-sutra, 1, 4, 5, 8, 12

Should Worldly Involvement Be Avoided?

The world is the bountiful creation of a benevolent God, who means for us to live positively in it, facing karma and fulfilling dharma. We must not despise or fear the world. Life is meant to be lived joyously. ¶The world is the place where our destiny is shaped, our desires fulfilled and our soul matured. In the world, we grow from ignorance into wisdom, from darkness into light and from a consciousness of death to immortality. The whole world is an ashrama in which all are doing sannyasin. We must love the world, which is God's creation. Those who despise, hate and fear the world do not understand the intrinsic goodness of all. The world is a glorious place, not to be feared. It is a gracious gift from God Himself, a

playground for His children in which to interrelate young souls with the old—the young experiencing their karma while the old hold firmly to their dharma. The young grow; the old know. Not fearing the world does not give us permission to become immersed in worldliness. To the contrary, it means remaining affectionately detached, like a drop of water on a lotus leaf, being in the world but not of it, walking in the rain without getting wet. The *Vedas* warn, "Behold the universe in the glory of God: and all that lives and moves on Earth. Leaving the transient, find joy in the Eternal. Set not your heart on another's possession."

The Lord created the world, the dwelling place of man. How shall I sing His majesty? He is as mighty as Mount Meru, whence He holds sway over the three worlds; and He is the four paths of Saivam here below. ¶Those who tread the path of Shuddha Saivam stand aloft, their hearts intent on Eternal Para, transcending worlds of pure and impure maya, where pure intelligence consorts not with base ignorance and the lines that divide Real, unreal and real-unreal are sharply discerned.

Tirumantiram 1419 & 1420

This Lord of Maya-world that has its rise in the mind, He knows all our thoughts, but we do not think of Him. Some be who groan, "God is not favorable to me," but surely God seeks those who seek, their souls to save. ¶"How is it they received God Siva's grace?" you ask. In the battle of life, their bewildered thoughts wandered. They trained their course and, freed of darkness, sought the Lord and adored His precious, holy feet.

What Is Liberation?

Having lived many lives, each soul eventually seeks release from mortality, experiences the Divine directly through Self Realization and ultimately attains liberation from the round of births and deaths. All Hindus know this to be their eventual goal, but the means of attainment and understanding of the ultimate state vary greatly. The point in evolution at which the individual earns release and exactly what happens afterwards is described differently in each of the Hindu denominations. Within each sect there are also distinct schools of thought. These are the subtle, profound and compelling perspectives we explore below.

The Hindu View of Liberation

The dawn of freedom from the cycle of reincarnation is called moksha (liberation), and one who has attained the state of liberation is called a *jivanmukta* (liberated soul). While some schools of Hinduism teach that liberation comes only upon death, most recognize the condition of *jivanmukti,* a state of liberation in which the spiritually advanced being continues to unfold its inherent perfection while in the embodied state. It is said of such a great one that "he died before he died," indicating the totally real, not merely symbolic, demise of the ego, or limited self-sense. Some schools hold the view that liberated beings may voluntarily return to the physical universe in order to help those who are as yet unliberated.

The Sanskrit word *moksha* derives from the root *muk,* which has many connotations: to loosen, to free, release, let loose, let go and thus also to spare, to let live, to allow to depart, to dispatch, to dismiss and even to relax, to spend, bestow, give away and to open. Philosophically, *moksha* means "release from worldly existence or transmigration; final or eternal emancipation." But moksha is not a state of extinction of the conscious being. Nor is it mere unconsciousness. Rather it is perfect freedom, an indescribable state of nondifferentiation, a proximity to, or a oneness with, the Divine. Moksha marks an end to the earthly sojourn, but it may also be understood as a beginning, not unlike graduation from university. *Apavarga* and *kaivalya* are other apt terms for this ineffable condition of perfect detachment, freedom and oneness.

Hinduism is a pluralistic tradition. On any given subject it offers a variety of views that reflect different human temperaments and different levels of emotional, intellectual, moral and spiritual development. So, too, on the subject of liberation, various learned opinions exist. Since liberation involves transcending time and space, and yet is a state that can be achieved while in a body, it defies precise definition. For this reason, some have argued that different views of liberation simply reflect the built-in limitations of language and reason.

Many Paths

The *Vedas* themselves present a number of approaches to liberation. Some of these are agnostic; others involve various monistic and theistic views. The main classical text on Self Realization within the Vedanta tradition, the *Brahma Sutra* of Badarayana, mentions a number of then current views: that upon liberation the soul (*jiva*) attains nondifference from Brahman (IV.4.4); that it gains the attributes of Brahman (IV.4.5); that it exists only as pure consciousness (IV.4.6); that even though it is pure consciousness from the relative standpoint, it can still gain the attributes of Brahman (IV.4.7); that through pure will alone it can gain whatever it wishes (IV.4.8); that it transcends any body or mind (IV.4.10); that it possesses a divine

body and mind (IV.4.11); and that it attains all powers except creatorship, which belongs to Ishvara alone (IV.4.17). Generally, the view that the soul attains the Absolute only is more represented by the *Brihadaranyaka Upanishad*, while the *Chandogya Upanishad* mentions liberation along with the attainment of lordly powers. Most later ideas of moksha are variations on these same Vedic views.

At one end of this metaphysical spectrum are the *jnanis* who follow the yoga of knowledge and who ascribe to the view that the Ultimate Reality is formless and unqualified (*nirguna*). At the other end are the bhaktas who follow the yoga of devotion and commonly believe that the individual being (*jiva*) remains in communion with its beloved (Bhagavan). Thus, devotees believe that they will come to inhabit the divine realm, or *loka,* of their chosen Deity, Siva, Vishnu, Kali, etc. Each metaphysical view has given rise to a distinct practical approach to reaching Oneness and Liberation.

Later Advaita Vedantins, such as Shankaracharya, spoke of two types of liberation. The first is complete or direct liberation, which they regarded as the highest state. The second is a gradual liberation that occurs wherein the individual being goes, after death, first to the heaven of Brahma and then gains liberation from there without having to return to the physical world.

Ramana Maharshi, the great sage of South India, observed that three types of liberation are mentioned in Hinduism: without form, with form, and both with and without form. He considered true liberation as transcending all such concepts (*Saddarshana* 42).

All schools are agreed that liberation is the ultimate fulfilment of human life, whose purpose is spiritual growth, not mere worldly enjoyment (*bhoga*). Having lived many lives and having learned many lessons, each conscious being seeks release from mortality, which then leads to glimpses of our divine origin and finally Self Realization. This consists in discovering our true nature, beyond body and mind, our identity in the incomprehensibly vast ultimate Being. Upon this discovery, we are released from the round of births and deaths and realize eternal freedom, untold bliss and supreme consciousness.

Having realized the Self, the rishis, perfected souls, satisfied with their knowledge, passion-free, tranquil—those wise beings, having attained the Ominipresent on all sides—enter into the All itself.
Atharva Veda, Mundaka Upanishad 3.2.5

finally becoming a *jivanmukta* in that or a future birth.

What distinguishes the *mukta* from the nonliberated individual is his total freedom from all selfishness and attachments, his permanent abidance in the all-pervading Divine Presence, his lucid, witnessing consciousness and his wisdom (*jnana*), revealed in spontaneous utterances.

Even after attaining perfect liberation, a being may, after passing into the inner worlds, consciously choose to be reborn to help others on the path. Such a one is called an *upadeshi*—exemplified by the benevolent *satguru*—as distinguished from a *nirvani*, or silent ascetic who abides at the pinnacle of consciousness, whether in this world or the next, shunning all worldly involvement.

The Nature of Soul and God

The concept of *moksha* for every Hindu school of thought is informed and modified by its understanding of the individual and its relationship to God. Most Hindus believe that after release from birth and death the innermost being will exist in the higher regions of the subtle worlds, where the Deities and spiritually mature beings abide. Some schools contend that the soul continues to evolve in these realms until it attains perfect union and merger with God. Others teach that the highest end is to abide eternally and separately in God's glorious presence. Four distinct views, reflected in the primary Hindu denominations, are explored below.

Smarta Hinduism

Smartism (the teaching following smriti, or tradition) is an ancient brahmanical tradition reformed by Adi Shankara in the ninth century. This liberal Hindu path, which revolves around the worship of six fundamental forms of the Divine, is monistic, nonsectarian, meditative and philosophical. Ishvara and the human being are in reality the singular absolute Brahman. Within maya, the soul and Ishvara appear as two. *Jnana*, spiritual wisdom, dispels that illusion.

Most Smartas believe that *moksha* is achieved through *jnana* yoga alone. This approach is defined as an intellectual and meditative but non-kundalini yoga path. Yet, many Advaitins also recognize the kundalini as the power of consciousness. Ramana Maharshi and Swami Shivananda of Rishikesh did, and Shankara wrote on tantra and kundalini as in the *Saundarya-Lahiri*. Guided by a realized guru and avowed to the unreality of the world, the initiate meditates on himself as Brahman to break through the illusion of maya. The ultimate goal of Smartas is to realize oneself as Brahman, the Absolute and only Reality. For this, one must conquer the state of *avidya*, ignorance, which causes the world to appear as real.

For the realized being, *jivanmukta*, all illusion has vanished, even as he lives out life in the physical body. If the sun were cold or the

A Natha Saivite View of Realization and Liberation

To attain liberation while living, the realization of the Self has to be brought through into every aspect of life, every atom of one's body. This occurs after many experiences of *nirvikalpa* samadhi. Through harnessing the power of sannyasin and *tapas*, the adept advances his or her evolution. Only great *tapasvins* achieve *jivanmukti*, for one must be proficient in *brahmacharya*, yoga, pranayama and the varied *sannyasins*. It is a grace made possible by guidance of a living *satguru* and attained by single-minded and strong-willed discipline, worship, detachment and purification.

Thus, it is possible to realize the Self—as in *nirvikalpa* samadhi—and still not reach the emancipated state. If this happens, the being reincarnates in the physical world after death and in his new body has the opportunity to build upon past virtues and realizations until

moon hot or fire burned downward, he would show no wonder. The *jivanmukta* teaches, blesses and sets an example for the welfare of the world. At death, his inner and outer bodies are extinguished. Brahman alone exists and he is That forever, all in All.

For Smartism, liberation depends on spiritual insight (*jnana*). It does not come from recitation of hymns, sacrificial worship or a hundred fasts. The human being is liberated not by effort, not by yogic practices, not by any self-transformation, but only by the knowledge gained from scripture and self-reflection that at its core the being is in fact Brahman. However, all such practices do help purify the body and mind and create the aptitude (*adhikara*) without which *jnana* remains mere theory or fantasy. *Jnana* yoga's progressive stages are scriptural study (*shravana*), reflection (*manana*) and sustained meditation (*nididhyasana* or *dhyana*). Practitioners may also choose from three other nonsuccessive paths in order to cultivate devotion, accrue good karma, and purify the mind. These are bhakti yoga, karma yoga and raja yoga, which some believe can also bring enlightenment, as they lead to *jnana*.

Scripture teaches that "for the great-souled, the surest way to liberation is the conviction that 'I am Brahman'" (*Shukla Yajur Veda, Paingala Upanishad* 4.19). Sri Jayendra Saraswati of Kanchi Peedam, Tamil Nadu, India, affirms, "That state where one transcends all feelings is liberation. Nothing affects this state of being. You may call it transcendental bliss, purified intuition that enables one to see the Supreme as one's own Self. One attains to Brahman, utterly liberated."

Vaishnava Hinduism

The primary goal of Vaishnavites is *videhamukti*, disembodied liberation, attainable only after death when the "small self" realizes union with God Vishnu's infinite body as a part of Him, yet maintains its pure individual personality. God's transcendental Being is a celestial form residing in the city of Vaikuntha, the home of all eternal values and perfection, where the inner being joins Him when liberated. Beings, however, do not share in God's all-pervasiveness or power to create.

Most Vaishnavites believe that dharma is the performance of various devotional disciplines (bhakti *sannyasins*), and that the human being can communicate with and receive the grace of Lord Vishnu, who manifests through the temple Deity, or icon. The paths of karma yoga and *jnana* yoga are thought to lead to bhakti yoga. Through total self-surrender, called *prapatti*, to Lord Vishnu, one attains liberation from the world of change (samsara). Vaishnavites consider the moksha of the Advaita philosophies a lesser attainment, extolling instead the bliss of eternal devotion. There are differing categories of souls that attain to four different levels of permanent release: *salokya*, or "sharing the world" of God; *samipya*, or "nearness" to God; *sarupya*, or "likeness" to God; and *sayujya*, or "union" with God. *Jivanmukti* exists only in the case of great souls who leave their place in the divine abode to take a human birth for the benefit of others and return to God as soon as their task is done.

There is one school of Vaishnavism, founded by Vallabhacharya, which takes an entirely different view of moksha. It teaches that upon liberation the soul, through its insight into truth revealed by virtue of perfect devotion, recovers divine qualities suppressed previously and becomes one with God, in identical essence, though the soul remains a part, and God the whole. This relationship is described by the analogy of sparks issuing from a fire.

Swami Prakashanand Saraswati of the International Society of Divine Love, Texas, offers a Vaishnava view, "Liberation from maya and the karmas is only possible after the divine vision of God. Thus, sincere longing for His vision is the only way to receive His grace and liberation."

Shakta Hinduism

Shaktas believe that the soul is one with the Divine. Emphasis is given to the feminine aspect of the ultimate reality—Shakti. The Divine Mother or Goddess Power, Shakti, is the mediatrix bestowing this advaitic moksha on those who worship Her. Moksha is complete identification with the transcendental Divine, which is achieved when the kundalini shakti—the individuated form of the divine power—is raised through the *sushumna* current of the spine to the top of the head where it merges with Siva.

The spiritual practices in Shaktism, which is also known as tantra or tantrism, are similar to those in Saivism, though there is more emphasis in Shaktism on God's power as opposed to mere Being or Consciousness. Shakta practices include visualization and rituals involving mantras, hand gestures (mudras), and geometric designs (yantras). The body is viewed as a temple of the Divine, and thus there are also numerous prescribed techniques for purifying and transforming the body. Philosophically, Shaktism's yogic world view embraces all opposites: male-female, absolute-relative, pleasure-pain, cause-effect, mind-body. Shamanistic Shaktism employs magic, trance mediumship, firewalking and animal sacrifice for healing, fertility, prophecy and power. In "left-hand" tantric circles an antinomianism is evident, which seeks to transcend traditional moral codes.

The state of *jivanmukti* in Shaktism is called *kulachara* or "the divine way of life," which is attained through sannyasin and grace. The liberated soul is known as a *kaula-siddha*, to whom wood and gold, life and death are the same. The *kaula-siddha* can move about in the world at will, even returning to earthly duties such as kingship, yet remaining liberated from rebirth, as his actions can no longer bind him.

The Goddess, Devi, gives both *mukti* and *bhukti*—liberation and worldly enjoyment. Dr. Sarvepalli Radhakrishnan explained, "The *jiva* under the influence of maya looks upon itself as an independent agent and enjoyer until release is gained. Knowledge of Shakti is the road to salvation, which is dissolution in the bliss effulgence of the Supreme." Shri Shri Shivaratnapuri Swami of Kailas Ashram, Bangalore, India, declares, "My message to mankind is right thought, right living and unremitting devotion to the Divine Mother. Faith is the most important thing that you should cultivate. By faith does one obtain knowledge."

Saiva Hinduism

The path for Saivites is divided into four progressive stages of belief and practice called *charya*, *kriya*, yoga and *jnana*. The soul evolves through karma and reincarnation from the instinctive-intellectual sphere into virtuous and moral living, then into temple worship and devotion, followed by internalized worship or yoga and its meditative disciplines. Union with God, Siva, comes through the grace of the *satguru* and culminates in the soul's maturity in the state of *jnana*, or wisdom. Saivism values both bhakti and yoga, devotional and contemplative *sannyasins*.

Moksha is defined differently in Saivism's six schools. 1) Pashupata Saivism emphasizes Siva as supreme cause and personal ruler of the soul and world. It teaches that the liberated soul retains its individuality in a state of complete union with Siva. 2) Vira Saivism holds that after liberation the soul experiences a true union and identity of Siva and soul, called Linga and *anga*. The soul ultimately merges in a state of Shunya, or Nothingness, which is not an empty

Union: *Every soul's ultimate goal, in this life or another, is to realize its oneness with God. That union is depicted here as Lord Siva and a mature soul merging in oneness. Siva sits beneath a banyan tree, bestowing His Grace by touching the third eye of the seeker, who reaches up to embrace Divinity.*

the *Upanishads* like the *Chandogya* and the *Brahma Sutras.*

The sixth, Saiva Siddhanta, has two subsects. Meykandar's pluralistic realism teaches that God, soul and world are eternally coexistent. Liberation leads to a state of oneness with Siva in which the soul retains its individuality, like salt added to water.

Tirumular's monistic theism, or Advaita Ishvaravada, the older of the two schools, holds that evolution continues after earthly births until *jiva* becomes Siva; the soul merges in perfect oneness with God, like a drop of water returning to the sea. Scriptures teach, "Having realized the Self, the rishis, perfected souls, satisfied with their knowledge, passion-free, tranquil—those wise beings, having attained the Omnipresent on all sides—enter into the All itself "(*Mundaka Upanishad* 3.2.5). The primary goal of this form of monistic Saiva Siddhanta is realizing one's identity with God Siva, in perfect union and nondifferentiation. This is termed *nirvikalpa* samadhi, Self Realization, and may be attained in this life, granting moksha, permanent liberation from the cycles of birth and death. A secondary goal is *savikalpa* samadhi, the realization of Satchidananda, a unitive experience within superconsciousness in which perfect Truth, Consciousness and Bliss are known.

Conclusion, from the Monistic Saiva View

According to the Saiva Siddhanta philosophy of South India, to reach emancipation, beyond all pleasure and pain, all difference and decay, the being must successively remove the three fetters: karma, "the power of cause and effect, action and reaction;" maya, "the power of manifestation;" and *anava*, "the power of egoity or veil of duality." Once freed by God's grace from these bonds (which do not cease to exist altogether, but no longer have the power to bind), the being is in the permanent state of *sahaja* samadhi, or "natural, spontaneous ecstasy," the living illumination called *jivanmukti.* This is the realization of the timeless, spaceless and formless Reality beyond all change or diversity. Simultaneously it is the realization that all forms, whether internal or external, are also aspects of this Ultimate Reality.

Moksha does not mean death, as some misunderstand it. It means freedom from rebirth, before or at the point of death, after which souls continue evolving in the inner worlds, the Antarloka and Sivaloka, and finally merge with Lord Siva as does river water when returning to the ocean. Moksha comes when all earthly karmas have been fully resolved. Finally, at the end of each soul's evolution comes *vishvagrasa,* total absorption in Siva. The *Vedas* promise, "If here one is able to realize Him before the death of the body, he will be liberated from the bondage of the world."

All embodied souls—whatever be their faith or convictions, Hindu or not—are destined to achieve moksha, but not necessarily in this life. Hindus know this and do not delude themselves that this life is the last. Old souls renounce worldly ambitions and take up sannyasa, renunciation, in quest of Self Realization even at a young age. Younger souls desire to seek lessons from the experiences of worldly life, which is rewarded by many, many births on Earth. In between, souls seek to fulfil their dharma while resolving karma and accruing merit through good deeds. After moksha has been attained—and it is an attainment resulting from much sannyasin, self-reflection and realization—subtle karmas are made and swiftly resolved, like writing on water. "The Self cannot be attained by the weak, nor by the careless, nor through aimless disciplines. But if one who knows strives by right means, his soul enters the abode of God" (*Mundaka Upanishad* 3.2.4).

void. 3) Kashmir Shaivism teaches that liberation comes through a sustained recognition, called *pratyabhijna,* of one's true Self as nothing but Siva. After liberation, the soul has no merger in God, as God and soul are eternally nondifferent. 4) In Gorakhnath Saivism, or Siddha Siddhanta, moksha leads to a complete sameness of Siva and soul, described as "bubbles arising and returning to water." 5) In Siva Advaita, liberation leads to the "akasha within the heart." Upon death, the soul goes to Siva along the path of the Gods, continuing to exist on the spiritual plane, enjoying the bliss of knowing all as Siva, and attaining all powers except creation. This is a similar view to

This chart assembles and cor-relates four essential elements of Hindu cosmology: the planes of existence and consciousness; the *tattvas*; the chakras; and the bodies of man. ¶It is organized with the highest consciousness, or subtlest level of manifestation, at the top, and the lowest, or gross-est, at the bottom. In studying the chart, it is important to remember that each level includes within itself all the levels above it. Thus, the element earth, the grossest or outermost aspect of manifestation, contains all the *tattvas* above it on the chart. They are its inner struc-ture. Similarly, the soul encased in a physical body also has all the sheaths named above—*pranic*, instinctive-intellectual, cognitive and causal.

The three columns on the left side of the chart depict the inner and outer universe. Column one shows the three worlds: the causal, superconscious realm of the Gods; the astral realm of dreams, abode of non-embodied souls; and the physical world of the five senses. Endearing Icons of Mythology, Mysticism, Culture and Devotion

Column two gives a more detailed division in 14 planes and correlates these to the chakras, the force centers of consciousness resident within each soul. It shows three levels in the third world, cor-responding to the sahasrara, ajna and vishuddha chakras; and three levels of the second world, or astral plane, corresponding to the *ana-hata, manipura* and *svadhishthana* chakras. Note that the grossest of these planes, the Bhuvarloka or Pitriloka, has a secondary realm, called the Pretakoka, where abide

Chart of Hindu Cosmology:

३ लोक **3 WORLDS**	१४ लोक **14 PLANES (LOKA)**	**CHAKRAS**	५ कला **5 SPHERES (KALĀ)**
THIRD WORLD Śivaloka, "plane of God" and the Gods, also called Kāraṇaloka, the "causal plane"	**7. SATYALOKA,** "plane of reality," also called Brahma-loka, region of *sahasrāra chakra*	SAHASRĀRA	**5. ŚĀNTYATITAKALĀ** Śivānanda, superconsciousness expanded into endless inner space.
	6. TAPOLOKA, "plane of austerity," *ājñā chakra*	AJÑA	**4. ŚĀNTIKALĀ** *kāraṇa chitta,* superconscious forms made of inner sounds and colors
	5. JANALOKA, "creative plane," *viśuddha chakra*	VIŚUDDHA	
SECOND WORLD Antarloka, the subtle, or astral, plane [HIGHER ASTRAL PLANE] [DEVALOKA]	**4. MAHARLOKA** "plane of greatness," also called Devaloka, "angelic world," *anāhata chakra*	ANĀHATA	• LIBERATED SOULS • BOUND SOULS • **3. VIDYĀKALĀ** *anukāraṇa chitta,* • subsuperconscious awareness of forms in their totality in progres-sive states of manifestation • subsuperconscious cognition of the interrelated forces of the spiri-tual and magnetic energies
CYCLE OF REINCARNATION *saṃsāra* [MID-ASTRAL] [SVARLOKA]	**3. SVARLOKA,** "celestial plane," *maṇipūra chakra*	MAṆIPŪRA	**2. PRATISHṬHĀKALĀ** *buddhi chitta and manas chitta,* realm of intellect and instinct
[PITRILOKA]	**2. BHUVARLOKA,** "plane of atmosphere," *svādhishthāna chakra* — PITṚILOKA, "world of ancestors"	SVADHISHTHANA	
[LOWER ASTRAL] [PRETALOKA]	PRETALOKA, "world of the departed," of earth-bound souls. The astral duplicate of Bhūloka.		**1. NIVṚITTIKALĀ:** *jāgrat chitta, saṃskāra chitta* and *vāsanā chitta*—the conscious, subconscious and subsubconscious mind, the interrelated magnetic forces between people, people and their possessions
FIRST WORLD Bhūloka	**1. BHŪLOKA,** "earth plane," *mūlādhāra chakra*	MŪLĀDHĀRA	
Antarloka's netherworld: **NARAKA** [SUB-ASTRAL] [NARAKALOKA]	**NARAKALOKA** (7 hellish planes of lower consciousness): -1) Put *(atala chakra)*, -2) Avīchi *(vitala chakra)*, -3) Saṃhāta *(sutala chakra)*, -4) Tāmisra *(talātala chakra)*, -5) Ṛijīsha *(rasātala chakra)*, -6) Kuḍmala *(mahātala chakra)*, -7) Kākola *(pātāla chakra)*		

the Inner and Outer Universe

Parasíva (*atattva,* "beyond existence") ३६ तत्त्व 36 EVOLUTES (TATTVA)	३ शरीर 3 BODIES (ŚARĪRA)	७ कोश 5 SHEATHS (KOŚA)
ŚUDDHA MĀYĀ: PURE SPIRITUAL ENERGY 1) *Śiva tattva:* Parāśakti-*nāda,* Satchidānanda, pure consciousness 2) *Śakti tattva:* Parameśvara-*bindu,* Personal God	*viśvagrāsa:* final merger of the golden *ānandamaya kośa* (*svarṇaśarīra*) in Parameśvara	
3) *Sadāśiva tattva:* power of revealment 4) *Īśvara tattva:* power of concealment 5) *Śuddhavidyā tattva: dharma,* pure knowing, the powers of dissolution, preservation and creation—Rudra, Vishṇu and Brahmā	**SOUL BODY** **KĀRAṆA ŚARĪRA,** "causal body" or **ĀNANDAMAYA KOŚA,** "sheath of bliss"—the body of the soul, also called the actinic causal body	
ŚUDDHĀŚUDDHA MĀYĀ **SPIRITUAL/MAGNETIC ENERGY** 6) *māyā tattva:* mirific energy 7) *kāla tattva:* time 8) *niyati tattva:* karma 9) *kalā tattva:* creativity, aptitude 10) *vidyā tattva:* knowledge 11) *rāga tattva:* attachment, desire 12) *purusha tattva:* shrouded soul	**SŪKSHMA ŚARĪRA** the "subtle body," also called the astral body	**REFINED ASTRAL BODY** **VIJÑĀNAMAYA KOŚA** the "sheath of cognition," the mental or actinodic causal sheath
AŚUDDHA MĀYĀ: MAGNETIC/GROSS ENERGY 13) *prakṛiti tattva:* primal nature 14–16) *antaḥkaraṇa:* mental faculties 17–21) *jñānendriyas:* organs of perception 22–26) *karmendriyas:* organs of action 27–31) *tanmātras:* elements of perception		**GROSS ASTRAL BODY** **MANOMAYA KOŚA** the intellectual (odic-causal) and instinctive (odic-astral) sheath
32–36) *ākāśa tattva* (ether), *vāyu tattva* (air), *tejas tattva* (fire), *āpas tattva* (water), *pṛithivī tattva* (earth)		**PRĀṆAMAYA KOŚA** the "sheath of vitality" which enlivens the physical body
	STHŪLA ŚARĪRA, "gross body," or **ANNAMAYA KOŚA,** "food-made sheath" —the physical body or odic body	

earth-bound astral entities. The first world, or Bhuloka, corresponds to the *muladhara* chakra. Below it is depicted the part of the astral plane called the Narakaloka—the realm of lower consciousness, fear, anger, jealousy, etc. Looking back to column one, the dotted path indicates that regions two, three and four of the Antarloka are the domain from which souls are reborn. Column three provides a view of the *kalas,* which emphasize the states of mind or levels of consciousness associated with these strata.

Column four of the chart lists the 36 *tattvas. Tattvas* (literally "that-ness") are the primary principles, elements, states or categories of existence, the building blocks of the universe. God constantly creates, sustains the form of and absorbs back into Himself His creations. Rishis describe this emanational process as the unfoldment of tattvas, stages or evolutes of manifestation, descending from subtle to gross. This column of the chart subdivides the tattvas into three levels of maya, manifest creation, as follows: *shuddha* maya (correlating to the Third World in column one); *shuddhashuddha* maya (corresponding to the Maharloka); and *ashuddha* maya (corresponding to the mid astral, lower astral and physical planes). Column five lists the three bodies of the soul: causal, subtle and physical (which correspond directly to the three worlds); and the five sheaths (*anandamaya, vijnanamaya, manomaya, pranamaya* and *annamaya*). Note the correlation of these and the worlds by reading across the chart to the left to the two columns named "3 worlds" and "14 planes." For more details on the subjects and terms in the chart, you can search for definitions at: www.himalayanacademy.com/resources/books/dws/DWSLexicon.html.

CHAPTER 4

A Hindu Primer

A Code of Practices, Beliefs and Attitudes Common to All Hindus

LOVING HINDU PARENTS WORLDWIDE, OF VARIOUS LINEAGES, HAVE CALLED FOR A common religious code to teach their sons and daughters. They have asked, "What is the minimum I must do to dispatch my duty to my religion and my children?" In response, and to convey the basics of Hinduism for devotees and seekers of all ages, we assembled this chapter. It contains 1) an overview of Hinduism; 2) nine basic beliefs; 3) four facts; five essential precepts; 4) five corresponding observances; 5) Hinduism from A to Z. The modern Hindu child raised up with these principles and practices will be a fully functioning human being, one who is tolerant, devotional, fair, fearless, obedient, secure, happy, selfless, pure and traditional. We apologize that, in our brevity, we have inevitably blurred over subtleties in the rainbow of Hindu views.

A Bird's-Eye View of a Family of Faiths

HINDUISM, ALSO KNOWN AS THE SANATANA DHARMA, or "Eternal Way," is our planet's original and oldest living religion, with no single founder. For as long as man has lived and roamed across Earth's land and water masses, breathed its air and worshiped in awe its fire, it has been a guide of righteous life for evolving souls. Today Hinduism has four main denominations: Saivism, Shaktism, Vaishnavism and Smartism, each with hundreds of lineages. They represent a broad range of beliefs, *sadhanas* and mystic goals.

While Hindus believe many diverse and exotic things, there are several bedrock concepts on which virtually all concur. All Hindus worship one Supreme Reality, though they call it by many names, and teach that all souls will ultimately realize the truth of the *Vedas* and *Agamas*. Hindus believe that there is no eternal hell, no damnation. They concur that there is no intrinsic evil. All is good. All is God. In contrast, Western faiths postulate a living evil force, embodied in Satan, that directly opposes the will of God.

Hindus believe that the universe was created out of God and is permeated by Him—a Supreme Being who both is form and pervades form, who creates, sustains and destroys the universe only to recreate it again in unending cycles. Hindus accept all genuine spiritual paths. Each soul is free to find his own way, whether by devotion, austerity, meditation, yoga or selfless service (*seva*). Hinduism's three pillars are temple worship, scripture and the guru-disciple tradition. Hinduism strongly declares the validity of the three worlds of existence—physical, astral and spiritual—and the myriad Gods and devas residing within them. Festivals, pilgrimage, chanting of holy hymns and home worship are dynamic practices. Family life is strong and precious. Love, nonviolence, good conduct and the law of dharma define the Hindu path. Hindus are generously tolerant of other faiths. Hinduism explains that the soul reincarnates until all karmas are resolved and God Realization is attained.

Hindus wear the sectarian marks, called *tilaka*, on their foreheads as sacred symbols, distinctive insignia of their heritage. This is a mystical religion, leading devotees to personally experience its eternal truths within themselves, finally reaching the pinnacle of consciousness where man and God are forever one. They prefer cremation of the body upon death, rather than burial, believing that the soul lives on and will inhabit a new body on Earth.

While we have many sacred scriptures, all sects ascribe the highest authority to the *Vedas* and *Agamas*, though their *Agamas* differ somewhat. Hinduism's nearly one billion adherents have tens of thousands of sacred temples and shrines, mostly in India, but now located around the world. Its spiritual core is its millions of holy men and women who have dedicated their lives to full-time service, devotion and God Realization, and to proclaiming the eternal truths of the Sanatana Dharma.

Children perform puja at an outdoor shrine as the Gods Ganesha and Murugan look on in approval

Nine Beliefs of Hinduism

1 Hindus believe in the divinity of the *Vedas*, the world's most ancient scripture, and venerate the *Agamas* as equally revealed. These primordial hymns are God's word and the bedrock of Sanatana Dharma, the eternal religion which has neither beginning nor end.

2 Hindus believe in a one, all-pervasive Supreme Being who is both immanent and transcendent, both Creator and Unmanifest Reality.

3 Hindus believe that the universe undergoes endless cycles of creation, preservation and dissolution.

4 Hindus believe in karma, the law of cause and effect by which each individual creates his own destiny by his thoughts, words and deeds.

5 Hindus believe that the soul reincarnates, evolving through many births until all karmas have been resolved, and moksha, spiritual knowledge and liberation from the cycle of rebirth, is attained. Not a single soul will be eternally deprived of this destiny.

6 Hindus believe that divine beings exist in unseen worlds and that temple worship, rituals, sacraments as well as personal devotionals create a communion with these devas and Gods.

7 Hindus believe that a spiritually awakened master, or *satguru*, is essential to know the Transcendent Absolute, as are personal discipline, good conduct, purification, pilgrimage, self inquiry and meditation.

8 Hindus believe that all life is sacred, to be loved and revered, and therefore practice ahimsa, "noninjury."

9 Hindus believe that no particular religion teaches the only way to salvation above all others, but that all genuine religious paths are facets of God's Pure Love and Light, deserving tolerance and understanding.

Four Facts of Hinduism: Karma, Reincarnation, All-Pervasive Divinity, and Dharma

1. Karma

Karma literally means "deed" or "act" and more broadly names the universal principle of cause and effect, action and reaction which governs all life. Karma is a natural law of the mind, just as gravity is a law of matter. Karma is not fate, for man acts with free will, creating his own destiny. The Vedas tell us, if we sow goodness, we will reap goodness; if we sow evil, we will reap evil. Karma refers to the totality of our actions and their concomitant reactions in this and previous lives, all of which determines our future. It is the interplay between our experience and how we respond to it that makes karma devastating or helpfully invigorating. The conquest of karma lies in intelligent action and dispassionate reaction. Not all karmas rebound immediately. Some accumulate and return unexpectedly in this or other births.

ART BY S. RAJAM

According as one acts, so does he become. One becomes virtuous by virtuous action, bad by bad action.

YAJUR VEDA, BRIHADARANYAKA UPANISHAD 4.4.5

A devotee prays to a small image of Ganesha, who hovers nearby in His subtle body, blessing her life and guiding her karmas.

2. Reincarnation

Reincarnation, *punarjanma,* is the natural process of birth, death and rebirth. At death we drop off the physical body and continue evolving in the inner worlds in our subtle bodies, until we again enter into birth. Through the ages, reincarnation has been the great consoling element within Hinduism, eliminating the fear of death. We are not the body in which we live but the immortal soul which inhabits many bodies in its evolutionary journey through samsara. After death, we continue to exist in unseen worlds, enjoying or suffering the harvest of earthly deeds until it comes time for yet another physical birth. The actions set in motion in previous lives form the tendencies and conditions of the next. Reincarnation ceases when karma is resolved, God is realized and moksha, liberation, is attained.

After death, the soul goes to the next world, bearing in mind the subtle impressions of its deeds, and after reaping their harvest returns again to this world of action. Thus, he who has desires continues subject to rebirth.

YAJUR VEDA, BRIHADARANYAKA UPANISHAD 4.4.6

In the center, we see a yogi. Behind him are depictions of how he looked and dressed in four earlier incarnations.

3. All-pervasive Divinity

As a family of faiths, Hinduism upholds a wide array of perspectives on the Divine, yet all worship the one, all-pervasive Supreme Being hailed in the *Upanishads*. As Absolute Reality, God is unmanifest, unchanging and transcendent, the Self God, timeless, formless and spaceless. As Pure Consciousness, God is the manifest primal substance, pure love and light flowing through all form, existing everywhere in time and space as infinite intelligence and power. As Primal Soul, God is our personal Lord, source of all three worlds, our Father-Mother God who protects, nurtures and guides us. We beseech God's grace in our lives while also knowing that He/She is the essence of our soul, the life of our life. Each denomination also venerates its own pantheon of Divinities, Mahadevas, or "great angels," who were created by the Supreme Lord and who serve and adore Him.

God's all-pervasive, immanent nature is portayed here. Siva is seated against a backdrop of swirling shakti. His body is made up of the elements, galaxies, mountains, rivers, animals and manifestations of all kinds, thus depicting Him as inherent in His creation.

He is the God of forms infinite in whose glory all things are— smaller than the smallest atom, and yet the Creator of all, ever living in the mystery of His creation. In the vision of this God of love there is everlasting peace. He is the Lord of all who, hidden in the heart of things, watches over the world of time.

KRISHNA YAJUR VEDA, SHVETASHVATARA UPANISHAD 4.14-15.

4. Dharma

When God created the universe, He endowed it with order, with the laws to govern creation. Dharma is God's divine law prevailing on every level of existence, from the sustaining cosmic order to religious and moral laws which bind us in harmony with that order. Related to the soul, dharma is the mode of conduct most conducive to spiritual advancement, the right and righteous path. It is piety and ethical practice, duty and obligation. When we follow dharma, we are in conformity with the Truth that inheres and instructs the universe, and we naturally abide in closeness to God. Adharma is opposition to divine law. Dharma is to the individual what its normal development is to a seed—the orderly fulfillment of an inherent nature and destiny.

Dharma embraces one's duties and obligations, and changes according to life's four natural stages of life: student, householder, elder advisor and religious solitaire, as show in this illustration.

Dharma yields Heaven's honor and Earth's wealth. What is there then that is more fruitful for a man? There is nothing more rewarding than dharma, nor anything more ruinous than its neglect.

TIRUKURAL 31-32

Five Precepts

THE MINIMAL HINDU BELIEFS. BY TEACHING THESE TO
SONS AND DAUGHTERS, PARENTS WORLDWIDE PASS ON
THE SANATANA DHARMA TO THEIR CHILDREN

ART BY A. MANIVEL

1. God Is All in all

The dear children are taught of one Supreme Being, all-pervasive, transcendent, creator, preserver, destroyer, manifesting in various forms, worshiped in all religions by many names, the immortal Self in all. They learn to be tolerant, knowing the soul's Divinity and the unity of all mankind.

Sarva
Brahman
सर्व ब्रह्मन्

2. Holy Temples

Mandira
मन्दिर

The dear children are taught that God, other divine beings and highly evolved souls exist in unseen worlds. They learn to be devoted, knowing that temple worship, fire ceremonies, sacraments and devotionals open channels for loving blessings, help and guidance from these beings.

3. Cosmic Justice

The dear children are taught of karma, the divine law of cause and effect by which every thought, word and deed justly returns to them in this or a future life. They learn to be compassionate, knowing that each experience, good or bad, is the self-created reward of prior expressions of free will.

Karma
कर्म

4. Liberation

Samsara,
Moksha
संसारा मोक्ष

The dear children are taught that souls experience righteousness, wealth and pleasure in many births, while maturing spiritually. They learn to be fearless, knowing that all souls, without exception, will ultimately attain Self Realization, liberation from rebirth and union with God.

5. Scripture and Preceptor

The dear children are taught that God revealed the *Vedas* and *Agamas*, which contain the eternal truths. They learn to be obedient, following the precepts of these sacred scriptures and awakened *satgurus*, whose guidance is absolutely essential for spiritual progress and enlightenment.

Veda, Guru
वोद गुरु

Five Practices

THE MINIMAL PRACTICES (ALSO KNOWN AS PANCHA NITYA KARMAS) TO NURTURE FUTURE CITIZENS WHO ARE STRONG, RESPONSIBLE, TOLERANT AND TRADITIONAL

1. Worship

The dear children are taught daily worship in the family shrine room—rituals, disciplines, chants, yogas and religious study. They learn to be secure through devotion in home and temple, wearing traditional dress, bringing forth love of the Divine and preparing the mind for serene meditation.

Upasana
उपासना

2. Holy Days

The dear children are taught to participate in Hindu festivals and holy days in the home and temple. They learn to be happy through sweet communion with God at such auspicious celebrations. *Utsava* includes fasting and attending the temple on Monday or Friday and other holy days.

Utsava

उत्सव

3. Virtuous Living

The dear children are taught to live a life of duty and good conduct. They learn to be selfless by thinking of others first, being respectful of parents, elders and swamis, following divine law, especially ahimsa, mental, emotional and physical noninjury to all beings. Thus they resolve karmas.

Dharma
धर्म

4. Pilgrimage

The dear children are taught the value of pilgrimage and are taken at least once a year for darshan of holy persons, temples and places, near or far. They learn to be detached by setting aside worldly affairs and making God, Gods and gurus life's singular focus during these journeys.

Tirthayatra

तीर्थयात्रा

5. Rites of Passage

The dear children are taught to observe the many sacraments which mark and sanctify their passages through life. They learn to be traditional by celebrating the rites of birth, name-giving, head-shaving, first feeding, ear-piercing, first learning, coming of age, marriage and death.

Samskara
संस्कार

Five Parenting Guidelines

BEHAVIORAL PRINCIPLES TO LIVE BY TO NURTURE CHILDREN AND TEACH THEM, VERBALLY AND BY EXAMPLE, TO FOLLOW THE PATH OF DHARMA

Pancha Kutumba Sadhana

पञ्च कुटुम्ब साधन

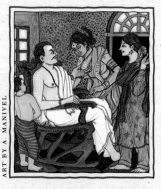

1. Good Conduct

Loving fathers and mothers, knowing they are the greatest influence in a child's life, behave the way their dear children should when adults. They never anger or argue before young ones. Father in a dhoti, mother in a sari at home, all sing to God, Gods and guru.

Dharmachara

धर्मचार

Dharma Svagriha

धर्मस्वगृह

2. Home Worship

Loving fathers and mothers establish a separate shrine room in the home for God, Gods and guardian devas of the family. Ideally it should be large enough for all the dear children. It is a sacred place for scriptural study, a refuge from the karmic storms of life.

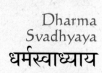

3. Talking about Religion

Loving fathers and mothers speak Vedic precepts while driving, eating and playing. This helps dear children understand experiences in right perspective. Parents know many worldly voices are blaring, and their dharmic voice must be stronger.

Dharma Sambhashana

धर्मसम्भाषन

4. Continuing Self-Study

Loving fathers and mothers keep informed by studying the *Vedas*, *Agamas* and sacred literature, listening to swamis and pandits. Youth face a world they will one day own, thus parents prepare their dear children to guide their own future progeny.

Dharma Svadhyaya

धर्मस्वाध्याय

5. Following a Spiritual Preceptor

Loving fathers and mothers choose a preceptor, a traditional *satguru*, and lineage to follow. They support their lineage with all their heart, energy and service. He in turn provides them clear guidance for a successful life, material and religious.

Dharma Sanga

धर्मसंग

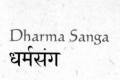

ART BY A. MANIVEL

Hinduism A to Z

A FUN, ILLUSTRATED ALPHABET DESIGNED AS TWENTY-SIX
MINI-LESSONS ON HINDU THOUGHT AND CULTURE

Dharma
Varnamala
धर्मवर्णमाला

A is for Aum, the three-syllabled mantra that represents the Sacred Mystery in sound and vibration.

D is for dharma, which is righteousness, cosmic order and duty, leading us on the right path.

B is for bhakti, deep devotion and love for the Divine which softens even hearts of stone.

E is for Earth, our lovely blue planet, which we treat as sacred, protecting all its wonderful creatures.

C is for culture, the beauty of Hindu music, fine arts, drama, dance, literature and architecture.

F is for family, the precious cornerstone of Hindu life, culture, service and tradition.

G is for guru, our enlightened master who, knowing Truth himself, can guide us there.

L is for lotus, the heart's inner shrine, where God dwells, ever serene, ever perfect.

H is for hatha yoga, healthful physical science for vitality, energy-balancing and meditation.

M is for *mauna*, not talking, the inner silence known when words, thoughts and actions are stilled.

I is for India, Bharata, Motherland to one-sixth of humanity, holy land for Hindus everywhere.

N is for non-attachment, the art of living the simple life, without too many needs or desires.

J is for *japa*, repetitive, prayerful mantras which quiet emotion and empower the mind.

O is for open-mindedness, the Hindu's tolerant freedom of thought, inquiry and belief.

K is for karma, the law of cause and effect by which we determine our experience and destiny.

P is for puja, mystic worship of the Divine in our home shrine and holy temples and places.

Q is for quest, seeking to know, "Who am I? Where did I come from? Where am I going?"

V is for *Vedas,* our oldest and holiest book, the word of God recorded in 100,000 Sanskrit verses.

R is for reincarnation, our immortal soul's journey from birth to rebirth. We do not fear death.

W is for wealth *(artha),* one of life's four goals, along with love, dharma and enlightenment.

S is for *samskaras,* sacraments sanctifying life's passages: name-giving, marriage, death and more.

X is for xerophily, the ability of certain plants and animals to thrive in India's hot, arid plains.

T is for *tilaka,* forehead marks worn in honor of our unique and varied lineages.

Y is for yoga, union of the soul with God which brings release from worldly bondage.

U is for *utsava,* our many home and temple festivals, full of bhakti, fun, feasting and family sharing.

Z is for zeal, the fervor with which we perform service, go on pilgrimage and greet our holy religious leaders.

CHAPTER 5

Who Is a Hindu?

Insights from Saints and Scholars on What Makes One a Hindu

EW PEOPLE TODAY PONDER THE SIGNIFI-cance of belief. Nevertheless, convictions constitute the foundation for every action. *Webster's* defines belief as a "confidence in the truth or existence of something not immediately susceptible to rigorous proof." But ask a Hindu what his all-important beliefs are, and the answer may well elude him. He is not accustomed to thinking of his religion as a clearly defined system, distinct and different from others, for it encompasses all of life.

Hinduism is so vast, so generously tolerant of conflicting concepts that to condense a brief list of basic beliefs might seem a vain enterprise. Some would assert that Hinduism could never be limited by such an ideological inventory—and they would be right. Still, an answer is required. Inside India, a clear answer prevents the erosion of "Hindu" into a mere geographical concept no different from "Indian;" elsewhere, it provides the necessary demarcation from other faiths in a pluralistic setting. The need for a precise list arises with the cognition that beliefs forge our attitudes, which determine our overall state of mind and the feelings we are predisposed to, and that these, in turn, directly determine our actions. Strong religious beliefs induce actions that weave uplifting patterns of daily conduct, furthering our unfoldment. In India, the defini-tion of who is a Hindu is critical in legal deliberations, and belief is the keystone of such determinations. Therefore, it is meaningful to catalog the convictions that all Hindus hold in common.

In 1926, Dr. S. Radhakrishnan eloquently elaborated the na-ture of Hindu belief in a series of lectures in Oxford, later pub-lished as *The Hindu View of Life.* "Hinduism is more a way of life than a form of thought. While it gives absolute liberty in the world of thought, it enjoins a strict code of practice. While fixed intel-lectual beliefs mark off one religion from another, Hinduism sets itself no such limits. Intellect is subordinated to intuition, dogma to experience, outer expression to inward realization. Religion is not the acceptance of academic abstractions or the celebration of ceremonies, but a kind of life or experience of reality." By em-phasizing conduct, Radhakrishnan did not deny belief. In fact, he provided one of the best extensive lists. His emphasis is on the absolute freedom of belief allowed within Hinduism—where the questioning mind is known as the seeking mind, rather than the errant mind.

The following definitions of Hinduism's shared central beliefs were garnered from prominent Hindu organizations and individu-als of the 20th century—evidence that the imperative to formalize conviction is a recent phenomenon. Overall, the lists and descrip-tions are surprisingly similar, echoing certain key concepts—gener-ally, that it is conduct, based upon belief in dharma, karma and reincarnation, which makes one a Hindu. Some of the beliefs listed are not shared by all Hindus—most prominently the concept of *ava-tar,* divine incarnation, which is a distinctive Vaishnava belief. We shall now cite what has been collected from distinguished scholars and saints.

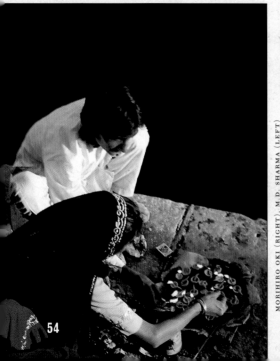

MORIHIRO OKI (RIGHT), M.D. SHARMA (LEFT)

54

Bal Ghangadhar Tilak, scholar, mathematician, philosopher and Indian nationalist, named "the father of the Indian Revolution" by Jawaharlal Nehru, summarized Hindu beliefs in his *Gitarahasya:* "Acceptance of the *Vedas* with reverence; recognition of the fact that the means or ways to salvation are diverse; and realization of the truth that the number of Gods to be worshiped is large, that indeed is the distinguishing feature of the Hindu religion." This oft-quoted statement, so compelling concise, is considered authoritative by Bharat's courts of law.

Sri K. Navaratnam, esteemed Sri Lankan religious scholar, enumerated a more extensive set of basic beliefs in his book, *Studies in Hinduism,* reflecting the Southern Saiva Agamic tradition. 1) A belief in the existence of God. 2) A belief in the existence of a soul separate from the body. 3) A belief in the existence of the finitizing principle known as *avidya* or *mala*. 4) A belief in the principle of matter—prakriti or maya. 5) A belief in the theory of karma and reincarnation. 6) A belief in the indispensable guidance of a guru to guide the spiritual aspirant towards God Realization. 7) A belief in moksha, or liberation, as the goal of human existence. 8) A belief in the indispensable necessity of temple worship in religious life. 9) A belief in graded forms of religious practices, both internal and external, until one realizes God. 10) A belief in ahimsa as the greatest dharma or virtue. 11) A belief in mental and physical purity as indispensable factors for spiritual progress.

Mahatma Mohandas K. Gandhi: "I call myself a Sanatani Hindu because I believe in the *Vedas,* the *Upanishads,* the *Puranas* and all that goes by the name of Hindu scriptures, and therefore in avatars and rebirth. Above all, I call myself a Sanatani Hindu, so long as the Hindu society in general accepts me as such. In a concrete manner he is a Hindu who believes in God, immortality of the soul, transmigration, the law of karma and moksha, and who tries to practice truth and ahimsa in daily life, and therefore practices cow protection in its widest sense and understands and tries to act according to the law of *varnashrama*."

Sri Pramukh Swami Maharaj of the Bochasanwasi Shri Akshar Purushottam Sanstha (Swaminarayan Faith) propounds: 1) *Parabrahman,* one supreme all-powerful God: He is the Creator, has a divine form, is immanent, transcendent and the giver of moksha. 2) *Avatarvad,* manifestation of God on Earth: God Himself incarnates on Earth in various forms to revive dharma and grant liberation. 3) *Karmavad,* law of action: the soul reaps fruits, good or bad, according to its past and present actions, which are experienced either in this life or future lives. 4) *Punarjanma,* reincarnation: the mortal soul is continuously born and reborn in one of the 8,400,000 species until it attains liberation. 5) Moksha, ultimate liberation: the goal of human life. It is the liberation of the soul from the cycle of births and deaths to remain eternally in the service of God. 6) *Guru-shishya sambandh,* master-disciple relationship: guidance and grace of a spiritually perfect master, revered as the embodiment of God, is essential for an aspirant seeking liberation. 7) Dharma, that which sustains the universe: an all-encompassing term representing divine law, law of being, path of righteousness, religion, duty, responsibility, virtue, justice, goodness and truth. 8) *Ved pramana,* scriptural authority of the *Vedas:* all Hindu faiths are based on the teachings of the *Vedas.* 9) *Murti-puja,* sacred image worship: consecrated images represent the presence of God which is worshiped. The sacred image is a medium to help devotees offer their devotion to God.

Sri Swami Vivekananda, speaking in America, said: "All Vedantists believe in God. Vedantists also believe the *Vedas* to be the revealed word of God—an expression of the knowledge of God—and as God is eternal, so are the *Vedas* eternal. Another common ground of belief is that of creation in cycles, that the whole of creation appears and disappears. They postulate the existence of a material, which they call akasha, which is something like the ether of the scientists, and a power which they call prana."

Sri Jayendra Saraswati: 69th Shankaracharya of the Kamakoti Peetham, Kanchipuram, defines in his writings the basic features of Hinduism as follows. 1) The concept of idol worship and the worship of God in His *nirguna* as well as *saguna* form. 2) The

Left to right: *Honoring ancestors on the Ganga; students of Vishva-bharati University celebrate Holi; Vaishnava Sadhu immersed in japa yoga; puja at the Siddhi Vinayagar temple in Malaysia*

SIAN DAVIES

LINDSAY HEBBERD

INDIVAR SIVANATHAN

wearing of sacred marks on the forehead. 3) Belief in the theory of past and future births in accordance with the theory of karma. 4) Cremation of ordinary men and burial of great men.

Dr. S. Radhakrishnan, renowned philosopher and president of India from 1962 to 1967, states in *The Hindu View of Life*: "The Hindu recognizes one Supreme Spirit, though different names are given to it. God is in the world, though not as the world. He does not merely intervene to create life or consciousness, but is working continuously. There is no dualism of the natural and the supernatural. Evil, error and ugliness are not ultimate. No view is so utterly erroneous, no man is so absolutely evil as to deserve complete castigation. There is no Hell, for that means there is a place where God is not, and there are sins which exceed His love. The law of karma tells us that the individual life is not a term, but a series. Heaven and Hell are higher and lower stages in one continuous movement. Every type has its own nature which should be followed. We should do our duty in that state of life to which we happen to be called. Hinduism affirms that the theological expressions of religious experience are bound to be varied, accepts all forms of belief and guides each along his path to the common goal. These are some of the central principles of Hinduism. If Hinduism lives today, it is due to them."

The Vishva Hindu Parishad declared its definition in a 1966 *Memorandum of Association, Rules and Regulations:* "Hindu means a person believing in, following or respecting the eternal values of life, ethical and spiritual, which have sprung up in Bharatkhand [India] and includes any person calling himself a Hindu."

The Indian Supreme Court, in 1966, formalized a judicial definition of Hindu beliefs to legally distinguish Hindu denominations from other religions in India. This list was affirmed by the Court as recently as 1995 in judging cases regarding religious identity. 1) Acceptance of the *Vedas* with reverence as the highest authority in religious and philosophic matters and acceptance with reverence of *Vedas* by Hindu thinkers and philosophers as the sole foundation of Hindu philosophy. 2) Spirit of tolerance and willingness to understand and appreciate the opponent's point of view based on the realization that truth is many-sided. 3) Acceptance of great world rhythm—vast periods of creation, maintenance and dissolution follow each other in endless succession—by all six systems of Hindu philosophy. 4) Acceptance by all systems of Hindu philosophy of the belief in rebirth and pre-existence. 5) Recognition of the fact that the means or ways to salvation are many. 6) Realization of the truth that numbers of Gods to be worshiped may be large, yet there being Hindus who do not believe in the worshiping of idols. 7) Unlike other religions, or religious creeds, Hindu religion's not being tied down to any definite set of philosophic concepts, as such.

The historic intermingling of myriad races, cultures and religions has exposed us to a kaleidoscopic array of beliefs and practices; yet threads of sameness and agreement bind them together. Taken as a whole, the definitions above, emphasizing the *Vedas*, dharma, karma and rebirth, can help us gain clarity and insight into our inmost convictions, offering the opportunity to freely and ably choose the same as our progenitors—or not. That "or not" may be the greatest freedom a seeker ever had or could ever hope for.

A scene from the movie Mystic India depicting the grand pagentry of the Hindu faith: devotees of Lord Swaminarayan pull a huge festival chariot

COURTESY BAPS

CHAPTER 6

12 Beliefs
Of Saivism

Devout followers bring abundant gifts, prayers and petitions in loving worship of Lord Siva

A Sacred Creed of One of Hinduism's Four Primary Denominations

EVERY RELIGION HAS A CREED OF ONE FORM OR AN-other, an authoritative formulation of its beliefs. Historically, creeds have developed whenever religions migrate from their homelands. Until then, the beliefs are fully contained in the culture and taught to children as a natural part of growing up. A creed is the distillation of volumes of knowledge into a series of easy-to-remember beliefs. A creed is meant to summarize the explicit teachings or articles of faith, to imbed and thus protect and transmit the beliefs. Creeds give strength to individuals seeking to understand life and religion. Creeds also enable members of one faith to express, in elementary and consistent terms, their traditions to members of another.

Though the vast array of doctrines within Hinduism has not always been articulated in summary form, from ancient times unto today we have the well-known creedal *maha-vakya*, "great sayings," of the Vedic *Upanishads*. Now, in this technological age in which village integrity is being replaced by worldwide mobility, the importance of a creed becomes apparent if religious identity is to be preserved. We need two kinds of strength—that which is found in diversity and individual freedom to inquire and that which derives from a union of minds in upholding the universal and shared principles of our faith.

Saivism is truly ageless, for it has no beginning. It is the precursor of the many-faceted religion now termed Hinduism. Scholars trace the roots of Siva worship back more than 8,000 years to the advanced Indus Valley civilization. But sacred writings tell us there never was a time when Saivism did not exist. Modern history records six main schools: Saiva Siddhanta, Pashupatism, Kashmir Saivism, Vira Saivism, Siddha Siddhanta and Siva Advaita. Saivism's grandeur and beauty are found in a practical culture, an enlightened view of man's place in the universe and a profound system of temple mysticism and yoga. It provides knowledge of man's evolution from God and back to God, of the soul's unfoldment and awakening guided by enlightened sages. Like all the Hindu sects, its majority are families, headed by hundreds of orders of swamis and sadhus who follow the fiery, world-renouncing path to moksha. The *Vedas* state, "By knowing Siva, who is hidden in all things, exceedingly fine, like film arising from clarified butter, the One embracer of the universe—by realizing God, one is released from all fetters."

The twelve beliefs on the following pages embody the centuries-old central convictions of Saivism, especially as postulated in Saiva Siddhanta, one of the six schools of Saivism. They cover the basic beliefs about God, soul and world, evil and love and more. On the last page is a glossary of words used in the twelve beliefs.

S RAJAM

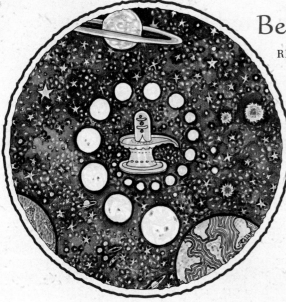

Belief One

REGARDING GOD'S UNMANIFEST REALITY

Siva's followers all believe that Lord Siva is God, whose Absolute Being, Parasiva, transcends time, form and space. The yogi silently exclaims, "It is not this. It is not that." Yea, such an inscrutable God is God Siva. Aum.

Belief Two

REGARDING GOD'S MANIFEST
NATURE OF ALL-PERVADING LOVE

Siva's followers all believe that Lord Siva is God, whose immanent nature of love, Parashakti, is the substratum, primal substance or pure consciousness flowing through all form as energy, existence, knowledge and bliss. Aum.

Belief Three

REGARDING GOD AS PERSONAL
LORD AND CREATOR OF ALL

Siva's followers all believe that Lord Siva is God, whose immanent nature is the Primal Soul, Supreme Maha-deva, Paramesvara, author of *Vedas* and *Agamas*, the creator, preserver and destroyer of all that exists. Aum.

ALL ART BY S RAJAM

Belief Four

REGARDING THE ELEPHANT-FACED DEITY

Siva's followers all believe in the
Mahadeva Lord Ganesha, son of
Siva-Shakti, to whom they must
first supplicate before beginning
any worship or task. His rule
is compassionate. His law is
just. Justice is His mind. Aum.

Belief Five

REGARDING THE DEITY KARTTIKEYA

Siva's followers all believe in the
Mahadeva Karttikeya, son of Siva-
Shakti, whose vel of grace dissolves
the bondages of ignorance. The yogi,
locked in lotus, venerates Murugan. Thus
restrained, his mind becomes calm. Aum.

Belief Six

REGARDING THE SOUL'S
CREATION AND IDENTITY WITH GOD

Siva's followers all believe that each
soul is created by Lord Siva and is
identical to Him, and that this identity
will be fully realized by all souls when
the bondage of *anava*, karma and
maya is removed by His grace. Aum.

Belief Seven

THE GROSS, SUBTLE AND CAUSAL PLANES OF EXISTENCE

Siva's followers all believe in three worlds: the gross plane, where souls take on physical bodies; the subtle plane, where souls take on astral bodies; and the causal plane, where souls exist in their self-effulgent form. Aum.

Belief Eight

REGARDING KARMA, SAMSARA AND LIBERATION FROM REBIRTH

Siva's followers all believe in the law of karma—that one must reap the effects of all actions he has caused—and that each soul continues to reincarnate until all karmas are resolved and moksha, liberation, is attained. Aum.

Belief Nine

REGARDING THE FOUR MARGAS, OR STAGES OF INNER PROGRESS

Siva's followers all believe that the performance of *charya*, virtuous living, *kriya*, temple worship, and yoga, leading to Parasiva through the grace of the living *satguru*, is absolutely necessary to bring forth *jnana*, wisdom. Aum.

Belief Ten

REGARDING THE GOODNESS OF ALL

Siva's followers all believe there is no intrinsic evil. Evil has no source, unless the source of evil's seeming be ignorance itself. They are truly compassionate, knowing that ultimately there is no good or bad. All is Siva's will. Aum.

Belief Eleven

REGARDING THE ESOTERIC PURPOSE OF TEMPLE WORSHIP

Siva's followers all believe that religion is the harmonious working together of the three worlds and that this harmony can be created through temple worship, wherein the beings of all three worlds can communicate. Aum.

Belief Twelve

REGARDING THE FIVE LETTERS

Siva's followers all believe in the Panchakshara Mantra, the five sacred syllables "Namasivaya," as Saivism's foremost and essential mantra. The secret of Namasivaya is to hear it from the right lips at the right time. Aum.

Veda study: *A father and his sons chant Vedic mantras together outside their adobe dwelling during their daily practice sessions*

The Path to Enlightenment

The path of enlightenment is divided naturally into four stages or *padas: charya,* virtue and selfless service; *kriya,* worshipful *sadhanas;* yoga, meditation under a guru's guidance; and jnana, the state of enlightened wisdom reached toward the path's end as a result of Self Realization through the Guru's grace. These four *padas* are quite similar to the four yogas of Vedanta: karma yoga, bhakti yoga, raja yoga and *jnana* yoga. However, there is one key difference. Whereas in Vedanta you can choose to follow just one of the yogas, in the Saiva Siddhanta school of Saivism we need to pass through all four stages, or *padas.*

Let's say the path of life is rocks across a shallow stream. Vedanta gives us four separate rock paths to choose from, one for each of the four yogas, all of which lead across the river. Saiva Siddhanta gives us one path for crossing the river which consists of four stones: *charya, kriya,* yoga and *jnana.*

The four stages are not alternative ways, but progressive, cumulative phases of a one path, much like the natural development of a butterfly from egg to caterpillar, from caterpillar to pupa, and then the final metamorphosis to butterfly. The four stages are what each human soul must pass through in many births to attain its final goal of moksha, freedom from rebirth. In the beginning stages, we suffer until we learn. Learning leads us to service; and selfless service is the beginning of spiritual striving. Service leads us to understanding. Understanding leads us to meditate deeply and without distractions. Finally meditation leads us to surrender in God. This is the straight and certain path, the San Marga, leading to Self Realization, the inmost purpose of life.

Charya Pada

Charya, literally "conduct," is the first stage of religiousness and the foundation for the next three stages. It is also called the *dasa marga,* meaning "path of servitude," for here the soul relates to God as servant to master. The disciplines of *charya* include humble service, attending the temple, performing one's duty to community and family,

honoring holy men, respecting elders, atoning for misdeeds and fulfilling the ten classical restraints called *yamas,* which are: noninjury, truthfulness, nonstealing, divine conduct, patience, steadfastness, compassion, honesty, moderate appetite and purity. It is the stage of overcoming basic instinctive patterns such as the tendencies to become angry and hurtful. Right behavior and self-sacrificing service are never outgrown. The keynote of *charya,* or karma yoga, is *seva,* religious service given without the least thought of reward, which has the magical effect of softening the ego and bringing forth the soul's innate devotion.

Kriya Pada

Saivism demands deep devotion through bhakti yoga in the *kriya pada,* the softening of the intellect and unfolding love. In *kriya,* the second stage of religiousness, our *sadhana,* or regular spiritual discipline, which was mostly external in *charya,* is now also internal. *Kriya,* literally "action or rite," is a stirring of the soul in awareness of the Divine, overcoming the instinctive-intellectual mind. We now look upon the Deity image not just as carved stone, but as the living presence of the God. We perform ritual and puja not because we have to but because we want to. We are drawn to the temple to satisfy our longing. We sing joyfully. We absorb and intuit the wisdom of the *Vedas* and *Agamas.* We perform pilgrimage and fulfill the sacraments. We practice diligently the ten classical observances called *niyamas* which are: remorse, contentment, giving, faith, worship of the Lord, scriptural listening, cognition, sacred vows, recitation and austerity. Our relationship with God in *kriya* is as a son to his parents.

Yoga Pada

Yoga, "union," is the process of uniting with God within oneself, a stage arrived at through perfecting *charya* and *kriya.* God is now like a friend to us. This system of inner discovery begins with asana—sitting quietly in yogic posture—and pranayama, breath control. *Pratyahara,* sense withdrawal, brings awareness into *dharana,* concentration, then into dhyana, meditation. Over the years, under ideal conditions, the kundalini fire of consciousness ascends to the higher chakras, burning the dross of ignorance and past karmas. Dhyana finally leads to enstasy—the contemplative experience of Satchidananda, God as energy-bliss, and ultimately to *nirvikalpa* samadhi, the experience of God as Parasiva, timeless, formless, spaceless. Truly a living *satguru* is needed as a steady guide to traverse this path. When yoga is practiced by one perfected in *kriya,* the Gods receive the yogi into their midst through his awakened, fiery kundalini, or cosmic energy within every individual.

Jnana Pada

Jnana is divine wisdom emanating from an enlightened being, a soul in its maturity, immersed in Sivaness, the blessed realization of God, while living out earthly karma. *Jnana* is the fruition of yoga and *tapas,* or intense spiritual discipline. Through yoga one bursts into the superconscious mind, experiencing bliss, all-knowingness and perfect silence. It is when the yogi's intellect is shattered that he soars into Parasiva and comes out a *jnani,* a knower. Each time he enters that unspeakable *nirvikalpa* samadhi, he returns to consciousness more and more the knower. He is the liberated one, the *jivanmukta,* the epitome of *kaivalya*—perfect freedom—far-seeing, filled with light, filled with love. One does not become a *jnani* simply by reading and understanding philosophy. The state of *jnana* lies in the realm of intuition, beyond the intellect.

Temple worship: *With Siva watching, devotees approach a temple traditionally with offerings of flowers, fruits and water*

CHAPTER 7

Hindu Scriptures

Ancient Holy Texts Revealed by God and Man

The Word, verily, is greater than name. The Word, in fact, makes known the *Rig Veda,* the *Yajur Veda,* the *Sama Veda,* the *Atharva Veda* as the fourth, and the ancient lore as the fifth: the Veda of *Vedas,* the ritual for ancestors, calculus, the augural sciences, the knowledge of the signs of the times, ethics, political science, sacred knowledge, theology, knowledge of the spirits, military science, astrology, the science of snakes and of celestial beings.

Sama Veda, Chandogya Upanishad 7.2.1.
The Vedic Experience, Panikkar, p. 111

Than whom there is naught else higher, than whom there is naught smaller, naught greater, the One stands like a tree established in heaven. By Him, the Person, is this whole universe filled.

Krishna Yajur Veda, Shvetashvatara
Upanishad 3.9, The Principal
Upanishads, Radhakrishnan, p. 727

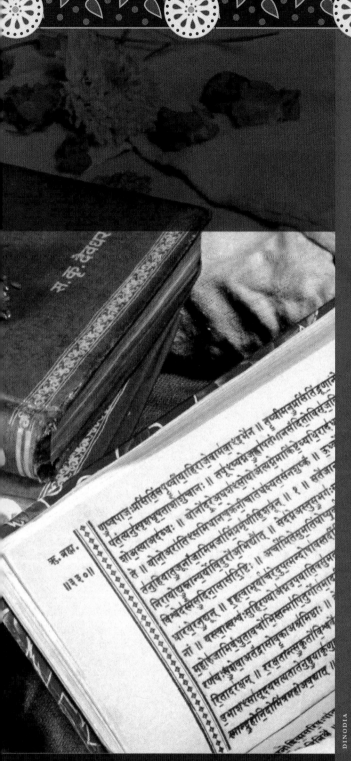

DINODIA

Presenting a mountaintop view of the vast library of wisdom that molds and influences Hindu life

Hinduism proudly embraces an incredibly rich collection of scripture. The holiest and most revered are the *Vedas* and *Agamas*, two massive compendia of *shruti* (that which is "heard"), both revealed by God to illumined sages centuries and millennia ago. The array of works known as smriti (that which is "remembered") is equally vast, the most prominent and widely celebrated of which are the *Itihasas* (epic dramas and history)—the *Ramayana* and *Mahabharata*—and the *Puranas* (mythology). The Vedic arts and sciences, including ayurveda, astrology, music, dance, architecture, statecraft, domestic duty and law, are reflected in an assembly of texts known as *Vedangas* and *Upavedas*. Moreover, through the ages God-realized souls, sharing their experience, have poured forth volume upon volume that reveal the wonders of yoga and offer passionate hymns of devotion. The creation of Hindu scripture continues to this day, as contemporary masters reiterate the timeless truths to guide souls on the path to Divinity. In this Educational Insight, we offer a simple overview of Hindu scripture and an anthology of verses from this luminous library of dharma.

The man who rejects the words of the scriptures and follows the impulse of desire attains neither his perfection, nor joy, nor the Path Supreme. Let the scriptures be, therefore, thy authority as to what is right and what is not right.

Bhagavad Gita 16.23-24, Mascaro, p. 111

The stack of books at left holds one bound volume from each of the four *Vedas* in the Sanskrit language. For centuries they have been the basis of philosophical discussion, study and commentary. The *Vedas* are also the subject of deep study and meditation, to realize the wisdom of the ancients within oneself. Their mantras are chanted and used in rites of worship, prayer and japa.

What Are Hindu Revealed Scriptures?

The *Vedas* and *Agamas,* revealed by God, are Hinduism's sovereign scriptures, called ***shruti,*** "that which is heard." Their timeless truths are expressed in the most extraordinarily profound mystical poetry known to man. Aum.

Above, God holds the holiest of scriptures, the *Vedas* and *Agamas.* Around these are an array of other scriptures, enscribed on stone, wood, pillars and scrolls. At left, we see a copy of the *Rig Veda Samhita.* In the dimmed background, lamps are offered, as prescribed in the *Agamas,* by priests at Nallur Kandaswamy Temple in Sri Lanka.

VEDA, FROM VID, "TO KNOW," MEANS "SUPREME wisdom or science." Similarly, *Agama,* which names the sacred sectarian revelations, means "descent of knowledge." The *Vedas* and *Agamas* are eternal truths transmitted by God through great clairaudient and clairvoyant rishis. They are Hinduism's primary and most authoritative scriptures, expounding life's sacredness and man's purpose on the planet. These psalms of wisdom were disclosed over many centuries, memorized and orally conveyed from generation to generation within priestly families, then finally written down in Sanskrit in the last few millennia. The subtly symbolic language of *shruti,* the cherished word of God, is lyrical and lofty. In imparting religious practice, rules and doctrine, the *Vedas* are general and the *Agamas* specific. The *Vedas* extol and invoke a multiplicity of Gods through elaborate fire rituals called *yajna.* The *Agamas* center around a single Deity and His worship with water, flowers and lights in sanctified temples and shrines. The *Tirumantiram* lauds, "Two are the scriptures that Lord Siva revealed—the primal *Vedas* and the perfect *Agamas.*" Aum Namah Sivaya.

What Is the Nature of the Veda Texts?

The holy *Vedas*, man's oldest scripture, dating back 6,000 to 8,000 years, are a collection of four books: the *Rig, Sama, Yajur* and *Atharva*. Each has four sections: hymns, rites, interpretation and philosophical instruction. Aum.

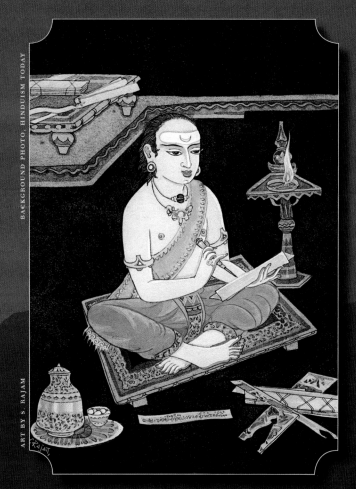

Above, using the traditional *elutani*, stylus, a pandit scribes memorized Vedic verses on dried palm leaves. For centuries the *Vedas* were passed on orally, then finally transcribed. Left, a devotee leafs through his holy text as he performs his morning *sadhana*.

THE OLDEST AND CORE PORTIONS OF THE *VEDAS* are the four *Samhitas*, "hymn collections." They consist of invocations to the One Divine and the Divinities of nature—such as the Sun, the Rain, the Wind, the Fire and the Dawn—as well as prayers for matrimony, progeny, prosperity, concord, domestic rites, formulas for magic, and more. They are composed in beautiful metrical verses, generally of three or four lines. The heart of the entire Veda is the 10,552-verse *Rig Samhita*. The *Sama* and *Yajur Samhitas*, each with about 2,000 verses, are mainly liturgical selections from the *Rig*, whereas most of the *Atharva Samhita's* nearly 6,000 verses of prayers, charms and rites are unique. The *Sama* is arranged for melodious chanting, the *Yajur* for cadenced intonation. Besides its *Samhita*, each *Veda* includes one or two *Brahmanas*, ceremonial handbooks, and *Aranyakas*, ritual interpretations, plus many inestimable *Upanishads*, metaphysical dialogs. In all there are over 100,000 Vedic verses, and some prose, in dozens of texts. The *Tirumantiram* confirms, "There is no dharma other than what the *Vedas* say. Dharma's central core the *Vedas* proclaim." Aum Namah Sivaya.

How Are the Vedas Significant Today?

The *Vedas*, the ultimate scriptural authority, permeate Hinduism's thought, ritual and meditation. They open a rare window into ancient Bharata society, proclaiming life's sacredness and the way to oneness with God. Aum.

Above, a young Smarta priest conducts a fire ceremony, *havana*, as decreed in the *Vedas*. At left, a Vaishnava priest blows a conch horn during prayers in Allahabad. Background photo, at Manikarnika Ghat in Varanasi, a priest performs *antyeshti*, the cremation ritual, last in the series of rites of passage prescribed in the *Vedas*.

IKE THE TAOIST TAO TE CHING, THE BUDDHIST *Dhammapada*, the Sikh *Adi Granth*, the Jewish *Torah*, the Christian *Bible* and the Muslim *Koran*, the *Veda* is the Hindu holy book. For untold centuries unto today, it has remained the sustaining force and authoritative doctrine, guiding followers in ways of worship, duty and enlightenment—*upasana*, dharma and *jnana*. The *Vedas* are the meditative and philosophical focus for millions of monks and a billion seekers. Their stanzas are chanted from memory by priests and laymen daily as liturgy in temple worship and domestic ritual. All Hindus wholeheartedly accept the *Vedas*, yet each draws selectively, interprets freely and amplifies abundantly. Over time, this tolerant allegiance has woven the varied tapestry of Bharata Dharma. Today the *Vedas* are published in Sanskrit, English, French, German and other languages. But it is the metaphysical and popular *Upanishads* which have been most amply and ably translated. The *Vedas* say, "Just as the spokes are affixed to the hub of a wheel, so are all things established in life, the *Rig* and *Yajur* and *Sama Veda*, sacrifice, the nobility and also the priesthood." Aum Namah Sivaya.

What Is the Nature of the Holy Agamas?

The *Agamas*, Sanatana Dharma's second authority, are revelations on sacred living, worship, yoga and philosophy. Saivism, Shaktism and Vaishnavism each exalts its own array of *Agamas*, many more than 2,000 years old. Aum.

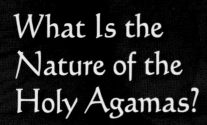

BACKGROUND: THOMAS KELLY

FRENCH INSTITUTE OF PONDICHERRY

FR. INSTITUTE OF PONDICHERRY

Above, Dr. Ganesan, a scholar at the French Institute of Pondicherry, India, shows the volumes of *Saiva Agamas* they have printed to date. They are keepers of 8,000 ancient manuscripts, mostly palm-leaf books, such as those seen stored on shelves on the left, which one day will be published to the world. In the background, a devotee offers flowers to the Lord.

N THE VAST AGAMIC LITERATURE, TRADITION counts 92 main *Saiva Agamas*—10 Siva, 18 Rudra and 64 Bhairava—77 Shakta *Agamas* and 108 *Vaishnava Pancharatra Agamas*. Most *Agamas* are of four parts, called *padas*, and possess thousands of metered Sanskrit verses, usually of two lines. The *charya pada* details daily religious observance, right conduct, the guru-*shishya* relationship, community life, house design and town planning. The *kriya pada*, commonly the longest, extols worship and temples in meticulous detail—from site selection, architectural design and iconography, to rules for priests and the intricacies of daily puja, annual festivals and home-shrine devotionals. The yoga *pada* discloses the interior way of meditation, of raja yoga, mantra and tantra, which stimulates the awakening of the slumbering serpent, kundalini. The jnana *pada* narrates the nature of God, soul and world, and the means for liberation. The *Tirumantiram* declares, "*Veda* and *Agama* are Iraivan's scriptures. Both are truth: one is general, the other specific. While some say these words of God reach two different conclusions, the wise see no difference." Aum Namah Sivaya.

How Are The Agamas Significant Today?

While the *Vedas,* with myriad Deities, bind all Hindus together, the *Agamas,* with a single supreme God, unify each sect in a oneness of thought, instilling in adherents the joyful arts of divine adoration. Aum Namah Sivaya.

Like millions of Hindus before them, the youth in these two photos are learning precise recitation of liturgy from the *Agamas* and *Vedas.* They will spend years perfecting this training, enabling them to perform ritual worship, puja, in temples around the world. In their priest school in Tirupati, India, they will memorize hundreds of mantras.

GOD IS LOVE, AND TO LOVE GOD IS THE PURE path prescribed in the *Agamas.* Veritably, these texts are God's own voice admonishing the samsari, reincarnation's wanderer, to give up love of the transient and adore instead the Immortal. How to love the Divine, when and where, with what mantras and visualizations and at what auspicious times, all this is preserved in the *Agamas.* The specific doctrines and practices of day-to-day Hinduism are nowhere more fully expounded than in these revelation hymns, delineating everything from daily work routines to astrology and cosmology. So overwhelming is Agamic influence in the lives of most Hindus, particularly in temple liturgy and culture, that it is impossible to ponder modern Sanatana Dharma without these discourses. While many *Agamas* have been published, most remain inaccessible, protected by families and guilds who are stewards of an intimate hereditary knowledge. The *Tirumantiram* says, "Nine are the *Agamas* of yore, in time expanded into 28, they then took divisions three, into one truth of Vedanta-Siddhanta to accord. That is Suddha Saiva, rare and precious." Aum Namah Sivaya.

Do Smriti And Sacred Literature Differ?

Hindu sacred literature is a treasury of hymns, legend, mythology, philosophy, science and ethics. From among this vast body of writings, each lineage recognizes a select portion as its secondary scripture, called **smriti**. Aum.

BACKGROUND PHOTO BY THOMAS KELLY

MANAS DAS

DINODIA

Above, Masako Ono voyaged from Japan to India to learn the ancient Odissi dance style and remained there to teach it. The many human arts are found in ancient scripture. At left, a collection of Hindu holy texts stacked in a Delhi store. In the background, two girls reverently touch the holy feet of Lord Vishnu at a shrine in Tirupati.

HILE THE *VEDAS* AND *AGAMAS* ARE SHARED AS part of every Hindu's primary scripture, *shruti*, each sect and lineage defines its own unique set of smriti. The sacred literature, *punya shastra,* from which smriti is drawn consists of writings, both ancient and modern, in many languages. Especially central are the ancient Sanskritic texts, such as the *Itihasas, Puranas* and *Dharma Sastras,* which are widely termed the classical smriti. In reality, while many revere these as smriti, others regard them only as sacred literature. Smriti means "that which is remembered" and is known as "the tradition," for it derives from human insight and experience and preserves the course of culture. While *shruti* comes from God and is eternal and universal, the ever-growing smriti canon is written by man. Hinduism's sacred literature is the touchstone of theater and dance, music, song and pageantry, yoga and *sadhana,* metaphysics and ethics, exquisite art and hallowed sciences. The *Vedas* inquire, "In whom are set firm the firstborn seers, the hymns, the songs and the sacrificial formulas, in whom is established the single seer—tell me of that support—who may He be?" Aum Namah Sivaya.

What Texts Amplify Vedas And Agamas?

Many texts support the *Vedas* and *Agamas*. *Vedangas* detail conduct, astrology, language and etymology. *Upavedas* unfold politics, health, warfare and music. *Upagamas* and *Paddhatis* elaborate the Agamic wisdom. Aum.

Above, a bride and groom are in the midst of their wedding; at left they hold an offering of sacred grasses. Wedding chants derive from the *Vedas*, *Agamas* and ancillary texts; attitudes and guidelines for family life are found in the *Sutras* and *Shastras*. In the background photo, a girl receives sacraments after a puja.

MUCH OF HINDUISM'S PRACTICAL KNOWLEDGE is safeguarded in venerable texts which amplify *shruti*. The *Vedangas* and *Upavedas* are collections of texts that augment and apply the *Vedas* as a comprehensive system of sacred living. *Jyotisha Vedanga* delineates auspicious timing for holy rites. *Kalpa Vedanga* defines public rituals in the *Srauta* and *Sulba Sutras*, domestic rites in the *Grihya Sutras* and religious law in the *Dharma Sastras*. Four other *Vedangas* ensure the purity of mantra recitation, through knowledge of phonetics, grammar, poetry and the way of words. The *Upavedas* expound profound sciences: *Arthaveda* unfolds statecraft; *Ayurveda* sets forth medicine and health; *Dhanurveda* discusses military science; *Gandharvaveda* illumines music and the arts; and *Sthapatyaveda* explains architecture. In addition, the *Kama Sutras* detail erotic pleasures. The *Agamas*, too, have ancillary texts, such as the *Upagamas* and *Paddhatis*, which elaborate the ancient wisdom. The *Jnaneshvari* says, "The *Vedas* in their perfection are as the beautiful image of the God of which the flawless words are the resplendent body. The smritis are the limbs thereof." Aum Namah Sivaya.

Does Hinduism Have Epics And Myths?

The *Mahabharata* and *Ramayana* are Hinduism's most renowned epic histories, called *Itihasa*. The *Puranas* are popular folk narratives, teaching faith, belief and ethics in mythology, allegory, legend and symbolism. Aum.

Above, a woman performs a dance depicting a scene from the *Ramayana* in Java, where the world-renowned epic is widely celebrated in gala dance and theater. At left, Sanskrit volumes of the famed poem are shown, along with Hinduism's other epic, the *Mahabharata*.

INDUISM'S POETIC STORIES OF RISHIS, GODS, heroes and demons are sung by gifted panditas and traveling bards, narrated to children and portrayed in dramas and festivals. The *Mahabharata*, the world's longest epic poem, is the legend of two ancient dynasties whose great battle of Kurukshetra is the scene of the *Bhagavad Gita*, the eloquent spiritual dialog between Arjuna and Krishna. The *Ramayana* relates the life of Rama, a heroic king revered as the ideal man. The *Puranas*, like the *Mahabharata*, are encyclopedic in scope, containing teachings on *sadhana*, philosophy, dharma, ritual, language and the arts, architecture, agriculture, magic charms and more. Of 18 principal *Puranas*, six honor God as Siva, six as Vishnu and six as Brahma. The witty *Panchatantra*, eminent among the "story" literature, or *katha*, portrays wisdom through animal fables and parables. The *Bhagavad Gita* proclaims, "He who reads this sacred dialog of ours, by him I consider Myself worshiped through the sacrifice of knowledge. And the man who listens to it with faith and without scoffing, liberated, he shall attain to the happy realm of the righteous." Aum Namah Sivaya.

Are There Other Types of Sacred Texts?

India's lofty philosophical texts expound diverse views in exacting dialectics. Yoga treatises unveil the mysterious path to ultimate samadhis. Intimate devotional hymns disclose the raptures of consummate divine love. Aum.

BACKGROUND PHOTO BY THOMAS KELLY

DINODIA

Above, a recluse, clearly immersed in his yoga *sadhana*, sits in meditation beneath a gnarled banyan tree. At left are displayed two primary yoga scriptures, *Yoga Sutras* and *Yoga Vashishtha*. In the background, a young lady lights a ghee lamp to offer in personal worship, as her ancestors have done for centuries.

IN ADDITION TO THE EPICS, LEGENDS AND SUPPLE-ments to the *Vedas* and *Agamas,* there is a wealth of Hindu metaphysical, yogic and devotional writings. Considered foundational are the early texts defining the six philosophical *darshanas:* the sutras by Kapila, Patanjali, Jaimini, Badarayana, Kanada and Gautama. Hailed as leading occult works on yoga, asanas, *nadis*, chakras, kundalini and samadhi are the *Yoga Sutras, Tirumantiram, Yoga Vasishtha, Siva Sutras, Siddha Siddhanta Paddhati, Jnaneshvari, Hatha Yoga Pradipika* and *Gheranda Samhita.* Widely extolled among the bhakti literature are the *Bhagavad Gita, Narada Sutras, Tiruvasagam,* the *Vachanas* of the Sivasharanas and the hymns of mystic poets like Surdas, Tukaram, Ramprasad, Mirabai, Andal, Vallabha, Tulasidasa, Tayumanavar, Lalla, Tagore, Auvaiyar and the saintly Nayanars and Alvars. *The Bhagavad Gita* explains, "As a blazing fire reduces the wood to ashes, O Arjuna, so does the fire of knowledge reduce all activity to ashes. There is nothing on Earth which possesses such power to cleanse as wisdom. The perfect yogin finds this knowledge in himself by himself in due time." Aum Namah Sivaya.

THOMAS KELLY

How Did the Sage of Kanchi Extol the Vedas?

Sri Chandrashekharendra Saraswati wrote, "The *Vedas* are eternal and are the source of all creation. Their greatness is to be known in many ways. Their sound produces in our *nadis* (subtle nerve channels), as well as in the atmosphere, vibrations that are salutary not only to our own Self but to the entire world—to the good of mankind as well as of all other creatures."

ART BY S. RAJAM

Sri Chandrashekharendra Saraswati [1894–1994], 68th pontiff of Kanchi Kamakoti Pitham, depicted above, walked throughout India teaching of the *Vedas*. Here he is shown before an image of Siva as Dakshinamurti, the silent guru seated beneath a banyan tree. Above left, an earthen mandala on a wall of Muktinath Temple in Nepal.

THE CONCERN FOR ALL CREATION THAT FINDS expression in the *Vedas* is not shared by any other religion. *Shanno astu dvipade shanchatushpade*—this occurs in a mantra. The *Vedas* pray for the good of all creatures including bipeds, quadrupeds, etc. Even grass, shrubs, trees, mountains and the rivers are not excluded from their benign purview. The happy state of all these sentient creatures and inert objects is brought about through the special quality of the *Vedas*.

"The *Vedas* are also notable for the lofty truths expressed in the mantras. The tenets of these scriptures have aroused the wonder of people of other lands, of other faiths. They are moved by the poetic beauty of the hymns, the subtle manner in which principles of social life are dealt with, the metaphysical truths embedded and expounded in them, and their moral instruction as well as scientific truths.

"There are mantras that are specially valuable for their sound but are otherwise meaningless. Similarly, there are works pregnant with meaning but with no mantric power. The remarkable thing about the *Vedas* is that they are of immeasurable value as much for their

As when a fire is lit with damp fuel, different clouds of smoke come forth. In the same way from this great Being are breathed forth the *Rig, Yajur, Sama* and *Atharva Vedas*.

Shukla Yajur Veda, Brihadaranyaka Upanishad 2.4.10

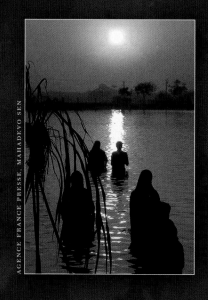

Above, an Indian boy piously pours ghee on the sacred fire, keeping the flame of devotion alive. At left, devotees worship the Sun in Bihar during Chhat festival, when, for one night and day, the people live on the banks of the river Ganga making offerings to Surya, the gracious Sun God, a primary Deity honored in the *Vedas*.

sound as for their verbal content. While they have the mantric power to do immense good to each one of us and to the world, they also contain teachings embodying great metaphysical truths.

"It must here be emphasized that on the doctrinal level the *Vedas* deal both with worldly life and the inner life of the Self. They teach how to conduct ourselves in such a manner as to create atmic well-being. And their concern is not with the liberation of the individual alone; they speak about the ideals of social life and about the duties of the public. How the brahmin ought to lead his life and how the king must rule his subjects and what ideals women are to follow: an answer to these—stated in the form of laws—is to be found in these scriptures.

"My duty is to impress upon you that it is your responsibility to keep the Vedic tradition alive. If in India the *Vedas* retain their original vitality even today, it is because they are being continuously repeated by students and teachers of the *Vedas*, and the purity of the sounds and accents of the words are retained in that process. But it is only by practicing the Vedic injunctions that we can obtain the grace of God, both for our individual welfare and for the welfare of the whole world."

Life Illumined with Scriptural Wisdom

Gurudeva, Sivaya Subramuniyaswami, founder of HINDUISM TODAY, was once asked, "What can I say if a missionary comes to my door and asks, 'Does Hinduism have a Bible?'" He answered, "You can say, 'Yes, we have the *Vedas* and *Agamas*, plus a hundred other scriptures that serve us very well, thank you.'" Indeed, this diverse body of knowledge is unlike the one Holy Book of other world faiths. It is diverse, a bit neglected, some nearly lost, some actually lost, but all of it precious. Yet, it defines and colors Hindu life like the genetic code that makes a starfish a starfish. It is reflected in the beautiful Hindu style of music, art, drama, dance, work ethics, law, domestic values, spiritual striving, relationships, rites of passage, astrology, medicine, games, love and business, architecture and storytelling, government and diplomacy, and the working together of this physical world with the heavenly realms of existence. This grand legacy helps make Hindus the gracious people they are, with qualities of humility, appreciation, love of God, forbearance, joy and soulful depth of character.

marriage & family

blessings

The soul is born and unfolds in a body, with dreams and desires and the food of life. And then it is reborn in new bodies in accordance with its former works. The quality of the soul determines its future body—earthly or airy, heavy or light.

Shvetashvatara Upanishad, 5.11–12.
The Upanishads, Mascsaro, p. 94

With earnest effort hold the senses in check. Controlling the breath, regulate the vital activities. As a charioteer holds back his restive horses, so does a persevering aspirant restrain his mind.

Shvetashvatara Upanishad, 2.9. The Upanishads,
Prabhavananda & Manchester, p. 192

The guru who has attained Self Realization can alone help the aspirant in acquiring it.

Siva Sutras 2.6, Jaideva Singh, p. 102

If daily to his home the friends who love him come, and coming, bring delight to eyes that kindle bright, a man has found the whole of life within his soul.

Panchatantra, Ryder, p. 218

In the beginning of worship, at the conclusion of the rite, in the offering of water, in the anointing of the image, in the bathing of the image, in the offering of light, in the sprinkling of the image with sandal, in the bathing of the image with consecrated liquids, in the offering of incense, in the act of worship, and in all other things to be done, the Sivacharya should strike the great bell.

Karana Agama 190-191, Motivations of Temple
Architecture in Saiva Siddhanta, p.160

diet, ayurveda

festivals

music

venerating gurus

home blessings

love of nature

Mantra yields early success due to practice done in previous life. Self-fulfilling, too, is the mantra which is received according to the line of tradition, with due *diksha*, obtained in the right way. Innumerable are the mantras; they but distract the mind. Only that mantra which is received through the grace of the guru gives all fulfillment.

Kularnava Tantra 11.3, Woodroff & Pandit, p. 112

O thou who pervades all space, both now and hereafter, as the Soul of souls! The *Vedas*, *Agamas*, *Puranas*, *Itihasas* and all other sciences inculcate fully the tenet of nonduality. It is the inexplicable duality that leads to the knowledge of nonduality. This is consonant with reason, experience, tradition, and is admitted by the dualists and nondualists.

Tayumanavar, 10.3, The Poems of Tayumanavar, Coomaraswamy, p. 44

By overthrowing the aggregate of the six enemies [lust, anger, greed, vanity, haughtiness and overjoy], he shall restrain the organs of sense; acquire wisdom by keeping company with the aged; see through his spies; establish safety and security by being ever active; maintain his subjects in the observance of their respective duties by exercising authority; keep

up his personal discipline by receiving lessons in the sciences; and endear himself to the people by bringing them in contact with wealth and doing good to them.

Book I, Chapter 7, The Life of a Holy King, Kautilya's Arthashastra, R. Shamasastry

Once Rama asked Hanuman, "How do you look at Me?" And Hanuman replied: "O Rama, as long as I have the feeling of 'I', I see that Thou art the whole and I am a part; Thou art the Master and I am Thy servant. But when, O Rama, I have the knowledge of Truth, Then I realize that Thou art I, and I am Thou."

From the Ramayana, as quoted by Sri Ramakrishna Paramahamsa

Let us have concord with our own people, and concord with people who are strangers to us. Aśvins, create between us and the strangers a unity of hearts.

Atharva Veda Samhita, 7.52.1

In him who is pure of mind, intellect and ego, the senses and their perceptions are pure, in fact, and he finds everything pure as well.

Sarvajnanottara Agama, Atma Sakshatkara 62, Collected Works of Ramana Maharshi, p.110

pilgrimage

devotional art

nurturing children

One who is established in the contemplation of nondual unity will abide in the Self of everyone and realize the immanent, all-pervading One. There is no doubt of this.

Sarvajnanottara Agama, Atma Sakshatkara 14, Collected Works of Ramana Maharshi, p.107

The Self resides within the lotus of the heart. Knowing this, consecrated to the Self, the sage enters daily that holy sanctuary. Absorbed in the Self, the sage is freed from identity with the body and lives in blissful consciousness.

Sama Veda, Chandogya Upanishad 8.3.3-4, The Upanishads, Prabhavananda & Manchester, p. 122

With the help of the gardeners called Mind and Love, plucking the flower called Steady Contemplation, offering the water of the flood of the Self's own bliss, worship the Lord with the sacred formula of silence!

Lalla, The Sources of Indian Tradition, p. 360

The Lord of Appati is both inside and outside, form and no form. He is both the flood and the bank. He is the broad-rayed sun. Himself the highest mystery, He is in all hidden thoughts. He is thought and meaning, and embraces all who embrace Him.

Tirumurai 4.48.7. Poems to Siva, The Hymns of the Tamil Saints, Peterson, p. 114

At the time of the sacrifice, O Lord of the wood [Agni], the worshipers smear you with sacred oil. When you stand upright or when you repose on Earth's bosom, you still will grant us good fortune. Set up to the East of the sacred fire, you accept our prayer, intense and unflagging. Hold yourself high to bring us prosperity. Drive far away dearth of inspiration. Lord of the wood, take now your stance on this, the loftiest spot of all Earth. Well-fixed and measured one, give to the worshiper, who brings a sacrifice, honor and glory.

Rig Veda 3.8.1-3, The Vedic Experience, Pannikar, p. 373-374

There is no difference between devotion and perfect knowledge. A person who is engrossed in devotion enjoys perpetual happiness. And perfect knowledge never descends in a vicious person averse to devotion.

Siva Purana, Rudra Samhita. 23.16, Ancient Indian Tradition and Mythology, vol 1, p. 380

As wide Earth, as fire and water, as sacrificer and wind that blows, as eternal moon and sun, as ether, as the eight-formed God, as cosmic good and evil, woman and man, all other forms and His own form, and all these as Himself, as yesterday and today and tomorrow, the God of the long, red hair stands, O Wonder!

Tirumurai 6.308.1. Poems to Siva, The Hymns of the Tamil Saints, Peterson, p.113

meditation

penance

dance

in the military

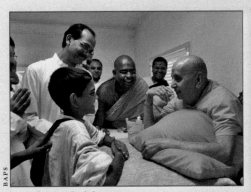

guiding children

monastic life

S RAJAM

CHAPTER 8

The Vedic Experience

A Bouquet of Verses from the *Vedas*, Hinduism's Most Venerated Scripture

ONE OF THE BEST OF THE MANY TRANSlations of the Vedas into the English language comes from an unexpected source, the famed Catholic theologian Raimon Panikkar. For twelve years, with the help of a team of Hindu pandits and Sanskrit scholars in Banaras, India, he struggled to bring the ancient texts into clear, accurate and inspired English. The result is a monumental scholarly achievement. The following seven pages of excerpts are drawn from *The Vedic Experience,* which Professor Panikkar wrote while living at the Catholic diocese in Banaras on the Ganga River from 1964 to 1976. The verses presented here were selected to give a sense of the variety and beauty of content throughout the *Vedas.* They follow Panikkar's creative and insightful ordering of the ancient texts into seven sections, corresponding to seven parts of an Earth day, a human life and a cosmic cycle. This provides a useful structure to the extremely diverse collection of hymns which comprise the *Veda.* The entire text is available at www.himalayanacademy.com/books/vedic_experience/VEIndex.html. Panikkar's seven sections excerpted over the next seven pages are:

1. Dawn: The preparation for birth into existence, fertile ground ready for planting.

2. Germination: The beginning, the striving, the affirmation of identity in the realm of existence.

3. Blossoming: The attainment of plenitude, of maturity, the zenith of a life well spent.

4. Fall and Decay: The beginning of the downward path, the natural decline of life, the discovery that nothing resists time.

5. Death: The destiny of all existing things, and the natural close of a physical life cycle.

6. New Life: The marvelous re-emergence of life out of the ordeal of death, the disclosure that life is immortal, that being is unfathomable, and that bliss and reality are capable of self-renewal.

7. Twilight: The last part of the anthology, like a bouquet ribbon, binds the six in summary.

Raimon Panikkar during a visit to Hinduism Today headquarters in Hawaii in 1991

To illustrate these magnificent translations, special art was commissioned by HINDUISM TODAY from renowned artist S. Rajam of Chennai in South India.

Raimon Panikkar was born in Barcelona, Spain, in 1918 of an Indian Hindu father and a Spanish Roman Catholic mother. Information on his early years is sketchy. He was a brilliant student and studied philosophy and chemistry in Barcelona, Madrid and Bonn, and theology in Madrid and Rome. He earned an astounding three doctorates in philosophy, chemistry and theology. He was ordained a Catholic priest in 1946, serving as a scholar and theologian, and not, apparently, as a parish priest. In 1953 Panikkar left Spain to live in India where he taught at the Universities of Mysore and Banaras, specializing in Indian philosophy and Christian-Hindu understanding. He has been a professor at the Universities of Madrid, Rome, Harvard and the University of California at Santa Barbara.

Panikkar played a key roll in the writing of *Nostra Aetate,* the "Declaration on the Relation of the Church to Non-Christian Religions," released by the Second Vatican Council in 1965. Though most certainly a devout Christian, he championed the concept of respect for other faiths, so much so that some call him the "apostle of interreligious dialogue." To this day the Catholic Church's relationship to other religions as defined in *Nostra Aetate* remains a delicate issue both inside and outside the Church. It was just after participating in Vatican II, which changed the face of modern Catholicism, that he departed to India to write *The Vedic Experience.*

He has written more than 30 books and 900 articles, including the following: *The Trinity and the World's Religions; Blessed Simplicity; Worship and Secular Man; The Silence of God: The Answer of the Buddha.* Panikkar makes his home in the mountains of Catalunya, Spain.

Dawn

At first was neither Being nor Nonbeing. There was not air nor yet sky beyond. What was its wrapping? Where? In whose protection? Was Water there, unfathomable and deep?

There was no death then, nor yet deathlessness; of night or day there was not any sign. The One breathed without breath, by its own impulse. Other than that was nothing else at all.

Darkness was there, all wrapped around by darkness, and all was Water indiscriminate. Then that which was hidden by the Void, that One, emerging, stirring, through power of Ardor, came to be.

In the beginning Love arose, which was the primal germ cell of the mind. The Seers, searching in their hearts with wisdom, discovered the connection of Being in Nonbeing.

A crosswise line cut Being from Nonbeing. What was described above it, what below? Bearers of seed there were and mighty forces, thrust from below and forward move above.

Who really knows? Who can presume to tell it? Whence was it born? Whence issued this creation? Even the Gods came after its emergence. Then who can tell from whence it came to be?

That out of which creation has arisen, whether it held it firm or it did not, He who surveys it in the highest heaven, He surely knows or maybe He does not!

RIG VEDA 10.129

Here, we see the dawn of manifestation, the preparation for emergence into existence. In the foreground new life in the form of a child is urged forth from the hands of God while in the background fields are fertile and ready for planting.

The Primal man is, simply, All. What is and what shall be, He is the Lord of Immortality

ATHARVA VEDA 19.6.4

O God, grant us of boons the best—a mind to think and a smiling love, increase of wealth, a healthy body, speech that is winsome and days that are fair.

RIG VEDA 2.21.6

Germination

Praise to the Breath of Life! He rules this world, master of all things, on which all things are based.

Praise, Breath of Life, to your uproar! Praise to your thunder! Praise to your lightning! Praise, Breath of Life, for your rain!

When Breath of Life with his thunder roars o'er the plants, then, pregnant with pollen, the flowers burst forth in abundance.

The plants converse with this Breath, drenched by his moisture: "Our life is prolonged, for you have made us all fragrant."

Breath of Life clothes all beings with care as a father his son; master of all things, whether they breathe or breathe not.

Breath of Life is Queen, is Guide, revered by all things; he is sun, he is moon; he is also the Father of all.

A man breathes in, he breathes out, within the womb. Quickened by you, to birth he comes once more.

The mighty Wind they call him, or Breeze. The future and the past exist in him. On Breath of Life all things are based.

Breath of Life, do not forsake me. You are, indeed, I. Like the Embryo of the Waters I bind you to me that I may live

ATHARVA VEDA 11.4

As the sun rises, striving begins in the realm of existence. The child, now a young man, learns the ways of community and faces his fresh potential. In the background the fields are bedecked with new growth, as in spring.

Blossoming

When a man is born, whoever he may be, there is born simultaneously a debt to the Gods, to the sages, to the ancestors, and to men.

When he performs sacrifice, it is the debt to the Gods which is concerned. It is on their behalf, therefore, that he is taking action when he sacrifices or makes an oblation.

And when he recites the *Vedas*, it is the debt to the sages which is concerned. It is on their behalf, therefore, that he is taking action, for it is said of one who has recited the *Vedas* that he is the guardian of the treasure store of the sages.

And when he desires offspring, it is the debt to the ancestors which is concerned. It is on their behalf, therefore, that he is taking action, so that their offspring may continue, without interruption.

And when he entertains guests, it is the debt to man which is concerned. It is on their behalf, therefore, that he is taking action if he entertains guests and gives them food and drink. The man who does all these things has performed a true work; he has obtained all, conquered all.

YAJUR VEDA, SHATAPATHA BRAHMANA 1.7.2

The sacrifice is man. It is man [who offers it] because it is man who spreads it out and because, in being spread out, it assumes exactly the same stature as man. For this reason, the sacrifice is man.

YAJUR VEDA, SHATAPATHA BRAHMANA 1.3.2.1

The sun reaches its zenith in the the attainment of plenitude, which our artists shows in the harvesting of fields in the background, and as a man in the foreground in the prime of life, experiencing fulfillment and self mastery.

Diffusing glory with your rays, you have scaled the shining realm of heaven. By you are supported all things that are, O God, All-Creator, essence all-divine.

RIG VEDA 10.170.4

Fall & Decay

Just as an overloaded cart lumbers along creaking, in the same way the self in this body, loaded by the Self of wisdom, lumbers along creaking when its breath is getting heavy.

When he becomes reduced, whether by old age or by disease, then, just as a mango fruit or a fig or a pipal fruit [detaches itself from its stem], so this person, being released from his limbs, returns to Life, to the place whence he has come.

Just as, when a king is arriving, the guards, the officers, the drivers, and the village elders await him with food, drink, and a place for his dwelling, saying, "Here he comes, here he comes!" even so all beings await him who knows this [saying]: "Here comes Brahman, here he comes!"

Just as the guards, the officers, the drivers, and the village elders gather around the king at his departure, even so all the powers of life gather around this self at the end of his time, when his breath is getting heavy.

YAJUR VEDA, BRIHADARANYAKA UPANISHAD 4.3

When a man, my dear, is stricken with disease, his relatives come near to him, asking: "Do you recognize me?" As long as his speech has not merged in his mind, his mind in his breath, his breath in light, and the light in the supreme Godhead, so long does he recognize them.

But when his speech has merged in his mind, his mind in his breath, his breath in light, and the light in the supreme Godhead, then he does not recognize them.

SAMA VEDA, CHANDOGYA UPANISHAD 6.15

Only when men shall roll up space as if it were a simple skin, only then will there be an end of sorrow without acknowledging God.

YAJUR VEDA, SHVETASVATARA UPANISHAD 6.20

Then comes life's afternoon, the solar source descending. It represents the inevitable waining of the life force, and the discovery that nothing resists time, and all cycles must conclude. The background shows fall moving into winter, as a man falls prey to the varied hazards encountered in one's latter years.

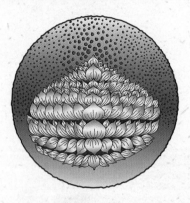

Death

When this atman becomes weak and unconscious, then all the life powers collect around him. Then he gathers to himself all the particles of light and descends into the heart. When the person in the eye withdraws from him, he no longer recognizes forms.

"He is becoming one," they say, "he does not see." "He is becoming one," they say, "he does not smell." "He is becoming one," they say, "he does not taste." "He is becoming one," they say, "he does not speak." "He is becoming one," they say, "he does not hear." "He is becoming one," they say, "he does not think." "He is becoming one," they say, "he does not feel." "He is becoming one," they say, "he does not understand."

The tip of his heart gets illumined and, being illumined, the atman departs through the eye or the head or some other part of the body. As he departs, the breath of life departs after him; and when the breath of life departs, all other breaths follow. He then is reunited with consciousness and departs together with consciousness. His knowledge and his works and his past experiences accompany him.

YAJUR VEDA, BRIHADARANYAKA UPANISHAD 4.4

From unreality lead me to reality; from darkness lead me to light; from death lead me to immortality.

YAJUR VEDA, BRIHADARANYAKA UPANISHAD 1.3

Just as a cucumber is removed from its stalk, so from Death's bonds may I be removed, but not from Immortality!

RIG VEDA 1.10.115

Finally come night and death, the irreversible destiny of all sentient things, the conclusion of one cycle of life. Pictured here is a traditional cremation ceremony, with the eldest son lighting the pyre. Behind, Lord Siva's spreads His arems in blessing.

Desireless, wise, immortal, self-existent, full of bliss, lacking in nothing, is the one who knows the wise, un-aging, youthful atman; he fears not death!

ATHARVA VEDA 10.8.44

That is Fullness, this is Fullness; from
Fullness comes Fullness. When Fullness is
taken from Fullness, Fullness remains.

YAJUR VEDA, BRIHADARANYAKA UPANISHAD 5.1

New Life

Eye cannot see him, nor words reveal
him; by the senses, austerity, or works he
is not known. When the mind is cleansed
by the grace of wisdom, he is seen by
contemplation—the One without parts.

MUNDAKA UPANISHAD 3.1.8

In the beginning this was Brahman,
One and infinite, infinite in the East,
infinite in the South, infinite in the
West, infinite in the North, infinite
above and below, infinite in every
direction. For him there are, of course,
no directions such as the East and so
on, no across, no above, and no below.

Inconceivable is this supreme atman,
immeasurable, unborn, inscrutable,
unthinkable, he whose Self is space. He
alone remains awake when the universe
is dissolved, and out of this space he
awakens [again] the world consisting of
thought. By him alone is all this thought
[into being] and in him it dissolves
again. His shining form is that which
burns in the sun; it is the multiform
light that shines in the smokeless fire
and it is that which digests the food in
the body. For thus it has been said:

He who dwells in the fire, he who dwells
in the heart, he who dwells in the sun,
he is One. The man who knows this, he
verily attains the Oneness of the One.

YAJUR VEDA, MAITRI UPANISHAD 6.17

For me there is no earth, no water, and no
fire. For me there is neither wind nor ether.
The one who has discovered the supreme
atman dwelling in the heart, without parts,
without a second, the universal witness,
neither being nor nonbeing, attains
the pure form of the supreme atman.

ATHARVA VEDA, KAIVALYA UPANISHAD 23

S RAJAM

*In this painting we see the marvelous reemergence of life out of the ordeal
of death even beyond the setting sun. Indeed, reality is capable of self-
renewal into an awareness of the oneness of all beings and things.*

United your resolve, united your hearts, may your spirits be at one, that you may long together dwell in unity and concord!

RIG VEDA 10.191.4

Twilight

At many a dawn of shining splendor has the Lord presided. Come on your chariots, far-ranging Spirits, come to our sacrifice.

Suffusing light for every creature, the Inspirer God rises. The Sun has filled heaven and earth with his radiance disclosing his presence.

Rosy Dawn advances, adorned with the brightness of many a beam. She pursues her way on her well-equipped chariot arousing Men to joy.

Come, O twin Spirits, at break of day on your powerful chariots. We offer in sacrifice this honey-sweet draught for your delectation.

How is it that, united and unsupported, he does not fall down? By what inner power moves he? Who has seen? A firm pillar, he protects heaven's vault.

RIG VEDA SAMHITA 4.14

I hail you, Goddess, Dawn of light! To her let us offer the homage of our songs! She imparts to us sweetness, she steadies the Heaven and lavishes abroad her radiant splendor.

Our songs have awakened this Daughter of Heaven. Equitable, generous, she has scaled the two worlds. Toward Dawn, O Fire, when she comes in her brightness, you advance, eager to share her fair treasures.

The Mighty One, firm-based on Order, speeds after each dawn and makes his debut in the worlds. Great are the powers of Mitra and Varuna. Dawn in all directions diffuses her splendor!

RIG VEDA 111.61

The seventh and last part of Professor Panikkar's anthology is a summary of the rest. In this illustration, shimmering in the twilight of existence, Siva is worshiped as the endless light in a pillar of fire, signifying completion of the seven-part cycle in the Ultimate.

Table of the Vedas

This table shows the correlation of various books of the *Vedas*, listing for each *Veda* the corresponding *Saṁhitās* (hymn collections), *Brāhmaṇas* (ceremonial handbooks), *Āraṇyakas* (forest treatises) and *Upanishads* (metaphysical dialogs). The bracketed titles under *Saṁhitās* are names of some of the different Śākhās (branches), versions or recensions of the same texts. The parentheses indicate synonymous titles. This is not a complete list of all *Veda* texts, but it does include those translated in *The Vedic Experience*. Note that the bracketed terms in the Saṁhitā column are names of the different *śākhās*, which are versions or recensions of the same texts. Terms in parenthesis indicate synonymous titles.

ॐ	SAṀHITĀ	BRĀHMAṆA	ĀRAṆYAKA	UPANISHAD
RIG VEDA	Ṛig Veda [Śakala] [Bāskala]	Aitareya Kaushitaki (Śāṅkhāyana)	Aitareya	Aitareya Kaushitaki
ATHARVA VEDA	Atharva Veda [Śaunaka] [Paippalāda]	Gopatha		Muṇḍaka Praśna Māṇḍūkya Kaivalya
SĀMA VEDA	Sāma Veda [Kauthama] [Rāṇayanīya] [Jaiminiya]	Jaiminiya Taṇḍya Mahā (Pañchaviṁśa)	Jaiminiya Upanishad Brāhmaṇa (Talavakāra)	Çhandogya Kena (Talavakāra)
KRISHNA YAJUR VEDA	Taittirīya (Apastambīya) Maitrāyani	Taittirīya	Taittirīya	Taittirīya Kaṭha Śvetāśvatara Mahānārāyaṇa Maitrī Prāṇāgnihotra
ŚUKLA YAJUR VEDA	Vājasaneyi [Kāṇva] [Mādhyamdina]	Śatapatha		Bṛihadāraṇyaka Īśa Jābāla Paiṅgala Sūrya

CHAPTER 9

Sacred Symbols

Endearing Icons of Mythology, Mysticism and Devotion Adorn Hindu Art, Architecture and Culture

ART BY S. RAJAM; BACKGROUND PHOTO OF TIRUVANAMALAI BY THOMAS KELLY ymbols adorn our world at every turn, in our spiritual, social and political experience. A ring or gold pendant silently strengthens and attests to wedded love. A sign with a truck silhouette on an angled line warns drivers of steep grades ahead. The red cross signifies aid in crises. Golden arches tell vegans to beware. The best known symbols are simple numerals: 0 through 9, which originated in India in the ancient Brahmi script. Historic images are etched in the mass mind; the mushroom cloud of the atom bomb forever represents nuclear destruction. But it is our sacred symbols, icons of Divinity and higher reality, that wield the greatest power to inform and transform consciousness. Taoists gazing upon a yin-yang symbol, Navajo Indians "pouring" a feather symbol in a sand painting, Muslims embroidering the crescent moon and star, Buddhists contemplating a mandala, Christians kneeling before the cross, Hindus meditating on the Aum, Pagans parading the ankh at Stonehenge—all these are potent meditations on cosmic symbols that are gateways to inner truths. To societies of prehistory, living fully in nature's raw splendor and power, symbols stood for supernatural states and beings—as they still can for us today. A stylized image of a snake coiled round a clay vase, for example, represented cosmic life and regeneration. Wielded as tools by mystic shamans, symbols can shape the forces of nature and invoke astral beings. To conjure power, a medieval alchemist would enclose himself in a magic circle filled with geometric pictograms symbolizing inner realities. Today, as in olden times, religious symbols derive from the world around us. The sun appears in motifs across cultures from Mexico to Mongolia, including the Hindu swastika and the wheel of the sun, honored by Buddhists as the eight-spoked dharma wheel. Hinduism has amassed a vast range of icons from thousands of years back. Coins found in the Indus Valley carry emblems of the cow and of a meditating yogi across a 6,000-year corridor of time. Images from the Vedic age are popular motifs in Kashmiri carpets and Chidambaram saris. These often serve to identify and distinguish members of a sect or community. The simple red dot worn on the forehead is both a mark of our dharmic heritage and a personal reminder that we must see the world not only with our physical eyes, but with the mind's eye, the third eye, the eye of the soul. India's adepts and seers have excelled at symbolic imagery, transforming mudras (hand gestures) into instantly recognized emblems and transmitters of a Deity's power or a particular frequency of energy. Each accoutrement of the dozens of Deities in the Hindu pantheon conveys a cosmic function or force. Today this ancient magic is with us everywhere, from the temple priest's invocation to the Indian housewife's drawing of multi-colored designs, called *kolams* or *rangoli*, on the ground as auspicious auguries, household blessings and greetings.

. . . .

Left, a deva holds above his head a golden vajra (a "thunderbolt" representing indestructibility), a celestial weapon wielded by the Vedic God Indra and other Deities. Other symbols, clockwise: shakti *vel*, cudgel, sword, noose, flag, mace, chakra with four flames, an umbrella and trident. In the background, a scene at night of the magnificent Meenakshi Sundareshwara Temple of Madurai, a bastion of Hindu culture.

वट

Vata, the banyan tree, *Ficus indicus*, symbolizes Hinduism, which branches out in all directions, draws from many roots, spreads shade far and wide, yet stems from one great trunk. Siva as Silent Sage sits beneath it. Aum.

ART BY A. MANIVEL

स्वस्तिक

Swastika is the symbol of auspiciousness and good fortune—literally, "It is well." The right-angled arms of this ancient sun-sign denote the indirect way that Divinity is apprehended: by intuition and not by intellect. Aum.

प्रणव ॐ

Pranava, Aum, is the root mantra and primal sound from which all creation issues forth. It is associated with Lord Ganesha. Its three syllables stand at the beginning and end of every sacred verse, every human act. Aum.

மயில்

Mayil, "peacock," is Lord Murugan's mount, swift and beautiful like Karttikeya Himself. The proud display of the dancing peacock symbolizes religion in full, unfolded glory. His shrill cry warns of approaching harm. Aum.

गणेश

Ganesha is the Lord of Obstacles and Ruler of Dharma. Seated upon His throne, He guides our karmas through creating and removing obstacles from our path. We seek His permission and blessings in every undertaking. Aum.

त्रिपुण्ड्र

Tripundra is a Saivite's great mark, three stripes of white *vibhuti* on the brow. This holy ash signifies purity and the burning away of *anava,* karma and maya. The *bindu,* or dot, at the third eye quickens spiritual insight. Aum.

ART BY A. MANIVEL

नन्दि

Nandi is Lord Siva's mount, or *vahana.* This huge white bull with a black tail, whose name means "joyful," disciplined animality kneeling at Siva's feet, is the ideal devotee, the pure joy and strength of Saiva Dharma. Aum.

नटराज

Nataraja is Siva as "King of Dance." Carved in stone or cast in bronze, His *ananda tandava,* the fierce ballet of bliss, dances the cosmos into and out of existence within a fiery arch of flames denoting consciousness. Aum.

बिल्व

Bilva is the bael tree. Its fruit, flowers and leaves are all sacred to Siva, liberation's summit. Planting *Aegle marmelos* trees around home or temple is sanctifying, as is worshiping a Linga with *bilva* leaves and water. Aum.

पद्म

Padma is the lotus flower, *Nelumbo nucifera,* perfection of beauty, associated with Deities and the chakras, especially the 1,000-petaled *sahasrara*. Rooted in the mud, its blossom is a promise of purity and unfoldment. Aum.

महाकाल

Mahakala, "Great Time," presides above creation's golden arch. Devouring instants and eons, with a ferocious face, He is Time beyond time, reminder of this world's transitoriness, that sin and suffering will pass. Aum.

अंकुश

Ankusha, the goad held in Lord Ganesha's right hand, is used to remove obstacles from dharma's path. It is the force by which all wrongful things are repelled from us, the sharp prod which spurs the dullards onward. Aum.

अञ्जलि

Anjali, the gesture of two hands brought together near the heart, means to "honor or celebrate." It is our Hindu greeting, two joined as one, the bringing together of matter and spirit, the self meeting the Self in all. Aum.

गो

Go, the cow, is a symbol of the Earth, the nourisher, the ever-giving, undemanding provider. To the Hindu, all animals are sacred, and we acknowledge this reverence of life in our special affection for the gentle cow. Aum.

மாங்கோலம்

Mankolam, the pleasing paisley design, is modeled after a mango and associated with Lord Ganesha. Mangos are the sweetest of fruits, symbolizing auspiciousness and the happy fulfillment of legitimate worldly desires. Aum.

होमकुण्ड

Homakunda, the fire altar, is the symbol of ancient Vedic rites. It is through the fire element, denoting divine consciousness, that we make offerings to the Gods. Hindu sacraments are solemnized before the *homa* fire. Aum.

षड्कोण

Shatkona, "six-pointed star," is two interlocking triangles; the upper stands for Siva, *purusha* and fire, the lower for Shakti, prakriti and water. Their union gives birth to Sanatkumara, whose sacred number is six. Aum.

मुषिक

Mushika is Lord Ganesha's mount, the mouse, traditionally associated with abundance in family life. Under cover of darkness, seldom visible yet always at work, Mushika is like God's unseen grace in our lives. Aum.

ART BY A. MANIVEL

घण्टा

Ghanta is the bell used in ritual puja, which engages all senses, including hearing. Its ringing summons the Gods, stimulates the inner ear and reminds us that, like sound, the world may be perceived but not possessed. Aum.

கொன்றை

Konrai, Golden Shower, blossoms are the flowering symbol of Siva's honeyed grace in our life. Associated with His shrines and temples throughout India, the *Cassia fistula* is lauded in numberless *Tirumurai* hymns. Aum.

गोपुर

Gopuras are the towering stone gateways through which pilgrims enter the South Indian temple. Richly ornamented with myriad sculptures of the divine pantheon, their tiers symbolize the several planes of existence. Aum.

कलश

Kalasha, a husked coconut circled by mango leaves on a pot, is used in puja to represent any God, especially Lord Ganesha. Breaking a coconut before His shrine is the ego's shattering to reveal the sweet fruit inside. Aum.

குத்துவிளக்கு

Kuttuvilaku, the standing oil lamp, symbolizes the dispelling of ignorance and awakening of the divine light within us. Its soft glow illumines the temple or shrine room, keeping the atmosphere pure and serene. Aum.

कमण्डलु

Kamandalu, the water vessel, is carried by the Hindu monastic. It symbolizes his simple, self-contained life, his freedom from worldly needs, his constant *sadhana* and *tapas,* and his oath to seek God everywhere. Aum.

திருவடி

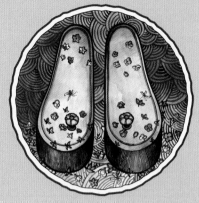

Tiruvadi, the sacred sandals worn by saints, sages and *satgurus,* symbolize the preceptor's holy feet, which are the source of his grace. Prostrating before him, we humbly touch his feet for release from worldliness. Aum.

त्रिकोण

Trikona, the triangle, is a symbol of God Siva which, like the Sivalinga, denotes His Absolute Being. It represents the element fire and portrays the process of spiritual ascent and liberation spoken of in scripture. Aum.

சேவல்

Seval is the noble red rooster who heralds each dawn, calling all to awake and arise. He is a symbol of the imminence of spiritual unfoldment and wisdom. As a fighting cock, he crows from Lord Skanda's battle flag. Aum.

रुद्राक्ष

Rudraksha seeds, *Eleocarpus ganitrus*, are prized as the compassionate tears Lord Siva shed for mankind's suffering. Saivites wear *malas* of them always as a symbol of God's love, chanting on each bead, "Aum Namah Sivaya."

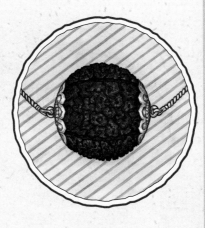

चन्द्र सूर्य

Chandra is the moon, ruler of the watery realms and of emotion, testing place of migrating souls. *Surya* is the sun, ruler of intellect, source of truth. One is *pingala* and lights the day; the other is *ida* and lights the night. Aum.

ART BY A. MANIVEL

வேல்

Vel, the holy lance, is Lord Murugan's protective power, our safeguard in adversity. Its tip is wide, long and sharp, signifying incisive discrimination and spiritual knowledge, which must be broad, deep and penetrating. Aum.

त्रिशूल

Trishula, Siva's trident carried by Himalayan *yogis*, is the royal scepter of the Saiva Dharma. Its triple prongs betoken desire, action and wisdom; *ida*, *pingala* and *sushumna;* and the gunas— sattva, rajas and tamas. Aum.

नाग

Naga, the cobra, is a symbol of *kundalini* power, cosmic energy coiled and slumbering within man. It inspires seekers to overcome misdeeds and suffering by lifting the serpent power up the spine into God Realization. Aum.

ध्वज

Dhvaja, "flag," is the orange or red banner flown above temples, at festivals and in processions. It is a symbol of victory, signal to all that "Sanatana Dharma shall prevail." Its color betokens the sun's life-giving glow. Aum.

कालचक्र

Kalachakra, "wheel, or circle, of time," is the symbol of perfect creation, of the cycles of existence. Time and space are interwoven, and eight spokes mark the directions, each ruled by a Deity and having a unique quality. Aum.

शिवलिङ्ग

Sivalinga is the ancient mark or symbol of God. This elliptical stone is a formless form betokening Parasiva, That which can never be described or portrayed. The *pitha*, pedestal, represents Siva's manifest Parashakti. Aum.

मोदक

Modaka, a round, lemon-sized sweet made of rice, coconut, sugar and spices, is a favorite treat of Ganesha. Esoterically, it corresponds to siddhi (attainment or fulfillment), the gladdening contentment of pure joy. Aum.

पाश

Pasha, tether or noose, represents the soul's threefold bondage of *anava*, karma and maya. *Pasha* is the all-important force or fetter by which God (Pati, envisioned as a cowherd) brings souls (*pashu*, or cows) along the path to Truth. Aum.

हंस

Hamsa, vehicle of Brahma, is the swan (more accurately, the wild goose *Anser indicus*). It is a noble symbol for the soul, and for adept renunciates, Paramahamsa, winging high above the mundane and diving straight to the goal. Aum.

Family Life and

The Spiritual Ideals of Hinduism's

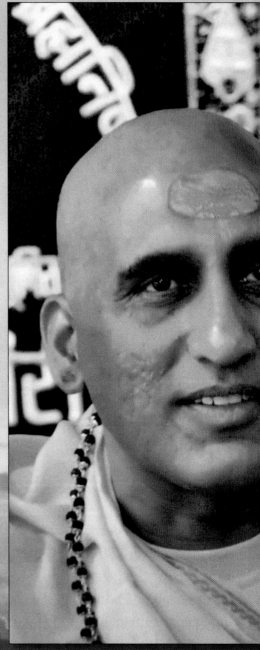

Exemplars of dharma's two paths: *(left) writer and homemaker Vatsala Sperling of Vermont, USA, with her son Mahar; (right) respected leader of Juna Akhara, Acharya Avdheshananda Ji*

EHUD SPERLING

Monastic Life

Two Noble Paths of Dharma

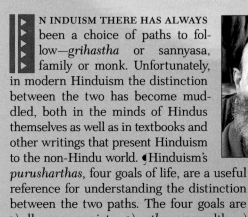

I**N INDUISM THERE HAS ALWAYS** been a choice of paths to follow—*grihastha* or sannyasa, family or monk. Unfortunately, in modern Hinduism the distinction between the two has become muddled, both in the minds of Hindus themselves as well as in textbooks and other writings that present Hinduism to the non-Hindu world. ◖Hinduism's *purusharthas*, four goals of life, are a useful reference for understanding the distinction between the two paths. The four goals are 1) dharma, or piety; 2) *artha*, or wealth; 3) *kama*, or pleasure; and 4) moksha, or liberation. Those on the *grihastha* path pursue all four goals, and the way they do so changes according to their age or *ashrama* in life. Those on the sannyasa path renounce *artha*, *kama* and family dharma in one-pointed pursuit of moksha—liberation from rebirth on Earth through intense personal experience of God. ◖For the *grihastha*, in the first *ashrama*, *brahmacharya*, age 12-24, the primary focus is on studying at school and preparing for profession and married life. In the second *ashrama*, *grihastha*, age 24-48, the primary focus is raising a family and fulfilling a career. The third *ashrama*, *vanaprastha*, age 48-72, is a time of transition from family and career to one of elder advisor to the younger generation. The fourth *ashrama*, *sannyasa*, age 72 onward, is a time in which the primary focus is on moksha, meaning that religious practic-es are the main activity of one's day. The sannyasin directly enters the fourth *ashrama* at the time of his initiation, no matter what his age, skipping over the other phases of life. ◖One of the most common ways the two paths have been muddled in modern Hinduism is in the classic textbook notion that Hindus believe the world is unreal and that this is why there is so much poverty in India. This, of course, is an incorrect perception. The accurate statement is that those on the path of the monk are trained to look at the world as impermanent, or unreal or fleeting. *Grihasthas*, however are not. They pursue the same ideals of success, family and wealth as do families in Western society. ◖Many thoughtful Hindu lay leaders lament the lack of trained Hindus who can speak out in a knowledgeable way about Hinduism. One trend is to train Hindu priests for this capacity, which in the Western world is called a minister. Said another way, Hinduism needs more ministers to TEACH and counsel. Of course, t✳is is one of the roles that Hindu monks traditionally fulfill. Thus, another solution is to produce and train more swamis and sadhus to serve as competent ministers. ◖This 16-page Educational Insight is drawn primarily from Gurudeva's Master Course trilogy (www.gurudeva.org/resources/books/).

Bodhinatha Veylanswami

The Two Paths of Dharma

From the Sacred Teachings of Satguru Sivaya Subramuniyaswami

There are two traditional paths for the devout Hindu of nearly every lineage. The first is the path of the renunciate. The second is the path of the householder, who guides human society and produces the next generation. The ancient rishis evolved well-defined principles for both, knowing that unmarried aspirants would most easily unfold by adhering to principles of nonownership, noninvolvement in the world and *brahmacharya* (celibacy), while married men and women would uphold the more complex and material family dharma. Though the principles or guidelines for these two paths are different, the goal is the same: to establish a life dedicated to spiritual unfoldment, hastening the evolution of the soul through knowledge of the forces at work within us, and wise, consistent application of that knowledge.

THE PATH OF RENUNCIATION

The two fundamental objectives of sannyasa, renunciation, are to promote the spiritual progress of the individual, bringing him into God Realization, and to protect and perpetuate the religion. Sannyasa life has both an individual and a universal objective. At the individual level, it is a life of selflessness in which the sannyasin has made the supreme sacrifice of renouncing all personal ambition, all involvement in worldly matters, that he might direct his consciousness and energies fully toward God. Guided by the satguru along the *sadhana marga*, he unfolds through the years into deeper and deeper realizations. Ultimate-

ly, if he persists, he comes into direct knowing of transcendent Reality. At the universal level, the sannyasins foster the entire religion by preserving the truths of the Sanatana Dharma. Competent swamis are the teachers, the theologians, the exemplars of their faith, the torchbearers lighting the way for all.

Among those on the renunciate path, there are two lifestyles. In our *Holy Orders of Sannyasa*, these two lifestyles are described as follows. "Some among them are sadhus, anchorites living in the seclusion of distant caves and remote forests or wandering as homeless mendicants, itinerant pilgrims to the holy sanctuaries of Hinduism. Others dwell as cenobites, assembled with their brothers, often in the ashrama, *aadheenam* or *matha* of their *satguru*, but always under the guru's aegis, serving together in fulfillment of a common mission. These devotees, when initiated into the order of sannyasa, don the saffron robes and thereby bind themselves to a universal body of Hindu renunciates, numbering today three million, whose existence has never ceased, an assembly of men inwardly linked in their mutual dedication to God, though not necessarily outwardly associated."

There are three primary currents in the human nerve system. The aggressive-intellectual current is masculine, mental in nature and psychically seen as blue in color. This current is termed in Sanskrit *pingala*. The passive-physical current is feminine, material in nature. This current, which is pink or red, is known as *ida*. The third

Voices on Hindu Family Life

LEADERS OF THE UNITED NATIONS DEDICATED 1994 AS THE international Year of the Family. They were seeking to counter a global failure of the family unit and the by-products of such a breakdown: crime, delinquent youth, disobedient children, divorce and other household miseries, in other words the basic problems of social instability. They decided to inquire of the major religions of the world as to what their views were and are today on family life, all planned for a multi-lingual United Nations publication, *Family Issues as Seen by Different Religions,* a unique vision of family from the point of view of Jews, Christians, Muslims, Buddhists, Hindus and Baha'is. The UN approached us at HINDUISM TODAY magazine to define and describe the traditional family values of the Hindu. In creating the Hindu chapter for the UN book, we joined forces with two of our HINDUISM TODAY correspondents, Archana Dongre of Los Angeles and Lavina Melwani of New York. Their comments provide

the "voices" of experience throughout the text. We include excerpts from the resulting article here as a sidebar to this Educational Insight on the two paths of Hindu dharma.

THE HINDU VIEW OF FAMILY

Hindu families all over the world are struggling—some failing, most succeeding. Our experience is that those most rooted in their Hinduness cope better and are the better survivors. Hindu households, sheltering one-sixth of the human race, are being threatened. What if the concept of family itself were dying? What if the very institution, the cauldron of our cultural and spiritual consciousness, were struck by some fatal disease and perished? Who could measure such a tragedy? Who could

S. RAJAM

current is spiritual in nature and flows directly through the spine and into the head. Being yellowish-white, the *sushumna*, as it is called, is the channel for pure spiritual energies that flood into the body through the spine and out into the 6,000 miles of nerve currents. Depending on the nature and dharma, each individual's energy expresses itself as predominantly physical or intellectual—passive or aggressive—or spiritual. However, in the sannyasin the two forces are so precisely balanced that neither is dominant, and he therefore lives almost totally in *sushumna*. The monastic, whether a monk or a nun, is in a sense neither male nor female, but a being capable of all modes of expression.

Brahmacharya for the monastic means complete sexual abstinence and is, of course, an understood requirement to maintain this position in life. Transmutation of the sexual energies is an essential discipline for the monastic. Transmutation is not a repression or inhibition of natural instincts, but a conscious transformation of these energies into life-giving forces that lend vigor and strength to the body and provide the impetus that propels awareness to the depths of contemplation. This process of transmutation begins with the sexual instincts but encompasses transmutation of all instinctive forces, including fear, anger, covetousness, jealousy, envy, pride, etc. True purity is possible only when these base instincts have been conquered.

The renunciate fosters the inner attitude, strictly maintained, that all young women are his sisters and all older women his mother. He does not view movies that depict the base instincts of man, nor look at books, magazines or websites of this nature. The principle with which he is working is to protect the mind's natural purity, not allowing anything that is degrading, sensuous or low-minded to enter into the field of his experience.

At times, the renunciate's *sadhana* is austere, as he burns layer after layer of dross through severe *tapas*. He wears the saffron robe, studies the ancient ways and scriptures. He chants the sacred mantras. He reflects

In a scene from olden days in India, a priest and his wife sit before a sannyasin to receive his blessings. They present to him a difficulty they face, and he gives advice from tradition.

With that in mind, let us embark on an exploration of some of the Hindu family's truly remarkable strengths.

VOICES: *My grandma never tired of reminding us that the Hindu religion always glorified sacrifice. It was considered heroic to make sacrifice for the family members. Hindu epics like* Ramayana *and* Mahabharata *purport that even great beings like Lord Rama and noble kings like the Pandavas had to endure trying circumstances and make sacrifices. "So what's wrong if ordinary folks had to make some sacrifices?" she would say. Parents often make great sacrifices to give a good education to their children. Many Hindu parents have gone hungry to afford quality education for their children. The children in turn curtail their freedom and luxury when parents grow old and infirm and*

weep sufficient tears? Yet, that is precisely the path which we are semi-consciously following, a path leading to the demise of the traditional Hindu family, the source of our strength, the patron of our spirituality, the sole guarantor of our future.

Is it our fault that the family is disintegrating? Perhaps. Does it portend uncertainty? Be certain that it does. Is it inevitable? Probably not. A final eulogy for the Hindu family may be premature.

constantly on the Absolute. He lives from moment to moment, day to day. He is always available, present, open. He has neither likes nor dislikes, but clear perceptions.

Having stepped out of his ego shell, the sannyasin is a free soul. Nothing binds him. Nothing claims him. Nothing involves him. Without exclusive territory, without limiting relationships, he is free to be himself totally. If he has problems within himself, he keeps them silently within and works them out there. If he speaks, it is only to say what is true, kind, helpful or necessary. He never argues, debates, complains. His words and his life always affirm, never negate. He finds points of agreement, forsaking contention and difference. No man is his enemy. No man is his friend. All men are his teachers. Some teach him what to do; others teach him what not to do. He has no one to rely upon except God, Gods, guru and the power within his own spine. He is strong, yet gentle. He is aloof, yet present. He is enlightened, yet ordinary. He speaks wisely of the Vedic scriptures and ancient shastras and lives them in his own example. Yet, he consciously remains inconspicuous, transparent.

He is a man on the path of enlightenment who has arrived at a certain subsuperconscious [intuitive] state and wishes to stay there. Therefore, he automatically has released various interactions with the world, physically and emotionally, and remains poised in a contemplative, monastic lifestyle. The basic thought behind the philosophy of being a sannyasin is to put oneself in a hot-house condition of self-imposed discipline, where unfoldment of the spirit can be catalyzed at a greater intensity than in family life, where the exterior concerns and overt responsibilities of the world predominate.

The sannyasin is the homeless one who remains detached from all forms of involvement—friends, family, personal ambition—finding security in his own being rather than attaching himself to outward manifestations of security, warmth and companionship. He is alone, but never lonely. He lives as though on the eve of his departure, often abiding no more than three nights in the same place. He may be a pilgrim, a wandering sadhu. He may be a monastic contemplative living in a cloistered monastery or semi-cloistered ashrama.

OUR CENTER GALLERY ALTERNATELY FEATURES SCENES OF HOUSEHOLDERS AND

ROHINI KUMAR

SESHU BADRINATH/PIPAL PRODUCTIONS

BABY PHOTOS OF JAFFNA

When family life possesses love and virtue, it has found both its essence and fruition. TIRUKURAL, VERSE 5

Scenes from
Family Life

need support from the younger generation. A Hindu never pities a sacrifice, but glorifies it with appreciation. Grandma made a big point to us about hospitality. She took it as a spiritual duty to serve guests as if they were God. This helped a lot in tying her community together and gave the family a loving way to greet the outside world. If a guest comes to a family, even unannounced, he is invited in warmly and asked about his well being. He is also served the best food in the house, even to the extent that family members may go hungry to ensure that the guest is well fed. Hinduism taught us the love of all living creatures. At lunch time, my mother would say a silent prayer and set aside a portion to be fed to the cows. If a hungry man came to the door at mealtime, he was fed and given a few coins.

VOICES: Growing up a Hindu in India, I found that pleasure and pilgrimage, religious rituals and daily life were intricately intertwined. Religion was always associated with joy and pleasure, never moralistic teaching. Every weekend we were taken to the beautiful sandstone Birla Mandir—cold marble below bare feet,

the softness of the marigolds and rose petals in our hands, the smiling faces of Krishna, Siva and Vishnu, the harmonium and cymbals and the sheer faith of hundreds of devotees. Afterwards, there were joy rides in the temple complex, trinkets and holy pictures and a cold soda. For us, it was a spiritual Disney World.

VOICES: Where I grew up, mothers ruled the house, even though they did not go out in the olden days to earn. Sisters were respected and given gifts on at least two religious occasions. The rituals like Raksha Bandhan and Bhau Bij are woven around pure love between a brother and a sister and bonding of that relationship. In the former, the sister ties a specially made bracelet around her brother's wrist, requesting him to protect her if need be, and in the latter, the sister does arati (a worshipful expression of love and devotion through a tiny lighted ghee lamp) to her brother, wishing him long life and prosperity. The brother gives her gifts and sweets on both occasions. The Hindu religious principles emphasize that women should be respected. A Sanskrit saying goes, "Yatra naryastu pujyante, ramante tatra devatah." It

In preparation for sannyasa, the aspirant leaves behind family, former friends and old acquaintances and steps out into a new pattern of subsuperconscious living. He strives to be all spine-power, all light. When we see him trying, although he may not be too successful at it if he is going through some inner turmoil or challenge, we know he is striving, and that is an inspiration to us. His very existence is his mission in life. He has dedicated himself to live a life of total commitment to the path of yoga, and by doing so he sustains the spiritual vibration for the householders. It is the renunciate who keeps the Vedic religions alive on the Earth. He keeps the philosophy vibrant and lucid, presenting it dynamically to the householders.

Monks of every Hindu order are guided and guarded by unseen beings who look after their lives as if they were their own. Families are blessed who share in and support the renunciation of their sons born through them to perform a greater dharma than the *grihastha* life could ever offer. It is the monastic communities worldwide, of all religions, that sustain sanity on this planet. It is the monks living up to their vows who sustain the vibration of law and order in the communities and nations of the world. This is how the devonic [angelic]

world sees each monastic community worldwide. This is how it is and should always be. This is how humanity balances out its experiential karmas and avoids destroying itself as it passes through the darkness of the Kali Yuga. The monastic communities that surround the planet, fulfilling their dharma, compensate for the adharma that is so prevalent, thus ensuring that humanity does not self-destruct in these trying times. We must, for the sake of clarity, state here that monastic communities are either strictly male or strictly female. Coed mixed-group ashramas are not monastic communities, but classed traditionally as communes.

Path-Choosing

The two paths—householder and renunciate—every young man has to choose between them. In Hindu tradition the choice is made before the marriage ceremony, and, if not, during the ceremony itself. Though guided by the advice of parents, elder family members and religious leaders, the choice is his and his alone as to how his soul is to live through the birth karmas of this incarnation. Both paths take courage, great courage, to step forward and embrace the responsibili-

RENUNCIATES ENGAGED IN WORSHIP, SERVICE, FELLOWSHIP AND LIFE'S MANY JOYS

A mother applies a forehead mark for her daughter during puja; a beautifully adorned woman outshines the roses in a Singapore garden; a youth carries *kavadi* during festival time at Nallur Temple in Sri Lanka; children in Nepal offer lamps during the Chaith festival; a Jaffna-born couple marry in London; a royal priest pours sandalwood paste over a crystal Sivalinga during puja

means that wherever the women are honored, those are the places where even the Gods rejoice.

How is the Hindu concept of family experienced differently from that of other faiths? Only in the faiths of India does one encounter the tenet that we all experience a multitude of families in our journey toward God. In birth after birth we evolve, our tradition assures. In family after family we grow and mature and learn. Thus, in the Hindu family we find that the past and the future are intricately bound together. How intricately? We know a Sri Lankan family who is certain that their daughter, now nine, is the father's deceased grandmother. In this community it is considered a very great blessing—especially if one has the privilege of being part of a fine, noble family—for a departed relative

A family study teachings of their lineage

to be born again into its midst. There is a profound intuition that when relatives pass they will return, perhaps soon and perhaps in the very same home. So, everyone watches for the telltale signs.

How wonderful, the family feels, to care for Grandma as she once cared for us!

Thus, the spiritual insight into rebirth extends the family concept beyond the present, binding the present to the past, and promising further continuity with the future. Many Hindu families are aware of such relationships. Many others will consciously seek to be born into a particular family, knowing that life there will be fulfilling, secure and high-minded.

VOICES: *When a married daughter visits her parents' family, she is revered like a guest but showered with love like a daughter, with blessings and all the nice clothes as well*

ties of adult life.

In making this decision in our tradition we have found it valuable for the young man to spend time in a Hindu monastery where he can live the monk's life for a period of six months or more and receive spiritual and religious training that will enhance his character for a positive future, no matter which path he chooses. Only by living for a time as a monk will he come to truly understand the monastic path and be empowered to make a knowledgeable choice between that path and the traditional dharma of the householder, raising a family and serving the community. One of the best times for this sojourn apart from the world, setting aside life's usual concerns, is just after high school or during an interim break. Then, after the time in the monastery, a firm and positive consideration should be made, in consultation with family and elders, as to which of the two paths he wishes to pursue.

Path-choosing is a beginning, pointing a direction, declaring an intention. Marriage becomes a lifetime commitment only when the final marriage vows are spoken. This is preceded by months or even years of choosing a spouse, a process that calls forth the wisdom of the two families, community elders, religious leaders and those who are trained to judge astrological compatibilities. Renunciate life in our Natha tradition and many others becomes a lifetime commitment only when final, lifetime vows of renunciation of the world are voiced. In some lineages, no formal vows are even taken, but there are traditionally understood norms of conduct, proprieties and protocol to be adhered to.

We might say that one does not choose renunciation, but rather is chosen by it, when the soul is matured to the point when the world no longer holds a binding fascination. While considerations of the order that one will join are practical realities, it is vital that the young man choosing renunciate life does so not seeking place or position in a particular order, but sets out as a free spirit, unencumbered, under the guidance of his *satguru*, willing to serve everywhere and anywhere he is sent, be it in his guru's central ashrama, a distant center, a monastery of another guru or alone on an independent *sadhana*. The clear path is to define the path itself. Then, proceed with confidence.

Know it with a certainty beyond question that the path of renunciation is life's most grand and glorious path, and the singular path for those seeking life's ultimate goal, Realization of God as

THOMAS KELLY

COURTESY BAPS

THOMAAS KELLY

THOMAAS KELLY

Attempting to speak of the renunciate's magnitude is like numbering all the human multitudes who have ever died. TIRUKURAL, VERSE 22

Scenes from
Renunciate Life

as food the family can give. I had such a wonderful homecoming in India after I had lived for many years in the West. Such a homecoming of a few days is an emotionally gratifying, soul-satisfying event for the girl, who carries those fond memories for life.

Hinduism teaches a constellation of principles which, if followed by husband and wife, make the bold assertion that preserving the marriage and the integrity of the family holds rewards that far outweigh benefits they might expect from separation. We work with families on a daily basis, solving their problems, helping them to individually follow their path and to mutually work together. Hinduism teaches them the ideals of dharma, which includes duty, selflessness, virtue and faith. When dharma is the shared ideal of every

Leaving her body at death, a soul is received by devas

A. MANIVEL

family member—as opposed to self-fulfillment or social-economic objectives—it is easier to navigate troubled waters, easier to persist in seasons of loss or lack, in times of emotional or mental difficulty.

VOICES: *Looking back to my early years, it was the scriptures that tied our family together. I would hear father and grandfather chanting the Vedic mantras together in the early hours of each day. Everyone I know held the highest esteem for the* Vedas, *the very voice of God, elders would say. I knew they were old, and everyone said they were profound. But it was not until I was in my teens that I really discovered the* Upanishads. *Such beauty, such profundity, such humor and insight I had never before or since known. I would spend hours with the texts, talking with my parents and friends, wondering*

timeless, formless, spaceless Absolute Reality, that mystic treasure reserved for the renunciate. Know, too, that renunciation is not merely an attitude, a mental posture which can be equally assumed by the householder and the renunciate. Our scriptures proclaim that a false concept. My order supports the scriptural doctrine that the two paths—householder and renunciate—are distinct in their dharmas and attainments, affirming that true renunciation may not be achieved by those in the world even by virtue of a genuine attitude of detachment. The householder may attain great and profound spiritual depths during his life, unfolding the mysteries of existence in his or her states of contemplation and, according to our ancient mystics, perhaps experiencing total God Realization at the hour of death, though this attainment is reserved for the ardent, sincere and devout *grihasthi*. Many years ago, my *satguru*, Yogaswami of Jaffna, Sri Lanka, wrote the following poem to honor those valiant souls on the path of renunciation.

Hail, O sannyasin, love's embodiment!
Does any power exist apart from love?
Diffuse thyself throughout the happy world.
Let painful maya cease and ne'er return!

Day and night give praise unto the Lord.
Pour forth a stream of songs to melt the very stones.
Attain the sight where night is not nor day.
See Siva everywhere, and rest in bliss.
Live without interest in worldly gain.
Here, as thou hast ever been, remain.
Then never will cruel sorrow venture nigh.

Best of sannyasins, of one-pointed mind!
Morning and evening worship without fail
The holy feet of the Almighty Lord,
Who here and hereafter preserves and safeguards thee.
Cast aside the fetters of thy sins!
By steadfast concentration of thy mind
Awareness of a separate self thou must extirpate.
Conquer with love all those that censure thee.
Thou art eternal! Have no doubt of this!
What is not thou is fancy's artifice.
Formless thou art!
Then live from all thought free!

An ash-covered sadhu in prayer; Pramukh Swami, head of BAPS, initiating a new sadhu in Bhuj; Swami Tejomayananda with devotees; sadhus sit for a simple meal served on banana leaves; a score of men during initiatory rites in Ujjain to enter the Avahan Akhara; two Vaishnava yogis perform fire tapas, encircled by burning coals; a holy woman of Juna Akhara at the Ujjain Kumbha Mela

myself how these men, so many thousands of years ago, had gained all that wisdom—more, it seemed to me then, than people had today. Through the years I have seen so many families whose lives revolve around the sacred texts. While all honor the Vedas, for some the heart is moved by the Gita, the epics, the Tirumurai or maybe their own family guru's writings composed only decades ago. Whatever texts they are, it's quite clear in my experience that sacred texts do much to bind a family together in thought.

Then there is faith in karma. The Hindu family believes, in its heart, that even life's difficulties are part of God's purpose and the fruition of each member's past karmas. To go through things together is natural, expected, accepted. Breaking up, divorcing, separating—such reactions to stress don't resolve karmas that were brought into this life to go through. In fact, they make things worse, create new, unseemly karmas and thus further need for perhaps even more sorrowful births. The belief in karma—the law by which our thoughts, words and deeds reap their natural reactions—helps hold a family together, not unlike the crew of a storm-tossed ship would never think of jumping overboard when the going gets rough, but work together to weather the crisis, with their shared goal lying beyond the immediate difficulty.

Thus, difficult experiences can be serenely endured by the practicing Hindu. Knowing this in her heart, a Hindu wife in Kuala Lumpur can find solace in the midst of the death of a child. Knowing this in his heart, a Hindu father in Bangalore can sustain periods of privation and business failure. Each finds the strength to go on.

VOICES: *There is a beautiful word in the Hindi language, shukur, which means acceptance. Sometimes it's very hard to accept the cards life deals one, yet the Hindu belief in the acceptance of God's will makes it possible to bear incredible hardships. A young friend of my husband went into a coma after going in for preventive surgery. They gave him too much chloroform, and he never came out of the coma. He was a young man, his children were young. In the beginning, his wife was frantic, weeping all the time. Yet, her beliefs were solid as a rock within her, gradually calming her. It's now five*

THE IDEALS OF FAMILY LIFE

If both husband and wife are on the spiritual path, the householder family will progress beautifully and deeply. Their love for one another and their offspring maintains family harmony. However, the nature of their *sadhana* and unfoldment of the spirit is different from that of the sannyasin. The family unit itself is a magnetic-force structure, a material structure, for they are involved in the objects and relationships of the world. It is the family's effort to be "in the world but not of it" that gives the impetus for insight and the awakening of the soul. The struggle to maintain the responsibilities of the home and children while simultaneously observing the contemplative way, in itself, provides strength and balance, and slowly matures innate wisdom through the years.

The successful Hindu householder family is stable, an asset to the larger community in which it lives, an example of joyous, contented relationships. Members of the family are more interested in serving than being served. They accept responsibility for one another. They are pliable, flexible, able to flow freely like water. They worship and meditate daily without fail and strictly observe their individual *sadhanas*. Their insight is respected and their advice sought. Yet, they do not bring the world into the home, but guard and protect the home vibration as the spiritual center of their life. Their commitments are always first to the family, then to the community. Their home remains sacrosanct, apart from the world, a place of reflection, growing and peace. They intuitively know the complex workings of the world, the forces and motivations of people, and often guide others to perceptive action. Yet, they do not display exclusive spiritual knowledge or put themselves above their fellow man.

Problems for them are merely challenges, opportunities for growth. Forgetting themselves in their service to the family and their fellow man, they become the pure channel for love and light. Intuition unfolds naturally. What is unspoken is more tangible than what is said. Their timing is good, and abundance comes. They live simply, guided by real need and not novel desire. They are creative, acquiring and using skills such as making their own clothing, growing food, building their own house and furniture. The inner knowing awakened by their meditations is brought

The virtuous householder supports the needs of renunciates, ancestors and the poor. TIRUKURAL, VERSE 41

Scenes from
Family Life

years later, and she's picked up the pieces of her life. Yet she never forgets to have her pujas; her husband's picture is always there in the ritual ceremonies. His presence is there in the family. She seems to know that the soul cannot die, that his spirit lives on. Every year on his death anniversary, we all gather for the ritual ceremonies. Everybody feels the grief, and each religion teaches you to cope in a different way. Her belief in the undying soul gives her a little solace. She constantly has the prayers and the satsangas at home, and they help her in the changing patterns of her life.

There are many other ideals that help a family survive in Hinduism. An important one is that father and mother are the children's first guru, first teacher of things of the spirit. This brings a deep honoring to the parent-child relationship. Such a tie transcends the physical, emotional, intellec-

A Saivite father shares the teachings with his wife and children

tual relationship that is the sum of some family bonds. It brings an air of sacredness into the interactions, a deeper reverencing which powerfully connects a daughter or son to his mother and father. One sees this expressed so beautifully in the traditional family when young ones gently and lovingly touch the feet of their parents. They are worshiping the Divine in their parents and thus being prepared to see God in everyone.

In the strict Hindu family, there is a clear and well-understood hierarchy, based fundamentally on age. Younger members are taught to respect and follow the directions from their elders, and to cherish and protect those younger than themselves. Even differences of a few months are respected. Many problems that could arise in less-structured families— and do, as proven in the modern nuclear family—simply never come up. There is less vying for attention, less ego conflict, less confusion

directly into the busy details of everyday life. They use the forces of procreation wisely to produce the next generation and not as instinctive indulgence. They worship profoundly and seek and find spiritual revelation in the midst of life.

Maintaining a Balance of Forces

Within each family, the man is predominantly in the *pingala* force. The woman is predominantly in the *ida* force. When the energies are the other way around, disharmony is the result. When they live together in harmony and have awakened enough innate knowledge of the relation of their forces to balance them, then both are in the *sushumna* force and can soar into the Divinity within. Children born to such harmonious people come through from the deeper chakras and tend to be highly evolved and well balanced.

Should the woman become aggressively intellectual and the man become passively physical, then forces in the home are disturbed. The two bicker and argue. Consequently, the children are upset, because they only reflect the vibration of the parents and are guided by their example. Sometimes the parents separate, going their own

ways until the conflicting forces quiet down. But when they come back together, if the wife still remains in the *pingala* channel, and the husband in the *ida* channel, they will generate the same inharmonious conditions. It is always a question of who is the head of the house, he or she? The head is always the one who holds the *pranas* within the *pingala*. Two *pingala* spouses in one house, husband and wife, spells conflict.

The balancing of the *ida* and *pingala* into *sushumna* is, in fact, the pre-ordained spiritual *sadhana*, a built-in *sadhana*, or birth *sadhana*, of all family persons. To be on the spiritual path, to stay on the spiritual path, to get back on the spiritual path, to keep the children on the spiritual path, to bring them back to the spiritual path, too—as a family, father, mother, sons and daughters living together as humans were ordained to do without the intrusions of uncontrolled instinctive areas of the mind and emotions—it is imperative, it is a virtual command of the soul of each member of the family, that these two forces, the *ida* and *pingala*, become and remain balanced, first through understanding and then through the actual accomplishment of this *sadhana*.

Father and daughter arrive at a temple in Sri Lanka; women pray at a shrine in Ujjain; ladies throw colored powder during the jubilant Holi festival; shopping at a roadside market in Jaffna, Sri Lanka; a mom and dad reading to their son; taking a stroll in sunny Tirupati; a young couple wait in queue for darshan of Sri Venkateshwara

about everyone's role and place. With the lines of seniority known to all, regulations, changes and cooperative exchanges flow freely among family members.

VOICES: *In the family life, thousands of years ago, a Hindu was told, "Matridevo bhava, pitridevo bhava, acharya devo bhava." This Sanskrit dictum means, "Be the one who respects his mother as God, his father as God and his guru or teacher as God." Such an ultimate reverence for the elders creates a profound, serene feeling and certainly prepares the mind to receive the good and loving advice from them in the proper spirit. Bowing down before the elders in respectful salutation and touching their feet is an exclusively Hindu custom. When such a deep respect is accorded to family members, no wonder the family bonds are strong and they remain unified.*

Daily worship in the home is a unique Hindu contribution to family sharing. Of course, faith is a shared experience in all religious households. But the Hindu takes it a step further, sanctifying the home itself with a beautiful shrine room—a kind of miniature temple right in the house. The father or oldest son is the family's liturgist, leading others in daily ritual. Others care for the sacred

implements, gather fresh flowers for the morning rites and decorate for holy days or festivals. In Hindu culture, family and spirituality are intimately intertwined.

VOICES: *Every Hindu family in our village had a home shrine where the family members worship their Gods. Even the poorest set aside a place for this. Rituals are periodic celebrations which are religious and spiritual in character, and they address the inward feelings rather than outward. Such pujas and rituals give an individual a chance to pause, look inward and concentrate on something more meaningful, more profound, than mere materialism and the daily drudgery of life. Worships and rejoicings in the name of God, fasting and observances of special days enable people to look beyond the day-to-day life to a larger scheme of things. In the best homes I know, the father performs the rites daily, and the family joins and assists. I guess it's like the old adage, "The family that prays together stays together." Even in the busy rat race of life in cosmopolitan cities like Mumbai or Los Angeles, there are many Hindus who perform at least a mini puja daily. They claim that even the small ritual of a few minutes a day makes them concentrate, feel*

One thing to remember: the family man is the guru of his household. If he wants to find out how to be a good guru, he just has to observe his own *satguru*, that is all he has to do. He will learn through observation. Often this is best accomplished by living in the guru's ashrama periodically to perform *sadhana* and service. Being head of his home does not mean he is a dominant authority figure, arrogantly commanding unconditional obedience, such as Bollywood and Hollywood portray. No. He must assume full responsibility for his family and guide subtly and wisely, with love always flowing. This means that he must accept the responsibility for the conditions in the home and for the spiritual training and unfoldment of his wife and children. This is his *purusha* dharma. To not recognize and not follow it is to create much *kukarma*, bad actions, bringing back hurtful results to him in this or another life.

When the wife has problems in fulfilling her womanly duties, *stri* dharma, it is often because the husband has not upheld his duty, nor allowed her to fulfill hers. When he does not allow her to or fails to insist that she perform her *stri* dharma and give her the space and time to do so, she creates *kukarmas* which are equally shared by him. This is because the *purusha* karmic duty and obligation of running a proper home naturally falls upon him, as well as upon her. So, there are great penalties to be paid by the man, husband and father for failure to uphold his *purusha* dharma.

Of course, when the children "go wrong" and are corrected by the society at large, both husband and wife suffer and equally share in the *kukarmas* created by their offspring. In summary, the husband took the wife into his home and is therefore responsible for her well-being. Together they bring the children into their home and are responsible for them, spiritually, socially, culturally, economically, as well as for their education.

What does it mean to be the spiritual head of the house? He is responsible for stabilizing the *pranic* forces, both positive, negative and mixed. When the magnetic, materialistic forces become too strong in the home, or out of proper balance with the others,

The scriptures exalt above every other good the greatness of virtuous renunciates. TIRUKURAL, VERSE 21

Scenes from
Monastic Life

elevated spiritually, brings their minds on an even keel, enabling them to perform better in their line of work.

Another family tradition is the *kulaguru*, or family preceptor. Though it is not required that every member of a Hindu family have the same *guru*, it often happens that way. This gives all members a shared spiritual point of reference, a voice whose wisdom will be sought in times of decision, difference or unclarity, a voice that will also be listened to, its advice followed. That means that there is a kind of outside counselor, a mediator to work out deadlocks, a referee to arbitrate and settle disputes. Thus, the family need never be stuck in some irresolvable impasse. The *kulaguru's* counsel can be trusted to transcend the personalities involved, to be impersonal and just. And that simple practice can bring a family through many a quandary.

Hindu heritage gives a strong defini-

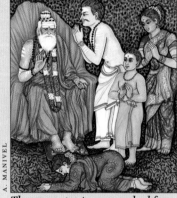

The preceptor is approached for blessings, and guidance

tion to the growth and maturing of family members, through the application of the *ashramas*. Every member in a family is expected to spend the first twenty-four years or so in the *brahmacharya*, or student, stage. It's a time of learning, studying, serving and growing up. Then comes the stage of the *grihastha*, or householder, and with it marriage, children and social responsibilities. These stages are informally defined in nearly every culture, but in Hinduism the definitions are elaborately detailed beyond raising the family. Sometime around fifty, every member enters the *vanaprastha ashrama*, a stage of advisor and elder. By formalizing this stage, the Hindu family gives a place of prominence and usefulness to its senior citizens. They do not just retire, and they certainly are not sent off to a retirement home. Rather, their advice is sought, their years of experience drawn upon. Thus, Hinduism gives a place to those who have served the family in their youth but,

he has to work within himself in early morning *sadhana* and deep meditation to bring through the spiritual forces of happiness, contentment, love and trust. By going deep within himself, into his soul nature, he uplifts the spiritual awareness of the entire family into one of the higher chakras.

The family woman has to be a good mother. To achieve this, she has to learn to flow her awareness with the awareness of the children. She has been through the same series of experiences the children are going through. She intuits what to do next. As a mother, she fails only if she neglects the children, takes her awareness completely away, leaving the children to flounder. But if she stays close, attends to each child's needs, is there when he or she cries or comes home from school, everything is fine. The child is raised perfectly. This occurs if the wife stays in the home, stabilizing the domestic force field, where she is needed most, allowing the husband to be the breadwinner and stabilizer of the external force field, which is his natural domain.

The Hindu woman is trained to perform her *stri* dharma from the time she is a little girl. She finds ways to express her natural creativity within the home itself. She may write poetry or become an artist. Perhaps she has a special talent for sewing or embroidery or gardening or music. She can learn to loom cloth and make the family's clothing. If needed, she can use her skills to supplement the family income without leaving the home. There are so many ways for a Hindu wife and mother to fully use her creative energies, including being creative enough to never let her life become boring. It is her special blessing that she is free to pursue her religion fully, to study the scriptures, to sing bhajana and keep her own spiritual life strong inside.

If each understands—or at least the family man understands, for it is his home—how the forces have to be worked within it, and realizes that he, as a man, flows through a different area of the mind than does his wife in fulfilling their respective, but very different, birth karmas, then everything remains harmonious. He thinks; she feels. He rea-

Sadhvis meditating in Hardwar; Swami Arunagirinatha, head of Madurai Aadheenam; Swami Chidananda Saraswati, head of Divine Life Society, giving darshan; a yogi in bliss; sadhus of Swaminarayanan Fellowship (BAPS) with their guru; Swami Gautamananda, head of Chennai's RK Mission; Swami Achalanand Ji Maharaj of Jodhpur offers words of wisdom

with age, can no longer serve in that same way. They have a new place. Far from being a lesser function, it is a place of greater honor. This is one of the greatest gifts that the traditional Hindu family offers, thus averting one of the greatest tragedies: depriving elders of due recognition.

VOICES: *My mother-in-law, right up till she died in her seventies, was the head of the household. She could do anything with my children, and I wouldn't have the guts to tell her no. She would put kohl, mascara, adorning their eyes and oil in their hair, and their eyes would be black and their hair greasy, but I wouldn't say anything to her. She would bribe the kids with candy, and they loved her for it. It's a loving relationship, because you do something for someone and they do something for you. The blessings do come on you because she felt very wanted and happy. She taught me the sanctity of the family unit and respect for elders.*

It is significant that Hindus, numbering over one billion today, constitute sixteen percent of the human race. One out of every six people on the planet is a Hindu. So, the ability of that large community to preserve its strengths, to pass on its values and cultural treasures, to protect its members and keep them well and fulfilled

is important. Important does not suffice. Crucial, really. On the optimistic side, as much as eighty percent of Hindus live in rural India, in the 700,000 small villages which remain less affected by outside influences and thus retain the promise of carrying on the traditional ways, including language, religion and custom. As all the foregoing amply indicates, the Hindu concept of family is unique in many ways.

There is a more cosmic definition taught by every grandma and village elder, that in truth all of us on Earth are the creation of the One Great God; thus, in the broadest sense, we belong to a single family. *Vasudhaiva kutumbukam*—"The whole world is one family." That's not an innovative notion derived from New Age insights or Gaia ecology. It's been part of Indian folk culture for thousands of years.

VOICES: *I was always taught that we as Hindus must have a magnanimous attitude, that our Hindu religion visualizes the entire Earth as one family. But while looking at all human beings as one family, I also saw that elders deeply considered the smaller family unit, the dynamism of its members' relationships with one another, and the pivotal role the institution of family plays in building the society.*

sons and intellectualizes, while she reasons and emotionalizes. He is in his realm. She is in her realm. He is not trying to make her adjust to the same area of the mind that he is flowing through. And, of course, if she is in her realm, she will not expect him to flow through her area of the mind, because women just do not do this.

Usually it is the man who does not want to, or understand how to, become the spiritual head of his house. Often he wants the woman to flow through his area of the mind, to be something of a brother and pal or partner to him. Therefore, he experiences everything that goes along with brothers and pals and partners: arguments, fights, scraps and good times. In an equal relationship of this kind, the forces of the home are not building or becoming strong, for such a home is not a sanctified place in which they can bring inner-plane beings into reincarnation from the higher celestial realms. If they do have children under these conditions, they simply take "potluck" off the lower astral plane, or Pretaloka.

A man goes through his intellectual cycles in facing the problems of the external world. A woman has to be strong enough, understanding enough, to allow him to go through those cycles. A woman goes through emotional cycles and feeling cycles as she lives within the home, raises the family and takes care of her husband. He has to be confident enough to understand and allow her to go through those cycles.

Rather than arguing or talking about their cycles, the man who is spiritual head of his house meditates to stabilize the forces within himself. He withdraws the physical energies from the *pingala* and the *ida* currents into *sushumna* in his spine and head. He breathes regularly, sitting motionless until the forces adjust to his inner command. When he comes out of his meditation, if it really was a meditation, she sees him as a different being, and a new atmosphere and relationship are created in the home immediately. The children grow up as young disciples of the mother and the father. As they mature, they learn of inner things. It is the duty of the mother and the father to give to the child at a very early age his first religious training and his education in attention, concentration, observation and meditation.

He who rightly pursues the householder's life here on Earth will be rightfully placed among the Gods there in Heaven. TIRUKURAL, VERSE 10

Scenes from
Family Life

India's Venerable Renunciate Tradition

Renunciation and asceticism have been integral components of Hindu culture and religion from the earliest days, the most highly honored facet of the Hindu Dharma. The ideal of the life-long celibate monastic, living within the social order and yet freed from worldly obligation that he might find and shed his spiritual light, started before the Mohenjodaro and Harappa civilizations of five thousand years ago and traces its development in the references in the *Rig Veda*; to the *munis* and the *yatis*, men who wore long hair and yellow robes, such men as Sanatkumara, Dattatreya and others, all *naishtika brahmacharis* [lifelong celibates]. Later in the *Vedas* the sannyasa *ashrama*, or last stage of the four-fold division of life, became formalized, and many references are made to those who after age seventy-two relinquished all in search of the Absolute.

The ancient shastras recognize four justifiable motivations for entering into sannyasa: *vidvat, vividisha, markata* and *atura*.

Vidvat ("knowing; wise") sannyasa is the spontaneous withdrawal from the world in search for Self Realization which results from karma and tendencies developed in a previous life. *Vividisha* ("discriminating") sannyasa is renunciation to satisfy a yearning for the Self developed through scriptural study and practice. *Markata* sannyasa is taking refuge in sannyasa as a result of great sorrow, disappointment or misfortune in worldly pursuits. *Atura* ("suffering or sick") sannyasa is entering into sannyasa upon one's deathbed, realizing that there is no longer hope in life.

Renunciation of the world found a high expression in the monastic principles of Jainism and Buddhism, both religions founded by illustrious sons of India. Siddhartha Gautama, the Buddha, was born and died a Hindu in the seventh century bce. He himself cherished, lived and promulgated the ascetic ideal within the compass of Hinduism, and his followers made a separate religion of his teachings after his death. It is only in Hinduism and the

The parents must be fully knowledgeable of what their child is experiencing. During the first seven years, the child will go through the chakra of memory. He will be learning, absorbing, observing. The second seven years will be dedicated to the development of reason, as the second chakra unfolds. If theirs is a boy child, he is going through the *pingala*. If a girl child, she is going through the *ida* current and will go through emotional cycles.

Religion begins in the home under the mother's influence and instruction. The mother goes to the temple to get strong. That is the reason Hindus live near a temple. They go to the temple to draw strength from the shakti of the Deity, and they return to the home where they maintain a similar vibration in which to raise the next generation to be staunch and wonderfully productive citizens of the world, to bring peace on Earth, to keep peace on Earth. There is an ancient South Indian proverb which says one should not live in a city which has no temple.

By both spouses' respecting the differences between them and understanding where each one is flowing in consciousness, there is a give and take in the family, a beautiful flow of the forces. The *acharyas* and swamis work with the family man and woman to bring them into inner states of being so that they can bring through to the Earth a generation of great inner souls. It is a well-ordered cycle. Each one plays a part in the cycle, and if it is done through wisdom and understanding, a family home is created that has the same vibration as the temple or a contemplative monastery.

A contemplative home where the family can meditate has to have that uplifting, temple-like vibration. In just approaching it, the *sushumna* current of the man should withdraw awareness from the *pingala* current deep within. That is what the man can do when he is the spiritual head of the home.

From the point of view of the Second World, or astral plane, the home is the family temple, and the wife and mother is in charge of that spiritual environment. The husband can come into that sanctum sanctorum but should not bring the world into it. He will naturally find a refuge in the home if she is doing her duty. He will be able to regain his peace of mind there, renew himself for the next day

DINODIA / THOMAS KELLY / REUTERS/JAYANTA SHAW / KUMAR BHOOBUN

A tiny infant in loving arms; women at the market in Nepal; boys meditate at the Tirunavakarasu Ashram/Gurukulam in Sri Lanka; a family perform havan, the Vedic fire ceremony; a young family, heads shaven as an act of penance, enjoy rice and curry prasadam at Tirupati Temple; a devotee sings devotional hymns; renowned dancer Paolomi Ashwinkumar

Hindu-inspired religions of Jainism and Buddhism that asceticism is a vibrant and valued mode of life, a part of the natural dharma. Though the homeless sadhu and the wandering mendicant existed before, it was Gautama Buddha who around six hundred years bce, organized what had been an individual *sadhana* into a monastic order, which he termed the *sanga*. In the early 9th century, Adi Shankaracharya, the great exemplar of the ideals of sannyasa who revitalized and restored the ancient ways during his short life of thirty-two years, organized the Hindu monastics of his day. In his travels throughout India, he assessed the existing traditions and finally validated ten orders of ascetics, at the same time establishing four religious centers or *pithas* in the North, East, South and West of India, known respectively as Jyotih, Govardhana, Sringeri and Sharada. Each *dashanami* order is loosely associated with one of the four centers. A fifth prominent *pitha*, associated with Sringeri Matha, is in Kanchipuram, also in the South. Thus, the ancient order of sannyasa extends back to time immemorial, structurally influenced by Gautama Buddha about twenty-five centuries ago and revitalized in its present form by Adi Shankaracharya around

twelve hundred years ago.

Today the total number of monks in India and the world is not known for sure. Estimates range from one million to as high as five million, as there is naturally no official census or way of counting those who live this reclusive life. One of the largest of Hindu orders is the sadhu order known as Juna Akhara, which has 150,000 sadhus. *Sadhu* means "virtuous one," and is a holy man dedicated to the search for God. There are thirteen such sadhu *akharas*. The Juna Akhara and Niranjani Akhara are the most prominent. Others include the Agan, Alakhiya, Abhana, Anand, Mahanirvani and Atal. Most of these orders are considered Saivite; three are Vaishnavite (formed beginning in 1299 by Saint Ramananda Ji) and a few are Sikh orders patterned after the Hindu monastic system. *Akhara* is a Hindi term meaning "wrestling arena." It can mean either a place of verbal debate or one of physical combat. Sadhus of the various *akharas* may also hold allegiance to one of the ten *dashanami* orders: Sarasvati, Puri, Bana, Tirtha, Giri, Parvati, Bharati, Aranya, Ashrama and Sagara. Thus, the *akharas* overlap with the *dashanami* system. The *akharas'* dates of found-in the stressful situations that the outside world is full of. In this technological age a man needs this refuge. He needs that inner balance in his life. When he comes home, she greets him at the entrance and performs a rite of purification and welcome, offering *arati* to cleanse his aura. This and other customs protect the sanctity of the home. When he enters that sanctuary and she is in her soul body and the child is in its soul body, then he becomes consciously conscious in his soul body, called *anandamaya kosha* in Sanskrit. He leaves the conscious mind, which is a limited, external state of mind and not a balanced state of mind. He enters the intuitive mind. He gets immediate and intuitive answers to his worldly problems.

A woman depends on a man for physical and emotional security. She depends on herself for her inner security. He is the guide and the example. A man creates this security by setting a positive spiritual example. When she sees him in meditation, and sees light around his head and light within his spine, she feels secure. She knows that his intuition is going to direct his intellect. She

knows he will be decisive, fair, clear-minded in the external world. She knows that when he is at home, he turns to inner and more spiritual things. He controls his emotional nature and he does not scold her if she has a hard time controlling her emotional nature, because he realizes that she lives more in the *ida* force and goes through emotional cycles. In the same way, she does not scold him if he is having a terrible time intellectually solving several business problems, because she knows he is in the intellectual force, and that is what happens in that realm of the mind. She devotes her thought and energies to making the home comfortable and pleasant for him and for the children. He devotes his thought and energies to providing sustenance and security for that home.

The man seeks understanding through observation. The woman seeks harmony through devotion. He must observe what is going on within the home, not talk too much about it, other than to make small suggestions, with much praise and virtually no criticism. He must remember that his wife is making a home for him, and he should appreciate the vibration she creates. If

PRADIP GUPTA/DINODIA

RAJESH JANTILAL

HINDUISM TODAY

THOMAS KELLY

Domestic life is rightly called virtue. The monastic path, rightly lived beyond blame, is likewise good. TIRUKURAL, VERSE 9

Meetings of the Ways

ing range from the sixth to the fourteenth century, though large monastic orders have existed throughout India's long history. Several *akharas* run hundreds of ashramas, schools and service institutions.

The majority of sadhus live in various *akhara* camps scattered all over India. Holy cities, including Rishikesh, Haridwar, Nashik, Prayag, Varanasi, Vrindavan and Ujjain have permanent *akhara* camps. Many sadhus move constantly from one camp to another. Those swamis and sadhus who are not a part of an *akhara* live in independent *mathas* and ashramas situated all over the country, or wander as mendicants. There is also the important *aadheenam* tradition, not associated with the *dashanami* orders, a series of ancient monastery-temple complexes in Tamil Nadu.

A large number of *sadhvis*, women monks, perhaps as many as 100,000, are a part of the *akhara* system, though they live separately from the men, and even during the massive Kumbha Mela festivals they have separate camps.

There are also sannyasin orders, such as the Nathas, that exist

outside the *dashanami* and *akhara* systems.

Additionally, several large cenobitic orders have branches outside India, such as the Ramakrishna Mission, with 1,000 sannyasins; Swaminarayan Gadi, with 1,500 sadhus; BAPS Swaminarayan Sanstha, with 700 sadhus and *brahmacharis*; and the Chinmaya Mission, with 100 swamis and swaminis.

The famed Kumbha Mela is fundamentally a gathering of the great monastic orders of India. At the high point of the Mela festivals, hundreds of thousands of renunciate monks travel in grand procession to a nearby river's edge for the *shahi snan*, "royal bath," while pilgrims line the streets to receive their blessings. The Kumbha Mela is a time to elect new *akhara* leadership, discuss and solve problems, consult with the other *akharas*, meet with devotees and initiate new monastics.

There are countless sadhus on the roads, byways, mountains, riverbanks, and in the ashramas and caves of India. They have, by their very existence, a profound, stabilizing effect on the consciousness of India and the world. It is well known that through their austerity and renunciation, the sadhus and sannyasins help

he is doing well in his inner life, is steady and strong, and she is devoted, she will flow along in inner life happily also. She must strive to be one with him, to back him up in his desires and his ambitions and what he wants to accomplish in the outside world. This makes him feel strong and stand straight with head up. She can create a successful man of her husband very easily by using her wonderful intuitive powers. Together they make a contemplative life by building the home into a temple-like vibration, so blissful, so uplifting.

In the home, the mother is likened to the Shakti Deity. She is the power, the very soul of the home. None other. So she has to be there. She has to be treated sensitively and kindly, and with respect. She has to be given all the things she needs and everything she wants so she will release her shakti power to support her husband, so that he is successful in all his manly endeavors. When she is hurt, depressed, frustrated or disappointed, she automatically withdraws that power, compromising his success in the outside world along with it. People will draw away from him. His job, business or creative abilities will suffer. This is her great *siddhi*, her inborn power, which Hindu women know so well.

How can he not be successful in his *purusha* dharma in the outside world when he has the backing of a good wife? She is naturally perceptive, naturally intuitive. She balances out his intellect, softens the impact of the forces which dash against his nervous system from morning to night. Encouragement and love naturally radiate out from her as she fulfills her *stri* dharma. Without these balancing elements in his life, a man becomes too externalized, too instinctive.

It is the man's duty, his *purusha* dharma, to provide for her and for the children. The husband should provide her with all the fine things, with a good house which she then makes into a home, with adornments, gold and jewels and clothes, gold hanging down until her ears hurt, more bracelets, more things to keep her in the home so she is feeling secure and happy. In return she provides a refuge, a serene corner of the world where he can escape from the pressures of daily life, where he can regain his inner perspective, perform his religious *sadhana* and meditations, then enjoy his family. Thus, she brings happiness and peace of mind to her family, to the community and to the world.

Sadhus march with dandas at the Kumbha Mela; Swamis in South Africa conclave with lay leaders; Satguru Sivaya Subramuniyaswami chats with a young seeker; Swami Avdheshananda Ji Giri speaks on Hinduism; the mayor of Bratislava, Slovakia, cuts the ribbon with Swami Maheshwarananda to his new yoga center; sadhus in procession; saints give blessings

consume and balance out the karma of the community at large. They are honored for the unseen benefits in the wise culture of India, and many people help support them with donations.

Today, Hindu monastics and their institutions are, for the most part, growing, thriving, while monastic traditions in other faiths are facing an erosion of numbers. This bodes well for the future of Hinduism, for the monastics are the spiritual guides and inspirers.

While Hindu monasticism is not a centralized system, it does have a competent and substantial organized leadership of gurus revered by their followers. There are also various oversight bodies. Among the *akharas*, for example, there is the Akhara Parishad and the Chatur Sampradaya. The

Delhi-based assembly, the Acharya Sangam, is a voice for some 15,000 sadhus.

Contrary to modern misconceptions, Hindu monks and families are closely associated, each helping the other in their chosen expression of dharma. Many sadhus and swamis personally guide the lives of hundreds of families. Many run institutions that provide social service. Even orders that keep their distance from society work to bring the philosophical teachings to the masses. Others live a strictly reclusive life, going deep to the source of existence in their meditations and uplifting mankind through their mere existence in elevated states of consciousness.

CHAPTER 11

A Creed of Monasticism

A. MANIVEL

Swami Vivekananda's "Song of the Sannyasin" Boldly Defines the Ideals of Monastic Life

HINDUISM TODAY

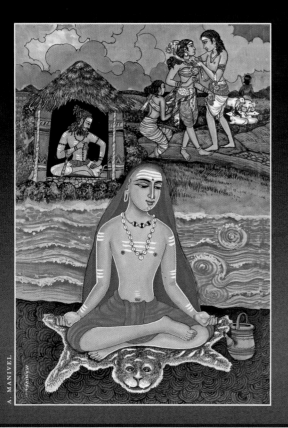

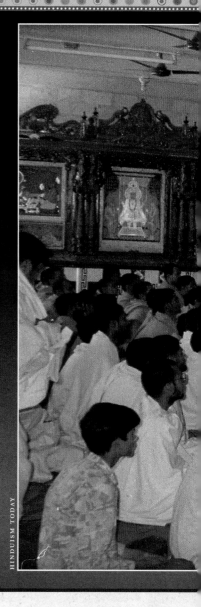

Steadfastnesse: *In the painting at left a young sadhu sits near a river, recalling his choice in life (depicted in the scene behind him) between being a solitary monk (left) and a married man (right). In the photo to the right, ashramites at the BAPS Sarangpur Sadhu school listen in rapt attention to Sivaya Subramuniyaswami's wisdom regarding monastic life during a gathering in 1995.*

THERE WAS A TIME, NOT TOO LONG AGO, WHEN CHILDREN and young men in India were taught that to renounce the world in the quest for God realization, in service to God, was the noblest human path. Parents would explain to boys that sannyasa, the way of the renunciate monk, was open to them. They would explain that, if they chose it, they would have the greatest chance of knowing once and for all the divine purpose and Ultimate Truth of life. Hindu scriptures clearly and abundantly proclaim sannyasa to be the highest dharma. But how many believe this anymore? How many parents encourage a child to consider sannyasa as a life pattern? How many young men honestly feel they will be respected more for donning orange robes and serving God than for wearing a white smock and amassing money? Still, there are bastions of hope. Notable are the Ramakrishna Mission and the Swaminarayan monastic orders—among India's three million mendicants. But today, more and more, if one proposed to Hindu parents that their son might become a swami, the response would be quiet disregard, indicating that "there are much better things the boy could do."

Swami Vivekananda held firm to the time-honored Hindu scriptural view of sannyasa. He lived it fully and experienced its every nuance. Yet, he is so revered for his latter few years—traveling and promoting Hinduism in the West—that details of his ascetic life prior to his trip to America are not commonly recanted. Perhaps Vivekananda anticipated that renunciates might one day lose esteem, or perhaps he saw it happening in his lifetime, for, in 1895, during a seven-week stay at Thousand Island Park, on the St. Lawrence River in New York State, he composed the eloquent "Song of the Sannyasin," a 13-verse ode to the supremacy of renunciation.

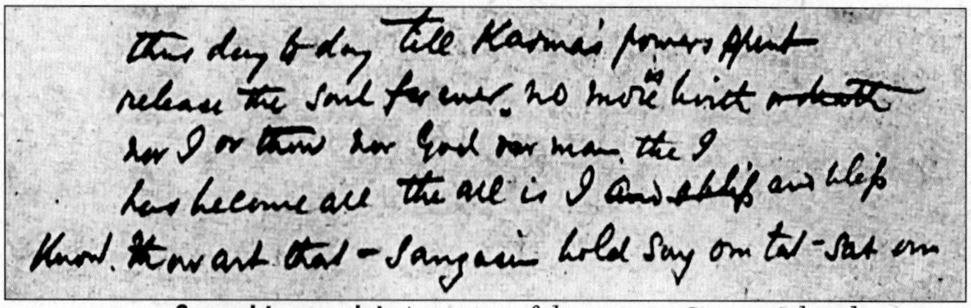
thus day by day till Karma's powers spent
release the soul for ever. No more is birth nor death
nor I nor thou nor God nor man. The I
has become all the all is I and bliss and bliss
Know. Thou art that – Sannyasin bold Say Om tat-sat om

Sacred transcript: *A portion of the poem in Swamiji's hand*

Vivekananda and his song have inspired many saints of this century. Sage Yogaswami of Sri Lanka was deeply touched by Swami Vivekananda's public address given during a brief stay in Colombo

in 1897. Vivekananda's opening words, "The time is short and the subject is vast," impacted the young Yogaswami profoundly. Yoga-swami quoted the phrase like a mantra, endeavoring to impress upon devotees not to waste time in idle pursuits of the world, but immediately begin working for their liberation from the cycle of birth and death.

Satguru Sivaya Subramuniyaswami, Yogaswami's successor, was infused with the urge to renounce the world upon reading "Song of the Sannyasin" when just a teenager.

Today each of the hundreds of Ramakrishna monks glean inspiration and encouragement from this poem and by studying Swami Vivekananda's life. But the song was not his only declaration on sannyasa's supremacy. Swami is well known for saying, "Never forget and teach to your children that as is the difference between a firefly and the blazing sun, between the infinite ocean and a little pond, between a mustard seed and the mountain Meru, such is the difference between the householder and the sannyasin!"

Vivekananda was arguably the most renowned Hindu spiritual leader of this century (even though he died in 1902 at the early age 39). It is the spirit of his renunciation, and the profound wisdom and insights into human experience gained from his dedicated life, that the "Song of the Sannyasin" presents in poetic beauty and compelling command.

The remarkable philosopher-monk was only 32 years old at the time of his visit to the Park, but he was already a celebrity in America. He had arrived in the United States two years earlier, in July 1893, journeying from India to Chicago at the urging of his fellow monks and admirers to represent Hinduism at the World Parliament of Religions. His humble yet electrifying address, at the end of an opening day of sectarian speeches, completely transformed the tenor of the conference. *The New York Herald* noted: "He is undoubtedly the greatest figure in the parliament."

Exhausted by nearly two strenuous years of lecturing throughout the US, Vivekananda was grateful to find refuge at the Park. Feeling rejuvenated, he gathered his spiritual power to train the twelve students who followed him there. His thoughts and teachings were transcribed into "Inspired Talks," a compilation which merged the spirituality of Ramakrishna with Swamiji's deep concern for the political freedom and material well-being of humanity. Swami said he was "at his best" at Thousand Island Park. The ideas and visions he refined and expressed there grew during later years into institutions in India and elsewhere.

Vivekananda's song presents a bold message, one sorely needed in today's world. We present it here in honor of the Ramakrishna renunciates, and for all courageous youth who yet today dare to wonder if life may have more to offer. Here is assurance that it does.

Song of the Sannyasin

Wake up the note! the song that had its birth
Far off, where worldly taint could never reach,
In mountain caves and glades of forest deep,
Whose calm no sigh for lust or wealth or fame
Could ever dare to break; where rolled the stream
Of knowledge, truth, and bliss that follows both.
Sing high that note, sannyasin bold! Say,
"Om Tat Sat, Om!"

Strike off thy fetters! bonds that bind thee down,
Of shining gold, or darker, baser ore—
Love, hate; good, bad; and all the dual throng.
Know slave is slave, caressed or whipped, not free;
For fetters, though of gold, are not less strong to bind.
Then off with them, sannyasin bold! Say,
"Om Tat Sat, Om!"

Let darkness go, the will-o'-the-wisp that leads
With blinking light to pile more gloom on gloom.
This thirst for life forever quench; it drags
From birth to death, and death to birth, the soul.
He conquers all who conquers self.
Know this and never yield, sannyasin bold! Say,
"Om Tat Sat, Om!"

"Who sows must reap," they say, "and cause must bring
The sure effect: good, good; bad, bad; and none
Escapes the law. But whoso wears a form
Must wear the chain." Too true; but far beyond
Both name and form is atman, ever free.
Know thou art That, sannyasin bold! Say,
"Om Tat Sat, Om!"

They know not truth who dream such vacant dreams
As father, mother, children, wife and friend.
The sexless Self—whose father He? whose child?
Whose friend, whose foe, is He who is but One?
The Self is all in all—none else exists;
And thou art That, sannyasin bold! Say,
"Om Tat Sat, Om!"

There is but One: the Free, the Knower, Self,
Without a name, without a form or stain.
In Him is maya, dreaming all this dream.
The Witness, He appears as nature, soul.
Know thou art That, sannyasin bold! Say,
"Om Tat Sat, Om!"

Where seekest thou? That freedom, friend, this world
Nor that can give. In books and temples, vain
Thy search. Thine only is the hand that holds
The rope that drags thee on. Then cease lament.
Let go thy hold, sannyasin bold! Say,
"Om Tat Sat, Om!"

Say, "Peace to all. From me no danger be
To aught that lives. In those that dwell on high,
In those that lowly creep—I am the Self in all!
All life, both here and there, do I renounce,
All heavens and earths and hells, all hopes and fears."
Thus cut thy bonds, sannyasin bold! Say,
"Om Tat Sat, Om!"

Heed then no more how body lives or goes.
Its task is done: let karma float it down.
Let one put garlands on, another kick
This frame: say naught. No praise or blame can be
Where praiser, praised, and blamer, blamed, are one.
Thus be thou calm, sannyasin bold! Say,
"Om Tat Sat, Om!"

Truth never comes where lust and fame and greed
Of gain reside. No man who thinks of woman
As his wife can ever perfect be;
Nor he who owns the least of things, nor he
Whom anger chains, can ever pass through maya's gates.
So, give these up, sannyasin bold! Say,
"Om Tat Sat, Om!"

Have thou no home. What home can hold thee, friend?
The sky thy roof, the grass thy bed, and food
What chance may bring—well cooked or ill, judge not.
No food or drink can taint that noble Self
Which knows Itself. Like rolling river free
Thou ever be, sannyasin bold! Say,
"Om Tat Sat, Om!"

Few only know the truth. The rest will hate
And laugh at thee, great one; but pay no heed.
Go thou, the free, from place to place, and help
Them out of darkness, maya's veil. Without
The fear of pain or search for pleasure, go
Beyond them both, sannyasin bold! Say,
"Om Tat Sat, Om!"

Thus day by day, till karma's power's spent,
Release the soul forever. No more is birth,
Nor I, nor thou, nor God, nor man. The "I"
Has All become, the All is "I" and Bliss.
Know thou art That, sannyasin bold! Say,
"Om Tat Sat, Om!"

"Song of the Sannyasin" by Swami Vivekananda is quoted, with written permission, from Inspired Talks, My Master and Other Writings; copyright 1958 by Swami Nikhilananda, trustee of the estate of Swami Vivekananda; published by the Ramakrishna-Vivekananda Center of New York.

The Author: *Swami Vivekananda in his days as a wandering ascetic; the renovated cottage at Thousand Island Park, New York, where Swamiji composed the "Song of the Sannyasin"*

CHAPTER 12

Ten Questions
people ask
About Hinduism
...and ten terrific answers!

Humanity's most profound faith is now a global phenomenon. Students, teachers, neighbors and friends are full of questions. Misconceptions prevail. Here are ten thoughtful answers you can use to instill correct understanding and set the record straight.

HAVE YOU EVER BEEN PUT ON the spot with a provocative question about Hinduism, even one that really shouldn't be so hard to answer? If so, you are not alone. It takes some good preparation and a little attitude adjustment to confidently field queries on your faith—be they from friendly co-workers, students, passersby or especially from Christian evangelists. Back in the spring of 1990, a group of teens from the Hindu Temple of Greater Chicago, Lemont, sent a request to HINDUISM TODAY for "official answers" to nine questions they were commonly asked by their peers. These questions had perplexed the Hindu youth themselves; and their parents had no convincing answers. Satguru Sivaya Subramuniyaswami took up the challenge and provided the following answers to the nine questions. Perusing the list for this edition of the magazine, we thought it crucial to add a tenth dialog on caste, since that is the most relentless criticism Hinduism faces today.

Let's begin with advice on the attitudes to hold when responding. First, ask yourself, "Who is asking the question?" Millions of people are sincerely interested in Hinduism and the many Asian religions. So, when asked about Hinduism, don't be defensive, even if the questioner seems confrontational. Instead, assume that the person really wants to learn. Of course, some only want to harass, badger and turn you to their view. If you sense this is the case, feel free to smile and courteously dismiss yourself without any attempt to answer, lest you simply add fuel to his fires.

With all this in mind, it is still best never to answer a question

Above, a visitor to India questions an elder about temple ceremonies and customs. Right, Lord Vishnu stands with the vast ocean of truth behind Him. In the sky above, ten birds—symbolizing persistent misconceptions about Hinduism—take flight as we tackle ten common questions about our faith.

about religion too boldly or too immediately. That might lead to confrontation. Offer a prologue first, then come to the question, guiding the inquirer toward understanding. Your poise and deliberateness gives assurance that you know what you are talking about. It also gives you a moment to think and draw on your intuitive knowing. Before going deeply into an answer, always ask the questioner what his religion is. Knowing that, you can address his particular frame of mind and make your answer most relevant. Another key: have confidence in yourself and your ability to give a meaningful and polite response. Even to say "I am sorry. I still have much to learn about my religion and I don't yet know the answer to that" is a meaningful answer. Honesty is always appreciated. Never be afraid to admit what you don't know, for this lends credibility to what you do know.

Here are four prologues that can be used, according to the situation, before you begin to actually answer a question. 1) "I am really pleased that you are interested in my religion. You may not know that one out of every six people in the world is a Hindu." 2) "Many people have asked me about my tradition. I don't know everything, but I will try to answer your question." 3) "First, you should know that in Hinduism, it is not only belief and intellectual understanding that is important. Hindus place the greatest value on experiencing each of these truths personally." 4) The fourth type of prologue is to repeat the question to see if the person has actually stated what he wants to know. Repeat the question in your own words and ask if you have understood his query correctly.

If it's a complicated question, you might begin by saying, "Philosophers have spent lifetimes discussing and pondering questions such as this, but I will do my best to explain."

Have courage. Speak from your inner mind. Sanatana Dharma is an experiential path, not a dogma, so your experience in answering questions will help your own spiritual unfoldment. You will learn from your answers if you listen to your inner mind speak. This can actually be a lot of fun. The attentive teacher always learns more than the student.

After the prologue, address the question without hesitation. If the person is sincere, you can ask, "Do you have any other questions?" If he wants to know more, then elaborate as best you can. Use easy, everyday examples. Share what enlightened souls and scriptures of Hinduism have said on the subject. Remember, we must not assume that everyone who asks about Hinduism is insincere or is challenging our faith. Many are just being friendly or mak-

ing conversation to get to know you. So don't be on the defensive or take it all too seriously. Smile when you give your response. Be open. If the second or third question is on something you know nothing about, you can say, "I don't know. But if you are really interested, I will find out, mail you some literature or lend you one of my books." Smile and have confidence as you give these answers. Don't be shy. There is no question that can be put to you in your birth karmas that you cannot rise up to with a fine answer to fully satisfy the seeker. You may make lifelong friends in this way.

Each of the ten answers is organized with a short response that can be committed to memory, a longer answer, and a detailed explanation. Many questioners will be content with the short, simple answer, so start with that first. Use the explanation as background information for yourself, or as a contingency response in case you end up in a deeper philosophical discussion. Additional resources can be found at: www.himalayanacademy.com/basics/.

Why does Hinduism have so many Gods?

Hindus all believe in one Supreme God who created the universe. He is all-pervasive. He created many Gods, highly advanced spiritual beings, to be His helpers.

Contrary to prevailing misconceptions, Hindus all worship a one Supreme Being, though by different names. This is because the peoples of India with different languages and cultures have understood the one God in their own distinct way. Through history there arose four principal Hindu denominations—Saivism, Shaktism, Vaishnavism and Smartism. For Saivites, God is Siva. For Shaktas, Goddess Shakti is supreme. For Vaishnavites, Lord Vishnu is God. For Smartas—who see all Deities as reflections of the One God—the choice of Deity is left to the devotee. This liberal Smarta perspective is well known, but it is not the prevailing Hindu view. Due to this diversity, Hindus are profoundly tolerant of other religions, respecting the fact that each has its own pathway to the one God.

One of the unique understandings in Hinduism is that God is not far away, living in a remote heaven, but is inside each and every soul, in the heart and consciousness, waiting to be discovered. This knowing that God is always with us gives us hope and courage. Knowing the One Great God in this intimate and experiential way is the goal of Hindu spirituality.

Elaboration: Hinduism is both monotheistic and henotheistic. Hindus were never polytheistic, in the sense that there are many equal Gods. Henotheism (literally "one God") better defines the Hindu view. It means the worship of one God without denying the existence of other Gods. We Hindus believe in the one all-pervasive

Hindus all worship the One Supreme God, called by various names, depending on their denomination, and they revere a multitude of angelic beings, which they call Gods. Above, the central figure is Lord Siva, worshiped as the Supreme Being by Saivites and many other Hindus. Cradled in His hands are other great beings, known as Gods, including Lord Ganesha.

is the natural universe and nothing more. It is also different from strict theism which says God is only above the world, apart and transcendent. Panentheism is an all-encompassing concept. It says that God is both in the world and beyond it, both immanent and transcendent. That is the highest Hindu view.

Hindus also believe in many Gods who perform various functions, like executives in a large corporation. These should not be confused with the Supreme God. These Divinities are highly advanced beings who have specific duties and powers—not unlike the heavenly spirits, overlords or archangels revered in other faiths. Each denomination worships the Supreme God and its own pantheon of divine beings.

What is sometimes confusing to non-Hindus is that Hindus of various sects may call the one God by many different names, according to their denomination or regional tradition. Truth for the Hindu has many names, but that does not make for many truths. Hinduism gives us the freedom to approach God in our own way, encouraging a multiplicity of paths, not asking for conformity to just one.

There is much confusion about this subject, even among Hindus. Learn the right terms and the subtle differences in them, and you can explain the profound ways Hindus look at Divinity. Others will be delighted with the richness of the Indian concepts of God. You may wish to mention

God who energizes the entire universe. We can see Him in the life shining out of the eyes of humans and all creatures. This view of God as existing in and giving life to all things is called panentheism. It is different from pantheism, which is the belief that God that some Hindus believe only in the formless Absolute Reality as God; others believe in God as personal Lord and Creator. This freedom makes the understanding of God in Hinduism, the oldest living religion, the richest in all of Earth's existing faiths.

Do Hindus believe in reincarnation?

Yes, we believe the soul is immortal and takes birth time and time again. Through this process, we have experiences, learn lessons and evolve spiritually. Finally we graduate from physical birth.

*C*arnate means "of flesh," and *reincarnate* means to "reenter the flesh." Yes, Hindus believe in reincarnation. To us, it explains the natural way the soul evolves from immaturity to spiritual illumination. Life and death are realities for all of us. Hinduism believes that the soul is immortal, that it never dies, but inhabits one body after another on the Earth during its evolutionary journey. Like the caterpillar's transformation into a butterfly, physical death is a most natural transition for the soul, which survives and, guided by karma, continues its long pilgrimage until it is one with God.

I myself have had many lives before this one and expect to have more. Finally, when I have it all worked out and all the lessons have been learned, I will attain enlightenment and *moksha*, liberation. This means I will still exist, but will no longer be pulled back to be born in a physical body.

Even modern science is discovering reincarnation. There have been many cases of individuals' remembering their past lives. These have been researched by scientists, psychiatrists and parapsychologists during the past decades and documented in good books and videos. Young children speak of vivid past-life memories, which fade as they grow older, as the veils of individuality shroud the soul's intuitive understanding. Great mystics speak of their past lives as well. So do our ancient scriptures, the *Vedas*, reveal the reality of reincarnation.

Reincarnation is believed in by the Jains and the Sikhs, by the Indians of the Americas, and by the Buddhists, certain Jewish sects, the Pagans and the many indigenous faiths. Even Christianity originally taught reincarnation, but formally renounced it in the twelfth century. It is, in fact, one of the widest held articles of

Each soul evolves by experiencing many varied lives through reincarnation, called punarjanma *in Sanskrit, the process wherein the soul repeatedly takes on a physical body through being born on Earth. Here, a soul, represented by the ray of light, is shown in seven successive lives. Reincarnation is a purposeful maturing process governed by the law of karma.*

faith on planet Earth.

Elaboration: At death the soul leaves the physical body. But the soul does not die. It lives on in a subtle body called the astral body. The astral body exists in the nonphysical dimension called the astral plane, which is also the world we are in during our dreams at night when we sleep. Here we continue to have experiences until we are reborn again in another physical body as a baby. Each reincarnating soul chooses a home and a family which can best fulfill its next step of learning and maturation.

After many lifetimes of following dharma, the soul is fully matured in love, wisdom and knowledge of God. There is no longer a need for physical birth, for all lessons have been learned, all karmas fulfilled. That soul is then liberated, freed from the cycle of birth, death and rebirth. Evolution then continues in the more refined spiritual worlds. Similarly, after we graduate from elementary school we never have to go back to the fifth grade. We have gone beyond that level in understanding.

Thus, life's ultimate goal is not money, not clothes, not sex, not power, not food or any other of the instinctive needs. These are natural pursuits, but our real purpose on this Earth is to know, to love and to serve God and the Gods. That leads to the rare and priceless objects of life: enlightenment and liberation. This Hindu view of the soul's evolution answers many otherwise bewildering questions, removing the fear of death while giving assurance that each soul is evolving toward the same spiritual destiny, for the Hindu believes that karma and reincarnation are leading every single soul to God Realization.

What is karma?

Karma is the universal principle of cause and effect. Our actions, both good and bad, come back to us in the future, helping us to learn from life's lessons and become better people.

Karma is one of the natural laws of the mind, just as gravity is a law of matter. Just as God created gravity to bring order to the physical world, He created karma as a divine system of justice that is self-governing and infinitely fair. It automatically creates the appropriate future experience in response to the current action. *Karma* simply means "action" or "cause and effect." When something happens to us that is apparently unfortunate or unjust, it is not God punishing us. It is the result of our own past actions. The *Vedas,* Hinduism's revealed scripture, tell us if we sow goodness, we will reap goodness; if we sow evil, we will reap evil. Thus we create our own destiny through thought and action. And the divine law is: whatever karma we are experiencing in our life is just what we need at the moment, and nothing can happen but that we have the strength to meet it. Even harsh karma, when faced in wisdom, can be the greatest catalyst for spiritual growth. Understanding the way karma works, we seek to live a good and virtuous life through right thought, right speech and right action. This is called dharma.

Elaboration: Karma is basically energy. I throw energy out through thoughts, words and deeds, and it comes back to me, in time, through other people. Karma is our best teacher, for we must always face the consequences of our actions and thus improve and refine our behavior, or suffer if we do not. We Hindus look at time as a circle, as things cycle around again. Professor Einstein came to the same conclusion. He saw time as a curve, and space as well. This would eventually make a circle. Karma is a very just law which, like gravity, treats everyone the same. Because we Hindus understand karma, we do not hate or re-

One of the best examples of karma is that you can't give anything away but that generosity will return to you, with interest. In the upper scene, a lady gives clothing to a youth. Below, she receives an unexpected gift from a neighbor as the karma of her good deed brings its natural reward. By wisely heeding karma's ways, we tread the path of dharma.

sent people who do us harm. We understand they are giving back the effects of the causes we set in motion at an earlier time. The law of karma puts man at the center of responsibility for everything he does and everything that is done to him.

Karma is a word we hear quite often on television. "This is my karma," or "It must have been something I did in a past life to bring such good karma to me." We hear karma simply defined as "What goes around, comes around." In some schools of Hinduism, karma is looked upon as something bad—perhaps because we are most aware of this law when we are facing difficult karma, and not so aware of it when life is going smoothly. Even some Hindus equate karma with sin, and this is what evangelical Christians preach that it means. Many people believe that karma means "fate," a preordained destiny over which one has no control, which is also untrue.

The process of action and reaction on all levels—physical, mental and spiritual—is karma. Here is an example. I say kind words to you, and you feel peaceful and happy. I say harsh words to you, and you become ruffled and upset. The kindness and the harshness will return to me, through others, at a later time. This is karma. An architect thinks creative, productive thoughts while drawing plans for a new building. But were he to think destructive, unproductive thoughts, he would soon not be able to accomplish any kind of positive task even if he desired to do so. This is karma, a natural law of the mind. We must also be very careful about our thoughts because thought creates, and thoughts make karmas—good, bad and mixed.

Why do Hindus worship the cow?

Hindus don't worship cows. We respect, honor and adore the cow. By honoring this gentle animal, who gives more than she takes, we honor all creatures.

Hindus regard all living creatures as sacred—mammals, fishes, birds and more. We acknowledge this reverence for life in our special affection for the cow. At festivals we decorate and honor her, but we do not worship her in the sense that we worship the Deity.

To the Hindu, the cow symbolizes all other creatures. The cow is a symbol of the Earth, the nourisher, the ever-giving, undemanding provider. The cow represents life and the sustenance of life. The cow is so generous, taking nothing but water, grass and grain. It gives and gives and gives of its milk, as does the liberated soul give of his spiritual knowledge. The cow is so vital to life, the virtual sustainer of life, for many humans. The cow is a symbol of grace and abundance. Veneration of the cow instills in Hindus the virtues of gentleness, receptivity and connectedness with nature.

Elaboration: Who is the greatest giver on planet Earth today? Who do we see on every table in every country of the world—breakfast, lunch and dinner? It is the cow. McDonald's cow-vending golden arches and their rivals have made fortunes on the humble cow. The generous cow gives milk and cream, yogurt and cheese, butter and ice cream, ghee and buttermilk. It gives entirely of itself through sirloin, ribs, rump, porterhouse and beef stew. Its bones are the base for soup broths and glues. It gives the world leather belts, leather seats, leather coats and shoes, beef jerky, cowboy hats—you name it. The only cow-question for Hindus is, "Why don't more people respect and protect this remarkable creature?" Mahatma Gandhi once said, "One can measure the greatness of a nation and its moral progress by the way it treats its animals.

Hindus do not worship cows, but they do revere them as the perfect example of Divinity in all forms of life. Here a girl garlands a cow whose horns are painted and adorned with tassels and brass tips. Her sister offers fresh grass. In India, the cow is honored and protected as a symbol of wealth, strength, abundance, selfless giving and a full Earthly life.

Cow protection to me is not mere protection of the cow. It means protection of all that lives and is helpless and weak in the world. The cow means the entire subhuman world."

In the Hindu tradition, the cow is honored, garlanded and given special feedings at festivals all over India, most importantly the annual Gopashtama festival. Demonstrating how dearly Hindus love their cows, colorful cow jewelry and clothing is sold at fairs all over the Indian countryside. From a young age, Hindu children are taught to decorate the cow with garlands, paint and ornaments. Her nature is epitomized in Kamadhenu, the divine, wish-fulfilling cow. The cow and her sacred gifts—milk and ghee in particular—are essential elements in Hindu worship, penance and rites of passage. In India, more than 3,000 institutions called Gaushalas, maintained by charitable trusts, care for old and infirm cows. And while many Hindus are not vegetarians, most respect the still widely held code of abstaining from eating beef.

By her docile, tolerant nature, the cow exemplifies the cardinal virtue of Hinduism, noninjury, known as ahimsa. The cow also symbolizes dignity, strength, endurance, maternity and selfless service.

In the *Vedas*, cows represent wealth and joyous Earthly life. From the *Rig Veda* (4.28.1;6) we read. "The cows have come and have brought us good fortune. In our stalls, contented, may they stay! May they bring forth calves for us, many-colored, giving milk for Indra each day. You make, O cows, the thin man sleek; to the unlovely you bring beauty. Rejoice our homestead with pleasant lowing. In our assemblies we laud your vigor."

Are Hindus idol worshipers?

Hindus do not worship a stone or metal "idol" as God. We worship God through the image. We invoke the presence of God from the higher, unseen worlds, into the image so that we can commune with Him and receive His blessings.

The stone or metal Deity images in Hindu temples and shrines are not mere symbols of the Gods. They are the form through which their love, power and blessings flood forth into this world. We may liken this mystery to our ability to communicate with others through the telephone. We do not talk to the telephone; rather we use it as a means of communication with another person. Without the telephone, we could not converse across long distances; and without the sanctified icon in the temple, we cannot easily commune with the Deity. Divinity can also be invoked and felt in a sacred fire, or in a tree, or in the enlightened person of a *satguru*. In our temples, God is invoked in the sanctum by highly trained priests. Through the practice of yoga, or meditation, we invoke God inside ourself. *Yoga* means to yoke oneself to God within. The image or icon of worship is a focus for our prayers and devotions.

Another way to explain icon worship is to acknowledge that Hindus believe God is everywhere, in all things, whether stone, wood, creatures or people. So, it is not surprising that they feel comfortable worshiping the Divine in His material manifestation. The Hindu can see God in stone and water, fire, air and ether, and inside his own soul. Indeed, there are Hindu temples which have in the sanctum sanctorum no image at all but a *yantra*, a symbolic or mystic diagram. However, the sight of the image enhances the devotee's worship.

Elaboration: In Hinduism one of the ultimate attainments is when the seeker transcends the need of all form and symbol. This is the yogi's goal. In this way Hinduism is the least idol-oriented of all the religions of the world. There is no religion that is more aware of the transcendent, timeless, formless,

A devotee looks within and beyond the bronze dancing Siva to behold God in His spiritual body of light. Dressed in traditional Hindu garb, the man is performing his daily puja *in his home shrine—chanting Sanskrit mantras, offering fruit, water, flowers, incense and light—worshiping devoutly, beseeching God to send blessings through the enshrined image.*

causeless Truth. Nor is there any religion which uses more symbols to represent Truth in preparation for that realization.

Humorously speaking, Hindus are not idle worshipers. I have never seen a Hindu worship in a lazy or idle way. They worship with great vigor and devotion, with unstinting regularity and constancy. There's nothing idle about our ways of worship! (A little humor never hurts.)

But, of course, the question is about "graven images." All religions have their symbols of holiness through which the sacred flows into the mundane. To name a few: the Christian cross, or statues of Mother Mary and Saint Theresa, the holy Kaaba in Mecca, the Sikh *Adi Granth* enshrined in the Golden Temple in Amritsar, the Arc and Torah of the Jews, the image of a meditating Buddha, the totems of indigenous and Pagan faiths, and the artifacts of the holy men and women of all religions. Such icons, or graven images, are held in awe by the followers of the respective faiths. The question is, does this make all such religionists idol worshipers? The answer is, yes and no. From our perspective, idol worship is an intelligent, mystical practice shared by all of the world's great faiths.

The human mind releases itself from suffering through the use of forms and symbols that awaken reverence, evoke sanctity and spiritual wisdom. Even a fundamentalist Christian who rejects all forms of idol worship, including those of the Catholic and Episcopal churches, would resent someone who showed disrespect for his Bible. This is because he considers it sacred. His book and the Hindu's icon are much alike in this way.

Are Hindus forbidden to eat meat?

Hindus teach vegetarianism as a way to live with a minimum of hurt to other beings. But in today's world not all Hindus are vegetarians.

ur religion does not lay down rigid "do's and don'ts." There are no commandments. Hinduism gives us the wisdom to make up our own mind on what we put in our body, for it is the only one we have—in this life, at least. Vegetarians are more numerous in the South of India than in the North. This is because of the North's cooler climactic conditions and past Islamic influence.

Priests and religious leaders are definitely vegetarian, so as to maintain a high level of purity and spiritual consciousness to fulfill their responsibilities, and to awaken the refined areas of their nature. Soldiers and law-enforcement officers are generally not vegetarians, because they have to keep alive their aggressive forces in order to perform their work. To practice yoga and be successful in meditation, it is mandatory to be vegetarian. It is a matter of wisdom—the application of knowledge at any given moment. Today, about twenty percent of all Hindus are vegetarians.

Elaboration: This can be a touchy subject. There are several ways to respond, depending on who is asking and the background in which he was raised. But the overlying principle that defines the Hindu answer to this query is *ahimsa*—refraining from injuring, physically, mentally or emotionally, anyone or any living creature. The Hindu who wishes to strictly follow the path of noninjury naturally adopts a vegetarian diet. It's a matter of conscience more than anything else.

Vendors at a market are selling fruits, vegetables, grains, spices and sweets—a potpourri of foods that great cooks creatively combine in one of the world's most sumptuous cuisines. Hindus understand the sound reasons against eating meat, and many abstain entirely. With such a savory and healthy diet, there is no need to consume flesh.

like. Many Hindu swamis advise followers to be well-established vegetarians prior to initiation into mantra, and to remain vegetarian thereafter. But most do not insist upon vegetarianism for those not seeking initiation. Swamis have learned that families who are vegetarian have fewer problems than those who are not.

Poignant scriptural citations counsel against eating meat. The *Yajur Veda* (36.18) calls for kindliness toward all creatures living on the Earth, in the air and in the water. The *Tirukural*, a 2,200-year-old masterpiece of ethics, states, "When a man realizes that meat is the butchered flesh of another creature, he will abstain from eating it" (257). The *Manu Dharma Shastras* state, "Having well considered the origin of flesh and the cruelty of fettering and slaying corporeal beings, let one entirely abstain from eating flesh," and "When the diet is pure, the mind and heart are pure."

For guidance in this and all matters, Hindus also rely on their own guru, community elders, their own conscience and their knowledge of the benefits of abstaining from meat and enjoying a wholesome vegetarian diet. Of course, there are good Hindus who eat meat, and there are not-so-good Hindus who are vegetarians.

Today in America and Europe millions of people are vegetarians because they want to live a long time and be healthy. Many feel a moral obligation to shun the mentality of violence to which meat-eating gives rise. There are good

When we eat meat, fish, fowl and eggs, we absorb the vibration of the instinctive creatures into our nerve system. This chemically alters our consciousness and amplifies our lower nature, which is prone to fear, anger, jealousy, confusion, resentment and the

books on vegetarianism, such as *Diet for a New America*, by John Robbins. There is also a fine magazine called *Vegetarian Times*. Mr. Robbins' insightful "How to Win an Argument with a Meat-Eater" is included in chapter 43 of this book

Do Hindus have a Bible?

Our "Bible" is called the *Veda*. The *Veda*, which means "wisdom," is comprised of four ancient and holy scriptures which all Hindus revere as the revealed word of God.

ike the taoist *Tao te Ching*, the Buddhist *Dhammapada*, the Sikh *Adi Granth*, the Jewish *Torah*, the Christian *Bible* and the Muslim *Koran*—the *Veda* is the Hindu holy book. The four books of the *Vedas*—*Rig*, *Yajur*, *Sama* and *Atharva*—include over 100,000 verses. The knowledge imparted by the *Vedas* ranges from earthy devotion to high philosophy. Their words and wisdom permeate Hindu thought, ritual and meditation. The *Vedas* are the ultimate scriptural authority for Hindus. Their oldest portions are said by some to date back as far as 6,000 BCE, orally transmitted for most of history and written down in Sanskrit in the last few millennia, making them the world's longest and most ancient scripture. The *Vedas* open a rare window into ancient Indian society, proclaiming life's sacredness and the way to oneness with God.

Elaboration: For untold centuries unto today, the *Vedas* have remained the sustaining force and authoritative doctrine, guiding followers in ways of worship, duty and enlightenment. The *Vedas* are the meditative and philosophical focus for millions of monks and a billion seekers. Their stanzas are chanted from memory by priests and laymen daily as liturgy in temple worship and domestic ritual. All Hindus wholeheartedly accept the *Vedas*, yet each draws selectively, interprets freely and amplifies abundantly. Over time, this tolerant allegiance has woven the varied tapestry of Indian Hindu Dharma.

Each of the four *Vedas* has four sections: *Samhitas* (hymn collections), *Brahmanas* (priestly manuals), *Aranyakas* (forest treatises) and *Upanishads* (enlightened discourses). The *Samhitas* and *Brahmanas* affirm that God is immanent and transcendent and pre-

The Vedas are revealed scripture, meaning they were issued forth by God through enlightened sages, or rishis. This divine transmission is depicted here as Lord Siva bestows the four books of the Veda to four rishis. The sacred knowledge, passed orally for most of history, was finally scribed in Sanskrit on palm leaves to share and preserve it.

A. MANIVEL

scribe ritual worship, mantra and devotional hymns to establish communication with the spiritual worlds. The hymns are invocations to the One Divine and to the Divinities of nature, such as the Sun, the Rain, the Wind, the Fire and the Dawn—as well as prayers for matrimony, progeny, prosperity, concord, protection, domestic rites and more.

The *Aranyakas* and *Upanishads* outline the soul's evolutionary journey, provide yogic philosophical training and propound realization of man's oneness with God as the destiny of all souls. Today, the *Vedas* are published in Sanskrit, English, French, German and other languages. But it is the popular, metaphysical *Upanishads* that have been most amply and ably translated.

The *Vedas* advise: "Let there be no neglect of Truth. Let there be no neglect of dharma. Let there be no neglect of welfare. Let there be no neglect of prosperity. Let there be no neglect of study and teaching. Let there be no neglect of the duties to the Gods and the ancestors" (*Taittiriya Upanishad* 1.11.1). "United your resolve, united your hearts, may your spirits be one, that you may long together dwell in unity and concord!" (*Rig Veda* 10.191.4). "There, where there is no darkness, nor night, nor day, nor being, nor nonbeing, there is the Auspicious One, alone, absolute and eternal. There is the glorious splendor of that Light from whom in the beginning sprang ancient wisdom" (*Shvetashvatara Upanishad* 4.18).

"Taking as a bow the great weapon of the *Upanishad*, one should put upon it an arrow sharpened by meditation. Stretching it with a thought directed to the essence of That, penetrate that Imperishable as the mark, my friend" (*Mundaka Upanishad* 2.2.3).

Why do many Hindus wear a dot near the middle of their forehead?

The dot worn on the forehead is a religious symbol. It represents divine sight and shows that one is a Hindu. For women, it is also a beauty mark.

The dot worn between the eyes or in the middle of the forehead is a sign that one is a Hindu. It is called the *bindi* in the Hindi language, *bindu* in Sanskrit and *pottu* in Tamil. In olden days, all Hindu men and women wore these marks, and they both also wore earrings. Today it is the women who are most faithful in wearing the *bindi*.

The dot has a mystical meaning. It represents the third eye of spiritual sight, which sees things the physical eyes cannot see. Hindus seek to awaken their inner sight through yoga. The forehead dot is a reminder to use and cultivate this spiritual vision to perceive and better understand life's inner workings—to see things not just physically, but with the "mind's eye" as well. The *bindi* is made of red powder called *sindur*, traditionally made from powdered turmeric and fresh lime juice, or from sandalpaste or cosmetics.

In addition to the simple dot, there are many types of forehead marks, known as *tilaka* in Sanskrit. Each mark represents a particular sect or denomination of our vast religion. We have four major sects: Saivism, Vaishnavism, Shaktism and Smartism. Vaishnava Hindus, for example, wear a v-shaped *tilaka* made of white clay. Elaborate *tilakas* are worn by Hindus mainly at religious events, though many wear the simple *bindi*, indicating they are Hindu, even in the general public. By these marks we know what a person believes, and therefore know how to begin conversations.

For Hindu women, the forehead dot is also a beauty mark, not unlike the black mark European and American women once wore on the cheek. The red *bindi* is generally a sign of marriage. A black *bindi* is often worn before marriage to ward off the evil eye.

Decorating the face and body with colorful paints is a universal human practice, often a cultural rite expressing one's tribe, beliefs and identity. The forehead dot shows that one is proud to be a Hindu and bespeaks mystical seeing beyond the five senses. Here, in a simple, daily act, a woman obligingly applies a red bindi *to her sister's forehead.*

A. MANIVEL

As an exotic fashion statement, the dot's color complements the color of a lady's sari. Ornate *bindis* are even worn by actresses in popular American TV shows.

Elaboration: Men and women of a particular religion wishing to identify themselves to one another often do so by wearing distinctive religious symbols. Often these are blessed in their temples, churches or synagogues. Christians wear a cross on a necklace. Jewish boys wear small leather cases that hold scriptural passages, and the round cap called *yarmulka*. Sikh men wear their hair in a turban. In many countries, Muslim women cover their head with a scarf, called *hajib*.

Do not be ashamed to wear the *bindi* on your forehead in the United States, Canada, Europe or any country of the world. Wear it proudly. The forehead dot will distinguish you from all other people as a very special person, a Hindu, a knower of eternal truths. You will never be mistaken as belonging to another nationality or religion. The sacred forehead dot is an easy way of distinguishing Hindus from Muslims. And don't be intimidated when people ask you what the dot means. Now you have lots of information to give a good answer, which will probably lead to more questions about your venerable religion.

For both boys and girls, men and women, the dot can be small or large depending on the circumstance, but should always be there when appropriate. Naturally, we don't want to flaunt our religion in the face of others. We observe that many Christian men and women take off or conceal their crosses in the corporate business world. Some communities and institutions disallow wearing religious symbols entirely.

Are the Gods of Hinduism really married?

It is true that God is often depicted with a spouse in our traditional stories. However, on a deeper, philosophical level, the Supreme Being and the Gods are neither male nor female and are therefore not married.

In popular, village Hinduism God is represented as male, and God's energy, or Shakti, is personified as His spouse—for example, Vishnu and Lakshmi. In Hindu temples, art and mythology, God is everywhere seen as the beloved, divine couple. Philosophically, however, the caution is always made that God and God's energy are One, and the metaphor of the inseparable divine couple serves only to illustrate this Oneness.

Hinduism is taught on many levels to many different people, and to uneducated people who are not able to understand high philosophy, Hinduism is taught in story form. Because the temple is the center of every Hindu community, and everyone is focused on the temple and the Gods within it, the Gods are the major players in these stories. Hindus who understand the higher philosophy seek to find God on the inside while also worshiping God in the temples. Simple folk strive to be like a God, or like a Goddess. These tales, called *Puranas*, have long been the basis of dance, plays and storytelling around the fire in the homes to children as they are growing up. The stories illustrate how a family should live, how they should raise their children, and much more. Before the printing press, there were few books, and Hinduism was conveyed orally through stories and parables. While these often violent children's tales should not be perpetuated, there remains much of value in the extensive writings of the *Puranas*.

Through history Hindus have depicted God as Ardhanarishvara, which literally means "half-female Lord"—Siva as male on the right and female on the left. This vision of the Divine as our Mother-Father God supersedes the popular, mythological notion of marriage of a God and Goddess, declaring that God and His energy are one.

currents, *ida* and *pingala*, into the spiritual current, *sushumna,* in the center of the spine within each individual.

Hindus know that the Gods do not marry, that they are complete within themselves. This unity is depicted in the traditional icon of Ardhanarishvara, Siva as half man and half woman, and in the teaching that Siva and Shakti are one, that Shakti is Siva's energy. Siva is dearly loved as our Father-Mother God. Yet, sexual gender and matrimonial relations are of the physical and emotional realms, whereas the Gods exist in a stratum that far supersedes these levels of life. For that matter, the soul itself is neither male nor female.

Some modern swamis now urge devotees not to pay any attention to Puranic stories about the Gods, saying that they have no relationship with the world today—that they are misleading and confusing and should no longer be taught to the children. Instead, they encourage followers to deepen themselves with the higher philosophies of the Vedic *Upanishads* and the realizations of Hindu seers.

Other faiths sometimes criticize the Hindu religion as a sort of comic-book religion, and we should not be part of perpetuating that image by passing on such misconceptions as the marriage of the Gods. Other religions move and adjust with the times. Hinduism must also do so. It must offer answers to the questions about God, soul and world—answers that are

Elaboration: Those who learn the higher Hindu philosophies know that Gods are neither male nor female. In fact, attaining to that Godly level of being is one of the mystical goals of yoga. This is accomplished by blending the feminine and masculine reasonable, that can be understood and accepted even by a child, that are coherent, sensible and strictly in accord with scripture and tradition. This is necessary in the technological age, necessary in order that Hinduism will be a religion of the future, not of the past.

What about caste and untouchability?

Caste is the hereditary division of Indian society based on occupation. The lowest class, deemed untouchables, suffer from discrimination and mistreatment. It is illegal in India to discriminate against, abuse or insult anyone on the basis of caste.

Caste, from the Portuguese *casta*, meaning "clan" or "lineage," refers to two systems within Hindu society. The first is *varna*, the division of society into four groups: workers, business people, lawmakers/law enforcers and priests. The second is *jati*, the thousands of occupational guilds whose members follow a single profession. *Jati* members usually marry within their own *jati* and follow traditions associated with their *jati*. In urban areas they often enter other occupations, but still usually arrange marriages within the *jati*.

Wealth, especially in urban areas, often trumps caste. Industrialization and education have greatly altered India's *jati* system by eliminating or changing the professions upon which it was originally based, and opening new employment options. The *jatis* are evolving to function today less like guilds and more like large clans of related families. At the bottom are the so-called untouchables, who perform the dirtiest jobs and have suffered much like the black people of America, who were freed from slavery just 138 years ago. Strong laws have been passed in India to end caste-based discrimination. Modern Hindus rightly deplore caste abuse and are working to set matters right. Just as in the US, it is a difficult task that will take decades, especially in the villages.

Elaboration: Caste is, no doubt, the biggest stick that Hindus get beaten with. It is taught as the defining attribute, or fatal flaw, of Hinduism in Western schools. Untouchability as a formal system shocks Westerners. One response we can make is to separate social stratification from the issue of racial/class discrimination.

First issue: social stratification. India is one of the world's oldest

Representatives of the four castes, or varnas, are shown here surrounding Lord Ganesha. They are: worker, businessman, general and priest. These are natural divisions which appear in all nations and societies as shown by the universal existence, in some form, of labor unions, businessmen's associations, armies and police forces, and religious ministers.

A. MANIVEL

societies. It has sustained a continuity of culture and religion for thousands of years. Europe, on the other hand, has seen millenniums of upheaval. Still, one only has to go back to before the 17th-century industrial revolution to find a social system that is similar to caste. European society then comprised the landed elite (including royalty, a hereditary caste maintained to this day), merchants, artisans and peasants. The artisans formed guilds, occupation-based organizations that served both as closed unions and marketing monopolies. The guild legacy remains in Western surnames such as Smith, a metal worker. There was no public education system, and each generation learned at home the family occupation. There was little technological change, so jobs were static. Industrialization and public education altered (but did not destroy) this class system in the West, just as they are changing caste and *jati* in India today.

Second issue: racial/class discrimination. Most Indians are unfamiliar with the extent of discrimination in the West today. In America, for example, hundreds of thousands live destitute and homeless on city streets, as true "untouchables." US cities are more racially segregated than before the 1950s Civil Rights Movement because of "white flight" to the suburbs. Black Americans receive harsher sentences than white Americans for the same crime. Many Native American Indians live at the bottom of society, destitute and alcoholic, on barren Indian reservations. This kind of response—we can call it the "You're one, too" defense—doesn't mean Hindus should not work much harder to end caste discrimination. But it reminds others that no country in the world is yet free from racial discrimination.

CHAPTER 13

How to Become a

The remarkable personal stories of men and women who entered the Hindu religion, shrugging off the myth that "You must be born a Hindu to be a Hindu"

ONVERSION REMAINS A VITAL ISSUE AND A POTENT TOPIC in the press today. On one hand, Hindus continue to lament the impact of Christian missionaries in India. On the other hand, Hindus are criticizing Hindus about the lack of rights given to tribals who are converted back to Hinduism. But, as an undercurrent during the last two decades, a little-known trend has been gaining momentum. People are becoming staunch, proud Hindus, not by birth, not by coercion, but through a careful process of ethical conversion.

Here are true histories of individuals and families who formally entered Hinduism over the years. These inspiring real-life stories have been excerpted from *How to Become a Hindu: Stories of Ethical Self-Conversion,* by Satguru Sivaya Subramuniyaswami. Their tales illustrate the six steps of ethical conversion as detailed in the book. They are: 1) joining a Hindu community; 2) creating a point-counterpoint of the beliefs of Hinduism and one's previous religion; 3) severing from former mentors; 4) legally adopting a Hindu name; 5) having a *namakarana* samskara, the traditional Hindu name-giving ceremony and 6) publicly announcing the severance and name change. Each story is written from a delightfully different angle and describes one or more of the six steps. The second testimony tells the tale of how a born Hindu strayed from, then rediscovered his religion. In addition, the book was sent to 86 Hindu religious leaders and scholars around the world. The book inspired spontaneous commentaries revealing their views about conversion to Hinduism. Their messages are included at the end.

I'm So Proud to Be a Hindu

Asha Alahan, 50, lives in the East San Francisco Bay Area, California. She formally entered Saivism in 1985 at Kauai Hindu Temple. Asha, whose husband and children are also Hindus, is a wife, mother and housewife and a home-school teacher to all her children.

My mother was a devout Catholic, and my father had converted to Catholicism right before they were married. I was a happy child, believing in God, loving God and doing as I was told. But when I reached my teens, I started to question the beliefs and became disillusioned with the Church. So I left and became nothing!

At eighteen I moved away from my parents' home to live with my older sister in Santa Barbara, California. I loved God and knew that something was really missing, but did not quite know where to begin searching. My subconscious was so programmed that it was the Catholic Church or nothing. As children we were not even allowed to enter other places of worship; it was

considered a sin. So I just did nothing! It wasn't until I was twenty-one that I knew my life was on a down-hill spiral and I had to do something. I returned to my parents' home and tried going to the local Catholic Church again. But I still felt that their religion did not hold the answers for me.

It was not long after that I was married to my wonderful husband, and he introduced me to Hindu teachings. It was all so new and exciting. The words were so true. It was a whole new way of perceiving the world and beyond—almost a little scary, as my subconscious mind kept trying to remind me of all the previous programming from early childhood and the Catholic school I had attended.

We continued our studies and proceeded to follow the steps towards severance. I had been confirmed in the Catholic Church so I

Hindu

Embraced: *A modern, newly converted Hindu family is honored and warmly welcomed into the traditional Hindu community*

• •

needed to go back to the original parish where this had taken place and talk to the priest, have him understand my position and ask if he would please write a letter of severance for me. By the time I had finished speaking with him, he was unsure of what to say to me. He denied me the letter and suggested that I speak with the Archbishop of that diocese. I felt since I was going to a higher authority than the local priest that this should be easier. I was wrong. The Archbishop was not at all happy (even on the verge of anger) and totally refused to let me explain myself. So I left, wondering where I might go next.

In the area where we lived there were some old California mis-

sions that were still functional (as places of worship) so I decided to speak with a priest at the nearby mission. I knew the moment I walked into this priest's office that I had been guided by divine beings—he was the one to speak with. He had symbols of the major world religions hanging on his walls. We spoke for a while, and then he wrote me a letter stating that he understood that I wished to sever all previous ties with the Catholic Church and would soon be entering the Hindu religion and then wished me well.

I came to Kauai's Kadavul Hindu Temple to have my *namakarana* samskara. It was magical. At the time I don't think I realized the deep profoundness of that experience, finally finding the place where my soul knew it belonged. I am so proud to be a Hindu. Jai!

How I Became a Hindu
Sita Ram Goel, of Delhi, was a well-known renaissance writer on Hindu issues. He was associated with the Voice of India, a publishing house which guides understanding through enlightening tracts, books and articles. His testimony below was excerpted from his book, How I Became a Hindu. *His friend, Ram Swarup (1920-1998) was a distinguished social observer, author and spokesman of renascent Hinduism which, he believed, can also help other nations in rediscovering their spiritual roots.* The Word as Revelation, Names of God *is Swarup's best-known book.*

I was born a Hindu. But I had ceased to be one by the time I came out of college at the age of twenty-two. I had become a Marxist and a militant atheist. I had come to believe that Hindu scriptures should be burnt in a bonfire if India was to be saved. It was fifteen years later that I could see this culmination as the explosion of an inflated ego. During those years of self-poisoning, I was sincerely convinced that I was engaged in a philosophical exploration of cosmic proportions. How my ego got inflated to a point where I could see nothing beyond my own morbid mental constructions is no exceptional story. It happens to many of us mortals. What is relevant in my story is the seeking and the suffering and the struggle to break out of that spider's web of my own weaving.

In my family, our women did keep some fasts, performed some rituals and visited the temple and the Sivalinga, but the menfolk were mostly convinced about the futility of image worship and did not normally participate in any rituals. The brahmin priest was not seen in our homes, except on occasions like marriage and death. I remember vividly how lofty a view I took of my own *nirguna* doctrines and how I looked down upon my classmates from Sanatanist families whose ways I thought effeminate. I particularly disliked their going to the annual *mela* (festival) of a Devi in a neighboring town. God for me was a male person. Devi worship was a defilement of the true faith.

But as my moral and intellectual life was preparing to settle down in a universe of firm faith provided by Mahatma Gandhi, my emotional life was heading towards an upheaval. I started doubting if there was a moral order in the universe at large and in the human society in which I lived. The sages, saints and thinkers whom I had honored so far were sure that the world was made and governed by a God who was Satyam (Truth), Sivam (Good), Sundaram (Beauty). But all around me I saw much that was untrue, unwholesome and ugly. God and His creation could not be reconciled.

This problem of evil arose and gripped my mind, partly because of my personal situation in life. In spite of my pose of humility, learned from Mahatma Gandhi, I was harboring a sense of great self-esteem. I was a good student who had won distinctions and scholarships at every stage. I had read a lot of books, which made me feel learned and wise. I was trying to lead a life of moral endeavor, which I thought made me better than most of my fellow men. Standing at the confluence of these several streams of self-esteem, I came to believe that I was somebody in particular and that the society in which I lived owed me some special and privileged treatment.

Now I was in a desperate hurry to get a good knowledge of the doctrine of socialism. A desire to read Karl Marx now became irresistible. First, I read the *Communist Manifesto*. It was simply breathtaking in the breadth and depth of its sweep over vast vistas of human history. It was also a great call to action, to change the world and end exploitation and social injustice for all time to come.

At the same time I concluded that God as a creator of this world could be conceived only in three ways—either as a rogue who sanctioned and shared in the roguery prevalent in his world, or as an imbecile who could no more control what he had created, or as a sannyasin, who no more cared for what was happening to his creatures. If God was a rogue, we had to rise in revolt against his rule. If he was an imbecile, we could forget him and take charge of the world ourselves. And if he was a sannyasin, he could mind his business while we minded our own. The scriptures, however, held out a different version of God and his role, one that was supported neither by experience nor by logic. The scriptures should, therefore, be burned in a bonfire, preferably during winter when they could provide some warmth.

Four years after leaving college, I was ready to join the Communist Party of India. I conveyed my decision to my friend Ram Swarup, whom I had met after leaving college and who was to exercise a decisive influence on my intellectual evolution. He wrote back immediately: "You are too intelligent not to become a communist. But you are also too intelligent to remain one for long."

This was a prophecy which came true. It was only a year and a few months later that I renounced Marxism as an inadequate philosophy, realized that the Communist Party of India was a fifth column for the advancement of Russian Imperialism in India, and denounced the Soviet Union under Stalin as a vast slave empire.

The promise made by Sri Aurobindo, on the other hand, regarding the ultimate destiny of the human race was far more stupendous than that held out by Marx. Howsoever vague and inchoate my vision might have been at that time, I did feel that Sri Aurobindo was talking about fundamentally different dimensions of the universe and human life. The gulf between my mundane interests and the grand aspirations dictated by Sri Aurobindo's vision was very wide, and I could hardly muster the care or the courage to cross over. But in the inner recesses of my mind, I did become curious about the nature of the universe, man's place in it and a meaningful goal of human life.

I was present in the Second Party Conference of the Communist Party of India which was held in the Maidan at Calcutta in February, 1948. My friend Ram Swarup suddenly appeared on the scene and expressed his intention to stay with me for quite some time. I was very happy because he was my nearest and dearest in the whole world. I did not know that he had by now come to regard communism as a great evil threatening to engulf the future of mankind. After I failed to put my three best communist friends against Ram Swarup, I had to face him myself and all alone. The discussions spread over several months. Most of the time I repeated party slogans, sometimes very vehemently. Ram Swarup dismissed them with a smile.

Finally, I was back to square one. My faith in Gandhism had lost the battle to Marxism. Now I was no longer a Marxist. I asked myself again and again: Where do I go from here?

It was at this time that I fell seriously ill and lost a lot of weight. A Catholic missionary whom I had known earlier came to visit me. He was a good and kindly man and had a strong character. The Father, as I called him, found me in a difficult condition, physically as well as financially. He felt sure that it was in such times that Jesus Christ came to people. He asked me if I was prepared to receive Jesus. I did not understand immediately that he was inviting me to get converted to Catholicism. My impression was that he wanted to help me with some spiritual exercises prescribed by Christianity. Moreover, I had always admired Jesus. I had, therefore, no objection to receiving him. Only I was doubtful if someone was really in a position to arrange my meeting with Jesus. I became aware of the Father's true intentions as I traveled with him to a distant monastery.

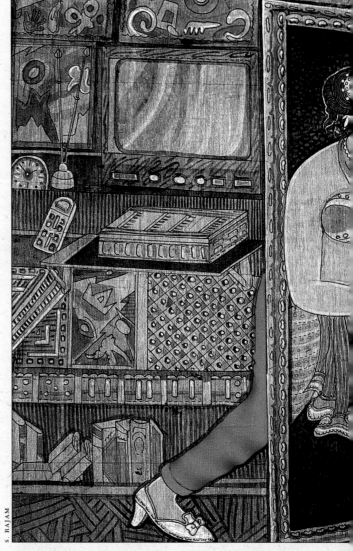

S. RAJAM

He asked every other missionary he met on the way to pray for his success.

At this monastery, which was a vast place with very picturesque surroundings, I was advised by the Father to go into a retreat. It meant my solitary confinement to a room. I was not supposed to look at or talk to anyone on my way to the bathrooms or while taking my morning and evening strolls on the extensive lawns outside. And I was to meditate on themes which the Father prescribed for me in the course of four or five lectures he delivered to me during the course of the day, starting at about 6:30 in those winter mornings. I was not used to this way of life. I had never lived in such solitude by my own choice. My only solace was that I was allowed to smoke and provided with plenty of books on the Christian creed and theology.

I tried to read some of the books, but I failed to finish any one of them. They were full of Biblical themes and theological terminology with which I was not familiar. Most of the time they made me recall Ram Swarup's observation about mere cerebration. Or they were simplistic harangues to love Christ and join the Catholic Church. They had a close similarity to communist pamphlets which I had read in plenty. The Father had asked me again and again to invoke Christ and meditate upon him. But he had not told me how to do it. I had no previous practice in meditation. I did not know how to invoke Christ, or any other godhead for that matter.

During a lecture about creation, the Father said that God in His wisdom and kindness had made all fishes and animals and birds

• •

is baptized in the Church of Christ. He is the only savior. No one outside His fold can claim salvation. The only thing the heathens can look forward to is eternal hell-fire."

My new job in Delhi gave me a lot of leisure. But what mattered most was that I could now spend all my evenings with Ram Swarup. He was now spending long hours sitting in meditation. His talks now centered round the *Vedas*, the *Upanishads*, the *Gita*, the *Mahabharata* and the Buddha. In the long evenings I spent with Ram Swarup I compared with him my notes on the *Mahabharata*. But Ram Swarup's way of looking at the *Mahabharata* was quite different. He related it directly to the *Vedas*. He expounded how the mighty characters of this great epic embodied and made living the spiritual vision of the Vedic seers. What fascinated me still more was Ram Swarup's exposition of dharma as enunciated in the *Mahabharata*. To me, dharma had always been a matter of normative morals, external rules and regulations, do's and dont's, enforced on life by an act of will. Now I was made to see dharma as a multidimensional movement of man's inner law of being, his psychic evolution, his spiritual growth and his spontaneous building of an outer life for himself and the community in which he lived.

The next thing I did was to read and reread the major works of Aurobindo and discuss his message with Ram Swarup day after day. Aurobindo would have remained an abstract philosopher for me had not Ram Swarup explained to me how this seer was the greatest exponent of the Vedic vision in our times. Aurobindo's message, he told me, was in essence the same old Vedic message, namely, that we are Gods in our innermost being and should live the life of Gods on this Earth. He made me see what Aurobindo meant by the physical, the vital, the mental and the psychic. He related these terms to the theory of the five *kosas* in the *Upanishads*.

I now requested Ram Swarup to initiate me into meditation. He told me that I could sit and meditate with him whenever I liked, wait and watch, go within myself as far as I could manage, at any time, dwell on whatever good thoughts got revealed in the process, and the rest would follow. I acted upon his simple instructions with some measure of skepticism in my mind. But in the next few days I could see some results, which encouraged me.

One day I meditated on ahimsa, which had remained an abstract concept for me so far. After a while I found myself begging forgiveness from all those whom I had hurt by word or deed, or towards whom I had harbored any ill will. It was not an exercise in generalities. Person after person rose into my memory, going back into the distant past and I bowed in repentance before each one of them. Finally I begged forgiveness from Stalin, against whom I had written so much and upon whom I had hurled so many brickbats. The bitterness which had poisoned my life over the long years was swept off my mind in a sudden relaxation of nerves. I felt as if a thousand thorns which had tormented my flesh had been taken out by a master physician without causing the slightest pain. I was in need of no greater assurance that this was the way on which I should walk.

One day I told Ram Swarup how I had never been able to accept the Devi, either as Sarasvati or as Lakshmi or as Durga or as Kali. He smiled and asked me to meditate on the Devi that day. I tried my best in my own way. Nothing happened for some time. Nothing came my way. My mind was a big blank. But in the next moment the void was filled with a sense of some great presence. I did not see any concrete image. No words were whispered in my ears. Yet the rigidity of a lifetime broke down and disappeared. The Great Mother was beckoning her lost child to go and sit in her lap and feel safe from all fears. We had a record of Dr. Govind Gopal Mukhopadhyaya's sonorous *stuti* to the Devi. As I played it, I prayed to Her.

My progress was not fast; nor did I go far. But I now felt sure that

for man's consumption. I immediately rose in revolt. I told him very emphatically that I was a Vaishnava and a vegetarian and that I had absolutely no use for a God that bestowed upon man the right to kill and eat His other creatures simply because man happened to be stronger and more skilled. I added that in my opinion it was the duty of the strong and the more skilled to protect the weak and the less wily.

The Father also suddenly lost his self-possession. He almost shouted: "I can never understand you Hindus who go about seeking a soul in every lice and bug and cockroach that crawls around you. The Bible says in so many words that man is God's highest creation. What is wrong with the higher ruling over the lower?"

On our way back to the big city where his mission was housed, he became his old normal self again. There was not a trace of bitterness on his face or in his voice as we talked and joked and discussed several serious and not so serious matters. Now I took my courage in both my hands and asked him my final question: "Father, am I not already a Christian? I do not normally tell a lie. I do not steal. I do not bear false witness. I do not covet my neighbor's wife or property. What more can a man do to demand God's grace and kinship with Christ? Why should you insist on a formal conversion which in no way helps me to become better than what I am?" His reply was very positive and it estranged me from the Christian creed for good. He said: "It is an illusion that you can become a Christian if you practice Christian virtues. One cannot claim to be virtuous unless one

this was the method by which I could rediscover for myself the great truths of which the ancients had spoken in Hindu scriptures. It was not the end of my seeking, which had only started in right earnest. But it was surely the end of my wandering in search of a shore where I could safely anchor my soul and take stock of my situation.

The soul's hunger for absolute Truth, absolute Good, absolute Beauty and absolute Power, I was told, was like the body's hunger for wholesome food and drink. And that which satisfied this hunger of the human soul, fully and finally, was Sanatana Dharma, true for all times and climes. A votary of Sanatana Dharma did not need an arbitrary exercise of will to put blind faith in a supernatural revelation laid down in a single scripture. He did not need the intermediacy of a historical prophet nor the help of an organized church to attain salvation. Sanatana Dharma called upon its votary to explore his own self in the first instance and see for himself the truths expounded in sacred scriptures. Prophets and churches and scriptures could be aids, but never the substitutes for self-exploration, self-purification and self-transcendence.

I had come back at last, come back to my spiritual home from which I had wandered away in self-forgetfulness. But this coming back was no atavistic act. On the contrary, it was a reawakening to my ancestral heritage, which was waiting for me all along to lay my claim on its largesses. It was also the heritage of all mankind, as proved by the seers, sages and mystics of many a time and clime. It spoke in different languages to different people. To me it spoke in the language of Hindu spirituality and Hindu culture at their highest. I could not resist its call. I became a Hindu.

My Whole Family Became Hindus

Isani Alahan, 52, (photo at right) lived in Chennai, India, for several years, where she worked in the home, cooking South Indian ayurvedic meals for her family of five, and did home-schooling with her youngest daughter. She also studied Carnatic music, Sanskrit, hatha yoga and the Kerala health system known as Kalaripayattu. She returned with her family to live in Kauai in June, 2000.

I was introduced to Hinduism in 1970 through a local hatha yoga class in Carson City, Nevada. As time went on, I read more about yoga and the wonderful benefits for the body and mind. At this time I decided to become a vegetarian. I was sixteen years old. In 1972 my interest in meditation manifested. I attended weekly satsanga in Virginia City, Nevada. During the first satsanga, I had a memorable vision of Lord Siva Nataraja on the banks of the sacred Ganga. My life had changed.

In 1975 I married my husband of 25 years. My husband was accepting of my beliefs, but wasn't interested in studying. I continued on my own, and in 1980 I legally changed my name to Isani Alahan from Ardith Jean Barton, but kept my husband's last name, Pontius.

In December of 1982 I completed my conversion to Hinduism. I prepared a statement of apostasy and took it to the local priest. He looked at it and agreed to sign my formal release from the Catholic Church. As I took a deep sigh of relief, he hesitated and asked me to leave the room. When I returned, he had changed his mind. He told me he had called the Bishop in Reno and was told he could not

Acceptance and release: *(above) Isani Alahan's family was featured on the cover of a Tamil magazine during their stay in Chennai, South India. Clockwise: husband Durvasa, Isani, Priya, Neesha and Sitara. (right) The letter of release for Peshanidevi Dandapani reveals the angst many pastors feel when confronted with conversion out of their church.*

• •

sign the paper. Later I learned this was not true, and the Bishop had been out of town. I tried another priest in the town where I was born. He was understanding, but also declined. Within a few weeks, I called the Bishop to make an appointment to meet with him. He told me to go back to the original priest, who would sign my declaration of apostasy. I returned to the local rectory and met a priest of Chinese descent. He was very warm and accommodating. He explained how he understood the Hindu concept of ethical conversion. He signed my declaration and wished me the best.

I had my *namakarana* samskara at Kauai's Hindu Temple on December 25, 1982, with my two-year-old daughter, Neesha. Then we were off for six weeks of pilgrimage, visiting temples and ashrams throughout Malaysia, Sri Lanka and Tamil Nadu, India. It was a fantastic spiritual experience that continues to reverberate in my mind.

At the time, my husband was not a Hindu, but our three daughters were given Hindu first names at birth, while keeping his family name. We raised the children according to Hindu Dharma and our guru's guidance. In 1984 we moved to the Seattle area. During the ten years we lived in Seattle, my children and I gathered with the other local Hindus for weekly satsanga. We also met with the local Hindu community for festivals. We studied Bharata Natyam and Carnatic vocal music. My children attended Hindu summer camps in Hawaii.

All through these years, with his permission, I prayed that my husband would become a Hindu. Then, in 1993 my husband formally adopted Hinduism, legally changed his name from Victor Dean Pontius to Durvasa Alahan. He became a vegetarian, stopped smoking and gave up catch-and-release fishing, which was his favorite hobby. He had his *namakarana* samskara in 1994.

In November, 1996, my husband and eldest daughter went on pilgrimage to India for a month. My daughter was interested in studying Bharata Natyam, and my husband left my daughter in India so that she could attend Kalakshetra College of Fine Arts and get a diploma in Bharata Natyam. She started college in June of 1997, and the rest of the family, my husband, myself and two younger daughters, moved to Chennai, Tamil Nadu, in November of 1997. The past three years have had their moments of difficulty, but overall they have been a peak experience of my life, a fulfillment of my heart's desires.

My Husband and I and Our Lifelong Quest

Amala Seyon, 58, entered Hinduism in May, 1975. A homemaker on Kauai, she and her husband live within walking distance of the Kadavul Hindu Temple.

My first introduction to Hinduism was when I met my husband. He had been going through a very soul-searching time, asking God why the Vietnam war, why the rioting in the streets of America, and what does materialism have to offer the soul? While going through this trying time and praying, a born Hindu man came to his world religion class and talked about the Hindu religion. All the concepts of Hinduism were the truths my husband was looking for. This Hindu man had a meditation center and invited anyone in the class to come. My husband started going on a regular basis.

During this time, my husband asked me to marry him. He explained to me about the Hindu religion and took me to the meditation center. I was so happy to hear some of the concepts, like God is within you, the law of karma, the evolution of the soul. I felt like I had been in a cage, like a bird, and someone opened the door, and I was able to fly into something much bigger and deeper.

My husband told me that if we got married this was the path he wanted us to take. I accepted that and supported it fully. This started the process of a confrontation of Western and Eastern philosophies. Our first encounter was in finding someone to marry us. My husband went to the Hindu meditation center and asked this saintly man if he could marry us. His visa did not allow him to perform the ceremony. So we went to my family's Christian minister and asked him to marry us. He asked my husband a series of questions. Do

Our Lady of the Ozarks Catholic Church
P. O. Box 639
FORSYTH, MISSOURI 65653
Ph. 417/546-5208

January 17, 1995

Dear Francine,

It is with a heavy heart, and some reluctance, that I write this letter. I had hoped that you would be able to be an active and happy person as a Catholic. Even after your first marriage failed, I held out the hope that you could find a solution in your life to once more be active.

But this last move, it is so shocking that I could not react as I might have with more time. After your visit ended here, and you had gone, the impact of your decision became more scary. I can't imagine someone, who having been given the gift of Faith, could just set it aside. To make such a drastic change in your life makes one think that you have been brainwashed in some fashion. All that you guided your life by, is no longer revelant or has any meaning. I must confess to being amazed and not a little depressed. In a world that so desperately needs Our Savior, and needs to follow His teachings as a solution to the ills that we are enduring, to turn away from Him for a man-made philosophy is unbelievable. There has got to be another reason.

I can only hope that your desire to repair the errors of the past, has not led you to this decision. The past is past. It will never come again. The mistakes we made in the past can only be repented for, and the lessons we have learned by the wrong we have done, can and should guide our future decisions. But to so completely abandon the one saving supernatural mode of life for one that is based on natural knowledge, is to step backward into a realm of myth and conjecture.

I acknowledge that you are making this change in your life, and are embracing Saivite Hinduism. I do not approve. I do not give permission. I know this will not stop you in your determination to take this step. I also know that this step excommunicates you from the Catholic Church. I will pray every day that you come to your senses and return to the only true religion, The Catholic Faith.

I hope you will keep in touch as you promised to do. May the Blessing of Almighty God, Father, Son and Holy Spirit descent on you and remain forever.

Love and Prayers,

Father Mark Ernstmann

RECEIVED JAN 2 1 1995

Father Mark Ernstmann

you believe Jesus Christ is the only Son of God? Do you believe that the *Holy Bible* is the only word of God? The questioning went on for some time, and at the end of the interview he told my husband that not only could he not marry us but he was going to call my parents and tell them that he was against having me marry someone who was not a Christian.

We then had to confront my mother, who was very much a Christian. This was all emotionally hard for her because of the belief that you could only be saved through the belief in Jesus Christ. She was very disappointed, and the issue caused a major disruption in our family. Finally, they accepted our marriage, and my husband located his past minister, who agreed to marry us.

After our marriage, we started reading all we could on Hinduism. My husband mistakenly followed the statements in Hindu scripture

that we now realize were intended for monks. We sold and gave away all our wedding gifts and went to live in very remote areas of British Columbia. He read from morning until night and sat by a river for hours on end, but we finally realized we were not making real spiritual progress, and I was lonely living in remote areas and even on a deserted island.

We started searching and praying, and one day someone invited us to meet our Gurudeva, Sivaya Subramuniyaswami. We recognized what a great soul he was immediately, and we started our studies with him. When our two daughters were five and three years old, we all had our name-giving together, formally entering the Hindu religion.

My children were raised in the Hindu religion, and we spent a lot of years living near the Flushing, New York, Ganesha Temple, learning the culture and mixing with born Hindus. We learned so much and felt so naturally a part of the Hindu heritage. We followed a curriculum for teaching our children in the home until they were twelve years old. Our daughters are now both married and are wonderful mothers who stay home and care for their children. Our oldest daughter is married to a wonderful Hindu man from Mauritius in an extended family that showers her with love. We now live on the little island of Kauai and serve the community and the broader Hindu family through our many activities. We are so very grateful.

From the Masonic Order and Roman Catholicism

Shyamadeva and Peshanidevi Dandapani, both age 60, live in Anchorage, Alaska. Shyamadeva is a commercial real estate broker specializing in site acquisitions and leasing for local, regional and national real estate clients. Peshanidevi is a retired nurse, "domestic engineer" and homemaker.

We pilgrimaged to Kauai in November of 1994 for Krittika Dipam. During this pilgrimage, we truly began to embrace the Sanatana Dharma and returned home to Alaska to talk to our family and friends about becoming Hindus, and to begin merging with the Hindu community in Anchorage. For the most part, everyone was tolerant of our enthusiasm about becoming Hindus.

We had already leased out our house in preparation for moving to Kauai, so we rented an apartment, continued our studies and began the conversion and severance process. It was our in-depth study to review our lives, to determine our true beliefs, where they came from and if they were still valid for us. There were many rewrites and surprises. We returned to our previous influences (myself to the Freemasons and Peshanidevi to the Catholic Church), studying and participating with them again to be positive that we wanted to change our path. I returned to the Masonic Lodge and fully embraced Freemasonry for the next thirty days. I attended the lodge and participated fully in all its ceremonies and rituals. At the end of the thirty days, I was completely convinced that I no longer held the inherent beliefs of the Masonic Order. Even with all the years of being a very active Mason I knew it was neither my belief nor my path. The Masons say, "Once a Mason, always a Mason." The only way to sever the vows was to become a self-imposed apostate. I prepared a letter declaring that I was a self-imposed apostate to the Masonic vows and beliefs, and that I was converting fully to Hinduism. I read the letter in open lodge before all the members present and a copy was given to the secretary to be recorded into the minutes of the meeting on June 8, 1995, at Kenai Lodge No. 11.

Peshanidevi returned to the Midwest to attend mass and meet with the priest who had given her instructions for being baptized a Catholic. Two hours of discussion did not produce a letter of release, because, he said, "Once a Catholic, always a Catholic." He took it very personally but promised a letter to follow. A month later it arrived (above left). The fire was strong but the bond was broken.

We applied for our legal name change and announced it in the newspapers. On the auspicious day of July 9, 1995, in Kadavul Hin-

du Temple we made the irrevocable step of having our *namakarana samskara.* We felt the blessings of Lord Siva pour forth on us as we sat before God, Gods and our guru and took this momentous, life-changing step. We had come home to the religion of our souls. We experienced so much love, joy and emotion, and it affirmed our beliefs that we are Hindu souls.

The name change made our conversion very real to others, and many were quite alarmed. Our daughter was visibly frightened to enter our shrine room, and she forbid her young children to spend the night with us anymore. She was willing to use our new names and said that whatever we wanted to do was okay, but it was not for her. She would not accept any literature or talk about Hinduism. The two sons said about the same but were less rigid. My parents and siblings felt total rejection because of the family name, and they disowned us. They said that if their name was not good enough for us, then they had no son and daughter.

My wife's grandmother and her brother were the only family members who were really happy for us. And they showed it by immediately beginning to learn how to pronounce and then use our new names. In my work, a few close friends fully accepted our new names and life without question. However, there was a period of about one year where I faced a lot of fire and testing.

Our Release from Judaism

Vel Alahan, 58, is a partner in a home building center in Vail, Colorado. His wife is Valli Alahan.

I was nervous as I sat with my former rabbi to discuss my change of religion. We explained what we were doing, and he gave arguments in response. He wanted us to give him a chance to start over. But I explained what we had been through and that we could not refute the inner knowing that had come from within about the truth of our Hinduism. We told him that based on our own inner experience we believed in Hinduism. Based on the fact that I was a normal person, successful in the business world, with a family and children, he believed what I said and respected my convictions.

I explained to him why I had come: because I needed to A) test myself in the face of my former religious commitments and B) in the presence of my former rabbi and Jewish inner plane hierarchy, in the Jewish institution, state my inner commitment and my desire to leave Judaism. He had his arguments. We just had to stay strong. I held fast to my inner commitment. My outer mind was fluxing and swaying a bit, but I always had the inner part to hold onto.

He would not write a letter of severance. He felt that by writing such a letter he would be doing a wrong act himself. But he wished us well, gave his blessings and complimented us on a fine intellectual knowledge of our religion and of Judaism. I introduced the witness and explained why we had brought a witness, so that in the event that the rabbi would not write a letter, the witness could write a letter stating what had happened. We were well prepared, and that is a key point. If one were to go unkempt, unemployed, he would not get the respect. And if you are unprepared, you will fumble a bit.

After the meeting was over, I felt a sense of release. I felt wonderful. And we did not hurt the rabbi's feelings; though he did say he was sad to lose one of his fold and expressed his view that "Once a Jew, always a Jew." But he had never faced anything like this before.

When we reached the stage to contact the Hindu community, we made an appointment to meet with the Gangadharam family, Pattisapu and Sakunthala. They talked with us and took us into the community. They became our *appa* and *amma* and treated us very nicely. We explained that we intended to have a *namakarana* samskara later, and they immediately said, "We will do it. We insist. It will be good for the community as a whole."

Mrs. Gangadharam planned the day according to Hindu astrology. And a priest was there from the Pittsburgh Temple, Panduranga Rao. Many people were there. A new sari was given to my wife

S. RAJAM

to wear and a shirt and veshti was given to me. It was very nice the way they took care of us. During the ceremony, our "parents" signed our names in rice and repeated the required words before the community and Gods. Then we walked around and touched the feet of anyone who was an elder and gestured *namaskara* to anyone younger. Food was served afterwards, *prasadam* from the *puja.*

Being Refused Communion Was the Test

Aran Sendan, 56, is a builder and general contractor from Canada living in the Hawaiian islands. He and his wife Valli entered Hinduism formally on February 14, 1980.

I was in the process of formally converting from Roman Catholicism to Hinduism. I had resolved that, indeed, I felt more comfortable with Hindu beliefs than those of Catholicism or Christianity. I needed a clean break with Catholicism, so went back to Sacred Heart Church, the parish in which I was baptized, confirmed and received my first holy communion. I had an appointment with the monsignor and met with him in the rectory office.

I would have preferred a frank and rational discussion along the lines of the point-counterpoint; I was ready for that, but we were not going there. He was non-plussed by my statements, like it really wasn't happening, and said that, well, Buddhists or whatever

Comments from Hindu Leaders on Becoming a Hindu

"All those who find their roots in the Vedas, who believe that India is a pious land, who have sympathy and believe in protecting the cow can become Hindus, while keeping others' welfare in mind, and is acceptable to His Holiness as a Hindu. Those who have been proselytized by deceptive methods or by physical force must be permitted to go back to their original religion on the principles of human rights."

Srimadjagadguru Shankaracharya, Goverdhan Math, Puri, Orissa, India, Sri Swami Nischalananda Saraswatiji Maharaj

"Revered Maharaj points out that the doors of Hinduism had been kept closed to 'outsiders' for centuries. Swami Vivekananda himself gave his famous call to Hindus to broaden their outlook. There are many devotees associated with the Ramakrishna Order who were not born into the Hindu faith but have accepted Hindu names of their own accord. Scores among them have gone on to take, and faithfully keep, formal lifelong vows of *brahmacharya* and sannyasa."

Swami Asimatmananda, for Srimat Swami Ranganathanandaji, President, Belur Ramakrishna Math and Mission, West Bengal, India

"The Hindu religion has a long history of accepting anyone and everyone who is on the path toward eternal truth. Hinduism does not discriminate against any sincere seeker. Whosoever is devoted to the search for that Eternal Truth is embraced by Hinduism. Therefore, it is perhaps the most universal and welcoming faith of all time."

H.H. Sri Swami Satchidananda, Founder/Spiritual Head of Satchidananda Ashram; Founder, Light of Truth Universal Shrine (LOTUS); Yogaville, Virginia

"True conversion is not a mere change of label but an inner transformation of mind and heart. The great task that lies ahead of us is that of converting Hindus—in India and abroad—into true Hindus, acutely aware of the rich heritage that belongs to them. When the Hindus bear witness in deeds of daily living to the great ideals of Sanatana Dharma, then indeed will India shine once again in the splendor of the new morning sun. Hindus have forgotten how to live as Hindus. They need to be taught the truths proclaimed by their prophets and *avataras*. Millions of Hindus are waiting to be converted into true Hindus. I am one of them."

H.H. Dada J.P. Vaswani, head of the worldwide Sadhu Vaswani Mission, renowned Sindhi religious leader and lecturer, Pune, India

"Hinduism does not proselytize. However, nothing keeps it from defending itself from the obsessing and devouring invasion of those religions that live under the flag of proselytism. A line of defense can be the correct popularization of how you can become a Hindu and profess your religious beliefs appropriately. Hinduism would certainly be more solid and of greater utility for humanity if every Hindu professed his own religious beliefs with pride, asserting his spiritual principles, cultivating them in his own family and becoming an example for society. Or still, if every organization or group of Hindu devotees in the world collaborated with one another, without egoism and exaggerated pride, to carry out a common task of spreading Hinduism, its spiritual traditions and culture, without superficiality."

Sri Svami Yogananda Giri, Founder and Spiritual Head of Unione Induista Italiana, Sanatana Dharma Samgha, Gitananda Ashram, Carcare, Italy

The ethical method: *The key steps of ethical conversion, clockwise from center right: study of the creed and philosophy; learning cultural customs and dress; beginning worship of Lord Ganesha; severance from former spiritual mentors and the namakarana samskara, Hindu name-giving sacrament*

were good people, too, and if I wanted to study, that it was alright with him. I insisted that he write "declared apostate" next to my name in the Parish record book where my baptism, confirmation and first holy communion dates were recorded. He wouldn't do it, but allowed me to. I wrote "declared apostate" and dated it. I left the meeting unsatisfied by the interaction and felt that I needed to do something else.

I decided to attend mass the next morning and went up to the communion rail where the same priest was giving out holy communion to the faithful. It seemed to me that his faith would prevent him from giving me holy communion and thus my point would be made. At the rail he asked if I "believed in Jesus Christ as the son of God and the savior of mankind." I said that I didn't and that he couldn't give me holy communion. At that moment it became real.

I could feel the Catholic angels withdrawing from me as clearly as I could feel the wind. I now understood Catholicism better than I had ever understood it before. It isn't a religion of belief. It's a religion of faith, and clearly not my faith. I was no longer a Catholic.

CHAPTER 14

Hinduism & Buddhism

Buddhism sprang from the Hindu heart and heartland, then pioneered its own distinct vision. Now, 2,500 years later, how similar is Buddha's way?

ASIA'S TWO SPIRITUAL TITANS, HINDUISM and Buddhism, have exerted profound influence on the planet and its people since their beginnings. They are unique in offering imperative moral direction alongside esoteric knowledge of the yogas leading to transcendent states of consciousness and ultimately to Liberation. Taken together, Buddhist and Hindu adherents and enthusiasts would roughly account for one-quarter of the entire world population. Both religions have spread from the same soil, India, to countries far and wide. Buddhism especially has settled abroad, while its once powerful presence in India has dwindled to fewer than five million adherents (.5 percent of the population). Despite significant similarities and lasting philosophical affinities, profound and undeniable differences remain between them, differences that sincere seekers of either tradition must eventually cognize, understand and resolve to agree or disagree with, thus essentially choosing one religion or the other. This feature is in three parts. First, New Delhi's *doyen* of Dharma, Ram Swarup, offers a thought-provoking overview of Hindu-Buddhist kinships and boldly proposes how the Buddha can be "explained" in a Hindu context. Second, New Mexico's Vamadeva Shastri (David Frawley) eloquently calls for a deeper understanding among Western seekers who cling to misconceptions about both of these great rivers of righteousness. Lastly, nine essential beliefs of both traditions are presented.

COREL

BY RAM SWARUP, NEW DELHI

BUDDHISM IS RETURNING HOME TO INDIA AFTER A LONG exile of a thousand years. Religious tolerance of the average Hindu partly explains the warm reception. But a more important reason is the fact that Buddha and Buddhism form an intimate part of Hindu consciousness. Buddha was a Hindu, and Buddhism is Hindu in its origin and development, art and architecture, iconography, language, many of its beliefs, psychology, names, nomenclature, religious vows and spiritual disciplines. Hinduism is not all Buddhism, but Buddhism forms part of the ethos which is essentially Hindu.

Buddha's transcendence is the highlight and essence of his teachings and the justification of his claim to be a great world teacher and guide. Similarly, Buddha's compassion was not merely secular or even humanistic. Rather, it was a deep and loving concern of the "Enlightened One" for worldly creatures caught in the wheel of existence—birth, disease, decay, old age, death. The peace he taught was the Upanishadic "peace beyond understanding," not merely civic and political truce amongst men and nations. The joy he taught was the joy of emancipation from the web of repeated births.

To understand the relationship of Buddhism with Hinduism is to understand the deepest questions relating to spiritual theology as well as a whole gamut of *yogic* practices and spiritual disciplines. However, this relationship has been clouded, misunderstood and its intimacy minimized for two reasons. One reason is Buddha's silence over such fundamental questions as Brahman, God and soul, questions which occupy the center of interest in the Upanishadic literature. The other reason is Buddha's individual nuances and emphases. These nuances are not lacking in the *Upanishads*, but there they form only a part of a larger whole and therefore do not create the same one-sided impression of escapism and the painfulness of existence.

Nirvana: *painting inside a temple at Sarnath, India, depicting Buddha's enlightenment there and the forces he vanquished to reach it*

But was Buddha just an anomaly? Or was he a mighty representative, a leader of a well-authenticated spiritual tradition such as is so highly developed in the *Upanishads* and confirmed by great teachers and seers of ancient times? Thus posed, the question is not difficult to answer. His spiritual experience could not be random, arbitrary and personal. It must have been of a character universal and necessary, and there is reason to believe that his spiritual experience was wholly in the Vedantic tradition. Buddha's spiritual experience of enlightenment confirms and closely agrees with the Upanishadic teaching regarding the nature of the Ultimate Reality. He belonged to the Upanishadic heritage, and he cannot be understood in any other sense. The attempt to understand him in isolation, divorced from that tradition which he confirmed, enriched and represented, has only led to misunderstanding and distortion of his teachings. He himself claimed no originality, only to have "Seen an ancient way; followed an ancient road." What Buddha experienced was the vision celebrated in the *Upanishads* that the world of man divorced from Godhead, the phenomenal world conceived independently of the transcendental principle, is nothing; it is an illusion, maya, an imposition, a house of cards, a castle of sand. But the nature of Buddhist Nothingness should not be misunderstood. In fact, there is nothing peculiarly Buddhist about this Nothingness. It is the process of self-noughting enjoined by all mystical religions and yogic disciplines. For going into spiritual regions above, it is necessary to pass through the doors of Nothingness. This is why an arhat has been defined as one in whom all outflows, all desires, all sense-life have ceased.

In Buddhism, as in Vedanta, self-abnegation was to precede transcendental experience. Not only in the self-noughting of the phenomenal but also in the characterization of the transcendental, Buddha follows the *Upanishads*. The nihilistic rendering by which Buddhism is known today is caused by his future followers like Nagasena, but there is nothing in the teachings of the Master himself to support this negativism. Nirvana was described as a state in which there is "neither old age, nor fear, nor disease, nor birth, nor death, nor anxiety." This is virtually the language of the Vedanta, the "That" of the *Upanishads*, declared to be imperishable, deathless, free, unborn, self-existent and formless by the *Isha Upanishad*. This is called nirvana by Buddha and Brahman by Vedanta.

Still, there are differences to be accounted for. As one studies the early Buddhist literature, one encounters a certain atmosphere of dryness, of narrow and laborious self-culture, of strenuousness. One misses the atmosphere of effortlessness, fullness, ease and self-abandonment which one comes across, say, in reading Chaitanya, Mira, the Alvar saints and the other devotional figures of Hinduism. In Buddhism one is particularly struck by the omission of any reference to God or soul, those mighty facts of spiritual experience which figure so much in the *Upanishads*, the *Gita*, the *Mahabharata* and in the religious consciousness of the country in general. Other differences of nuances and emphases generally relate to the misery and transitoriness of this life. These are why a reading of Hindu and Buddhist literatures leaves two distinctly different impressions on the mind.

But let us not stress the differences too far. As we have seen, there is an important tradition of the Vedanta which is very much akin to the life denying trends in Buddhism. Similarly, there are many schools of Buddhist philosophy and Buddhist methods of *sadhana* which are akin to the more affirmative tradition of Hinduism. In these schools one does not pass into a void or Sunya effected through negation of all thought-forms or thought-complexes and through detachment from the world. Buddhism in these developments is no longer dry or flat, but rich and even luxuriant, though these powerful developments in Buddhism are not found in the earliest records and are not agreed upon by all schools.

Probably, in its world excursion, Buddhism followed the trail of Hinduism. It went where Hinduism was already known and honored. There it made a permanent niche in the affections of the people and destroyed nothing. Nourished by their psyche, it acquired a new wealth and became thoroughly indigenous. It was not governed by a distant mother-church. Instead, it drew its sustenance from the soil of its adoption. This prevented it from becoming the handmaid of imperialism, exploited from afar. Its center and authority was always local. It thus became the genuine voice of the people who lived by it.

Recapturing their lost identity, regaining their sense of the Divine and transcendent and uniting into a mighty force of living spirituality, let Hinduism and Buddhism, the two sister-religions, come forward and offer their healing message to a troubled world. In the absense of this message, inferior ideologies and life-philosophies are having a field day and are doing immense damage to humanity.

Yoga and Buddhism

By Vamadeva Shastri (David Frawley), New Mexico

It is not surprising that many of us born in the West, particularly after an initial exposure, are apt to regard Yoga and Buddhism as more or less the same. The differences that have existed between the two systems historically are less obvious to us than their commonalities. However, the tendency to find commonality between these two great spiritual traditions is not limited to the West. Swami Vivekananda, the first great figure to bring yoga to the West, examined the Buddhist Mahayana scriptures (sutras) and found much similarity between their key teachings and those of Vedanta. In recent years, with the influx of Tibetan refugees, including the Dalai Lama, into India since the Chinese occupation of Tibet, there has been a new dialogue between the two traditions that is bringing about greater respect between them.

Various syncretic Hindu-Buddhist teachings have existed through history. Buddha himself was born a Hindu and some scholars have argued that Buddhism as a religion apart from Hinduism did not arise until long after the Buddha had passed away. A Siva-Buddha teaching existed in Indonesia in medieval times. Buddha became accepted as an avatar of Vishnu during the period when Buddhism was still flourishing in India, and many Hindus still consider that we live in the age of the Buddha-avatar. Most Hindus accept Buddha, even if they do not accept all Buddhist teachings.

However such syncretic trends did not exclude disagreements and debates between the two traditions, which were quite common historically. Nor did they ever succeed in fully uniting them. Their traditions and lineages remain separate to the present day. Generally, the Hindu Yoga tradition sought to absorb Buddhism into itself by reinterpreting Buddha in a more Hindu light. Buddhism, however, strove to maintain its separate identity. Most Hindu and Buddhist teachers, including those of the Yoga school of Hinduism, found it necessary to discriminate their doctrines, particularly on subtle levels of practice and insight. Hence, while we can honor the connections between these two systems, we cannot overlook their differences.

The Yoga Tradition: By Yoga here we mean primarily the classical Yoga system as set forth by Patanjali in the *Yoga Sutras.* However, Patanjali was not the inventor of Yoga, as many people in the West are inclined to believe, but only a compiler of the teaching at a later period. Classical Yoga was always part of the greater Hindu Vedic tradition. It clearly deals with the nature of the soul, God and immortality, which are the main topics of religion throughout the world. Its main concern is religious and by no means merely exercise or health.

The Buddhist schools, of which there are four in classical Indian philosophy, though they shared many ideas with Vedic spirituality, like karma and rebirth, did not accept the authority of the *Vedas* and rejected a number of key Vedic principles. All Buddhist schools employ meditation, but some add more specific yogic practices, like pranayama and mantra. Such systems may be called Buddhist yoga by modern writers. However, *yoga* as a term is lacking in early Buddhist texts, particularly of the Theravadin type, and becomes prominent mainly in the Buddhist tantric tradition that developed later, particularly as practiced in Tibet.

The Buddhist Mahayana tradition, particularly in its tantric forms, uses breathing exercises, mantras, visualizations and deities, much like the Yoga tradition. The Theravadin tradition has less in common with Yoga, though it does use similar meditation and concentration methods. It generally rejects devotional worship and the use of deities such as occurs in yogic paths. In fact, it could be argued that Tibetan Buddhism, with its mantras, deities and yogic teachings, is closer to Hinduism in its teachings than to such Buddhist schools.

Buddhism grew up in a cultural cauldron of Hinduism. For this reason, Indian and Tibetan Buddhism have included ayurvedic medicine, Hindu astrology, Sanskrit, the same rules of iconography, the same forms of temple worship and other common factors. A number of Hindu Gods and Goddesses, like Ganesha and Sarasvati, appear in the Buddhist tradition. Some figures, like the Goddess Tara, appear in both. Yet, as Buddhism moved to other countries, many of these connections were either lost or their basis forgotten. Nepal has remained one region of the Indian subcontinent in which both these religions have continued. In this regard Nepalese Hindus and Buddhists respect one another but seldom combine the teachings of these two different religions by way of their actual practices. They tend to follow one tradition or the other, but seldom both.

In the *Yoga Sutras,* only three sutras out of two hundred deal with asana, yogic postures. The great majority deal with meditation, its theory and results. Unfortunately, however, yoga today is most known for its asana tradition—the most popular, visible and outward form of the system. Buddhism, by comparison, is known as a tradition of meditation, as in the more popular forms of Buddhist meditation like Zen and Vipassana. Many people who have studied yoga in the West look to Buddhist teachings for meditation practices, not realizing that there are yogic and Vedantic forms of meditation which are traditionally not only part of the yogic system but its core teaching!

Yoga and Buddhism are both meditation traditions devised to help us transcend karma and rebirth and realize the truth of consciousness. They see the suffering and impermanence inherent in all birth—animal, human or Godly—and seek to alleviate it through developing a higher awareness. Both emphasize the need to dissolve the ego, the sense of me and mine, and return to the original reality that is not limited by the separate self. Both traditions emphasize enlightenment or inner illumination to be realized through meditation.

Both systems recognize dharma, the principle of truth or natural law, as the basic law of the universe we must come to understand. Buddhism defines itself as Buddha Dharma or the dharma of the enlightened ones, which is seen as a tradition transcending time or place. Yoga defines itself as part of the Hindu tradition called Sanatana Dharma, the universal or eternal dharma, which is not defined according to any particular teacher or tradition.

Divergence: The main differences between the two systems are over their cosmic view and way of practice. Vedic systems are built upon fundamental principles like the Self (Atman), the Creator (Ishvara) and Godhead (Brahman). Buddhism rejects all such ontological principles as mere creations of the mind itself. Apart from such philosophical differences, both systems share the same basic ethical values, like nonviolence, truthfulness, nonattachment and nonstealing. The vows that Buddhist monks take and those that monks and sadhus take in the yoga tradition are the same, as are those of the Jains.

Vedanta defines the Absolute as a metaphysical principle, Being-consciousness-bliss, Satchidananda or Brahman, in which there is perfect peace and liberation. [Though some would say that Satchidananda is *saguna* brahman and the transcendent absolute is *nirguna brahman*]. Buddhism does recognize an Absolute which is non-dual and beyond all birth and death, however, Buddhism generally does not allow it any definition and regards it as a void. It is sometimes called the Dharmakaya, or body of dharma, though Sanskrit Buddhist texts never call it Brahman.

Buddhism generally rejects the Self (Atma or Purusha) of yoga-Vedanta and emphasizes the non-Self (*anatman*). It says that there is no Self in anything and therefore that the Self is merely a fiction of the mind. Whatever we point out as the Self, the Buddhists state, is merely some impression, thought or feeling, but no such homogenous entity like a Self can be found anywhere. Even so, a number of Buddhist traditions, particularly traditions outside of India, like the Chan and Zen of China, have used terms like "Self-mind, one's original nature, the original nature of consciousness" or "one's original face," which are similar to the Self of Vedanta. But by and large,

Buddhism has tended to lump the Self of Vedanta as another form of the ego or the misconception that there is a Self.

In contrast, the yoga-Vedanta tradition emphasizes Self-realization, or the realization of our true nature. Yoga-Vedanta discriminates between the Self, which is our true nature as consciousness, and the ego (*ahamkara*), which is the false identification of our true nature with the mind-body complex. The Atman of Vedanta is not the ego but is the enlightened awareness which transcends time, form and space.

Is there a God? The Yoga tradition is based upon a recognition of, respect for and devotion to God or the creator, preserver and destroyer of the universe. One of its main principles is that of surrender to God (Ishvara-pranidhana), which is said to be the most direct route to Self-Realization. This is perhaps the main point of difference between Yoga and Buddhism. Buddhism rejects God (Ishvara) or a cosmic lord and creator. It sees no need for any creator and considers that living beings arise through karma alone. Yoga emphasizes devotion and surrender to God as one of the main spiritual paths, bhakti yoga, through which we open our hearts to God and surrender to the divine will. As Buddhism does not recognize God, devotion to God does not appear. That is why we don't find any significant tradition of great devotees and singers of divine love in Buddhism like Chaitanya, Ramakrishna, Tulsidas or Mirabai in the Hindu tradition. Buddhism does recognize devotion to the Buddha. However, devotion to great teachers does not quite strike the human heart with the same significance as devotion to the Divine Father and Mother of the universe.

If we equate the One Mind of the Buddhists with the One Self of Vedanta, make Buddha and God the same, give the Buddha the power of creation of the universe and make other such correlations, both traditions could be synthesized. However, prominent Buddhist leaders have yet to make such statements. Until they do, we cannot dismiss such differences as unnecessary, but must respect them. If you believe not only in karma and rebirth but also the existence of God or the Creator, you would be a Hindu, not a Buddhist in your views.

It is crucial that such meditation traditions as Yoga and Buddhism form a common front in light of the needs of this materialistic age. Their common values of protecting the Earth, nonviolence, recognition of the law of karma, and the practice of meditation are perhaps the crucial voice to deliver us out of our present crisis.

Left to right: *Monks and lamas at the week-long summer festival at Chongra in the Derge district of eastern Tibet; a Buddhist* thangka *painting of the Deity Ganesha; Dai Pagoda, Xishaung Banna, Thailand; Buddhist monks at the Sakya center, Dehra Dun, India*

COREL

RENU AND DEV RAJ AGARWAL

Core Beliefs

A Creedal Summary of Hinduism and Buddhism

Veneration: *Buddhist monks worship before the massive brick stupa at Deer Park in Sarnath, India, the site of the Buddha's first sermon*

Buddhism

BUDDHISTS BELIEVE THAT THE SUPREME is completely transcendent and can be described as Sunya, a void or state of nonbeing.

BUDDHISTS BELIEVE IN THE FOUR Noble Truths: 1. that suffering exists; 2. that desire is the cause of suffering; 3. that suffering may be ended by the annihilation of desire; 4. that to end desire one must follow the Eight-Fold Path.

BUDDHISTS BELIEVE IN THE EIGHT-FOLD path of right belief, right aims, right speech, right actions, right occupation, right endeavor, right mindfulness and right meditation.

BUDDHISTS BELIEVE IN DHARMA (the way), karma (cause and effect), reincarnation, the sanga (brotherhood of seekers) and the passage on earth as an opportunity to end the cycle of birth and death.

BUDDHISTS BELIEVE THAT LIFE'S AIM IS to end suffering through the annihilation of individual existence and absorption into nirvana, the Real.

BUDDHISTS BELIEVE IN THE "Middle Path," living moderately, avoiding extremes of luxury and asceticism.

BUDDHISTS BELIEVE IN THE SANCTITY of the Buddha and in the sacred scriptures of Buddhism: the *Tripitaka* (Three Baskets of Wisdom) and/or the *Mahayana Sutras*.

BUDDHISTS BELIEVE IN THE GREATNESS of self-giving love and compassion toward all creatures that live, for these contain merit exceeding the giving of offerings to the Gods.

BUDDHISTS BELIEVE THAT MAN'S TRUE nature is divine and eternal, yet his individuality is subject to the change that affects all forms and is therefore transient, dissolving at liberation into nirvana.

Hinduism

HINDUS BELIEVE IN A ONE, all-pervasive Supreme Being who is both immanent and transcendent, both Creator and Unmanifest Reality.

HINDUS BELIEVE IN THE DIVINITY OF the *Vedas*, the world's most ancient scripture, and venerate the *Agamas* as equally revealed. These primordial hymns are God's word and the bedrock of Sanatana Dharma, the eternal religion which has neither beginning nor end.

HINDUS BELIEVE IN KARMA, the law of cause and effect by which each individual creates his own destiny by his thoughts, words and deeds.

HINDUS BELIEVE THAT THE SOUL reincarnates, evolving through many births until all karmas have been resolved, and moksha, spiritual knowledge and liberation from the cycle of rebirth, is attained. Not a single soul will be eternally deprived of this destiny.

HINDUS BELIEVE THAT THE UNIVERSE undergoes endless cycles of creation, preservation and dissolution.

HINDUS BELIEVE THAT DIVINE BEINGS EXIST in unseen worlds and that temple worship, rituals, sacraments as well as personal devotionals create a communion with these devas and Gods.

HINDUS BELIEVE THAT A SPIRITUALLY awakened master, or *satguru*, is essential to know the Transcendent Absolute, as are personal discipline, good conduct, purification, pilgrimage, self-inquiry and meditation.

HINDUS BELIEVE THAT ALL LIFE IS sacred, to be loved and revered, and therefore practice ahimsa, "noninjury."

HINDUS BELIEVE THAT NO PARTICULAR religion teaches the only way to salvation above all others, but that all genuine religious paths are facets of God's Pure Love and Light, deserving tolerance and understanding.

© THOMAS L. KELLY

Hinduism vis-à-vis Christianity

HINDUISM TODAY and CHRISTIANITY TODAY compose a point-counterpoint

N 1993, OUR EDITORS WERE CONTACTED BY CHRISTIANITY TODAY MAGAZINE TO BE INTERviewed for a major story called *Hindus in America*. Thus began a series of dialogs that added to their article crucial and often corrective insights to dispel common myths and misinformation about the world's oldest religion. Perhaps most significantly, they agreed to publish our own nine fundamental Hindu beliefs. The editors of CHRISTIANITY TODAY counter-composed nine parallel Christian convictions, written just before press time in a series of grueling sessions by the best theologians they could assemble. The resulting point-counterpoint—whose brevity is both its strength and its weakness—summarizes the cosmic perspective of two of the world's largest faiths. Christians seeking to understand Hinduism often ask how it compares with their faith. This comparison answers that question in a nutshell.

1

HINDUS BELIEVE IN THE DIVINITY OF THE VEDAS, the world's most ancient scripture, and venerate the *Agamas* as equally revealed. These primordial hymns are God's word and the bedrock of Sanatana Dharma, the eternal religion which has neither beginning nor end.

CHRISTIANS BELIEVE THAT THE BIBLE IS THE uniquely inspired and fully trustworthy word of God. It is the final authority for Christians in matters of belief and practice, and though it was written long ago, it continues to speak to believers today.

2

HINDUS BELIEVE IN A ONE, ALL-PERVASIVE SUPREME Being who is both immanent and transcendent, both Creator and Unmanifest Reality.

CHRISTIANS BELIEVE IN ONE GOD IN THREE PERSONS. He is distinct from his creation, yet intimately involved with it as its sustainer and redeemer.

3

HINDUS BELIEVE THAT THE UNIVERSE undergoes endless cycles of creation, preservation and dissolution.

CHRISTIANS BELIEVE THAT THE WORLD WAS CREATED ONCE by the divine will, was corrupted by sin, yet under God's providence moves toward final perfection.

4

HINDUS BELIEVE IN KARMA, THE LAW OF CAUSE AND effect by which each individual creates his own destiny by his thoughts, words and deeds.

CHRISTIANS BELIEVE THAT, THROUGH GOD'S GRACE AND FAVOR, lost sinners are rescued from the guilt, power and eternal consequences of their evil thoughts, words and deeds.

5

HINDUS BELIEVE THAT THE SOUL REINCARNATES, evolving through many births until all karmas have been resolved, and *moksha*, spiritual knowledge and liberation from the cycle of rebirth, is attained. Not a single soul will be eternally deprived of this destiny.

CHRISTIANS BELIEVE THAT IT IS APPOINTED FOR HUMAN beings to die once and after that face judgment. In Adam's sin, the human race was spiritually alienated from God, and those who are called by God and respond to his grace will have eternal life. Those who persist in rebellion will be lost eternally.

6

HINDUS BELIEVE THAT DIVINE BEINGS EXIST IN UNSEEN WORLDS and that temple worship, rituals, sacraments as well as personal devotionals create a communion with these *devas* and Gods.

CHRISTIANS BELIEVE THAT SPIRIT BEINGS INHABIT the universe, some good and some evil, but worship is due to God alone.

7

HINDUS BELIEVE THAT A SPIRITUALLY AWAKENED master, or *satguru*, is essential to know the Transcendent Absolute, as are personal discipline, good conduct, purification, pilgrimage, self-inquiry and meditation.

CHRISTIANS BELIEVE THAT GOD HAS GIVEN US A CLEAR revelation of Himself in Jesus and the sacred Scriptures. He has empowered by his Spirit prophets, apostles, evangelists, and pastors who are teachers charged to guide us into faith and holiness in accordance with his Word.

8

HINDUS BELIEVE THAT ALL LIFE IS SACRED, to be loved and revered, and therefore practice ahimsa, "noninjury."

CHRISTIANS BELIEVE THAT LIFE IS TO BE HIGHLY ESTEEMED but that it must be subordinated in the service of Biblical love and justice.

9

HINDUS BELIEVE THAT NO PARTICULAR RELIGION teaches the only way to salvation above all others, but that all genuine religious paths are facets of God's Pure Love and Light, deserving tolerance and understanding.

CHRISTIANS BELIEVE THAT JESUS IS GOD INCARNATE and, therefore, the only sure path to salvation. Many religions may offer ethical and spiritual insights, but only Jesus is the Way, the Truth and the Life.

Hindu Metaphysics

The esoterics of the satguru, chakras, the human aura, death, rebirth and astrology

A lotus flower in full bloom, representing the glorious illumination and divine maturity that is the destiny of all souls, without exception

CHAPTER 15

The Satguru

Exploring the centrality of the enlightened master in Hinduism, with verses from the *Kularnava Tantra* on reverence for one's preceptor

EVERYONE NEEDS A TEACHER, A MODEL TO LOOK UP TO AND FOLLOW, A MASTER OF HIS art, a champion in his field, one who sets the standards of aspiration. These days, heros are often rock stars, athletes or actors, but there is, indeed, a class of souls of a higher calling. For century upon century, Hindu society has been uniquely inwardly oriented, ever intrigued with the deeper realities of existence, fascinated with the search for Truth, the control of mind and realization of the Self, God, within, through the practice of yoga. Thus, it honors the great rishis, gurus, *sants* and *mahatmas* as the greatest heros of all. These are beings who walk with God and hold truth in the palm of their hand, who seem to know everything, because they do, because they have discovered the source of all knowing. Though perhaps rare, such awakened beings still walk among us today. All too often amid the pace of modern life, humans are too busy to recognize and honor these pure souls until after they have departed this earthly stage. Only in their absence is their greatness apparent to many, in the vacuum of their prodigious presence, which had filled with faith and courage the voids of doubt and discouragement for everyone they touched. This chapter offers wisdom from Satguru Sivaya Subramuniyaswami on the role and importance of the illumined master, or *satguru*, in Hindu culture, as well as select verses from the *Kularnava Tantra*, an ancient text extolling the guru as the embodiment of God and speaking boldly of the necessity to strive for spiritual progress in this lifetime.

Precious Darshan of the Illumined Master

If you were to travel through India on a spiritual pilgrimage, you would undoubtedly hear much about the Sanskrit word *darshan*. The religious leaders of the Orient are categorized according to the darshan they give, for there are various kinds of darshan. Darshan is the vibration that emanates from the illumined soul as a result of his inner attainment, be he a yogi, pandit, swami, guru or a rishi. Usually the yogi, swami, saint or sage attracts his following not so much by what he says as by the darshan he radiates. Hindus travel for miles to receive the darshan of an illumined soul established in his enlightenment. Perhaps he doesn't even speak to them. Perhaps he scolds some of them. Perhaps he gives the most inspired of talks to them. In any case, they feel the darshan flooding out from him.

A great soul is always giving darshan. Hindus believe that the darshan coming from a great soul helps them in their evolution, changes patterns in their life by cleaning up areas of their subconscious mind that they could not possibly have done for themselves. They further believe that if his darshan is strong enough, if they are in tune with him enough, by its power the kundalini force can be stimulated enough that they can really begin to meditate. This is called the grace of the guru. The ability for one to meditate comes from this grace. You must have it before you can begin to meditate, or you must do severe austerities by yourself instead. Darshan is not well understood in the West, because the West is outwardly refined but not necessarily inwardly refined. The peoples of the Orient, by their heritage, are inwardly sensitive enough to understand and appreciate darshan.

One who is closed on the inside of himself misses the darshan of the awakened soul. He sees in the greater soul just another ordinary person like himself. The darshan is there, but he is too negative to feel it. But the darshan permeates him just the same. He goes away from the garden not having smelled a rose, but carrying the perfume of the rose himself. If you stand away from the rose, you smell less of its fragrance.

Bring yourself really close, and more of its strong and sweet scent will penetrate your body.

Darshan from a great soul, like the pollen of the flowers, can stimulate healthy sneezing and cleansing if one's subconscious happens to be congested. Call it, if you like, an allergy to flowers. Some people have allergies to gurus, too. The guru's darshan lifts repressed subconscious patterns that have been out of the flow of the cosmic pattern of regenerative life, bringing them up before one's conscious attention. Instead of feeling wonderful, the visitor to the garden feels miserable, as the fire is brought up from within, releasing his awareness to view the polluted state of the subconscious mind.

Some people are more sensitive to fragrance than others. Others are so selfless and sensitive, they can become the fragrance itself for a time. In such a person, the rose smells sweet through every pore of his body. He is not in the least aware of any subconscious congested area of the mind. He sits in the garden and goes deep into meditation on the subtle fragrance of the flowers. The same principle relates to the unfolded soul. Darshan pours forth from within the unfolded soul just as fragrance flows from the rose—stronger at some times than at others because some devotees are more in tune than others. For them, the room begins to ring and vibrate. Some people are so sensitive that when a great soul comes to the same town, they feel his presence. This shows their inner attunement to the constant flowing power of the darshan.

Everyone has some feelings radiating from within, but they are emanations that fluctuate. Because you feel these vibrations coming from them, you can intuit how they are feeling. They do not emanate a constant or a building flow. It is a fluctuating flow of emotional, or astral, energy. The darshan I am explaining is really the energies flowing from the deeper chakras, sahasrara and ajna, the seventh and sixth chakras, or psychic force centers, in the head, through the kundalini force within the spine. These energy flows do not fluctuate as the emotional odic-force energies do. They go on day and night and night and day through the illumined soul. Those devotees who are in tune with the guru can feel his physical presence when he enters their town because the darshan gets stronger. And it feels to them more ethereal when he is farther away.

These energy flows are very important to study, because it is possible to draw and enjoy a great darshan from an illumined soul if you approach him in just the right way. If you can become as a sponge when you approach him, you will draw out inspiring talks and gracious blessings from him. The Hindu is conscious that he is drawing darshan from his rishi or his *satguru*, just as you are conscious of drawing the perfume of

ART BY A. MANIVEL

At the sage's hermitage: Yogaswami sits outside his Sri Lankan hut, emjoying the darshan of Siva as Ardhanarishvara. Some devotees have come to worship, sing, listen, seek his counsel, and have his grace uplift their life.

the rose into your body. When approaching a soul who is known to give darshan, be in the same area of the superconscious mind that you feel he must be in. The guru does not have to be necessarily functioning in that same area. He could be externalized in consciousness at the time. This is not important. It does not stop his darshan at all. The guru, feeling you draw the darshan, would immediately go within and enjoy it himself. Once darshan is there in him, it is always there.

Hindu devotees are very careful not to upset their guru, for they do not want his forces strongly directed at them. It is the same darshan, however. At a time such as this, it is like a distilled perfume from the rose. It becomes too potent. Therefore, the devotee tries to maintain a good atmosphere around the guru so that his darshan is pleasant and natural. The darshan of a guru is the power that stabilizes the devotee on the path. The philosophies, teachings and practices that he is given to do are important, but it is the power of darshan that is his stabilizing influence, enabling him to unfold easily on the path of enlightenment.

Darshan is a mystical power emanating from the adept who has gone deep enough within to awaken this power. By stabilizing that power, he gives psychic protection to his disciples and devotees, even during their sleep at night. Devout Hindus sit before a *satguru* and, in seeing him, draw the darshan vibration from him, absorbing it into themselves. They are sensitive enough to distinguish the vibration of darshan from the other vibrations around the guru. They also believe that any physical thing the *satguru* touches begins to carry some of his darshan or personal vibration, and that when away from him they can just hold the article to receive the full impact of his darshan, for the physical object is a direct link to the *satguru* himself. It is darshan vibration that makes a human being a holy person. When we say someone is holy or saintly we are feeling the radiations of that divine energy flooding through him and out into the world.

The inner life of a devotee has to be stabilized, cherished and well protected by the guru. The guru is able to do this through his well-developed facilities of darshan, even if his devotee lives at great distances from him. Unless the inner vibratory rate of the devotee is held stable, he will not come into his fullness in this life. If a plant is transplanted too often, it won't come into its full growth. If the bud is picked before it blooms, it will not flower or give forth its redolent fragrance. Yes, the grace of the *satguru* fires the ability to meditate in the seeker, the erudite Hindu believes.

The satguru is like the sun. He is just there, radiating this very pure energy like the sun evaporates water. The satguru hardly does anything at all. It is the seeker who opens himself to the great accumulated power of darshan which the guru inherited from his guru and his guru's guru, as well as the natural darshan he unfolded from within himself through his evolution and practices of sadhana and tapas. It's all up to the aspirant at first.

Why We Worship The Feet of the Guru

The uninitiated may wonder why the feet of holy ones are so reverently worshiped in the Hindu faith. According to tradition, the totality of the *satguru* is contained within his feet. All nerve currents terminate there. The vital points of every organ of his bodies—inner astral, inner mental and soul—are there. Touch the feet and we touch the spiritual master.

Mystics teach that the big toe on the left foot exudes the most grace. The left leg is the revealing grace, and the big toe of that leg connects to the guru's pituitary gland, the entrance to the door of Brahm, deep within the *sahasrara* chakra where, in contemplation, he merges with Siva. The vibration of the *satguru* can be subtly felt through gently touching his sandals. In doing so, one tunes in to the feet of the preceptor's physical, pranic, astral, mental and soul bodies.

In deep spirituality there is little presumption of ego. All that one hopes for, all that one prays for, all that one strives for is to touch the Divine in the most modest of ways. Worship of the feet epitomizes this humble attitude. Devotees worship the feet of the guru as the feet of God Siva, the attainable attainment, seeking to partake of, absorb into themselves, the vibration of their guru, ultimately to become like their guru, who has realized his oneness with God Siva.

Satguru Sivaya Subramuniyaswami wrote, "Practices to advance spiritual unfoldment include prostrating before God, Gods and guru, full body, face down, arms and hands outstretched, and in that act, total giving up, giving up, giving up, giving up. What are these devoted ones giving up? By this act they are giving the lower energies to the higher energies. It is a merger, a blending. When one is performing this traditional devotional act, awakening true *prapatti*, it is easy to see the lower energies from the base of the spine, the *muladhara* chakra, rising, rising, rising up the spine through all six chakras above it and out through the top of the head. It is transmuting, changing the form of, the base energies which breed conflict and resistance, 'mine and yours' and 'you and me,' division, insecurity and separateness, into the spiritual energies of 'us and we,' amalgamation, security, togetherness. Once the giving up of the lower is total—body and face on the ground, hands outstretched before the image of God, Gods or guru—those energies are surrendered into the higher chakras within the devotee, and it is a blissful moment, into the consciousness of 'us and ours,' 'we and oneness,' and inseparable love, thus claiming their individuality, not as a separate thing, but as a shared oneness with all. Thereafter, these devoted ones, having been transformed, are able to uplift others, to harmonize forces around them that they work with day after day, year after year after year. This total surrender,

A devotee falls humbly at his guru's feet, prayerful that training, protection may come. The satguru's mind is on Siva within, who blesses with a garland of jasmine flowers.

and adopting his revelation of the Sanatana Dharma as their own. Therefore, choose your spiritual model carefully, because you are going to become like that model if you worship that guru's feet. There is yet another meaning of the holy feet. When a person walks upon the Earth, only the feet touch the ground. Similarly, when God and guru contact the Earth, it is the esoteric feet, the lowest part of consciousness, which make that contact. This, then, becomes the locus of communion with the Divine. In India the greatest of all initiations is for the *satguru* to place his holy feet upon the worthy disciple's head.

VERSES FROM SCRIPTURE

The Ancient Kularnava Tantra

Around 1150 ce, a scripture was recorded, called the *Kularnava Tantra,* that pours forth exaltation to such spiritual lights and admonishes seekers to raise slumbersome eyelids and recognize their glory. Among its messages is that the guru is like a deep well from which one can and should draw forth wisdom and blessings, taking advantage of his rare presence, his radiant darshan, to advance oneself on the spiritual path. This tantra of guru devotion and protocol gives guidance that is as practical and poignant today as it was when first scribed on palm leaves and etched in stone long, long ago.

The *Kularnava Tantra* is an important and authoritative text of the Shakta Agamic tantra tradition and a major statement of Hindu spiritual thought. It focuses unequivocally on the quest for God Realization calling on us to leave aside our attachments, our desires, our misapprehensions and to live a divine life, a holy life, on this Earth and seek for the Self within.

The original, first translated from the Sanskrit and published in English in 1878, contains 2,058 verses on many profound subjects, of which a small fraction dealing with the *guru-shishya* (teacher-disciple) relationship are excerpted here. This translation was completed in 1916 by Sri M.P. Pandit and Sir Arthur Avalon in north India. The selected verses have been slightly edited for this presentation.

The scripture opens with a single question posed by Shakti, the Mother of the universe, as to how all souls may attain release from sorrow, ignorance and birth. Lord Siva answers, speaking out the verses of the *Kularnava Tantra.*

prapatti, is the meaning of Siddhanta. This is the true meaning of Vedanta. The combination of both, and the pure practice of *prapatti* as just described brings out from within the deeper meanings of Vedanta, the Vedic philosophy, without having to depend on the path of words, lectures and debates."

Devotees are admonished to choose their guru carefully, forsaking all previous beliefs, religious inclinations and aspirations

Devotion to the Guru

Lord Siva said: There is One Real. Call it Siva. This Parabrahman is formless, stainless, one without a second, changeless, beyond the highest. This Mahesvara is all-knowing, all-doing, sovereign of all, self-luminous, without beginning or end. All embodied souls, *jivas*, all the born creatures, are portions of Me, like sparks of the fire. But human birth is the most important, for it is then that one becomes awake, aware of his state of bondage and the necessity of release. It is then that one is in a position to take steps for his liberation from bondage's hold.

Humans have a self-will and are not totally subject to the impulses and drives of nature, as are other creatures. It is only on this Earth—and that, too, in a human body endowed with a soul—that one can choose one's path for spiritual progress. But not all are aware of the precious opportunity afforded by human birth, which is truly the ladder to Liberation. The Self is to be realized only here in this life. If here you do not find it and work out the means for your Liberation, where else is it possible? It is possible nowhere else. It has to be worked out by yourself from within yourself.

The world you reach after the physical body is shed is determined by the level of consciousness reached while in the body. So, as long as the body lasts, exert yourself towards the goal of Liberation. Remember, the physical body does not last forever. Age prowls like a leopard; diseases attack like an enemy. Death waits not to see what is done or not done. Before the limbs lose their vitality, before adversities crowd in upon you, take to the auspicious path.

Therefore, choose, then worship a *satguru*. Worship his feet. Cherish the very sandals (*paduka*) which hold his feet. All knowledge is founded on those *paduka*. Remember and cherish those *paduka*, which yield infinitely more merit than any number of observances, gifts, sacrifices, pilgrimages, *mantra-japa* and rituals of worship.

It is these feet, when remembered, that protect in times of distress, danger or calamity. Study, remembrance, knowledge, donations, sacrifices and worship are truly done by him who ever remembers the *satguru's* feet. Look toward the direction in which the lotus feet of the *satguru* lie and bow down to them every day with devotion. There is no mantra higher than that of his feet, no merit higher than his worship.

All fear of distress, grief, avarice, delusion and bewilderment exist only as long as one does not take refuge in the *satguru*. All wanderings in the ocean of births, called samsara, fraught with grief and impurity, last as long as one has no devotion to a holy Sivaguru. As the boon-giving guru gives the mantra in contentment and beatitude, try to please him with devotion, wealth, your very life.

The *shishya* who has complete devotion, steady and constant, what has he to worry about? *Moksha* is in the hollow of his palm. For him who remembers, "My *satguru* is Siva Himself who grants Liberation," fulfillment is not far off. As the steady devotion for the *satguru* grows, so grows one's knowledge. The sacred *paduka* of the guru are the ornament. Remembrance of his name is *japa*. Carrying out his command is duty. Service to him is worship.

The guru offers blessings as his devotee experiences the bliss of beholding the inner clear white light and hearing the vina-like tones of the high "eee"

Serving the Preceptor

Why the pains of long pilgrimage? Why observances that emaciate the body? All the fruit anticipated from such austerities can be easily obtained by motiveless service to the holy *satguru*. Therefore, bear your karma for the sake of the guru. Acquire wealth for the sake of the guru. Exert yourself for the guru, regardless of your own life.

Service to the *satguru* and his mission is fourfold: service with your own hands, service by wealth or through others, service by spiritual enthusiasm and service by happy feeling. Service done with devotion, according to one's means, has the same merit whether little or much, whether by the rich or by the poor.

With your mind dedicated to selfless service, please the *satguru*. The fruit obtained is the same as from great rituals. Such service invites the grace of the Mother of the Universe.

In the service of the guru, either expressed or unexpressed by him, do not be unmindful. Be always in service of the guru, ever in his presence, giving up desire and anger, humble and devoted, lauding in spirit, upright in doing his work.

If service is accompanied by *santosha* (happy devotion), it brings with it all fulfillment. Sins dissolve away and merit grows by leaps and bounds.

Power of the Guru

When the entire universe is looked on as pervaded by the Sivaguru, what mantra can fail to achieve its purpose for the *shishya*? When the *satguru* is present, no *tapas* is necessary, neither by fasting nor observances, neither pilgrimage nor purificatory bath. What he speaks is as scripture.

Feel one with your guru and not separate from him, and do good to all as your own. Whatever is beneficial to yourself, term that beneficial to him. Whether moving or standing, sleeping or waking, performing *japa* or making offerings, carry out only the injunctions of your guru with your inner being dwelling in him.

As in the vicinity of fire, butter gets melted, so in the proximity of the holy Sivaguru all bad karmas dissolve. As lighted fire burns up all fuel, dry and moist, so the glance of the Sivaguru burns up in a moment the karmas of the *shishya*. As the heap of cotton blown up by a great storm scatters in all the ten directions, so the heap of negative karmas is blown away by the compassion of the Sivaguru. As darkness is destroyed at the very sight of the lamp, so is ignorance destroyed at the sight of the holy Sivaguru.

I tell you now that there can be no Liberation without *diksha*, initiation. Nor can there be initiation without a preceptor. Hence the dharma, the *shakti* and the tradition come down the line of masters, called *parampara*.

Without a *satguru* all philosophy, knowledge and mantras are fruitless. Him alone the Gods praise who is the *satguru*, keeping active what is handed down to him by tradition. Therefore, one should seek with all effort to obtain a preceptor of the unbroken tradition, born of Supreme Siva.

ART BY A. MANIVEL

A knower of God strides along the path of enlightenment. Having lived many lives, mastered his energies and resolved his karmas, he has reached Siva consciousness, which symbolically surrounds him as the Ganges water flowing from Siva's hair.

The Guru's Inner Nature

Lord Siva said: At the root of dhyana, meditation, is the form of the *satguru*. At the root of puja, worship, is the feet of the *satguru*. At the root of mantra, incantation, is the word of the *satguru*. At the root of all Liberation is the grace of the *satguru*. In this world all holy actions are rooted in the *satguru*. Therefore, he is to be constantly served with devotion for fulfillment.

For the *shishya* who devotedly remembers, "My guru is actually Siva Himself who grants Liberation," fulfillment is not far off. Look upon your *satguru* as mother, as father, as Siva. The *satguru*, it is to be declared in unmistakable terms, is the very Lord Himself. To approach the *satguru*, to worship the *satguru*, is to approach Siva, to worship Siva.

Why should I choose to manifest through the *satguru*? Why should I not act directly? I am really all-pervading, subtle, above the mind, with and without form, imperishable, of the form of ether, eternal and infinite. How can such a One be worshiped? That is why, out of compassion for My creations, I take the form of the *satguru*, and when so worshiped in devotion grant Liberation and fulfillment.

Because I have no binding form that is perceived by the human eye, I protect the *shishya*, revealing the dharma in the form of the guru. Therefore, the *satguru* is none other than the Supreme Siva enclosed in a human skin. Within him I walk the Earth concealed.

To the *jivas*, embodied souls laden with beclouding karmas, the *satguru* appears to be merely human. But to them whose karmas are auspicious, meritful, the *satguru* appears as Lord Siva Himself. The less fortunate do not recognize the *satguru* as the embodiment of Supreme Truth even when face to face with him, like the blind before the arisen sun.

But verily, the *satguru* is none other than Sadasiva. This is the truth.

I Myself am the Truth. Otherwise, who is it who gives fulfillment and Liberation? There is no difference between God Siva and Satsivaguru. It is ignorance to make such a distinction.

Gurus are of six kinds: 1) *preraka* is the "impeller" who instigates interest that leads to initiation; 2) *suchaka* is the "indicator" who describes the *sadhana* in which interest has been awakened; 3) *vachana* is the "explainer" who describes the process and its object; 4) *darshaka* is the "shower" who definitely points out the working and aims of the path in greater detail; 5) *shikshaka* is the "trainer" who actually instructs how to do *sadhana*; 6) *bodhaka* is the "illuminator," the *satguru* who lights in the *shishya* the lamp of spiritual knowledge. He is the cause of the other five.

The *Vedas* and shastras are many, but life is very short. Moreover, in this life there are millions of hindrances. Therefore, one should acquire only the essence of all shastras, just as the swan takes the milk out of water with which it has been mixed.

Neither the *Vedas* nor the philosophies are causes of Liberation. Realization alone is the cause of Liberation. Better it is to bear even a single life-inspiring great mantra taught by a *satguru* than to carry a load of lifeless blocks of wood which are various forms of worldly knowledge.

Only from the mouth of a *satguru* can a *jiva* realize the one immutable Brahman which has been taught by Siva Himself. Such knowledge cannot be attained through the study of even ten million shastras.

Many are the gurus who, like lamps, offer light in a house. But rare is the *satguru* who illumines the village like the sun. Many are the gurus who are proficient to the utmost in the *Vedas* and shastras. But rare is the *satguru* who has attained Parasiva. Many are the gurus on Earth who give what is other than the Self. But rare is the *satguru* who brings the atma to light. Many are the gurus who rob *shishyas* of their wealth. But rare is the *satguru* who removes the afflictions of the *shishya*.

He is the *satguru* in whose very presence there flows the supreme bliss called ananda. The intelligent person will choose such a one as *satguru* and none other.

FROM CHAPTER SIX

Guru Protocol

When entering the presence of a *satguru*, be calm of mind and devoted in the extreme. Dress traditionally or conservatively. Leave outside your sandals, umbrella, fan, make-up and other stimulating things.

If the spiritual preceptor speaks harshly, take it as a benediction. Whatever objects of enjoyment there be, offer these first to the guru and enjoy only what he leaves as *prasadam*.

To the *satguru* you shall not command or talk to as an equal. Do not enter into argument with those who deny your guru, nor even talk to them. Avoid them from afar. Do not sit in their company at any time. They are to be shunned.

What you hear elsewhere regarding mantras, tantras, *sadhana*, spiritual advice and scriptures, report to him and accept only what is approved by your guru, and reject what is not.

A satguru *sits in samadhi, immersed in pure consciousness, having withdrawn his awareness from the swirling forces of the world that surround him, radiating blessings and stabilizing humanity on Earth*

When he bestows confidential knowledge, do not speak of it to others, for sacred is secret. To talk of it is to weaken the *guru-shishya* understanding.

Even your own wealth you shall utilize only after mentally offering it to your *satguru*.

Do not lend your ear to any censure of your guru. Where such criticism appears, close your ears, leave immediately and chant his name to counteract.

Do not disrespect the retinue of a *satguru*. Do not criticize his traditions, whether based on the *Vedas*, *Agamas* or other scriptures.

In the presence of a *satguru*, take care to avoid dozing, harsh speech, ordering others, frivolous laughter, uncontrolled weeping, loosening or tightening of the clothes, informal or immodest dress, stretching of the legs toward him; debate, expressing hatred or blame. Avoid contortion of the body, whistling, striking of the hands in command, amusements, playful wrestling, smoking and the like. Such acts invoke the asuras in dreams and visions and invite calamity in your life.

To speak falsehood before the *satguru* is to commit the highest sin. In the absence of the *satguru* who is away or in distress, do not abandon him. Go wherever he commands.

When he stands below, do not yourself stand above. Do not walk or drive in front of him. Do not sit when he stands up. Do not sleep in his presence. Unless directed by him, do not speak, do not read, do not sing, do not eat there. Do nothing without bowing to him. Never fail to carry out his injunctions.

In the presence of your guru's guru, bow to your own guru mentally. Should you eat food without first mentally offering it to your *satguru*, it becomes impure. Do not approach him empty-handed. Offer in the measure of your capacity fruit, flowers, cloth and the like.

Guru Urgency

If atma itself does not keep atma from injury, then where in the world is the benefactor who can deliver atma from this sea of samsara? He who in this world does not undergo treatment for that disease which leads to lower-world states, what will he do with such disease when he goes to the next world, in which there is no medicine for this ailment?

The supreme Truth should be sought from the *satguru* so long as this body exists. Who is there so perverse as to commence the excavation of a well with a view to extinguish a fire which has already caught his house? Like a tigress, old age waits with open mouth to swallow the *jiva*.

As water continually exudes from a broken vessel, so is the period of life constantly being shortened. Diseases constantly inflict wounds like enemies laying siege to a fortress. Hence one should, as early as possible, engage in the working of good to oneself and *satguru*. Good work should be done in times when there is no sorrow or danger, and when the senses are not disabled.

Time passes in various involvements, but the *jiva* remains unaware of its passing. Happiness and sorrow born of samsara slay the *jiva*, but even then he does not awaken to the path of the welfare of the atma. How many *jivas* are born, fall into dangers, become subject to suffering and sorrow, and die? Even the sight of such does not enlighten the *jiva*, maddened as he is by drinking the wine of delusion as to what is his own good. Prosperity is like a dream, youth is short-lived like a flower, and life passes like a flash of lightning.

How can one be satisfied who has seen all of this? The utmost period of one's life is a hundred years. Half of it is passed in sleep, and the remaining half is made useless by childhood, disease, old age, sorrow and other causes.

Utterly indifferent to the spiritual work which ought to be begun by all means, sleeping during the time he should be awake, and imagining danger when he should have firm faith—alas! How can such a *jiva*, cherishing the fleeting samsara so dear to him, live without

Four Self-realized sages gather in a mango grove, radiant auras displaying their purity and refined consciousness. One among them may be a satguru.

In the presence of the *satguru* remain poised. Do not enter with desire. Serve him looking at his face. Do what he says. Honor wholeheartedly what he says and, when understood, do it without questioning.

Intensely devoted to the *satguru*, do not commission others for his work if you yourself can do it, even though you may have any number of attendants. Do not be proud because of class, learning or wealth. Knowing the mind of the *satguru*, be by his side, humble and cheerful of countenance.

Should you do anything in the presence of a *satguru* which is normally prohibited, it is extremely blameworthy. Do not, therefore, out of disregard, hear with the face turned away what the *satguru* says, whether it is beneficial or otherwise.

fear in this body which is as evanescent as a bubble of water, enduring no longer than the stay of a bird on the branch of a tree?

He seeks benefit from things which do him injury, thinks the impermanent to be permanent, sees the highest good in that which is evil, and yet he does not see that death is coming upon him.

Deluded by the great maya, the *jiva* looks and yet sees not, reads and yet knows not. The whole of this world is at each moment sinking into the deep sea of time infested with the great alligators of death and disease.

We speak of "my son," "my wife," "my wealth" and "my friend," but even as we indulge in such senseless talk, death seizes the body like a tiger. Death seizes a person while still engaged in doing this thing or that thing. Seeing all this, the awakened *jiva* does today the works of tomorrow, and in the forenoon the work of the afternoon, for death is indifferent to the finishing or unfinishing of any work.

The slumbering *jiva* does not see approaching him before his very eyes death's terrible army of diseases guided by old age and with orders from death himself. Death devours people after piercing them with the roasting skewer of thirsting desire, smearing them with the ghee of mundane objects, and barbecuing them in the fire of attachment and dislike. Death brings all under Yama's rule, both boy or youth, old man, or child in the womb. The visible world and all classes of beings therein thus remain vulnerable to death and subject to Yama, My emmissary.

Therefore, *jivas* awakened to the path should be prompt in doing with all their heart such things as are calculated to benefit their *satguru* and themselves in this world and hereafter.

FROM CHAPTER NINE

Divine Manifestation

Lord Siva said: How can My subtle perfection, which is one, omnipresent, attributeless, indifferent, undecaying, unattached like space, unbeginning and unending, be an object of worship for the dualistic mind? Hence it is that I, as the Supreme Guru, have entered into the bodies of human *satgurus*.

Even My gross aspect, being full of light and energy, is imperceptible to human eyes. For this reason I have assumed the form of the *satguru* in the world, and thus protect the race of *shishyas*.

As Mahesvara, in human body I secretly wander on the Earth in order to favor *shishyas*. As Sadasiva, I assume the modest and merciful form for the protection of *sadhakas*. Though remaining above samsara, yet I appear and act in this world as though I were a man of samsara.

When the fruits of sin predominate, *satguru* is seen as a person. And when the fruits of virtuous acts prevail, *satguru* is seen as Siva. Like blind men deprived forever of seeing the sun, unfortunate *jivas* are unable to see the real *satguru*, the embodiment of Mahesvara, though He is present before their eyes. It is undoubtedly true that Satguru is Deva Sadasiva Himself, for who is it that grants Liberation to seekers if *satguru* be not Siva Himself?

O Beloved, there is not the least difference between Deva Sadasiva and Sriguru. Whoever makes a distinction between them commits a sin. For by assuming the form of a preceptor, the Gurudeva severs the multitude of bonds which bind *jivas* to the state of *pashu* and enables them to attain the Self, Parasiva.

ART BY S. RAJAM

On the banks of the Ganga, a Sivaguru places his hands on the head of a swami candidate. A homa fire burns where the initiation rites will occur, after which the youth will don the orange cloth and holy beads being held by his spiritual brothers.

CHAPTER 16

The Chakras

Exploring the 14 Mystical Force Centers that Govern Awareness

There are fourteen great nerve centers in the physical body, in the astral body and in the body of the soul. These centers are called chakras in Sanskrit, which means "wheel." These spinning vortices of energy are actually regions of mind power, each one governing certain aspects of our inner being, and together they are the subtle components of people. When inwardly perceived, they are vividly colorful and can be heard. In fact, they are quite noisy. When awareness flows through any one or more of these regions, the various functions of consciousness operate, such as memory, reason and willpower. The physical body has a connection to each of the seven higher chakras through plexuses of nerves along the spinal cord and in the cranium. As the kundalini force of awareness travels the spine, it enters each of these chakras, energizing them and awakening in turn each function. By examining the functions of these great force centers, we can clearly cognize our own position on the spiritual path and better understand our fellow man.

In any one lifetime, one may predominantly be aware in two or three centers, thus setting the pattern for the way one thinks and lives. One develops a comprehension of these seven regions in a natural sequence, the perfection of one leading logically to the next. Thus, though we may not psychically be seeing spinning forces within ourself, we nevertheless mature through memory, reason, willpower, cognition, universal love, divine sight and spiritual illumination.

There are six chakras above the *muladhara*, which is located at the base of the spine. When awareness is flowing through these chakras, consciousness is in the higher nature. There are also seven chakras below the *muladhara*, and when awareness is flowing through them, consciousness is in the lower nature. The lower chakras are located between the coccyx and the heels. In this age, the Kali Yuga, most people live in the consciousness of the seven force centers below the *muladhara*. Their beliefs and attitudes strongly reflect the animal nature, the instinctive mind. Thus, the *muladhara* chakra, the divine seat of Lord Ganesha, is the dividing point between the lower nature and the higher. It is the beginning of religion for everyone, entered when consciousness arrives out of the realms below Lord Ganesha's holy feet. Through personal *sadhana*, prayer, meditation, right thought, speech and action and love of God, we lift our own consciousness and that of others into the chakras above the *muladhara*, bringing the mind into the higher nature.

The functions of the chakras are aspects of our being that we use every day. In the same way, we use our arms and hands everyday without thinking. Yet, if we study the physiology of the hands, we encounter layer after layer of intricate interrelationships of tissues, cells, plasma. We examine the engineering of the structural system of bones and joints, the energy transmission of the muscular system, the biochemistry of growth and healing, the biophysics of nerve action and reaction. Suddenly a simple and natural part of human life seems complex. Similarly, we use the various functions of consciousness, the chakras, every day without even thinking about them.

The chakras do not awaken. They are already awakened in everyone. It only seems as if they awaken as we become aware of flowing our energy through them, because energy, willpower and awareness are one and the same thing. To become conscious of the core of energy itself, all we have to do is detach awareness from the realms of reason, memory and aggressive, intellectual will; then turning inward, we move from one chakra to another. The physical body changes as these more refined energies flow through it. And the inner nerve conduits, *nadis,* inwardly become stronger.

It may help, as we examine each of these centers individually, to visualize ourselves as a seven-storied building, with each story being one of the chakras. Awareness travels up and down in the elevator, and as it goes higher and higher, it gains a progressively broader, more comprehensive and beautiful vista. Reaching the top floor, it views the panorama below with total understanding, not only of the landscape below, but also of the relation of the building to other buildings and of each floor to the next. Venturing below the *muladhara*, we enter the basement levels of consciousness.

Planetary Patterns: During each predominant age throughout history, one or another of the chakras has come into power. When the Greek God Cronus, the God of time, was worshiped, the mass consciousness came into memory—the *muladhara* chakra—with its new-found concern for time, for a past and a future, dates and records. Next the mass consciousness came into the *svadhishthana* and its powers of reason. Reason was a God in the Golden Age of Greece. Discourse, debate and logic all became instruments of power and influence. If it was not reasonable, it was not true. Next the chakra of will came into power. Man conquered nations, waged wars, developed efficient weapons. Crusades were fought and kingdoms established. Our world was experiencing force over force. Direct cognition, the *anahata* chakra, came when man opened the doors of science within his own mind. He cognized the laws of the physical universe: mathematics, physics, chemistry, astronomy and biology. Then he unfolded the mind sciences by looking into his subconscious mind, into the chakras where he had previously been. With man's look into his own mind, psychology, metaphysics and the mind-religions were born.

Now, in our present time, the mass consciousness is coming into *vishuddha*—the forces of universal love. The forerunners of this emerging Sat Yuga, popularly called the New Age, are not worshiping reason as the great thing of the mind or trying to take over another's possessions through the use of force. They are not worshiping science or psychology or the mind religions as the great panacea. They are looking inward and worshiping the light, the

1 Sahasrara

2 Ajna

3 Vishuddha

4 Anahata

5 Manipura

6 Svadishthana

7 Muladhara

8 Atala

9 Vitala

10 Sutala

11 Talatala

12 Rasatala

13 Mahatala

14 Patala

ART BY A. MANIVEL

Chakra man: *(right) The chakras are shown in their locations within the inner bodies of man, along with the attribute of each force center. The seven principal chakras are depicted as multi-petalled wheels or lotuses situated along the spinal cord, and the seven lower chakras as colored circles within the subtle body in regions below the spine, down to the feet. Above in the painting, is the heavenly realm of devas and Gods. Below is the Naraka realm of asuras.*

. . . .

established hierarchies founded on power or intellectual acumen. With that one needed balance, everything on the Earth will quiet down, because the *vishuddha* chakra is of the new age of universal love, in which everyone sees eye to eye, and if they do not, there will always be someone there to be the peacemaker. Look back through history and you will see how these planetary influences, these great mind strata of thought, have molded history and people.

Personal Patterns: The same cyclical pattern of development in human history is evident even more clearly in the growth of the individual. In the seven cycles of a person's life, beginning at the time of birth, awareness automatically flows through one of these chakras and then the next one, and then the next, provided a pure life is lived, following Sanatana Dharma under the guidance of a *satguru*. Each one experiences the chakras somewhat differently, depending upon the amount of kundalini force that is released. Non-religious people, who have a minimal amount of kundalini released, may experience the chakra only in its physical and emotional manifestation. Those who perform *sadhana* will experience the chakras in a much deeper way. Yogis performing *tapas*, serious austerities, would likely experience each chakra in the depths of their soul body.

In reality, most people never make it into the higher four chakras, but instead regress back time and again into the chakras of reason, instinctive will, memory, anger, fear and jealousy. Nevertheless, the natural, ideal pattern is as follows. From one to seven years of age, one is in the *muladhara* chakra learning the basics of movement, language and society. The patterns of the subconscious are established primarily in these early years. From seven to fourteen one is in the *svadhishthana* chakra. One reasons, questions and refines the ability to think for oneself. Between fourteen and twenty-one, one comes into willpower. The personality gets strong. Likes and dislikes solidify. Generally, about this time one wants to run away from home and express oneself. From twenty-one to twenty-eight one begins realizing responsibilities and gaining a new perspective of themselves and the world. Theoretically, one should be in *anahata*, the chakra of cognition, but a lot of people never make it.

If awareness is mature and full, however, having incarnated many, many times, one goes on at twenty-one to twenty-eight into the *anahata* chakra. Here we begin to understand "what it's all about." We comprehend our fellow men and women, their relationships, the world around us. We seek inwardly for more profound insight. This chakra is stabilized and smoothly spinning once one has raised one's family and performed one's social duty, and though one may yet continue in business, one would find the energies withdrawing nat-

Divinity, within their own body, within their own spine, within their own head, and they are going inward into a deep spiritual quest which is based on direct experience, on compassion for all things in creation.

As the forces of the *vishuddha* chakra come into prominence in the New Age, it does not mean that the other centers of consciousness have stopped working. But this new one coming into prominence is claiming the energy within the mass consciousness. When the center of divine love gains a little more power, everything will come into a beautiful balance. There will be a natural hierarchy of people based on the awakening of their soul, just as previous ages

Labels on illustration (top to bottom):
Illumination
Divine sight
Divine love
Direct cognition
Willpower
Reason
Memory
Fear & lust
Raging anger
Retaliatory jealousy
Prolonged confusion
Selfishness
Consciencelessness
Malice & murder

urally into the chest. It is most often the renunciate, the *mathavasi*, the *sannyasin*, who from twenty-eight to thirty-five or before, depending on the strictness of his *satguru*, comes into the *vishuddha* chakra, into inner light experiences, assuming a spiritual responsibility for himself and for others. This awakening soul appreciates people, loves them. His heart and mind broadly encompass all of humanity. He is less interested in what people do and more in what they are. It is here that, having withdrawn from the world, the world begins to renounce him. Then, from thirty-five to forty-two or before, he perfects his *sadhanas* and lives in the *ajna* chakra, experiencing the body of the soul, that body of light, awareness traveling within naturally at that time, withdrawing from mundane matters of the conscious mind. From forty-two through forty-nine he is getting established in the *sahasrara* chakra in a very natural way, having met all of the responsibilities through life.

Esoterically, there are seven more chakras above and within the *sahasrara*. Agamic Hindu tradition cites them as seven divisions of *Paranada*, inner sound. They are, from highest to lowest: *Unmana, Samana, Anasrita, Anatha, Ananta, Vyomanga* and *Vyapini*. These chakras are a conglomerate of *nadis* that slowly develop as a result of consistent and repetitive Self-Realization experiences.

The Seven Chakras of Higher Consciousness

Here we present a brief overview of each of the seven principal chakras, followed by the seven chakras below the *muladhara*.

1. Muladhara: The memory center, *muladhara*, located at the base of the spine, creates a consciousness of time through the powers of memory. Whenever we go back in our memory patterns, we are using the forces of the *muladhara*. It has four petals or aspects, one of which governs memories of past lives. The other three contain the compiled memory patterns and interrelated karmas of this life. This chakra is associated also with human qualities of individuality, egoism, physicality (including sexuality), materialism and dominance. A person lives predominantly in this chakra during the first seven years of life, acquiring language skills, relationships and cultural ways.

2. Svadishthana: Once the ability to remember has been established, the natural consequence is reason, and from reason evolves

the intellect. Reason is the manipulation of memorized information. We categorize it, edit it, rearrange it and store the results. People in this six-petaled chakra research, explore and wonder, "Why? Why? Why?" They propose theories and formulate rational explanations. They often form a rigid intellectual mind based upon opinionated knowledge and accumulated memory, reinforced by habit patterns of the instinctive mind. It is in this chakra that the majority of people live, think, worry and travel on the astral plane. We open naturally into this chakra between ages 8 and 14. This center controls the *muladhara*, as does each progressively higher chakra control those that lie below it.

3. Manipura: The third chakra is represented in the central nervous system by the solar plexus, where all nerves merge to form the "second brain." Of its ten petals, five face up and five face down. Correspondingly, depending on how the energy is flowing, the forces of willpower from this chakra add power either to worldly consciousness through the first two centers or to spiritual consciousness through the fourth and fifth centers. When awareness is confined to the realms of memory, reason and aggressive willpower, men and women are instinctive in nature. They are quick to react and retaliate, quick to have their feelings hurt and quick to pursue the conquest of others while fearing their own defeat. In these states of mind, the ego rises to its greatest prominence, and emotional experiences are extremely intense. Young adults from 14 to 21 discover willpower, willfulness and individuality as this chakra unfolds.

4. Anahata: The center of perception and insight is often referred to as "the lotus of the heart." Its 12 "petals" imply that cognition can be expressed in twelve distinct ways or through as many masks or personae. People abiding here are generally well-balanced, content and self-contained. Even when in day-to-day life they become involved in the seemingly fractured parts, they are able to look through it all and understand. They have a deep understanding of human nature, which brings effortless tolerance and an innate ability to help others, to resolve conflicts and confusions. Between ages 21 and 28, perceptions deepen and understanding matures for those who enter this chakra. Many people regress back into reason and memory. But, if awareness is mature, having incarnated many times, and well-trained all through youth, the soul proceeds smoothly into *anahata* consciousness.

5. Vishuddha: Universal or divine love is the faculty expressed by the *vishuddha* chakra. Whenever people feel filled with inexpressible love for and kinship with all mankind, all creatures large and

Castles of consciousness: *(counterclockwise from above) The* muladhara, svadishthana, manipura, anahata, vishuddha, ajna *and* sahasrara *chakras, showing their presiding deity and seed syllable*

small, they are vibrating within the sixteen-petaled *vishuddha*. When deeply immersed in this state, there is no consciousness of being a person with emotions, no consciousness of thoughts. One is just being the light or being fully aware of oneself as radiant force flowing through all form. One may sometimes see light throughout the entirety of the body. The exceptional soul who resides fully in this center, usually between the ages of 28 and 35, is able for the first time to withdraw awareness totally into the spine, into *sushumna*, the central spiritual current. Ultimately, he realizes that the inner being is the reality of himself.

6. Ajna: The sixth force center is called *ajna*. It is the "third eye," the center of divine sight and direct congition. Of its two "petals" or facets, one is the ability to look into the lower worlds or states of mind and the other is the perception of the higher worlds, or spiritual states, of consciousness. It, therefore, is the connecting link, allowing the awakened soul to relate the highest consciousness to the lowest in a unified vision. We open naturally into this chakra between ages 35 and 42.

7. Sahasrara: The seventh center at the top of the head is called the crown chakra. According to the ancient mystics, it governs 1,008 aspects or attributes of the soul body. These personae are transparent, a crystal-clear white light, ever present, shining through the circumference of the golden soul body. Here the soul dissolves even blissful visions of light and is immersed in pure space, pure awareness, pure being. Within the *sahasrara* is the Brahmarandhra, or "door of God," an aperture in the *sushumna nadi* through which the kundalini exits the body, catapulting the mind beyond and into *nirvikalpa* samadhi, and the truly pure spirit escapes the body at death. We open naturally into the crown chakra between ages 42 and 49.

Often when people get older, if they have not learned to sustain consciousness in the higher chakras, they start to drop in consciousness, returning to reason and trying to understand why all the things that happened to them in their lifetime happened as they did. They get stuck in the *muladhara* and spend years just remembering the past, reliving old experiences, good and bad alike. But more mature souls rightly fullfill life's two final stages: senior advisor and religious solitaire. They utilize their golden years to manifest higher-chakra faculties of love, light, inner vision and God Realization through service, *sadhana*, pilgrimage, worship and meditation.

The Seven Lower Chakras

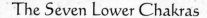

1. Atala: The first lower chakra, located in the hips, governs the state of mind called fear, which is truly a bottomless abyss. Someone in this consciousness fears death, fears life, even fears God and other people. This center is also the home of lust and promiscuity.

2. Vitala: Here anger predominates, and burning resentment. Anger comes from despair, confusion, frustration or lack of understanding. People in the consciousness of this chakra, centered in the thighs, are always wrathful, mad at the world, even angry at God.

3. Sutala: This chakra, found in the knees, governs jealousy, wanting what one can't have. Jealousy is a feeling of inadequacy, inferiority and helplessness. People in *sutala* consciousness covet everything, often deny the existence of God and are contentiously combative.

4. Talatala: Prolonged confusion dominates here, giving rise to instinctive willfulness: to get rather than give, to push others around and pursue materialistic advancement over all else. Greed and deceit prevail in this dog-eat-dog state of mind, centered in the calves.

5. Rasatala: This chakra of the ankles is the true home of the animal nature. Unmitigated selfishness prevails, of seeing to the well-being of "number one" first. The suffering of others is of no concern. Jealousy, anger and fear are intense, even high, states of consciousness.

6. Mahatala: This is the realm of conscience-lessness, or inner blindness to the effect of one's actions, of negativity and deep depression. Those living in this chakra of the feet steal freely, taking what they justify as theirs anyway, feeling that the world "owes them a living."

7. Patala: Here, in the soles of the feet, is the abode of destructiveness, revenge, murder for the sake of murder, torture and hatred expressed through harming the properties, minds, emotions and bodies of others. Hatred and scorn abide here. Malice reigns supreme. Reason seldom reaches this state of mind.

This is the story of our evolution through the mind—from the gross to the refined, from darkness into light, from a consciousness of death to immortality. We follow a natural pattern that is built right in the nerve system itself: memory; reason; will; direct cognition; inner light perceptions of the soul which give a universal love of all mankind; psychic perceptions through divine sight; and the heavenly refinement of being in the thousand-petaled lotus.

Recommended Resources: Tools for Tantra and Chakras: Energy Centers of Transformation, by Harish Johari, Inner Traditions International, Ltd., Rochester, Vermont 05767 USA; Theories of the Chakras: Bridge to Higher Consciousness, by Hiroshi Motoyama, and The Chakras, by C.W. Leadbeater, Theosophical Publishing House, 306 West Geneva Road, Wheaton, Illinois 60187 USA; The Chakra Handbook, by Shalila Sharamon and Bodo J. Baginski, Lotus Light, PO Box 2, Wilmot, Wisconsin 53129 USA

CHAPTER 17

Our Subtle Energy Highways

THERE ARE TWO BASIC ENERGY CURRENTS within our subtle body. These are *ida* and *pingala*, which surround a central major current, *sushumna*. The *ida* current is feminine and the channel of physical-emotional energy. When energy is flowing through *ida*, we are more conscious of the physical body. We are not in the world of thought but in the world of feeling. We feel strongly and experience strong emotions. The *pingala* current is masculine and the channel of intellectual-mental energy. When energy is flowing through the *pingala*, we are aware in the mind. We are inquisitive. We like to talk a lot. We tend to argue and to reason. *Sushumna* is the central energy current, rising through the spine up to the crown of the head. The life force within the *sushumna* becomes very powerful when the *ida* and *pingala* forces are balanced. Through yoga, the kundalini energy is awakened and made to rise up *sushumna* through each chakra to the *sahasrara* at the top of the head.

. . . .

Energy flow: *The* ida *current, pink in color, begins on the left side of the body, while the* pingala *current, blue, begins on the right. The* ida *and* pingala *cross at the chakras. The yellow current in the middle is the* sushumna, *the central source of energy. The kundalini energy can flow through the* ida *and* pingala. *This energy flow appears psychically like two serpents.*

A. MANIVEL

Insights from Scriptures, Saints And Scholars

The *sushumna* ascends upward and conducts prana. It is separated between the two sides of the palate. Uniting the prana with the syllable Om and the mind, the yogi ascends upward. And as he turns the tip of his tongue towards the palate and collects the sense-organs into a unity, he sees greatness. Through that he attains to the state of selflessness, and does not participate in joy or sorrow.

Krishna Yajur Veda, Maitrayana Upanishad 20

Where on the left guards *ida* and on the right the *pingala*. Between them is the chief spot. He who knows it, knows the Veda. Dustless, entering into Brahman, the *sushumna* is related to it. It's the pillow on which rest the 72,000 arteries.

Atharva Veda, Kshurika Upanishad 16-17

When the breaths of *ida*-moon and *pingala*-sun course their way unhindered through the spinal channel, your body will be imperishable, and abiding joys shall arise even here in this world below. This is the true way of Siva yoga. *Tirumantiram, verse 883*

The yogi ascends along the *sushumna* from chakra to chakra. The ascent is made gradually by patient efforts. Even a mere shaking of the opening of *sushumna* causes a great deal of bliss. You become intoxicated. You will entirely forget the world. When the opening of *sushumna* is shaken a bit, the kundalini *shakti* tries to enter *sushumna*. Great dispassion comes in. You will become fearless. When the *sushumna nadi* is working, i.e., when the breath flows through both the nostrils, meditation proceeds with ease and joy. The mind then is calm. When the mind is in the *sushumna*, the yogi is shut out from the objective, physical consciousness of the world. He is practically dead to the world, sees various visions and moves in the mental, ethereal space. Samadhi starts. *Swami Sivananda*

The *ida* and *pingala nadis* govern, on the physical level, responses of the sympathetic and parasympathetic nervous systems. Through controlled breathing in which life force is guided along the *pingala*, yogis can speed up their heart rate and metabolism and improve eyesight and hearing. And, through controlled breathing in which the life force is conducted along the *ida*, yogis can greatly slow down their metabolism. This can be pushed to the point where expert yogis can remain underground in an airtight container for hours, even days.

Georg Feuerstein, in The Yoga Tradition

A CURIOUS CORRELATION TO THE IDA, PINGALA AND SUSH-*umna* currents is found in the caduceus of Greek mythology. The caduceus was a winged staff with two serpents twined around it, carried by Hermes, messenger of the Gods, as a symbol of peace. Romans believed serpents discovered the secret of eternal life, interpreting shedding of skin as a return to youth. In modern times the caduceus was adopted as the physician's symbol and as the emblem of the US Army Medical Corps.

CHAPTER 18

The Human Aura

Understanding and Improving Your Colorful Emotional-Energy Field

The human aura extends out around the body from three to four feet, even from five to six feet in the case of more evolved souls. It is made up of a variety of vibratory rates or colors. Each area of the mind that awareness flows through reflects a change in these vibratory rates of colors in the human aura. When you have developed a certain psychic sight, by seeing through the eyes of the soul, you will be able to look at a person, see the aura around him and know immediately the area of the instinctive, intellectual or superconscious mind he is aware in at that particular time.

For instance, if someone's awareness was flowing through the realms of depression, that is, the area within the vast mind substance that contains the vibratory rate of depression, his aura would look rather gray, dim and dismal. If he was aware in the feeling of a beautiful love for all humanity, his aura would look light blue, fringed and tinged with yellow. However, if his love for humanity was of a superficial, emotional nature, being more idle talk and emotion than subsuperconscious compassion; his aura would be pink or reddish, telling you there was still a lot of instinctive fire, and should an upsetting circumstance occur, he could easily forget about universal love and become quite angry. Then the pink would turn to flaming red streaked with black. After this, if he were to feel remorseful about the emotional upheaval, the aura would turn to dark blue, and you could hardly see his face for the deep blue mist that would form around his body. If awareness was flowing through the area of the mind of inferiority and jealousy, the aura would be dark grayish-green in color. Someone with healing inclinations would have a pale green aura. A student increasing his intellectual knowledge would have an aura of brilliant yellow. The combinations are almost endless.

Several colors often appear in the aura at the same time. For example, the red of suppressed desire and seething anger might

appear along with the yellow of intellectual involvement. This person's head would be surrounded in yellow, and the lower part of his body streaked in red. Even a touch of very dark green might appear, showing that jealousy caused his anger. A devotee sitting in meditation, diligently working within himself, will in the course of half an hour change the colors of his aura from three to four to five times, as he moves his awareness from the instinctive-intellectual areas into the brilliancy of subsuperconscious realms. His aura will take on shades of light blue and light yellow interlaced with white. Then as he moves into superconsciousness, rays of light from the central source of energy will begin to emerge from the core of his spine and flood out through his aura and penetrate the atmosphere of the room. You feel his presence as darshan. The sub of the subconscious mind, the home of deep-seated, often emotionally charged impressions, has an aura of its own deep within the outer aura that we have been describing. It is seen "within" the physical body itself and is different from the daily emotional-intellectual aura which appears around the physical body as a result of awareness being in one area of the mind or another. All the reactionary conditions of our past which are currently reacting in our subconscious mind are reflected in the colors of this inner subconscious aura.

The big question always arises, "How do we know whether or not we are seeing an aura, or if it is just our imagination?" The colors around the person are first seen within your own mind. You would not clearly see them around their physical body. Later, after becoming adjusted to this new form of sight, you may see colors around an individual's physical body. Where do these colors come from? All things in the mind are sound and color. Look around you and observe each vibratory rate of every physical object as having a sound as well as a color. Everything is sound. Everything is color. Everything is shape. Therefore, in the refined areas of the mind, all things are color and all things are sound, recognizable through the sixth sense of the all-seeing eye. This faculty is always awake. You only have to learn how to be aware of and use it, in a similar way an artist must learn to distinguish with his physical eyes between one shade of color and another and between the dimensions in a painting. The mystic learns how to use his already developed sixth sense, his third eye. It is used all the time, constantly, day in and day out, though not consciously. For example, someone may walk into your home. You look at them and say, "You are not feeling very well today. You seem disturbed." How do you know? Inside yourself you are seeing their aura. If they enter looking bright and shiny, you know how they feel inside because you see their aura.

Some people are born with psychic sight and maintain it

malice, hatred
service
pure spirituality
anger, rage
high devotion
selfish desire
superficial emotion
jealousy, envy
lust, sensuality
high intellect
devotion
healing inclination
universal love
religious teachings

ILLUSTRATION ORIGINALLY APPEARS IN HANDS OF LIGHT (TM), BY BARBARA BRENNAN (SM), ILLUSTRATED BY JOS A. SMITH, BANTAM BOOKS

throughout their lifetime. As this faculty was developed in a prior birth, the wisdom and understanding of its proper use comes naturally to them. But more commonly, psychic sight develops slowly, almost imperceptibly, through an unbroken continuity of *sadhana*. Through the unveiling grace of Lord Siva we are allowed to see what needs to be seen at the proper time in our life when we can sustain the resultant reactions. Generally, if you do have this awakened inner perception of auras, you would only notice someone's aura if it were peculiarly dull or strongly radiant. A mystic who has control of this faculty does not generally see auras all of the time, but just when he wants to.

Auric Cleansing: You as a devotee have often gone to the temple with your problems and placed them at the feet of the Deity. In the unseen world of the Devaloka what actually happens is that the Deity and His many devas work with your problems by working with your aura, most especially the inner aura, by disintegrating or clearing up any congestion they find. From the inner sanctum, they lighten the darker colors, which were created by traveling through troubled states of mind, infusing them with rays of white and violet light. We rarely see this happening, but we can certainly feel it, and we depart the temple feeling relieved and freed from congestion and worry.

You can also flood your aura with rays of white and violet light, just like the Deities and devas do. If you are in a negative mood because of having just become angry with somebody because you were jealous of them, there is a remedy that you can perform for yourself. Your aura is now brownish with murky, dirty green, possibly accented with black and red sparks. To counteract this heaviness, just add white. Visualize white light flooding out from the center of your spine into and through your aura. Visualize violet rays flooding into your new white aura, invigorating and cutting through the darkness. When you go, as pure awareness, right into the center of your spine and flood white mind-substance out into your aura, the white mixes with the black, and gray appears in your aura. Immediately you experience fear, but this emotion soon passes as more white enters the aura. The gray soon disappears. As still more white enters the aura, the flaming red of anger turns to the pink shades of tolerance and compassion. The dark browns and the murky dark green of jealousy turn to the emerald green of confidence and humility. A feeling of peace and contentment comes as the new colors react back on the emotions. It takes but a little effort on your part, a little concentration, persistence and faith in your ability to change your own mood by a positive effort of will. You have no doubt experienced difficulty in getting up in the morning. What is the remedy for this? Flood your aura with red, of course. A nice, bright red. It doesn't take much effort to visual-

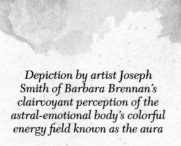

Depiction by artist Joseph Smith of Barbara Brennan's clairvoyant perception of the astral-emotional body's colorful energy field known as the aura

Reading: Man Visible and Invisible, C.W. Leadbeater, The Theosophical Publishing House, 306 West Genevea Road, Wheaton, Illinois 60187 USA. **Hands of Light,** Barbara Ann Brennan, Bantam Books, 666 Fifth Avenue, New York, New York 10103 USA. **The Raiment of Light, A Study of the Human Aura,** David Tansley, Routledge & Kegan Paul, Ltd., 11 New Fetter Lane, London, EC4P 4EE, London, United Kingdom.

ize the color red. You will know that you have succeeded when all of a sudden your physical vitality awakens and you feel invigorated and ready to jump up for a wonderful day. All of us at one time or another experience mental laziness. What is the remedy? Simply flood your aura with yellow by visualizing yellow light all around you, and soon you will be drawn into the thinking area of the mind and be able to progressively pursue your studies. Visualizing orange strengthens your intellectual aggressiveness because red is added to the yellow.

If your child is crying uncontrollably and you can't get to sleep, what color would you bless him with? Would you get angry and yell, "Why don't you go to sleep! I told you, you're disturbing your father!" Flashes of red? The child would be terrified. No, you would harmonize the child's emotions with shades of blue and pale green. Beating, berating and insulting of children does permanent damage to their aura. C.W. Leadbeater described one case of a child tormented by a teacher. "The child's aura changed and twisted about horribly, and when it was still again, all the beautiful little shoots of lovely color had disappeared, and in their place were innumerable little scars, harm done which could not be cancelled in the present life." The colors of deep red, representing suppressed anger, and the grays and black of fear and hatred would now permanently predominate.

You can familiarize yourself with the individual physical, mental and spiritual effect of each color by simply looking at one color after another and experiencing the results. Each color and the emotions it reflects are like two sides of the same coin. Learn them so well that the thought of one immediately brings the idea of the other. For example, how do you feel when you enter a room that is painted blue? White? Yellow? Place before you a piece of paper of the color you wish to visualize. Look at the paper and then close your eyes and try to see the exact same color in your mind. Then open your eyes and look at the paper again and, with eyes still open, turn your head away from the paper and try to see the color in your conscious mind. Literally fill your mind with the color of the paper. After you have accomplished this exercise with one color, repeat it with another, then another and then another.

Protecting Your Aura: Each color has its own special protective qualities, which can be chosen to counteract or balance out the particular vibrations you are or will be experiencing. Let's take the example of protecting yourself from the auric emanations of persons

Barbara Brennan's Hands of Light

SUSAN ORISTAGLIO

As a child, Barbara Brennan would practice walking blindfold in the woods of her family's Wisconsin farm. "I would feel the trees long before I could touch them," she recalls. "They were larger than they appeared to the visible eye." She learned to see this energy field, as well as that around small animals. Later in life she earned a master's degree in atmospheric physics and then worked for NASA for a number of years. Unsatisfied, she trained as a counselor and started helping people. Her forgotten ability to see energy fields returned. "I became skeptical and confused. Were they really there? Did they have meaning? Was it wishful thinking, or was I experiencing another dimension of reality that had meaning, was orderly and was very helpful in understanding my present life circumstances and, in fact, life as a whole?" She persevered and sought out the esoteric literature, such as that of the great theosophist, C.W. Leadbeater, which confirmed her experiences.

Her clairvoyant ability to see auras helped her counseling work immensely, for she was able to diagnose physical, emotional, mental and spiritual difficulties just by observing the aura of her patients. Especially she could see how a person's disease was actually caused by emotional and mental blocks. Some of what she has seen is depicted in the paintings below. As with other clairvoyants, who can always be found among the general population, she teaches that anyone can develop the ability; indeed, everyone already possesses it to some extent.

who are ill, a condition you will encounter if you visit a hospital. You can easily counteract this influence by flooding your aura with colors of health and physical strength. This will not only protect you, but it will also improve the condition of those around you. How do you do this? Become aware of your spine and visualize a stream of white light in its center, from the base to the top of your head. Then mentally draw from this pure white light warm red and vibrant pink. As a healing power, visualize pale green surrounding the patient, a color many modern hospitals have adopted to invoke healing. To increase your vitality even more, visualize yourself effortlessly performing some strenuous physical or athletic feat, and you will soon feel the energy rising within you.

Bright oranges and yellows will bring a new energy which will enhance your intellect and protect you from being overpowered by the intellectual force of someone else. This is also a way to help overcoming shyness. Surrounded by a vibrant aura, charged with bright orange and yellow, you are a secure and confident individual, able to enter into discussion with a new self-assurance. The vibrations of others tend to rebound from your aura. You are relaxed and friendly, and intelligence pours forth uninhibitedly from you.

The colors used to harmonize and protect the emotional nature are light blue and violet. By flooding your aura with beautiful sky blue and vivid violet, you quiet your own lower emotions and feelings and become impervious to the negative feelings and moods of those around you. With the advent of these colors, your individual awareness is transported into the more refined, uplifting realms of the superconscious mind. Always remember that by flooding your aura with bright sky-blue and lavender you are automatically building an armor to protect yourself from their lower feelings and passions, such as anger, jealousy, hatred and lust. So, now make a study of bright, clear blues and violets and select the ones that appeal to you the most. Intuitively you will know which shades are best for you. Beautiful shades of blue and violets will always be found in the auras of successful teachers, missionaries, social workers and those who work among those of lesser emotional and mental refinement than their own. When someone becomes angry at you, or you become angry with someone, they are actually cursing you astrally, or you them. This is because powerful

From Barbara Brennan's Perceptions

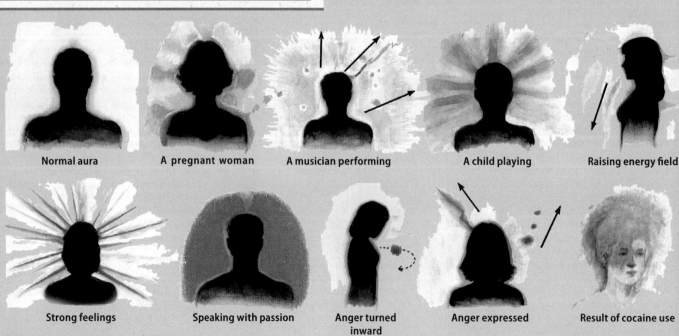

Normal aura

A pregnant woman

A musician performing

A child playing

Raising energy field

Strong feelings

Speaking with passion

Anger turned inward

Anger expressed

Result of cocaine use

THE ABOVE ILLUSTRATIONS ORIGINALLY APPEAR IN HANDS OF LIGHT (TM), E
BARBARA BRENNAN (SM), ILLUSTRATED BY JOS A. SMITH, BANTAM BOOK

vibrations of red and black, grays and muddy, brownish greens are being sent from one person to another. Truly, this hurts, and bad karma is made.

Our holy scriptures tell us that we must purify our intellects. That means that we must lighten up the colors that are within our subconscious and sub of the subconscious mind. When the intellect is finally purified, the outer aura shows many pastel colors in and through it. The permanent, inner aura will be filled with beautiful patterns of golden yellow, blue and lavender. But once the intellect is purified, good mental maintenance must occur daily so that congested areas are not recreated out of habit. This is the great value of a regulated religious life and daily *sadhana*.

To keep the colors of our subconscious and sub-subconscious refined, our religion tells us to go on a long pilgrimage once a year. This means we take our inner aura that has been building up through the year and place it at the feet of the Deity at some far-off temple. While on the pilgrimage, we are able to collect all its colors, emotions and deep feelings and leave them, along with our offering of fruit and flowers, at the God's holy feet to be disintegrated by Him. To keep the colors of our subconscious and sub-subconscious refined, our religion tells us to read scriptures daily because their high-minded thoughts and concepts bring purple, lavender, pink and yellow into our aura.

To keep the colors of our subconscious and sub-subconscious refined, our religion tells us to perform puja daily to personally invoke the higher beings in the Devaloka at our own home shrine and obtain their blessings. It may interest you to know that such blessings lighten not only the aura of each one in the household but also the physical building itself. To keep the colors of our subconscious and sub-subconscious refined, our religion tells us to provide the essential sacraments in life for the children so that the permanent impressions of these special combinations of color and sound are placed into the inner aura of the sub-subconscious mind and added to the ones that are already there from previous impressions.

The Occult World of C.W. Leadbeater

IN HIS BOOK *MAN VISIBLE and Invisible,* published in 1925, the great psychic and theosophist C.W. Leadbeater illustrated and explained at length his profound experience of the human aura. His was not a new discovery. But in the past such psychic revelations, which have been experienced by individuals of all religions, were largely kept secret, spoken of privately and passed from guru to disciple. Leadbeater and fellow theosophists Annie Besant and Madam Blavatsky, who had advanced clairvoyant abilities, were among the first write about and attempt to illustrate the human aura, the chakras and thought forms. At about the same time, Swami Panchadasi of India came to America and published in 1912 *The Human Aura*, a profound exposition.

Leadbeater sought not to establish a new religion. Rather, he wrote, he wanted to awaken "the inner faculties as yet latent in the majority of mankind" so that each person could independently investigate and verify the worlds beyond the physical plane.

"I am perfectly aware that the world at large is not yet convinced of the existence of this power of clairvoyant sight," wrote Leadbeater. "But I also know that all who have really studied the question have found the evidence for it irresistible. To those who are daily in the habit of exercising this higher vision in a hundred different ways, the denial of the majority that such sight is possible naturally seems ridiculous. It is as if a blind man came up to us and assured us there was no such thing as ordinary physical sight, and that we were deluded in supposing that we possessed this faculty."

From C.W. Leadbeater's Perceptions

The aura of a devotional person, with lower portions betraying selfishness

A wave of strong and pure affection sweeping over a person

A person consumed in Intense anger

A person in love. Lust and jealousy show in the lower half with affection and devotion in upper areas.

CHAPTER 19

Death and Dying

The Hindu View of the Grand Departure and Its Sacred Rites of Passage

EAD ME FROM DARKNESS TO LIGHT, FROM DEATH to immortality." This famed Vedic prayer proclaims the human urge to survive, to conquer death and to know the joys of illuminated consciousness. People often pilgrimage to an isolated place in expectation of a vision, be it a jungle of fauna and foliage or cement and glass. Every person is on a vision quest. But for all souls, at the time of the great departure, *mahaprasthana,* a vision comes as a tunnel of light at the end of which are beings of divine nature.

Many, having had a near-death experience, have sworn their testimony of such transforming encounters. An American woman who "died" during childbirth, but was brought back to life by quick medical action, recounted: "It was an incredible energy—a light you wouldn't believe. I almost floated in it. It was feeding my consciousness feelings of unconditional love, complete safety and complete, total perfection. And then, and then, a piece of knowledge came in—it was that I was immortal, indestructible. I cannot be hurt, cannot be lost, and that the world is perfect." Hundreds of people report similar experiences, affirming what Hinduism has always taught—that death is a blissful, light-filled transition from one state to another, as simple and natural as changing clothes, far from the morbid, even hellish alternatives some dread. A Vedic funeral hymn intones: "Where eternal luster glows, the realm in which the light divine is set, place me, Purifier, in that deathless, imperishable world. Make me immortal in that realm where movement is accordant to wish, in the third region, the third heaven of heavens, where the worlds are resplendent" (*Rig Veda,* **Aitareya Aranyaka** 6-11).

Most often, before our own death, we encounter its reality in the passing of friends or family. Our thoughts during the rites, termed *antyeshti* samskara in Sanskrit, turn to God. We witness the end of another's life and ask, "What am I going to do with the remaining years of my own life?" All that is said during these times reminds us that life on earth is temporary. All our possessions, power, ego and learning will end. Seeing this truth we turn the mind toward God, toward life's ultimate goal, moksha, liberation, and toward the path of dharma that will take us there. We do this not in trepidation, but in assurance, faith and gratitude for the opportunity to progress spiritually in this physical incarnation.

Death is defined differently according to what people believe themselves to be. If they are only the body and brain (as with humanists or atheists), then death is the end of sensory experience, of self. If we live once, death ends our only sojourn on Earth and is naturally dreaded. If we are born again and again, it loses its dread in light of the soul's pilgrimage to eternity. No matter how ill, how infirm our condition, there is a serene and consoling center of our being to which we can adjourn, the Source within. It is more us than our body, more us than our mind and emotion. It will not die. It does not hurt or fear. As physical debility and death draw near, we seek this center, whether we call it Paramatma, God, Self or Divine Consciousness. In the *Krishna Yajur Veda, Katha Upanishad,* Yama, Lord of Death, explains: "Death is a mere illusion

SUBODH MAHESWARI

which appears to those who cannot grasp Absolute Reality. The soul is immortal, self-existent, self-luminous and never dies."

It is the soul's subtle body, *linga sharira,* that stores the "thought-energy" experiential impressions of life, called samskaras. When the body dies, this nonphysical sheath continues as a constellation of subtle elements—dispositions, memories, desires, etc. It is within this subtle body that the soul, if needed, reincarnates, as described in the *Shukla Yajur Veda, Brihadaranyaka Upanishad* (4.4.5-6): "A man acts according to the desires to which he clings. After death he goes to the next world bearing in his mind the subtle impressions of his deeds; and after reaping there the harvest of his deeds, he returns again to this world of action. Thus, he who has desires continues subject to rebirth." Death, according to

Hinduism, is not the contradiction of life. Death and birth are two sides of life's cosmic cycle. The culmination of that cycle is liberation. As the venerable Satguru Yogaswami of Sri Lanka taught: "By getting rid of desire, man can put an end to birth altogether."

Resolving Karmas: Many who have had a near-death experience speak of having come back to complete unfinished obligations to children, parents or friends. It is a great blessing to know of one's impending transition. A Hindu approaching death works diligently to finish all his "business" of this lifetime, the allotted portion of his total karma carried into this birth to face and resolve. If death

Grand departure: *A soul detaches from the body (dressed in red) at the time of death in its subtle body (draped in blue). Keeping vigil, a swami reads from Hindu scripture.*

has entered life's final stage, that of the renunciate, or sannyasin.

Making the Transition Consciously: Knowing that a conscious death is the ideal, the Hindu avoids excessive drugs or mind-numbing medical measures. He cultivates detachment as death approaches, knowing that loss is not suffered when something is given up voluntarily, only when it is taken from us by force. He is grateful for life, but not angry with or fearful of death. Dying is not unlike falling asleep. We have all experienced death many times in past lives. The astral body separates from the physical body, just as in sleep. The difference is that the silver cord connecting the two breaks at the moment of transition, signaling the point of no return.

Scriptures speak of leaving the body through one chakra or another, departing in a level of consciousness of a particular chakra, which then determines where in the inner worlds a person will find himself after death. Those who depart full of hatred and resentment go to the world of those who also died in lower consciousness. Those with love in their heart enter a world where abide others with similar attainment. Therefore, during transition a person must strive to be in the highest possible state of consciousness, concentrating on the top of the head and holding to lofty thoughts as he succumbs. A woman in California narrated: "Shortly before my husband died, he held my hands and asked me to recite the *Lalitha Sahasranama* and to say the mantra we were initiated into. He repeated after me in a loud voice when suddenly his face began to shine with a luster, and he became overjoyed and beaming. He started almost shouting in joy that he was seeing the temple and the Deities—Siva, Ganesha and Murugan—smiling at him. In this glowing way he passed away shortly thereafter while I recited the mantra in his ear."

Those who die suddenly, through accident or murder, have no time to prepare. Traditionally, full death rites are not performed after such deaths, because rebirth is expected almost immediately. For the same reason, rites are not accorded children who die young, before adolescence. In India, bodies of accidental-death victims and children are buried in a common grave or put in a river. Since neither is possible in Westernized countries, cremation is accepted.

Funeral and Memorial Rites: Hindus traditionally cremate their dead, for swifter, more complete release of the soul. Burial, which preserves the bond, is generally forbidden. Death's anniversary is called Liberation Day. For saints, it is celebrated rather than the day of birth. To some extent, the funeral rites serve to notify the departed soul that he has, in fact, died. It is possible for a disoriented soul, not understanding that he is on the other side, to linger close to the physical plane. He can still see this material world, and even observe his own funeral. Some of the ritual chants address the deceased, urging him to relinquish attachments and continue the journey. The rites are also for the living, allowing the family to say a respectable and dignified "farewell," to express grief, loss and the mosaic of emotions they naturally encounter. The deepest significance of the funeral rites lies in their yoking the inner and outer worlds, Bhuloka and Devaloka, and their recognition that a family consists not just of its living generations, but its ancestors as well. Often a group of souls will sequentially incarnate into the same extended family, so that, for example, a grandson may be the returned soul of the father. In this way collective karma and dharma are worked through. Those in the inner worlds help relatives living in the outer world. When their turn comes in the outer world, they strive to attain spiritual progress that is only possible in physical incarnation. Ceremonial uniting of the deceased with his forefathers and yearly honoring of ancestors keep open the inner communication which makes the family prosperous and preserves its longevity.

The *Vedas* proclaim, "When a person comes to weakness, be it through old age or disease, he frees himself from these limbs just as a mango, a fig or a berry releases itself from its stalk" (*Shukla Yajur Veda, Brihadharanyaka Upanishad* 4.3.36).

comes while loose ends remain (misunderstandings unresolved, misdeeds unatoned for or obligations unfulfilled), another lifetime may be required to expire that karma. Thus, an aging or ailing Hindu will be seen going around to friends and enemies, giving love, help and blessings, working to resolve conflicts and differences, offering apologies and fulfilling all known obligations. Ideally, he executes his own will, distributing his properties and duties to heirs, charities and endowments, not leaving such tasks to others.

That done, he turns to God, reads scriptures, attends temple and amplifies meditation and devotion. He may pilgrimage to sacred spots or retire to a secluded place to practice *japa* and yoga *sadhanas*. The family takes care not to disturb these efforts, nor his retirement from social obligation or interaction, realizing he

Rites of Transition

HINDU DEATH RITU-als in all traditions follow a fairly uniform pattern drawn from the *Vedas,* with variations according to sect, region, caste and family tradition. Most rites are fulfilled by the family, all of whom participate, including the children, who need not be shielded from the death. Certain rites are traditionally performed by a priest but may also be performed by the family if no priest is available. Here is a simple outline of rites that can be performed by Hindus in any locality. Variations are noted and suggestions made for Hindus in Western countries.

1. As Death Approaches
Traditionally, a Hindu dies at home. Nowadays the dying are increasingly kept in hospitals, even when recovery is clearly not possible. Knowing the merits of dying at home among loved ones, Hindus bring the ill home. When death is imminent, kindred are notified. The person is placed in his room or in the entryway of the house, with the head facing east. A lamp is lit near his head and he is urged to concentrate on his mantra. Kindred keep vigil until the great departure, singing hymns, praying and reading scripture. If he cannot come home, this happens at the hospital, regardless of institutional objections.

2. The Moment of Death
If the dying person is unconscious at departure, a family member chants the mantra softly in the right ear. If none is known, "Aum Namo Narayana" or "Aum Nama Sivaya" is intoned. (This is also done for sudden-death victims, such as on a battlefield or in a car accident.) Holy ash or sandal paste is applied to the forehead, Vedic verses are chanted, and a few drops of milk, Ganga or other holy water are trickled into the mouth. After death, the body is laid in the home's entryway, with the head facing south, on a cot or the ground—reflecting a return to the lap of Mother Earth. The lamp is kept lit near the head and incense burned. A cloth is tied under the chin and over the top of the head. The thumbs are tied together, as are the big toes. In a hospital, the family has the death certificate signed immediately and transports the body home. Under no circumstances should the body be embalmed or organs removed for use by others. Religious pictures are turned to the wall, and in some traditions mirrors are covered. Relatives are beckoned to bid farewell and sing sacred songs at the side of the body.

3. The Homa Fire Ritual
If available, a special funeral priest is called. In a shelter built by the family, a fire ritual (*homa*) is performed to bless nine brass *kumbhas* (water pots) and one clay pot. Lacking the shelter, an appropriate fire is made in the home. The "chief mourner" leads the rites. He is the eldest son in the case of the father's death and the youngest son in the case of the mother's. In some traditions, the eldest son serves for both, or the wife, son-in-law or nearest male relative.

4. Preparing the Body
The chief mourner now performs *arati,* passing an oil lamp over the remains, then offering flowers. The male (or female, depending on the gender of the deceased) relatives carry the body to the back porch, remove the clothes and drape it with a white cloth. (If there is no porch, the body can be sponge bathed and prepared where it is.) Each applies sesame oil to the head, and the body is bathed with water from the nine *kumbhas,* dressed, placed in a coffin (or on a palanquin) and carried to the *homa* shelter. The young children, holding small lighted sticks, encircle the body, singing hymns. The women then walk around the body and offer puffed rice into the mouth to nourish the deceased for the journey ahead. A widow will place her *tali* (wedding pendant) around her husband's neck, signifying her enduring tie to him. The coffin is then closed. If unable to bring the body home, the family arranges to clean and dress it at the mortuary rather than leave these duties to strangers. The ritual *homa* fire can be made at home or kindled at the crematorium.

5. Cremation
Only men go to the cremation site, led by the chief mourner. Two pots are carried: the clay *kumbha* and another containing burning embers from the *homa.* The body is carried three times counterclockwise around the pyre, then placed upon it. All circumambulating, and some *arati,* in the rites is counterclockwise. If a coffin is used, the cover is now removed. The men offer puffed rice as the women did earlier, cover the body with wood and offer incense and ghee. With the clay pot on his left shoulder, the chief mourner circles the pyre while holding a fire brand behind his back. At

---

Kasi, the holiest place to die: *A man awaits his great departure; at the moment of death Ganga water is trickled into the mouth at the Mukti Bhavan free hospice; cremation grounds; women in mourning.*

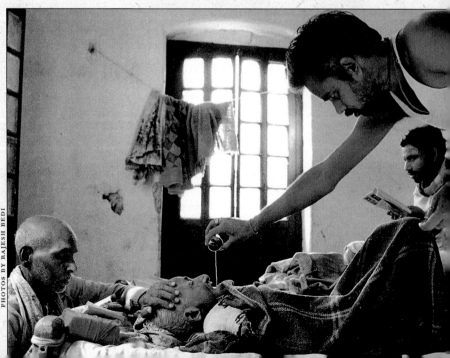

PHOTOS BY RAJESH BEDI

ach turn around the pyre, a relative knocks a hole in the pot with a knife, letting water out, signifying life's leaving its vessel. At the end of three turns, the chief mourner drops the pot. Then, without turning to face the body, he lights the pyre and leaves the cremation grounds. The others follow. At a gas-fueled crematorium, sacred wood and ghee are placed inside the coffin with the body. Where permitted, the body is carried around the chamber, and a small fire is lit in the coffin before it is consigned to the flames. The cremation switch then is engaged by the chief mourner.

. Return Home; Ritual Impurity

Returning home, all bathe and share in cleaning the house. A lamp and water pot are set where the body lay in state. The water is changed daily, and pictures remain turned to the wall. The shrine room is closed, with white cloth draping all icons. During these days of ritual impurity, family and close relatives do not visit others' homes, though neighbors and relatives bring daily meals to relieve the burdens during mourning. Neither do they attend festivals and temples, visit swamis, nor take part in marriage arrangements. Some observe this period up to one year. For the death of friends, teachers or students, observances are optional. While mourning is never suppressed or denied,

scriptures admonish against excessive lamentation and encourage joyous release. The departed soul is acutely conscious of emotional forces directed at him. Prolonged grieving can hold him in earthly consciousness, inhibiting full transition to the heaven worlds. In Hindu Bali, it is shameful to cry for the dead.

7. Bone-Gathering Ceremony

About 12 hours after cremation, family men return to collect the remains. Water is sprinkled on the ash; the remains are collected on a large tray. At crematoriums the family can arrange to personally gather the remains: ashes and small pieces of white bone called "flowers." In crematoriums these are ground to dust, and arrangements must be made to preserve them. Ashes are carried or sent to India for deposition in the Ganges or placed them in an auspicious river or the ocean, along with garlands and flowers.

8. First Memorial

On the 3rd, 5th, 7th or 9th day, relatives gather for a meal of the deceased's favorite foods. A portion is offered before his

photo and later ceremonially left at an abandoned place, along with some lit camphor. Customs for this period are varied. Some offer *pinda* (rice balls) daily for nine days. Others combine all these offerings with the following *sapindikarana* rituals for a few days or one day of ceremonies.

Yama: Lord of Death

BADRI NARAYAN

9. The 31st-Day Memorial

On the 31st day, a memorial service is held. In some traditions it is a repetition of the funeral rites. At home, all thoroughly clean the house. A priest purifies the home, and performs the *sapindikarana,* making one large pinda (representing the deceased) and three small, representing the father, grandfather and great grandfather. The large ball is cut in three pieces and joined with the small *pindas* to ritually unite the soul with the ancestors in the next world. The *pindas* are fed to the crows, to a cow or thrown in a river for

the fish. Some perform this rite on the 11th day after cremation. Others perform it twice: on the 31st day or (11th, 15th, etc.) and after one year. Once the first *sapindikarana* is completed, the ritual impurity ends. Monthly repetition is also common for one year.

10. One-Year Memorial

At the yearly anniversary of the death (according to the moon calendar), a priest conducts the *shraddha* rites in the home, offering *pinda* to the ancestors. This ceremony is done yearly as long as the sons of the deceased are alive (or for a specified period). It is now common in India to observe *shraddha* for ancestors just prior to the yearly Navaratri festival. This time is also appropriate for cases where the day of death is unknown.

Hindu funeral rites can be simple or exceedingly complex. These ten steps, devotedly completed according to the customs, means, and ability of the family, will properly conclude one earthly sojourn of any Hindu soul.

Recommended Resources: **Caring for Your own Dead,** Lisa Carlson, Upper Access Publishers, PO Box 457, Hinesburg, Vermont 05461. **Dialogue with Death,** Eknath Easwaran, Nilgiri Press, Box 477, Petaluma, California 94953. **Funeral and Other Sacraments After Death,** Jnana Prabodhini, 510 Sadashiv Petha, Pune 411 030, India. **Grihya Sutras,** Sacred Books of the East Series, Motilal Banarsidass, Bungalow Road, Jawaharnagar, New Delhi 7, India. **Hindu Samskaras,** Dr. Raj Bali Pandy, Motilal Banarsidass. **Life After Life,** Raymond A. Moody, Bantam Books, 1540 Broadway, New York, New York 10036. **Meditation and the Art of Dying,** Pandit Usharbudh Arya, Himalayan Institute, Honesdale, Pennsylvania 18431. **The Transition Called Death,** Charles Hampton, Theosophical Publishing House, 306 West Geneva Rd, Wheaton, Illinois 60187. **Dilemmas of Life and Death,** S. Cromwell Crowley, SUNY Press, Albany, New York 12240.

CHAPTER 20

Life After Death

Hindu Metaphysics' Answers to
Universal Questions about the "End of Life"

ART BY A. MANIVEL; BACKGROUND PHOTO, COREL

Death is the most fateful experience of each of our lives. But no Hindu really fears death, nor does he look forward to it. Death for the Hindu is merely transition, simultaneously an end and a new beginning. Over two thousand years ago Saint Tiruvalluvar wrote that "Death is like falling asleep, and birth is like awakening from that sleep." In one of the ancient languages of our religion, the physical body had a name which literally meant "that which is always dropping off." When key truths are understood and accepted about the nature of the soul and the cycles of birth, life, dying, death, afterlife and rebirth, all sense of foreboding and fear of death perish. Here we explore those realities.

What is the Eastern perspective on Death?

For Hindus, death is nobly referred to as *mahaprasthana,* the "great journey." When the lessons of this life have been learned and karmas reach a point of intensity, the soul leaves the physical body, which then returns its elements to the earth. The awareness, will, memory and intelligence which we think of as ourselves continue to exist in the soul body. Death is a most natural experience, not to be feared. It is a quick transition from the physical world to the astral plane, like walking through a door, leaving one room and entering another. Knowing this, we approach death as a *sadhana,* as a spiritual opportunity, bringing a level of detachment which is difficult to achieve in the tumult of life and an urgency to strive more than ever in our search for the Divine Self. At death we drop off the physical body and continue evolving in the inner worlds in our subtle bodies, until we again enter into birth. We are not the body in which we live but the immortal soul which inhabits many bodies in its evolutionary journey.

What is this "soul" which never dies?

Our individual soul is the immortal and spiritual body of light that animates life and reincarnates again and again until all necessary karmas are created and resolved and its essential unity with God is fully realized. Our soul is God's emanational creation, the source of all our higher functions, including knowledge, will and love. Our soul is neither male nor female. It is that which never dies, even when its four outer sheaths change form and perish as they naturally do. The soul body has a form just as the astral body has a form, but it is more refined and is of a more permanent nature. It is this body which reincarnates, creating around itself new physical and astral bodies, life after life after life. This process matures and develops the body of the soul. The body of the soul is pure light, made of quantums. It is indestructible. It cannot be hurt or damaged in any way. It is a pure being, created by God, maturing its way to Him in final merger. The body of the soul is constant radiance. Its mind is superconsciousness, containing all intelligence, and is constantly aware, does not sleep and is expanding awareness as the soul body matures. The body of the soul lives in the eternity of the moment, simultaneously conscious of past and future as a one cycle. The true nature, everlasting secure personal identity, is realizing oneself as the soul body. This is truly finding our roots, our source, our indestructible, ever-maturing soul.

• •

In the illustration at left, a woman has just died. Her immortal soul, above the physical body, is releasing itself to continue its evolution in the inner worlds and to assume its next reincarnation at the right time. Lord Siva gives blessings at this crucial moment of transition.

What are the five bodies?

In Sanskrit, the bodies of our being are called *kosa,* which means "sheath, vessel, container or layer." They are the sheaths through which the soul functions simultaneously in the various planes of existence. The *kosas,* in order of increasing subtlety, are as follows: —*annamaya kosa:* "Sheath composed of food." The physical body, coarsest of sheaths. —*pranamaya kosa:* "sheath composed of *prana* (vital force)." Also known as the etheric or health body, it coexists within the physical body as its source of life, breath and vitality, and is its connection with the astral body. —*manomaya kosa:* "Mind-formed sheath." The lower astral body. The instinctive-intellectual sheath of ordinary thought, desire and emotion. —*vijnanamaya kosa:* "Sheath of cognition." The mental or cognitive-intuitive sheath. It is the vehicle of higher thought, understanding, knowing, direct cognition, wisdom, intuition and creativity. —*anandamaya kosa:* "Body of bliss." The intuitive-superconscious sheath, the ultimate foundation of all life, intelligence and higher faculties. *Anandamaya kosa* is not a sheath in the same sense as the outer *kosas.* It is the soul itself.

The term "astral body" names the subtle, nonphysical body in which the soul functions in the astral plane. The astral body includes the *pranamaya kosa,* the *manomaya kosa* and the *vijnanamaya kosa.*

What happens at the point of death?

As the physical forces wane, all the gross and subtle energy goes into the mental and emotional astral body. If the person was prepared for death, sudden or otherwise, his mental and emotional astral body would have already been well schooled in readiness. Sudden death to such a soul is a boon and a blessing. At death, the soul slowly becomes totally aware in its astral/mental bodies, and it predominantly lives through those bodies in the astral dimension. The soul functions with complete continuity in its astral/mental bodies. It is with these sensitive vehicles that we experience dream or "astral" worlds during sleep every night.

When the physical body dies, this automatically severs the subtle silver cord that connects the astral and physical bodies. This cord is an astral-pranic thread that connects the astral body through the navel to the physical body. It is a little like an umbilical cord. During out-of-the-body experiences, this silver cord is often seen as a cord of light connecting the physical, astral and spiritual bodies. When the cord is cut at the death of the physical body, the process of reincarnation and rebirth begins. The *Vedas* say, "When a person comes to weakness, be it through old age or disease, he frees himself from these limbs just as a mango, a fig or a berry releases itself from its stalk."

It is painful to the astral body to have the physical body cut or disturbed seriously within seventy-two hours after death. The soul can see and feel this, and it detains him from going on. As soon as you tamper with his physical body, he gets attached, becomes aware that he has two bodies, and this becomes a problem. Ideally when you die, your physical body goes up in flames, and immediately you know it's gone. You now know that the astral body is your body, and you can effortlessly release the physical body. But if you keep the old body around, then you keep the person around, and he is aware that he has two bodies. He becomes earthbound, tied into the Pretaloka, and confused.

What are the inner worlds?

The Sanskrit, *loka,* means "world, habitat, realm or plane of existence." Hinduism describes three primary *lokas,* as follows. —*Bhuloka:* "Earth world." The world perceived through the five senses, also called the gross plane, as it is the most dense of the worlds. —*Antarloka:* "Inner or in-between world." Known in English as the subtle or astral plane, the intermediate dimension between the physical and causal worlds, where souls in their astral bodies sojourn between incarnations and when they sleep. —*Karanaloka:* "World of God," and of the Gods and highly evolved souls, existing deep within the Antarloka at a higher level of vibration. It is a world of superconsciousness and extremely refined energy, the quantum level of the universe. Subdivisions of the Antarloka are: —*Devaloka:* "Place of radiant be-

ings." The higher astral plane, or mental plane, the realm of "angels." —*Pretaloka:* "World of the departed." The realm of earth-bound souls, or ghosts. It is an astral duplicate of the physical world and closest to it. —*Narakaloka:* Abode of darkness. The lower worlds, realm of "demons." Equivalent to the Western term "hell," a gross region of the Antarloka. A congested, distressful area where beings suffer the consequences of their own misdeeds in previous lives. Described as a place of torment, pain, darkness, confusion and disease. Narakaloka is not a place where souls reside forever. Hinduism has no eternal hell.

What determines where one goes after death?

Where the soul goes in the astral plane at sleep or death is dependent upon his earthly pursuits and the quality of his mind. If the soul body itself is evolved, it will occupy the astral/mental bodies in the Devaloka. If somebody dies in the states of anger and fear, he goes into the lower worlds of those states of consciousness. And in that realm there would be hundreds of thousands of people in that same state of consciousness. The thoughts at death are the next *samskaras* of the astral body. Even if you have the thought, "When you're dead you're dead," your astral body might just float over your physical body and be "dead." A lot of people who are about to die do not believe in life after death, so they remain hovering over their physical body when it is lifeless. Astral-plane helpers have to come and "wake them up" and tell them that their physical body is dead and explain that they are all right and are alive in their astral body. It is often not easy getting them readjusted.

At death you leave through a nerve ganglia of consciousness, a chakra. Each chakra is a window, and at death it becomes a portal, a doorway. The tunnel of light that is experienced by so many people at the point of death is the portal they are going through, the window, the chakra. Passing through the tunnel is leaving this world and going into another. So, it is the state of mind at death that gets you into one *loka* or another. At the moment of death, you have the opportunity to stabilize yourself in the highest chakra you have experienced in this life. The dying should always remember that the place where one will reincarnate is the place that he is thinking about prior to death. So, choose your desires wisely. The last thoughts just before death are the most powerful thoughts in creating the next life. Secret questionings and doubt of Hindu belief, and associations with other belief systems will automatically place him among like-minded people whose beliefs are alien to Hinduism. A nominal Hindu on Earth could be a selfish materialist in the astral world. The Hindu also knows that death must come naturally, in its own course, and that suicide only accelerates the intensity of one's karma, placing one in a

In between: *Having experienced death, a woman continues her spiritual journey in a refined area of the subtle worlds. Below her are depicted the lower regions of fear, anger and hurtfulness. The heavenly realm of the Gods is shown above and to her left.*

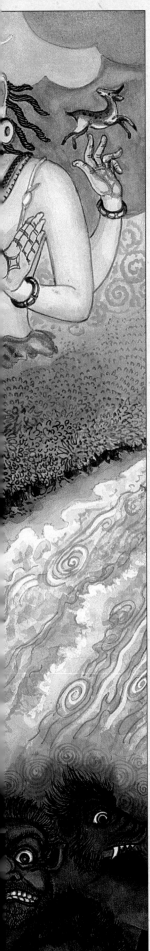

lengthy earth-bound limbo state in the astral plane, bringing a series of immediate lesser births and requiring several lives for the soul to return to the exact evolutionary point that existed at the moment of suicide, at which time the still-existing karmic entanglements must again be faced and resolved.

What should one do to prepare for death?

Everyone is prepared to die, and whether it happens suddenly or slowly, intuitively each individual knows exactly what he is experiencing and about to experience. You don't need any counseling. It is a blessing to know when you are going to die, because then you can prepare for it, make a decision whether you are going to be reborn, do intense *sadhanas*, make preparations. When one knows he is going to depart the physical body, he should not hesitate to tell his relatives he is going to die, and that is a wonderful blessing for them, as they can prepare for his great departure. In turn, family and friends should release him, be happy. Don't cry; you will make him unhappy. The sadness at death comes from Western attitudes. Western thought has to be reversed. He should consciously go over his wealth, his properties, be the executor of his own will, taking care of everybody, not leaving these things to others to deal with after his passing. After everything is settled, all personal possessions disposed of, then he begins meditation and awaits the fruitful hour, trying to exit through the highest chakra of the attainment of this life.

The ideal is to leave through the top of the head, through the door of Brahman, to get into the highest heaven and not have to come back. The dying person should, at the time of transition, concentrate awareness at the top of his head and willfully draw up into it all the energies from the left and right legs and arms, one after another, then the energy within the entire torso, and all the energies within the spine, from the *muladhara* chakra, up into the third eye and crown chakras. With all the energies gathered at the top of his head, he will leave through the highest chakra he experienced this lifetime. This would put him in a great place in the inner world.

Prolonging the life of the individual body must be done by the individual himself. Medical assistance is needed to cauterize wounds and provide the numerous helpful things that are available, but to prolong life in the debilitated physical body past the point that the natural will of the person has sustained is to incarcerate, to jail, to place that person in prison. Ayurvedic medicine seeks to keep a person healthy and strong, but not to interfere with the process of death.

Should I fear death?

Our soul never dies; only the physical body dies. We are not the physical body, mind or emotions. We are the immortal soul, *atman*. We neither fear death nor look forward to it, but revere it as a most exalted experience. Life, death and the afterlife are all part of our path to perfect oneness with God. People wonder whether death is a painful process, such as in the case of cancer victims. Cancer, which produces a lot of pain, is a process of life which results in death, but death itself is not pain-

ful. Death itself is blissful. Death is like a meditation, a samadhi. That's why it is called *maha* (great) samadhi. A Hindu is prepared from childhood for that *mahasamadhi*. Remember, pain is not part of the process of death. That is the process of life, which results in death. Death takes place in a short period, but is a foreboding affair to those who have never meditated. But dying is not such a dramatic experience really. Every night you "die" and leave your physical body. It is very similar.

The fear of death is a natural instinctive reflex. We encounter it sometimes daily, once a month, or at least once a year when we come face to face with the possibility of obliteration of our personality and of leaving the conscious mind. The fear of change or fear of the unknown is an ominous element in the destiny of a human being. The study and comprehension of the laws of reincarnation can alleviate this fear and bring an enlightened vision of the cosmic rhythms of life and death. It is a simple process, no more fantastic than other growth problems we experience daily. Death, like birth, has been repeated so many times that it is no mystery to the soul. The only problem comes with conflicting beliefs, which produce fear and anxiety about death. This temporary ignorance soon subsides when the failing forces of the physical body reach a certain level. At this point, the superconscious intelligence, the soul itself, is there.

Why must we return to a physical body?

Certain karmas can be resolved only in the physical world. This is due to the fact that on the refined inner planes only three or four of the higher chakras are activated; the others are dormant. For *nirvikalpa* samadhi, all seven chakras, as well as the three major energy currents, have to be functioning to sustain enough kundalini force to burst through to the Self. At the right time, the soul is reborn into a flesh body that will best fulfill its karmic pattern. In this process, the current astral body—which is a duplicate of the last physical form—is sloughed off as a lifeless shell that in due course disintegrates, and a new astral body develops as the new physical body grows. This entering into another body is called reincarnation, "re-occupying the flesh." Generally, the soul, at the time of conception, chooses the body he will inhabit but does not actually enter the womb until the infant body takes life and begins to move and kick.

During our numerous Earth lives, a remarkable variety of life patterns is experienced. We exist as male and female, often switching back and forth from life to life as the nature becomes more harmonized into a person exhibiting both feminine nurturing and masculine intrepidness. Therefore, the Hindu knows that the belief in a single life on Earth, followed by eternal joy or pain is utterly wrong and causes great anxiety, confusion and fear. Hindus know that all souls reincarnate, take one body and then another, evolving through experience over long periods of time. Like the caterpillar's metamorphosis into the butterfly, death doesn't end our existence but frees us to pursue an even greater development. Reincarnation ceases when dharma has been well performed, earthly karma is resolved, God is fully realized and moksha, liberation, is attained.

ANSWERS COMPILED FROM DANCING WITH SIVA: HINDUISM'S CONTEMPORARY CATECHISM AND MERGING WITH SIVA: HINDUISM'S CONTEMPORARY METAPHYSICS, BY SATGURU SIVAYA SUBRAMUNIYASWAMI, PUBLISHED BY HIMALAYAN ACADEMY, 107 KAHOLALELE ROAD, KAPAA, HAWAII 96746 USA. TEL: 808-240-3108; FAX: 808-822-4351; WWW.MINIMELA.COM

CHAPTER 21

Hindu Astrology's Lunar Mansions

The 27 Nakshatras and Their Impact On Human Nature and Behavior

In the upper background photo we see Krittika, the six bright stars of the Pleiades, a nakshatra division that spans Aries and Taurus. The cluster contains more than 4,000 stars and lies 400 light years, or 2,400 trillion miles, from Earth. Life's various activities and pursuits, as represed in the scene below from ancient India, flow more smoothly when in tune with the Moon's vibration.

HAT'S YOUR SIGN?" PEOPLE IN AMERICA ASK, MEANING, "What was the position of the Sun in the zodiac when you were born?" But in India, when the temple priest queries, "What's your *nakshatra?*" he wants to know the position of the Moon at your birth. The difference is not superficial. In Western astrology, the birth position of the Sun is considered paramount, while in Hindu astrology, the Moon's placement is most critical. While both systems use (with important differences) the zodiac, or *rasi*, division of twelve parts (Aries, Pisces, etc.), Hindus further refine this to 27 *nakshatras*—literally, "star clusters," also know as the "lunar mansions" (Ashvini, Bharani, etc.). The moon passes through all 27 in the course of a lunar month, at the rate of about one a day. The division is ancient. The list of the 27 *nakshatras* given in the *Krishna Yajur Veda* (*Taittiriya Samhita 2.4.10*) as part of the construction of the sacred fire altar was likely recorded in the second millennium, BCE. Each *nakshatra* is governed by a Vedic Deity—Krittika by Agni, Rohini by Prajapati, and so forth.

A *nakshatra* is male or female, as well as sattvic, rajasic or tamasic in nature. Sattva is the quality of spirituality and purity. Rajas is high-energy activity. Tam*as* has the basic quality of dullness, inertia and darkness. A specific symbol [see pages 178–179], animal species, sex, caste, temperament and primary motivation—*dharma* (life purpose), *artha* (wealth), *kama* (pleasure) and *moksha* (enlightenment)—is associated with each *nakshatra*. An individual is born when the Moon is in a *nakshatra* suited to his destined experiences of that lifetime. Astrological interpretations are based both on the *nakshatra* and the *rasi* [zodiac sign] of each planet, but for both the Moon and the planets it is the *nakshatra* that has the deeper effect.

Nakshatras are of primary importance in *muhurtha*, or electional astrology, estimating the optimal timing to undertake any new venture, such as starting a new business, building a new home or choosing an auspicious wedding date.

Nakshatras (as well as *rasis*) mentioned in ancient texts provide clues of great historical value. In scriptures, such as the *Vedas*, *Puranas* and *Mahabharata*, are found references that at the equinox (or solstice), the Sun was in a particular *nakshatra*. Because of the precession of the equinoxes, the Sun slowly changes *nakshatras* at the equinox—so one can calculate backward to arrive at the date of the scripture, accurate to within a few hundred years. For example, in the *Atharva Veda* (19.7) and *Shatapatha Brahmana*, the solstice is in Magha, the period of 2700–1900BCE. This fact is used to trace the beginning of the later Vedic age.

Applying Star Knowledge to Daily Life

AKSHATRAS PROVIDE AN EFFECTIVE MEANS TO FIND auspicious times for every imaginable human activity. They're also useful for avoiding actions on a day when results are likely to be frustrated. In order to find that date when the cosmic vibrations will be just perfect for you to make that big career move, buy a car or plant your garden, you need a *panchangam*—an astrological calendar—calculated for your region [see resources]. The Moon's *nakshatra* is the same all over the world at the same moment, but the human conventions of time zones and the international date line make the calendars produced in one place inapplicable to another. *Panchangam* in hand, you can proceed to research dates according to the following recommendations. In general, activities will bear more productive fruit if the Moon is waxing, that is, moving in the brightest phase toward full moon day. The *nakshatras* are grouped into seven categories:

Light: Ashvini, Pushya and Hasta are especially good constellations for travel, sports activities, doing healing work or administering medicines, opening a business, sales, trade and borrowing and repaying.

Soft: Mrigashira, Chitra, Anuradha and Revati are excellent for learning music, dance and drama, performing auspicious ceremonies such as marriage, buying and wearing new clothes, the enjoyment of pleasure, romance, conception of a child and making of friends.

Fixed: Rohini, Uttaraphalguni, Uttarashadha and Uttaraprostapada are good for permanent works such as making vows or taking oaths of office, building homes and laying the foundations of cities, plowing the land, planting and purchasing farms.

Moveable: Purnarvasu, Svati, Shravana, Dhanishtha and Satabhishak are good for buying vehicles, for parades, gardening, change of residence or career, travel and other major life changes.

Sharp: Ardra, Aslesha, Jyeshtha and Mula. Their vibration contributes to separation from spouse or friends, argument, the working of black magic, exorcism, punishment and harm to others. These are good days for doing things requiring a harsh, strong or cutting force.

Dreadful: Bharani, Magha, Purvaphalguni, Purvashadha, and Purvaprostapada. All stir the mind, leading to evil deeds such as setting fires, poisoning and destruction, also imprisonment or confinement. Purvaprostapada is good for repentance and penance.

Mixed: Krittika and Vishakha are best for mundane daily activities. Krittika can be good for fire ceremonies due to its Deity, Agni. Excellent for meditation.

Dr. B.V. Raman wrote that "the constellation of Pushya is the most favorable of all the *nakshatras*. It is said to neutralize almost all *doshas* or flaws arising out of a number of adverse combinations. Pushya, the constellation par excellence, has the power to overcome negative forces and assert its benefic nature. Despite all its positive influence, Pushya is still considered inauspicious for a marriage ceremony." The days from the third quarter of Dhanishtha, the 23rd *nakshatra*, to the end of Revati, the 27th, are unsuitable for any kind of auspicious work, except Uttara Prostapada. Each *nakshatra* has a set of syllables which should be used to begin the name of a person born under that *nakshatra*. This gives a name in harmony with the person's nature, and also is an easy way to record one's *nakshatra*.

By consulting an astrologer, or studying books on the subject, one can determine auspicious times for celebrating *samskaras* (rites of passage), medical treatment, beginning of education, etc. This more complex analysis, involving your own birth chart, the location of the planets during the time period in question, can more precisely bring your desired aims into harmony with universal energies—something that is not necessarily going to happen when you schedule activities only according to a convenient day of the week. Those who live by this ancient lunar calendar swear it empowers their life. One way to find out is to try it. On the next two pages we outline the 27 *nakshatras*, how they relate to the 12 *rasis* and the basic qualities of a person born under each *lunar mansion*.

Contributors to this introduction include Devendra Trivedi, B.V. Raman, Dennis Harness, Vamadeva Shastri and Linda Johnsen.
RESOURCES: PANCHANGAMS: HINDUISM TODAY HTTP:// WWW.HINDU.ORG/ SCIENCES/PANCHANGAM.HTML; PALANI PANCHANG, 4831 PIPER STREET, FREMONT, CALIFORNIA 94538, USA. EDUCATIONAL SCIENCES CORPORATION OF AMERICA, PO BOX 88852 WORLD WAY CENTER, LOS ANGELES, CA 90009, USA. BOOKS: MYTHS AND SYMBOLS OF VEDIC ASTROLOGY, BY BEPIN BEHARI, PASSAGE PRESS, PO BOX 21713, SALT LAKE CITY, UTAH 84121-0713, USA; NAKSHATRAS BY DENNIS HARNESS P.O. BOX 2149, SEDONA, ARIZONA 86339 USA; NAKSHATRA, BY K.T. SHUBHAKARAN, SAGAR PUBLICATIONS, 72 JANPATH, VED MANSION, NEW DELHI 110 001 INDIA [ON THE TECHNICAL SIDE]; LIGHT ON LIFE, BY HART DEFOUW, AVAILABLE FROM JDR VENTURES, 918 DOUGLAS DRIVE, WOOSTER, OH 44691 USA.

Character Influences Of the Nakshatras

A terse summary of the nature and tendencies of persons born when the moon is located in each of the 27 lunar mansions

1. Ashvini (Beta Arietis): Passionate, impulsive, attractive and intelligent, people whose birth Moon is in Ashvini can also be headstrong and extravagant. They enjoy travel, are often skilled workers, and may have healing abilities. The Ashvins are Vedic gods of light, healing and inspiration.

2. Bharani (41 Arietis): Bharani folk are usually healthy, happy, skillful and conscientious. They also tend to be somewhat impatient and self-indulgent, and find it hard to forgive. Setbacks can shift their priorities from material preoccupation to spiritual transcendence.

3. Krittika (Alcyone 2-Pleiades): Krittika types are fiery, full of creative energy, highly ambitious, dedicated to divine service, self-motivated and "think big." They stand out in a crowd and can become quite famous. They're prone to eating too much.

4. Rohini (Aldebaran): Rohini gives a loving, truthful disposition, serenity, a sense of responsibility and a love of the arts, beauty and culture. If the Moon is afflicted, they may be prone to stubbornness, anger, selfishness and fault-finding.

5. Mrigashira (Lambda Orionis): Gentle, sensitive, highly perceptive, drawn to romance, music and the arts, Mrigashiras prefer a quiet, comfortable life, can be very hard working and are frequently drawn to spiritual life. Some are haunted by self-doubt or egoity.

6. Ardra (Betelguese 7): Full of vitality, good athletes, Ardras live life with enthusiasm and intensity. Sympathetic and helpful, they're often drawn to the study of esoteric laws. If the Moon is afflicted, they can be cruel, lashing out at others unfairly at times.

7. Punarvasu (Pollux 11): Good-natured, generous emotionally, prudent financially, content to live a relaxed, uncluttered life, self-disciplined, yet playful. They need to guard against complacency and watch their health. They make good friends.

8. Pushya (Delta Cancri): They are stable, easy going personalities, prosperous, well educated, popular, virtuous, nice looking, forthright, intelligent and wise. Can be overly rigid, selfish and arrogant. Productive and caring people who make good teachers.

9. Ashlesha (Epsilon Hydrae): Self-reliant, excellent communicators, capable of great concentration and penetrating insight. Their candor can turn to tactlessness, and they may manipulate truth to protect themselves. Don't humiliate them; they will never forget it.

10. Magha (Alpha Leonis): Regal, ambitious, pleasure loving, physically strong, they easily rise to leadership positions, honor tradition and pursue noteworthy projects. They enjoy being served more than serving, and they can fall prey to a voracious desire for sex.

11. Purva Phalguni (Delta Leonis): Magnanimous, loyal, delightful conversationalists, earthy, attractive. They get their way without intimidating others. Often they are wanderers, drawn to the arts, and enjoy life to the full. The body is usually healthy, but the mind is so active and creative, they tend to leap before looking.

12. Uttara Phalguni (Beta Leonis): Likeable, generally well-to-do, earning substantial salaries through their exceptional intelligence. Make wonderful friends, and are always ready to help their companions. Success, courage and love of adventure may appear, but romantic escapades may lead to trouble.

13. Hasta (Delta Corvi): Hard working, industrious and exceptionally resourceful, they make fine artisans, specialists, business people and teachers, but are not often leaders. May display intelligence, a sharp wit and healing ability, also a lack of patience, and a determined effort to manipulate others for their own ends.

14. Chitra (Spica 16): Charming and stylishly dressed, drawn to anything new or out of the ordinary. Magnets to the opposite sex, often artistically gifted, they surround themselves with beautiful things. May at times become self-indulgent. These are intelligent,

With Earth in the center, this diagram depicts the 12 rasis, or signs, of the zodiac, surrounded by the 27 nakshatras, according to their relative location in the heavens as seen from Earth. Each nakshatra has a symbol related either to its subtle vibration or to the shape of a nearby constellation of stars. The Moon's location at birth along this ancient division of the ecliptic, says Hindu astrology, is a prime indication of a person's basic characteristics There are also four equal divisions within each nakshatra, making a total of 108 expressions of human nature. Noted next to each nakshatra name in the descriptions below is the star with which it is associated. There are 2-1/4 nakshatras per zodiac sign.

styles, but have a deep spiritual nature. They value family and friends, enjoy organizing projects and managing people. The less mature are prone to jealousy and depression.

18. Jyeshtha (Antares 18): Deeply passionate, able leaders, renowned for their adherence to virtue—and their testy temperaments! Generally cheerful, but quite irascible when provoked, they gladly fight to defend the helpless.

19. Mula (Lambda Scorpii): Set in their ways, clever, soft and happy disposition, but somewhat suspicious of other people's motivations. They tend to find their way to money, or money finds its way to them.

20. Purvashadha (Delta Sagittarii): Patient, independent minded, convincing in speech, proud, lucky in love, outgoing people who will stick with their friends. Value their own opinions over other's.

21. Uttarashadha (Pi Sagittarii): Popular, idealistic, influential, stable, introspective and ethical. Good both at starting projects and completing them. Drawn to work which uplifts others. The less mature may be lazy, easily distracted or stressed out.

22. Shravana (Altair 20): Intelligent, well-educated, and prosperous. A degree of fame usually comes their way. They love to learn, make good teachers and enjoy traveling. Often drawn to religious life, or a life of service, but they may become rigid or fanatical.

23. Dhanishtha (Alpha Delphini): Courageous, generous, often prosperous, upbeat, ambitious and with a universal outlook. They bring people together for a worthy cause. Not easily fooled, they carefully analyze any proposition put to them. Can be aggressive, rash or overly conservative.

24. Satabhishak (Lambda Aquarii): Blunt but honest, disinclined to conform, almost always get their way. Drawn to fields requiring penetrating insight such as science or philosophy. Can become a mindless workaholic, private, hiding their real thoughts. Most devoted to service of humanity, whether recognized or not.

25. Purva Prostapada (Beta Pegasi): Fine speakers, good business skills, can make money and hang onto it. Generally fairly serious people, yet may act impetuously or have a hard time sticking to a decision. The less mature can be phobic, cynical or may strike out vindictively at others.

26. Uttara Prostapada (Gamma Pegasi): Well-balanced and ethical people, kindly, self-sacrificing, supportive, very convincing in discussions. They sincerely enjoy family life and like to help others. When conflicts or competition arise, they are likely to hold the winning hand. Young souls can be lazy, irresponsible and envious.

27. Revati (Zeta Piscium): Healthy, intelligent, with a sweet disposition and artistically gifted, they love people, wish harm to no one and nourish those in need. While they don't seek much for themselves, wealth and joy are often spontaneously bestowed on them. The less mature may display an inferiority complex, a servile nature, or fall prey to continual disappointments.

honest, efficient, substantial people.

15. Svati (Arcturus 17): Independent, generally quiet, nice people who control themselves in public. They are helpful, pleasant conversationalists and rarely hold grudges. Like travel and strongly attracted to religion or philosophy. Sometimes they experience chronic discontent.

16. Vishakha (Alpha 2 Libra): Purposeful, forceful, commanding in appearance. Excellent public speakers who enjoy making money. Courage, ambition and one-pointedness carry them quickly to their goals. They revel in turmoil and enjoy a good argument.

17. Anuradha (Delta Scorpio): Well-to-do, they dislike austere life-

How Hindus Worship

The home shrine room, "my friend
Lord Ganesha," visiting a temple, and
an overview of Hindu festivals

In the photo we see a typical arati lamp held by a temple
priest, or pujari. At the height of the puja, he will pass
it before the Deity image in adoration, then present it to
gathered devotees so they may pass their hands through
the flame and draw the God's blessings to their eyes.

CHAPTER 22

The Home Shrine

How and Why to Establish a Holy Room for Worship and Meditation

WHAT IS THE CENTER OF YOUR HOME? THE KITCHEN, the workshop, the living room, the den? The ancients designated the crucial part of the home as a sacred sanctuary, a fortress of purity to which dwellers could retreat before dawn each day, to commune with their higher nature and with God and the Gods. This center of spiritual force is called *devatarchanam,* the "place for honoring Divinity." Sacred architecture places it in the northeast corner, the realm of Isana, where its potency naturally flourishes. Scriptures speak but little of this tradition, perhaps because its necessity is taken for granted. Nevertheless, the custom has lived on, and every prominent devout Hindu home has a holy shrine room, often opulent, sometimes austere, the domiciles' most auspicious quadrant, reserved for religious pursuits, and like a miniature temple, radiating blessings constantly through the abode and out to the community.

Love and joy come to Hindu families who worship God in their home through the traditional ceremony known as puja, meaning adoration or worship. Through such rites and the divine energies invoked, each family makes the house a sanctuary, a refuge from the concerns and worries of the world. The center of that sanctuary, the site of puja, is the shrine, mystically tied to the temple to which they pilgrimage weekly. Puja is performed daily—usually in the early morning, but also in the afternoon or evening—generally by the head of the house. All members of the family attend. Rites can be as simple as lighting a lamp and offering a flower at the Lord's holy feet, or they can be most elaborate and detailed, with myriad Sanskrit chants and offerings. The essential and indispensable part of

any puja is devotion. Without love and reverence in the heart, outer performance is of little value. But with true devotion even simple gestures become sacred ritual.

As in a temple, the images or icons of God and Gods are the focus of the shrine room. These are called *murti* in Sanskrit, worshiped and cared for as the physical body of the the Divine. Hindus do not worship these "idols" per se. They worship God and the Gods who by their infinite powers spiritually hover over and indwell the image. *Murtis* of the Gods are sanctified forms through which their love, power and blessings flood forth to bless the family. The God's vibration and presence can be felt in the image, and the Divinity can use the images as a temporary physical-plane body or channel. Hindus believe and expect that the God is actually present and conscious in the *murti* during puja, aware of thoughts and feelings and even sensing the worshiper's gentle touch on the metal or stone. The great Adi Shankaracharya, while espousing a strict monism, wrote, "Although Parabrahman is all pervading, to attain Him one should accept that He is 'more' present in one particular place, just as we see Vishnu in the Shaligrama, a small round stone." The Vaishnava saint Ramanuja similarly stated, "Although the Lord is all pervading, using His omnipotent powers He appears before devotees to accept their devotion through an image."

The Science of Ritual: Puja is a ceremony in which the ringing of bells, passing of flames, presenting of offerings and chanting of mantras invoke the devas and Gods, who then come to bless and help the devotees. Puja is holy communion, full of wonder and tender affections. Thus the home shrine is a place of tremendous

A Saivite shrine: *Husband offers arati (flame), wife rings the bell and son blows a conch before their altar to Siva Nataraja, Ardhanarishvara, Sivalinga, Ganesha and Muruga.*

importance, made more and more sacred by the culmulative power of prayer. Daily puja is the axis of religious life, and the puja room is the heart of the home. Chanting the Vedas is the magic enlivener. In the words of Sri Chandrasekharendra Saraswati, "The *Veda* mantras being the root cause of creation, the mere chanting of *Veda* mantras would, by their vibrations, make the Devas appear in person."

The home shrine is also the locus for private and group meditation, prayer, mantra recitation and devotional singing. Its sanctity is protected by never using it for other purposes. This space is meticulously cared for, kept immaculate and elaborately decorated to look like a small temple. It should be well-lit and free from drafts and household disturbances. The altar is generally close to the floor, since most

of the puja is performed while seated. But when there are small children in the home it is often higher, as to be out of their reach. Pictured in the large illustrations are "typical" altars (slightly larger than life) of the four major Hindu denominations: Saivism, Vaishnavism, Saktism and Smartism. In truth, Hinduism consists of ten thousand lineages and more, each with its unique traditions, and as many variations in home altars as well. Yet, there are many similarities.

At a Ganesha shrine, for example, an icon, or *murti*, of the elephant-headed God is placed at the center of the altar. A metal or stone image is considered best, but if not available there are two traditional alternatives: 1) a framed picture, preferably with a sheet of copper on the back, or 2) A *kumbha*, which is a symbol of Ganesha

Do Hindus Worship Idols?

FROM THE MOMENT THE VEDIC rites are completed and a statue or painting of the image manifests all His glory and grace, He accepts various devotions. He listens to prayers and woes. He is at once a confidante and giver of blessings. Thus, an image cannot be said to be merely a beautiful statue or doll, nor an excellent painting. The image *is* God.

Said Swami Vivekananda, "It has become a trite saying that idolatry is bad, and everyone swallows it at the present time without questioning. I once thought so, and to pay the penalty of that, I had to learn my lessons sitting at the feet of a man who realized everything from idols. I allude to Ramakrishna Paramahansa. Yet, idolatry is condemned. Why? Some hundreds of years ago, some man of Jewish blood happened to condemn it. He happened to condemn everybody else's idols except his own. If God is represented

in any beautiful form or any symbolic form, said the Jew, it is awfully bad; it is sin. But if He is represented in the form of a chest with two angels sitting on either side, it is the holiest of holies. If God comes in the form of a dove, it is holy. But if He comes in the form of a cow, it is heathen superstition, condemn it…"

Over the centuries, in their condescending haste and missionary fervor to convert the rest of the world to the "One and only correct faith, and to commit the souls of the otherwise damned to God," various religions have condemned image worship with fanatic zeal. This has led to a shallow refutal of image worship and a misinterpretation of the Hindu image

So lifelike: *Icon of Santoshi Ma, Orissa*

© STEPHEN P. HUYLER

worshiped. To complicate the issue, image worship is also frowned on by some professing Hindus.

The question of image worship will be debated for years to come. Here it suffices to say that with the ancient Hindus image worship was not left to be treated as an ignorant and useless practice fit only for the ignorant and spiritually immature; even the greatest visited mandirs and worshiped images, and these thinkers did not do so blindly or unconsciously. A human necessity was recognized, the nature of the necessity was understood, its psychology systematically analyzed, the various phases of image worship, mental and material, were defined. The modern Hindu follows in footsteps of his forebearers. Through the image, the eye is taught to see God, and not to seek God. The first lesson received at the sanctum is to be applied everywhere: see God in everything!

A Shakta shrine: *In a large joint-family home, womenfolk clean and decorate the shrine room and prepare offerings to Kali Ma, the fierce image of the Goddess. Flower garlands are hung to create the feeling of a small temple.*

SHRINE ART BY A. MANIVEL

made by placing a coconut on a brass pot of water with five mango leaves inserted between the coconut and the pot. The coconut is husked but the tuft of fibers at the top is not removed. Most shrines also honor a picture of the guru of the family lineage, either on the altar or adorning the walls.

Bathing the God's image is often a central part of puja. For this, special arrangements are established at the altar to catch the sacred water or milk as it pours off the icon. Most simply, the *murti* may be placed in a deep tray to catch the water. After the bath, the tray is removed and the *murti* dried off, then dressed and decorated. More elaborately, a drain is set up so the water flows into a pot at the side

of the altar. If devotees are in attendance, this blessed water is later served by the pujari (the person performing the ritual) who places a small spoonful in each devotee's right palm.

Holy Accoutrements: Puja implements for the shrine are kept on large metal trays. On these are arranged *ghee* lamps, bells, cups, spoons and pots to hold the various sacraments. Available from Indian shops, these are dedicated articles, never used for purposes other than puja. Their care, cleaning and polishing is considered a sacred duty. Usual items include: 1) water cups and a small spoon for offering water; 2) a brass vessel of unbroken, uncooked rice (usually mixed with turmeric powder), also for offering; 3) tray or basket of freshly

Harmonious Home Design According to Vastu

In INDIAN ARCHITECTURE, THE DWELLING is itself a shrine. A home is called *manush-yalaya,* literally, "human temple." It is not merely a shelter for human beings in which to rest and eat. The concept behind house design is the same as for temple design, so sacred and spiritual are the two spaces. The "open courtyard" system of house design was the national pattern in India before Western models were introduced. The order introduced into the "built space" accounts for the creation of spiritual ambience required for the indweller to enjoy spiritual well-being and material welfare and prosperity.

At right is a typical layout of a square building, with a grid of 9x9=81 squares, meant for family persons (for yogis, scientists and artists, a grid of 8x8=64 is prescribed). The space oc-

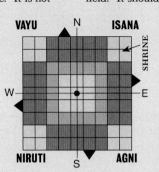

House grid: *With sloping roof and open courtyard*

cupied by the central 3x3=9 squares is called Brahmasthanam, meaning the "nuclear energy field." It should be kept unbuilt and open to the sky so as to have contact with the outer space (*akasha*). This central courtyard is likened to the lungs of the human body. It is not for living purposes. Religious and cultural events can be held here—such as yajna (fire ritual), music and dance performances and marriage.

The row of squares surrounding the Brahmasthanam is the walkway. The corner spaces, occupying 2x2=4 squares, are rooms with specific purposes. The northeast quarter is called Isana, the southeast Agni, the southwest Niruthi and northwest Vayu. These are said to possess the qualities of four respective devatas or Gods—Isa, Agni, Niruthi and Vayu. Accordingly—with due respect to

A Vaishnava shrine: *Mother and daughter sing devotional hymns as father offers fruits, flowers and light to Radha and Krishna, before whom are enshrined Lord Hanuman and five Shaligrama stones. Traditional sweets have been prepared; incense and small ritual fire have been lit.*

picked flowers (without stems) or loose flower petals; 4) a standing oil lamp, *dipastambha*, that remains lit throughout the puja; ideally kept lit all day; 5) a *dipa* (or lamp with cotton string wick) for waving light before the Deity; 6) a small metal bell, *ghanta*; 7) an incense burner and a few sticks of incense, *agarbhatti*; 8) sacraments of one's tradition, such as holy ash, *vibhuti*; sandalwood paste, *chandana; and* red powder, *kumkuma* (these are kept in polished brass or silver containers); 9) *naivedya*, an offering for the Deity of fresh fruit and-or a covered dish of freshly cooked food, such as rice (never tasted during preparation); 10) a camphor (*karpura*) burner for passing flame before the God at the height of puja; 11) brass or silver pots for bathing the *murti*; 12) colorful clothing for dressing the *murti*; 13) flower garlands; 14) additional oil lamps to illumine and decorate the room; 15) a CD or tape player.

Purity: Before entering the shrine room, all attending the ceremony bathe and dress in fresh, clean clothes. It is a common practice to not partake of food at least an hour or more before puja. The best time for puja is before dawn. Each worshiper brings an offering of flowers or fruit (prepared before the bath). Traditionally, women during their monthly period refrain from attending puja, entering the home shrine or temple or approaching swamis or other holy men. Also during this time women do not help in puja preparation, such as picking flowers or making *prasada* for the Deity. Use of the home shrine is also restricted during periods of retreat that follow the birth or death of a family member.

Worshipful Icons: As seen in the main illustrations, the images enshrined on home altars vary according to lineage and denomination. All icons, however, are either anthropomorphic, meaning human in appearance; theriomorphic, having animal characteristics (for example, Lord Hanuman, the monkey God); or aniconic, meaning without representational likeness, such as the element fire, or the smooth Shaligrama stone, worshiped as Lord Vishnu. Other objects of enshrinement include divine emblems or artifacts, including weapons, such as Durga's sword; animal mounts, like Siva's bull; a full pot of water, indicating the presence of the Devi; the sun disk, representing Surya; the holy footprints or sandals of a God or saint; the standing oil lamp; the fire pit, mystic diagrams called *yantra;* water from holy rivers; and sacred plants, such as the tulsi tree. All these are honored as embodiments of the God or Goddess. The *Vedas* enjoin: "The Gods, led by the spirit, honor faith in their worship. Faith is composed of the heart's intention. Light comes through faith. Through faith men come to prayer, faith in the morning, faith at noon and at the setting of the sun. O Faith, give us faith!"

The "built space:" *The ideal position of each aspect of the home is enhanced by that place's inherent nature. This knowledge is given in the* Vastu Shastras, *a study of the dynamics of time and space, by Mayan, the architect and town planner of ancient India. About 60% of Indian homes still follow this paradisiacal design.*

ecological friendliness with the subtle forces of the spirit—those spaces (quarters) are assigned as follows: northeast for the home shrine, southeast for the kitchen, southwest for master bedroom and northwest for the storage of grains. The spaces lying between the corner zones, measuring 2x5=10 squares, are those of the north, east, south and west. They are meant for multi purposes.

For home worship, *griha* puja, the Deity icon should be smaller in size than in a temple. The agreeable and generally recommended height of the standing image without pedestal is one's own fist (*mushti*) size, measured with the thumb raised.

By V. Ganapati Sthapati, *Master Architect, Chennai*

CATION

Shrine Room

ENTRY

EAST

Living Space

Kitchen

orridor and Porch

A Smarta shrine: *A brahmin chants the* Vedas *as his father meditates after morning puja. Pictures honor major Deities of the Hindu pantheon. Ritual ablution has just been performed to five small Shaligrama stones (see inset) now encased in an ornate chest; Sivalinga (center), Devi (clockwise from top), Vishnu, Sun and Ganesha.*

SHRINE ART BY A. MANIVEL

MANIVEL

CHAPTER 23

My Friend, Lord
Ganesha

Above, devotees offer a ghee flame to the elephant-faced Deity during Ganesha Chaturthi in India. Top of page, HINDUISM TODAY founder Satguru Sivaya Subramuniyaswami holds a stone murti of Lord Ganesha. He gifted three dozen such murtis to budding temples outside India to encourage initial patterns of worship.

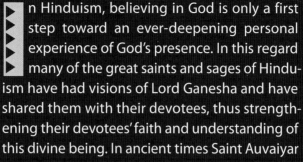

n Hinduism, believing in God is only a first step toward an ever-deepening personal experience of God's presence. In this regard many of the great saints and sages of Hinduism have had visions of Lord Ganesha and have shared them with their devotees, thus strengthening their devotees' faith and understanding of this divine being. In ancient times Saint Auvaiyar wrote of her experience of the elephant-faced God in her devotional poem "Vinayaga Ahaval:""Desiring to make me yours this instant, you, like a mother, have appeared before me and cut the delusion of unending births." In modern times, my Gurudeva, Sivaya Subramuniyawami, had many experiences of Lord Ganesha, whom he considered a dear friend. He observed, "There are a great many liberal Hindus and/or Western-influenced Hindus who don't think of Ganesha as a real being. To them He is a symbol, a superstition, a way of explaining philosophy to children and the uneducated. But this has not been my experience of our loving Lord. I have seen Him with my own eye. He has come to me in visions several times and convinced my lower mind of His reality." Of course, the *murti*, or form, of Lord Ganesha does contain important symbols, such as the noose and the goad, which relate to His creating and removing obstacles. And it is true we can learn a great deal about Ganesha and the other Deities through studying such symbols, but what is even more important is to know that Ganesha is a real being whom we can know and love. ¶We have arranged group pilgrimages to India since 1969, and some pilgrims on various programs definitely had visions of Lord Ganesha, as well as other Deities. Some witnessed the stone or bronze *murti* moving and smiling at them or turning into a human-like figure. Others, with eyes closed, saw the Deity's face as real as any living person. The more common way we experience the Gods and devas is as an uplifting, peaceful, divine energy, or shakti, that radiates out from the image. It is easiest to feel their blessings at the high point of the puja when the flame is held high. The shakti of Lord Ganesha is a gentle, loving force which has the power to move the devotees' awareness into a peaceful, contented state, free of any worry, fear, anger or other negative emotion. ¶This Educational Insight is drawn from Gurudeva's book, *Loving Ganesha* (www.gurudeva.org/resources/books/lg/), delving into the nature of the elephant-faced Deity, what He is like, what functions this great God performs and how each seeker can make Him a vital part of daily life on the path of experience.

Satguru Bodhinatha Veylanswami

The Benefits of Befriending Ganesha

We sincerely hope that this chapter will serve to bring you closer to Lord Ganesha. We are deeply grateful to Gurudeva for his inspiring words of wisdom, drawn from his book, *Loving Ganesha*, which fill the following 13 pages. One comment that he makes especially stands out to me as central: "Among all the wonderful Hindu Deities, Lord Ganesha is the closest to the material plane of consciousness, most easily contacted and most able to assist us in our day-to-day life and concerns." In giving this some thought, I developed a list of eleven ways in which Ganesha can benefit your everyday life. These benefits were written for youth, as that is the best time to develop a closeness with Ganesha, but they apply equally to adults.

- ❀ strengthen memory
- ❀ stimulate intelligence
- ❀ solve problems easier
- ❀ study well in school
- ❀ stabilize emotions
- ❀ improve your character
- ❀ experience good timing
- ❀ increase domestic harmony
- ❀ increase self control
- ❀ remove obstacles in your path
- ❀ be more successful in life

Through the worship of Lord Ganesha, we feel better about life, rising above the lower emotions of insecurity, fear, anger and jealousy and instead experiencing peace and contentment. Tuning in to His shakti and being, through attending puja at the temple or even just visualizing Him in your mind, helps raise you up into the *muladhara* chakra and therefore out of anger and fear into a calm state of mind. In fact, you can slowly seal off these lower states of mind and keep awareness permanently lifted above the animal instincts of fear and anger through the regular worship of Lord Ganesha. He sits on the chakra of memory; and when we are stable in that chakra, focused and concentrated, our memory is strong and our intellect keen.

Lord Ganesha's worship can enable us to tune in to the natural flow of events that allows us to be in the right place at the right time. Have you noticed that some days our timing is excellent and yet other days everyone we go to see has just left, the store just closed, we missed our bus by one minute? The worship of Ganesha quiets the aggressive intellect, allowing you to be guided by intuition, which can change a day of bad timing to one of perfectly good timing. Everyone knows Lord Ganesha is the Lord of Obstacles, able to both place a barrier in our path when our direction is less than perfect and to remove barriers that keep us from achieving our highest aspirations in life. By bringing our consciousness close to Him, we give permission for Him to positively influence our life in these subtle, often unseen, ways.

When you start each day's study, or come upon a difficult subject, pray for Ganesha's clear mind. See and feel a bright yellow light around your head. Feel smart. Strongly desire to understand. When you have a problem in life, at school, home or work, Lord Ganesha will help you. Ganesha knows everything about you and everybody you know, from the past into the future. But you must ask for His help. See Ganesha's majestic face and with mental force ask for help and explain the problem. Lord Ganesha will send you ideas and thought power, introduce you to new attitudes, help you to understand other people, help you use wisdom and not emotions to face life's many experiences, and when that happens you will be more successful in all you undertake.

It is very clear that worshiping Lord Ganesha can benefit our life in many ways, provided we have developed a closeness with Him to the point where He is our friend. Ganesha is then able to help us become happier, more successful and more cultured Hindus who value the temple as an indispensable part of our life.

Knowing that the Gods are real beings and that the purpose of going to the temple is to experience their blessings is what transforms the temple from a cultural hall to a truly sacred place.

For the full, online version of *Loving Ganesha,* go to www.himalayanacademy.com/resources/books/lg/

A. MANIVEL

The great Lord Ganesha has been prayed to, worshiped and adored in one form or another since time began; and time itself began with His creation. He, above all others, is the God, the great Mahadeva, to be invoked before every act and especially worshiped and prayed to when changes occur in our lives as we move from the old established patterns into new ones. Lord Ganesha is always there to steady our minds and open the proper doors as we evolve and progress. He never, ever fails. He is always there for us when we need Him.

Hindus around the world pray to Ganesha for help and guidance as He leads us out of an agricultural age through the technological and information eras and on into the new age of space. Many are still on the farms; others are in the offices and in the factories; while still others land on the moon and orbit through space. With a mind more intricate than the most complicated computers in the world all hooked together, but as simple as an on-and-off switch, Ganesha knows all aspects of these transitions, in unfailing continuity, from one era to another. He is totally aware, at every point in time, of the mother in her home, the farmer in his field, the astronaut orbiting this planet, the corporate worker at his desk and the factory technician performing his tasks.

For thousands of years in the villages of Vedic India, Lord Ganesha has been and is today in towns and cities in many countries, a powerful and immediate presence in everyone's lives. He was and is the one prayed to when starting a business or an enterprise of any kind. Today factory workers approach a small shrine dedicated to Him before commencing their daily work, so that nothing might go wrong. Businessmen beg His help in adjusting the stock market to their advantage, and farmers, of course, chant His 108 names while planting their seeds, rice, other crops, or trees. When no rain comes, images of our loving Lord are seen throughout Bharat land submerged in water up to His neck, so that His great mind may become impressed with the people's crying needs. When Grandma is sick or the crops are not coming in on time, when the children are growing up wrongly by adopting alien ways, Hindus diligently pray to our loving God for help in restructuring their lives. He is the supreme Lord of Dharma, and we pray to Him for guidance in the direction of our lives.

Worship of Lord Ganesha is immediate. One has but to think of His form to contact His ever-present mind. Close your eyes for a second, visualize His large elephant head and experience the direct communication that has immediately begun. This is similar to punching in a code at a personal computer terminal which gives immediate access to the entire network of computers, large and small. On this remarkable and universal Innernet, obscure and necessary information and answers to every question are now available as needed through the direct link with Lord Ganesha. Wherever we are, whatever we are doing, we can use the computer terminal of our own brain and code in the divine image of Lord Ganesha and gain complete access to His vast computer-like mind. Ganesha's mind has been programmed by the history of experience over eons of time and naturally encompasses the intricacies of the universe and the cycles of life in all their rami-

Adopted by the Elephant God

Seekers of Truth come from many backgrounds, many religions, and have trod many paths. Having become acquainted with Lord Ganesha, they may wonder how their past can participate in their present aspirations. "What am I doing worshiping an elephant-faced God and loving it?" they may wonder. "What do I do now to harmonize this unfoldment with my previous upbringing?"

There is a way to reconcile this subconscious dilemma. Let's not "pack it away in denial," as they say; let's face up to the spiritual awakening. Truth is, you have a loving friend in Ganesha, who, if we may use the word, is the pope of the Hindu religion. And you are by no means alone. One fourth of the human race is acquainted with Ganesha—twenty-five percent of the people on this planet—1.25 billion, and that number is growing year by year.

Our loving Ganesha leads his devotees deep into the oldest religion on planet Earth. There are two ways to come into Hinduism. One is to be born into the Hindu religion and be carried in your mother's arms to the temple, there to be inwardly and psychically connected to our loving God, Ganesha. So strong are those early impressions and samskaras that they carry you through life. Another way is to unfold naturally to the point of being ready to formally enter Hinduism, to supplicate, to sincerely entreat the guardians of that religion to allow you to be a part of that immense and ancient tradition. You have to want to be a Hindu so strongly, so sincerely, that Lord Ganesha lifts you out of the fog of the materialistic conscious mind, establishing a connection and a relationship with you. This is a personal relationship with the Deity. There is nobody in-between—just you and the God, Lord Ganesha. It's like being adopted, in a way. If you were an orphan or abandoned on the streets of São Paulo or Chennai or on the streets of wherever there are little kids running around, you would be "free." You could go through life listening to no one and exercising unrestricted free will, free instinctive will. If you had a developed intellect, then you could exercise an intellectual will. You could do anything that you wanted to do, absolutely anything. Of course, you would find that as you attempted to fulfill your

fications and simplicities. Our great God Ganesha sits contentedly upon the *muladhara* chakra. This chakra controls the forces of memory within every creature. Worship of Him strengthens your memory, builds character and brings knowledge from the within. It also protects you from the lower forces which reside in the little-known chakras below the *muladhara*. These darker chakras govern fear, anger, jealousy and the confused thinking centered around self-preservation.

Wherever His devotees are—in the home, the factories, the offices, the hospitals, the marketplace, orbiting in space or tilling the soil on the farm—Lord Ganesha is ever there. Intimate access is acquired by simply loving Ganesha and holding His robust image in your mind. Carefully visualize the large head and ears, His long trunk, massive body, big belly and the objects He holds in His many hands. Look into Ganesha's eyes. Train yourself to see Him within your own mind with your eyes closed. This is the key. Hold His form steady in your mind through the power of visualization. Now you can talk to Him. Pronounce the words mentally into His ear. He is listening, though He will never speak back but take into His vast mind your prayer and slowly work it out. You must simply

Right, devotees immerse a large image of Ganesha during His grand departure festival in Mumbai. Above, a devotee shows off the clay Ganesha she has made for the festival. Below right, a man dances in ecstatic devotion as Ganesha hovers nearby in His subtle body.

PHOTOS BY SHANA DRESSLER

"Adopted" continued . . .

below the *muladhara* chakra. Anguish is there.

It is the same when you evolve a relationship, a personal relationship, with the Deity Lord Ganesha. He will not allow you to use your free will to get into difficulties. Guiding you carefully and protecting you along your way in your natural karma through life is His concern. Someone once said, "I worship Lord Siva. I worship Lord Murugan, but I have never really gotten acquainted with Lord Ganesha." I responded, "You worship Siva and Lord Murugan, and that is wonderful. But unless you have established a personal relationship with Lord Ganesha, your worship of any of the Gods is probably more according to your own thoughts and fancy than true worship. Until you have established a rapport with Lord Ganesha, you cannot establish a relationship with Krishna, Ayyappan, Amman, Vishnu, Rama, Hanuman, Lakshmi, Sita, Radharani, Siva

desires, you were limited, sometimes prevented, by the natural forces within and without. But you could attempt anything.

If you were fortunate enough, foster parents might come along to help you. They would adopt you and take you into their home. Your new mother would begin to lovingly guide and direct your life. You are a part of their family now, and your well-being, your education, your training all now come under their will, to which you must adjust yourself and obey. They will watch over you and discipline you morning and night. They will protect you from getting into trouble with your "free will." The modern concept of freedom leads to the darker chakras

speak all of your questions and your problems into His right ear. When you are finished, open your eyes. Go on with your day and go on with your life. Wherever you are, remember this simple way of making contact with Lord Ganesha and as a good seeker exercise this psychic power, this siddhi.

Starting today and in the days to come, you will notice how He answers questions and solves problems for you through the course of your daily life. You will notice how He influences events and decisions slowly and subtly, in unseen ways. Situations will change for you, unexpected doors will open, and accustomed ones will close as you are propelled through His grace toward your inevitable glorious future. Read and reread the above formula for immediate access to Lord Ganesha until it is firmly implanted in your subconscious memory patterns, and then begin to make contact with Him often through each day wherever you are and whatever you are doing. Yes! Lord Ganesha is immediate, and you have immediate access to Him. Wherever you are, remember this and as a seeker on the path through life's experiences exercise this siddhi. It is your right to do so.

Once a psychic connection is made with Lord Ganesha—the Deity who manifests in several forms, including the elephant-headed Lord of Categories and Remover of Obstacles—one is brought slowly into the mysteries of the Sanatana Dharma. Such an inner connection, which can be as subtle as a feeling, as tenuous as a dream or as bold as a

personal visit, is also an entering into one's own *muladhara* chakra, governed by the planet Mercury, for every opening into a new chakra is also an introduction to the Deity who governs that state of consciousness and the planet to which that chakra is connected.

The Sanatana Dharma, known today as Hinduism, is the only living religion on the planet that does not look to a human founder for its source of inspiration, scripture or historical beginning. It is timeless and ageless. Sanatana Dharma, the root religion of humankind, looks inward for its origins, into the subtle, superconscious realms within the microcosm, which it calls the Karanaloka, Sivaloka or Third World. This great religion has no single organized headquarters on the material plane. Nor does it have a one hierarchy. Who then is in charge of Hinduism? Why, it is none other than our loving Ganesha! He doesn't live in Rome, nor in Salt Lake City. Lord Ganesha lives simultaneously everywhere Hindus worship and pray within themselves. He doesn't have to be reappointed from time to time, because yugas and yugas ago He was permanently and irrevocably appointed when He was created for this work.

Ganesha, the Gatekeeper

Yes, it is the Great Ganesha who is the gateway for seekers into the world's most ancient faith. He is the inner authority, the guardian, the one who grants access to the spiritual mysteries of the Sanatana Dharma. All Hindus worship Him, regardless of their sectarian or philosophical positions. He truly binds them together in His love. This great God is both the beginning of the Hindu religion and the meeting ground for all its devotees. And that is only proper, inasmuch as Ganesha is the personification of the material universe. The universe in all of its varied and various magnificent manifestations is nothing but the body of this cheerfully portly God.

Ganesha sits on the psychic lotus of the *muladhara* chakra, the ganglia of nerves at the base of the spine within everyone. This chakra governs time, matter and memory. As the spiritual aspirant

or Murugan, outside of your own limited concepts. It is Ganesha who introduces you to the millions of Gods of the Hindu pantheon, no one else. That is the way it works."

Yes, little by little, slowly, imperceptibly, a relationship evolves, a very personal, loving relationship, between the devotee and the elephant-faced God. Psychic protection is granted; physical protection, mental and emotional protection are all granted as boons by Him. He will not allow His devotees to use their free, instinctive willfulness to make more negative karma by getting into difficulties. Rather, He will guide them carefully, protecting them every moment along the way so that their natural birth karmas may be worked through and good karma created by right living. This is His main concern. Lord Ganesha loves and cares for His devotees. Once the devotee is connected to Him through the awakening of the *muladhara* chakra, loneliness is never experienced.

Ganesha is a truly wonderful, loving God. He has an

A. MANIVEL

extraordinary knack for unweaving complicated situations and making them simple. He can unweave His devotees from their karma, simplifying and purifying their lives. But this only happens after they have established a personal relationship with Him. Soon thereafter, changes begin to happen in their lives; and when they go through difficult times, they no longer become angry or live in fear or worry. When difficult times come, they know it is because they are being unwound from accumulated and congested, difficult karmas, or being turned in a new direction altogether. They know that at such a time they have to consciously surrender their free, instinctive willfulness and not fight the divine happenings, but allow the God's divine will to guide their life. Such is the spiritual path of total surrender, known as *prapatti*.

is lifted up from fear and confusion into conscious awareness of right thought, right speech and right action, the *muladhara* chakra becomes activated. It is then that the seeker, with heart filled with love, encounters the holy feet of Lord Ganesha. As the spiritual seeker worships the loving elephant-faced God, clearness of mind comes more and more as he automatically and very slowly enters the Hindu path to enlightenment. Once the connection is firmly established between the devotee and Ganesha, all of the currents of the devotee's mind and body become harmonized. After that strong connection is made, should he falter on the spiritual path, he has gained divine protection.

But the seeker loses one thing. He loses his free, instinctive willfulness. It is lost forever. Yet it is not a great loss. Man's own personal willfulness, his animalistic free will, is a feeble and insignificant force when compared to Lord Ganesha's divine will. When beholden to God Ganesha and inwardly awakened enough to be attuned to His will, it is then quite natural that the instinctive will bows down. Personal likes and dislikes vanish. Limited faculties of reason and analysis are overpowered and subdued by a greater will, a cosmic will, the will of dharma. When sufficient humility has been awakened, it is easy to surrender personal, instinctive willfulness to the greater subsuperconscious will of dharma. It happens most naturally, but very slowly, because Lord Ganesha, of all the many Gods, proceeds with methodic deliberation. He is the careful, loving guide on the inner path of all seekers.

Among all the wonderful Hindu Deities, Lord Ganesha is the closest to the material plane of consciousness, most easily contacted and most able to assist us in our day-to-day life and concerns. In His hands Ganesha wields a noose and a goad. With the noose He can hold you close or hold obstacles close. Ganesha can capture and confine both blessings and obstacles. With the goad, Ganesha can strike and repel obstacles. This Lord is called the Remover of Obstacles; but He also places obstacles in our way, for sometimes his devotees are proceeding in the wrong direction, and His obstacles block their progress and guide them slowly back onto the straight path of dharma. When instinctive willfulness causes the seeker to decide to step out of the boundaries of dharma, the Lord of Obstacles is there to block the way. His emblem is the swastika, symbolizing His circuitous course in guiding the seeker through life's perplexing experiences.

The Meaning of Grace

"What about the grace of the Deity?" seekers ask. Grace is received from the God when you are consistent in your worship, consistent in your discipline, consistent in your bhakti, your devotion. With such a foundation in your life, a great shakti, a force or power, will come from Lord Ganesha. This is grace. It is uplifting. It comes unexpectedly. When grace comes, your mind may change and your heart may melt. Your sight will become clear

The Milk-Drinking Miracle of 1995

It all began on September 21, 1995, when an otherwise ordinary man in New Delhi dreamt that Ganesha, the elephant-headed God of wisdom, craved a little milk. Upon awakening, he rushed in the dark before dawn to the nearest temple, where a skeptical priest allowed him to proffer a spoonful of milk to the small stone image. Both watched in astonishment as it disappeared, magically consumed by the God. Within hours, news spread like a brush fire across India that Ganesha was accepting milk offerings. Tens of millions of people of all ages flocked to the temples. The unworldly happening brought worldly New Delhi to a standstill, and its vast stocks of milk, more than a million liters, sold out within hours. Just as suddenly as it started in India, it stopped, in just 24 hours. But it was just beginning elsewhere, as Hindus in India called their relatives in other parts of the world. Soon our HINDUISM TODAY offices were flooded with reports from around the world. Everywhere the story was the same. A teaspoonful of milk offered by touching it to Ganesha's trunk, tusk or mouth would disappear in a few seconds to a few minutes—not always, but with unprecedented frequency. Reuters news service quoted Anila Premji, "I held the spoon out level, and it just disappeared. To me it was just a miracle. It gave me a sense of feeling that there is a God, a sense of Spirit on this Earth." Not only Ganesha, but Siva, Parvati, Nandi and the Naga, Siva's snake, took milk. This "milk miracle" may go down in history as the most important event shared by Hindus this century, if not in the last millennium. It has brought about an instantaneous religious revival among nearly one billion people. No other religion has ever done that before! It is as if every Hindu who had, say, "ten pounds of devotion," suddenly has twenty

Miracles witnessed by many people happen from time to time in Hinduism as in other faiths, but they're rare. As a young boy, the tenth-century saint, Nambi Anbar Nambi, inspired Lord Ganesha to actually eat the offerings placed before Him. Saint Jnaneshvara

Temples mobbed after 'milk miracle'

By Rahul Bedi in New Delhi

THOUSANDS of people mobbed temples in the Indian capital of New Delhi yesterday after a rumour that idols of Hindu gods were drinking milk brought as offerings.

Traffic was halted as police struggled to control crowds who gathered outside hundreds of temples with jugs and saucepans of milk for the marble idols of Ganesh, the Hindu god of wisdom and learning, and Shiva, his father, the god of destruction.

The rumours began around midnight after a Hindu in south Delhi claimed that the Ganesh idol in his neighbourhood had drunk a cup of milk.

By early morning the story had spread beyond New Delhi to most other north Indian towns, bringing life to a virtual standstill as people rushed to temples to see for themselves.

Across Delhi, society ladies with silver jugs and tumblers full of milk could be seen standing alongside uneducated labouring women in mile-long queues, awaiting their turn. They claimed that small the god in milli across the coun drinking offeri milk.

"It is a mira have come dow solve all our pr Mrs Shakun housewife, out south Delhi tem

Another wor waited almost feed a white ma Ganesh, said world is conv and maybe the to help us."

The priest th than 5,000 peop his temple to r of milk and se "We are havin managing the c Indians are stitious and sa though not unknown, are u in their reach hoods or villag themselves.

Sceptics ye missed the cla and criticised

NEWS □ LOCAL

Statue of Hindu God, Ganesha, drinks milk

Phenomenon witnessed in Fiji and around the world

By Hari Gaunder

HINDUS in Fiji and throughout the world are witnessing a phenomenon which has been creating an international coverage through various television and radio stations.

According to the reports, Hindus all over the world that in their houses installed their consecrated statues of Lord Ganesha have been consuming milk.

People who have witnessed this have offered prayers and returned to their homes.

A fortnight ago Hindus worldwide thronged temples and other work this phenomenon seems to have taken place, first in India and then in various parts of the world wherever Hindus offered prayers to Lord Ganesha.

The belief nowadays gave a wide coverage of the miracle on Saturday night covering temples and other centres in

EVENING STANDARD

Believers thirst for a miracle from Hong Kong to Southall

The Edmonton Sunday Sun, September 24, 1995

Wonder of milk

By PHILIP LEE-SHANOK Staff Writer

The pilgrimage to see an idol that appears to drink milk has swelled as thousands of Alberta Hindus jammed an Edmonton temple for the second day.

Since Friday evening, milk held up to the black marble statue of the Hindu Lord Ganesha has been disappearing - as if the elephant-headed idol is drinking the milk.

"I've never done anything like life," said Pardeep Sethi after h teaspoon of milk beneath the stat "I feel like God has come to me."

Thousands of Albertans from a as Drumheller and Fort McMurray pilgrimage yesterday at the Ganesh 1603 111 St.

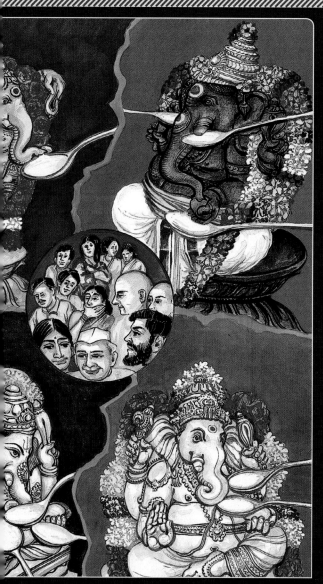

...st's depiction of the milk miracle: devotees lined up in long ...s and took turns offering spoons full of milk to statues of ...nesha, small and large, around the world. Magically, the ...k would vanish as if being sipped by an invisible being.

and penetrating. You may say, "I have been graced to see everything differently." New doors will begin to open for you, and as you go through them, your life will become more full, more wonderful. And the grace of it is that it would not have ordinarily happened to you.

By grace we are directed deeper into spiritual life, pointed in the right direction, carefully guided on the San Marga, the straight path to our supreme God. After grace has been received, our thoughts are enlivened, our life is inspired with enthusiasm and energy, and we live daily in the joyous knowledge that everything is all right, everything is happening around us in accord with our karma, our dharma and God's gracious will.

The Gods Are Real Beings, Not Mere Symbols

Many people look at the Gods as mere symbols, representations of forces or mind areas. Actually, the Gods are beings, and down through the ages ordinary men and women, great saints and sages, prophets and mystics in all cultures have inwardly seen, heard and been profoundly influenced by these superconscious, inner-plane, inner-galactic beings. Lord Ganesha is just such a being. He can think just as we can think. He can see and understand and make decisions—decisions so vast in their implications and complexity that we could never comprehend them with our human faculties of limited understanding.

In recent history, missionaries and others from the Western religions have told the Indian people over and over again that their Gods are not real beings, but merely symbols of spiritual matters—

to the Hindustan Times: "I am a senior scientist of the Indian Agriculture Research Institute, New Delhi. I found my offerings of milk in a temple being mysteriously drunk by the Deities. How can the scientists explain the copper snake absorbing the milk I offered with a spoon kept at a good distance away from it?" Scientific or not, gallons of milk were disappearing with hardly a trace. A leading barrister in Malaysia was dumbfounded when he watched a metal Ganesha attached to an automobile dashboard absorb six teaspoons of milk. In Nepal King Birendra himself made offerings to the God. Deities in Kenya and other countries took gallons of milk while sitting in shallow metal trays with no drains.

The worldwide press coverage was nearly as amazing as the miracle itself. Of course, the event dominated the news in India for days. But once it started outside India, local and leading national papers, such as the New York Times and Washington Post in America, and the Financial Times in UK, picked up the story. The international wire services, Reuters and Associated Press, carried a dozen articles a day on what had now been named the "Milk Miracle." Many in India are unaware of how warmly the Western press embraced the miracle. In many countries reporters came to the temples and personally offered milk.

...f Maharashtra became famous 600 years ago for having a water buffalo ...ecite the *Vedas* before a group of arrogant priests.

Naturally there are skeptics—10 percent of Hindus, according to our ...ery unscientific poll, all of whom moved swiftly to distance themselves ...rom the phenomenon. "Capillary action," coupled with "mass hysteria," ...s the correct explanation, concluded many scientists within a few hours. ...parna Chattopadhyay of New Delhi replied to these scoffers in a letter

and unfortunately many have begun to believe this and look at their Gods in this way. Even among Hindus there are quite a few who don't believe in inner-world beings. Their belief is restricted to the people they see in the physical world, and that is all. You dare not tell them differently. It is very difficult, but not impossible, to introduce them to the grand philosophy which is based solely on worship, meditation, inner discipline and the search for Absolute Truth. But this is too high-minded for those living in the everyday materialistic consciousness. For the knowledge of inner worlds to become accepted, a personal realization has to occur. This is a slow process for the materialist, a very slow process, and only Lord Ganesha can help it along. To contact Lord Ganesha, it is imperative that the materialist visit one of His temples or shrines, to make initial contact. It only takes one meeting.

Around the World

Maha Ganapati, of course, belongs to all mankind, not to Hindus alone. To the Chinese He is embodied in the form of a massive dragon, whose physical immensity depicts His incredible and irresistible force. To some Chinese He is Kuan-shi t'ien or Ho Tei, the large-bellied God of Happiness. To the Polynesians in Hawaii He is God Lono.

The South Indian and Sri Lankan Tamils call him by the affectionate term Pillaiyar, "Noble Child." The Tibetans know Him as Ts'ogsbdag, and the Burmese worship Maha-Pienne. In Mongolia His name is Totkharour Khaghan. Cambodians offer worship to Prah Kenes, and the Japanese supplicate Vinayaksa or Sho-ten. By some He is envisioned as the feminine Mother Nature, and even

Mantras to Ganesha—Using the Magic of Sound

Japa, or recitation, is the spiritual practice of devotedly repeating a mantra, generally a specified number of times, such as 108, often while counting on a strand of beads, called a *japa mala,* while conscientiously concentrating on the meaning of the mantra. The repetition should be dutifully slow. This brings *punya,* merit, to the devotee. It should not be thoughtlessly mechanical or hurried, the so-called rapid-fire or machine-gun *japa.* Such casual, nonchalant negligence and disregard for contemplative traditions brings *papa,* demerit, to the devotee, creating internal strife, community opposition and turmoil for all concerned.

Japa is a form of devotional worship, invocation, supplication, praise, adoration, meditation and direct, experiential communion. Unless we are actually in a state of samadhi (total absorption), which is rare for most people, *japa* provides a means to disengage from our racing thoughts and our memories of the past—mostly the bad ones. The repetition of positive, uplifting, spiritual mantras over and over again lifts consciousness and causes the *muladhara* chakra to spin clockwise. We feel uplifted. Life does not look so bad, and neither does the past. A sense of forgiveness comes and the future looms bright. The past is forgiven and forgotten.

Top of page, a gallery of Ganesha images, from greeting cards, posters and temples; right, Ganesha in the Aum; above, a devotee performs japa.

A. MANIVEL

What is important for us to realize is that each Mahadeva can be experienced, expressed, in a mantra form that corresponds to that Being. This phenomenon is akin to remembering someone by his name rather than his face. When we utter such a mantra, we call forth the Mahadeva or cause a particular inner truth to rise up in our minds. Then we feel His presence and enjoy.

Repeating mantras slowly purifies the mind, like running fresh water continually into a container of discolored water. A fresh stream of water causes the mud at the bottom of a container to rise and flow out over the top edges, eventually to be completely replaced by crystal-clear water. Similarly, *japa* cleanses the mind of impurities as the pure vibrations of the mantras loosen and wash away the impure vibrations.

Lord Ganesha is invoked through the mantra Aum. The *Mandukya Upanishad* elucidates the inner meaning of Aum, which embodies the highest wisdom. Aum has three syllables. A represents the waking state. U represents the dreaming state. M represents the state of deep sleep. Aum in its entirety, plus the moment of silence which follows it, represents the shanti, the peace beyond understanding. Thus, Aum *japa* performed as an invocation to Lord Ganesha, the Lord of Wisdom

nonbelievers seek to understand Him through personifying His great powers as Fate, Destiny or Numen. The ancient Egyptians may have known Him as a minor but very popular Deity, Bes, grotesque, pot-bellied and cheerful. The Romans called Him Janus and sought His blessings at the outset of any new venture. On His festival on the first of January (the month named after Him) He was treated with special cakes; mutual good wishes were exchanged and people made presents of sweets to one another for a good omen for the new year. In the West He is ubiquitous as the corpulent jolly Santa Claus, the dispenser of boons and gifts, especially to children, who knows our thoughts, words and deeds and bestows rewards accordingly. The Buddhists and Jains also honor Ganesha. In one form or another, He is honored throughout the world.

Hindus worship the great God Ganesha at countless pujas per-

formed daily on every continent. In temples and home shrines Lord Ganesha is worshiped today in India, Sri Lanka, Nepal, Malaysia, Java, Bali, Borneo, Tibet, Myanmar, Siam, Afganistan, the Middle East, China, Indo-China, Japan, the Caribbean, Trinidad and Tobago, Hawaii and the Pacific Islands, Africa, Mauritius, Reunion, Europe, Australia, Canada, South America, the United States and elsewhere.

Every Hindu village and community has an image of the God Ganesha, and one of the many forms of Ganesha is found in every Hindu temple. The eminent scholar M. Arunachalam wrote, "Ganesha is usually installed at the entrance to the central sanctum, at the south, and also at the southwestern corner in the first court, of every Siva temple. Besides, He is placed on the first eastern *goshta* (niche) on the other southern wall of the *ardha mandapa* (secondary hall) in the dancing pose, known as

and Knowledge—while love is welling up from our hearts and tears are for no reason flowing simultaneously—calls forth the knowledge of the entirety of our existence in these four categories of consciousness. These are realms that God Ganesha rules over as Lord of Categories, and this is the knowledge that He can grant devotees who perform Aum *japa* and meditation on the meaning of Aum.

For Aum *japa* to be effective, the mantra must be pronounced correctly. The first syllable is A, pronounced as the English word "awe," but prolonged: "aaa." The second syllable is U, as in "roof," pronounced "oo" but prolonged: "ooo." The third syllable is M, pronounced "mm" with the front teeth gently touching and the sound prolonged: "mmmm." Each repetition is sounded for about seven seconds, with two seconds on A, two seconds on U and three seconds on M, with a silence of about two seconds before the next repetition. The three syllables are run together: AAUUMM (silence), AAUUMM (silence), AAUUMM (silence). On the first syllable, A, we feel the solar plexus and chest vibrating. On the second syllable, U, the throat vibrates. The third syllable, M, vibrates the top of the head. Thus, proper chanting of Aum is a high form of yoga, moving energy from the lower chakras of the body up to the highest chakra, or energy center—the *sahasrara* chakra at the crown of the head.

Another traditional way to do this *japa* is to take a full breath and then chant the AUM three times as you exhale. The first repetition is

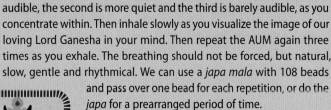

audible, the second is more quiet and the third is barely audible, as you concentrate within. Then inhale slowly as you visualize the image of our loving Lord Ganesha in your mind. Then repeat the AUM again three times as you exhale. The breathing should not be forced, but natural, slow, gentle and rhythmical. We can use a *japa mala* with 108 beads and pass over one bead for each repetition, or do the *japa* for a prearranged period of time.

Two other Ganesha mantras are commonly used. One is Aum Shri Ganeshaya Namah, meaning "Praise to Lord Ganesha." This is the mantra of invocation, adoration and worship. It is repeated at the beginning of pujas, and it can be used for *japa* to invoke Ganesha's blessings for the auspicious beginning of a task, project, change of life, community undertaking or simply to offer Him our praise. Another special mantra is Aum Gam Ganapataye Namah. This is Lord Ganesha's *mula* ("root") mantra. It is also known as His *bija* mantra, for it combines Ganesha's *bija* ("seed") sound, *Gam*, with the phrase, "Praise be to Ganapati." This mantra is used for yoga *sadhana* in which we invoke Ganesha and merge ourself with His supreme knowledge and peace.

When the *ganas* and *devas* of Lord Ganesha are finally attracted to the home shrine, the room will feel filled with spiritual energy. This feeling indicates that Ganesha's *ganas* are present, eager and willing to do whatever they can to maintain shanti, peace, within the home and bind the family together.

Nartana Ganapati, in many temples. The tip of His trunk will curve to the left and touch the *modaka*, generally held in the left hand. In a few rare cases the trunk will curve to the right to touch the *modaka* on a right hand. Here He is called Valampuri (right turned) Vinayaga" (*Festivals of Tamil Nadu*, 1980, p. 112).

While Ganesha shrines are found at all Hindu temples, they often stand alone as well. They are often quite humble, not uncommonly a simple roadside shrine such as the one between Jaffna and Anuradhapura in Sri Lanka or along the roadsides here and there in South India. Here travelers stop to break a coconut and burn a bit of camphor before the Lord of Obstacles to pray for a safe and successful journey. There is a similar shrine near the university in Chennai. Many years ago a young man discovered a tree that formed the shape of Ganesha's head in its gnarled trunk. He began worshiping and soon took a vow not to leave the site. Travelers and students about to take their exams come to the shrine to seek Lord Ganesha's blessings. Such tree shrines enjoy the patronage of thousands of worshipers annually.

Historically His image is often found in places of danger, such as steep slopes, river crossings or where two roads cross. Here His *murti* may be a rough-hewn stone or even a trunk of a bo or banyan tree which has taken the form of the God Ganesha. A natural stone, or *svayambhu* ("self-created") *murti*, may also be the object of worship. Researcher Alice Getty wrote: "The most celebrated *svayambhu murtis* of Ganesha are found in Kashmir, where there are three famous and most powerful formless stones which from ancient times have drawn pilgrims to their shrines. One, which is near the village of Ganesh-bal, is in the river Lidar near its right bank, and is still an important place of pilgrimage.... Another rock in Kashmir which has been worshiped from most ancient times as a symbol of Ganesha under the name of Bhimasvamin is at the foot of the hill Hari-Parbat near Srinagar.... The most

remarkable of these *svayambhu murtis* in Kashmir is the one on a cliff along the Kishen-Ganga known as Ganesh-Gati" (*Ganesha, a Monograph on the Elephant-Faced God*, by Alice Getty, 1971, p. 22-23).

Perhaps the most famous Ganesha temple in India is the Uchi Pillaiyar Koyil at Trichy. Uchi means "at the top." This large temple (also known as the Rock Fort Temple), built on a hilltop, commands a breathtaking view of the city and of the river Kaveri. Another large Ganesha temple is the Pillaiyarpatti Temple near Karaikudi in Ramanathapuram District, also in Tamil Nadu. In New Delhi there is the Siddhi Buddhi Vinayagar temple situated in Vinayanagar. The Mukkuruni Pillaiyar inside the huge Meenakshi Temple complex in Madurai, India, is also quite famous. This *murti* is ten to twelve feet tall. Mukkuruni refers to a large measure of rice (about forty pounds). Here the priests cook a huge *modaka* ball for Ganesha using this measure. Hence the name Mukkuruni Pillaiyar. Also in Madurai, Lord Ganesha is worshiped as Vyaghrapada Ganeshani, in female form with tiger feet. The Ganeshani *murti* in *sukhasana* pose resides at Suchindram. There are two other temples in India with the female Ganesha form. One is at a tenth-century temple dedicated to sixty-four yoginis in Bheraghat, a village near Jabalpur. The other is the Tanumalaya Swami Temple in Suchindrum, Kerala. In Tibet She is worshiped as Gajanani.

A five-headed Ganesha mounted on a lion resides at Nagapattinam. At Vellore, India, Ganesha is enshrined as Valampuri Vinayakar, with his trunk

Festivals for Ganesha ॐ

Opulent Hindu festivals are times of joyous celebration marked by special observances. There are many festivals each year, several to each of the Gods. Festivals are characterized by acts of piety—penance, fasting, *sadhana*, pilgrimage—and spiritual rejoicing: singing, dancing, musical performance, parades, feasting, storytelling, scripture-reading and elaborate pujas. Here we briefly present the major festivals that honor Lord Ganesha.

Ganesha Chaturthi

Ganesha Chaturthi, also known as Vinayaka Chaturthi, is the festival day celebrating the birth of Lord Ganesha. One of the great national festivals of India, and the foremost annual festival to Ganesha, it is celebrated on the *chaturthi*, or "fourth day" after the new moon, in August/September. We decorate the temple and home shrine with banana leaves, sugarcane and strings of mango leaves, making it look like a small for-

Children bring offerings during Pancha Ganapati. The five colored rays above Ganesha represent his five shaktis.

est. We bring baskets of fruits and sweets, especially *modaka* balls, and place them before the sanctum. He receives special pujas throughout the day and often a festival parade. Each year we obtain or make a small or large soft clay image of Ganapati and use it for worship at home for two to ten days after Ganesha Chaturthi. Then we bid Him fond farewell, honoring His departure, or *visarjana*, with a grand parade, as we carry Him to the water's edge on a palanquin bedecked with flowers and accompanied by puja, music, dancing and celebration. Clay images of Ganesha specifically prepared for the event are ceremoniously dissolved in the ocean or other body of water at this time by devotees all over the world, signifying His withdrawal into all-pervasive consciousness. This final day is known as Ganesha Visarjana.

Vinayaka Vratam

Vinayaka Vratam is a 21-day festival honoring Lord Gane-

CAROLE KAHN

Above, a parade in Mumbai; left, a devotee prays intently and offers incense; below, a graceful Ganesha in granite carved in Bangalore

turned to the right instead of to the left. This *murti* is considered very auspicious. Highly revered Ganesha shrines are also found in the Siva temple of Tirunelveli, in the Kanyakumari temple at the southern tip of India, and in Rameshvaram and Chidambaram. Our loving Ganesha is especially beloved in Maharashtra, where eight temples form one of His most sacred pilgrimages, and dozens of other sites are designated for his adoration. (Go to www.gurudeva.org/resources/books/lg/lg_ch-13 for an extensive list of prominent Ganesha citadels.) It is said that to make a visit on hardship pilgrimage (third-class on trains, on foot or by crawling) to 108 Ganesha temples and roadside shrines is most auspicious to smooth out the karmas of the future by dissolving, through His grace, the negative karmas and mistakes of the past, made knowingly or unknowingly. Penance of this sort deliberately condenses into a short period, or puts all in one place, the suffering that would otherwise be encountered over a long span of time.

The garden island of Sri Lanka has fourteen well-known Ganesha temples. There is an unusual Vinayaka at the Siva temple in Central Java, which is presently an archeological tourist site being restored by the Indonesian government. Lord Ganesha here sits with the soles of His feet pressed together, much like a child would sit, or as a yogi might sit in deep samadhi.

Shri H. Krishnamurthi writes in *Tattvaloka* (Feb.-March 1990): "Several images of Ganesha have been discovered in the excavations of Central America and Mexico. It is said that in Mexico the name of Ganesha is

fruits and incense are offered to Pancha Ganapati, ideally prepared and presented by the children. Puja is performed and hymns and bhajanas are sung in His praise. Each day gifts are given to the children, who place them unopened before Pancha Ganapati, to open on the fifth day.

On each day the family focuses on one of Ganesha's five shaktis, through discussion, gift-giving, apology and appreciation. On day one we draw forth Ganesha's first shakti to create a vibration of love and harmony among immediate family members. On day two we draw forth Ganesha's second shakti to establish a vibration of love and harmony among neighbors, relatives and close friends. On day three we strive to create love and harmony among business associates, the casual merchant and the public at large. On day four we draw forth the vibration of joy and harmony that comes from music, art, drama and the dance. On day five we strive to bring forth the special rewards and fulfillments that only religion brings into our life. We focus this day on our connection with Ganesha, the Lord of Dharma, by holding five special pujas for Him through the day. After the grand evening puja, gifts are distributed and joyously opened. Happy children. Happy parents. Happy God.

sha beginning on the full moon day in the month of Karttikai—November/December. During these days, *Vinayaka Purana,* or stories, are recited in the temples, and special pujas are conducted at every Ganesha temple. Many devotees observe the *vrata* (vow) of attending daily puja at a Ganesha temple and taking only one meal a day, in the evening.

Pancha Ganapati

Pancha Ganapati is a modern festival of the Five-Faced (*pancha* means "five") Ganesha held in Hindu homes from December 21 through 25. Pancha Ganapati is a Hindu expression of this natural season of worship, gift-giving and celebration. A festive shrine is created especially for the five-day event in the main living room of the home. Each day sweets,

Virakosha." India's Birla Science Institute announced a new find: "A piece of evidence was connected with the legend of Ganesha's writing down the [*Mahabharata*] epic to the dictation of Vyasa. A metal plate depicting the elephant-headed Deity holding an etching stylus has been found in Luristan in Western Iran and has been dated to around 1200 BCE (Motilal Banarsidass Newsletter Dec. 1993)."

Among the most renowned of Ganesha's temples in Malaysia are the Siddhi Vinayagar temple of Petaling Jaya and the Kotta Malai Pillaiyar Temple of Kuala Lumpur on the busy street of Paduraya. The latter is a small temple, but extremely powerful, said to be the most popular Ganesha temple in the land. Also notable are the Jalan Pudu (Pasar Road) Pillaiyar Temple and the Poyyata Vinayagar Temple of Melaka. In Hawaii our Kadavul Hindu Temple has a three-ton, six-foot-tall Ganesha. At the Saiva Dharmashala at Riviere du Rempart, Mauritius, we have dedicated a Spiritual Park and erected a grand pavilion around a five-ton, nine-foot tall, five-faced *murti* of Ganesha, Panchamukha Ganapati, in a mango grove. In Edmonton, Canada, New Zealand and Nandi, Fiji, Seattle, Salt Lake City, Bethesda, Denver, Scottsdale, Sebastian, Anchorage and Chicago there are exquisite stone *murtis* of the elephant-faced God, gifted by my *aadheenam* to the born Hindu communities, conferring blessings for new temples. In Great Britain Ganesha is enshrined at each of the nation's several new temples, including the Shree Ganapati Temple in Wimbledon, and is the presiding Deity at the and at temples in Switzerland, Germany and Denmark.

The religion of the earliest known North American Indians bears many analogies to and apparently has sprung up from the same ultimate sources as our own venerable Sanatana Dharma, a fact that is evidenced by their rituals and religious beliefs and symbols. One of Lord Ganesha's oldest symbols, the swastika, was one of the central motifs used in the designs and patterns of many American Indian tribes and is still seen today in their beautiful blankets and pottery. So the great God Ganesha is not really new to the Western countries, but quite old. His recent coming into prominence is more our remembering Him in lands where He has always been. But it is in this twentieth century, in the decades of the 70s and 80s, that Lord Ganesha came to be traditionally enshrined in magnificent multi-million-dollar Hindu temples. We find Him in New York, Pittsburgh, Chicago, Concord, Livermore, Fremont, Denver, Houston, Nashville, Edmonton in Canada and hundreds of other places. These shrines have brought forth the *murti*, or physical image, of Ganesha as Gajanana, the Elephant-Faced. Ganesha's presence in North America at the beginning of the growth of Agamic Hinduism in the West ensures its success.

As Hinduism emerged in North America in the twentieth century, Ganesha led the way. One of the first traditional temples to be built was the large Maha Ganapati Temple in Flushing, New York. As each community sought guidance and direction in establishing religious roots, I constantly urged the trustees of each temple society, who came seeking guidance from Kauai's Hindu Monastery in the Hawaiian Island chain, to first begin their congregations in the worship of Ganesha in order for their temple to come up quickly.

We would often present the group with large or small stone image of the great God and give them the blessings for His worship to begin. Thus, at

Connecting with Ganesha through Puja

Love and joy come to Hindu families who worship Lord Ganesha in their home through the traditional ceremony known as puja. By means of such sacred rites and the divine energies invoked, each family makes their house a sacred sanctuary, a refuge from the concerns and worries of the world. Pujas can be as simple as lighting a lamp and offering a flower at the Lord's holy feet; or they can be elaborate and detailed, with many chants and offerings. The indispensable part of any puja is devotion. Without love in the heart, outer performance is of little value. But with true devotion, even simple gestures are sacred ritual. Every morning, all around our planet, millions of Hindus perform puja in their home.

A superb definition of puja is given in *South Asian Folklore: An Encyclopedia*. "A puja is a ritual performance that honors a being or an object and provides the context for the transaction between worshiper and deity in which a visual and substantive connection can occur. The most common expression in theistic Hinduism today, pujas are done outdoors, in homes, temples, at natural sites, and within a devotee's mind and body.

The external focus of a puja is a *murti* (form), which may be a respected living being, such as a teacher or guru; a stone, wood, or metal icon of a deity; an aniconic image, such as the Ganges River; plants; animals; the implements of one's profession or subsistence; or any form to which devotion and a relationship of dependence is to be demonstrated" (Routledge, 2002).

One need not be initiated to perform simple puja invoking our Loving Ganesha. All that is required is that the celebrant believe in the laws of karma and reincarnation, which are the cornerstones of Hindu ethical and philosophical doctrine. Ganesha worship is enjoyed by all, Hindus and non-Hindus alike, as He is the first God to be worshiped. It is not wise for an *ardha*-Hindu, or half Hindu, to centralize worship on Siva or Murugan or other Gods until full commitment has been made through receiving the traditional sacraments, called samskaras. Home puja is performed at least once a day, usu-

many a new temple site, a Ganesha image was established in a small shrine while construction and fund raising proceeded. This occurred in Fiji, Edmonton, Livermore, Fremont, Salt Lake City, Houston, Denver, Chicago, Lansing, Bethesda, London, Germany and elsewhere. Priests were brought from India, devotees flocked to the shrines, the worship began, and the funds to construct the temple began to flow. This practice has now become a tradition in the West as Hindus have learned from experience that once Lord Ganesha is worshiped, it is actually He who builds the temple in a most wonderful and inspiring way, and they are His helpers.

Visions of Ganesha

Lord Ganesha's vivified presence in the Western world has already culminated in many special visions of Him by both born and formally converted Hindus living in North and South America. In hopes of spiriting onward the worldwide fellowship of Hindus around the globe, a few such visions will be included here anonymously.

Lord Ganesha has been worshiped here and there in North and South America in many small ways by devotees from India for

Left, this stunningly ornate Ganesha shrine at Bangkok's World Trade Center is a favorite place of worship for Thai Hindus and Buddhists. Below, Bodhinatha receives an elephant's blessing in Madurai. Below left, a devotee performing puja perceives Ganesha as a real, living being.

HINDUISM TODAY

ally in the early morning. It is traditional to not partake of food at least three hours before puja, so puja is usually done prior to meals.

All Hindus attend puja at their local temple at least once a week and maintain a sacred shrine at home, which esoterically functions as an extension of the temple. The shrine room is meticulously cared for and not used for purposes other than worship, prayer, *japa* yoga, scriptural study and meditation. Here puja, home liturgy, is performed daily, generally by the head of the house. All members of the family attend.

Creating a home shrine is not difficult. The altar should be close to the floor, since most of the puja is performed while seated, or when there are small children in the home it is often higher, out of their reach. For a Ganesha shrine, an image, or *murti*, of Lord Ganesha is placed at the center of the altar.

The entire puja, of which this is a summary, can be learned in the following chapter. Puja is a ritual welcoming of a holy person or deity, to whom all precious substances and comforts are offered. Offerings are made with the right hand.

The offering of food is an important part of puja, such as cooked rice or freshly cut fruit. After the puja, the food offerings—along with holy ash (*vibhuti*), sacred water (*tirtha*), sandalwood paste (*chandana*), red powder (*kunkuma*) and flowers (*pushpa*)—are passed out and enjoyed as *prasada*, for they have been imbued with the blessings of the God.

After the sacraments are passed out, everyone present can chant Aum three times and then sit quietly and direct their worship to God within themselves. Externalized worship traditionally is followed by internalized worship, yogic quietude enjoyed in the aftermath of the puja. The simple practice of mentally chanting Aum followed by a period of meditation and self-reflection makes devotees strong enough to face the external world with enhanced willpower, true confidence and a heart filled with love, realizing that we are truly one world, one family.

many years since the turn of the century. But not until events in the early 1970s brought about the building of a large Ganesha temple in New York did Lord Ganesha take up a formal public residence. The sequence of events affirmed the ancient tradition wherein the Deity Himself decides when and where His temple is to be built. It is not a man or a woman or a group of people who make that decision on personal inspiration. Rather, the Deity, the God, informs us that the time has come for His temple to come up and then we, in turn, proceed to help Him manifest it in the material world. The message from the God containing the direction of when and where to build His home is traditionally given by Him to holy men, gurus, swamis or sants who are respected by the community and are in personal touch with the Gods. Such religious leaders also have spiritual insight into the religious progress of the community. Lord Ganesha may strengthen the instructions of such holy men through a dream or vision to a devotee.

The Maha Ganapati Temple in Flushing, New York, began with two gentlemen from India who had been living in New York for several years. One of these hailed from a long line of temple builders; the other was a devout man who performed regular religious and yoga *sadhana*. This man had returned to India. He had a vision one night. He found himself soaring high above New York City until he came above an abandoned church in an area near his former residence. He came over the steeple, which opened as he moved down to land in front of the altar. Lo! There on the altar was Lord Ganapati Himself, who said nothing to him but just smiled. Immediately upon awakening, with his heart filled with love and the vision of the Great God still fresh in his inner mind, this sant phoned the temple builder who was then serving at the United Nations in New York.

The temple builder asked him to come to New York right away. Travel arrangements were made, and within 24 hours the two of them were driving around the Queens section of New York in search of Lord Ganapati's new home. They finally came upon the

A. MANIVEL

old church that was the very one seen in the vision and which was for sale at the time! There could be no doubt that Ganesha had shown where to put His temple. The building was subsequently purchased. After many years of hard work, with the blessings and sanction of Shrilashri Pandrimalaiswami, Ganesha was installed and consecrated in an orthodox shrine to receive traditional public worship.

Since 1972 many other devotees have seen Lord Ganesha in their visions and dreams. For example, several pilgrims on the 1981 India Odyssey, a spiritual pilgrimage to the holy lands of ancient Bharat (India), had life-altering visions of Lord Ganesha at the Shri Kumbalavalai Temple in Jaffna, Sri Lanka. Such visions of Lord Ganesha clarify much about the way this great Lord works. While the visions took place within the subtle minds of His devotees, or our microcosm, this subtle space is in fact enormous and quite a macrocosm of its own.

Just as Lord Ganesha's vehicle, the tiny rodent, ferrets out every secret space and hidden area of the house, so does this Great Mahadeva have the ability to move within the seemingly most obscure and intricate areas of our minds. He is the master of both the big and the small, the macrocosm and the microcosm. Lord Ganesha's great girth is the entire

INDIVAR SIVANATHAN

Personal Testimony about Ganesha

Kamala Garneau, Edmonton, Canada. "During the last year of my degree, I was facing a very important interview for entrance into an internship program. As the interview drew near, I went to the temple and sat and prayed to Lord Ganesha. I told Him that I would make coming to see Him daily a priority in my life for a minimum of two weeks and as long as I could after that, and prayed for Him to remove any obstacles blocking my path from having a successful interview and being accepted into the program. The next day I woke up early and went to the temple for the puja. This routine continued, and the day of the interview drew near. On the day of the interview, I was reviewing some possible interview questions my family and I had prepared. Later, as I was brushing my teeth, three different interview questions just entered my mind. They were somewhat unusual and a little complicated to answer, so I mentally prepared answers to them as I drove to the interview. As it turned out, I was asked all three of those questions in exactly the same way they came to me. Thanks to Lord

Ganesha, I had already prepared my answers and was easily able to handle them and finish the interview successfully. That night I went to the temple and thanked Lord Ganesha for helping me. A few months later I was accepted into the program."

Sheela Venkatakrishnan, Chennai. "Ganeshas in myriad shapes and forms sit around my home, reminding me of who I am and what I can become! Tears wash away with just one look in the sheer joy that emanates from every form He took. Acceptance becomes a way of life. Surrender comes as a shield from strife. It becomes easy to amble along with the heart singing a sweet, sweet song! Ganesha, my friend, my guide, stands strong when all seems wrong. He lights up the way every day and shatters all that stands in the way of what I will become one day! A shining soul such as He. You are Him, and He is me!"

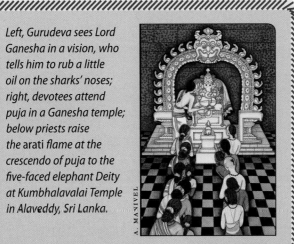

Left, Gurudeva sees Lord Ganesha in a vision, who tells him to rub a little oil on the sharks' noses; right, devotees attend puja in a Ganesha temple; below priests raise the arati flame at the crescendo of puja to the five-faced elephant Deity at Kumbhalavalai Temple in Alaveddy, Sri Lanka.

A. MANIVEL

manifestation of all that is, of the five elements of earth, air, fire, water and ether. Thus, He pervades all, not from the outside in but from the inside out. He does not move to pervade, for all form in its purest state is together, not far apart. Seated unmoving on the broad, four-petalled lotus of the *muladhara* chakra, Lord Ganesha records and governs the movements of vast inner oceans of actinodic energy that appear to our physical eyes to manifest as forms so many millions of miles apart. He is at work through all the outwardly gross forms of nature, and yet mounted on his tiny mouse He can, in utter minuteness, travel about within His devotees' minds as if they were great, well-lit caverns. Such is the mystery of the pompous elephant-faced God, the embodiment of form who rides the mouse.

The final vision to recite is one that I had in the mid-1980s of Lord Ganesha walking from His temple attended by two priests. He was about to take a bath in the beautiful Indian Ocean in the country of Mauritius where the river meets the sea. I was standing in the water with several sharks swimming around me. Lord Ganesha, accompanied by two priests, looked at me and said, "Just rub some oil on their noses and they will not harm you." This vivid mystic experience is illustrated on this page (above left).

Remember, such visions of this great Lord do not come only to the meditating yogis, but to sincere *bhaktas* as well —those who by virtue of their good karma receive this special grace at particularly auspicious times in their lives.

more meaningful as I began to analyze what Sanatana Dharma is. I began to meditate, or rather sit down quietly to get some concentration. I began to buy books on spiritual life. Then one day, my group of friends brought me to a powerful consecration rite for a nearby Pillaiyar temple. During the visits to Pillaiyar in this temple my spiritual life

Vikneswaran, Kuala Lumpur. "Since my teens, I have been acquainted with this beautiful God. He was my guide since then. I first got to know Him when I saw His *svayambhu* form in an old tree where people used to pray to Him. I would go and burn camphor to Him whenever I could. I wasn't a devout person, and I was very much attached to the ideologies of the West. Still, my daily life somehow was centered around Him. I used to sit at the tree simply watching His beautifully formed face with its huge trunk. He somehow communicated with me whenever I was there with Him, and gradually my life turned deepened. I am still learning about Lord Ganesha, still communicating with Lord Ganesha, still loving my Lord Ganesha. Every single obstacle that I face in my life, Pillaiyar removes for me; even the littlest problems are solved by Him."

Chamundi Sabanathan, California. "My most vivid experience with Lord Ganesha occurred at the old temple on Sacramento Street in San Francisco, not long after His *murti* was installed. I was seated at the back of the room, but suddenly had the experience of being at His feet, prostrating with overwhelming devotion."

CHAPTER 24

Home Puja

A Simple, Traditional Worship Ceremony to Lord Ganesha that Anyone Can Perform—with English Translation, Illustrations And Internet Resources to Facilitate Learning the Chants

T HE HINDU FORM OF HOME WORSHIP, KNOWN AS puja, is unique in all the world. Quite fittingly, it arises from the magnanimous spirit of hospitality that Hindu people are famous for. All guests are received and treated as God in the Hindu home, and God is no exception. During this daily morning rite, family members gather in their well-appointed shrine room to honor God as their royal guest. They receive Him warmly, offer a seat, serve water to quench His thirst, bathe and dress Him in beautiful clothes, burn the finest incense for His enjoyment, honor Him with light and flowers and feed Him a sumptuous meal. It is an intimate, personal interaction with God. Throughout the puja, the officiant chants sweetly to the Deity in Sanskrit, describing these kindly acts and beseeching His blessings. Finally, he thanks the Deity for His presence, bids Him farewell and humbly apologizes for any errors he may have committed. It is a ritual performed daily in millions of homes. In a sense, each Hindu has a private temple right in the home, and invites God to abide there, close to the family. Mystically, it keeps open the channels to the superconscious, divine areas of the inner worlds, bringing peace, health, prosperity and happiness to family members. Intellectually, it keeps religious beliefs strong. Emotionally, it cultivates a burgeoning love of God, known as bhakti. ¶Puja literally

means "worship, adoration." Home puja is a personal version of the public puja performed in temples by priests. The forms of puja vary widely between Hinduism's four main denominations and its hundreds of lineages, but all puja finds its basis in sixteen offerings, *shodasha upachara.* These also vary somewhat, depending on the scriptural source that is followed, but one popular list is the following: 1) *Āvāhanam,* invoking; 2) *Āsanam,* offering a seat; 3) *Pādyam,* offering water for cleansing feet; 4) *Arghyam,* offering water for cleansing the palms; 5) *Āchamanīyam,* sipping water; 6) *Snānam,* ceremonial bath; 7) *Vastram,* offering vestments; 8) *Yajñopavītam,* offering sacred thread; 9) *Chandanam,* offering sandalwood paste; 10) *Pushpam,* offering flowers; 11) *Dhūpam,* burning incense; 12) *Dīpam,* waving lighted camphor; 13) *Naivedyam,* offering food; 14) *Añjali,* praying with folded hands; 15) *Pradakshinā,* circumambulation; 16) *Udvasanam,* farewell. Lord Ganesha is the God honored and worshiped by all Hindus, so here we present a puja for this universally beloved, boon-giving Lord of Beginnings and Ruler of Obstacles, which can be performed by anyone, young and old, Hindu or non-Hindu, Vaishnava or Shakta, Saiva or Smarta. It is Lord Ganesha who bridges all distinctions and unifies all peoples, and it is through His worship that we ultimately come to know all the other Gods.

A young Hindu family share in morning worship, as father performs the traditional rite of worship called puja, honoring and invoking the blessings of the Elephant-Headed Lord of Dharma, the Deity worshiped by Hindus of all lineages.

Family members have donned traditional clothing and gathered in their shrine room for morning worship. They are just completing their preparations and are about to begin the daily ritual that keeps their home safe, harmonious and spiritually vibrant.

Instructions for Establishing a Home Shrine And Performing Puja to Lord Ganesha

In performing the puja, preparation is of utmost importance— gathering flowers, cleaning the altar and puja tray, making ready the oil lamps and preparing the fruit and/or cooked food offering. It is common to chant a Ganesha mantra or softly sing devotional songs while performing these tasks. This quiets the mind and brings one's awareness close to Him. Indeed, all this preparation is an integral part of worship.

As you see in the photos, there are a number of traditional implements needed for the puja, such as a metal tray, holy water cups and spoons, ghee lamp, camphor lamp, as well as puja supplies, like holy ash and sandalwood paste. These are now available at Indian grocery stores, and online at www.minimela. com. For more information on setting up an altar, see Chapter 22, "Hindu Home Sanctuary"

Before beginning the puja, check the altar to make sure all necessary articles are there, so that you don't have to interrupt the flow of puja to get a missing item. Arrange all the items the same way for each puja so you can reach automatically when needed, with those most frequently used closest at hand.

Hold the attitude that, as *pujari*, you are a servant of the Gods, a channel for the spiritual energies. Only thoughts of God are on your mind as you perform puja, thus enhancing the outpouring of divine blessings. Tradition provides a caution: you should never perform puja during or within 31 days of experiencing severe anger or other deep emotional upset, but it is all right to attend.

Also, puja is not performed or attended by women during their menses, or by anyone who has a wound that is bleeding. Puja is a yoga, or link, between this and inner worlds. Therefore, you must be at your best in mood and emotion to assist in making this connection. Before performing puja, you should be freshly dressed, clean and undistracted by daily concerns. Having bathed beforehand, enter the shrine room and prostrate.

The form of prostration differs for men and women. Men perform "eight-limbed obeisance," *ashtanga pranama,* a fully prone pose in which hands, chest, forehead, knees and feet touch the ground. Women perform "five-limbed obeisance," *panchanga pranama,* a kneeling pose in which hands, head and knees touch the ground (with ankles crossed, right over the left).

When everything is ready, take your seat in a cross-legged posture in front of and to the left of the altar, facing the Deity but turned slightly to the right. Close your eyes, sit quietly for a moment and tune your nerve system to God Ganesha and the sacred puja you are about to perform. If others are attending, be careful not to sit directly in front of the Deity, thereby blocking their view of the altar. Generally one remains seated throughout the ritual, though in some shrines it may be more comfortable to stand during the *arati* or throughout the puja. When small children are in the home, the shrine room is locked so they do not disturb the contents. If a lockable room is not available, the altar is raised so as to be out of reach, and the puja is performed

PHOTOS COURTESY YALE UNIVERSITY PRESS/STEPHEN P. HUYLER

Unlike the puja we are presenting in this chapter, some home pujas are long and elaborate. Here a priest performs a long Siva puja in an Indian home shrine during Mahasivaratri.

Puja, the worship of a murti through water, lights and flowers in temples and shrines, is the Agamic counterpart of the Vedic yajna rite, in which offerings are conveyed through the sacred homa fire. These are the two great streams of adoration and communion in Hinduism, drawn from Hinduism's two massive compendiums of revealed scripture—the Vedas *and the Agamas.*

standing up. Those attending will usually sit during most of the ceremony, then stand during the final *arati*. However, this again may be left to individual discretion in consideration of the height of the shrine.

During the ritual, you will be making many offerings. Most offerings are made with the right hand, never just the left, though there are occasions when both hands are used.

The offering of food is an important part of puja. Traditionally a simple dish of cooked rice is prepared especially for the Deity, with cooking utensils reserved for this purpose alone. If cooked food is not offered, then freshly cut fruit may be substituted. Keep the offering covered until the point in the puja when the pranas (life energies) of the food are offered to the Deity. Keeping the food covered helps to preserve purity and contain the pranas, which the Gods and *devas* can see, absorb, enjoy and reflect back to cleanse the auras of devotees. After the puja, the food offerings—along with holy ash (*vibhuti*), sacred water (*tirtha*), sandalwood paste (*chandana*), red powder (*kumkuma*) and flowers (*pushpa*)—are passed out and enjoyed as *prasada*.

A recording of sacred chanting from the *Vedas* may be played softly before the puja begins. At the high point, as the *arati* is presented, loud drums and *nagasvaras* resound. As the sacraments are passed out by the *pujari*, the divine musical ragas are heard softly played on the vina, or Vedic chanting or devotional songs may be played.

After the sacraments are passed out, encourage everyone to sit quietly for a while to enjoy the *sannidhya*, the ever-present feeling of the Divine, that the God, Gods, inner-plane gurus and *devas* suffuse in the shrine room. Such internalized worship naturally follows a puja. Those who perform daily *japa* will find this an ideal time for that *sadhana*.

Internalizing worship in this way gives you and all members of the family strength to face the outside world, its daily challenges and, yes, school tests. Internalizing worship is the core of the Sanatana Dharma. It is the root, stem and blossom of the highest chakra, the 1,000-petalled lotus. It is the force that gives the strength to resist temptation, to turn others from their bad ways and to face up to and live through birth karmas, *prarabdha* karmas, that are brought with you in this life. It gives the courage to resist making new, especially unwanted, karmas to be faced at a later date. It gives the willpower needed in this Kali Yuga to survive. It gives the love which provokes the understanding to overlook and forgive, then forget. Finally, internalized worship gives the peace of mind, the shanti, in which all saints, sages, mahatmas and great seers dwell, in their *jnana*, their wisdom, of how things work in their universe of which we are a vital part.

Many people are hesitant to do puja, specific, traditional rites of worship, because they feel they don't have enough training or don't understand the mystical principles behind it well enough. Most Hindus depend on the priests to perform the pujas and sacraments for them, or to train them to perform home puja and give them permission to do so through initiation, called *diksha*. However, simple pujas, such as this one, may be performed by anyone wishing to invoke grace from God, Mahadevas and *devas*. Mothers, daughters, aunts, fathers, sons, uncles, all may perform puja within their own home, and do, as the Hindu home is considered to be nothing less than an extension of the nearby temple.

The Ganesha puja presented on the following pages consists of a series of Sanskrit chants to be intoned while performing the indicated actions and visualizations. Each chant is given in three forms, first in Sanskrit's traditional Devanagari script, second in transliterated for those who speak English, and third in a

Te presents a ghee lamp to Siva, Shakti and Ganesha during a long ritual in which he baths the Deities with water, hooney and other precious substances.

freely-rendered English translation. Each translation is followed by detailed instructions to guide the *pujari's* actions.

The chants of the simple Ganesha puja given here are in Sanskrit, Hinduism's ancient scriptural language. Time spent mastering the pronunciation is time well spent. Ideally, training is received personally from a priest, pundit or other person proficient in Sanskrit, so that you can chant the verses properly. Such a teacher will generally begin by teaching the alphabet and will offer training in reading in the Devanagari script, as well as the transliteration to help English-speaking students. Learning Sanskrit is not mandatory, and for those who do not have a teacher, we have a voice recording of this entire puja for learning the mantras properly. It is available at www.himalayanacademy. com/audio/chants/. A key to Sanskrit pronunciation for the transliteration system used in this puja is available online at www. himalayanacademy.com/resources/sanskrit/.

Devotion During Sacred Rituals

While correct chanting is important, the essential part of any puja is devotion. Without love of God and the Gods, outer performance is of little value. But with true devotion, even the simplest puja can be a profoundly sacred experience. Devotion is facilitated by the belief that you really are communing with the Divine through puja, that the Gods and *devas* do actually hear your prayers, enjoy your intonations and respond by sending blessings that purify your aura and protect your home. Though you can't see them with your physical eyes, they are there nonetheless. As you perform or attend puja, visualize the Deity sitting before you, accepting your offerings, pleased to be in your company, delighted with your love and hospitality. Think of the God as a part of your fam-

ily, a grand being who is concerned with your welfare. Through strong visualization and sincere devotion, your sensitivity to the darshan will grow and your relationship with the Deity will become strong and close.

Cultivating devotion is called bhakti yoga. Satguru Sivaya Subramuniyaswami stressed its importance in this way, "Bhakti yoga is love on all levels of consciousness—physical, mental, emotional and spiritual. The greatest inhibiting factor in practicing bhakti yoga is the doubting, cynical, intellectual mind. Doubt and skepticism harden the heart and narrow the mind. The bloom of bhakti softens the heart and relaxes the intellect. Through bhakti yoga, the yoga of devotion, the combative mind becomes erased, absorbed into the consciousness of the One Self, the Being permeating all beings. With the help of devotion, you can soar within. You can not only pull away detachedly from unwholesome areas of the mind, but it is possible to keep yourself in an inward state of expanded consciousness."

Use and Care of the Shrine Room

Keep the shrine spotlessly clean, and decorate it for festivals and special holy days. Visit your shrine before you leave the home, seeking blessings and protection as you leave its shelter, and go there again for purification upon returning. Worship in heartfelt devotion, so the Gods' grace flows freely toward you and loved ones. Make the shrine a refuge for all family members, a haven where they can find peace and solace, where they can connect with the Gods, offer their praise and pray for practical needs. Train your children to worship in the shrine before each important event in life, such as a major exam at school or when faced with a personal challenge or problem.

आचमनम् *Āchamanam*	*Water Sipping By the Pūjāri*

ॐ सुमुखाय स्वाहा
ॐ एकदन्ताय स्वाहा
ॐ गजकर्णकाय स्वाहा

Aum sumukhāya svāhā
Aum ekadantāya svāhā
Aum gajakarṇakāya svāhā

Aum! Hail to the God whose face is always shining!
Aum! Hail to the God who has only one tusk!
Aum! Hail to the God with huge elephant ears!

Holding the spoon with your left hand, take a spoonful of water from the cup and place it in the right palm to rinse the hand, letting the excess fall onto the floor or a tray. Put another spoonful of water into the right hand, intone "Aum sumukhāya svāhā" and sip the water. Repeat for the second and third lines, then rinse the right hand again.

विघ्नेश्वर प्रार्थना *Vighneśvara Prārthanā*	*Gaṇeśa Invocation*

ॐ शुक्लांबरधरं विष्णुं शशिवर्णं चतुर्भुजम् ।
प्रसन्न वदनं ध्यायेत् सर्वविघ्नोपशान्तये ॥

Aum śuklāmbaradharam vishṇum
śaśivarṇam chaturbhujam
prasanna vadanam dhyāyet
sarvavighnopaśāntaye

Aum. O Lord dressed in splendid white, pervading the universe, shining radiantly like rays of the full moon, having four mighty arms and a charming, happy face, we meditate on you that all obstacles may be quelled.

Salute Lord Gaṇeśa by holding hands in añjali mudrā, the prayerful pose. Then, while reciting the verse, tap your temples lightly with your knuckles three times, as in the photo. Alternatively, you may cross your arms before your face, the left hand tapping the right temple and vice versa. Return your hands to añjali mudrā while reciting the last words of the chant.

संकल्पम् *Saṅkalpam*	*Dedication of Pūjā, Statement of Purpose*

ॐ अद्य पूर्वोक्त एवंगुणसकल
विशेषेण विशिष्टायां अस्यां शुभतिथौ
ॐ महागणेश्वरं उद्दिश्य महागणेश्वरप्रीत्यर्थं
महागणेश्वरप्रसादसिद्ध्यर्थं
यथा शक्ति (name of city) देशे (period of day)
ध्यानावाहनादि गणेशपूजां करिष्ये ।
ॐ अप उपस्पृश्य

Five periods of the day *(insert one in chant)*

उषः काल	ushaḥ kāla, dawn
प्रातः काल	prātaḥ kāla, morning
मध्याह्नकाल	madhyāhnakāla, noon
सायङ्काल	sāyaṅkāla, evening
ऊर्ध्व यामकाल	ūrdhvayāmakāla, night

Aum adya pūrvokta evaṅguṇasakala
viśeshena viśishṭāyām asyām śubhatithau
Aum Mahāgaṇeśvaram uddiśya
Mahāgaṇeśvara prītyartham
Mahāgaṇeśvara prasāda siddhyartham
yathā śakti (chant city) deśe (insert the time of day)
dhyānāvāhanādi Gaṇeśa pūjām karishye
Aum apa upaspṛiśya

At this particularly auspicious moment, time and place, on this auspicious day, so that we may realize the fullness of your grace, to the best of our ability this (insert time of day) Gaṇeśa pūjā we shall now perform. Aum. By touching pure water we become pure.

While reciting this statement of purpose, take a pinch of rice and hold it at chest height in your closed right palm, with open left hand underneath. Insert the time of day and the place where indicated. As you chant the last word, karishye, gently toss the rice toward the base of the image. Then, with

the left hand, place a spoonful of water into your right palm and ritually wash both hands with the water by wiping the palms together a few times as you recite "Aum apa upa spriśya." Once the saṅkalpam has been chanted, the pūjā must not be interrupted or abandoned until the concluding mantras are recited.

WORSHIP AND OFFERINGS BEGIN

आवाहनम् आसनम्
Āvāhanam, Āsanam

Welcoming and Offering a Seat

ध्यायामि । आवाहयामि ।
रत्नसिंहासनं समर्पयामि ।

dhyāyāmi, āvāhayāmi, ratnasinhāsanaṁ samarpayāmi

We now meditate on you, O Lord, and invite you to sit upon the jewel-studded, lion throne we have prepared for you.

Offer a pinch of rice to the Deity as you chant each of the three words before "samarpayāmi." Visualize Gaṇeśa seated on a gem-studded throne before you, smiling, full of blessings, waiting to be honored as a guest in your home.

अर्घ्यम्
Arghyam

Washing the Lord's Feet and Hands

पादयोः पाद्यं समर्पयामि ।
हस्तयोः अर्घ्यं समर्पयामि ।

pādayoḥ pādyam samarpayāmi
hastayoḥ arghyam samarpayāmi

We now humbly bathe each of your white lotus feet and gently wash each of your precious hands, Lord Gaṇeśa.

With your right hand offer a spoonful of pure water by holding it up before the Deity momentarily and then placing it in the tīrtha cup. This is how all water offering is done throughout the pūjā. As you chant the first line, visualize yourself bathing the feet of Gaṇeśa. Offer a second spoonful of pure water as you intone the next line and visualize yourself washing His hands.

आचमनम्
Āchamanam

Offering Water to Quench His Thirst

ॐ भूर्भुवः सुवः आचमनीयं समर्पयामि ।

Aum bhūr-bhuvaḥ suvaḥ āchamanīyaṁ samarpayāmi

Aum! In all three worlds, we humbly offer you fresh, pure water for sipping.

Offer a spoonful of pure water to Gaṇeśa. Visualize His accepting it in His Hand and sipping it.

स्नानम्
Snānam

Ritual
Bathing

ॐ सुरसिन्धुसमानीतं सुवर्णकलशस्थितम् ।
स्नानार्थं गृह्यातां शम्भो सलिलं विमलं गणेश ॥
गङ्गास्नानं समर्पयामि

Aum surasindhu samānītam suvarṇakalaśāsthitam |
snānārtham gṛihyatām śambho salilam vimalam gaṇeśa ||
gangāsnanam samarpayami

We now bathe you, beloved Lord Gaṇeśa, the pure one, with the water that was brought from the Ganges in the golden pot. We have bathed you in sacred Gaṅgā water.

While ringing the bell and reciting this verse, dip a flower into the tīrtha water and gently sprinkle the Deity. Do this three times or more. Hold the flower in your right hand in the mṛigi mudrā, the stem between your third and fourth fingers. If the altar design allows, you may pour water over the mūrti, rather than sprinkling it during this chant.

अलङ्कारम्
Alaṅkāram

Adornment and
Offerings

वस्त्रार्थं मङ्गलाक्षतान् समर्पयामि
उपवीतार्थं मङ्गलाक्षतान् समर्पयामि
ॐ गन्धं गृहाण सुरभिमन्धकासुरसूदन ।
कुङ्कुमदिसमायुक्तं कुलाचलनिकेतन ॥
दिव्य परिमल विभूति चन्दन कुंकुमम् समर्पयामि

vastrārtham maṅgalākshatān samarpayāmi
upavītārtham maṅgalākshatān samarpayāmi

Aum gandham gṛihāṇa surabhim andhakā surasūdana,
kuṅkumadi samāyuktam kulāchalaniketana
divya parimala vibhūti chandana
kuṅkumam samarpayāmi

We give you this auspicious unbroken rice, our magnificent Lord, that you may enjoy resplendent clothing. We give you auspicious unbroken rice, Lord Gaṇeśa, that you may be handsomely adorned with a white, cotton sacred thread. Aum. O Lord, the destroyer of the demon Andhakāsura, you who resides in the Himālayas, please accept the good smelling *chandana* with *kuṅkuma* and choice offerings.

Dress the Deity. Offer a pinch of unbroken rice while chanting each of the first two lines. Repeat the third and fourth lines over and over as you decorate the Deity with flowers. The last line is recited once while applying vibhūti (holy ash), chandana (sandalpaste) and kuṅkuma. (red powder).

पुष्पम्
Pushpam

Offering
Flowers

तदुपरि मङ्गलाक्षतान् समर्पयामि ।
पूजार्थं नानाविधपत्र पुष्पाणि समर्पयामि ।

tadupari maṅgalākshatān samarpayāmi
pūjārtham nānāvidhapatra pushpāṇi samarpayāmi

We now offer this auspicious unbroken rice. And for the fulfillment of our devotion, we offer many kinds of fresh, blooming flowers, our peerless Lord.

A pinch of rice is offered with the first line. A handful of flowers is offered with the second.

धूपम्
Dhūpam

Offering
Incense

ॐ वनस्पत्युद्भवैः दिव्यैः नानागन्धसमन्वितैः ।
आघ्रेयधूपदीपानां धूपोऽयं प्रतिगृह्यताम् ॥
दशाङ्गं गुग्गुलोपेतं सुगन्धं सुमनोहरम् ।
आघ्रेयःसर्वदेवानां धूपोऽयं प्रतिगृह्यताम् ॥
धूपमाघ्रापयामि धूपानन्तरमाचमनीयं समर्पयामि
मङ्गलाक्षतान् समर्पयामि

Aum vanaspatyudbhavaiḥ divyaiḥ
nānāgandhasamanvitaiḥ,
āghreyadhūpadīpānām dhūpo-yam pratigṛihyatām.
daśāṅgam guggulopetam sugandhan sumanoharam,
āghreyaḥ sarvadevānām dhūpo-yam pratigṛihyatām.
dhūpamāghrāpayāmi
dhūpānantaram āchamanīyam samarpayāmi
maṅgalākshatān samarpayāmi

The finest incense, of magical qualities, of full and varied fragrances, Lord Gaṇeśa, we set aflame and offer to you in this, our home. Incense of the finest resins and perfumes, incomparable in sweetness and aroma, to be inhaled and enjoyed by you and all the Gods and *devas*, we offer to you in this, our home. Eagerly we offer to you, our resplendent Lord, fine resin incense, of heavenly odor, bewitching to the mind, rising out of a ghee-fed flame. We offer it to you in this, our home. This fine incense we have duly offered for your pleasure. And we again offer you cool, sweet water for sipping and auspicious unbroken rice.

During this chant, make three circles before the Deity with lighted incense held in your right hand while ringing the bell with your left hand. Complete the third circle and trace an Aum as you chant the fifth line, dhūpamāghrāpayāmi. At that point raise the incense higher and ring the bell louder. Put the incense down, and recite the next two lines. With the first, water is offered, with the second, a pinch of rice.

दीपम् Dīpam	Offering The Light

Aum! Salutations to all the Gods invoked! This divine, auspicious light we offer to you. After that, we offer you pure water for sipping and auspicious unbroken rice.

Offer the oil light to Lord Gaṇeśa and ring the bell as you chant this hymn. As with the incense, circle three times then draw the Aum with the flame. Then raise the flame and ring the bell louder, then stop ringing. Offer water, then a flower or a pinch of rice.

ॐ साज्यवर्तित्रयोपेतं प्राज्यमङ्गलदायकं ।
दीपं पश्य दयाराशे दीनबन्धो नमोऽस्तु ते ॥
ॐ आवाहिताभ्यः सर्वाभ्यो देवताभ्यो नमः ।
दिव्य मङ्गलदीपं सन्दर्शयामि ।
दीपान्तरमाचमनीयं समर्पयामि ।
मङ्गलाक्षतान् समर्पयामि ।

aum sājyavarti trayopetam prājyamaṅgala dāyakam,
dīpam paśya dayārāśe dīnabandho namo-stu te.
aum āvāhitabhyaḥ sarvabhyo devatabhyo namaḥ,
divya maṅgala dīpaṁ sandarśayāmi,
dīpānantaramāchamanīyaṁ samarpayāmi,
maṅgalākṣatān samarpayāmi

O the Compassionate, the friend of devotees! See this lamp offered which is lighted with ghee and three wicks and which is the provider of abundant auspiciousness. Salutations to you!

नैवेद्यम् Naivedyam	Offering Food

ringing the bell, circle a spoonful of water over the food and offer it to the Deity. While ringing the bell softly, gently waft the aroma and vital essences of the food or fruit toward the Deity. Do this by sweeping the right hand over the food with a flower held between your fingers, stem upward. The palm is facing downward as it moves over the food, then rotates upward as the sweep approaches the Deity, bringing the aroma and prāṇa toward His nose and mouth. As you complete the third line, gently toss the flower toward the feet of the Deity at the end of the sweep with all the love in your heart.

सत्यं त्वर्तेन *(chant in morning)*
ऋतं त्वा सत्येन *(chant if evening)* परिषिञ्चामि ।
ॐ अमृतमस्तु अमृतोपस्तरणमसि स्वाहा ।
ॐ गणेशाय स्वाहाँ । ॐ गणेशाय स्वाहाँ ।
ॐ गणेशाय स्वाहाँ ।

satyaṁ tvartena   *(chant if in morning)*
ṛitaṁ tvā satyena   *(if evening)* parishiñchāmi
Aum amṛitamastu amṛitopastaraṇamasi svāhā
Aum gaṇeśāya svāhā̃, Aum gaṇeśāya svāhā̃,
Aum gaṇeśāya svāhā̃

We add Truth to Truth. Aum. May this sweet and pungent food be transformed into nectar. We humbly offer to you this food.

While reciting the first part of the mantra, uncover the food offering. Then, while chanting the last line and

ॐ आवाहिताभ्यः सर्वाभ्यो देवताभ्यो नमः ।
नानाविधमहानैवेद्यं निवेदयामि ।
यथाशक्तिसमर्पितमहानैवेद्यम् कृपया स्वीकुरु ।

Aum āvāhitābhyaḥ sarvābhyo devatābhyo namaḥ,
nānā vidha mahānaivedyaṁ nivedayāmi,
yathāśakti samarpita mahānaivedyam kṛipayā svīkuru

Aum! Salutations to all the Gods invoked! Because
we are offering you our very best, Lord Gaṇeśa, in all
sincerity and love, please consider the essence of this
food as among the finest meals you have ever received.
To the best of our ability in the worship of you, we offer
this food and humbly beg that you will receive it.

Ringing the bell loudly as you recite
the above chant, pick up a flower or
a pinch of rice and hold it at chest
height in the fingertips of the right
hand. As the last word is spoken,
gently release the rice or flower
at the feet of the Deity. Then put
down the bell and raise your hands
above your head in devout prayer
that Gaṇeśa will accept the meal.
While your hands are raised, close
your eyes and visualize Gaṇeśa accepting and partaking of the meal.
After a moment, lower your
hands and intone Aum quietly.

विघ्नेश्वराष्टोत्तर
शतनामावलिः
*Vighneśvarāshṭottara
Śatanāmāvaliḥ*
**Chanting Gaṇeśa's
108 Names**

In this section of the pūjā, chant the "garland of
Gaṇeśa's 108 names." As you intone each name, offer with your right hand a flower, some flower petals or a pinch of rice. The names are attributes of the
Deity, each delineating an aspect of His wondrous
nature. Each name is preceded by the mantra Aum
and followed by namaḥ, meaning "obeisance, adoration or homage to." Thus the first line is chanted Aum
Vināyakāya Namaḥ (pronounced, "na-ma-ha").

विनायकाय	**Vināyakāya** ...... *the remover (of obstacles)*	सर्वात्मकाय	**Sarvātmakāya** .... *the soul of all*
विघ्नराजाय	**Vighnarājāya** .... *the ruler of obstacles*	सृष्टिकर्त्रे	**Sṛishṭikartre** .... *the creator*
गौरीपुत्राय	**Gaurīputrāya** .... *the son of Gaurī*	देवाय	**Devāya** .... *the resplendent one*
गणेश्वराय	**Gaṇeśvarāya** .... *the lord of categories*	अनेकार्चिताय	**Anekārchitāya** ...*worshiped by multitudes*
स्कन्दाग्रजाय	**Skandāgrajāya** ....*Skanda's elder brother*	शिवाय	**Śivāya** .... *the auspicious one*
अव्ययाय	**Avyayāya** ..... *the inexhaustible one*	शुद्धाय	**Śuddhāya** .... *the pure one*
पूताय	**Pūtāya** .... *the pure one*	बुद्धिप्रियाय	**Buddhipriyāya** ..... *who loves intelligence*
दक्षाय	**Dakshāya** .... *the dexterous one*	शान्ताय	**Śāntāya** .... *the peaceful one*
अध्यक्षाय	**Adhyakshāya** ....*the great presider*	ब्रह्मचारिणे	**Brahmachāriṇe** .... *the celibate one*
द्विजप्रियाय	**Dvijapriyāya** .... *who loves the twice-born*	गजाननाय	**Gajānanāya** .... *the elephant's faced*
अग्निगर्वच्छिदे	**Agnigarvacchide** ..*who destroyed fire's ego*	द्वैमातुराय	**Dvaimāturāya** ..... *who has two mothers*
इन्द्रश्रीप्रदाय	**Indraśrīpradāya** *who restored Indra's wealth*	मुनिस्तुताय	**Munistutāya** .... *who is praised by sages*
वाणीप्रदाय	**Vāṇīpradāya** .... *who gives eloquence*	भक्तविघ्नवि नाशनाय	**Bhaktavighna vināśanāya** ...... *who destroys devotees' obstacles*
अव्ययाय	**Avyayāya** .... *the inexhaustible one*	एकदन्ताय	**Ekadantāya** ....*who has one tusk*
सर्वसिद्धिप्रदाय	**Sarvasiddhipradāya** ...*giver of fulfillment*	चतुर्बाहवे	**Chaturbāhave** ....*who has four arms*
सर्वतनयाय	**Sarvatanayāya** .... *the son of Śiva*	चतुराय	**Chaturāya** .... *the ingenious one*
शर्वरीप्रियाय	**Śarvarīpriyāya** .... *loved by Pārvatī*		

शक्तिसंयुताय	Śaktisaṁyutāya	united with power
लंबोदराय	Lambodarāya	who has a large belly
शूर्पकर्णाय	Śūrpakarṇāya	with fan-like ears
हरये	Haraye	destroys evil with lion-like courage
ब्रह्मविदुत्तमाय	Brahmaviduttamāya	foremost knower of God
कालाय	Kālāya	the master of destiny
ग्रहपतये	Grahapataye	lord of planets
कामिने	Kāmine	who is love
सोमसूर्याग्नि लोचनाय	Somasūryāgni lochanāya	whose eyes are the moon, sun and fire
पाशाङ्कुश धराय	Pāśāṅkuśa dharāya	who holds a noose and a goad
चण्डाय	Chaṇḍāya	who is fierce-looking
गुणातीताय	Guṇātītāya	who transcends qualities
निरञ्जनाय	Nirañjanāya	who is without blemish
अकल्मषाय	Akalmashāya	who is without impurity
स्वयंसिद्धाय	Svayaṁsiddhāya	self-fulfilled, perfect
सिद्धार्चित पदाम्बुजाय	Siddhārchita padāmbujāya	whose lotus feet sages worship
बीजपूर फलासक्ताय	Bījapūraphalāsaktāya	who is fond of pomegranates
वरदाय	Varadāya	the boon giver
शाश्वताय	Śāśvatāya	the eternal, unchanging one
कृतिने	Kritine	the skillful one
द्विजप्रियाय	Dvijapriyāya	fond of the twice-born
वीतभयाय	Vītabhayāya	who is fearless
गदिने	Gadine	who wields the mace
चक्रिणे	Chakrine	who wields a discus
इक्षुचापधृते	Ikshuchāpadhrite	who holds a sugarcane bow
श्रीदाय	Śrīdāya	the bestower of wealth
अजाय	Ajāya	the unborn one
उत्पलकराय	Utpalakarāya	who holds a proud blue lotus flower
श्रीपतये	Śrīpataye	the Lord of wealth
स्तुतिहर्षिताय	Stutiharshitāya	who delights in praise
कुलाद्रिभृते	Kulādribhrite	who supports Himālaya, His family's mountain
जटिलाय	Jaṭilāya	who has matted hair
कलिकल्मष नाशनाय	Kalikalmasha nāśanāya	the destroyer of sins in the Kaliyuga
चन्द्रचूडामणये	Chandrachūḍāmaṇaye	who wears a moon upon his head
कान्ताय	Kāntāya	the beloved, loving one
पापहारिणे	Pāpahārine	the consumer of sins
समाहिताय	Samāhitāya	absorbed in meditation
आश्रिताय	Āśritāya	who is our refuge
श्रीकराय	Śrīkarāya	who manifests prosperity
सौम्याय	Saumyāya	the amiable one
भक्तवाञ्छित दायकाय	Bhaktavāñchita dāyakāya	the grantor of devotees' desires
शान्ताय	Śāntāya	the peaceful one
कैवल्य सुखदाय	Kaivalya sukhadāya	bestower of unsullied liberation
सच्चिदानन्द विग्रहाय	Sacchidānanda vigrahāya	embodiment of existence-knowledge-bliss
ज्ञानिने	Jñānine	the great wisdom
दयायुताय	Dayāyutāya	full of compassion
दान्ताय	Dāntāya	who has self-control
ब्रह्मद्वेष विवर्जिताय	Brahmadvesha vivarjitāya	who is free from aversion to knowledge
प्रमत्तदैत्य भयदाय	Pramattadaitya bhayadāya	who brings terror to demons
श्रीकण्ठाय	Śrīkaṇṭhāya	with beautiful throat
विबुधेश्वराय	Vibudheśvarāya	Lord of the Wise
रामार्चिताय	Rāmārchitāya	worshiped by Rāma
विधये	Vidhaye	who is the destiny of all
नागराज यज्ञोपवीतवते	Nāgarāja yajñopavītavate	whose sacred thread is a king cobra
स्थूलकण्ठाय	Sthūlakaṇṭhāya	of stout neck
स्वयं कर्त्रे	Svayaṁkartre	who is self-created
सामघोषप्रियाय	Sāmaghoshapriyāya	who loves the sound of Sāma Veda

परस्मै	Parasmai .... who is supreme
स्थूलतुण्डाय	Sthūlatuṇḍāya ..... who has a stout trunk
अग्रण्ये	Agraṇye .... the leader
धीराय	Dhīrāya .... the courageous one
वागीशाय	Vāgīśāya .... the Lord of speech
सिद्धिदायकाय	Siddhidāyakāya ... bestower of fulfillment
दूर्वाबिल्व प्रियाय	Dūrvābilva priyāya .... who loves dūrvā grass and bilva leaves
अव्यक्तमूर्तये	Avyaktamūrtaye ....the manifestation of the Unmanifest
अद्भुतमूर्तिमते	Adbhutamūrtimate ... of wondrous form

शैलेन्द्रतनुजोत्सङ्ग खेलनोत्सुकमानसाय

Śailendratanujotsaṅga khelanotsukamānasāya
*who is happy to play in the lap of His mother,
Pārvatī, daughter of the mountain Lord*

स्वलावण्यसुधासारजित मन्मथविग्रहाय

Svalāvaṇyasudhāsārajita manmathavigrahāya
... who defeated Manmatha, the God of love, by His sweet beauty

समस्त जगदाधाराय	Samasta jagadādhārāya .... the supporter of all the worlds
मायिने	Māyine ....the source of illusory power
मूषिकवाहनाय	Mūshikavāhanāya .. who rides the mouse
हृष्टाय	Hrishṭāya ....the joyful one
तुष्टाय	Tushṭāya .... the contented one
प्रसन्नात्मने	Prasannātmane *the bright kindly-souled one*
सर्वसिद्धि प्रदायकाय	Sarvasiddhi pradāyakāya .... the grantor of all fulfillment

ALL PHOTOS BY DINODIA

मन्त्र पुष्पम्
Mantra Pushpam

Worship With Flowers

ॐ यो॒ऽपां पुष्पं॑ वेद॑ ।
पुष्प॑वान् प्र॒जाव॑ान् पशु॒मान् भ॑वति ।
च॒न्द्रम॒ा॒वा अ॒पां पुष्प॑म् ।
पुष्प॑वान् प्र॒जाव॑ान् पशु॒मान् भ॑वति ।
य ए॒वं वेद॑ । यो॒ऽपाम॒ाय॑त॒नं वेद॑ ।
आ॒य॒त॑नवान् भवति ॥
ॐ श्री महागणेश्वराय नमः
मन्त्रपुष्पाञ्जलिं समर्पयामि ।

Aum yo-pām pushpaṁ veda,
pushpavān prajāvān paśumān bhavati,
chandramāvā apām pushpam,
pushpavān prajāvān paśumān bhavati,
ya evaṁ veda, yo-pāmāyatanaṁ veda,
āyatanavān bhavati.

Aum Śrī Mahāgaṇeśvarāya namaḥ
mantra pushpāñjaliṁ samarpayāmi

The one who understands the beauty of the blooming powers of the Supreme Being is blessed with beautiful, blooming life, progeny and cattle. The moon is certainly the bloom of those powers. One who realizes the qualities of the moon, which are nothing but the blooming divine powers, is blessed with a blooming, beautiful life of perfection, progeny and cattle. One who realizes this principle and realizes the source from whom all these powers have come himself becomes the abode of those divine powers. Aum, salutations, Lord Mahāgaṇeśa, we respectfully offer you this flower mantra.

While chanting this mantra, hold a handful of flowers before you in añjali mudrā, hands cupped loosely around the flowers at chest height. Recite the verses with adoration. As you intone the last word, samarpayāmi, lower your hands (as shown in the photo) and toss the flowers into the air above the murti, sending a shower of blossoms upon the God with feelings of gratitude and loving devotion.

आरती
Ārati

Worship
With Flame

ॐ साज्यं त्रिवर्त्तिसंयुक्तं वह्निना योजितं मया ।
गृहाण मङ्गलारतिं ईशपुत्र नमोऽस्तु ते ॥
ॐ आवाहिताभ्यः सर्वाभ्यो देवताभ्यो नमः ।
दिव्यमङ्गलदीपं सन्दर्शयामि ।
आचमनीयं समर्पयामि ।
मङ्गलाक्षतान् समर्पयामि ।

aum sājyaṁ trivartisaṁyuktam vahninā yojitaṁ mayā,
gṛihāṇa maṅgalāratim īśa putra namo-stu te.
aum āvāhitābhyaḥ sarvābhyo devatābhyo namaḥ
divya maṅgaladīpaṁ sandarśayāmi
āchamanīyaṁ samarpayāmi
maṅgalākshatān samarpayāmi

O Gaṇapati, Son of God Śiva, please accept this auspicious *ārati* prepared by me with ghee, three wicks and fire. My salutations to you! Aum! Salutations to all the Gods invoked! This divine, auspicious light we offer to you. After that, we offer you pure water for sipping and auspicious unbroken rice.

During this chant, hold the lit oil lamp or camphor burner in your right hand and the bell in your left. While ringing the bell and slowly reciting the ārati mantra, make three circles clockwise before Gaṇeśa with the flame. Stop at the top of the third circle, lower the lamp slightly and trace the symbol of Aum in Sanskrit or in your native language.

Then lift the flame slightly above the Aum that you placed in the ākāśic ether and ring the bell louder for all three worlds to hear. Keep ringing loudly while chanting the above two-line salutation to the devas ("āvāhitābhyaḥ … sandarśayāmi"). Put down the bell and the lamp and then, with the flame still burning, offer a spoonful of water with "āchamanīyaṁ samarpayāmi," then a pinch of rice with "maṅgalāshatān samarpayāmi."

रक्षधारणम्
Rakshadhāraṇam

Prayer for
Protection

इन्द्र स्तोमेनपञ्चदशेन
मध्यमिदं वातेन सगरेण
रक्ष रक्षां धारयामि ।

indra-stomena pañchadaśena
madhyamidaṁ vātena sagareṇa
raksha rakshāṁ dhārayāmi

O Indra, Lord of material and spiritual prosperity, please protect the space between the heavens and earth as well as the mind between the body and the soul with the help of fifteen noble powers and virtues (five *prāṇas*, five *jñānendriyas* and five *karmendriyas*). Your protection and blessings sustain me.

As you recite this mantra, make three circles above the burning flame with a flower held in the right hand, stem upward (photo next page). With the last words, toss the flower gently toward the Deity and place your hands in añjali mudrā while facing the altar. Now offer the flame at chest level to all present, allowing each to draw both hands through it and lightly touch the eyes three times (photo next page, upper right). The Gods and devas can see us

through the flame and send blessings. If especially honored persons are present, such as one's guru, parents or teacher, take the flame first to them. Then proceed clockwise to the others. In some cases, the pujārī may stand near the altar while devotees come forward to receive the flame. If no one is attending the pūjā, you may personally draw blessings from the flame, but not otherwise. Finally, present the flame once more to the Deity, then extinguish it with a wave of the right hand or by snuffing it out with a flower.

अर्पणम्
Arpaṇam

Final
Consecration

अनया यथा शक्ति कृत
(state period of day)
पूजया भगवान् सर्व देवात्मकः
श्री महागणेश्वराः सुप्रीतः
सुप्रसन्नो वरदो भवतु

anayā yathā śakti kṛita
(state period of day from list on page I-4)
pūjaya bhagavān sarva devātmakaḥ
śrī mahāgaṇeśvaraḥ suprītaḥ
suprasanno varado bhavatu

To the best of our ability we have performed this (state time of day) *pūjā* and worshiped you, dear Lord, the brightest of all the Gods. May it please you. May it be enjoyed by you. Surrounded by your presence, we place ourselves in your care, loving Gaṇeśa.

Before reciting the above verse, place a pinch of rice in your left palm, then transfer it to the right palm. Add to the rice three spoonfuls of water and close the hand (left photo). Hold the rice before you as you face the Deity, the left hand under the right hand, and recite the mantra. As you intone the last words, let the rice and water fall into the *tīrtha* cup (right photo). The sacraments may then be given out in the following order: holy ash, blessed water, sandalpaste, red powder, food and flowers. If no one is attending the *pūjā*, you may partake of the sacraments yourself, but not otherwise. If many devotees are attending, a second person may help pass out the sacraments, except for the holy ash, which is always given by the person who performed the *pūjā*.

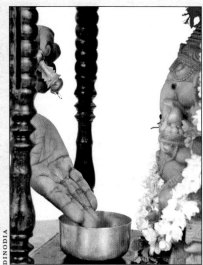

Sharing the blessed offerings: at left holy ash is distributed, a small pinch into the right hand of each devotee; at right, the father of this household applies the sacred dot on his daughter's forehead.

Below, the family offers final prayers at the conclusion of their morning puja.

THOMAS KELLY

DINODIA

विसर्जनम्
Visarjanam

Farewell and Apologies

ॐ आवाहनं न जानामि न जानामि विसर्जनम् ।
पूजाञ्चैव न जानामि क्षम्यतां परमेश्वर ॥
मन्त्रहीनं क्रियाहीनम् भक्तिहीनं सुरेश्वर ।
यत् पूजितं मया देव परिपूर्णं तदस्तु ते ।
अन्यथा शरणम् नास्ति त्वमेव शरणम् मम ।
तस्मात् कारुण्यभावेन रक्ष रक्ष गणेश्वर ॥
ॐ तत् सत् ॐ

Aum āvāhanaṁ na jānāmi na jānāmi visarjanam,
pūjāñchaiva na jānāmi kshamyatāṁ parameśvara.
mantrahīnaṁ kriyāhīnam bhaktihīnaṁ sureśvara,
yat pūjitam mayā deva paripūrṇam tadastu te,
anyathā śaraṇam nāsti tvameva śaraṇam mama,
tasmāt kāruṇyabhāvena raksha raksha gaṇeśvara.
Aum tat sat Aum.

O Lord, we do not know the proper means of inviting you or, when taking our leave, how to wish you farewell. A full knowledge of priestly rites has not been imparted to us, so you must overlook and forgive any mistakes or omissions. We know little of mantras or pious conduct, and we are strangers to true bhakti. Nonetheless, please forgive us and regard our attempts as exact and complete—because you are our only refuge. With your compassionate nature, Lord Gaṇeśa, we beseech you, please protect those who pray. That which is Truth is Aum.

DINODIA

This concluding apology is recited with hands in añjali mudrā. It is a formal and devout end to the worship service. As the final words, "Aum tat sat Aum," are spoken, it is customary to clap your hands together three times. All may now prostrate.

It is traditional and most uplifting to meditate for a few minutes after the pūjā, rather than rushing offer to daily duties. There is great personal benefit in such internalized worship, eyes closed, mind still, following, deep within yourself, the prāṇas that the pūjā has created. Externalized worship is the bhakti path; internalized worship is the yoga path. Both together make the complete circle that sustains devotees in their spiritual life, making them strong and kindly in moving the forces of the world in their daily life. This dual-pronged effort towards self-transformation and right living is the very foundation for the final goal of all seekers: moksha, freedom from rebirth.

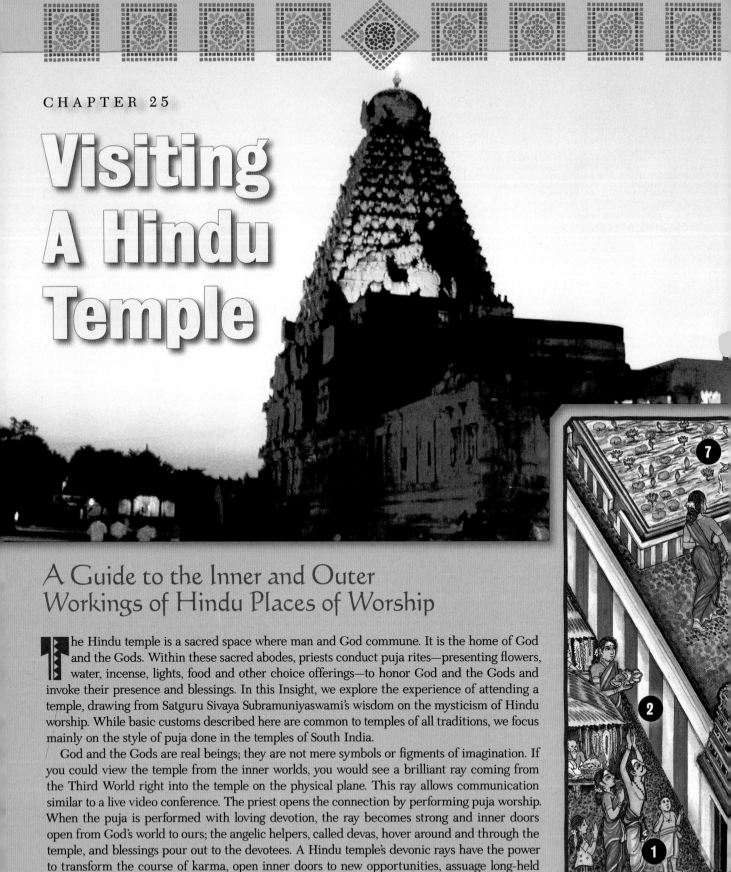

CHAPTER 25

Visiting A Hindu Temple

A Guide to the Inner and Outer Workings of Hindu Places of Worship

The Hindu temple is a sacred space where man and God commune. It is the home of God and the Gods. Within these sacred abodes, priests conduct puja rites—presenting flowers, water, incense, lights, food and other choice offerings—to honor God and the Gods and invoke their presence and blessings. In this Insight, we explore the experience of attending a temple, drawing from Satguru Sivaya Subramuniyaswami's wisdom on the mysticism of Hindu worship. While basic customs described here are common to temples of all traditions, we focus mainly on the style of puja done in the temples of South India.

God and the Gods are real beings; they are not mere symbols or figments of imagination. If you could view the temple from the inner worlds, you would see a brilliant ray coming from the Third World right into the temple on the physical plane. This ray allows communication similar to a live video conference. The priest opens the connection by performing puja worship. When the puja is performed with loving devotion, the ray becomes strong and inner doors open from God's world to ours; the angelic helpers, called devas, hover around and through the temple, and blessings pour out to the devotees. A Hindu temple's devonic rays have the power to transform the course of karma, open inner doors to new opportunities, assuage long-held hurts and provide inner visions equaling the fullness of devotion.

Devotion in Hinduism is known as bhakti. It is an entire realm of knowledge and practice unto itself, ranging from the child-like wonder of the unknown and the mysterious to the deep reverence which comes with understanding of the esoteric interworkings of the three worlds.

A MANIVEL

218 WHAT IS HINDUISM?

In the mural below, we depict the myriad goings-on in a large temple courtyard. Here is a key to the numbered activities.

1. A family worships at the temple entrance. Vendors sell garlands, incense, rosewater, coconuts and other traditional offering items.

2. A woman approaches with an offering tray.

3. A merchant at a stall watches after devotee's footwear for a small fee.

4. A husband and wife prostrate at the flag pole.

5. A father and son receive blessings from the elephant, who lightly touches their forehead with his trunk.

6. A devotee breaks a coconut near the Ganesha shrine while praying for a new job.

7. A man bathes and worships at the temple tank as an act of purification.

8. Led by musicians, the festival Deity is pulled around the temple in a special chariot.

9. A youth meditates in a quiet corner.

10. A child, held by his father, is having his ears pierced by a trained priest.

11. A family sings devotional hymns in praise of God and the Gods.

12. At the main shrine, a pujari offers the lighted oil lamp before the Sivalinga at the height of puja.

13. Hovering over the temple in the inner worlds, Lord Siva gives forth blessings.

14. A woman circumambulates the Siva shrine.

15. A girl joyfully rings the big temple bell.

16. Two boys listen as their teacher chants the *Vedas*.

17. A man gives coins to a group of sadhus.

18. After enjoying the morning at the temple, a family partakes of picnic lunch.

19. At the Murugan shrine, a woman beseeches the Deity for help with a difficult problem.

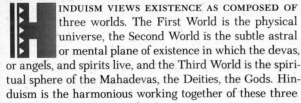

INDUISM VIEWS EXISTENCE AS COMPOSED OF three worlds. The First World is the physical universe, the Second World is the subtle astral or mental plane of existence in which the devas, or angels, and spirits live, and the Third World is the spiritual sphere of the Mahadevas, the Deities, the Gods. Hinduism is the harmonious working together of these three worlds. Religion blossoms for the Hindu as he awakens to the existence of the Second and Third Worlds. These inner worlds naturally inspire in man responses of love and devotion and even awe. They are that wonderful.

Devotion in Hinduism occurs on many levels and at different cycles of time in the evolution of the soul. All forms of devotion are equally valid, and none claims itself as the only proper form of worship. There is devotion to the tribal Deities, to the scriptures, to the saints and to the *satguru*. But the most prevalent expression of worship for the Hindu comes as devotion to God and the Gods. In the Hindu pantheon there are said to be 330 million Gods. Even so, all Hindus believe in one Supreme Being who pervades the entire universe.

The many Gods are perceived as divine creations of that

one Being. These Gods, or Mahadevas, are real beings, capable of thought and feeling beyond the limited thought and feeling of embodied man. So, Hinduism has one God, but it has many Gods. There are only a few of these Gods for whom temples are built and pujas conducted. Ganesha, Siva, Subramaniam, Vishnu and Shakti are the most prominent Deities in contemporary Hinduism. Of course, there are many others for whom certain rites or mantras are done in daily ceremony, often in the home shrine. These include Brahma, Surya, Sarasvati, Lakshmi, Agni, Chandra, Ayyappan, Hanuman, Mariyamman and others.

Worship is pouring all your energy into one-pointedly adoring the God or Goddess...

The Hindu traditionally adopts an Ishta Devata. This is a personal Deity chosen from the many Hindu Gods, often according to the devotee's family background or the feeling of closeness to one form of divine manifestation. It is the unique and all-encompassing nature of Hinduism that one devotee may be worshiping Ganesha while his friend worships Subramaniam or Vishnu, and yet both honor the other's choice and feel no sense of conflict. The profound understanding and universal acceptance that are unique in Hinduism are reflected

Approaching the Temple

Look and Feel Your Best

You will want to look and feel your best when you go to the temple, God's home. Prepare yourself by bathing and putting on clean clothing. Traditional dress is best—saris or *punjabis* for ladies, long dresses for girls, and *kurta* shirt and *dhoti* or pants for men and boys. But any nice, modest clothing suitable for sitting on the floor is acceptable.

Prepare Mentally; Bring a Gift

Prepare your mind by thinking about God in anticipation of your visit. Bring an offering, such as fruits and flowers. Prostrate and walk around the temple where possible. Hands pressed together in namaskara, greet the Deities at their shrines, starting with Ganesha, and present your offerings. Inwardly feel God's uplifting presence, called *sannidhya*.

ALL ART BY A. MANIVEL

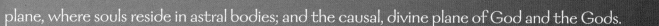

plane, where souls reside in astral bodies; and the causal, divine plane of God and the Gods.

in this faculty for accommodating different approaches to the Divine, allowing for different names and forms of God to be worshiped side by side within the temple walls. It may even happen that one may adopt a different personal Deity through the years according to one's spiritual unfoldment and inner needs.

The Hindu religion brings to us the gift of tolerance that allows for different stages of worship, different and personal expressions of devotion and even different Gods to guide our life on this Earth. Yet, it is a one religion under a single divine hierarchy that sees to the harmonious working together of the three worlds. These intelligent beings have evolved through

> *...feeling your loving sincerity, the Deity responds with life-changing blessings.*

eons of time and are able to help mankind without themselves having to live in a physical body. These great Mahadevas, with their multitudes of angelic devas, live and work constantly and tirelessly for the people of our religion, protecting and guiding them, opening new doors and closing unused ones. The Gods worshiped by the Hindu abide in the Third World, aided by the devas that inhabit the Second World.

It is in the Hindu temple that the three worlds meet and devotees invoke the Gods of our religion. The temple is built as a palace in which the Gods reside. It is the visible home of the Gods, a

sacred place unlike every other place on the Earth. The Hindu must associate himself with these Gods in a very sensitive way when he approaches the temple.

Though the devotee rarely has the psychic vision of the Deity, he is aware of the God's divine presence. He is aware through feeling, through sensing the divine presence within the temple. As he approaches the sanctum sanctorum, the Hindu is fully aware that an intelligent being, greater and more evolved than himself, is there. This God is intently aware of him, safeguarding him, fully knowing his inmost thought, fully capable of coping with any situation the devotee may mentally lay at His holy feet. It is important that we approach the Deity in this way—conscious and confident that our needs are known in the inner spiritual worlds.

The physical representation of the God, be it a stone or metal image, a yantra or other sacred form, simply marks the place that the God will manifest in or hover above in His etheric body. It can be conceived as an antenna to receive the divine rays of the God or as the material body in or through which the God manifests in this First World. Man takes one body and then another in his progression through the cycles of birth and death and rebirth. Similarly, the Gods in their subtle bodies inhabit, for brief or protracted spans of time, these temple images. When we perform puja, a religious ritual, we are attracting the attention of the

TEMPLE MANNERS: *Remove your shoes before entering. Be respectful of God and the Gods at all times, as if approaching the benevolent leader of a great realm. Bring your problems, wishes or your sorrows but leave improper manners outside as you enter this holy sanctuary. Do not enter the shrines without invitation. Do not sit with your feet pointing toward the Deities, the guru or another person. Hugging and other demonstrations of affection between adults are not appropriate. Refrain from gossip and worldly talk. Treat the priests with respect.*

Prostrate to the Deity

Prostrating is a traditional expression of worshipful surrender and adoration. The form of prostration differs for men and women. Men perform a fully prone pose, called *ashtanga pranama*, in which hands, chest, forehead, knees and feet touch the ground. Women perform a kneeling pose, *panchanga pranama*, in which hands, head and legs touch the ground.

Worship Wholeheartedly

Ardent worship takes many forms in a temple. You can be immersed in the joys of devotion, in prayerful communion, seeking solace for a loss, singing hymns, chanting mantras or celebrating a rite of passage. Meditation is appropriate, especially after the puja, and emotion is not out of place. God will receive your devotion, however you offer it.

PHOTO BY
THOMAS
KELLY

Religion is the harmonious working together of the three worlds. This harmony can be

devas and Mahadevas in the inner worlds. That is the purpose of a puja; it is a form of communication. To enhance this communication, we establish an altar in the temple and in the home. This becomes charged or magnetized through our devotional thoughts and feelings, which radiate out and affect the surrounding environment.

Chanting and satsanga and ceremonial rituals all contribute to this sanctifying process, creating an atmosphere to which the Gods are drawn and in which they can manifest. By the word *manifest*, I mean they actually come and dwell there and can stay for periods of time, providing the vibration is kept pure and undisturbed. The altar takes on a certain power. In our religion there are altars in temples all over the world inhabited by the devas and the great Gods. When you enter these holy places, you can sense their sanctity. You can feel the presence of these divine beings, and this radiation from them is known as darshan. The reality of the Mahadevas and their darshan can be experienced by the devotee through his awakened *ajna* vision, or more often as the physical sight of the image in the sanctum coupled with the inner knowing that He is there within the microcosm. This darshan can be felt by all devotees, becoming stronger and more defined

as devotion is perfected. Through this darshan, messages can be channeled along the vibratory emanations that radiate out from the Mahadevas, as well as from their representatives, the Second World devas who carry out their work for them in shrines and altars.

To understand darshan, consider the everyday and yet subtle communication of language. You are hearing the tones of my voice through the sensitive organ, your ear. Meaning comes into your mind, for you have been trained to translate these vibrations into meaning through the knowing of the language that I am speaking. Darshan is a vibration, too.

You can go into the temple with problems and lay them at the feet of the Deity,

It is first experienced in the simple physical glimpse of the form of the Deity in the sanctum. Later, that physical sight gives way to a clairvoyant vision or to a refined cognition received through the sensitive ganglia within your nerve system, the chakras. Through these receptors, a subtle message is received, often not consciously. Perhaps not immediately, but the message that the darshan carries, direct from the Mahadeva—direct from Lord Ganesha, direct from Lord Murugan,

Attending the Puja Ceremony

ALL ART BY A. MANIVEL

Conducted by a trained priest called a pujari, a Hindu worship service or puja, literally *"adoration,"* is similar to a grand reception for a king. Pujas can last from ten minutes to several hours, but all follow one basic pattern. First, the pujari purifies himself, the sacred implements and the place of worship. He chants in Sanskrit the time, place and nature of this particular puja. Through hand gestures *(mudras)* and chants, he beseeches the Deity to come and dwell in the image. Ringing a bell and chanting mantras and hymns from the ancient *Vedas* and *Agamas*, the pujari then offers pre-

cious substances to the Deity, including water, uncooked rice with turmeric powder, holy ash, sandalwood paste and kumkum. Sometimes water, sesame oil, turmeric water, saffron, milk, yogurt, ghee, honey, lime juice, *vibhuti*, sandalwood paste, *panchamritam* (mixture of five fruits), coconut water and rosewater are poured over the Deity in a ritual bath called *abhishekam*. Devotees are seated during most of the puja, in some traditions, men on the right and women on the left. After *abhishekam*, the Deity is dressed in new clothes and beautifully decorated with

flowers. At this point, devotees may sing devotional songs. After decorating the Deity, the pujari offers incense, oil lamps and food. He offers flowers while chanting 108 names of the God. At the high point of the puja, a large, sacred lamp is waved before the Deity and the temple bells are rung loudly as God sends His power through the holy image of Himself. When the lamp is lowered, everyone prostrates to the Divine. The lamp is then carried out to bless the worshipers, who often leave a donation on the tray (or later in the temple offering box). Finally, depending on the tradition, sacraments such as holy ash, holy water, sandalwood paste, kumkum, fruit, sweets and flowers are passed out to bless all present. These include a portion of the offerings— flowers, cooked food and more—brought by devotees. Devotees may then sit in meditation, basking in the blessings invoked by the puja.

created through temple worship, wherein the beings of all three worlds can communicate.

direct from Lord Siva Himself—manifests in your life. This is the way the Gods converse. It is a communication more real than the communication of language that you experience each day. It is not necessary to understand the communication immediately. The devotee may go away from the temple outwardly feeling that there was no particular message, or not knowing in his intellectual mind exactly what the darshan meant. Even the words you are now reading may not be fully cognized for days, weeks or even months. The depth of meaning will unfold itself on reflection.

Visiting a Hindu temple, receiving darshan from the majestic Gods of our religion, can al-

> *...and later leave feeling uplifted, hardly remembering what was bothering you.*

together change the life of a worshiper. It alters the flow of the pranas, or life currents, within his body. It draws his awareness into the deeper chakras. It adjusts his beliefs and the attitudes that are the natural consequence of those beliefs. But the change is slow. He lives with the experience for months and months after his visit to the temple. He comes to know and love the Deity. The Deity comes to know and love him, helping and guiding his entire evolutionary pattern. Darshan coming from the great temples of our Gods can change the patterns

of karma dating back many past lives, clearing and clarifying conditions that were created hundreds of years ago and are but seeds now, waiting to manifest in the future. Through the grace of the Gods, those seeds can be removed if the manifestation in the future would not enhance the evolution of the soul.

Devotees ask, "Why do we circumambulate the temple?" When we come to the temple out of the world, off the street, we are often shrouded by negative vibrations, which can actually be seen in our aura. Our nerve system may be upset, especially now, in the technological age, when we often suffer from stress and strain, the insecurity of so many changes and the rapid pace of life. In order to prepare ourselves to enter the sanctum sanctorum of the temple, the great *mandapam* inside, we walk clockwise around the temple very slowly. In this way we prepare our mind. We consciously drop off worldliness, letting the sufferings go, letting all disturbances leave our mind the best we can, and trying to reach deep inside of ourselves where peace exists eternally. We become as celestial as we can during the time we are walking around the temple, so that we can communicate with the celestial beings within the temple.

In a Hindu temple there is often a multiplicity of simultaneous proceedings and ceremonies. In one corner, an extended family,

Partaking of the Sacred Flame

The sacramental lamp which has just been offered at the high point of the puja is sometimes passed among the devotees. The devas can see and bless you through this flame as it lights up your face. Sometimes you, too, can glimpse into their world. When the priest comes to you with the lamp, hold your hands a few inches apart with your palms down. Reach out and pass both hands devoutly over the flame. Then bring your hands back, turn your palms toward your face and touch your eyes with your fingertips to receive the Deity's blessings. At Lord Vishnu's shrine, the priest may bring out the silver or gold crown of the Deity and lightly touch it to the head of each devotee as a personal blessing.

Receiving Holy Ash & Water

A sacrament offered in many temples is holy ash, *vibhuti,* by burning dried cow dung cakes with ghee, flowers, yogurt and and other ingredients. It symbolizes the purity we attain by burning the bonds of ego, karma and maya to reveal the soul's natural goodness. The priest will put a pinch of ash into your right palm. (Accept all offerings with your right hand.) Transfer the *vibhuti* into your left palm, then apply it to your forehead using your right hand, generally three broad stripes for men, one short stroke for ladies. Next, a small spoonful of holy water, or *tirtham,* is placed into your cupped right hand, which you then sip, afterwards touching the right palm to the crown of your head.

PHOTO BY
THOMAS
KELLY

Pray first to Ganesha. When in the temple, take every opportunity to serve
in simple ways, sweeping the floor, polishing the brass, making flower garlands.

or clan, with its hundreds of tightly knit members, may be joyously celebrating a wedding. At another shrine a lady might be crying in front of the Deity, saddened by some misfortune and in need of solace. Elsewhere in the crowded precincts a baby is being blessed, and several groups of temple musicians are filling the chamber with the shrill sounds of the *nagasvaram* and drum. After the puja reaches its zenith, brahmin priests move in and out of the sanctum, passing camphor and sacred ash and holy water to hundreds of worshipers crowding eagerly to get a glimpse of the Deity. All of this is happening at once, unplanned and yet totally organized. It is a wonderful experience, and such a diverse array of devotional ceremonies and such an intensity of worship can only be seen in a Hindu temple. There is no place on Earth quite like a Hindu temple.

Esoterically, the Gods in the temple, who live in the microcosm, can work extraordinarily fast with everyone. There is so much going on that everyone has the sense of being alone. The weeping woman is allowed her moment of mourning. No one feels that she is upsetting the nearby wedding. No one even notices her. The temple is so active, so filled with people, that each one is left to worship as he needs that day—to cry or to laugh or to sing or to sit in silent contemplation in a far-off corner.

Like the Hindu religion itself, the Hindu temple is able to absorb and encompass everyone. It never says you must worship in this way, or you must be silent because there is a ceremony in progress. It accepts all, rejects none. It encourages all to come to God and does not legislate a single form of devotion.

Hindus always want to live near a temple so they can frequent it regularly. When we go to the temple, we leave with our mind filled with the *shakti* of the Deity. We are filled and thrilled with the *shakti* of the temple in every nerve current of our body. When we return to our home, we light an oil lamp, and that brings the power of the temple into the home. This

It is from worship in the temple that the culture arises—refined living, selfless giving,

simple act brings the devas in the Second World right into your home, where they can bless the rest of the family who perhaps did not go to the temple. Each Hindu temple throughout the world has its own rules on how to proceed and what to do within it. In some temples, in fact most temples in South India, all the men are required to take off their shirts and enter bare-chested. However, if you are in a business suit in the South Indian temple in New York, that's all right. You are not required to take off your shirt. Every temple has its own rules, so you have to observe what everybody else is doing the first time you go.

In the beginning stages of worship, a Hindu soul may have to

Accepting Other Sacraments

Chandanam, or sandalwood paste, is a traditional precious substance, valued for its wonderful scent. A small dab is placed in your hand by the priest, which you transfer to your left palm with a wiping motion. Dip your right-hand ring finger into the paste and apply it with a small circular motion between the eyebrows. Kumkum, a red powder, is next. The priest will either place a small pinch in your right hand or invite you to take some from the container which he holds for you. Apply the kumkum on top of the sandalwood, creating a dot, bindi, which represents the third eye of spiritual seeing.

Internalizing Your Worship

The bhakti of uncompromising surrender, *prapatti*, to the God during a temple puja awakens the amrita. The amrita is the sweet essence from the *sahasrara* chakra. It is the binding yoke to the Divine. Sit down in the lotus posture after the puja and internalize all the feeling that you had for the God during the worship. Draw into yourself the pranas you feel around your body. Then draw those energies up the spine into the head. This is done with the mind and with the breath. Devotees who want to awaken the higher chakras and sustain that awakening on the safe path will throw themselves into becoming uncompromising bhaktars.

wrestle with disbelief in the Gods. He may wonder whether they really exist, especially if his own intuition is obscured by assimilation of Western, existentialist beliefs and attitudes. Yet, he senses their existence, and this sensing brings him back to the temple. He is looking for proof, immersed in the process of coming to know the Gods for himself. He is heartened and assured by hundreds of saints and rishis who have fathomed and found close and enduring relationships with the Gods, and who then extolled their greatness in pages of scripture and chronicle.

The devotee stands before the sanctum and telepathically tells the Gods a problem, and

harmony, integrity, music, art, drama, dance and other aspects of spiritual conduct.

with hopeful faith leaves and waits. Days or weeks later, after he had forgotten about his prayer, he suddenly realizes the problem has disappeared. He attempts to trace the source of its solution and finds that a simple, favorable play of circumstance and events brought it about. Had the Gods answered his prayer, or would it have happened anyway? He brings another prayer to the Gods, and again in time an answer appears in the natural course of his life. It appears to him that the Gods are hearing and responding to his needs. Trust and love have taken root. He goes on, year after year, bringing the Gods into his secular affairs, while just as carefully the Gods are bringing him into their celestial spheres, enlivening his soul with energy, joy and intelligence.

The Hindu looks to the Gods for very practical assistance. He devoutly believes that the Gods from their dwelling in the Third World are capable of consciously working with the forces of evolution in the universe and they could then certainly manage a few simpler problems. He devoutly believes that the Gods are given to care for man on the planet and see him through his tenure on Earth, and that their decisions are vast in their implications. Their overview spans time itself, and yet their detailed focus upon the complicated fabric of human affairs is just as awesome.

The Gods of Hinduism create, preserve and protect mankind. It is through their sanction that all things continue, and through their will that they cease. It is through their grace that all good things happen, and all things that happen are for the good. Now, you may wonder why one would put himself under this divine authority so willingly, thus losing his semblance of freedom. But does one not willingly put himself in total harmony with those whom he loves? Of course he does. And loving these great souls comes so naturally. Their timeless wisdom, their vast intelligence, their thoroughly benign natures, their ceaseless concern for the problems and well-being of devotees, and their power and sheer godly brilliance—all these inspire our love.

Invoking Special Blessings

An *archana* is a short puja for an individual, usually done after the main puja. It is a way of asking God for something specific, such as success in school or business, or to express thanks for good fortune. Inform the priest that you want an *archana*. You should bring fruit and flowers, as well as the *archana* fee, on an offering tray, which can also have a coconut, incense, kumkum, camphor and sandalwood paste. As you stand before the shrine, the priest will ask your name, *gotra* (family lineage), and *nakshatra* (birthstar). During the *archana*, pray for your special needs. Afterwards the priest will return part of your blessed offerings to take home.

Celebrating Rites of Passage

A central part of every Hindu's life, *samskaras* are sacred rites of passage. You can arrange for a *samskara* with the temple priest. There is a charge for these rites, which usually include a puja and *homa*, or fire ceremony. The priest will set an auspicious time, explain how to prepare and what to bring, as well as what you do during the ceremony. The principal *samskaras* held in temples, homes or halls are: name-giving (11 to 41 days old for a child, or anytime for an adult entering Hinduism); first solid food (6 months old); ear-piercing (1, 3 or 5 years old); head shaving (1 to 4 years old); first learning (4 years old); initiation into Vedic study (9 to 15 years old); marriage and funeral.

ALL ART BY A. MANIVEL

CHAPTER 26

Holy Festivals

Insights into the Annual Celebrations Hindus Enjoy the World Over

WHEN IT COMES TO HINDU FESTIVALS, NEPAL EXCELLS. THE NEPALESE CELEBRATE 19 per year on their official calendar, three of them exclusively for women. India, by contrast, sets aside just two Hindu days a year on its national calendar—Navaratri and Dipavali. But whatever official calendars say, Hindus miss no opportunity to set mundane matters aside and join with friends, neighbors and strangers alike in invocation of the One Supreme God and the many Gods, in honor of the guru or in celebration of the passing of the seasons. These are times when all three worlds—of men, of devas and of Gods—come close and commune with each other. While anthropologists generally assign mere social significance in our cycles of festivals, the devout Hindu knows these are times of profound mystical connection to the inner worlds, times when God and the Gods touch our world, revitalize our very souls, lighten our karmas and bless our families. In this chapter we present the nine most popular Hindu festivals. While a few are celebrated by all Hindus, most are specific to one or more of the four main denominations.

In celebration: *(left) one million Hindus gather at Batu Caves, Malaysia, to celebrate Thai Pusam in honor of Lord Murugan; (below) family and neighbors in North India join in kirtan, ecstatic religious singing, for Janmashtami, the birthday of Lord Krishna*

The nine festivals described here are celebrated India-wide—or rather, worldwide, wherever Hindus live. There are also many regional festivals, some of which are locally celebrated on an even grander scale than some of these nine.

Ram Navami

Lord Rama, the seventh incarnation of Vishnu, was born on *navami*, the ninth lunar day, or *tithi*, of the bright half of Meena, or Pisces (Chaitra—the lunar month of March/April). Devotees observe this day with non-stop recitation of the *Ramayana*, the story of Rama's life. In the evening, crowds attend Ramalila, dramatic performances recounting Rama's deeds. Every home will resound with devotional singing. This festival is especially popular in Uttar Pradesh, where Rama's ancient kingdom of Ayodhya was situated. Sometimes Ramalila and other devotional observances are done during the nine days before or after *navami*. People will keep fasts or eat only fruit or a special *prasadam* prepared for the day. If celebrated for nine

Of brothers and Gods: *(below) women toss colored powders in the air at each other in celebration of Holi; (right top) A sister ties the rakhi around her brother's wrist; (right below) a huge crowd escorts Lord Ganesha to the ocean in Mumbai on Ganesha Chaturthi*

days, it is common to remain awake the whole ninth night, engaged in devotional practices. Devotees also contribute generously to temples and other charitable organizations on Ram Navami. Lord Rama is honored not only as an incarnation of God, but also as an ideal man who exemplified the virtues of reverence, obedience and duty.

Raksha Bandhan

On the full moon of Karkata, or Cancer (Sravana—July/August), sisters tie a *rakhi* around the wrist of their brothers, who in return give a present of clothing, cash or jewelry and become obligated for the safety of the sister. The *rakhi* can also be given to anyone chosen as an "adopted brother," even outside the Hindu community. It signifies that she is praying for his welfare and that he is determined to give protection to her. Originally the *rakhi* was a handspun cotton thread dyed yellow with turmeric, but now many colors and materials are used. Three knots are made in the thread to signify protection in thought, word and deed. This day is also celebrated as Narali Purnima, "coconut full moon," when coconuts are offered to Varuna, God of the Sea, by throwing them into the ocean. It is also called Avani Avittam, the ceremony of changing of the sacred thread among the brahmins. This tradition dates back to Vedic times when the year's studies were commenced on this day.

Ganesha Chaturthi

The fourth lunar day of the bright half of Simha, or Leo (Bhadra—August/September), is celebrated around the world as the birthday of Ganesha, the elephant-headed God of Wisdom and Lord of Obstacles. As with other festivals, the homes and temples are elaborately decorated for the day. The special activity is the making of clay images of Ganesha, reverently formed and decorated. Some are huge works of art created by craftsmen, others are tiny icons painted and decorated by children. At the end of the day, or seven or ten days later, these images are ceremoniously immersed in the ocean or a nearby stream or lake, signifying the creation of Ganesha from the Earth and His return and dissolution in the ocean of universal consciousness. So intense has been His presence at this time that even grown men weep at His auspicious departure. His worship on this day removes obstacles and ensures smooth progress in all ventures through the year. As Ganesha is common to all Hindu sects, this festival is serving both inside and outside of India as a day to celebrate Hindu solidarity and unity.

Dipavali (or Diwali)

The festival of lights, Dipavali, or Diwali, takes place on the fourteenth lunar day of the dark half of Tula, or Libra (Karttika—October/November), with related festivities on adjacent days. It is the most widely celebrated Hindu festival in the world, and possibly related to the European Celtic festival of Samhain, observed at the same time of the year with huge bonfires set on hilltops. This is the day that Rama returned to Ayodhya after spending 14 years in exile, though many other reasons for the day are cited. It is a celebration of renewal as the New Year commences in the Vikram calendar. Everyone takes a special bath in the early morning and puts on new clothes. Houses are cleaned, painted and decorated. Goddess Lakshmi is invoked for prosperity, and Her presence is felt in every home. Businesses close out their books for the past year and open new ones, even conducting a mock first business deal of the year. In the evening, every house, store, temple and wall is decorated with thousands of small lamps, while fireworks are set off overhead and firecrackers by the hundreds of thousands below. Family bonds are renewed, especially between brothers and sisters, and forgiveness is requested from friends for any misunderstandings during the previous year. Of all festivals, Dipavali holds a special place, and is the premier international one, holding official holiday status in nine countries—India, Nepal, Fiji, Mauritius, Guyana, Malaysia, Sri Lanka, Trinidad and Singapore, with attempts being made to add more countries where Hindus live.

Holi

Bonfires and the splashing of friends and strangers alike with brightly colored waters, powders and paints mark this most high-spirited of Hindu festivals. It is celebrated on the full moon day of Kumbha, or Aquarius (Phalguna—February/March), and in many places for the several days preceding. Giant bonfires are built by neighborhood boys, where effigies of various demons are consumed. Friends are visited and presents of sweets exchanged. This is essentially a celebration of spring, at which different events are commemorated. This is the day the infant Krishna killed the demoness Putana; the day that Lord Vishnu's devotee Pralada, son of the demon Hiranyakasipu, survived a fire intended to kill him, and the day that Siva burnt Kama, the God of Love, to ashes. Holi is very popular among devotees of Krishna at Mathura, Krishna's birthplace. Also known as Hutasani, "fire consuming," Holi signifies the triumph of good over evil, the beginning of the new agricultural season and the renewal of relationships.

Guru Purnima

In ashrams around the world, the spiritual preceptor is honored on this full moon day of July with garlands, gifts and donations to show love and gratitude for his wisdom through the year. Devotees renew their commitment to following his teachings and guidance for the coming year. The traditional worship is *pada* puja, ceremonial bathing of the guru's feet (or, in his absence, his sandals) with water, milk, honey, sandalwood paste and offering gifts of precious items including 108 gold coins. This day is also known as Vyasa Puja, in honor of Sage Vyasa, codifier of the *Vedas* and author of the *Mahabharata* and *Puranas*. He is honored in temples with offerings of limes and rice, the latter being taken home by devotees and mixed with their own store of rice. This is also a day for reading religious books while remembering the auspicious form of the *satguru* through whom God grants the grace of enlightenment to seekers.

Krishna Janmashtami

Lord Krishna, eighth incarnation of Vishnu, was born on the eighth lunar day (*ashtami*) of the dark half of Karkata, or Cancer (Sravana—July/August). Devotees fast the preceding day until midnight, the time that Krishna was born to Vasudeva and Devika in the Mathura kingdom's prison 5,000 years ago. At midnight, amist grand ceremony the temple priest places the image of the newborn Krishna in a swinging crib. Among the traditional observances, pots of sweets, curd and butter are hung near homes, on trees and street poles in recollection of Krishna's love for these things. Teenage boys dressed as cowherds form human pyramids to reach and break the pots. The following day is again one of festivity, including puja, storytelling and the Ras Leela, a folk theater depicting major events of Krishna's life. "Dark as a rain cloud," reads one account of His birth, "He made the prison glow with the splendor of His crown, His jewelry and His yellow silk robes. He was the Lord God incarnate."

Navaratri

The festival of "Nine Nights," Navaratri, honoring the Goddess, begins on the first lunar day of the bright half of Kanya, or Virgo (Asvina—September/October). Three days are devoted each to Durga (Goddess of valor), Lakshmi (Goddess of wealth) and Sarasvati (Goddess of knowledge). In eastern India the festival is known as Durga Puja. There, images of the Goddess are created,

• •

God, Gods and guru: *(above) priest offers holy ash to the guru's sacred sandals on Guru Purnima; (below) North Indian devotees crowd about a Sivalinga to offer milk and garlands during Mahasivaratri; (far right) a pyramid of daring youth attempt to knock a pot down strung high above the street in this competition held in imitation of the child Lord Krishna's stealing butter*

worshiped for ten days, then immersed in the sea. In southern India, houses are decorated with displays of dolls, toys and images of the Gods. In western India, the traditional *garbha* dance is performed nightly. On the fifth day (Lalita Panchami), all books of a household are gathered, sacred lamps lit reverently by their side and the blessings of Sarasvati invoked. Artisans give their tools a "day of rest," worship and seek blessings for them. Day ten, variously known as Vijaya Dasami, Dasara and Dussehra, marks the commencement of learning. In many localities huge effigies of Ravana are burnt to celebrate Rama's conquest of the demon.

Mahasivaratri

On "Siva's Great Night," Mahasivaratri, the fourteenth day of the dark half of Kumbha, or Aquarius (Phalguna—February/March), devotees fast all day in preparation to worship Lord Siva from evening until early dawn—bathing the sacred Siva Linga with water, milk, honey and saffron water, then offering bilva leaves while chanting *Sri Rudram*, the pre-eminent Vedic hymn to Siva, or reciting His 1,008 names are the highpoints of the all-night vigil. Only when the last puja is finished in early morning do devotees break their fast by eating the sacred *prasadam* offered earlier to the Lord. The following day is one of feasting and gaiety, especially at grand fairs held in many parts of India. On Siva's night we contemplate Siva as the Unmanifest Reality. We dive deep in yogic meditation on His endless/beginningless Radiance.

Setting Festival Dates

Most festivals are held on astrologically auspicious times for a particular deity in the same zodiac sign of the Sun each year. Ram Navami, for example, takes place in the sign of Meena or Pisces, which corresponds to the north Indian month of Chaitra or the Tamil month of Panguni. Each festival day is designated on a particular lunar day, or *tithi*, during a particular sign. There are 30 *tithis* from new moon to new moon. The month's "bright half" (*shukla paksha*) starts from the new moon (*amavasya*) to the full moon (*purnima*) and the "dark half" (*krishna paksha*) from the full moon to the new moon. Because the cycle of the Moon around the Earth (about 29.5 days) and the Sun through one zodiac sign (about 30.4 days) do not match, the month may begin on varying *tithis. Tithis* also vary in length from 20 to 26 hours, because of the Moon's orbit in relation to the sun. When a *tithi* occurs twice in one month, the second is chosen for the festival. Because a *tithi* is not the same as a 24-hour day and the calculations depend on location, one must consult a Hindu calendar (*panchanga*) computed for a particular place to determine a festival date. One cannot simply go by the dates for India. Some festivals are calculated using the *nakshatra* system. There are many regional variations in calendars and hence even dissent on festival calculations.

DINODIA/D. BANERJEE

COMMENTARY

The Inner Light

Amidst the parties and fireworks, let us not forget the real meaning of Dipavali

BY RAMA DEVAGUPTA

"FROM FALSEHOOD LEAD ME TO TRUTH, FROM DARKNESS lead me to light, from death lead me to immortality." Nowhere else is the symbolism of these lines from the *Brihadaranyaka Upanishad* better expressed than in the celebration of Dipavali. Popularly known as the Festival of Lights and abbreviated to Diwali in contemporary usage, Dipavali is the most important festival for the world's Hindu population. With its arrays of lighted lamps, firecrackers and festivities, Dipavali transforms the desolate, fall moonless skies by filling them with laughter, happiness and radiance.

Like other religious festivals of the world, Dipavali is associated with several different legends and has deep social and spiritual significance. It is primarily known for the worship of the Goddess Lakshmi, who symbolizes wealth and prosperity. In North India, it

is a commemoration of Lord Rama's triumphant return to Ayodhya after vanquishing the forces led by Ravana. In South India, Dipavali is celebrated in remembrance of Lord Krishna's victory over Narakasura. In addition, it marks the end of the rainy season and the harvesting cycle, and therefore it is also the festival of the Kharif or new crop.

Whichever story one might prefer, Dipavali celebrations all over the world are universally marked by majestic fireworks, a variety of cultural programs, a spirit of sharing and brotherhood, and, most importantly, the lighting of lamps (*dipas*) in several rows (*vali*) inside and outside the house. It is these luminous *dipas* that contain the essence of Dipavali. Just as light dispels the darkness of the night and shows the right path to a weary traveler, the lighting of lamps on the night of Karttik Amavasya, when the new moon is in Tula or Libra, symbolizes the victory of goodness over evil, justice over injustice, light over darkness and wisdom over ignorance.

Since the beginning of time, spiritual aspirants have sought light as the culmination of their journey. What is this internal, divine light of which the *dipas* on Dipavali night, or those set before the family deity during morning and evening prayers, are only an external representation?

One of the most illustrious conversations on this subject can be found in the *Brihadaranyaka Upanishad*, wherein King Janaka of Videha, whose courtroom was famed for spiritual discussions con-

Dipavali: *(left) devotee contemplates her offering tray and sacred lamps; (right) traditional clay lamp is set upon the drawing of a swastika and other auspicious symbols made with colored rice flour*

• •

ducted by the most distinguished rishis of his time, once asked of Sage Yajnavalkya: "Revered Sage, enlighten me! What is the light of man? What is it that allows him to function in this world?"

Yajnavalkya gave a simple and straightforward answer. "The sun is his light, O King!" he said. "If there were no sunlight, people would be unable to perform their duties in this world. By the light of the sun activity is possible, and it is by the light of the sun that one sits, moves about, completes all work and becomes content." In a series of questions, Janaka presses the sage on the issue, finally asking what light there would be in the absence of all external manifestations. Yajnavalkya gave a very revealing answer. "O King Janaka!" he said. "Know that when everything else fails, the Soul, the inner Self, will be the guide. It is the Self that will be the light."

This light, which is equated with the Supreme and supposed to be the consciousness of life, is expressed as follows in the *Chandogya Upanishad* (3.13.7): "There is a Light that shines beyond all things on Earth, beyond us all, beyond the heavens, beyond the highest, the very highest, heavens. This is the Light that shines in our heart."

Unfortunately, we are oblivious to it most of the time. Even when we read and hear about its presence, we are unable to see the Light, mainly because this flame, which the *Vedas* say is tinier than the tiniest of atomic sparks and hidden in the innermost chamber of the human heart, is now covered by layers of grossness, complexities and impressions. Also, due to our outward-turning senses, tendencies and attachments to the fruits of action, we are unable to turn our eyes inward—at least not until compelled by external circumstances. But we must be able to do so somehow, if the lower self is to become one with the Ultimate Being. But this union is not as easy as it appears in words. The journey is filled with obstacles: darkness and ignorance, misleading visions.

In Arjuna's vision of Lord Krishna in His Cosmic Form on the battlefield of Kurukshetra, the experience of the transcendental Reality is associated with brilliance, splendor and light: "If a thousand suns should rise all at once in the sky, such splendor would resemble the splendor of that great Being…. Then Arjuna, who was filled with amazement, whose hair was standing on end, bowing his head to the Lord with joined palms, said: … 'With infinite power, without beginning, middle or end, with innumerable arms, the Moon and Sun being Your eyes, I see You, the blazing fire Your mouth, burning all this universe with Your radiance.'"

Fascinating and awesome as such visions might be, even the experience of light ought not be the final goal. If that were so, the *Bhagavad Gita* would have ended with the Eleventh Teaching. But it does not. According to Krishna Himself, the supreme state is that which the Sun does not illumine, nor the Moon, nor the fire, for it is the Light of Pure Consciousness. These words are analogous to those found in the *Svetasvatara* (6.14) and *Katha Upanishad* (5.15). "There the Sun shines not, nor the Moon, nor the stars; lightnings shine not there and much less earthly fire. From His light all these give light, and His radiance illumines all creation."

In the modern era, Shri Ram Chandra of Shahjahanpur for almost fifty years taught meditation on the "divine light in the heart," according to the Sahaj Marg system of Raja Yoga. In *Voice Real*, he writes, "Every saint has used the word *light* … and that is the best expression for Reality. But that creates some complication, because when we talk of light, the idea of luminosity becomes prominent, and we begin to take it

as glittering. The Real Light carries with it no such sense and may be represented as 'light without luminosity.' It refers only to the real substance or, more appropriately, to 'substanceless substance,' which is associated with neither light nor darkness, but beyond both."

It is painfully evident that words and descriptions of spiritual Light can convey only so much. As Babuji says, understanding comes by intuitive capacity and practical experience in the spiritual field.

We should be celebrating the Festival of Lights in renewal of our quest for that spiritual Light. But today, few, if any, attach such reverence to the occasion. Instead, it has become a night of entertainment, gambling, pleasure and consumption. Just as the candles and electric lights of modern society have gradually replaced the traditional *dipas*, the focus of the prayers has shifted from the journey from darkness to light to the quest for fortune and wealth.

To appreciate the spirit behind this festival and pass on its significance to others, one needs only to consider the traditional lamps that are popular even today in the small towns and villages of India. These *dipas* represent the four essential elements that are required in the seeker: detachment (the clay container), devotion to the Lord (the oil), prayer and meditation (the cotton wick), and spiritual wisdom (the matchstick to light the lamp). It is noteworthy that on Dipavali the first lamp is lit with a matchstick, after which that lamp is used to light the whole array of lamps inside and outside the house. The first lamp symbolizes divine effulgence, while the other lighted lamps represent the light in individual hearts. Together, they reiterate the eternal truth pronounced in the *Vedas*: "The One willed to become the Many."

As the flames of all these lamps burn brightly and reach upward through the entire night, they show the possibility that, with the removal of darkness, grossness and ignorance, the tiny flickering light in our hearts can also shine brightly, illumining the whole universe. May we all progress speedily to the highest levels of spirituality—from darkness to light, and beyond.

Rama Devagupta, Ph.D. in bioorganic chemistry from Texas A&M University, is a full-time mother and freelance writer on parenting issues and spirituality. She teaches the Sahaj Marg system of Raja Yoga as a preceptor of Shri Ram Chandra Mission (www.srcm.org), and lives in Houston, Texas, with her family.

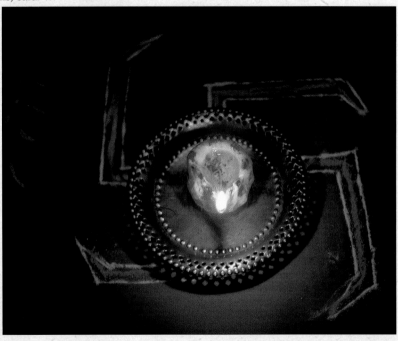

CHAPTER 27
Home Festivals

Annual Observances That Uplift the Family & Spiritualize the Household

INDUISM IS A CELEBRATORY RELIGION, AND NOWHERE CAN THIS BE SEEN MORE clearly than in the yearly cycle of home festivals. In 1998, renowned Chennai artist S. Rajam sought to immortalize the sights, sounds and foods of the Saivite and Vaishnavite festivals of Tamil Nadu in 12 pieces of art, one falling in each month of the year by the Tamil calendar. A few of these are specific to South India, but most have counterparts in all of Bharat. In each he depicted typical scenes one might encounter during the festival day, as well as the Gods and Goddesses worshiped. The explanations of the art were dictated by the artist himself. At family gatherings, parents, grandparents and relatives can elaborate from their childhood experiences.

PAINTINGS BY S. RAJAM

Thai (mid-January/mid-February)

At left the Sun God, Surya, is being worshiped with the outdoor cooking of a large pot of rice from the recent harvest. The overflowing of the dish is called "pongalo-pongal," and thus this festival is known as Thai Pongal. Other crops, like sugarcane, bananas and turmeric, are also offered. *Kolams* (hand-made rice flour patterns) are drawn in the form of the chariot, with the Sun and Moon in the center. On this day cows and other animals are decorated and fed special foods, and their owners prostrate to them. Crows and other birds are offered food on leaves of turmeric. Sisters pray for the welfare of brothers, and elders bless the children. Thai Pongal is celebrated by the poorest farmers and the wealthiest householders.

Masi (February/March)

Above, this is the month of Mahasivaratri, Siva's great night. In the above painting four stories associated with the festival are told. At lower left a hunter has been cornered in a tree-top by wild beasts, where he must spend the night. To avoid sleep, he plucks leaves from the bilva tree, sacred to Lord Siva, and drops them upon a Sivalinga below—a traditional form of worship. Many undertake fasts and stay awake the whole night, praying to Lord Siva both at home and in temples (lower right). The home observance of Karadainombu (upper right) derives from the story of Savitri and her husband, Satyavan. They enter a forest, where he dies. When Lord Yama, the God of Death, comes to take his life, Savitri persuades Yama to let him live. The intent of the observance is that wives not be separated from their husbands. Another explanation of this festival (upper left) is that on this day Lord Siva tied a thread to Parvati's right hand after their marriage as a sign of protection and fidelity.

● ●

PAINTINGS BY S. RAJAM

Panguni (March/April)

This month brings the popular nine-day festival of Ram Navami, celebrating the birthday of Lord Rama, an incarnation of Lord Vishnu. When the full moon rises, Vishnu in the form of Satyanarayana is worshiped before a decorated kumbha pot with a branch of mango leaves placed in its mouth and a coconut on top. Rice is spread on banana leaves and the sacred vessel is completed with a tray of fruits, flowers an betel leaves and nuts. This month is also known for Sita's marriage to Rama. King Janaka, Dasaratha and priests surround the sacred fire, as Sita garlands Rama in Janaka's royal palace.

. . . .

Chitrai (Apirl/May)

This month (right) begins with he completion of Ram Navami, the nine days of celebration of Lord Rama's birth ages ago, which started in the previous month. At the upper left we see a decorated picture of Lord Rama's coronation. Next (proceeding clockwise) comes a Vaisnava priest telling the stories of Lord Rama's birth and life; behind him are great pots of *paanagan,* a delicious drink of sugar and ginger, and a basket of *sundal,* spiced chickpeas, served to the storyteller's guests, who also receive palm fans, as this is the hot season. Tamil New Year often falls on April 14 (as does the New Year of several other communities). The lady at upper right is shown with the new clothes and jewelry which are part of the celebration, as well as bananas, mangos and the ingredients for *vipon pu pachadi,* a combination of bitter neem blossoms, sugar and mango—a reminder to face the unpleasant in life with a sweet smile. At lower left is the marriage of Siva and Parvati, Meenakshi Kalyanam, with brother Vishnu pouring the sacred Ganga water on their joined hands. At lower right is the dark form of Yama, Lord of Death, who figures in three stories associated with this month; that of Savitri, who won her husband back from Yama in a battle of wits; Nachiketas, the boy who extracted three boons from Him and Markandeya, who won eternal youth from Lord Yama through the worship of the Sivalinga.

. . . .

Vaikasi (May/June)

This month is devoted to the worship of Lord Murugan, who is honored on Vaikasi Visakham (above). He is shown at far left as Palani, the renunciate, dressed in loincloth, wearing a necklace of rudraksha beads, sacred ash covering His body and holding the sannyasin's staff. To the right He is shown as a prince, with His peacock, and farther to the right as the six-headed Arumugam. Devotees approach Him doing penance by piercing their bodies with small spears and carrying various offerings, including pots of milk and a *kavadi*, a kind of portable arched shrine. At lower right is depicted Naga Chaturthi, celebrating an ancient story in which a young boy bit by a cobra was saved from death when his sister's prayers caused the sands of the cobra's anthill to counteract the poison.

Ani (June/July)

This is the one month of the year when there are no home festivals—coinciding not uncoincidentally with an intense month of agricultural effort. However, during Ani, major temple festivals are held for Lord Siva as Nataraja, King of Dance (above left), and for Siva and Parvati.

• • • • • • • • • • • • • • • •

PAINTINGS BY S RAJAM

Adi (July/August)

There are two major home festivals this month. The first is Adi-Perukku, in honor of the Kaveri River. Women and girls go to the nearest river where they place offerings on a bamboo tray (upper left) into the water, then have a feast upon the riverbank. Varalakshmi Vratam ("vow to bring Lakshmi") is also a ladies' festival, in which paintings of the Goddess of Wealth are made upon the walls (upper right), kumbha pots intended for worship are decorated with Her image. Beside the pot are placed various cosmetics, comb, beads, etc., and worship is done. Then the ladies sing songs inviting the Goddess to their home. Kozhukkatai, rice and jaggary cakes, are a favorite of the day. In the evening, friends are invited to the home and given clothing, coconuts and sweets.

• • • • • • • • • • • • • • • • • • •

Avani (August/September)

This is a busy month, with two major festivals celebrated both at home and at the temple. Krishna Jayanthi, the birth of Lord Krishna, comes first. In the painting at right is the rescue of the baby Krishna, who was born in a prison. His father carries him across a swollen stream while the seven-headed serpent, Adi Seshan, protects the incarnation of Lord Vishnu from the storm. In the home, offerings of butter and yogurt are made to Krishna's image, and footprints made with red powder reveal his path from the home's front door to the shrine room, suggesting that Krishna has come to participate. Ganesha Chaturthi is a mammoth festival across all of India, ten days in celebration of His manifestation. Shown in the center of the painting is a statue of Lord Ganesha and a devotee offering obeisance by pulling his ears and bobbing up and down, a practice called *thopukarannam* in Tamil, done only for Ganesha—one explanation being that it is to make the Baby Ganesha laugh. The icon of Ganesha is made by the devotees from river clay and painted and decorated. At festival's end is the Visarjana, or departure, when the clay icon is placed into the river the Deity is bid farewell. In North India Visarjana is celebrated by millions of people. At far right in the art is depicted

the story of Ganesha consuming so many sweet offerings that He had to tie a snake around his belly to keep it from bursting. Ganesha chastised the Moon for laughing at His predicament, and as penance the Moon has ever since waxed and waned through the month instead of remaining constantly bright.

● ●

Purattasi (September/October)

Navaratri ("nine nights") is the principal festival this month (above left). The Goddess is worshiped in Her many forms, and on the ninth day, Sarasvati (center of the painting) is invoked to bless musical instruments, account books, agricultural instruments and home tools (upper left). On Vijaya Dasami, the day following Navaratri, Goddess Durga is invoked as children are given their first instruction, worship their school books and honor their teacher (bottom left). A decorated display of dolls (lower right) is displayed through the nine days, then dismantled and stored on the tenth day. Vijaya Dasami is also the birthday of Lord Venkateshwara (upper right), presiding Deity of Tirupati Temple in Andhra Pradesh, India's wealthiest temple.

● ●

Aippasi (October/November)

Skanda Shasti is the first festival of this month (right), commemorating the victory of Lord Murugan over the demon Sura, of the higher, spiritual self over the lower nature. Dipavali is the major event of Aippasi, celebrated everywhere Hindus live and by Buddhists and Jains, too. In one story of its origins, Vamana, the dwarf avatar of Lord Vishnu, requests the amount of land from King Bali that He can cover in three steps. Granted the request, Vamana covers with his first step all of the Earth, with the second all of the sky, and then asks the king where to take the third step. The king offers his own head (lower left), and in commemoration of the king's humility,

PAINTINGS BY S. RAJAM

the day was established. In another story, Lord Vishnu (center) kills the demon Nagagasvaran with His discus. The various observances (lower right) of Dipavali include an oil bath, gifts of new clothes, fireworks (sufficiently indulged in Chennai to rattle dishes off the kitchen shelves), oil lamps for display and abundant pots of delicious food. The early morning bath is always considered to be in the Ganga itself, so one greeting of the day is, "Did you have the Ganga bath?"

Karttikai (November/December)

Krittika Dipa (right) is a joyous one-day festival held on the Krittika nakshatra (when the moon is in Pleiades constellation). Also called Sivalaya Dipa, it is celebrated most famously at Tiruvannamalai (upper left in the painting), on top of Arunachala Hill, home of saint Ramana Maharshi. A bonfire is lit on top that can be seen for miles around. Karthigai Purnima, the full-moon day, honors Lord Murugan. In one traditional story, six sparks from Siva's third eye became six babies (lower left), later gathered into one six-headed Arumugam (center) by Parvati. Celebrations include lighting hundreds of oil lamps, especially the standing lamp (right) of the home. On this day in Orissa, devotees make banana leaf boats and float them in the river with oil lamps (lower left).

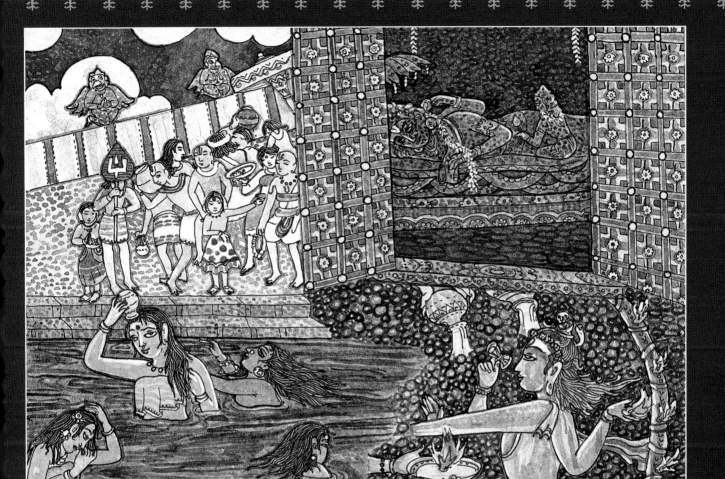

Markali (December/January)

During Tirupuval (below, in upper left of painting), people bathe (lower left) and gather in the early morning to go on procession singing devotional Vaishnava songs (upper left). Especially popular are those of the 9th century lady saint Andal, venerated as one of South India's greatest devotional poets. On Vaikunth Ekadasi, the 11th day of the lunar month, the doors of the huge temple of Srirangam are opened to devotees from morning to night for darshan of Rangam, an aspect of Lord Vishnu, sleeping on Adishani, the serpent king (upper right). Another famed festival is Ardra Darshana, when Siva Nataraja is decorated and taken from the temple in procession throughout the community (lower right). Especially the ill and those of old age seek to have a glimpse of Nataraj. A renowned sweet, aururda kalli, is made with vegetables on this day.

• •

S. Rajam concluded his descriptions by saying, "All of these festivals are earnestly conducted. People wait for the day with their mind on God. The purpose is to gather in the home and worship for the prosperity of the family and of all mankind."

• •

CHAPTER 28

Kumbha Mela

Cosmic Alignment and Divine Presence Empower Humanity's Grandest Religious Observance

T HE TENS OF MILLIONS OF HINDUS who came to the Kumbha Mela at Haridwar this year were nearly all of modest means. After days of travel, many spent a mere 24 hours in the holy city at the gateway to the Himalayas. They chanted *Jai Ganga Ma*—"Hail Mother Ganga"—took their sacred bath in the frigid river, collected a pot of holy Ganga water and then headed home. One typical pilgrim, an illiterate woman, traveled with her family by crowded bus from West Bengal, slept in the open and ate at the free feeding tents. "We are poor, but we have enough. I asked God not for money but for peace and salvation"—so easily did this humble villager capture the essence of the world's greatest act of pilgrimage, the Kumbha Mela.

For her and millions of others, the religious ritual of pilgrimage—one of the five obligatory duties of every Hindu—began with the first plans to attend, and encompasses the entire process of getting ready, freeing oneself from worldly affairs, traveling to the site, taking the bath, meeting the sadhu-mendicants or just observing them from a distance, and the return home. At nearly every *mela*, pil-

grims have been killed in one mishap or another, so each who came duly considered the possibility, however small, that they might not return. For the true devotee, pilgrimage is among the most profound religious practices, one in which material gain—so often the motivation for their prayers at local temples—is superceded by higher aspirations.

The Kumbha Mela takes place every three years in rotation at Haridwar, Prayag (Allahabad), Nasik and Ujjain, according to the placement of Jupiter in the Zodiac. A modern innovation, there are also popular half-*melas*, *ardha-kumbhas*, every six years at Haridwar and Prayag. It is at Prayag, where the Yamuna River joins the Ganga, that the largest number of human beings in history gathered—15 million on February 6, 1989. Haridwar, logistically less convenient, managed ten million on April 14, 1998. Still, that's five times this year's two million Muslim pilgrims who journeyed to Mecca for the Haj, the second largest gathering.

Every religion, as a matter of doctrine or custom, engages in the practice of pilgrimage to holy places. Among the world's prime des-

Contested prize: *After eons of churning, depicted in this painting by Harish Johari, the Ocean of Milk yielded the Amrita Kumbha, pot of the nectar of immortality. As angelic beings flew off with the pot, drops fell at four places—Haridwar, Prayag, Ujjain and Nasik—forever empowering them as sites of the Kumbha Mela.*

coveted result—the pot (*kumbha*) of nectar (*amrita*), by consuming which anyone would become immortal. As they churned mightily, the first substances to be released were deadly fumes and gases. These Lord Siva took upon Himself to consume and neutralize, thus saving the world's inhabitants from certain death. These poisons turned His throat blue and resulted in His name, *Nilakantha*. After many aeons of churning, the ocean yielded a series of treasures, the last of which was Dhanvantari, the great healer, who held in his hands the desired chalice of ambrosia.

The asuras immediately demanded their share of the prize, but the devas reneged on their agreement, knowing that if their rivals were to drink the nectar they would be eternally unbeatable, and too great a power to keep in check. The asuras, sensing their position, snatched the *kumbha* and fled. With the asuras momentarily distracted by Lord Vishnu, the devas retrieved the pot and fled. In their haste they let one drop of nectar fall at Haridwar, Prayag, Ujjain and Nasik.

"Since the beginning," explains Sri Mahant Rudra Giri Ji, of the Atal Akhara, "the Kumbha Mela was attended by 350 million devas and 88,000 rishis. It was started to promote and propagate our ancient heritage. Even now these devas and rishis participate." A few of the angelic beings, devas, are able to return with each pilgrim to their home, carried, in a mystical sense, in the pot of Ganga water that each pilgrim collects and places on his home altar. Thus the blessing of the pilgrimage is extended months, even years, beyond the actual event.

Esoterically, it is taught that the *kumbha* represents higher consciousness, the *sahasrara* chakra. The *amrita* that it holds symbolizes mankind's attainment of that higher reality—the true source of immortality.

According to researcher Subhas Rai, the cosmic alignments associated with the festival are chosen so as to increase the efficacy of the pilgrims' bathing. He believes the combined power of river Ganga and the auspicious planetary positions generates unique purifying power.

Pilgrimage to sacred rivers is an ancient practice, believed by historian S.B. Roy to exist in India as far back as 10,000 BCE. Megasthanes, the 4th century BCE Greek visitor to India, described what could have been a Kumbha Mela, but the likeliest first reference is by the Chinese pilgrim Hiuen-Tsang, who resided in India from 629 to 645 CE. He wrote that King Harshavardhan attended, on every fifth year of his reign, a month-long, "ageless festival" at Prayag that attracted up to half a million people from all walks of life.

When references to the Kumbha Mela appear clearly in the 14th century, the *mela* has all of its modern characteristics—the places, the bathing, the hoards of pilgrims and legions of mendicants. Many believe its organization to be the work of Adi Shankara, the great 8th-century Indian saint, though nothing in his writings supports the assertion. By the 14th century the presence of large numbers of militant sadhu orders was also a clear feature, especially after the wholesale slaughter of Mela pilgrims in 1398 by Muslim general Tirmur, shortly after he leveled Delhi because the reigning sultan was "too tolerant" of Hindus. Similar martial monastic orders have developed in other religions, such as the 12th-century Christian Knights Templar and Hospitalers in Europe—also to protect pilgrims against Muslim oppression—the Shao Lin monks of Kung Fu martial arts fame in China, the Buddhist monastic police of Tibet and the Zen master archers and swordsmen of Japan. Sadly, through the centuries mendicant militancy has led to frequent murderous Kumbha

tinations are Bodh Gaya, where Buddha attained enlightenment; Jerusalem, sacred to three religions; Lourdes in France; Amritsar; the Ise Shrine in Japan; and the various Jain sites throughout India.

The Kumbha Mela is unique for its sheer size, and for being a meeting both of ascetics and lay people. Some of the ascetics are *naga* sadhus, naked monks who practice the severest austerities and leave the mountains and jungles only for the *mela*. Just the sight of them—and there are thousands—is a blessing to the lay pilgrims.

Within the several-month period of the *mela* are set auspicious bathing days, usually coinciding with festivals of the period. Most important are the days for the *shahisnan*, "royal bath," in which the holy men, *naga* sadhus first, go in procession to the river.

Asked the origin of the event, nearly every pilgrim will narrate the ancient story from the *Puranas* of the time when the devas (gods or angels) and the asuras (their rivals) cooperated to "churn the Ocean of Milk"—an act which promised to yield countless treasures. With Mount Meru as the post and the serpent Shesha as the churning rope, they set about their task. They agreed to share the most

Mela battles over who gets to bathe closest to the supremely auspicious moment—the very issue which caused this year's fight.

Many orders of sadhus gather at the Mela. A large portion are members of a dozen or more orders called *akharas,* the most prominent being the Juna and Niranjani—the two who tangled this year. Others include the Agan, Alakhiya, Abhana, Anand, Mahanirvani and Atal. Most orders are Saivite, three are Vaishnavite and a few are Sikh orders patterned after the Hindu monastic system. *Akhara* is Hindi for a "wrestling arena," and can mean either a place of verbal debate, or one of real fighting. Each *akhara* may contain monks of several different Dasanami orders—the ten designations—Saraswati, Puri, Bana, Tirtha, Giri, Parvati, Bharati, Aranya, Ashrama, and Sagara—regularized by Adi Shankara in the 8th century. Thus, the *akharas* overlap with the Dasanami system. There are also sannyasi orders, such as the Nathas, that exist outside the Dasanami system. The *akharas'* dates of founding range from the sixth to the fourteenth century. The development of the *akharas* and the Kumbha Mela took place over the same time span and are likely related. *Akharas* may include thousands, even tens of thousands, of sadhus. Several *akharas* run hundreds of ashrams, schools and service institutions.

The Kumbha Mela is a time to elect new *akhara* leadership, discuss and solve problems, consult with the other *akharas,* meet with devotees and initiate new monastics. During Muslim and British times, the *mela* gathering of pilgrims and sadhus was a significant force in the preservation of Hinduism and the continued identity of India as a Hindu nation. "Khumba weaves our nation into one," said Mahant Ganga Puri of the Mahanirvani Akhara.

One little-known purpose of the Mela is to review smriti, the codes (shastras) of law and conduct which govern Hindu society. Unlike the *Vedas* and other revealed scriptures, these codes are meant to be adjusted according to changes in time and circumstance. Rameshbhai Oza explained, "The saints from all over India should get together at the Mela to discuss not only religious and spiritual matters, but also the problems faced by the contemporary society. Their solutions offer a new system and a new smriti." Ramesh is a world renowned performer of *kathak* (preaching through song and sermon on the life of Lord Rama and other Hindu heros).

Many are the motivations and benefits for Hindus to attend the Kumbha Mela, the most popular pilgrimage of the day. It is a time to gain a new look on life, to purify oneself and to regain the sense of Godly aspiration as the central purpose for this earthly incarnation.

With **Jono Lineen,** *British Columbia*

RAJEEV GUPTA

TIMELINE

10,000 bce: Historian S.B. Roy postulates presence of ritual bathing.
600 bce: River *melas* are mentioned in Buddhist writings.
400 bce: Greek ambassador to Indian King Chandra Gupta reports on a *mela.*
ca 300 ce: Roy believes present form of *melas* crystalizes. Various *Puranas,* written texts based on oral traditions of unknown antiquity, recount the dropping of the nectar of immortality at four sites after the "churning of the ocean."
547: Earliest founding date of an *akhara,* the Abhana.
600: Chinese pilgrim Hiuen-Tsang attends *mela* at Prayag (modern Allahabad) organized by King Harsha on a five-year cycle.
ca 800: Adi Shankara believed to have reorganized and promoted *kumbha melas.*
904: Founding of Niranjani Akhara
1146: Founding of Juna Akhara
1300: Kanphata Yogi militant ascetics employed in army of King of Kanaj, Rajasthan
1398: Tirmur lays waste to Delhi to punish Sultan's tolerance toward Hindus, proceeds to Haridwar *mela* and massacres thousands. Hindu ascetics arm themselves.
1565: Madhusudana Sarasvati organizes fighting units of Dasanami orders.

1684: French traveller Tavernier estimates 1.2 million Hindu ascetics in India.
1760: Saivites battle with Vaishnava sects at Haridwar; 1,800 are killed.
ca 1780: British establish the order for royal bathing by the monastic groups (the same order is followed today).
1820: Stampede leaves 430 dead at Haridwar *mela.*
1906: British calvary intercede in *mela* battle between sadhus.
1954: Four million people, one percent of India's population, attend *mela* at Allahabad, hundreds perish in a stampede.
1989: *Guinness Book of World Records* proclaims 20-million-strong *mela* crowd at Allahabad on February 6 "the largest-ever gathering of human beings for a single purpose," a record soon broken by another Kumbha Mela.
1998: Haridwar Mela attracts 25 million pilgrims in four months, ten million on April 14.
2001: Most recent *mela* at Allahabad, attended by an astonishing 70 million pilgrims.
2003: Most recent *mela* at Ujjain and Nasik.
2007: *Ardha-mela* at Allahabad. Main bathing date: January 19.
2010: Next *mela* at Haridwar. Main bathing date: April 14.
2013: Next *mela* at Allahabad.

"In the midst of the Waters, the Lord is moving, surveying men's truth and men's lies. How sweet are the Waters, crystal clear and cleansing! Now may these great, divine Waters enliven me!"

Rig Veda VII.49.3

Haridwar: *With all but a few of Her devotees fast asleep by Her shores, the River Ganga silently rushes past Hari ki Pauri Ghat late at night. (below) Novitiate nuns in yellow saris meditate with ordained nuns before Goddess Durga at a Haridwar ashram.*

THOMAS KELLY

Spiritual

Managing and easing karma, harnessing anger, the practice of silence, hatha yoga and sacred pilgrimage

THOMAS KELLY

Practices

A panoramic night scene of the Kumbha Mela festival, the largest human event on the planet. The festival is held every three years, rotating between four cities: Haridwar (pictured here), Prayag, Nashik and Ujjain. Millions of devotees make the pilgrimage from all over the world, to bathe in the sacred waters and have darshan of India's holy men. The 2001 Mela in Prayag drew 150 million pilgrims.

Karma is Self-Generated: A man's actions create his future karmas to be experienced, just as if he carved himself out of a stone with his own hands—as the man in the painting is doing. In the background, Lord Ganesha, the Lord of Karma, confers blessings with His raised right hand.

Karma Management

A Step-by-Step Guide to Help You Effectively Deal with Your Karma

BY SATGURU BODHINATHA VEYLANSWAMI

THE CONCEPT OF KARMA HAS SPREAD BEYOND THE CONFINES OF THE ASIAN RELIGIONS that conceived it to become a core concept of today's yoga and New Age movements. It is now mentioned regularly on American mainstream television programs and in the movies. Last year in discussing the concept with a junior college class in Hawaii, a student expressed contemporary culture's astute definition of karma as "What goes around comes around." Unfortunately, most individuals' understanding of karma is at best limited to thinking about it as an abstract principle without applying it to their own life. This is equivalent to a student's learning and understanding all the laws of nutrition, being able to get an "A" on any test on the subject, but following a personal diet of junk food three times a day. What he learned is not influencing how he lives. The study of karma is effectively approached in a three-step process: 1) dispelling common misconceptions about karma; 2) acquiring a correct intellectual understanding of karma's key concepts; 3) managing your own karma by utilizing the correct understanding of karma to refine your actions and reactions in life.

Two Misconceptions

1 You have no doubt heard the most common false concept about karma on a number of occasions. It goes something like this: "Nothing but bad things happen to me. It's my karma, and even when I strive to do better, my striving has no effect upon it. So why should I even try to make my life amount to anything? It's truly hopeless."

This misconception must be rejected for two important reasons. The first is that you can actually change your karma through the principles of effective karma management. The second is that how you live in this life creates the karma you will face in your future lives. So, why not consciously use the law of karma to create a future that is filled with pleasant experiences rather than painful ones?

2 A second common false concept about karma, which you have probably also heard, goes like this: "My life is in a state of chaos. Everything is going wrong, and it all started three months ago when Saturn entered Taurus and my karma changed. I have been advised that if I can successfully appease Saturn through having a priest do regular Sani puja, my problems will go away.

Therefore, that has become the entire focus of my religious life at this time." The fallacy of this attitude is that, yes, karmic difficulties indicated by your astrology can be mitigated, but not simply by paying a priest to do Sani puja. If that is all you are doing to work with your situation, that's not enough. In working through the trying times of life, your primary powers are willpower, devotion and understanding. Such karma can be mitigated through specific actions performed by the individual, such as those outlined below, but not merely by giving over such duties to others.

A second reason this misconception must be rejected is that it attributes the cause of our problems to the planet Saturn rather than to our own actions in the past. It is like pleading with the jailer to release you from your cell simply because being incarcerated is an unpleasant experience, having forgotten about the crime you committed that put you in prison in the first place. Planets don't determine your karma, and neither do the actions of others. It is self-created, and you are the source of it all—good, bad and mixed.

Ten Correct Concepts

ONE: Karma means act or deed.

Let's begin with the word karma itself. What does it mean? Karma means "action" or "deed," such as in the common phrase karma yoga, "union through action."

TWO: The law of karma is the law of cause and effect.

When we say "the law of karma," we refer to the law of action and reaction, also called the law of cause and effect. This law states that what we sow we shall reap in this or future lives. Benevolent actions (*punyakarma* or *sukarma*) will bring loving reactions. Selfish, hateful acts (*papakarma* or *kukarma*) will bring suffering. Every action that we perform in life, every word we speak, even every thought that we think, has its reaction.

THREE: Karma is just and self-governing.

The law of karma is a divine, self-governing system of justice that automatically creates the appropriate future experience in response to the current action. However, unlike the justice systems of a country, which only punish the misdeeds of those who are caught, tried and found guilty, karma punishes misdeeds and rewards good deeds whether they are known or not. For example, if a man robs a bank and is never caught, no punishment is received through man's law. However, he will inevitably face the consequences of his crime through the law of karma. Similarly, the good deed of giving money regularly but anonymously to a charity will be rewarded, even though no one knows the giver's name.

FOUR: Karma is our teacher.

Through understanding the consequences of their actions, individuals sooner or later learn to refrain from committing a particular misdeed. Any good system of justice does not want repeat offenders. It wants individuals to understand the error of their ways and reform their behavior. You've heard Alexander Pope's famous phrase that to err is human, to forgive is divine. Well, we can adapt his adage and say to err is human but to err only once is divine, meaning those who are striving to live a religious life are self-reflective and learn quickly from their mistakes. This is what we mean by saying "Karma is our teacher." It teaches us to refine our behavior—hopefully sooner rather than later. One way to tell a young soul from an old soul is to observe how quickly he learns karma's lessons in life.

FIVE: We each have our individual karma.

Karma also refers to our individual karma that we carry from life to life, both the karma to be resolved in this life, and the karma to be resolved in a future life. To understand this better, let us reflect again on the criminal justice system. Justice is known for moving slowly. It can take a number of years before a convicted criminal receives his punishment. The law of karma is even slower. The consequences, or fruits of actions, known as *karmaphala*, may not come for a number of lifetimes. Thus, the karma we are born with is comprised of rewards and punishments from many past lives that have yet to manifest, and are yet to be resolved.

SIX: There are three types of individual karma.

Our individual karma is of three types: *sanchita*, *prarabdha* and *kriyamana*. *Sanchita* is the sum total of past karmas yet to be resolved. *Prarabdha* is that portion of *sanchita* karma scheduled to be experienced in the present life, shaping its events and conditions, including the nature of our bodies, personal tendencies and associations. *Kriyamana* is karma you are presently creating. While some *kriyamana* karmas bear fruit in the current life, others are stored for future births.

SEVEN: Astrology indicates the patterns of karma.

Prarabdha karma determines one's time of birth, which dictates one's astrology, which in turn delineates the individual life pattern by influencing the release of these karmas. Thus, an individual will experience certain astrological periods as difficult and other periods as auspicious and positive. Astrology does not dictate our karma, rather our karma determines our astrology, so understanding our horoscope helps us knowledgeably manage our karma as it arises to be faced.

EIGHT: Karmas are either active or inactive.

Sanchita, *prarabdha* and *kriyamana* karmas can each be divided into two categories: *arabdha*, "begun" or "undertaken" karma that is sprouting; and *anarabhda*, "not commenced," "dormant," or seed karma. An analogy can be drawn to a garden in which a variety of seeds have been planted. Some types of plants will sprout in a few days, others will take weeks and still others lie dormant for months. Similarly, some of our karmas will manifest in the next few years, some toward life's end and others in a future life.

NINE: We create our own future.

Our actions in the present are creating what we will experience in the future, even in future lives. The point here is that when we think of karma, we tend to think of the past. We reflect upon the rewards and punishments from the past that are now manifesting and what we must have done to create them. However, we must also think about our future in this life and lives to come. Our actions in the present are influencing that future, making it pleasant or unpleasant. Therefore, before acting, a wise person reflects on that action's karmic consequences and thereby consciously molds his future.

TEN: Life is all about resolving karma.

The ultimate future to consider is liberation from the cycle of birth and death, samsara. As long as we have karmas to resolve, we will be reborn on Earth. Thus, individuals who are intent upon spiritual progress take the creation and resolution of karma quite seriously. Not only do they strive to act wisely in the present, they perform extra religious practices to rid themselves in this life of karmas that would normally only manifest in future lives. This is a profound practice performed by sagacious sannyasins especially.

Ten Principles for Effective Karma Management

ALL ART BY A. MANIVEL

1 FOREGO RETALIATION: *The protest march led by Gandhi on May 21, 1930, is attacked by police as they approach Dharasana Salt Factory. The protestors did not retaliate or defend themselves, but allowed the injustice of the attack to recoil on the British administration that ordered it. In each of the paintings commissioned for this article, Lord Ganesha, who governs karma, looks on.*

BY SATGURU BODHINATHA VEYLANSWAMI

A FEW YEARS AGO, I WAS ONE OF TWO speakers at a lecture in perth, australia. i spoke on enlightenment, stressing that it is a gradual process, a deepening of the ability to experience God, starting with seeing God as the light in the eyes of everyone you look at. The second speaker, a prominent Malaysian Hindu leader, made the point that a modern trend of Hindus is to consider the traditional wisdom given by swamis as old-fashioned and not lend it much weight. Instead, many Hindus are fascinated with the modern, secular self-improvement-seminar approach, which quite often takes its principles from Hindu thinking but gives them a modern packaging. So, today we are taking that modern approach to karma. You've heard of stress management workshops? Well, this a karma management program, designed for workshops, in which we will learn the ten principles for effective karma management, drawn from the teachings of Satguru Sivaya Subramuniyaswami (Gurudeva). This fulfills the third step of learning about karma, which is to apply our understanding of karma to our own life and thus refine the way we act in and react to life. Gurudeva taught: "It is easy to study the law of karma and to appreciate it philosophically, but to realize it, to apply it to everything that happens to you, to understand the workings of it as the day goes by, requires an ability to which you must awaken."

FIRST PRINCIPLE
Forego Retaliation

1 There is no need for you to be the instrument to return a karmic reaction to someone else. For example, an individual is really nasty to you, so you feel the impulse to retaliate and be nasty to him. If you follow that tack, you will create a new unseemly karma to face in the future. Better to let the law of karma take its own course without your intervention, which will generally happen through some other person with less self-control who does not understand this law of life.

Let us take another example: a classic cowboy movie plot. Someone shoots and kills the hero's brother during a robbery, and the rest of the film is devoted to his chasing down the outlaw and shooting him in revenge. What, then, happens in the next life, the sequel? There is definitely a karma to be faced for killing in revenge. Perhaps another robbery will take place and the hero will be killed. Wisdom tells us that it is better to let the

CHAPTER 29: KARMA MANAGEMENT **251**

2 ACCEPT RESPONSIBILITY: *The lady is recovering from having her purse stolen by the fleeing robber. She is remembering a time when she stole a valuable necklace from another lady's purse, realizing that the karma of that theft has now caught up with her.*

3 FORGIVE THE OFFENDER: *Swami Sivananda was once attacked by a man wielding an axe. Devotees restrained the man and locked him in an ashram room. Sivananda came to the man, forgave him for the attack and let him go.*

. . . .

sheriff apprehend the outlaw and bring him to justice. The sheriff has taken an oath and is authorized to uphold the law and therefore creates no negative karma in capturing the outlaw, even if he has no choice but to kill him in the process.

Gurudeva said, "Retaliation is a terrible, negative force. When we retaliate against others, we build up a bank account of negative karma that will come back on us full force when we least expect it."

Tirukural: "Forget anger toward all who have offended you, for it gives rise to teeming troubles."

SECOND PRINCIPLE
Accept Responsibility

Karma generally manifests through other people, and thus it is easy to see the other person as totally responsible for what happens to us. For example, you are attacked by a mugger who strikes you and steals your valuables. You are quite upset with the malicious thief. However, the mystical perspective is to see yourself as responsible for whatever happens to you. You are, through your actions in the past, the creator of all that you experience in the present. You caused your loss; the thief is just the instrument for returning your karma to you.

Of course, it is easy to apply this principle when the effect is an enjoyable one (we know intuitively when we get good things that we deserve them) and not so easy to apply it when it is not enjoyable, but in both cases we are equally responsible. In the end, you have no one to praise but yourself when your life is filled with successes and no one to blame but yourself when your life is filled with difficulties.

Gurudeva said, "As long as we externalize the source of our successes and failures, we perpetuate the cycles of karma, good or bad. There is no one out there making it all happen. Our actions, thoughts and attitudes make it all happen. We must accept and bear our karma cheerfully."

Tirukural: "Why should those who rejoice when destiny brings them good moan when that same destiny decrees misfortune?"

THIRD PRINCIPLE
Forgive the Offender

Take as an example a teenage boy on the way home from school. One day a gang of boys teases him for being different in some way and beats him up. A common response is for the teenager to feel angry at the boys and harbor ill feelings toward them for years. This is problematic, however, as it keeps the lower emotions of anger constantly churning in his subconscious mind. Unless he forgives them, he perpetuates the event in his own mind, long after it is over.

Gurudeva often told the story of when a man attacked Swami Sivananda, hitting him forcefully in the head with an axe during evening satsang at his Rishikesh ashram. Swamiji's followers were outraged and angrily subdued the man. But Swami Sivananda responded with the opposite sentiment. He asked that the man not be punished or turned over to the police. The next day he met with his attacker and gave him a train ticket home, several spiritual books and money. Swami said, "Thank you so much for being the instrument to bring this karma back to me. Now I am free of it." He felt no anger toward the man whatsoever.

Tirukural: "If you return kindness for injuries received and forget both, those who harmed you will be punished by their own shame."

FOURTH PRINCIPLE
Consider the Consequences

Quite often our actions are based upon an emotional reaction to what someone has done or said to us. The consequences of such actions are often not clearly and carefully thought about. For example, someone insults you, so you insult them back. If you did reflect, you would see that the consequence of harming someone else with your words in the present is for you to be harmed again in the future by someone else's words. This behavior creates an endless cycle of being harmed and harming others, which is only stopped by considering the consequences before acting and not harming back. Mahatma Gandhi once said, "An eye for an eye makes the whole world blind." So, too, instinctive retaliation ultimately makes the whole world angry. The principle of considering the karmic consequences pertains equally to positive actions. The wisest approach is to not simply react to things that happen to us, but to take time to consider the karmic repercussions of all actions before we take them.

The habit of considering the consequences before acting can be developed at an early age when parents and teachers utilize positive discipline methods to help children face the natural and logical consequences of their actions. An insightful letter from Lord Ganesha on consequences in Gurudeva's book *Loving Ganesha* reminds us: "Keep track of your paces, for your walk makes marks. Each mark is a reward or a stumbling block. Learn to look at the step you have made and the step you have not made yet. This brings you close to Me."

Gurudeva elucidates our fourth principle: "It is our reaction to karmas through lack of understanding that creates most karmas we shall experience at a future time."

Tirukural: "All suffering recoils on the wrongdoer himself. Thus, those desiring not to suffer refrain from causing others pain."

FIFTH PRINCIPLE
Create No Negative Karmas

Now that we have a good grasp of the karmic consequences of various kinds of actions, what is needed next to progress even further in the management of karma is a firm commitment to refrain from actions that create new negative karma. Perhaps we should all take a pledge, such as "I promise henceforth to refrain from all actions that create negative karmas."

This is actually not as difficult as it sounds. How do we know if a specific action will create negative karma or not? Scriptures such as the Tirukural may make mention of it. We can ask a Hindu religious leader his or her opinion. We can ask our parents or elders. And once we get the knack of it, our own conscience will be able to provide the answer most of the time.

Gurudeva advises us: "Wise handling of karma begins with the decision to carry the karma we now have cheerfully, and not add to it. A firm decision to live in such a way as to create no new negative karmas is a sound basis for living a religious life, for following the precepts of dharma and avoiding that which is adharmic."

Tirukural: "What good is a man's knowledge unless it prompts him to prevent the pain of others as if it were his own pain?"

4 CONSIDER THE CONSEQUENCES: *This well-to-do lady didn't restrain herself from stealing a nice outfit in a department store, even though she could have afforded to buy it. Spotting her in the act, a security guard arrests her and leads her out in handcuffs to the waiting police van and a day in court.*

Seek Divine Guidance

6 We don't have to manage our karma totally on our own. Help is available, divine help, in fact. Such help comes from none other than Lord Ganesha, who has the duty of helping sincere devotees manage their karma in the best way possible.

Once, through sincere worship, an individual develops a personal relationship with Ganesha, he naturally drops off any remaining adharmic patterns of behavior and becomes fully established in a dharmic life. Lord Ganesha helps you not only become established in dharma, but in the best personal dharmic pattern for this life, known as *svadharma*, your natural occupation and duties to family, friends, relatives, deceased relatives, community, guru and temple.

When we seek His permission and blessings before every undertaking, Ganesha, as the Lord of Obstacles, guides our karmas through creating and removing obstacles from our path, similar to a mother's watching over her young children at play. He also has an extraordinary knack for unweaving complicated situations and making them simple. He can unweave His devotees from their karma, clarifying and purifying their lives. How can we invoke this divine guidance when we encounter karmic difficulties? Simply by chanting His name or a simple mantra, or placing a flower at His feet, visiting His temples for puja, meditating on Him or just visualizing His holy form and inviting Him mentally to help in our time of need. He will respond.

Gurudeva comments on *svadharma*, "Such a life is the fulfillment of all previous efforts and thus erases the uncomplimentary deeds and adds beneficial ones, so a next birth can be most rewardingly great and useful to the whole of mankind."

Tirukural: "Draw near the Feet of Him who is free of desire and aversion, and live forever free of suffering."

Mitigate Past Karma

7 Once we have stopped acting in ways that create new negative karma, our life will be sublime enough to focus on ridding ourselves of karmas of the past, mitigating them, meaning to make less harsh, painful or severe.

To better understand mitigation, let's make another comparison to the judicial system. A man commits armed robbery and receives a ten- to twenty-year sentence. But due to good behavior in prison, he is paroled after only five years. He has mitigated his sentence, made it less severe, through his good behavior.

Let's now take an example of karma that is mitigated. You are destined to lose a leg in this life because you caused someone to lose his in a past life. If you are living a selfish, low-minded kind of life, the karma would come full force and you would lose your leg. However, if you are a kindly person who regularly helps others, the karma would be mitigated and you might read in the morning paper about someone losing a leg and take on the emotion of that experience as if it had happened to you. Later on when hiking you stumble and your leg is injured, but not severely. The full force of the karma was softened by your kind and helpful actions.

There are several methods by which we can mitigate our karma:

Following dharma: Living virtuously, in itself, helps modulate the release of karmic seeds, evening out the ebb and flow of karma and minimizing "karmic explosions" that might otherwise occur. Thus

Try to live life as though you are walking in the rain without getting wet, or carefully writing on water. No ripples, no disturbance, no reactionary residue that has to be faced at some future dat

ALL ART BY A. MANIVEL

5 CREATE NO NEW NEGATIVE KARMA: *Satguru Subramuniyaswami often said we should "live like writing on water." He meant that our actions should be so considered that we pass through life without making ripples of bad karma that return to us in the future.*

negative karmas in one's individual pattern are naturally avoided or mollified and positive karmas accentuated and brought into fruition.

Karma yoga: Helping others—karma yoga, performing good deeds—and thus acquiring merit which registers as a new and positive karma is one way of alleviating the heaviness of some of our past karma.

Bhakti yoga: Worship, bhakti yoga, that is intense enough to cause us to receive the grace of the Gods can change the patterns of karma dating back many past lives, clearing and clarifying conditions that were created hundreds of years ago and are but seeds now, waiting to manifest in the future. The key concept here is intensity. Dropping by the temple for fifteen minutes on the way home from work is unlikely to accomplish such a transformation.

Pilgrimage: Pilgrimage is an excellent way to generate an intensity of worship. Over the years, Gurudeva's devotees have pilgrimaged to India, visiting major temples such as Chidambaram, Rameshvaram and Palani Hills. Many have come back transformed. They physically look a little different, behave differently and fit back into life in a more positive way than before. Their karma was changed by the grace of the Gods.

6 SEEK DIVINE GUIDANCE: *Seeking to clarify some difficult karmas he is facing, this devotee invokes Lord Ganesha. The Lord of Obstacles is able to bring simplicity to complex situations. After worshipping Him, our duty becomes clear, and the right course of action to resolve our situation unfolds to our inner intelligence.*

Vows: A vrata, or vow, can also generate an intensity of worship, such as fasting during the day and attending the temple on each of the six days of Skanda Shashthi or the 21 days of Vinayaga Viratam.

Penance: Penance, prayashchitta, is a sixth way to mitigate karma. This is like punishing yourself now and getting it over with instead of waiting for your karma to manifest a punishment in the future. A typical form of penance is to perform walking prostrations, such as around a sacred lake or mountain, up a sacred path or around a temple.

Often it is advised to perform penance that is directly related to a misdeed. Let's take the example of a teacher who frequently used corporal punishment to discipline students but now strongly feels hitting children for any reason, even for discipline, is wrong. An appropriate penance would be to print and distribute to teachers literature on alternatives to corporal punishment. This type of penance should only be undertaken after a certain degree of remorse is shown and the urgency is felt by the devotee to rid his mind of the plaguing matter.

Gurudeva said, "When pre-dawn morning pujas, scriptural reading, devotionals to the guru and meditation are performed without fail, the deeper side of ourselves is cultivated, and that in itself softens our karmas and prolongs life."

7 MITIGATE PAST KARMA: *In a fit of anger, this man beat his son earlier in the day, even though he vowed to his guru that he would never again strike his child. As he fasts in a self-imposed penance for his misdeed, he feels regretful and renews his resolve to raise the boy without violence.*

Tirukural: "Be unremitting in the doing of good deeds; do them with all your might and by every possible means."

EIGHTH PRINCIPLE
Accelerate Karma

Why wait twenty more births to achieve spiritual maturity when you could achieve it in two births? That is the idea behind accelerating karma. When we begin meditating and performing regular daily *sadhana*, preferably at the same time each day, our individual karma is intensified. In our first four or five years of striving on the path we face the karmic patterns that we would never have faced in this life had we not consciously intensified our spiritual practices. Those on the spiritual path resolve much more karma in a lifetime than others. They could be called professional karma managers.

Of course, family duties in the *grihastha ashrama* don't allow much time for *sadhana*. Thus, the principle of karma acceleration is best fulfilled in the stage called sannyasa, both by those following the path of the monk and by everyone after age seventy-two. Retirement can be more than playing golf. It is an opportunity to intensify our spiritual practices and thus accelerate our karma.

Gurudeva said, "By this conscious process of purification, of inner striving, of refining and maturing, the karmas come more swiftly, evolution speeds up and things can and usually do get more intense. Don't worry though. That is natural and necessary. That intensity is the way the mind experiences the added cosmic energies that begin to flow through the nervous system."

Tirukural: "Not allowing a day to pass without doing some good is a boulder that will block your passage on the path to rebirth."

8 ACCELERATE KARMA: *By intensifying our spiritual practices, we can accelerate our spiritual progress. The difference in rate of resolution of karma is as great as the difference in speed between a flying carpet and the ponderous bullock cart.*

ALL ART BY A. MANIVEL

NINTH PRINCIPLE
Resolve Dream Karma

Though some of our dreams are only the result of thoughts occurring in our own mind, other dreams are astral experiences, of being conscious in our astral body and interacting with others in their astral body. These astral-plane actions create karma, just as do our physical-plane actions. This is the basis of the Hindu ideal that one would not steal or injure even in a dream. Why? Because such transgressions create negative karma that will come back to you. These are real karmas that may eventually manifest on the physical plane. However, this can be avoided if you happen to have further dream experiences in which appropriate actions are taken to dissolve the karma. More commonly, though, we can resolve dream or astral-plane karmas in the same way we would physical-world experiences, by performing penance for them in our waking state, while remembering the high standards of virtue and good conduct that should always be maintained, even during sleep. For instance, if in an emotional dream you injured someone intentionally, you could perform a simple penance the next day to atone, such as fasting one meal.

Gurudeva said, "These kinds of dreams—when a person is in his astral body and can feel what he touches, emote to his experiences, think and talk—are not what is known as the dream state. This is an astral experience, similar to the death experience, but the astral body is still connected to the physical body."

Tirukural: "The highest principle is this: never knowingly harm anyone at any time in any way."

TENTH PRINCIPLE
Incinerate Karma

In the practice of yoga, we can burn up negative seed karmas without ever having to live through them. What we have to do is find the seed and dissolve it in intense inner light. Let's take the analogy of growing alfalfa spouts. You place the seeds in a jar and keep them moist until they sprout. But if you heat the seeds in a frying pan before putting them into the jar, they will no longer sprout. Similarly, karmas exposed to intense inner light are destroyed.

A meditation adept, having pinpointed an unmanifested karmic seed, can either dissolve it in intense light or inwardly live through the reaction of his past action. If his meditation is successful, he will be able to throw out the vibrating experiences or desires which are consuming the mind. In doing this, in traveling past the world of desire, he breaks the wheel of karma which binds him to the specific reaction which must follow every action. That experience will never have to happen on the physical plane, for its vibrating power has already been absorbed in his nerve system. This incineration of karmic seeds can also happen during sleep.

Gurudeva explains it in this way, "It is the held-back force of *sanchita* karma that the yogi seeks to burn out with his kundalini flame, to disempower it within the karmic reservoir of *anandamaya kosha,* the soul body."

Tirukural: "As the intense fire of the furnace refines gold to brilliance, so does the burning suffering of austerity purify the soul to resplendence."

Conclusion

No matter how deep our understanding of karma may be, actually applying our understanding of karma to the events in our daily life can still be a challenge. Why is this? Our humanness gets in the way; our ego is challenged and we react to preserve our self image; our emotions are stirred and we respond impulsively, without intellectual reflection; our attitudes are prejudicial against certain religious or ethnic groups and we feel justified in striking out at them, because they are not "our people."

How can such human weaknesses be overcome? It is by perfecting our character, which Gurudeva defined as "the ability to act with care." This is done through mastering Hinduism's Code of Conduct, the ten *yamas,* restraints, and the ten *niyamas,* observances. (See Chapter 42, "Hinduism's Code of Ethics.") With a strong character in place, the mastery of karma becomes natural to us. Gurudeva mystically summarizes this process as follows:

"Bhakti brings grace, and the sustaining grace melts and blends the karmas in the heart. In the heart chakra karmas are in a molten state. The throat chakra molds the karmas through *sadhana,* regular religious practices. The third eye chakra sees the karmas past, present and future as a singular oneness. And the crown chakra absorbs, burns clean, enough of the karmas to open the gate, the door of Brahman, revealing the straight path to merging with Siva."

9 RESOLVE KARMA IN DEEP SLEEP OR MEDITATION: *In her dream, a child is going through a traumatic experience and her deceased grandmother is comforting her. Karma can be experienced and resolved in such dream states.*

10 INCINERATE KARMA: *This yogi is joyously coming out of a deep meditation in which he has uncovered and "fried" the seeds of future karma, depicted as the human forms in the flames above him. He faced this karma on the subtle plane, before there would be a physical manifestation.*

CHAPTER 30

Karma and Reincarnation

Insights from Swami Vivekananda on How We Each Forge Our Own Destiny

JUST BEFORE THE TURN OF THE 20TH CENTURY, SWAMI VIVEKANANDA, A BRILLIANT young Hindu monk from India, preached about the great law of karma in the United States to all who drew near. He explained, "Any word, any action, any thought that produces an effect is called karma. Thus, the law of karma means the law of causation, of inevitable cause and effect. Whatever we see or feel or do, whatever action there is anywhere in the universe, while being the effect of past work on the one hand, becomes on the other, the cause in its turn and produces its own effect. Each one of us is the effect of an infinite past. The child is ushered into the world not as something flashing from the hands of nature, as poets delight so much to depict, but he has the burden of an infinite past. For good or evil, he comes to work out his own past deeds. This makes the differentiation. This is the law of karma. Each one of us is the maker of his own fate."

Through the ripening of the fruits of his actions he does not attain any rest, like a worm caught within a whirlpool. The desire for liberation arises in human beings at the end of many births, through the ripening of their past virtuous conduct.

YAJUR VEDA, PAINGALA UPANISHAD

2.22

A. MANIVEL

MANIVEL

We create our own destiny, moment by moment.

Swami Vivekananda's spiritual ardor was set ablaze by the great Ramakrishna Paramahamsa. Swamiji (1863–1902) is best known for his electrifying address to the World Parliament of Religions in 1893, to which he traveled without invitation to represent Hinduism but was invited to speak through a chance meeting with a Harvard professor. Thus began two years of inspired lectures that have influenced millions of seekers. Returning to India, he founded the Ramakrishna Mission, which thrives today internationally, with over 100 centers and nearly 1,000 sannyasins. Swamiji is credited—along with Tagore, Aurobindo, S. Radhakrishnan and others—with sparking the modern Hindu revival.

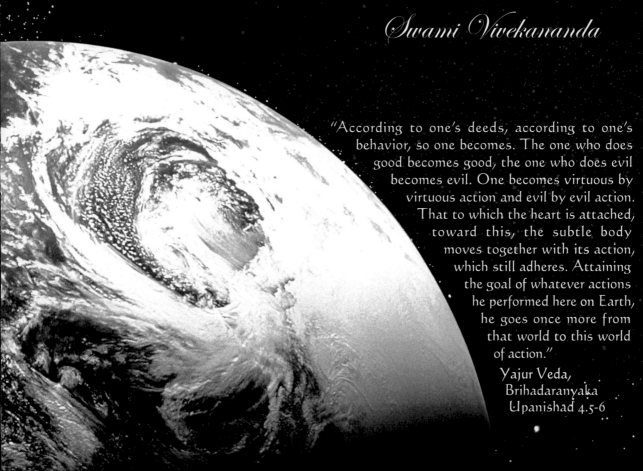

The idea of rebirth runs parallel with the doctrine of the eternity of the human soul. How is it that one man is born of good parents, receives a good education and becomes a good man, while another comes from besotted parents and ends on the gallows? How do you explain this inequality without implicating God? Then, too, what becomes of my freedom if this is my first birth? If I come into this world without experience of a former life, my independence would be gone, for my path would be marked out by the experience of others. If I cannot be the maker of my own fortune, then I am not free. But if this is not my first birth, I can take upon myself the blame for the misery of this life, which is the result of the evil I have committed in another, and say I will unmake it. This, then, is our philosophy of the migration of the soul: We come into this life with the experience of another, and the fortune or misfortune of this existence is the result of our acts in a former existence, and thus we are always becoming better, till at last perfection is reached."

Swami Vivekananda

"According to one's deeds, according to one's behavior, so one becomes. The one who does good becomes good, the one who does evil becomes evil. One becomes virtuous by virtuous action and evil by evil action. That to which the heart is attached, toward this, the subtle body moves together with its action, which still adheres. Attaining the goal of whatever actions he performed here on Earth, he goes once more from that world to this world of action."

Yajur Veda,
Brihadaranyaka
Upanishad 4.5-6

QUOTATIONS BY SWAMI VIVEKANANDA ARE REPRINTED
WITH PERMISSION FROM "VIVEKANANDA, A BIOGRAPHY,"
PUBLISHED BY THE RAMAKRISHNA-VIVEKANANDA CENTER OF
NEW YORK, COPYRIGHT 1953. VEDIC VERSES ARE FROM THE
PRINCIPAL UPANISHADS, S. RADHAKRISHNAN. BACKGROUND
PHOTO: © TONY STONE IMAGES/WORLD PERSPECTIVES

Penance is deeply enmeshed in the Hindu experience. In a story from the *Puranas*, Goddess Parvati performs severe penance for years in a forest.

CHAPTER 31

How to Ease Karma

Using the Power of Penance to Mitigate the Effects of Misdeeds

A FEW YEARS AGO, A DEVOUT HINDU COUPLE PULLED up TO the drive-in window of their local Taco Bell fast-food Mexican restaurant in Ventura, California, and ordered a bean burrito—one of the few items on the menu these strict vegetarians could eat. After a few bites, the man suddenly realized that his spicy burrito was made not with beans but ground beef—the first time in his life he had ever tasted the flesh of the sacred cow. Aghast, he did the American thing: he sued Taco Bell, demanding the company pay for his expenses to return to India to do penance: specifically, to bathe in the Ganga River. Unfortunately, he lost the suit on the technicality that he could not prove to the court's satisfaction that he had actually consumed any beef. Early in the proceedings, HINDUISM TODAY was contacted by an attorney in the case and asked about the need for purification. We explained that indeed the man's plight was quite real, and he did need to do something for having inadvertently eaten beef, a transgression codified in the Hindu law books.

We wrote to Swami Paramananda Bharati of Bangalore, our 1990 "Hindu of the Year," for advice. Swami, who is attached to Sringeri Mutt, replied by email, explaining that because the offense was unintentional, the *prayashchitta,* penance, could be relatively simple—the chanting of mantras for about half an hour a day for eleven days. Realizing that Hindus would like to better understand the ancient system of *prayashchitta,* we enlisted Swami's help in researching the concept. He, in turn, drafted Mrs. B.G. Sreelakshmi of Bangalore, with the approval of Sringeri Mutt, to research the texts. Mrs. Sreelakshmi submitted a lengthy analysis from which we have drawn this article. For her complete text see www.hindu. org/penance/.

Karmic Basis: The guiding principles of penance in Hindu philosophy are derived from the law of karma, the principle of cause and effect. The doctrine of karma is complex, with many subtle distinctions and categories. But for the purpose of understanding penance, we may consider karma as two-fold: the meritorious or good, called *punya or sukarma* in Sanskrit; and the undesirable or bad, termed *papa or kukarma. Papa* includes all forms of wrongdoing, from the simplest infraction to the most heinous crime. According to Patanjali's *Yoga Sutras* (2nd century BCE), man's inclination toward wrong action arises from the five *klesas* ("troubles" or "af-

flictions"): ignorance, ego, attachment, aversion and fear (or "will to live"). In the broadest sense, the entire system of reincarnation is an elaborate form of penance, for we are born with the body, family, circumstances and even longevity and propensity toward disease brought about by our past actions. *Prayashchitta* is, however, an act of limited aim, intended only to mitigate or avoid altogether the *karmaphala,* "fruit of action," of some action we have taken in this lifetime. Actions from our past lives are not considered within reach of ordinary *prayashchitta.* The karmas of past lives can only be assuaged or erased altogether by intense *tapas* or austerities under the guidance of a guru, or by the extraordinary grace of God. *Manu Dharma Shastras* 11.54 states, "Penances, therefore, must always be performed for the sake of purification, because those whose sins have not been expiated are born again with disgraceful marks." *Prayashchittas,* in other words, permit us to resolve the *papa* created in this life and not carry it into the next.

Dharma as Guide: *Papa* arises in two ways, from the commission of what is forbidden and the omission of what is ordained by dharma. "How does one become aware of dharma?" asks J.R. Gharpure in his book, *Teaching of Dharmasastra.* "To say it again in another way: not from books of law or ethics, nor from sacred scriptures, nor by means of scientific theories, nor because public opinion or a special group of people expect it from him. But an enlightened person becomes aware of an urge within himself and, because it demands satisfaction, he follows and obeys."

Failure to follow dharma occurs in three ways according to *Manu Dharma Shastras:* by the body, by the speech and by the mind. "Broadly speaking," states this *shastra,* "it is the mind that is the instigator of all actions. For example, coveting another's wealth by unfair means, desiring that evil befall another and adherence to false doctrines are evil mental actions. Abusing others, speaking untruth, detracting from the merits of all men and talking idly are four kinds of evil vocal sins. Taking what has not been given, injuring sentient beings against the injunction of the *shastras* and adultery are bodily sins. A man obtains the result of a good or evil mental act in his mind, that of a verbal act in his speech and that of a bodily act in his body. [*Manu* 12:3-8]"

Manu and the other *dharma shastras* contain long lists of actions for which *prayashchitta* is advised. These range from what the modern

Softening karma: *In a traditional analogy, karma is described in a bow and arrow analogy. The full complement of arrows in quivers represent sanchita karmas, all those possessed by a soul (frame one). The prarabdha karmas (frame two) are all the karmas a person brings into the present life. When a man is impelled to act* (frame three), he sets one of these karmas in motion (frame four). Should the action have unexpected negative consequences for which the man is remorseful (frame five), it is possible for him to do a penance (frame six, in this case, chanting of a mantra), resulting in the breaking of the karmic cycle (frame seven).

penal code calls "capital crimes," such as murder, to felonies such as adultery, theft and cow killing, to misdemeanors like gambling, and what could be termed "civil offenses" such as "living outside the four *ashramas*." *Manu* offers a general list of wrongdoings, which reads, in part: "Killing a brahmin, stealing, adultery, giving false information to the king, forgetting the *Veda*, reviling the *Vedas*, eating forbidden food, stealing a deposit, a horse or diamonds, incest, casting off one's teacher, mother, father or son, selling goods which one ought not to sell, injuring living plants, subsisting on the earnings of one's wife, sorcery, cutting down green trees for firewood, assault, killing an animal, accepting presents from blamed men, killing insects or birds, and stealing fruit, firewood or flowers." [Manu 11.55-71]. The list of transgressions is remarkable, differing only in details from modern penal codes, even though some of these lists are from books as old as the *Rig Veda* (c. 4000 BCE). They also contain very modern—for the West—concepts such as the protection of plants and animals. One special form of transgression is association with a person guilty of great crimes. The *papa* was considered transferred by sitting, sleeping, travelling, conversing or dining together—such association required half the penance of the actual crime.

Efficacy: Why should it be accepted that *prayashchitta* should destroy *papa*? This was a question even in ancient times. Some held that the *prayashchitta* did not actually destroy the *karmaphala*, but made the person fit for transaction with society. Others held, based on Vedic passages such as "One who performs the Aswamedha [horse] sacrifice is absolved of all sins," that *prayashchitta* actually fulfills the karma. Pleas to forgive transgressions of dharma were evident in the earliest *Vedas*, such as *Rig Veda* 7.89.5, "Varuna, whatever wrong we men have done against the divine beings, whatever rules of yours we have flouted through nonvigilance, do not on that account of sin strike us down." The ancient commentator Apararka, however, observed that repentance is less arduous than penance and not enough to destroy *papa*. He said repentance and not repeating the act are important aspects of *prayashchitta*, but they cannot independently take the place of penances for their efficacy.

Manu 11.228-234 makes the definitive declaration: "By confession, by repentance, by austerity and by reciting the *Veda* a sinner is freed from guilt, and, in case no other course is possible, by liberality. In proportion as a man who has done wrong, and himself confesses it, even so far he is freed from guilt, as a snake from its slough. In proportion as his heart loathes his evil deed, even so far is his body freed from that guilt. He who

What Is the Hindu View of Sin?

THE SANSKRIT WORD *PAPA* IS OFTEN translated as *sin*. According to the specific meaning of *sin*, "a transgression of religious or moral law, especially when deliberate," the translation is accurate. However, the concept of sin in the West carries certain theological baggage which does not reflect Hindu philosophy. For example, there is the idea of "original" or "inherent" sin, a result of Adam's disobedience to God in the Garden of Eden. This is, according to Christian theology, shared by all people, and can only be removed by faith in Jesus. Hinduism does not hold to this doctrine of original sin.

Western theologies tend to consider sin a crime against God, whereas Hinduism views it as an act against dharma, moral order and one's own self. The absence of reincarnation or karma in Christian thinking makes their understanding of sin far different from that of the Hindu.

What to do about sin created in the present life—known as "actual sin" as contrasted with original sin—created the great division between the Catholics and the Protestants.

The Protestants said that faith in Jesus is the only way to remove that sin too, while the Catholics adhered to a complex system of confession and penance. In the Middle Ages, there were "penitential books" in Europe listing sins and penances, plus the more dubious system of "indulgences" whereby one could escape bodily penances such as fasting by an appropriate donation to the church's building program. In the 17th century, Martin Luther declared that faith alone, not penance and especially not indulgences, was efficacious in absolving sin.

Hindu writers educated in Christian schools tend to mix in these Christian concepts of sin while discussing *papa*, or undesirable karma. At times, the idea of an original sin creeps in, one that cannot be erased or evolved out of. At other times, the Protestant scorn for penance appears, and doubt is thrown by the writer upon the whole concept of *prayashchitta*. Occasionally one will find Hindu priests or gurus disparagingly cast as akin to Catholic priests, somehow ordained to "forgive" sins, when they serve no such function.

PHOTOS BY THOMAS KELLY

has committed a sin and has repented is freed from that sin, but he is purified only by the resolution of ceasing to sin and by thinking 'I will do so no more.' Having thus considered in his mind what results will arise from his deeds after death, let him always be good in thoughts, speech and actions. He who, having either unintentionally or intentionally committed a reprehensible deed desires to be freed from the guilt of it must not commit it a second time. If his mind be uneasy with respect to any act, let him repeat the austerities prescribed as a penance for it until they fully satisfy his conscience."

Law and Order: Every society has evolved some system of punishment to check erring behavior, with the belief that fear of punishment would deter error in the future. Within the Hindu tradition, there are three sources of punishment: the king, the *parishad* (assembly of wise men) and the individual himself. *Prayashchitta* is the correct term for punishment originating from any of these three. However, in the present context, we shall explore only punishment that is self-inflicted, in consultation with one's guru or religious guide and guided by the scriptures. Societies recognize that self-correction is the best correction. It has been, for example, relatively fruitless to jail a few wife-beaters for their crimes, because there has been little impact upon the large number of such men whose transgressions remain unknown to the law. When wife-beating reaches epidemic levels, as it has, then law enforcement is powerless, and other methods must be employed to educate, raise awareness and provide the means for individuals to convince themselves to stop their wrong behavior and make amends.

Mitigating Circumstances: Just as in modern law, due consideration is given to the circumstances of any transgression of dharma. The penance differs first between an act intentionally committed and the one committed through ignorance (or unaware, as with our Taco Bell incident), and between an act done only once and one done repeatedly. Consideration is given to who instigated the act, who approved of it and who committed it. If these are different people, the most responsibility lies with he who performs it, according to *Apastambu Dharma Shastras 2.11.19*. *Prayashchittas* are of two kinds, for actions committed secretly and those committed

Prayer: *Vedic hymns include pleas to the Gods for forgiveness of transgressions*

THOMAS KELLY

openly. Manu and others hold that if a man's act is known only to himself, then he may perform secret expiation. If more than a year is allowed to pass, the penances would have to be double. Caste is also a factor, and the *Vishnu Samhita* states that the *prayashchitta* for a *kshatriya* (warrior), *vaishya* (businessman) and *sudra* (worker) should be three-quarters, one-half and one-quarter, respectively, of what is prescribed for the brahmin priest. Several texts provide for lesser punishments for the very old, the young and the ill. For a child below five, no punishment is suggested for any wrongdoing. For a child between five and eleven, his father, brother, relative or friend has to undergo the *prayashchitta* for him, an ancient acknowledgement of modern rediscoveries that families are responsible for children's behavior, even legally.

Administration of Prayashchitta: The sage Angiras writes, "Having committed a sin, one should not hide. If one hides, the sin increases. Controlled in speech, one should approach the *parishad*." The steps were then fourfold: confessing before the *parishad*, declaration by the *parishad* of the appropriate *prayashchitta*, actual performance of the penance, and the announcing by the *parishad* of the transgressor's freedom from crime or taint. The *parishad* was advised not to reduce penance through affection, greed, fear or ignorance, lest they themselves incur *papa*.

According to the *shastras*, one should follow the *prayashchitta* therein recommended to erase the *papa* incurred by an act. At first glance, some of these penances appear either too severe or too lenient, or not logically connected to the transgression. But it must be kept in mind that confession and repentance are required prerequisites to *prayashchitta*. From the Hindu point of view, the critical act is to repent and resolve to not repeat the transgression, thus to transform one's behavior, change one's ways permanently. The *prayashchitta* is only sometimes to make full amends for the crime. Principally it is

Means of atonement: *(from left to right) Yogini chants a mantra on rudraksha beads. Caves in Lubrak, northern Nepal, used for silent retreats. Hindu boys roll from temple to temple in the town of Sankhu, Nepal. A year earlier, this girl was brought gravely ill to this temple. Here she wears the healing neem leaves as she walks and prostrates toward the temple with her family in thanks. Nepalese women observe a yearly three days of penance through fasting and ritual bathing to ensure a happy and productive marriage. The observance is based on the penance of Goddess Parvati.*

to subvert the future karma which would otherwise result by forestalling the thoughts, words and deeds which create negative karma. *Prayashchitta* is not an "eye for an eye, tooth for a tooth" proposition. The penance serves both to assuage the guilty conscience by suffering some punishment, and in a subtle way, to thwart the future karma of one's act. The objective is repentance, not retribution.

Some of the *prayashchittas* given in the old texts were extremely severe, resulting in the painful death of the person. One can be put off by reading in *Manu Dharma Shastras* that such and such a sinner should be punished in such and such a horrendous manner. Punishment in all ancient societies tended to be harsh.

Contemporary Penances: In modern times, *prayashchitta* can be placed in nine categories: confession, repentance, *pranayama* (breath control), *tapas* (austerity and sacrifice, such as head shaving), *kriya yoga* (self study and worship of God), *homa* (sponsoring of expiating ceremony, especially the fire sacrifice), *japa* (recitation of scriptures and mantras), *danam* (gifts, such as to temples and priests), fasting (either complete or by abstaining from certain foods) and pilgrimage. It is likely that even in the early times these were also the most common *prayashchittas*, as each is described in the ancient scriptures.

Confession and repentance have been explained as prerequisites for any further *prayashchitta*. By *pranayama*, certain specific patterns of breath control, one regains control of his mind and emotions. This is applied for lesser offenses. *Tapas* or austerity includes, according to Gautama, celibacy, sleeping on the ground and bathing thrice daily. Another common austerity is prostrating repeatedly while encircling a temple. Much more arduous are the prostrations around an entire city, such as Vrindaban, or a mountain, such as Kailas. The carrying of *kavadi*, a kind of portable shrine on an arch, while having the skin pierced by numerous small spears is a popular austerity among South Indians today. Austerity is a frequent aspect of certain famous pilgrimages, especially those undertaken barefoot. The sponsoring of religious ceremonies, particularly the *homa* or fire sacrifice, as a *prayashchitta* is mentioned in the *Taittiriya Aranyaka*, a section of the *Krishna Yajur Veda*. *Japa* includes both the repetition of simple mantras, such as "Om," and the recitation of various *Upanishads*, or even the entire *Vedas*. *Dana* (gifting) is frequently mentioned, even as atonement for serious crimes. The gift of a cow to a priest or a temple is commonly required. As of April, 2000, a good milk cow in America sold for US$2,050, so one could translate these ancient fines given in number of cows to dollars. The construction by Lord Rama of the Rameshvaram Temple in South India as penance for the killing of his enemy Ravana, a brahmin, is an example of penance by religious gift. The later *shas-*

tras even prescribed bathing in the 22 wells of Rameshvaram as *prayashchitta* for killing a brahmin. Fasting is also a very common *prayashchitta*—it costs nothing to fulfill, and it even saves money! There are many kinds of whole and partial fasts described in the texts, some of which appear to be ayurvedic or medicinal remedies. Finally, pilgrimage is an especially favored *prayashchitta*, though the texts warn that a mere physical act of pilgrimage and a bath in holy waters without a change of heart would not be enough. Nor is anything to be gained, they warn, by abandoning one's duties and fleeing on pilgrimage. Certain pilgrimage destinations, especially Banaras, are renowned as places to rid oneself of *papa*.

In a list provided by Swami Paramananda Bharati, the *prayashchitta* for stealing food is fasting and Sun worship; that for stealing temple funds is fasting and giving gifts of gold, silver and clothes. Making false claims for a medicine can be remedied by fasting and public feedings. An act of ingratitude should be countered by fasting and the feeding of fifty persons, of backbiting by worship and gift of ghee.

Swami's Insights: Swami Paramananda Bharati states, "All sin originates from the love for the body and the ego. Otherwise, the *jivatma*, the individual soul, is by nature very pure. In this sense the real culprits in sin are only the body and the ego. So the cleansing process consists in punishing the body and the ego. That is, indeed, the logic unconsciously followed by the state when it punishes offenders. But the state does not understand the complexities of the soul and its progress. Therefore, it cannot decide the quality or the quantity of punishment, which differs from person to person for the same crime. It is only the *shastra* that can decide it. If the state gives punishment according to the *shastra*, the offender is fully redeemed. But we can never expect the state to be spiritual and follow the *shastra*. So this is to be done by the offender himself. When one inflicts punishment to oneself according to the *shastra*, it is called *prayashchitta*. In the absence of *prayashchitta*, the offender is bound to receive punishment either in the same life or in ensuing lives in the form of disease and other types of grief." In practice, one should consult one's guru, spiritual guide or a scholar of the *shastras* to receive recommendations for penance for a specific act.

Pilgrimage and prostration: *(left) Pilgrims feed a camphor burner at the famed Yellamma ("Universal Mother") shrine in Karnataka State, India. (right) Buddhist pilgrims circle Mount Kailas in the Himalayas. Wearing wooden gloves and a sheepskin apron, they will prostrate, stand, take two steps forward, and prostrate again along the full 33-mile path encircling the sacred mountain.*

A Satguru's Contemporary Experience

Hinduism Today's founder, Satguru Sivaya Subramuniyaswami, administrated penance to devotees for over 40 years. Here are his insights on the subject based on his decades of experience.

THE GURU HAS TO KNOW the devotee and his family karma over a long period of time before *prayashchitta* is given. Otherwise, it may have the wrong effect. Penance is for religious people, people who practice daily, know the philosophy and have a spiritual head of their family, people who genuinely want to reach a state of purity and grace. It is not for nonreligious people. Just as in the Catholic Church, penance is given to you by the spiritual preceptor. It is not a do-it-yourself, New Age kind of thing. Those who try to do it themselves may overdo it. It takes a certain amount of talking and counseling to gain an understanding of what is involved. Before doing any of the physical *prayashchittas*, I have devotees do the Maha Vasana Daha Tantra—"great purification of the subconscious by fire"—writing down and then burning ten pages of memories, good and bad, for each year of their life to the present day. This may automatically clear up events of the past. Also, I've experienced that sometimes just telling the confession to the guru is sufficient *prayashchitta* and nothing else is necessary. What they thought was bad was not bad at all, just normal happenings, but the conscience suffers until that fact is known.

This *prayashchitta* article [on the preceding five pages] we've done with great difficulty, the blessings of the Shankaracharya of Sringeri Mutt and the help of Swami Paramananda Bharati and Mrs. B.G. Sreelakshmi. It is just enough to know about *prayashchitta*. There is a lot in *Manu Dharma Shastras* which absolutely does not apply at this time.

Anger, I have observed, is the most difficult fault for people to overcome, because it comes in so many different forms—pouting, long silences, shouting, yelling, swearing. Some people are just angry all the time because they live in the lower nature, constantly engaged in mental criticism and arguments. Anger can eventually be controlled by putting a sum of money—$5.00, for example—in a jar each time one becomes angry and then donating that money to an orphanage or other charity. It soon

Preceptor in action: *Subramuniyaswami sharing how he administers penance*

gets too expensive to get angry. However, for devotees who are wealthy, that doesn't work. For them, I've found the penance of fasting for the next meal after they get angry works.

The "flower penance" has proven useful, especially to young people who have been beaten and abused by their parents. They put up a picture of the person who beat them—father, mother or teacher—and every day for 31 days place a flower in front of the picture and while doing so sincerely forgive the person in heart and mind. Some are able to see the experience as their own karma. They forgive their parents and experience a great deal of freedom. Others have so much hatred and resentment toward their parents they can't do it at all. This has also worked for someone who has a mental conflict with their employer. There is a severe penance, too, for him who beats his children, involving private self-punishment and public lectures against corporal punishment.

For wife-beating, I advise *kavadi*, putting small spears in the body and circumambulating the temple 108 times. This is a very serious matter, one which has broken up the home and created a rotten birth in the next life. To atone for that is very difficult. Without resolve and remorse, no penance will work.

CHAPTER 32

ANGER Management

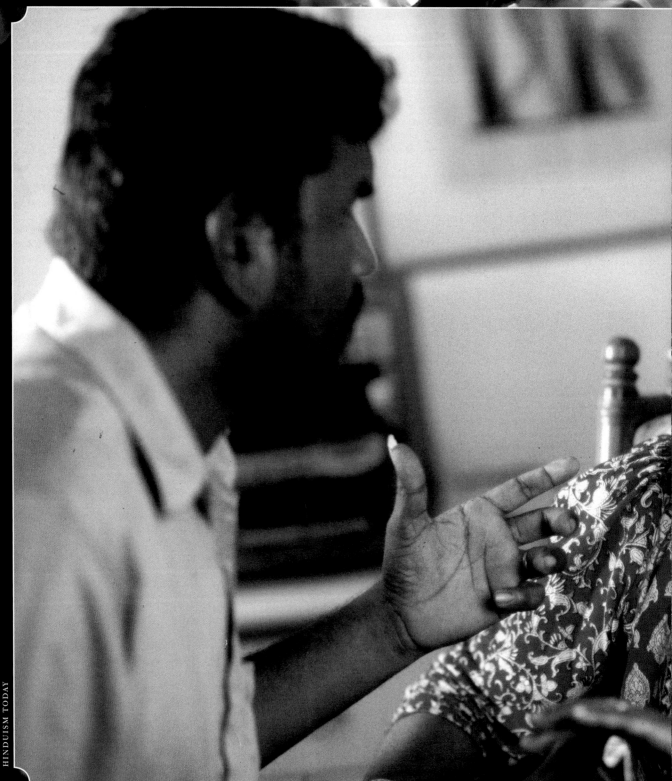

Seven Ways to Tame Your Most Destructive Emotion

By Satguru Bodhinatha Veylanswami

TWO CARS BANG FENDERS AT AN INTER-section; tempers flare and a fistfight breaks out. In a store nearby, a man stomps off in a fury, cursing the clerk for declining his credit card. In an apartment up the street, a mother screams at her daughter to clean up her room. Down the block, a schoolgirl pouts because her father won't let her date an older boy. Nearby, a man slaps his eight-year-old son because he won't sit still in the car. Anger is everywhere. It is the most powerful and hurtful emotion we possess. Yet, the average person succumbs to it helplessly, even willingly, lapsing into insane episodes now and again without thinking much about it. Many defend it as a tool they would not live without.

Anger is expressed in a wide range of ways. Low-minded individuals take delight in being angry with others and expressing that anger in aggressive and violent ways—gang wars, robbery, vandalism and more. They deliberately use anger and violence to get what they want from life. Then there are the mass of generally law-abiding people who live a normal, working life but are seriously angry on the inside about one thing or another and express that anger regularly in their words and actions. They are angry at life and have neither the means nor the motivation to eliminate this hurtful force from their lives.

The Perils Of Anger

The Tirukural   Chapter 32
By Saint Tiruvalluvar, 200 BCE

1 It is restraint that restrains rage when it can injure. If it cannot harm, what does restraint really matter?

2 Wrath is wrong even when it cannot cause injury, but when it can, there is nothing more evil.

3 Forget anger toward all who have offended you, for it gives rise to teeming troubles.

4 Anger kills the face's smile and the heart's joy. Does there exist a greater enemy than one's own anger?

Anger and the Spiritual Path: Finally, there are those who are striving to live a life following spiritual principles but are at times unable to control their anger and as a result end up hurting others and breaching Hinduism's core principal of nonviolence, *ahimsa*, as well as creating new negative karmas to live through in the future. It is to these individuals, who are striving to control anger, even eliminate it from their pattern of behavior, that this chapter is addressed.

To improve our understanding and control of anger, it is helpful to look at the concept of the threefold nature of man: 1) superconscious or spiritual, 2) intellectual or mental and 3) instinctive or physical-emotional. It is the instinctive nature, the animal-like nature, that contains the tendencies to become angry and harm others. The goal of living a religious life is to learn to control these animal instincts—as well as the ramifications of the intellect and the pride of the ego—and thereby manifest one's spiritual nature. Spiritual striving produces gradual improvement in harnessing and transmuting our instincts, intellect and ego, with the entire process of soul evolution spanning many lifetimes.

Anger is the instinctive behavior of responding to challenging situations by becoming frustrated, upset, enraged to the point of attacking others with words or fists. *Webster* compares the terms for anger as follows: "*Anger* is broadly applicable to feelings of resentful or revengeful displeasure; *indignation* implies righteous anger aroused by what seems unjust, mean or insulting; *rage* suggests a violent outburst of anger in which self-control is lost; *fury* implies a frenzied rage that borders on madness; *ire,* chiefly a literary word, suggests a show of great anger in acts, words, looks, etc.; *wrath* implies deep indignation expressing itself in a desire to punish or get revenge."

Learning to control anger is such an important part of harnessing the instinctive nature that the 2,200-year-old, South Indian scripture on ethics, the *Tirukural*, devotes an entire chapter to the subject. It is, in fact, the chapter that precedes "Avoidance of Injuring Others"—the order of these chapters itself suggesting that to successfully practice nonviolence we need to first control anger. The *Tirukural* warns that anger gives rise to teeming troubles. It kills the face's smile and the heart's joy. Left uncontrolled, it will annihilate you. It burns even friends and family who try to intervene, and easily leads to injuring others.

A few years ago we had a perfect opportunity to observe serious anger. Two carpenters were building a house next door to

Eight Rungs on the Ladder of Violence

1: Sneaky Anger

You act and speak normally but purposely neglect to do certain tasks others have asked you to do, pretending that you forgot all about the duties. Example: A teenage boy, upset with his father for firmly disciplining him, retaliates with sneaky anger by chronically "forgetting" to do his household chores.

2: The Cold Shoulder

You shun another person and make it clear you are mad about something. However, you absolutely refuse to let him or her know what it is. Example: A wife is upset with her husband for working late and, rather than talk the issue through, gives him the silent, cold shoulder for the entire evening.

ART BY A. MANIVEL

5 If a man be his own guard, let him guard himself against rage. Left unguarded, his own wrath will annihilate him.

6 Anger's fire engulfs all who draw near it, burning even friends and family who risk rescue.

7 As a man trying to strike the ground with his hand can hardly fail, just as surely will one who treasures his temper be destroyed.

8 Though others inflict wrongs as painful as flaming torches, it is good if a man can refrain from inflammatory tantrums.

9 If hostile thoughts do not invade his mind, all his other thoughts may swiftly manifest.

10 As men who have died resemble the dead, so men who have renounced rage resemble renunciates.

the monastery. One carpenter, James, was more prone to anger than the other. Every few minutes, when something didn't work out right, he would react by swearing loudly and at length. About once a week the two men would have a huge argument and James would drop his tools, stomp off the job and drive away with tires squealing in defiance. It was definitely an interesting study in anger and human nature, showing how anger is simply an accepted part of life for many people.

Swami Budhananda (1917-1983) of the Ramakrishna Mission noted in a series of talks on anger (published in *Vedanta Kesari*, www.sriramakrishnamath.org): "The evil effects of anger are innumerable. The first thing that happens to an angry person is that he forgets the lessons of wisdom he has learnt in life. After that, he loses control over his thoughts and emotions. He becomes overactive, with his highly charged ego as his only guide. He loses his power of discrimination, sense of proportion, and becomes aggressive in manner, hostile to his own welfare. When anger becomes the second nature of a person, physical health and equanimity of mind suffer, and inner peace vanishes in a trice. Anger can destroy friendships, families, business partnerships, professional prospects. Communal and ethnic riots, arsons, wars, suicides, murder and many other forms of crime are basically products of anger. In fact, anger makes even a handsome person look ugly. I suggested to a friend, who is remorseful about his flashes of anger, that he keep a large mirror facing his office desk. In case the anger-prone person has a lively sense of humor, this mirror-therapy is likely to work."

People's natures are quite different in their tendency to anger. Some are usually calm, but occasionally flare up. Others anger quite easily. Many people are quite selective about whom they get angry with—perhaps just their spouse.

My Gurudeva, Satguru Sivaya Subramuniyaswami, observed that anger is the most difficult fault to overcome, because it manifests in so many different forms: pouting, long silences, shouting, yelling, swearing and more. In *Living with Siva*, Gurudeva lists the eight forms of anger from the book *Angry All the Time* (see sidebar): 1) sneaky anger; 2) the cold shoulder; 3) blaming and shaming; 4) swearing and yelling; 5) demands and threats; 6) chasing and holding; 7) partly controlled violence; 8) blind rage. These are called the eight rungs on the ladder of violence, an analogy that Gurudeva found quite helpful in showing how anger can easily snowball. For example, an evening might start

"The *chitta-vrittis*, the thought-waves, which being gross, we can appreciate and feel. They can be more easily controlled, but what about the finer instincts? How can they be controlled? When I am angry, my whole mind becomes a huge wave of anger. I feel it, see it, handle it, can easily manipulate it, can fight with it; but I cannot succeed perfectly in the fight until I can get down to its causes." SWAMI VIVEKANANDA, *RAJA YOGA*

3: Blaming and Shaming

You fault others for something that happened and then tell them they are "no good" in order to make them feel shame. Example: an employee makes a simple mistake at work, and her boss is upset. Rather than help resolve the problem, he points blame at her, demeaning and intimidating her with personal criticisms.

4: Swearing, Screaming, Yelling

You lose control over your speech and scream and yell at others. Those who have a habit of swearing are most prone to this form of anger. Example: A teenage girl has admitted to a minor wrongdoing at school. Her teacher, known for his foul mouth, yells at her harshly, using cruel, out-of-control words to punish her.

with a mild expression of anger that seems harmless enough but soon escalates into shouting and swearing and culminates in physical violence.

Anger and the Chakras: We gain useful insights into the nature of anger and how to control it by relating it to the Hindu system of chakras, the subtle centers of consciousness within each individual (see sidebar). There are seven primary chakras along the spinal column and in the head. When our awareness is flowing through these chakras, consciousness is in the higher nature. The seven chakras, or *talas,* below the spine, down to the feet, are all seats of instinctive consciousness, the origin of fear, anger, jealousy, confusion, selfishness, absence of conscience and malice. The eighth rung on the ladder of violence—blind rage—corresponds to the second lower chakra, called *vitala.* Gurudeva explains, "Anger comes from despair or the threatening of one's self-will. When people are in the consciousness of this chakra, they are even angry at God. With their wrath, they often strike out at those around them, leaving a trail of hurt feelings behind them. From sustained anger arises a persistent, even burning, sense of resentment."

When someone goes into a blind rage, he has dropped far below the chakras of memory and reason—the *muladhara* and *svadhishthana.* Therefore it is no wonder that afterwards he may not even remember what happened. His consciousness was totally in the *vitala* chakra, having given up its normal faculties of memory and reason.

Many people think that sneaky anger and the cold shoulder are natural and harmless. Gurudeva warns that, while they are not as vicious as yelling and screaming or throwing objects against the wall, these practices stimulate the lower chakras and over time can easily lead to the more violent expressions of anger, as well as the experience of other lower-chakra emotions, such as fear and jealousy. For these reasons, it is best not to indulge in either sneaky anger or the cold shoulder. Sarcasm and cynicism can also be forms of anger. Gurudeva said, "People who are cynical are expressing their anger and contempt with snide remarks. They may seem to be joking, but their sharp feelings

come across anyway, which stimulates that lower chakra until one day their cynicism will turn into really good anger. Then they build up new karmas they never had before, which they will live with until they are faced with those karmas."

Swearing is even more problematic, as it stimulates the lower chakras to a greater degree than sneaky anger, the cold shoulder or cynicism. Therefore, it is quite important in managing anger to break the habit of swearing.

Step One for Conquering Anger: For those on the spiritual path who are striving to control anger, there is an important first step. That is to acknowledge that anger is a serious problem that easily leads to violence and is a quality that should be totally absent from those dedicated to making progress in their spiritual life.

I gave the following advice via e-mail to a devotee who was working to refrain from expressing occasional anger toward a parent: "Thank you for sharing the details regarding your angry encounters with your parent. I would suggest you reflect on the seriousness of disharmony in the home. It is taking a few steps backward in spiritual progress. When you do *sadhana,* you move forward. But if you become angry regularly, you step backward, and as a result you could end up standing still. It is like trying to save money for a special purpose. You save for a while, but then become angry, which is like spending what you saved for the last month. It is difficult to make your financial goal. By taking anger more seriously, you are more motivated to avoid it at all costs."

The devotee recently e-mailed again saying the advice had helped her cope with the force of anger. She had taken the first step—acknowledging that it is a serious problem, an unacceptable mode of behavior for those on the spiritual path.

Seven Remedies: With this resolve firmly in mind, she was ready to take the second step, which is to apply remedies to improve her behavior. On pages 274-277, in the illustrated sidebar, we offer seven remedies. The first is to affirm the Hindu philosophy that everything in the universe is perfect; the entire physical, mental, emotional and spiritual flow of events is moving in perfect harmony and exquisite coordination according to the divine laws of karma and dharma. Each happening is as perfect

5: Demands and Threats

You demand that others behave as you want them to or threaten you will do something drastic if they don't, such as hurt them or yourself. Example: An argument between two business partners gets out of hand and reaches the point where the younger threatens to beat up his associate unless he gets his way.

6: Chasing and Holding

You approach or pursue others and physically restrain them against their will and prevent them from leaving your presence. Example: A woman's fiancee has been accused of seeing another woman. Incensed, she follows him to work, grabs him desperately and insists they talk about the problem right now.

as an ocean wave or a butterfly's wing. Anger is an instinctive-emotional protest to what is happening at a particular moment. "Things are just not right!" anger declares. The source of peace and contentment is the opposite sentiment—a wholesome, intelligent acceptance of life's conditions, based on the understanding that God has given us a perfect universe in which to grow and learn, and each challenge or seeming imperfection we encounter is an opportunity for spiritual advancement. Gurudeva wrote: "We are all growing toward God, and experience is the path. Through experience we mature out of fear into fearlessness, out of anger into love, out of conflict into peace, out of darkness into light and union in God."

The second remedy is a first aid technique to apply during angry outbursts. It is to visualize light blue flooding out from the center of your spine into your aura, displacing the blackish reds that anger automatically displays in the colorful field of subtle energy radiating within and around your body. Mystically, this has the effect of moving your awareness out of the angry state of mind into a more peaceful mood. The third remedy is to worship Lord Ganesha, the elephant-faced Lord of Dharma, a compassionate God, ever available to assist embodied souls with immediate needs to further their evolution. Remedy four is a penance, setting aside a specified sum of money every time you experience anger. The fifth remedy is to skip the next meal if you become angry. These two sacrifices are designed to remold deep-seated subconscious patterns, called *vasanas*, convincing your subconscious that you are serious about controlling your anger, and gradually subduing any occurrence of wrath. Remedy six, the flower penance, is a way of letting go of angry feelings that you hold toward another person. Offering flowers with

Wheels of Consciousness

The fourteen chakras are centers of force and consciousness within the inner bodies of man—with corresponding nerve plexuses, ganglia and glands in the physical body. Where we reside in the range of chakras deeply influences our state of mind, our actions and reactions. Anger is the predominant consciousness of the *vitala* chakra, second among the seven lower chakras, all of which are instinctive realms of distress, darkness and confusion.

1 SAHASRARA... Illumination—CROWN OF HEAD

2 AJNA... Divine sight—THIRD EYE

3 VISHUDDHA... Divine love—THROAT

4 ANAHATA... Direct cognition—HEART

5 MANIPURA... Willpower—SOLAR PLEXUS

6 SVADISHTHANA... Reason—BELOW NAVEL

7 MULADHARA... Memory—BASE OF SPINE

8 ATALA... Fear & lust—HIPS

9 VITALA... Raging anger—THIGHS

10 SUTALA... Retaliatory jealousy—KNEES

11 TALATALA... Prolonged confusion—CALVES

12 RASATALA... Selfishness—ANKLES

13 MAHATALA... Consciencelessness—FEET

14 PATALA... Malice & murder—SOLES OF FEET

ART BY I. WAYAN MARYA

7: Partly Controlled Violence

You physically strike someone for the purpose of forcing him or her to do what you want, but without losing control. Example: A young boy is caught stealing at a neighbor's home. The owner, outraged, confronts the boy and swats him several times with a stick, wrongly thinking that this will reform the errant youth.

8: Blind Rage

You physically attack a person with total loss of control, to the extent that when you return to normal consciousness, you may not even remember the incident. Example: A sassy teenager deliberately insults an overweight stranger. Instead of just scowling, the fiery man flies into a blind rage and beats him mercilessly.

a loving heart has the effect of dissolving the resentment and awakening forgiveness—be it toward a parent, spouse, employer, sibling or friend. The seventh remedy is to perform three kindly acts toward someone who has disturbed you. For a loved one or close acquaintance, the acts can be performed openly. For others, such as business associates, employers or fellow employees, your good deeds may be done subtly, even without their knowledge. It may be difficult to fulfill this, as it requires you to go against the instinctive compulsion to hold on to hard feelings. But acting kindly toward offenders releases you from the grip of seething anger, as surely as the sun dispels a morning fog, dissolving it in the light of higher consciousness. The seven remedies are designed to help seekers objectify their anger, to see it in a clear, detached manner, as a force that they have the power to harness and transmute into higher forms of expression and ultimately be free of it altogether.

Diet and Ayurveda: What we eat influences our state of consciousness and where we are in the chakras more than most people realize. The Hindu ideal of following a strict vegetarian diet has many benefits, including lessening the tendency to become angry. Eating meat, fish, fowl and eggs, on the other hand, opens the door to lower consciousness and makes it harder to stay out of the states of fear, anger, jealousy and the subsequent remorseful emotions that follow. Temperament is largely a matter of diet. The *Chandogya Upanishad* (7.26.2) teaches: "When the food is pure, mind becomes pure. When the mind becomes pure, memory becomes

Anger's Rousing Threat

ANGER: "I will make the people blind and deaf. I will overpower them with wrath and suffocate them with rage. I will catch hold of even wise men. They shall neither harken to what concerns their own happiness, nor reflect what they had read in the scriptures. In a moment I can destroy even the learned, the famous, those who are attentive to duties, the charitable and the mighty

firm. And when a man is in possession of a firm memory, all the bonds which tie him down to the world are loosened." A vegetarian diet helps put us in touch with our higher consciousness and is therefore quite helpful in increasing our control over anger, as well as the other lower states of mind.

In the healthcare industry, anger is viewed as an insidious malady that, if not harnessed, leads to serious illness, causing high blood pressure, various diseases and even fatal heart attacks. It is addressed with prescription drugs, aromatherapy, massage

Seven Remedies for the Habit of Anger

1: Affirm: Everything Is Perfect!

Have you ever suggested to someone who was furious at you that he shouldn't get so angry? Perhaps you offered, "It certainly doesn't make me feel very good when you unleash that force on me! And it's not good for you either!" What was the result? He just got madder, right? "How dare you tell me not to get angry, you #%*$¿ !" The point is, no one can change a person except that person himself. We only change when *we* want to change. Are you ready? Controlling anger could well be viewed as the very first exercise in spiritual life, because it stands so squarely between the soul and peace of mind while living in a physical body. Nothing is more fundamental to conquer, and doing so unleashes great energy and provides emotional stability for all other endeavors. The work is well worth the effort. So, here are some sharp tools—powerful enough to make even a nice person nicer. They are philosophical, penitential, meta-

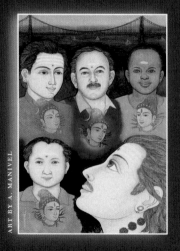

ART BY A. MANIVEL

From a mountaintop perspective, God is everywhere, in all things, and everything is in a state of balance and perfection at every point in time. Affirm this Hindu wisdom regularly to cultivate patience and wise acceptance, even of situations that tend to arouse anger. To do so, be seated, close your eyes, breathe deeply and affirm quietly to yourself, "I'm all right right now, and everything is as it should be from a mountaintop point of view."

and Retorts from Patience, Universal Love and Discrimination

potentates. I can infuse fury, resentment, wrath, indignation into the minds of all in the twinkling of an eye. I am very powerful. I will disturb the *tapas* of the aspirant and even yogis and destroy serenity. **ATMAN**, the soul, despaired, "Alas, who will help me now?" **KSHAMA**, the virtue of Patience, spoke up: "I will! I will pull out the venomous tooth of this demon, Anger." **VISHVA PREMA**, Universal Love, cried out, "I will! I am the water to quench the fire of anger." Finally, **VIVEKA**, Discrimination, roared: "I will! When I rise, anger dies."

Swami Sivananda founder, Divine Life Society

and homeopathy. The Hindu medical science, ayurveda, views anger as a primary sign of imbalance of the three bodily humors, known as *doshas*. Dr. Virender Sodhi of Bellevue, Washington (www.ayurvedicscience.com), explained, "Anger is under the control of the *pitta dosha*. *Pitta* is intelligence, anger, digestion, fire, sight and so on. At the mental level, we have four drives: anger, attachment, ego and desire for sex. Although all these are normal animal behaviors, imbalance in these leads to imbalance of their respective *doshas*. Just as attachment increases *kapha*, anger increases *pitta*. Imbalance in *pitta dosha* can cause excessive anger,

liver maladies, hypertension, etc. Balance is achieved by calming yoga, *shitali* pranayama, walks, mantra, self analysis and diverting the anger into a different form. Ayurvedic medicine also advises cooling foods and environment."

Dr. Vasant Lad, director of the Ayurvedic Institute (www.ayurveda.com) in Albuquerque, New Mexico, offers basic remedies for anger in *The Complete Book of Ayurvedic Home Remedies*:

"*Pitta* is necessary for right understanding and judgment, but when it gets disturbed or out of balance, it creates misunderstanding and wrong judgment, leading to anger and hostility. Here are several simple home remedies to cool down that hot *pitta* and keep tempers under control.

"**Diet:** Perhaps most important, a person who becomes angry easily or often should follow the *pitta*-pacifying diet, especially avoiding hot, spicy and fermented foods, citrus fruit and sour fruit. Favor simple, bland foods and cool drinks, and avoid alcohol and drinks with caffeine.

"**Keep Cool:** It's also not recommended for people with a *pitta* body type to take saunas or steam baths, to get overheated from exercise or sports, or to be in too much direct sun.

"**Oil Massage:** Rub some *bhringaraj* oil or coconut oil on your scalp and on the soles of the feet. That will help to bring down the excess *pitta*. You can do this every night before getting in bed to regularly moderate *pitta*.

"**Sandalwood Oil:** Another simple and effective way to help balance your emotions is to place a drop of sandalwood essential oil on the third eye area between your eyebrows, as well as on the throat, breastbone, navel, temples and wrists.

"**Herbal Teas:** Take ½ teaspoon of chamomile and 1 teaspoon of fresh, finely chopped cilantro leaves and steep them in 1 cup hot water for about 10 minutes. Allow this tea to cool before you drink it. You can drink it three times a day, after each meal.

"When your subconscious has been cleared of past reactionary patterns and reprogrammed thoroughly, you do not take exception to things that happen in the world. In understanding, you love everyone and embrace every event. You intuitively sense just what they are all going through, because you have in your memory banks knowledge of each happening acquired during all the lives you have ever lived." SATGURU SIVAYA SUBRAMUNIYASWAMI

2: Fill Your Aura with Light Blue

If you are overtaken by anger and resentment—emotions which fill your aura with blackish red, streaked with yellow—sit in meditation, breathe and visualize light blue entering your aura and surrounding your body. The light blue will neutralize the fiery reds, and before you know it the anger and resentment will be gone. Simply relax and visualize soothing blue radiating out from the center of your spine into your inner and outer aura.

3: Worship Lord Ganesha

The worship of Lord Ganesha is helpful in overcoming all emotional problems, including anger. As He is seated on the *muladhara* chakra, tuning in to His *shakti* helps raise us up into the *muladhara* chakra and therefore out of anger and fear into a calm, stable state of mind. In fact, you can slowly seal off these lower states of mind and keep awareness permanently lifted above fear and anger through the regular worship of Lord Ganesha.

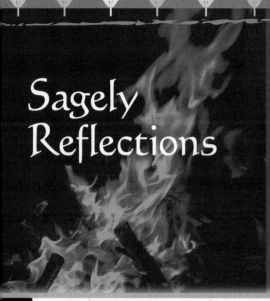

Sagely Reflections

I will permit no man to narrow and degrade my soul by making me hate him.

Booker T. Washington

If you are patient in one moment of anger, you will escape a hundred days of sorrow.

Chinese proverb

Nor he who owns the least of things, nor he whom anger chains, can ever pass through maya's gates. So, give these up, sannyasin bold! Say "Om Tat Sat, Om!"

Swami Vivekananda

There is nobody who lives happily with anger.

Shantideva

When we speak with hatred and anger, it leads to unhappiness pain and misery. So one should always be soft spoken.

Yajur Veda 3, 54

If we could read the secret histories of our enemies, we should find sorrow and suffering enough to disarm all hostility.

Longfellow

"**Ghee Nasya:** Dip your little finger into a jar of *brahmi* ghee (or plain ghee) and lubricate the inside of your nostrils with a small amount. (Make sure your nails are trimmed so you don't scratch yourself.) Then gently inhale the ghee upward. This sends a calming message to the brain.

"**Shitali Pranayama:** Make a tube of your tongue; breathe deeply through your mouth down into your belly, hold the breath for a few seconds; exhale through your nose. Do about 12 repetitions.

"**Yoga Postures:** Good yoga asanas for *pitta* include the camel, cobra, cow, boat, goat and bridge poses. Avoid the headstand or other inverted poses, such as the plow and shoulder stand.

"**Meditate:** There is an ancient method of meditation that involves watching your every emotion come and go, without either naming it or trying to tame it. As the feelings arise, breathe deeply and exhale the emotions out."

Anger and Spiritual Striving: Anger is a natural emotion, a protective function of the instinctive mind, not to be vilified or feared. It is a part of our nature, and it is normal to express

it—that is, if we are content to live on the instinctive level of our being, which many people are. But each soul inevitably reaches a point where it seeks to harness the natural instincts. Gurudeva explained, "Anger is also, like fear, an instinctive control, and at one time served its purpose. The onrush of anger served to protect man's private interests in critical situations by injecting adrenaline into his blood and thus preparing him for defense. But as man evolves closer to his real, actinic being, he discovers that actinic love, understanding, compassion and wisdom are higher qualities than anger."

Managing anger is important for anyone who seeks success at sophisticated endeavors and stable, wholesome relationships. For aspirants seeking self-transformation on the spiritual path, it is absolutely essential, for only when the lower nature is subdued can the divine nature be fully expressed.

Daily spiritual efforts designed to bring forth the divine nature are known as *sadhana*, such as *japa*, meditation and yoga. As Gurudeva wrote, *sadhana*, spiritual discipline, is "the mystical,

4: Pay for Each Burst of Ire

An effective and practical financial remedy is to put a sum of money, such as five dollars, in a jar each time you become angry, and later donate that money to a favorite orphanage or temple. Consistently performed, this penance soon makes it too expensive to get angry! This remedy impresses the subconscious mind that expressions of anger have karmic costs, and that anger can be completely eliminated by sincere efforts to overcome it.

5: Don't Eat the Next Meal

For those who can easily afford to put five dollars in a jar frequently, an alternate penance is fasting. Each time anger arises, simply skip the next meal. Denying yourself a meal has a potent impact, deeply impressing your subconscious mind. If you follow this without fail, the instinctive nature soon catches on that whenever it expresses anger it will soon experience hunger, and in this way is motivated to better control this destructive emotion.

ART BY A. MANIVEL

Suppose you have a weakness of getting angry easily. Now, what you should do is this: Once you become normal again, go and sit in the family shrine room if you have one, or sit in solitude; then regret and repent your own anger and sincerely pray to your beloved deity or to Mother Nature, seeking help to get rid of it.

Shri Mata Amritanandamayi Devi

To remove anger is not so difficult as to decide to remove it and to maintain that decision.

Sri Aurobindo

There should be no yelling in the home unless there is a fire.

David O. McKay

A nagging sense of discontent, a feeling of being dissatisfied, or of something being not right, is the fuel that gives rise to anger and hatred. Generally, this discontent arises in us when we feel that either we ourselves, or someone we love, or our close friends are being treated unfairly or threatened: people are being unjust toward us or our close friends.... The idea is to stop it at

an early stage, rather than wait for that anger or hatred to arise fully.

The Dalai Lama

Resentment is like taking poison and waiting for the other person to die.

Malachy McCourt

Worshipers of Siva who are victim to anger or hatred refrain from meditation, *japa* and kundalini yoga. They confess sins, do penance and engage in bhakti and karma yoga to raise consciousness. Aum Namah Sivaya.

Satguru Sivaya Subramuniyaswami

mental, physical and devotional exercise that enables us to dance with Siva by bringing inner advancement, changes in perception and improvements in character. *Sadhana* allows us to live in the refined and cultured soul nature, rather than in the outer, instinctive or intellectual spheres." But, Gurudeva warned, every time you become angry, you destroy one month's worth of spiritual striving and practice, or *sadhana*. So, if you don't control anger, performing *sadhana* is a waste of time. Hence, the number-one *sadhana* is anger management. Gurudeva is adamant that seekers refrain from any serious meditative practices until anger and other lower emotions have been harnessed. "Those who remain prone to anger should not do *raja* yoga or any form of intensive mantra, *japa*, or pranayama amplification of the energies into higher chakras—lest that collective energy plummet into the corresponding lower chakras and be vented through fear, anger and jealousy. Rather, they should perform the always healing *vasana daha tantra* [writing down and burning recollections of the past] and confine themselves to karma yoga, such as clean-

ing in and around the temple and picking flowers for the pujas. These simple acts of *charya* [humble service] are recommended, but should not be extended to intense worship. Then, and only then, their life will be in perspective with the philosophy of Sanatana Dharma and begin to become one with Siva's perfect universe. Brahmadvara, the door to the seven chakras below the *muladhara*, will then be sealed off as their experiential patterns settle into the traditional perspective of how life should be and each individual should behave within it."

When working to harness the instinctive nature, what is it that tells us how well we are doing? It is the subtle irritation, the seed of wrath, that precedes every form of anger, from the cold shoulder to blind rage. Viewed in this way, the impulse to anger is—at the beginning of the path, the intermediate stages and even subtly at the upper reaches—our astute teacher, signaling to us each split-second opportunity to be more patient, more understanding, more compassionate and to find a better way to cope with tense situations and keep closed the door to the lower chakras.

6: Offer Flowers

Put up a picture of the person you are angry with and for 31 days place a flower in front of the picture. While doing so, sincerely forgive the person in heart and mind. When it becomes difficult to offer the flower of forgiveness, because hurtful memories come up from the subconscious mind, write down the memories and burn the paper in a trash can. Say, "I forgive you, for I know that you gave back to me the karma that I set in motion."

7: Perform Three Kindly Acts

If you have gotten upset with another person, do three kindly acts to make up for it. This releases you from your anger and guilt even if he or she is unaware of your good deeds. Example: A husband shouts abusively at his wife after returning from work. After apologizing, he takes her dining to a place of her choosing, buys her an item that she needs for the kitchen and gives her some free time by taking care of the younger children for a half-day.

Silence Is Golden

Oasis: *The French Polynesian island of Bora Bora, a quiet citadel in the midst of the central South Pacific, the ocean called Peaceful*

ART WOLFE

Mind and Emotions Are Calmed As We Observe *Mauna,* Restraint of Speech

MANY THINK OF SILENCE SIMPLISTICALLY, AS JUST THE absence of noise, or not speaking words. But silence, like life itself, is more complex and subtle than that. We all seek silent moments, islands in the sea of sound, to reflect upon and reap the lessons from life's experiences. Usually our quest for quietude is an outer search. We vacation to paradise or hike into the hills to escape the daily din. While Hindu saints and scriptures do emphasize the importance of serene surroundings as an aid to introspection, they stress more the cultivation of silence within. Outer peace is simply a means to help us find inner silence. Ultimately, we learn to maintain and enjoy our innate serenity regardless of the cacophony that surrounds us. This is the basis of the Hindu practice of *mauna,* the vow to remain silent, and it is why some subdue speech altogether. *Mauna* is not the exclusive province of the sage. Brilliant orators and well-to-do intellectuals have also chosen to curb their speech. Mahatma Gandhi was perhaps the most prominent public figure to observe *mauna.* He tamed his tongue every Monday, communicating on that day only through writing.

The late Swami Nirmalananda of Karnataka had served the Army Postal Service in Europe during World War II. He later held various government posts in India. He travelled the globe and studied well the world's religions and philosophies. In the end, his burning search for truth culminated in silence. "If you desire to live in peace," he said, "hear all that falls on your ears, see all that appears before your eyes, realize that everything is in accordance with the eternal law of nature, and be silent." He did not speak for eleven years, and thereafter spoke sparingly. When he did, it was with clarity and conviction. "Wisdom to me is not a set of words, but freshness and emptiness of the mind. Empty the mind by self-observation, self-awareness and inner attention. Thus make the mind shine like a mirror. Then nothing is seen or known but the limitless radiance of eternity. This is a wonderful source of ever-renewed joy and inspiration beyond words."

Mauna is practiced in varying degrees by spiritual leaders, ascetics, aspirants and householders alike, throughout India and abroad. Still, popular belief holds that the vow of silence can be followed only by ascetics and sages, that it lies beyond the capability of ordinary mortals. HINDUISM TODAY correspondent, Choodie Shivaram of Bangalore, dispels this misconception, "I have seen ordinary people observing *mauna* in daily life. A very orthodox elderly cook in our house during my school days strictly observed *mauna* one day of the week. No matter how much we joked about her stony silence, she never budged. So, too, my great grand-aunt, Kadakka, observed *mauna* on certain days of the week. She insisted that we children keep perfect silence at least during meals. Of course, despite our valiant efforts, our childish giggles could not be contained."

Choodie continues, "In my childhood, an old friend of my father, Shri Chandrasekhar, would chat with me and my young friends. I had not seen him for many years, and I was shell-shocked last year when he refused to talk to me. Only later did I learn that he was observing *mauna.* Now in his eighties, Chandrasekhar spends most of his time at the Ramakrishna Math. He has been observing *mauna* for the past 17 years. Although with a wife and children, he speaks only for two hours on the first of every month. Even then, he is very choosy about to whom he speaks, and how much. Always clad in a white *dhoti* and half-sleeved white shirt, a sling bag over his shoulder, simplicity is his way of life."

Choodie heard Chandrasekhar's insights on his singular talking day last month: "Often people take me to be some worthless being, looking at my dress and silence. But it just does not matter to me. I began by talking for only one hour a day. After about one year, I began talking only once in a fortnight and gradually made it once a month. Now, I speak only two hours once a month. I plan to give it up totally. Besides talking, my communication is limited to written conversation with the *brahmacharis* in the ashram. That, too, is only done when I have to pass on some message or give instructions. I do not communicate with anyone else. I'm only a listener now. Silence teaches you to listen."

Prema Pandurang of Chennai is perhaps an unlikely candidate to have spontaneously taken a 41-day vow to remain mute. Prema is a famous religious lecturer in South India. She was a professor of English at Chennai's Presidency College for twenty-three years. She told HINDUISM TODAY's publisher how silence came to her. "For a long time, I had been a speaker. One day I woke up and said, 'Now. Let me see how it sounds—how it feels—if I don't speak.' It wasv not that anything in the world disgusted me. It was more the thought that there was so much sound around me, and I was creating most of it. I said, 'Let me be in silence and watch.'" Prema found the silence profound, and wrote down her inspirations in a small book, *Reflection on Silence*. She now continues her silence every Tuesday.

As austere as *maunis* may seem, most still shy away from the absolute vow. The strictest observance of *mauna*, utter silence, can seem unnatural to onlookers and impossible for those wishing to attempt it. Such a deliberate denial of human interaction is a stark withdrawal from a world structured and sustained with words. In *Sadhus, The Holy Men of India* (1991, Brijbasi, New Delhi), author Ramesh Bedi describes an encounter with a most extreme *mauni*. "Sadhus who take the vow of silence include those who will condescend to communicate with others by gesture or by writing things down and also those who take the absolute vow of silence, the *kashtha mauna* vow. *Kashtha* means wood. So this is the vow 'to be silent like a log of wood.' The *kashtha mauna* sadhu will partake in no communication at all with others. Only very penitential ones are capable of undertaking this vow. One such *sadhu* I encountered in 1938, in the foothills of the Shivalak Hills off Haridwar, even refused to accept the fruits and edibles offered to him. Having offered him a handful of mulberries once, I returned the next week to discover that these lay where I had left them. He didn't even look at them. Nearby villagers would regularly bring offerings of food, but the ascetic ate none of it, living on the wild fruits he found in the jungle."

More common are those who observe complete silence for shorter periods and those who communicate through writing. Baba Hari Dass of the Mount Madonna Center of California currently "talks" tersely through a book-sized chalkboard. But even he abandoned all outward expression for a period. "I was in *kashtha mauna* for one year. I did not use anything to communicate. There is always an advantage in removing the mind from worldly attachments, whatever the means. *Mauna* is one of the means." Baba gave up speaking over forty years ago. Sri Tiruchi Maha Swamigal of Kailash Ashram, Bangalore, undertook *mauna* for two years while living in a cave in the region of

Tayumaneshwarar Temple, Tamil Nadu. The purpose of his vow was to "contemplate deeply upon his upcoming divine mission." Swami tells stories of the many snakes encountered in the cave. As they passed him by harmlessly, he found that even wild animals are tamed by a true practitioner of *mauna*.

Quest for quiet: To abruptly stop speaking may be too stern a step for most. But the benefits of *mauna* can be obtained in less arduous ways (see the Seven Sadhanas of Silence, pp. 280-281). If you have the desire, dedicating some time to silence can be easy. Dada J.P. Vaswani advises, "First thing when you wake up in the morning, observe silence for at least ten minutes. This will help you to gather your thoughts." Sri Tiruchi Swami recommends that people with busy schedules fix a day or two in a week, or an hour or two in a day, for *mauna*. He elaborated to HINDUISM TODAY, "An ordinary devotee can observe *mauna* daily during, before or after the morning worship (personal or communal) for a duration of about one to three hours. One can also be silent for one to three hours during the evenings before or after sunset. Silence can be practiced one or two days a week while keeping aloof from one's normal schedules and activities. A visit to the temple can become extra special by including the discipline of not speaking. Also, one can make the vow of silence a part of one's pilgrimage. All days are suitable for *mauna*. The longer we can detach ourselves mentally from daily trivials, the better."

Recalling her own profound experience of silence, Prema Pandurang implores, "There is so much stress and tension today that everyone must observe silence—some time away from mother, father, child and wife, friends and everyone—at least a half-hour every day with no telephone calls in some corner of the house where one can see nature. Just sit and silently think about what you are doing. You'll be different. It is necessary. It brings your high blood pressure down, makes your pulse beat normally. You start recollecting whatever you've done and you start planning for what you're going to do. For this introspection you need silence, and that is why for the past eight years I've observed silence on Tuesdays."

One of the foremost reasons to curtail conversation is to conserve energy. Abstinence from speech transmutes the creative energies of the mind in the same way that sexual abstinence, *brahmacharya*, transmutes the physical energies. Baba Hari Dass explains, "We talk only by exhalation. The more we talk, the more we have to exhale and the more life energy we lose. Energy is lost primarily in two ways—by sex and by talking. The origin of both sound and sex is the *muladhara* chakra at the base of the spine. When we talk, we use tremendous energy. This can be felt if you stop talking for a few days and then start talking again. The energy we preserve through silence can be used for meditation."

A more mundane impetus for *mauna* is simply to stay out of

Stony silence: *Giant boulders study the Australian sky*

ART WOLFE

Speech needs company, silence needs solitude. Speech wants to conquer others, silence helps conquer oneself.

Speech makes friends or foes, silence befriends all. Speech demands respect, silence commands it.

Speech is earth-bound, silence is heaven-bound. Speech educates, silence exalts. Speech is subjective, silence objective.

Speech has regrets, silence none. Speech has limitations, silence is boundless. Speech needs effort, silence a lot more.

Speech is human, Silence is Divine. While speaking you are heard by creatures, in silence you hear the creator.

Silence leads to a stillness of the mind, then to introspection, then to self-cleansing, finally to liberation.

Prema Pandurang

trouble. Chandrasekhar confessed, "I have committed many mistakes. I have been harsh to people and have hurt many with my speech. Finally, I realized the importance of silence. In *mauna*, the mind projects all of our faults. They come like flashes. We begin to look within and see our mistakes. This helps us to rectify ourselves. This can solve many of life's petty problems. The natural mind is filled with compassion and Divinity. I think *mauna* is the first step towards realizing God. It detaches us from worldly pleasures."

In this regard, Rev. Swami Satchidananda, founder of Integral Yoga Institute, shares a Sanskrit proverb—"*Mauna kalaka nasti.*" He explains, "*Mauna* means silence; *kalaka* means problems or quarrels and *nasti* means nonexistent. So this saying tells us, 'When you are silent, there are no quarrels.' By talking, we create problems because we do not know how much to talk, how to talk, what to talk and when to talk. So, the immediate benefit of *mauna* is to avoid problems. The other benefits then follow. The silence of speech leads to the silence of mind, because if you decide not to speak, what good are thoughts? Every time a thought comes, you cannot express it with words, so the mind ultimately says, 'Alright, what is the point of my thinking?' You get into a thoughtless state. But there is one more *mauna*, the bodily silence. That means you don't move around. You stay in one place. That helps the silences of speech and mind also." Swami's institute holds occasional silent retreats where participants study yoga and meditation, all the while remaining silent. During one retreat, he jested in his jovial way, "Observe all, but refrain from talking. I will do all the talking for you. Whatever you want to say, just leave it to me...I think you cannot talk too much about silence."

The *Ribhu Gita* tells us, "Sitting in silence is the holy ablution. Sitting in silence is the *japa*. Sitting in silence is the worship. Sitting in silence is the highest. Read silently to yourself about the experience that all is Brahman. In a moment, all the *punya*, merit, which would result from a million *asvamedha*, horse sacrifices, can be obtained" (verses 16.42 and 33.29).

Vishvamitra: *Beyond words*

(image credit rotated: WATSON COLLECTION)

Quiet inspiration: *L to R: The ever-silent Baba Hari Dass of California. Karnataka's late Swami Nirmalananda, speechless for 11 years. The late Homi Baba of Banaras, silent for 40 years. A sadhu offers a mute blessing. Prema Pandurang, silent for 41 days in 1996.*

Seven Sadhanas of Silence

ome silence is golden, others are silver and a lot prove out just to be heavy metal—copper, iron, zinc or tin. A few kinds of silence are brazen brass. Silence can be learned. Let's begin at the bottom, by silencing the brass. To do this there is a *sadhana*, spiritual discipline, the first of the Seven Sadhanas of Silence.

The brass *sadhana* is to conquer jealousy, which bemoans, "She has more than I do. He gets everything he asks for, while I get nothing or very little. It's unfair." This noise goes on daily in the mind of those are in the jealousy chakra (*sutala*), located in the knees, which has to stop spinning in the astral areas of the inner mind to make way for peace of mind. How do we do this? It is easy. Just begin to stop talking to yourself about what is unfair. Let all mental arguments go. Drop the subject. Be silent about the issue. Such a silence provides a place for harmony of minds, while too much noisy complaining about "me and mine" gives no room for others.

The silence of tin is an even worse din. Have you ever heard a child beat on a tin can? That's how the force of anger sounds, "clank, clank, clank." Not musical, not melodious, not even nice. The noise of anger, which vibrates in the *vitala* chakra located in the thighs, has to be quieted to enjoy even the smallest sliver of silver peace. How do we do this? Well, it is expensive. A monetary sum is paid for each outburst or even unexpressed wave of anger. A jar, labeled "anger penance," is established in the shrine room, into which a monetary sum is placed each time anger is experienced—the greater the expression, the larger the sum. The money collected is sent to the charity of one's choice on the first day of each month.

The silence of zinc comes next. It is quieting the force of fear. Yes, fear can produce a very noisy mind. But it is not beyond being controlled and courted into obeyance. Fear creates. Often we create what we fear and make it happen by fearing that it might. We give it that energy, that possibility in our life. Fear vibrates in the *atala* chakra, located in the hips. To bring fear under control is a powerful accomplishment. How do we do this? One way is through the power of affirmation, reprogramming the subconscious mind. An affirmation is a series of positive words in line with a visual concept repeated time and time again. It can be repeated mentally or, pref-

erably, verbally. Here is an effective affirmation for overcoming fear. "I am the complete master of all my forces. My spiritual energies govern and control the force fields wherever I am for the highest good. Through understanding, being a pure soul, full of spirited life, I am filled and thrilled with unlimited power now and forever." While repeating this affirmation, visualize a bright white protective shell around your outer aura with a round opening at the top. As you persist, the trembling voice of fear will desist.

Now, the silence of iron. Many of us have strong memories, which become stronger as years go by. As strong as iron, they are there, rusting away in the *muladhara* chakra at the base of the spine. How do we silence memory? Write down or type in your computer all that you want to forget. Then burn up the paper. Writing down problems and burning them in any ordinary fire brings them from the subconscious into the external mind, releasing the suppressed emotion as the fire consumes the paper. The memory still exists, but it has lost its emotional power.

With the past thus stilled, we come to the silence of copper. We are climbing up the ladder of the chakras when we try to silence our reason, which in most of us is the noise of asking rhetorical and intellectual questions over and over again. Questions that have no answers. "Why did he do that? Does he not know better?" And on and on and on. It is important for seekers to silence the tendency to rationalize, to explain away, to excuse and defend the ego. To silence this *svadhishthana* chakra, located at the kidney level, some basic *yoga* must be done to empower the higher self. Controlled breathing, pranayama, helps harness and slow down the prana, energy, that spins this chakra, as does hatha yoga. Sit quietly with the spine in a straight line. Breathe naturally, as a baby breathes, by using the diaphragmatic muscles below the solar plexus. Inhale. The diaphragm pushes the stomach wall out, as the lower lungs inflate. Exhale. Relaxing the diaphragm, the air is expelled. Then pull the diaphragm in to push out the last bit of air. Nine counts in, hold one, nine counts out—this is a basic *sadhana* for the silence of copper.

With the intellect quieted a bit, we can seek the silence of silver, stilling the willpower located at the solar-plexus *manipura* chakra, which spins constantly, being the nerve center that interconnects all the forces of the physical and astral bodies. How to quiet willpower? Competitiveness and aggression must stop, for these direct the pranas, or energies, down to the lower chakras. The force of willfulness in its negative expression makes noises about self preservation— "Take care of me first and forget others." This can be counteracted by the practice of speaking only that which is true, kind, helpful and necessary. The silver *sadhana* is to use willpower positively to control the tongue, to be a helpmate to silence by speaking little, and never boasting of ambitions or attainments.

With the willpower subdued, the silence of gold comes into view—without the L, it is God. So get the L out of it. Here silence is truly the voice of God. To quiet the *anahata* chakra, heart center, of understanding, soul knowing, vision and peaceful thoughts is not to be a metaphysical know-it-all. It means not being a prophet or big ego in speaking about how others should live, but rather silently living the example of how one should be.

Then we come to the platinum *vishuddha* chakra, in the throat. Here resides the force of divine love. Love is understanding, forgiveness, compassion and benevolent, selfless giving. It is the chakra that the yogis enter to be truly silent. Here they cannot speak. Here they feel good and fulfilled. True, writing on a chalk board communicates the essentials; other than that, in a room alone such yogis are silent. Not blank in consciousness. Silence does not mean emptiness as much as divine fullness. They are all-seeing, for the *vishuddha* chakra energies stimulate the third eye—the *ajna* chakra, the all-seeing, never-sleeping sight of the soul. Here we are truly silent. In a room crowded with noise, we hear but a little of it. In meditation we soar beyond into the infinite of infinities.

How to quiet the highest chakras, which are quietness itself? The titanium metal of the *ajna* chakra of divine sight and the multifaceted gems of the *sahasrara* chakra at the top of the head? Do they speak, think, reason? Those who know and have experienced say no. These *jivanmuktas* are content in their silent knowing, not knowing all that they know. Their ever-watching presence on today's apparently hurting planet is an earned *sukarma*, good karma, for the human race. They are the beginning and end of all. They see the cosmic panorama of which the *Vedas* speak. "He contains all works, all desires, all perfumes and all tastes. He encompasses the whole universe; he is beyond speech and beyond desires. He is my atman within my heart, he is Brahman" (*Sama Veda, Chandogya Upanishad* 3.14.4.4). "Now, what people call 'the practice of silence' is really the disciplined life of a student of sacred knowledge, for only by leading such a life does one find the atman and meditate" (*Chandogya Upanishad* 5.5.4.3).

When to be silent then? Astrologers have an answer: one day each week, on the day ruled by one's current *mahadasha* planet— i.e., Monday for Moon *dasha*, Tuesday for Mars, etc. Some astrologers advise fasting and nonspeaking on that karmically critical day. If you don't know such details of your horoscope, an easy and pragmatic alternative is on the same day of the week you were born. Enough said.

© TONY STONE IMAGES/ANTHONY CASSIDY

DEVA RAJAN

CHAPTER 34

Hatha Yoga

A 24-Posture System of Body Tuning and Preparation for Meditation

HATHA YOGA IS A SYSTEM OF HANDLING THE PHYSI-cal body so that the mind and the nerve system are calmed and quieted. It is primarily a means to prepare oneself for meditation. Hatha yoga is founded on a principle of putting the physical body into a position so that the nerve currents in the physical body get tuned up to a perfect pitch. It is like tuning the strings on a violin; if you tune the violin just right, then each string will be in harmony with the other strings.

This chapter consists of original illustrations and instructions for 24 asanas organized in eight sets of three to be performed in series. While there are many more complex hatha yoga routines, these 24 relatively easy poses provide a good, balanced system for daily use. To prepare yourself for an effective meditation, this routine is all you will ever need. For the very best results, hatha yoga should be taught personally by a qualified teacher. The instructions and illustrations given here are a rudimentary aid. For more elaborate regimens, inquire at a recognized school specializing in hatha yoga.

Asanas elongate, tone and strengthen muscle tissue, massage the organs, stimulate the nerves and balance the *pingala* and *ida nadis*. From the hundreds of known asanas, these 24 affect all the major parts of the body. Each pose is to be held in relaxed stillness for 30 to 120 seconds, without straining. As maximum stretch and flexibility are approached, a subtle stimulation of the physical and psychic nerve system begins to occur.

Perform the postures daily in the privacy of your own room, without drawing attention to yourself. Naturally, they should not be performed after meals. Don't worry if you can't perform them perfectly, or if some are difficult for you. Do the best you can. Progress at your own pace, rather than in a competitive manner. With practice, you will find the body becoming more supple, reflecting the mind's flexibility, alertness and freedom from subconscious repressions.

By controlling breath we control thought and life energy, or prana. Yogis call this pranayama. The pranayama for these asanas is simple: breathe in for nine equal counts (ideally counting with *mathura*, the heartbeat), then hold one count, breathe out nine counts, hold one, and so on. Breathe deeply, fully and diaphragmatically, rather than shallowly expanding the upper chest. Harnessing the breath's three phases (inhalation, retention and exhalation) directs the flow of prana, calming and relaxing body and mind.

When physical tensions are released through hatha yoga, mental-emotional tensions are automatically dissolved. This is a great secret and a wonderful tool that you can use every day of your life. Free the mind of thoughts and tensions and you will be more aware, more alive, more serene. As you perform the hatha yoga asanas, put out of your mind all thoughts relating to your work, family, friends, associates, problems and challenges that normally concern you. Relax. Relax. Relax. Be completely at peace with yourself and fully enjoy this contemplative art.

Try to sense the inner and outer nerve system reaching a crescendo of energy as you sustain each pose. When this peak is felt, gracefully shift during the outbreath to the next asana. The whole series of 24 poses is like a dance; and a deliberate flow from one to the next is a key to perfect serenity. Each set includes a color visualization to quiet the mind and intensify healing. The color of the background wall in each illustration is the color to visualize while in that pose. Mentally fill your body with that color, from your head to your toes; or imagine yourself suspended in space, surrounded on all sides by the color shown with the pose. If tensions in the body or mind are discovered, visualize them flowing away with the outbreath. At the end, plunge into meditation. Tradition sets the best times for hatha yoga at dawn, noon and twilight. Minimally, only 12 minutes of time is needed.

An Important Caution: Individuals with neck or back problems should abstain from poses that place strain on the spine, such as the headstand, *shirshasana*, and the shoulder stand, *sarvangasana*.

SET 1

1. Bend the right leg back around the thigh and tuck the right foot along the contour of the buttocks. Bring the left leg in front of the torso, tucking it close to the groin. Hands are on the knees, palms up, thumb and index fingers touching, in the akasha mudra. Keep the spine (the powerhouse of the body) straight, the head erect and balanced at the top of the spine. 2. Next reverse leg positions. 3. In the third pose tuck the right leg into the groin area, then place the left leg in front of it, with the left heel in front of the right heel. This is a variation of the accomplished pose, *siddhasana*, सिद्धासन. Keep both legs resting fully on the floor. Visualize deep, ruby red for physical vitality during this first set.

SET 2

4. From the last pose of set one straighten the left leg, lean forward and grasp the left foot with the thumb and index fingers of both hands. This is the *janu shirshasana*, जानुशीर्षासन, head-to-knee pose. Relax into the position, letting the head drop lower and lower until it rests on the knee. In full flexibility the elbows lower to the floor, and the torso rests on the leg. 5. Repeat these steps on the right side. 6. Then extend both legs (a little bend is OK at first) into the forward bend, *pashchimottanasana*, पश्चिमोत्तानासन. Grasp the toes with the thumb and index fingers and let the head gently fall to the knees. With practice, the elbows will lower to the floor. In this set, visualize marigold orange for pure, selfless service.

ART BY A. MANIVEL

SET 3

7. Lying face-up on the floor, raise the legs and—with the hands in the mid-back region to support the body—raise the torso until the entire body is vertical over the shoulders. This is the shoulder stand, *sarvanga-sana*, सर्वाङ्गासन. Keep the spine straight, feet together, torso perpendicular to the floor. **8.** Lower the legs slowly over the head until the toes touch the floor.

Then lower the arms, palms down. This is the plough pose, *halasana*, हलासन. **9.** End the set with the corpse pose, *shavasana*, शवासन, by lowering the legs to the floor in front of you. Let the hands rest loosely by the sides, palms down. Every muscle is relaxed. Visualize sun-glow yellow for purified intellect during this third set.

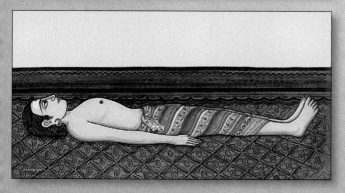

SET 4

10. Kneel and spread the feet apart, sitting between the ankles, hands on the knees, palms down. This is the heroic pose, *virasana*, वीरासन. **11.** Still kneeling, arch back as far as possible until the head touches the floor behind you in the couch pose, *paryankasana*, पर्यङ्कासन. Hold the palms together over the chest in namaskara. **12.** When you reach the right pitch of energy, bring the torso up (ideally without aid from the arms) and bend forward until the forehead touches the floor, palms down near the head, buttocks on the floor between the ankles. In this set, visualize emerald green for physical and emotional health.

SET 5

13. Move the upper body forward, inhale, arch the back slowly and extend the arms until straight, in the cobra pose, *bhujangasana*, भुजङ्गासन. Hold for two or three breaths, then lower the torso gracefully. **14.** Bring the legs up, reach back and clasp the ankles. Inhale as you pull the legs up and raise the head and upper body into the bow pose, *dhanurasana*, धनुगसन. Look up and back. Hold for two or three rounds of breathing. Exhale as you release the legs and lower to the prone position. **15.** Rise into a kneeling position, buttocks on the ankles, in the *panchanga pranamasana*, पंचाङ्गप्रणामासन, forehead on the floor, arms forward, palms down. In this set, visualize bright royal blue for peace of mind.

SET 6

16. From the last asana, move the body forward and form a triangle of forearms and head, hands clasped behind the head, fingers interwoven. The hairline touches the floor. Raise the body slowly, keeping the knees bent. Pause, then extend the legs vertically into the headstand, *salamba shirshasana*, सालम्ब शीर्षासन. Keep most of the body weight on the arms, not the head. **17.** When ready, bend and tuck in the knees and carefully lower into the curled pelvic pose for at least 8 cycles of breath to allow the blood to equalize. **18.** Slowly rise into the upright pelvic pose, hands on knees, palms down. Keep the head down momentarily against the chest in a *bandha*, or lock, and then straighten the neck. Visualize purple for the flooding forth of spiritual knowledge.

SET 7

19. Sit on the left hip and place the right foot over the left knee. Insert the left arm under the bent right knee. Extend the right arm behind the back and clasp the left hand with the right (as an easier alternative, grasp the right knee with the left arm). Keep the spine as straight as possible. This is the spinal twist, *matsyendrasana*, मत्स्येन्द्रासन. Turn the head slowly to the left each time you inhale, and back to the right as you exhale. **20.** Repeat the posture on the opposite side. **21.** Finally, bring the soles together and hold the feet with both hands in the bound-eagle pose, *baddha konasana*, बद्धकोणासन. Let the knees lower to the floor. Throughout this set visualize lavender to purify karma through divine sight.

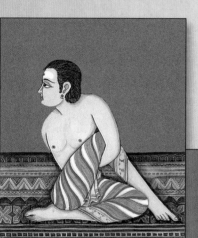

SET 8

22. Extend the right leg and place the left ankle high on the right thigh. Stretch forward and clasp the right foot with the thumb and index finger. This is a variation of the head-to-knee pose, *janu shirshasana*, जानुशीर्षासन. **23.** Repeat this same procedure on the left side, with the right foot on the left thigh.
24. Finally, assume the lotus posture, *padmasana*, पद्मासन. The right foot is already on the left thigh. To complete the lotus, carefully place the left foot on the right thigh. Spine straight with the hands resting in the lap, palms open, right hand on top, with the thumbs gently touching in *dhyana* mudra. Visualize white during this set to attain moksha, freedom from rebirth.

CHAPTER 35

Sacred Pilgrimage

Seeking God, Begging for Boons and Atoning for Misdeeds at 14 Holy Places

FIVE DUTIES, PANCHA KRIYA, FORM THE TRADITIONAL MINI-mal practices expected of every Hindu: *upasana* (worship); *utsava* (holy days); dharma (virtuous living); *tirthayatra* (pilgrimage); and samskara (rites of passage). Thus, most Hindus proceed on pilgrimage from time to time, choosing from among the seven sacred rivers or seven liberation-giving cities, the twelve Siva *mandirs* or the vast temple complexes of Mathura and Vrindavana, or thousands more holy places of India. Some visit the hallowed sanctuaries of Sri Lanka, Bali, Nepal and Bangladesh, Southeast Asia or the modern temples of Europe, America and Australia. How we follow the pilgrims' way is more important than where we go.

The concept of darshana is inextricably woven into *tirthayatra* (literally "journey to the river's ford") and all of its encounters, mundane and metaphysical. In fact, one cannot understand how a Hindu experiences pilgrimage without a deep appreciation for the not-so-obvious concept of darshana, which means "sight or vision." The direct encounter, or seeing, of the Divine, is the ideal that carries a Hindu on pilgrimage. He wants to *see* holy men and women, to *see* holy shrines, to *see* the images abiding in the ancient sanctums. Ultimately, he wants to see God, to have a personal, life-changing, bliss-engendering, karma-eradicating vision of Truth within himself. The pilgrim also wants to be seen by God, to reveal himself, uncover himself, stand before God and be known to Him. Darshana is the essence of every pilgrim's journey, the rationale, the inner and outer goal. Working diligently with himself, the pilgrim observes his yogas and his *sadhanas* (disciplines) so that his seeing may be pure and untainted. Traditional questors' practices of *snana*, the sacred bath, especially at the confluences of rivers, and *mundana*, shaving of the head, are part of attaining that purity.

Pilgrimage is a pan-human religious behavior, practiced by all cultures in much the same manner and for similar reasons—boons, expiation of sins, healing, nearness to God and enlightenment. A pilgrim of ancient Egypt testified, "I made myself a stranger to all vice and all Godlessness, was chaste for a considerable period, and offered the due incense in holy piety. I had a vision of God and found rest for my soul." The Aborigines of Australia travel to Ayer's Rock and other places of the continent. American Indian tribes undertake a "vision quest" at their sacred places. The Olympic Games were originally part of a pilgrimage to the temple of Zeus in Olympia, Greece. The Christians of the Middle Ages traveled to the holy city of Jerusalem, often at great personal peril. Muslims are expected once in their life to perform the *haj*, the visit to Mecca, holiest city of Islam—about 10 percent are able to do so.

Buddhists visit the four sanctified sites: Buddha's birthplace in Lumbini, Nepal; his place of enlightenment at Bodhgaya, India; Deer Park (Sarnath), where he gave his first sermon; and Kusinara, where he had his great departure. Jains pilgrimage to Mount Abu in Rajasthan and Parasnath in Bihar; Sikhs to the Golden Temple at Amritsar; Shintoists to Mount Fiji in Japan. There are numerous places in China sacred to Taoists and Confucianists. Catholics

are ardent pilgrims—four million a year to Lourdes in France, a million to Fatima in Portugal, to name just two destinations. Protestant Christians are possibly unique for rejecting the practice of pilgrimage as "childish and useless works;" but even they can be found at Lourdes or Jerusalem. Not only the practices but even the people are the same. What Hindu pilgrim would not recognize from his own experience the Christian characters of John Bunyan's novel *Pilgrim's Progress*—Mr. Worldly Wiseman, Mrs. Hopeful, Mr. Faithful, Mrs. Much-afraid and Mr. Ready-to-halt?

Pilgrimage is not a vacation, a chance to "get away from it all" and enjoy scenic vistas in far-off lands. The true blessing of pilgrimage comes with singlemindedness of purpose, rather than combining it (especially as a secondary purpose) with visits to relatives or the handling of business or professional concerns. Pilgrimage is a going toward holiness and a going away from worldly life. Sri Swami Satchidananda of the Integral Yoga Institute told HINDUISM TODAY, "There is a tradition that when you take a pilgrimage you temporarily become a *sannyasin* [renunciate]. It is called *yatra sannyasa*. You go as a *sannyasin,* doing with simple things and depending on God."

"Pilgrimages," explains Swami Chidanand Saraswati (Muniji) of Parmarth Niketan, in Rishikesh, "may be undertaken for realizing specific desires; as a *prayashchitta* (penance) for cleansing one's sins or for spiritual regeneration. Seekers go on pilgrimages in quest of knowledge, enlightenment and liberation. The great acharyas like Shankara, Ramanuja and Madhva went on pilgrimages to teach Sanatana Dharma." Pilgrims perform the *shraddha* rites at an auspicious place in honor of their ancestors. They seek the company of holy people. By such proximity, the pilgrim hopes to absorb a bit of the saint's religious merit, or maybe to capture a glimpse of the lofty state of the knower's consciousness.

The *Mahabharata*, in the *Tirthayatra* section, lists hundreds of holy destinations. Sage Pulastya describes to Bhishma a tour circumambulating all of India in a clockwise fashion, beginning from Pushkara in Rajasthan, then to Somnath and Dwarka in the West, to the Himalayas, across the top of India through Varanasi and Gaya to the mouth of the Ganges in the East, then southward to Kanyakumari, back up the western side of India to Gokarna in Karnataka, and ultimately returning to Pushkara. The existence of this pilgrimage route in ancient times proves, they say, that undivided India was a one culture unified by a one religion. In *Hindu Places of Pilgrimage in India*, Surinder Mohan Bhardwaj states, "The number of Hindu sanctuaries in India is so large and the practice of pilgrimage so ubiquitous that the whole of India can be regarded as a vast sacred space organized into a system of pilgrimage centers and their fields." The continuous circulation of tens of millions of pilgrims throughout India has forged a national unity of great strength. Swami Chidanand explains, "Pilgrimages have culturally and emotionally unified the Hindus. They have increased the generosity of people. Pilgrims learn and appreciate the many subcultures in the different regions, while also appreciating the overall unity."

The pilgrim, according to Sage Pulastya, must have content-

DEVRAJ AGARWAL

Pilgrims crowd along the edge of the Godavari River in central Nashik town during a main bathing day at the Kumbha Mela, one of the largest pilgrimage events in the world

ment, self-control and freedom from pride and anger. He must eat light, vegetarian food and regard all creatures as his own self. "The pilgrims," notes Ma Yoga Shakti, "should not entertain anything which is not spiritual. A pilgrim must go with total surrender, with a total faith in God, that it is only with God's grace that he can finish the pilgrimage." All along the way, there is help from others. "People know you are a pilgrim," Swami Satchidananda continued. "They say, 'We cannot go ourselves. We are all busy in the world. Please, by helping you, you can go and get some benefit, and parts of it will come to us.' " Pilgrims often sense a divine guidance during their journey, as obstacles unexpectedly disappear and needed assistance comes in a timely, unplanned fashion. Helping pilgrims is an important obligation. The *langar*, free vegetarian kitchen, and free rest houses at pilgrimage sites are common methods of assistance.

In addition to participation in the normal temple or festival events, the pilgrim's devotional practices include circumambulation, bathing, head shaving, *sraddha* offering to ancestors and prostration. Prostration and circumambulation are sometimes combined in the rigorous discipline of "measuring one's length"— prostrating, rising, stepping forward two paces and prostrating repeatedly around a sacred site. There are pilgrims who undertake this formidable penance the entire 33-mile path around Mount Kailas. Many destinations have a prescribed set of observances for pilgrims. Some, such as that to the temple of Lord Ayyappan in Sabarimala, have complex disciplines requiring months to complete.

Pilgrims pay obeisance to every Deity along their way. After worshiping at all the shrines in each temple, one finds a quiet place in meditation. *Manasa puja*, "mental ritual worship," is then performed to the Deity who stands out most strongly in one's mind, explained Swami Satchidananda. It is not enough to run from shrine to shrine taking darshana for "just five minutes," as the tour guides insist. One must also reflect internally in meditation and thus become open to receiving the gracious boons of the God. Even a life-changing vision of God may come to the pilgrim in his meditation, or later in a dream.

Swami Prakashanand, an ardent devotee of Radha-Rani, explains how to conclude a sacred journey. "Normally while going to a holy place people think of God, but as soon as they have the *darshan* of the Deity and they start back home, their mind is totally engrossed in business affairs. This is not correct. While coming back he should be further engrossed in feeling the closeness of God. Otherwise it is a sight-seeing trip." It is customary to return with holy water, *vibhuti* (holy ash) and other temple sacraments and place them upon the home altar after lighting a lamp. This establishes the holy places' blessings in the home and keeps the pilgrimage alive for months.

Divine Destinations

THE EARLIEST PILGRIMAGE DESTINATIONS ARE THOUGHT TO BE the *saptanadis* (seven holy rivers), hence the Sanskrit term for pilgrimage, *tirthayatra,* literally "journey to the river's ford." These seven rivers—Ganga, Yamuna, Godavari, Sarasvati, Narmada, Sindhu and Kaveri—remain preeminent among holy sites on their own accord and in association with the temples along their course. Each Hindu sect holds certain sites in high regard, though few Hindus would pass up the opportunity to visit any of the great sanctuaries. Paramount is the **Kumbha Mela,** the largest gathering of humans in the world, according to the *Guinness Book of World Records.* The 2001 *mela* at Prayag attracted 70 million pilgrims in six weeks, 30 million on January 24 alone. The month-long festival is held four times in each 12-year cycle of Jupiter, once each at **Haridwar, Prayag, Nashik** and **Ujjain.** A bath in India's sacred rivers yields immeasurable blessings. Hundreds of thousands of holy men emerge from caves and forests to bestow their blessings on humanity at the Kumbha Mela.

Haridwar, where the river Ganges enters the Gangetic Plain, is the gateway to the sacred Himalayan shrines, *tirthas* and ashrams. It attracts thousands of pilgrims year-round. The Kumbha Mela is held here when Jupiter is in Aquarius and the Sun in Aries—such as in January-February of 1998. **Prayag,** "place of sacrifice," attracts tens of millions who travel great distances and endure hardships for a purifying bath to absolve sins and seek *moksha,* freedom from rebirth, in the confluence of three rivers—Yamuna, Ganga and the invisible Sarasvati. This city holds the biggest Kumbha Mela of all when Jupiter is in Taurus and the Sun in Capricorn, last occurring in January-February of 2001. Near the source of the Godavari River in Maharashtra, **Nashik** is revered as Lord Rama's forest home during exile. One of ten cave temples here was Sita's abode, from which Ravana abducted her. Shrines of the area include the Kapaleshvara and Tryambakeshvara Siva temples. The Nashik *mela* (festival) is much smaller than those of Haridwar and Prayag. It occurred most recently in August-September 2003, when Jupiter and the Sun were

in Leo. Historic **Ujjain** is one of India's seven cities of liberation. This site of the Kumbha Mela on the Shipra River in Madhya Pradesh shelters an array of destinations, including the Mahakala Siva Temple and the Amareshvara Jyotir Linga. Its most recent *mela* was attended by 30 million pilgrims in April-May 2004, when Jupiter entered Leo with the Sun in Aries. A biannual Kumbha Mela of the South was begun in 1989 by Sri la Sri Tiruchi Mahaswamigal and Sri Sri Sri Balagangadharanathaswami of Bangalore at an auspicious site near Mysore.

Among the foremost religious retreats for Saivites is **Chidambaram,** the great Siva Nataraja temple, site of the Lingam of Akasha, located in Tamil Nadu. It was here that Lord Siva performed the Tandava dance of creation, overcoming the arrogance of the *rishis,* and where sage Patanjali later lived and wrote the *Yoga Sutras.* Here also lived Rishi Tirumular, author of the *Tirumantiram.* The glistening roof of the main sanctum contains 17,500 solid gold tiles, one for each breath a human takes in a day.

High north in Uttar Pradesh is **Kedarnath,** one of the twelve Jyotir Linga temples of Lord Siva. It was established at the foot of the Himalayas by the five Pandavas after the Mahabharata war to atone for their sins. Recent improvements have made the previously arduous ascent to this 12,000-foot sanctuary easier, but unfit trekkers are still cautioned about the cold and the 5,000-foot hike from Gaurikund, the last motorable outpost.

One of the greatest and most austere pilgrimages, **Mount Kailas,** Himalayan abode of Lord Siva, is sacred to five religions. Pilgrims perform a three-day, 33-mile circumambulation of the peak. At the foot of Kailas lies Lake Manasarovara, symbolizing a quieted mind, free from all thought. Kailas is the Mount Meru of Hindu cosmology, center of the universe. Within 50 miles are the sources of four of India's auspicious rivers.

The Ramanathaswamy Sivalinga Temple at **Rameshvaram** near India's southern tip was built by Lord Rama in penance for killing Ravana, a brahmin. Two Lingams (egg-shaped icons) are worshiped there, established by Sita and Hanuman. Each day the *abhishekam* (bathing) is performed with Ganges water. The temple is enormous in extent, with a mile of stone corridors. Pilgrims bathe in the sea and at 22 wells, each of which removes a particular kind of sin.

Pilgrims to **Varanasi,** Siva's City of Light, bathe at the *ghats* (river steps) along the River Ganges to cleanse the sins of a lifetime. Most pilgrims attend Sivalinga *puja* (devotional rites) at Kashi Vishwanatha, foremost of the 1,500 temples here. The devout journey here at life's end.

• •

Pilgrimage moments: *Elderly women hike 46 km to Amarnath cave in Jammu. Evening Ganga puja in Varanasi. Quiet moment of meditation before Lord Vishnu at Badami, Karnataka State. The infirm are carried by hired porters to difficult sacred destinations.*

One of the greatest Shakta temples is **Vaishno Devi.** Those who climb the mountain trail in the Trikuta mountains north of Jammu are rarely disappointed as they implore the Goddess for boons. It was here in the Himalayan foothills that Vaishno Devi, a devotee of Lord Vishnu, defeated the demon Bhaironatha. Though hidden within a cave, the shrine receives more than 20,000 pilgrims a day, even when wintery snows are piled deep outside.

At the very tip of India, where the Bay of Bengal, the Indian Ocean and the Arabian Sea meet, lies the ancient shrine of **Kanya-kumari,** Goddess Parvati as the eternal virgin. It was here that She defeated the demon Bana. Boats take pilgrims offshore to the Vivekananda Rock Memorial, erected where the young swami cognized his mission to begin a Hindu renaissance.

Pilgrim: *Searching for God*

Madurai, the Athens of India, holds the labyrinthine Meenakshi Sundareshvara temple. Here Siva came as Somasundarar to wed the Pandyan Princess Meenakshi, a manifestation of Parvati. Thus, this edifice encases two temples, one to Siva and another to Shakti. The towering entry gates, 1,000-pillared hall, sacred tanks and shrines vibrate with thousands of years of worship at this seven-walled citadel on the Vagai River.

Only a few centuries ago the **Kalighat** temple was established in what was then a remote jungle near the river Ganges. The now highly congested Calcutta expanded to envelope the shrine, which is filled daily with devotees' cries of "Kali Ma, Kali Ma," beseeching blessings from the incomparable Protectress and Mother of liberation.

Kamaksha is the Goddess of Love. Her holiest sanctuary is a small temple built on the rock of Nila Hill near Gauhati in Assam. The town and its legends are described in the *Mahabharata* and the *Kalika Purana.* This temple of magic for the sincere devotee contains no image of the Goddess, but in the depths of the shrine is a cleft in the stone, adored as the *yoni* of Sakti.

Vaishnavites revere **Ayodhya,** birthplace of Lord Rama, "Jewel of the Solar Kings." Here devotees worship and seek the blessings and boons of the seventh incarnation of God Vishnu. This orthodox Vaishnava town in Uttar Pradesh is among Hinduism's seven most sacred cities. Temples and shrines in every quarter honor famous sites of Rama's celebrated life, including the reclaimed Ram Janmabhoomi shrine and a temple to His devout servant, Hanuman.

Mathura is the birthplace of Lord Krishna, eighth incarnation of God Vishnu. Mathura and nearby Vrindaban and Gokula are an outdoor paradise for devotees visiting places of the Lord's youth. A ten-mile circumambulation of the city takes enchanted pilgrims to dozens of shrines and bathing spots for this beloved God's blessings.

Puri, in the state of Orissa, is the site of the famous Rathayatra, car festival, held around June each year at the sprawling, 900-year-old Jagannatha temple complex. A million pilgrims flock for darshana of God Vishnu as Lord of the Universe, and His brother and sister, Balabhadra and Subhadra. Using 500-meter ropes, throngs of devotees pull 40-foot-tall wooden chariots to the Gundicha temple.

Along with Yamunotri, Gangotri and Kedarnath, **Badrinath** lies in the area known as Uttarkhand, high in the Himalayas. During the half-year when not blocked by snow, hearty pilgrims climb 10,000 feet to the temple of Badrinarayana, where God Vishnu sits in meditation with a large diamond adorning His third eye and body bedecked with gems. Pilgrims take a purifying bath at the Tapt Kund, a sacred hot water pool.

India's richest and most popular temple, **Tirupati,** daily draws 25,000 pilgrims. They joyfully wait hours for a precious two seconds of darshana of the two-meter tall, jet-black image of the wish-fulfilling Sri Venkateshwara, or Balaji. His diamond crown is the costliest ornament on Earth. The temple is a Dravidian masterpiece of stonework, gold and jewels. Head-shaving here is a prized testimony of penance and devotion, and famed *laddu* sweets are the pilgrim's prized gift of blessed food.

In ancient times the *rishis* of the *Rig Veda* sang in praise of pilgrimage: "Flower-like the heels of the wanderer, his body grows and is fruitful; all his sins disappear, slain by the toil of his journeying." So meaningful is pilgrimage in the Sanatana Dharma, the world's oldest religion, that Hindus today have thousands of destinations, at which God awaits the pilgrim.

Recommended Resources: Hindu Places of Pilgrimage in India [comprehensive study for North Indian sites], Surinder Mohan Bhardwaj, University of California Press, 2120 Berkeley Way, Berkeley, California, 94720. **Pilgrimage Past and Present in the World Religions** [useful for Western faiths], Simon Coleman and John Elsner, Harvard University Press, 79 Garden Street, Cambridge, Massachusetts, 02138-1425. **Pilgrimages and Journeys,** [fine children's book], Katherine Prior, Thomson Learning, 115 Fifth Avenue, New York, New York, 10003. **A Historical Atlas of South Asia** [maps and historical accounts], Joseph E. Schwartzberg, Oxford University Press, 200 Madison Avenue, New York, New York, 10016. **Journeys to the Lands of the Gods** [a pilgrim's diary, especially good for South Indian sites], Rajalingam Rajathurai, Printworld Services Pte Ltd, 80 Genting Lane, #04-02 Genting Block, Ruby Industrial Complex, Singapore 349565

Family Life And Culture

Raising children as good Hindus, cues and clues for travelers, rites of passage, the duties of homemaking, and honoring Hindu heros

Above, a family celebrates Dipavali in their Toronto home, playing Hindu music and singing bhajanas. Hindu family life is strong and precious. Their dress and refinement exemplify one aspect of the traditions discussed in this section of *What Is Hinduism?*

CHAPTER 36

Hospitality

How Guests Are Treated As God in the Hindu Home

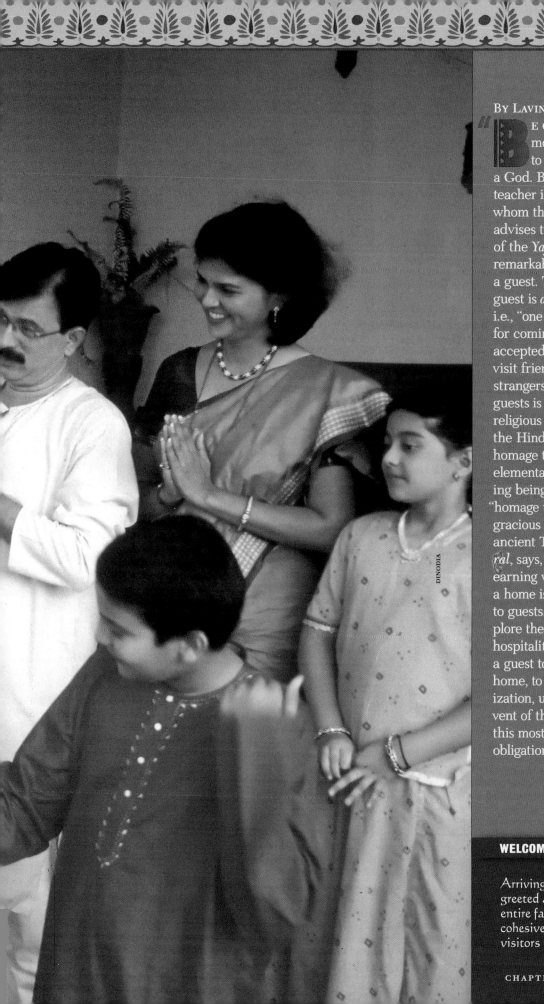

DINODIA

By Lavina Melwani, New York

"BE ONE TO WHOM THE mother is a God. Be one to whom the father is a God. Be one to whom the teacher is a God. Be one to whom the guest is a God." So advises the *Taittiriya Upanishad* of the *Yajur Veda*, affirming the remarkable Hindu reverence for a guest. The Sanskrit word for guest is *athithi*, "without time," i.e., "one who has no fixed day for coming." It remains today the accepted custom of Hindus to visit friends, relatives and even strangers without notice. Hosting guests is one of the five central religious duties or "sacrifices" of the Hindu householder: paying homage to seers, to Gods and elementals, to ancestors, to living beings and, *manushya yajna*, "homage to men," which includes gracious hosting of guests. The ancient Tamil scripture, *Tirukural*, says, "The whole purpose of earning wealth and maintaining a home is to provide hospitality to guests." In this article we explore the many facets of Hindu hospitality, from how to receive a guest to how to behave in the home, to the impact of modernization, urbanization and the advent of the nuclear family upon this most ancient and revered obligation of our faith.

WELCOME!

Arriving guests are warmly greeted at the entryway by the entire family. In a well-adjusted, cohesive family, receiving visitors is a joyous event.

Do you think you are the perfect Hindu host? Well, here's a story that will make you reevaluate your hospitality skills, for the host in this tale is none other than Lord Krishna. When his boyhood friend, Sudama—hungry, impoverished and in rags—arrived at the palace, the guards refused to allow him in. But Lord Krishna, overjoyed to see his old friend, received him with open arms and joyfully led him to his throne. He personally washed Sudama's feet and fed him with his own hands. Sudama had brought a humble gift, a handful of parched rice tied in the corner of his shawl and was too ashamed to give it to Lord Krishna in front of all the fine courtiers, but Lord Krishna opened it with delight and ate the grains with pleasure and appreciation. To him, the true value of this meager gift lay in the affection with which it had been offered. Similar stories abound in our scriptures and histories.

Although I did not grow up in a particularly religious household, the concept of hospitality was still very traditionally Hindu, both in giving and receiving. I remember we stopped at a friend's home in Mathura after a pilgrimage to Haridwar. The hosts received us like VIPs, with open hearts and minds. We ate a wonderful vegetarian meal in the cool evening air in their garden, and then, as the stars came out, the string beds were brought out into the open, for family and guests, each covered with a mosquito net to ward off insects.

Another time, I was with my older brother, who had to stop at an acquaintance's home in Old Delhi to pick up some paperwork. The family knew we were coming and had prepared a feast. In this very Hindu home, we removed our shoes, washed our hands and feet and sat on the immaculate kitchen floor with the hosts while a brahmin cook served us one of the most memorable meals I have ever eaten.

Indeed, you can never leave an Indian household without gaining a few ounces, for you will certainly be plied with some snacks, some tea at the very least, or a glass of cold rose sherbet in the heat of summer. In our home in New Delhi, family and friends came to us from everywhere, and they certainly got more than a glass of water: delicious meals, a comfortable bed, domestics hanging over their every need and, yes, even a guided tour of Delhi, and, sometimes, even Agra. Nor was the hospitality reserved just for visiting guests. Daily food was never eaten without my mother's consecrating a small portion to God, and a portion being given to a passing needy person or a cow.

Relatives came and were joyously received, especially on days of *shraddha* when the priest, uncles, aunts and cousins would descend on the house to honor the memory of ancestors. The house would take on an almost festive air, as scores of children erupted out of the arriving cars. After prayers and feeding the priest, the aroma of sizzling *puris* and *pakodas* wafted from the kitchen while elders embarked on a massive talkathon.

Sundari Katir of California told HINDUISM TODAY, "When I was growing up in Sri Lanka, guests would always be visiting us from different parts of the country and India. The whole household would jump into action. My mother would assemble the meal, and we children would get our rooms all ready, because we would give them up and sleep on mats on the floor. It was such a natural thing to do, and we were always delighted to have guests. Today my brother Ranjan is one of the few relatives left in Colombo, and he carries on the tradition. He treats everyone as God, with good food, comfortable beds and heartfelt hospitality. I have become a better hostess after observing him."

God as Guest: The most common Hindu form of worship, *puja*, is, in fact, an act of hosting. Rare is the Hindu home without a shrine for the Deities. From huge family temples of marble in the homes of the wealthy to modest shrines, Hindus revere their

Tips for Being a Good Guest

A GUEST MAY BE ANYONE FROM a close relative to a total stranger, and rules naturally vary accordingly. What is summarized here is for a visitor somewhere between the two extremes.

Arrival: It is traditional that a guest need not inform a host of his impending arrival. However, in today's busy world, more and more often guests do give advance notice. The host may insist that no advance notice is necessary, and close friends or relatives may even take advance notice as an affront, a disturbing sign that all may not be well with the relationship.

Duration: It is very impolite of the host to ask how long the guest is staying. But, as a guest, you should convey this information in an casual manner. In a gesture of hospitality, the host will naturally retort that you should really stay much longer.

Gifts: Gifts are always given to hosts by guests when staying overnight in a home. The value of the gift varies greatly, of course, depending on the guest's circumstances and resources.

DINODIA

Surprise: *Guests may even arrive unannounced*

It is proper to give a separate gift for the wife and the husband. The wife receives the nicest item. Small items should also be given for the children. In Sri Lanka, giving goes the other way as well. It is common for the host to give a gift to the guest, especially those poorer.

Helping: In a home without servants, considerate guests can help with housework and chores, as well as care for their quarters, even if the host insists it is not necessary. You can also help with cooking, as well as invite your hosts out for a meal.

Graciousness: It is an insult to refuse any offered drink or food. Blend into the family's rhythms. Be a genuine friend, taking real interest in the family's life and treating the children lovingly, as you would your own. Conversely, one should not meddle in family affairs, nor later make unflattering observations to others about one's hosts.

Thanks: After returning home, remember to send a warm and sincere thank-you letter, hand-written, mentioning some specific detail of your visit that you most appreciated.

Gods. Daily, images of the family Gods are bathed, clothed and offered fruit, flowers and incense, accompanied by chanting and the tinkle of the bell, all in the format of hosting a guest. The full 16-step *puja* begins with an invitation for God to come to the home, continues through offering of a seat, washing the feet with water, offerings of drink and food, garments and incense, flowers, etc., until finally the God is thanked and bid adieu. While the standard human guest would receive less adulation, a holy man visiting a family's home may well be welcomed and worshiped in this complete manner.

Festivals bring a more intense program to host God. At Dipavali, the Festival of Lights, when Goddess Lakshmi visits the homes of devotees, there is a frenzy of cleaning, sweeping and painting as homes are beautified and decorated with hundreds of earthen lamps to greet Her.

Guest as God: At the very heart of Hinduism is the belief that the Almighty permeates everything. Indeed, the Hindu belief in the presence of the Paramatma in every living thing transforms each one of us into God. The ancient Hindu texts say the guest has to be shown honor by the host's going out to meet him, offering him water to wash his feet, by giving him a seat, lighting a lamp before him, providing food and lodging and accompanying him some distance when he departs. Thousands of years have passed, but this code of etiquette remains little changed from the ancient scriptures.

In the *Manu Dharma Shastras*, for example, the host is directed thus: "All the food shall be very hot, and the guests shall eat in silence. Having addressed them with the question: 'Have you dined well?' let him give them water to sip, and bid farewell to them with the words: 'Now rest.'" K.T. Achaya in *Indian Food: A Historical Companion* points out that guests had an honored rank in Vedic society and, after being ceremoniously received, were offered the ambrosial beverage, *madhuparka*, consisting of ghee, curd, milk, honey and sugar.

According to the *Dharma Shastras*, hosting guests is one of the five obligatory sacrifices or duties of the householder. Anusasana states, "The host should give his eye, mind and agreeable speech to the guest, he should personally attend on him and should accompany him when he (the guest) departs; this sacrifice (*yajna*) demands these five fees."

The visit of a holy person is given extra special attention, and for good reason. *Vriddha Harita Dharma Shastra* says that if a *bramachari* ascetic stays as a guest in a householder's home for a single night, the latter's accumulated sins are destroyed, and when such an ascetic takes food at a man's house, it is Vishnu Himself who is fed.

Common Sense: It should be clearly stated that Hindu hospitality does not extend to being careless with the safety of one's family and home. Even Krishna's guards kept Sudama—a brahmin at that—outside the gates. When HINDUISM TODAY's founder, Satguru Sivaya Subramuniyaswami (Gurudeva), was in Sri Lanka as a young man, he experienced wonderful hospitality across the island from all the communities. Part of the time he stayed in the traditional Tamil village of Alaveddy at the home of Kandiah Chettiar, one of his teachers, receiving instructions on, among other things, the hosting of guests. One day, Chettiar had given food to a suspicious-looking man at the gate, rather than inviting him to the porch of the house. When the young Gurudeva asked why he didn't invite the man in, Chettiar replied, with characteristic frankness, "Because he would steal everything in the house." The *Dharma Shastras* discuss at some length the issue of unworthy or even dangerous guests, yet advising that, no matter what the circumstances, the visitor should at least receive food.

Village Traditions: Sheela Venkatakrishnan of Chennai, Tamil

Honing the Art of Hosting

HOSTING IS MORE AN ATTItude than a set of practices. The perfect host is truly open to guests and honestly delighted with their presence. That said, here are some specifics to keep your hosting up to par.

Welcome: Greet the guest with *namaskara*, invite him cheerfully into the house. Invite him to sit comfortably in the best surroundings. Speak pleasantly to him, inquiring about his welfare.

Refreshments: Always offer the guest something to eat and drink. Usually tea or juice is served, along with snacks. At least a glass of water is offered (with a smile and apology).

Hosting: Guests who are members of the extended family will just fit in to the family routine. When a bit more formality is called for, the father, if present, will speak with the guest. If not present, the mother and a son will fulfill this role, and if no son is present, the mother may act as hostess, but

Welcome! *A pleasant reception is the first step*

only with the accompaniment of someone close to the family. The children may go off to play among themselves, stay with the adults or come and go.

Wife Home Alone: If the lady of the house is home alone and a male visitor comes to see her husband, it is not proper for her to invite him in, or for him to expect to enter. Rather, he will leave a message and depart.

Punctuality: Life is generally more relaxed in the East than in the West. A good guideline is to not be surprised or offended if your guest arrives late or early. However, be punctual in your own engagements, as this is appreciated.

Duration of Stay: It is quite impolite to ask a guest how long he intends to stay, but it is good protocol for guests to make their plans and itinerary known from the outset.

Goodbyes: Always see your guest to his transport, and wave and watch until they are out of sight.

An enjoyable visit results when both guest and host are experts in the art of congenial conversation.

Nadu, told HINDUISM TODAY, "You offer your guest the same love and respect that you would offer to God. Simple! A striking example of hospitality is when the whole town of Kumbakonam, where my father hails from, turns host during the week of the Mahamaham." Thousands upon thousands of people come for the holy bath in the tank of the Kumbareswaran temple, and every home opens its doors to accommodate and feed all who reach its doorstep. No one is turned away.

Sheela explained, "Houses in the villages and towns of Tamil Nadu usually have a fairly large platform just outside their front door, called a *thinnai*. This serves two purposes. One is temporary storage of grain during the harvest and also an airy place to sleep during the hot and humid summers. It is not unusual for a traveller to use this as a resting place. You could open your front door in the morning and find someone sleeping on your *thinnai*. This is where you would find the strangers during Mahamaham. Of course, family and friends would be accommodated inside the house. But everyone is fed, irrespective of caste. It is possible that in the morning there is one set of people, in the afternoon another and a totally different group at night. The meals served would be according to whatever time of day it is. Also, the bath area often has a separate access from outside the house."

In her grandfather's day, Sheela noted, it was the practice for the head of the household to stand at his doorstep at mealtime and ask loudly, not once but thrice, "Is there someone who needs to be fed?" Sometimes a traveler or a poor man would come in for food. It was only after the guest had been fed that family would eat—one of the explicit instructions in the *Dharma Shastras*. The *Apastamba* says, "He who eats before his guest eats destroys food, prosperity, progeny, cattle and the merit of his own house."

Hospitality permeates Indian culture, both on a personal and institutional level. In Tamil Nadu, many of the bigger and older temples have the *annadanam* scheme—a daily free feeding. Recently, with the active patronage of the government, many more temples have revived this practice, where they feed a minimum

of 100 people each day at noon. Muslim *darghas* have adopted this practice, while the Sikh *gurudwaras* have always followed it. Mention also has to be made of the Hyderabadi brand of hospitality that has few parallels. Made famous by the Muslim *nawabs* of Lucknow, those on the receiving end enjoyed courtesy, food, drink and congeniality—all served with an elegant world-class flourish. Every ethnic and religious subculture of India puts a premium on hospitality.

Little wonder, then, that in multicultural India these varied streams of hospitality have coalesced to produce a generous and warm people. Visitors to India come away with awed stories of the way they were embraced and included in every family celebration—in fact, made part of a larger, extended family. Often these relationships last over the years.

You cannot go to even the humblest home without being honored with food and Indian drink, as Janet Chawla found out some years back. Chawla, an American who married a Sikh and now lives in New Delhi, believes the charm of India is in the graciousness of its people, although it is getting less so in the big cities. She feels there is a grace, a way of sitting together, singing together at weddings. People in small villages, she says, really are very giving, sharing the little they have.

"In America, if we were sitting and working together, and I had a sandwich—I would open it and eat it alone. An Indian would never do that," she says. "There is this kind of culturally prescribed sharing which I find very gracious." Janet didn't mention it, but some Westerners visiting India can find the level of hospitality discomfiting, especially the tradition of never leaving a guest alone. That impinges upon the Westerner's desire for privacy and "personal space"—concepts absent from the Indian milieu.

Hospitality at Home: Hindu tradition lays great stress on the respect due to guests. The greatest hurt for a guest is the thought that the host or hostess does not enjoy one's presence. Therefore, Hindus go out of their way to make each guest feel welcome. It is proper protocol to drop whatever one is doing, no matter how important, to entertain a visitor. One of the privileges of friendship in the East is being able to drop by any time without advance notice.

Mitesh Patel, whose family hails from Kathiawad region of Gujarat, says that in his hometown hospitality is extended to everyone: "When a guest comes to our house, we rarely let them go without offering a good meal. We don't feel that guests are a burden, whether they are staying for few hours or few days, and offer them full assistance."

He gives the example of his uncle who left the ancestral village 30 years ago to settle in the city of Rajkot. Three decades later, if anyone from the village comes for a medical checkup to the big hospital in the city, his uncle makes sure healthy, home-made meals go out to the patient every single day.

The level of hospitality depends upon several factors, the most obvious being family ties. Traditionally, any known or unknown member of one's extended family—and the Hindu extended family includes not only blood relatives to several degrees removed, but also all the in-laws by marriage—is basically treated just like a member of the immediate family. It would not be uncommon, for example, for a student at the university to stay with distant relatives throughout his entire schooling.

Then there are friends, business acquaintances, people from the same village or state and so on, all of whom have some connection to the host. They, too, may be treated just like a member of the extended family, as Janet Chawla experienced, though commonly a bit more formally. We can see from Sheela's description of her childhood village that the homes were designed to accommodate even total strangers in a convenient fashion.

The concept of hospitality extends to welcoming customers to business settings, where it certainly makes good sense. Go into a sari shop in crowded marketplaces and the owner will automatically offer you a soft drink in the heat. If you're shopping for an expensive wedding trousseau, they are even more solicitous—offering coconut water, a snack and drinks from the market. I recall my father in his jewelry store not only offering soft drinks, *paan* in silver containers and candy, but also giving the kids who came to the shop small items as gifts.

Untouchables: Yet, one does have to admit that Hinduism's glowing hospitality report card does have one very big black mark on it, something which the Gods probably did not ordain but which wily man has reinterpreted for his own gain—the treatment of the so-called lower castes. It is really quite inconceivable that a loving religion, which proclaims that God is in every living thing, would denigrate a whole class of human beings as untouchables.

The story of everyday village India is full of the low castes being turned away from village wells, being castigated for worshipping at the temple or merely for passing by the home of a brahmin. While things are improving in the big cities where caste and creed lose their importance in the great economic bazaar and where politicians see the lower castes as potential votes, the village scene remains woefully medieval. Buried in the back pages of newspapers are frequent stories of atrocities, which should shock us all from our complacency and our conceit of just how "hospitable" we may really be.

Loss of Tradition: In the larger hospitality picture, things seem to be changing for the worse as the time-honored extended family finally battles modernity. Dr. T. H. Chowdary of Hyderabad writes, "As people leave their villages and joint families break up and the educated move to flats in the cities, the old idea of hospitality is fast dying. In the villages and small towns in the past, in the evening when beggars came for food, whatever was left in the house would be given away. In those days of no refrigeration, food could not be kept. Now in the towns and cities, surplus is stored in refrigerators, which have thus come to be known as *garibmar*, the killers of the poor.

"Even when brothers and sisters and such near ones come, one silently wishes that they will stay in a hotel and, at best, they might come for a dinner or a breakfast," he goes on. "What to

Serving food is a host's duty. To omit this courtesy is a serious affront, as it is for the guest to refuse what is offered.

DINODIA

A fond farewell puts a sweet end to the guests' experience, and creates anticipation for the next visit

speak of caring for the parents or relatives when the wife and husband have no time even to talk to one another! Or when the one-year-old child, the only child, is put in a day-care center so that both the wife and husband can earn enough to satisfy their ideas of modern comforts, including that refrigerator or new TV

"What to speak of hospitality for friends and unknowns," says Chowdary, "when the nuclear family of wife and husband are saying that the old father must stay with one son and the old mother with another son? They want to separate the old parents, considering them burdens to be shared by the sons."

As Chowdary observes, with women joining the work force in large numbers, and time, effort and budgets stretched by modern life, the old-time hospitality is often compromised. Earlier, visitors could just drop in, but now hosts get agitated to find unexpected guests on the doorstep—a far cry from the hospitality of the village home's *thinnai*.

Sheela Venkatakrishnan agrees: "In recent years, the trend has become, as Gurudeva said, 'The women going out of their homes to work.' Living in nuclear families, who is there to take care of the home, leave alone a guest? You tend to think twice about visiting a friend or relative, not wanting to impose or inconvenience them in any way." Still, she points out that they have many relatives in joint families who welcome them with open arms. She herself lives in a joint family in Chennai where someone is always home: "The doors of our home and our hearts are open to God and all whom He chooses to send our way."

The Diaspora Adjusts: The picture, however, is bleaker in the diaspora, where immigrants struggle with the beliefs they grew up with and the pressures of their new environment. Most manage to keep the hospitality intact for family and close friends. Some go to extraordinary lengths, sponsoring relatives and even opening up their homes to them till they get settled.

The Gujarati community is particularly strong in this respect, and many continue to live in large, extended families abroad. This sense of caring is extended to the entire community and,

in fact, many Patels have managed to do so well in the motel business because of their unity and financial support of friends and relatives. No wonder the Gujaratis command a whopping portion of the motel industry. They are well-trained in the ways of hospitality, for as one of the successful hoteliers, H.P. Rama, affirms, "We Indians believe the guest is God."

Mitesh Patel, who lives in Edison, New Jersey, came to the US when he was 15, so he has seen life on both continents. Now 24, he believes that Hindu hospitality has lessened in the US, Canada and the UK, but not in India: "I believe the reason is quite simple. NRIs are busy making big bucks in these countries. Sometimes even family members don't see each other for a few days because they are busy working, so they feel that it's hard to accommodate a guest."

Indeed, living abroad, notions of hospitality do undergo a change. Also, abroad, one would never dream of dropping in on acquaintances without calling ahead. This is a culture where even children do not just play but have organized "play dates" scheduled out weeks in advance.

Indians living abroad do have to contend with housework, their jobs and the daily commute, all without the support of extended family or domestic helpers. So their standards of hospitality have diminished. Some compromise, putting guests in hotels or taking shortcuts in their care. Truly generous hospitality in any society or home depends on the strength, integrity and security of the family unit.

Changing Attitudes: Summer, especially, means an endless barrage of guests from India and points in the diaspora. Homes become as crowded as the Grand Central Terminal, and hosts are faced with a multitude of tasks. As one exhausted woman, whose house was full of summer guests, told me, "Houseguests are like fish: after three days, they stink."

She didn't know it, but this adage appeared in the 1736 edition of *Poor Richard's Almanac* by Benjamin Franklin, one of America's founding fathers. He said, precisely, "Fish and houseguests stink after three days." The statement, and the attitude behind it, stand in stark contrast to the Hindu view of the guest as God. And it's not just an American trait. Shakespeare wrote with a similar attitude in *King Henry VI, Part I*, "Unbidden guests are often welcomest when they are gone." In all fairness, there are many hospitable Americans and Britishers, but offering hospitality is not the religious obligation it is for Hindus. It is also relevant that, in the Hindu village, true strangers were served on the porch, or even at the compound gate, in order to preserve the sanctity and safety of the home.

While the pressures of life in the West are there for the hosts, to some extent their attitudes have also changed. The rhythms of the place where you live impact you. Leading frenetic lives in the West, people tend to become more brusque, more cynical. Like Franklin, they begin to regard the guest as an unwelcome nuisance. Standards of hospitality are indeed changing, and one wonders how far we should embrace modernization at the expense of true hospitality?

What to Do? Gurudeva once observed, "The guest is God, not an intruder. All Hindus have a heart to receive the guest as God. This is very important for us to remember, because guests come and guests go. Often, guests come and never come back, because of subtle inflections in the voice, because it was forgotten to serve even a glass of water, which is traditional in Hindu culture. The guest is God, not an intruder. When someone steps up to you, drop your work. People are more important than paper. People are more important than giving oneself to the computer. People are more important than anything else. People are the working out of your karma."

Yes, it may help to remember an old Indian saying: *Dane dane pe likha hai khane wale ka naam*—"On each grain is written the name of the eater." The people who turn up on your doorstep are meant to be there, part of your karma, part of the big cosmic play. Of course, it's hard to see it quite that way when you are under stress at work and still have to produce dinner for your guests by 7:00 PM!

For Hindus caught in the modern world of hurry and scurry,

it would be good to reaffirm their duty toward guests and to refresh their memories on how to be perfect hosts—and perfect guests. There is etiquette for both roles, and if each plays his part well, the whole experience can be rewarding.

Hosts should give of themselves with a generous and open heart, exerting every effort to make their visitors' stay a memorable one, where the kindnesses and warmth are vast, even if the budget is tight. They should do all they can to entertain and help visitors in a new and bewildering place.

Guests should attempt to be considerate, informing their hosts of their length of stay in advance. They should pick up after themselves and not add to the harried hostess' tasks. Bringing small gifts for the family members, entertaining the children or perhaps offering to take the family out to dinner are practical and appreciated gestures.

Hospitality is a virtue that has many benefits for the receiver and the giver, as these small kindnesses smooth social connections and build relations. It also shows the next generation the way to continue the beliefs of our ancestors. And of course, often the shoe is on the other foot—and the host himself becomes a guest. So he should treat his guests as he himself would like to be treated.

There are so many stories of God Vishnu himself donning beggar's raiment and coming to the door for alms. So, the next time the doorbell rings, welcome your guests with an open heart. Look beyond the facial features, the clothing and the physical bodies into the eternal soul which glows within each of us like the purest of gold. This is the Self that scripture says is immortal, the one that water cannot wet, sword cannot cut nor fire burn. And so, bending low, with folded hands, welcome the divine Paramatma, the God who is within each of us.

The author, **Lavina Melwani,** *a popular free-lance correspondent, was born in Sindh, grew up in New Delhi and has lived in Hong Kong and Africa. She currently resides in New York with her husband and two children.* **T. H. Chowdary,** *Information Technology Advisor: Government of Andhra Pradesh, contributed to this article.*

The Holy Kural on Hospitality

THE SOUTH INDIAN ETHICAL MASTER-piece, *Tirukural*, composed in Tamil couplets by Saint Tiruvalluvar (ca 200 bce), devotes an entire chapter to hospitality. This sagely compendium of practical advice, called "a bible on virtue for the human race," is so pithy, so profound and so sacred that it is sworn upon today in South Indian courts. Here now are verses 81 to 90.

The whole purpose of earning wealth and maintaining a home is to provide hospitality to guests.

When a guest is in the home, it is improper to hoard one's meal, even if it happens to be the nectar of immortality.

If a man cares daily for those who come to him, his life will never suffer the grievous ruin of poverty.

Wealth's Goddess dwells in the hospitable home of those who host guests with a smiling face.

If a man eats only after attending to guests' needs, what further sowing will his fertile fields require?

The host who, caring for guests, watches hopefully for more, will himself be a welcomed guest of those whose home is Heaven.

Charity's merit cannot be measured by gifts given. It is measured by measuring the receiver's merits.

Those who never sacrifice to care for guests will later lament: "We hoarded wealth, estranged ourselves, now none will care for us."

The poverty of poverties is having plenty yet shunning guests. Such senselessness is only found in senseless fools.

The delicate anicham flower withers when merely smelled, but an unwelcome look is enough to wither a guest's heart.

A. MANIVEL

CHAPTER 37

Raising Children As Good Hindus

Parents Are the First Gurus in Religion and Character Building

Many Hindu families visiting our Hawaii monastery, particularly those with young children, ask if I have any advice for them. I usually respond with one or two general suggestions. I always stress the importance of presenting Hinduism to their children in a practical way so that it influences each child's life for the better. Hindu practices should, for example, help children get better grades in school and get along well with others. Of course, there is not enough time in a short session to present all the many guidelines that a parent would find useful. Therefore, I decided to write up a full complement of suggestions to be handed to Hindu families in the future who want to know ways to present Hinduism to their kids. You hold the results in your hands: the parent's guidebook of minimum teachings to convey to children. It is based on the teachings of my satguru, Sivaya Subramuniyaswami, founder of HINDUISM TODAY, distilled from insights he gained from over 40 years of closely working with hundreds of families in a score of nations. This booklet presents a gridwork of character-building designed to augment any tradition or denomination. The key is this: start teaching early and don't stop until your children leave the home. Even if you did nothing more than what is outlined in these 16 pages, that would be enough to send them on their way as good Hindus, well-equipped to live as happy, effective citizens of the modern world.

Satguru Bodhinatha Veylanswami

Contents

DINODIA

Working together on projects is an ideal way to pass on your values, insights, skills and wisdom.

PART ONE

TEACH AND PRACTICE HINDUISM IN YOUR HOME

Take responsibility for being the primary teachers of Hinduism to your children.

It is wonderful that many temples have in place educational programs for the youth that are both effective and popular. However, it is important for parents to have the attitude that these programs supplement but do not replace the need for them to teach Hinduism to their children in the home. Parents are indeed the first guru. They teach in many different ways, such as by example, explanation, and giving advice and direction. The child's deepest impressions come from what the parents do and say. Therefore, if the parents follow a systematic approach to teaching the child Hinduism as he or she grows up, Sanatana Dharma will be fully integrated into his or her life, making it less likely to be sidelined or abandoned in adult years.

Without your help, there is no guarantee that your children will follow their faith as adults.

Look around at the younger generation of Hindus and you will find many who have no interest whatsoever in practicing the Hindu religion. One hundred years ago, before movies, television and computers, in the cities and villages of India and Hindu communities in other countries, the Hindu temple was the most interesting place in town. Besides the festivals, there were dramas, dances and musical concerts. The temple was a social and educational center as well. In our modern world we do have movies, television and computers, and many Hindu children would much rather spend their free time enjoying them with their friends rather than being at the temple. Why is this? There are many reasons. Families are not so close and trusting. And it used to be far easier to get children to come to the temple, since it was the center of village life. Times are different, and today's children often consider the temple boring compared to the all-pervasive and ever more compelling secular forms of entertainment that are available. So, parents are challenged more than ever to answer kids' puzzling queries—as grandparents did not have to do—by giving sensible, pragmatic explanations to temple worship and Hinduism's rich array of cultural and mystical practices. Kids today want answers that make sense to them. They are not at all content with "That's the way we have always done it." When parents are unable to meet this challenge, Hinduism does not become a meaningful and useful part of their children's lives. Many youth today do not view the practice of their faith as important to making their life happier, more religious and more successful. This is the challenge every Hindu parent faces. But all is not lost. New generations are eager to hear the lofty truths, and those truths can be explained in ways that engage and inspire young seekers, counterbalancing the powerfully magnetic influences of the modern world.

Establish a shrine in the home.

Hinduism is in no way more dynamically strengthened in the lives of children and the family than by establishing a shrine in the home. The home shrine works best when it is an entire room. That way it can be strictly reserved for worship and meditation, unsullied by worldly talk or other activities. This is the ideal. However, when that is not possible, it should at least be a quiet corner of a room, and more than a simple shelf or closet.

ALL PHOTOS BY DINODIA

CULTIVATE NINE SPIRITUAL QUALITIES

ALL PHOTOS BY DINODIA

Parents can consciously and systematically develop key qualities in their children that will help them to be happy, religious and successful when they reach adulthood. A wise mother wrote to me once on e-mail saying, "I truly believe we live out part of our karma through our children, and we grow and improve as they do." Though parents may think they are just helping their children be more happy, successful and religious, in truth parents cannot separate themselves from their children. The child's growth and spiritual evolution is the parents' as well. There are nine key qualities we want our children to possess. We will explore each of these to see what children should be taught, or not taught, by parents to develop that quality. The nine qualities are:

❖ **Positive Self-Concept**
❖ **Perceptive Self-Correction**
❖ **Powerful Self-Control**
❖ **Profound Self-Confidence**
❖ **Playful Self-Contentment**

❖ **Pious Character**
❖ **Proficiency in Conflict Resolution**
❖ **Parental Closeness**
❖ **Prejudice-Free Consciousness**

KIDS LEARN PRIMARILY THROUGH OBSERVATION

YOUR EXAMPLE AS A PARENT IS WHAT THEY LEARN FROM THE MOST

Naturally, as important as having a shrine is worshiping there daily. In the shrine room offer fruit, flowers or food. Visit your shrine when leaving the home, and upon returning. Worship in heartfelt devotion, clearing the inner channels to God and the Gods, so their grace flows toward you and loved ones. Make the shrine a refuge for all family members, where they can find peace and solace, where they can connect with the Gods and offer their praise, prayers and practical needs. Train your children to worship in the shrine before any important event in life, such as a major exam at school, or when faced with a personal challenge or problem. Following this simple, traditional practice in a sacred space within the home will do much to make Hinduism relevant to them on a day-to-day basis.

Worship together in the home shrine each morning.

A popular saying in English is "The family that prays together stays together." In Hinduism, ideally this refers to all members of the family participating in the morning worship in the home shrine before breakfast. The children can be trained to always bring an offering of a flower or at least a leaf. The exact routine followed depends on the family's religious background and lineage. Typical practices include a simple *arati* or a longer puja, singing devotional songs, repeating a mantra, reading scripture and then meditating or performing simple *sadhanas* and yogas. As the children get older, they can take on greater responsibilities during the morning worship. A number of Hindus have told us that what kept them a staunch, practicing Hindu, despite exposure in their youth to other religious traditions, at school and elsewhere, was the fact that the entire family practiced Hinduism together in the home.

I. DEVELOP A POSITIVE SELF-CONCEPT

A positive self-concept arises when we think of ourselves as a worthy individual deserving of a wonderful life. How is this accomplished? It is through being generous with your praise and appreciation, making children know they are loved and valued, that who they are makes a difference and life is full of promise. Unfortunately, many children reach adulthood with a negative self-concept, feeling that others are better than they are and life has little to offer. A negative self-concept is developed through verbally running down a child through teasing, joking or insulting remarks. This, of course, needs to be stopped and replaced with encouragement and praise. When it comes to correcting misbehavior, it is wise to distinguish between the person and the behavior. The behavior was foolish, not the person. For example, you can tell your children when they misbehave, "What you did was very foolish, but you are smart, and I'm sure you now know better and won't do that again." Parents should also not allow their children to call each other names, such as "fat" or "lame." Having a positive concept about one's outer self allows the child to accept the Hindu teaching that one's inner self is a divine being, a radiant soul. My Gurudeva wrote: "Praise your children. Celebrate their Divinity. Enjoy them and enjoy good times with them."

Worship together as a family at a local temple once a week.

Attending a puja at the temple every week allows us to experience the blessings of God and the Gods on a regular basis. This helps keep us pure as well as strong in our religious commitments. The religious vibration of the home shrine is also strengthened by going to the temple regularly. Specifically, some of the religious atmosphere of the temple can be brought home with you if you simply light an oil lamp in your shrine room when you return from the temple. This sacred act brings devas who were at the temple right into the home shrine room, where from the inner world they can bless all family members and strengthen the religious force field of the home.

DINODIA

PART TWO

TEACH ABOUT THE SOUL AND OUR PURPOSE ON EARTH

Teach that life's purpose is spiritual advancement.

The Hindu view of life is that we are a divine being, a soul, who experiences many lives on Earth, and that the purpose of our being here is spiritual unfoldment. Over a period of many lives we gradually become a more spiritual being and are thus able to experience spiritual consciousness more deeply. This eventually leads to a profound experience of God consciousness which brings to a conclusion our pattern of reincarnation on Earth. This is called moksha, liberation. A great lady saint of North India, Anandamayi Ma, stated the goal of God Realization quite beautifully: "Man is a human being only so much as he aspires to Self Realization. This is what human birth is meant for. To realize the One is the supreme duty of every human being."

Teach the four traditional goals of life.

The four traditional Hindu goals of life are duty (dharma), wealth (*artha*), love (kama) and liberation (moksha). The Hindu has the same ambitions as do others. He or she wants to experience love, family and children, as well as a profession, wealth and respect. Dharma enjoins the Hindu to fulfill these ambitions in an honest, virtuous, dutiful way. Although dharma, artha and kama are often seen as ends in themselves, their greatest value is in providing the environment and experiences which help the embodied soul mature over many lives into an ever deepening God consciousness—culminating in moksha, the fourth and final goal: liberation from the cycle of birth, death and rebirth.

2. DEVELOP PERCEPTIVE SELF-CORRECTION

Perceptive self-correction is evident when we are able to quickly learn the lesson from each experience and resolve not to repeat our mistakes. How do parents develop this quality in children? By teaching them that making mistakes is not bad. Everyone makes mistakes. It is natural and simply shows we do not understand something. It is important for the parent to determine what understanding the child lacks and teach it to him without blame. When parents discipline through natural and logical consequences, children are encouraged to learn to reflect on the possible effects of their behavior before acting. Such wisdom can be nurtured through encouraging self-reflection by asking the child to think about what he did and how he could avoid making that mistake again. Perceptive self-correction enables young ones to quickly learn from their inevitable mistakes, refine their still-developing behavior accordingly and thereby make more rapid progress on the spiritual path. Gurudeva observed: "Children are entrusted to their parents to be loved, guided and protected, for they are the future of the future. However, children can be a challenge to raise up into good citizenship. There are many positive ways to guide them, such as hugging, kindness, time spent explaining, giving wise direction and setting the example of what you want them to become."

Teach that, among humans, there are young souls and old souls.

Each soul is emanated from God, as a spark from a fire, and thus begins a spiritual journey which eventually leads it back to God. All human beings are on this journey, whether they realize it or not; and, of course, the journey spans many lives. One might ask, if all are on the same journey, why then is there such a disparity among men? Clearly some act like saints and others act like sin-

ners. Some take delight in helping their fellow man while others delight in harming him. The Hindu explanation is that each of us started the journey at a different time, and thus some are young souls, at the beginning of the spiritual path, while others are old souls, near the end. Our *paramaguru*, Jnanaguru Siva Yogaswami, in speaking to his devotees, described life as a school, with some in the M.A. class and others in kindergarten. Knowing the differences in spiritual maturity, he gave to each accordingly. Hindus do not condemn some men as evil and extol others as good but rather see all as divine beings, some young, some old and some in the intermediary stages. If children are taught this central Hindu principle, they will be able to understand and accept the otherwise confoundingly wide range of differences among people as part of God's cosmic plan of spiritual evolution.

Teach about man's threefold nature.

Man's nature can be described as three-fold: spiritual, intellectual and instinctive. One or more of these aspects predominate uniquely in each of us according to our maturity and evolution. The spiritual nature is the pure, superconscious, intuitive mind of the soul. The intellect is the thinking, reasoning nature. The instinctive aspect of our being is the animal-like nature which governs the physical body and brings forth strong desires and lower emotions such as anger, jealousy and fear. The goal is to learn to control these animal instincts as well as the ramifications of the intellect and the pride of the ego and to manifest one's spiritual nature.

It is the instinctive nature in man that contains the tendencies to harm others, disregard the prudent laws of society and stir up negativity within the home, the nation and beyond. Those who are expressing such tendencies are young souls who have yet to learn why and how to harness the instinctive forces. It may take such a person many lives to rise to a higher consciousness and live in his spiritual nature. Thus the Hindu approach to such a man, which children can be taught from an early age, is not to label him as evil, but rather to focus on restraining his hurtfulness and helping him learn to control these instincts and improve his behavior.

Gurudeva describes this in an insightful way: "People act in evil ways who are not yet in touch with their soul nature and live to-

3. DEVELOP POWERFUL SELF-CONTROL

Powerful self-control is the ability to restrain destructive emotions, such as anger, when we are tempted to express them. How is such control cultivated in children? It is through parents' never expressing such emotions themselves: children learn, by observing their parents, whether it's acceptable to behave emotionally or not. It is by referring often to the ten restraints (*yamas*) of Hinduism's Code of Conduct, finding illustrations of these ideals in daily life, on television and in movies. The *yamas* are noninjury, truthfulness, nonstealing, divine conduct, patience,

steadfastness, compassion, honesty, moderate appetite and purity. Self-control is also cultivated through emphasizing, from an early age, the traditional Hindu imperative to maintain chastity until marriage. Self-control leads to self-mastery, enabling one to be more successful in achieving outer and inner goals. Gurudeva noted: "Children who see their mother and father working out their differences in mature discussion or in the shrine room through prayer and meditation are at that moment given permission to do the same in their own life when they are older. They become the elite of society, the pillars of strength to the community during times of stress and hardship. These children, when older, will surely uphold the principles of dharma and will not succumb to the temptations of the lower mind."

tally in the outer, instinctive mind. What the ignorant see as evil, the enlightened see as the actions of low-minded and immature individuals."

Instill in your children a pride in Hinduism based upon its wise precepts for living.

Since the middle of the twentieth century, Hindu teachings have become more widely understood throughout the world. As a result, cardinal aspects of the Hindu approach to living have been taken up by many thoughtful individuals of diverse religions and ethnicities far beyond India. This is because they find them to be wise and effective ways of living. Hindu precepts that are being universally adopted in the 21st century include:

- ❖ **Following a vegetarian diet**
- ❖ **A reverence toward and desire to protect the environment**
- ❖ **Solving conflicts through nonviolent means**
- ❖ **Tolerance towards others**
- ❖ **Teaching that the whole world is one family**
- ❖ **The belief in karma as a system of divine justice**
- ❖ **The belief in reincarnation**
- ❖ **The practice of yoga and meditation**
- ❖ **Seeking to personally experience Divinity**

Teach your children how the unique wisdom of their born faith, especially in the principles listed above, is being more appreciated and adopted by spiritual seekers than ever before. Swami Chinmayananda, in his first public talk in 1951, made a powerful statement about the effectiveness of Hinduism: "The true Hinduism is a science of perfection. There is, in this true Hinduism, a solution to every individual, social, national and international problem. True Hinduism is the Sanatana Dharma of the *Upanishads*."

Children whose peers do not value Hinduism will take heart in Swami's pride-instilling words.

The traditional Hindu vegetarian diet has many benefits, both personal and planetary.

More and more individuals are switching from the meat-eating diet of their parents to a vegetarian diet as a matter of conscience based upon their personal realization of the suffering that animals undergo when they are fettered and slaughtered. This is, of course, also the Hindu rationale for a vegetarian diet. It is based on the virtue of ahimsa: refraining from injuring, physically mentally or emotionally, anyone or any living creature. The Hindu who wishes to strictly follow the path of noninjury naturally adopts a vegetarian diet. A common saying that conveys this principle to even the smallest child is, "I won't eat anything that has eyes, unless it's a potato."

A second rationale for vegetarianism has to do with our state of consciousness. When we eat meat, fish, fowl and eggs, we absorb the vibration of these instinctive creatures into our nerve system. This chemically alters our consciousness and amplifies our own instinctive nature, which is the part of us prone to fear, anger, jealousy, confusion, resentment and the like. Therefore, being vegetarian is a great help in attaining and maintaining a spiritual state of consciousness, and some individuals take up vegetarianism for this reason alone.

A third rationale for vegetarianism is that it uses the planet's natural resources in a much wiser way. In large measure, the escalating loss of species, destruction of ancient rain forests to create pasture lands for livestock, loss of topsoil and the consequent increase of water impurities and air pollution have all been traced to the single fact of meat in the human diet. No one decision that we can make as individuals or as a race can have such a dramatic

DINODIA

4. DEVELOP A PROFOUND SELF-CONFIDENCE

Profound self-confidence is exemplified when a child is confronted with a difficult task and his first response is the certainty that he can accomplish it. Unfortunately, many children reach adulthood lacking self-confidence and have as their first response the feeling that they will be unable to accomplish the task, as it is too difficult. How is profound self-confidence cultivated? Firstly, through being sure the child possesses a positive self-concept. Secondly, through helping the child be repetitively successful at progressively more difficult tasks as he or she grows up. A pattern of many successes going into our subconscious mind is what produces the sense of self-confidence and the feeling that we will be equal to any task. For example, a father teaches his son carpentry from age ten through eighteen. Each year the father helps the son make something that is more complex, never giving him a project that is too advanced, praising each achievement. Self-confidence is cultivated by watching for failures at school or at home and compensating for them. If the child is shy and has trouble at school with public speaking, work personally or through a tutor to overcome that shyness so he or she can speak comfortably before groups of people in any situation. Self-confidence makes developing youth magnetic to success in both outer and inner endeavors.

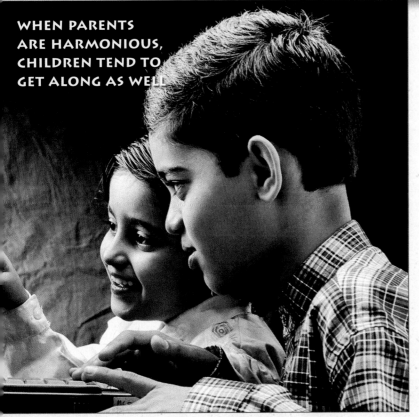

WHEN PARENTS ARE HARMONIOUS, CHILDREN TEND TO GET ALONG AS WELL

for man to kill or harm animals for food or sport. They believe that animals have a right to enjoy living on this planet as much as humans do. There is a Vedic verse in this regard that says: "Ahimsa is not causing pain to any living being at any time through the actions of one's mind, speech or body." Another Vedic verse states, "You must not use your God-given body for killing God's creatures, whether they are human, animal or whatever."

Hindus regard all living creatures as sacred—mammals, fishes, birds and more. They are stewards of trees and plants, fish and birds, bees and reptiles, animals and creatures of every shape and kind. We acknowledge this reverence for life in our special affection for the cow. Mahatma Gandhi once said about the cow, "One can measure the greatness of a nation and its moral progress by the way it treats its animals. Cow protection to me is not mere protection of the cow. It means protection of all that lives and is helpless and weak in the world. The cow means the entire subhuman world."

Many individuals are concerned about our environment and properly preserving it for future generations. Hindus share this concern and honor and revere the world around them as God's creation. They work for the protection of the Earth's diversity and resources to achieve the goal of a secure, sustainable and lasting environment. Children today, as never before, have a native understanding of the place of mankind as part of

effect on the improvement of our planetary ecology as the decision to not eat meat. Many seeking to save the planet for future generations have become vegetarians for this reason.

By teaching the value of a vegetarian diet to our youth, we protect their health, lengthen their lives, elevate their consciousness and preserve the Earth that is their home.

Hindus hold a deep reverence toward planet Earth and toward all living beings that dwell on it.

Many thoughtful people share the Hindu view that it is not right

the Earth, and it is our duty to reinforce this in their young minds.

Hinduism is respected for solving conflicts through nonviolent means.

Mahatma Gandhi's strong belief in the Hindu principle of ahimsa and his nonviolent methods for opposing British rule are well known throughout the world. The nonviolent approach has consciously been used by others as well. Certainly one of the best-known exponents of nonviolence was Dr. Martin Luther King Jr.. Dr. King, after decades of careful thought on the problem of racial

5. DEVELOP A PLAYFUL SELF-CONTENTMENT

Playful self-contentment is expressed when a child's usual mood is fun-loving, happy and satisfied. How is this developed? It is through the parents' living and verbalizing the philosophy that life is meant to be lived joyously. It is by holding the perspective that happiness does not depend on external circumstances but is a consciousness we can claim, whether life is free of or filled with challenges. It is by teaching the children to be satisfied with what they have in the present rather than dissatisfied about what

they don't have. It is nurtured by the family spending time together filled with play and laughter. The ability to remain playful, joyful, secure and content enables one to face with far greater equanimity the ups and downs of life. Gurudeva described the contentment, *santosha*, that we should teach children: "True *santosha* is seeing all-pervasiveness of the one divine power everywhere. The light within the eyes of each person is that divine power. With this in mind, you can go anywhere and do anything. Contentment is there, inside you, and needs to be brought out. It is a spiritual power. So, yes, do what makes you content. But know that contentment really transcends worrying about the challenges that face you. *Santosha* is being peaceful in any situation. The stronger you are in *santosha*, the greater the challenges you can face."

discrimination in the United States, selected the Hindu principle of ahimsa, as exemplified by Mahatma Gandhi's tactic of nonviolent resistance, as the most effective method for overcoming the unjust laws that existed in America at the time. In 1959 Dr. King even spent five weeks in India personally discussing with Gandhi's followers the philosophy and techniques of nonviolence to deepen his understanding of them before putting them into actual use.

Children learn conflict resolution at an early age, establishing patterns that will serve them throughout life. Some learn that fists, force and angry words are the way to work things out. Others are taught that diplomacy and kindly speech serve the same purpose more effectively and yield longer-lasting results. Children pick up these things largely through example in the home, by witnessing how mom and dad work out their differences.

Hinduism has great tolerance and considers the whole world to be a family.

In the world of the twenty-first century, a prime concern is the many wars and clashes between peoples of different religions, nationalities and ethnicities based on hatred on one or both sides. The opposite of hatred is tolerance, and in that Hinduism excels. The Hindu belief that gives rise to tolerance of differences in race and nationality is that all of mankind is good, we are all divine beings, souls created by God. Therefore, we respect and embrace the entire human race. The Hindu practice of greeting one another with "namaskara," worshiping God within the other person, is a way this philosophical truth is practiced on a daily basis.

Hindus do not believe that some individuals will be saved and others damned, nor in a chosen people, nor in a starkly divided world of good and evil filled only with the faithful and the infidels. Hinduism respects and defends the rights of humans of every caste, creed, color and sex, and it asks that those same rights be accorded its billion followers. Hindus think globally and act locally as interracial, international citizens of the Earth. They honor and value all human cultures, faiths, languages and peoples, never offending one to promote another.

This is taken one step further in the ancient verse "The whole world is one family." Everyone is family oriented. All our efforts are

CHILDREN NEED TO BE VALUED
AS PART OF THE FAMILY TEAM

DINODIA

6. DEVELOP A PIOUS CHARACTER

Pious character is evident when we naturally treat others with kindness, generosity and appreciation. It is fulfilled when we seek the blessings of God, Gods and guru throughout life. How can this be cultivated in children? It is through the parents' demonstrating these qualities themselves: children learn that this behavior is expected of them by observing their parents' actions. It is by referring often to the ten observances (*niyamas*) of Hinduism's Code of Conduct and pointing out their relevance in daily life, on TV and in movies.

The *niyamas* are remorse, contentment, giving, faith, worship of the Lord, scriptural listening, cognition, sacred vows, recitation and austerity. Pious character is nurtured by teaching the child to worship and pray in the home shrine or at the temple before important events, such as beginning a new school year or before final examinations. Pious conduct brings into our children's lives the joys of divine blessings. Gurudeva outlined the ideal: "Hindu children are always treated with great respect and awe, for one does not always know who they are. They may be incarnations of a grandmother, grandfather, aunt or uncle, dearly beloved mother, sister, brother, respected father, a yogi or rishi returned to flesh to help mankind spiritually. We must ask, 'Who are these souls? What is their destiny in this life? How can I help?' "

focused on benefiting the members of our family. We want them all to be happy, successful and religiously fulfilled. And when we define family as the whole world, it is clear that we wish everyone in the world happiness, success and religious fulfillment. The Vedic verse that captures this sentiment is "May all people be happy." By teaching our children this broad acceptance of peoples, even those who are very different from ourselves, we nurture in them a love for all and a compassionate tolerance that will serve them well throughout their lives.

Many people throughout the world firmly believe in karma and reincarnation.

In the second half of the twentieth century Hindu concepts became more and more popular and influential in the West. For example, every year thousands of Westerners take up the belief in karma and reincarnation as a logical explanation of what they observe in life. A contemporary expression of the law of karma is "What goes around comes around." Karma is the universal principle of cause and effect. Our actions, both good and bad, come back to us in the future, helping us to learn from life's lessons and become better people. Reincarnation is the belief that the soul is immortal and takes birth time and time again. Through this process, we have experiences, learn lessons and evolve spiritually. Finally, we graduate from physical birth and continue learning and evolving on inner planes of consciousness without the need for a physical body until, ultimately, we merge in God. The belief in karma and reincarnation gives children a logical explanation to what otherwise may seem an unjust, indifferent or Godless world. They can be taught that challenging questions such as the following all have logical explanations when viewed through the beliefs of karma and reincarnation.

❖ **Why do some innocent children die so young?**
❖ **Why are some people so much more talented than others?**
❖ **Why do some people act in evil ways?**
❖ **Why is it that a mean-spirited person may succeed and a good-hearted person fail?**

Belief in a single life makes it hard to reconcile such things, causing one to question how a just, benevolent God could allow them to happen. But an understanding of karma as God's divine law which transcends this one incarnation and brings to bear our actions from many past lives on Earth offers profound insight. That innocent child may have been a child murderer. That musical genius may have so perfected his art in a past life that he inherits a rare talent at birth and becomes a child prodigy.

The beliefs of karma and reincarnation give a spiritual purpose to our life. We know that the reason we are here on Earth is to mature spiritually and that this process extends over many lives. We know that karma is our teacher in this process, teaching us both what to do and what not to do through the reactions it brings back to us in the future. So, our current incarnation—the nature of our body, family, inclinations, talents, strengths and weaknesses—is specifically designed by us to help us face the fruits of our past actions, both positive and negative, and thus learn and evolve spiritually.

Hinduism boldly proclaims that man can experience God.

Throughout the world today, many who are on the mystical path want to have a personal spiritual experience. They want to see God. Hinduism not only gives them the hope that they can achieve their goal in this lifetime, but it gives them the practical tools, such as the disciplines of yoga and meditation, through which this goal eventually becomes a reality.

The focus of many religions is on helping those who do not believe in God to believe in God. Belief in God, in such faiths, is the beginning and the end of the process. Once you believe in God there is nothing more to do. However, in Hinduism belief is only the first step. Hindus want to move beyond believing in God to experiencing God. To the Hindu, belief is but a preparatory step to divine, daily communion and life-transforming personal realization.

There is a classic story from the life of Swami Vivekananda, one of Hinduism's best-known modern teachers, that illustrates the Hindu perspective of experiencing God. When Vivekananda was still a university student, he asked many of the foremost religious leaders in the Calcutta area where he lived if they had seen God. However, he never got a clear and authoritative answer from any

7. DEVELOP PROFICIENCY IN CONFLICT RESOLUTION

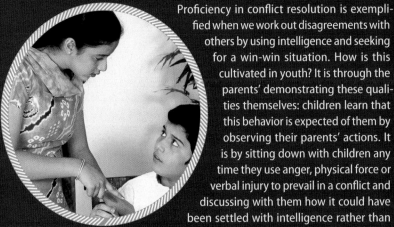

Proficiency in conflict resolution is exemplified when we work out disagreements with others by using intelligence and seeking for a win-win situation. How is this cultivated in youth? It is through the parents' demonstrating these qualities themselves: children learn that this behavior is expected of them by observing their parents' actions. It is by sitting down with children any time they use anger, physical force or verbal injury to prevail in a conflict and discussing with them how it could have been settled with intelligence rather than violence. It is through replacing the idea of "I want me to win and you to lose" with that of "I win when everybody wins." Kids can learn from parents that it is through taking a humble attitude, rather than a dominant position, that conflicts are resolved smoothly and easily. Illustrations of what to do and what not to do can be drawn from the people they see in television and movies. Proficiency in conflict resolution is nurtured by parents' following the wisdom of resolving their husband-and-wife disagreements before going to sleep, as this teaches by example the importance of facing and solving a conflict rather than fleeing from it. Mastery of resolving differences keeps our young one's lives sublime and their subconscious minds free of the disturbances caused by memories of unresolved disagreements.

one of them until he met Sri Ramakrishna. During his second meeting with Sri Ramakrishna he asked the great sage, "Sir, have you seen God?" Calmly Sri Ramakrishna replied, "Yes, I see Him as clearly as one sees an apple in the palm of the hand; nay, even more intently. And not only this, you can also see Him." This deeply impressed the young Vivekananda, who soon after accepted Sri Ramakrishna as his guru.

By teaching children about Hinduism's stress on personal Godly experience, we set them on a path of self-understanding, self-perfection and discovery of the Divine that does not rely on the beliefs or reports of others. This gives them an appreciation of each step in life—be it pleasant or unpleasant—as an integral part of a joyous spiritual journey.

PART FOUR
TEACH ABOUT HINDUISM AND THE OTHER WORLD RELIGIONS

Teach about the Vedic statement "Truth is One, sages describe it variously."

Hinduism is often misunderstood as being polytheistic, worshiping many Gods, none of which is supreme. It is important to correct this misconception in the minds of children. They can be taught that Hindus revere the great beings of light, called Mahadevas, just as the Catholics honor the Archangels of Heaven. But Hindus all worship the one Supreme Being, known in the various denominations by different names. Even more than that, Hindus believe that the immanent-transcendent Lord they worship is indeed the same God worshiped by all peoples of all faiths and religions of the world. As a country only has one king, we can school the young ones, so the universe has only one Supreme Being. The oneness of God is easily understood when we see that the different religions use various names to describe the same Truth. Teaching this to our young ones resolves many misconceptions, both within Hinduism itself and between Hinduism and the varied faiths of the world.

TAKING TIME TO TEACH AND SHARE BUILDS CLOSENESS AND TRUST

DINODIA

Teach the correct meaning of the Vedic statement "Truth is One, paths are many."

Some Hindus teach their children that all religions are one, thinking this is a way to describe Sanatana Dharma's broad vision. However, this is a problematic distortion of the Hindu belief that truth is one, paths are many. Teaching this to children will cause them to be half-hearted Hindus, never fully committed to their faith and not inspired to pass it on to their offspring. I have seen this attitude

8. DEVELOP PARENTAL CLOSENESS

Parental closeness finds fulfillment when children reach adulthood and choose to spend time with their parents because they really enjoy being with them. A strong bond of love and understanding exists. Sadly, the opposite is often the case. How then is parental closeness developed? It is through expressing love by hugging and saying often the three magic words "I love you." Distance is developed by never expressing love. Closeness is nurtured by correcting a child's misbehavior with positive discipline methods, such as time-out and appropriate, natural and logical consequences. The use of physical violence, anger, irrational punishments, blame and shame cause distance. Closeness comes when quality time is spent together in activities that all members of the family enjoy. It is developed by the father's binding with his sons and the mother's binding with her daughters, through developing common interests in hobbies or games and working on them together. It is protected when parents create in the home a nonthreatening atmosphere of love in which their children feel free to tell them everything they have done without fear of the consequences. They know their parents love them, no matter what. A loving parental closeness is powerfully reflected in all subsequent relationships children develop, even their relationship with God.

create indifferent Hindus who passively attend their non-Hindu spouse's church, presumably thinking it doesn't really matter, and who think it is best to raise their children "in both religions."

The correct teaching is that Hindus believe that all religions worship the same truth, the same Supreme Being. However, this does not mean that all religions are identical and it doesn't matter which religion you follow. The beliefs and practices of the world religions are, in fact, quite different. The God they worship is one, but each of the many paths is quite distinct. This knowledge will help children see the world's array of faiths in a realistic light while pursuing their Hindu path with full dedication.

Hindus believe that all of the major world religions are valid paths and everyone is well placed in their chosen faith.

Hindus do not proselytize, meaning they do not try to convert members of other religions to Hinduism. Proselytizing is based upon the belief that one's religion is the only true religion and therefore everyone in another religion should join it. Hindus hold the opposite point of view, which is that all faiths are good and the members of those religions are just fine remaining in the religions they are in. Each religion has its unique beliefs, practices, goals and paths of attainment, and the doctrines of one often conflict with those of another. Even this should never be cause for religious tension or intolerance. Hindus respect all religious traditions and the people within them. They know that good citizens and stable societies are created from groups of religious people in all nations.

However, it is important to teach children that while Hindus do not proselytize, Hinduism does, and always has, accepted new members into the religion who seek to participate at its deepest levels. It is simply not true, as uninformed commentators too often say, that you have to be born a Hindu to be a Hindu. When asked by a devotee about this idea, Swami Vivekananda responded, "Why, born aliens have been converted in the past by crowds, and the process is still going on."

Hindus who marry a non-Hindu spouse who is interested in the Sanatana Dharma wisely encourage him or her to study and eventually enter the faith so they can together raise their children as devout Hindus, rather than being torn between two faiths.

PART FIVE
TEACH HOW HINDUISM GRANTS EXPERIENCE OF GOD

Hinduism has advanced practices within it that many religions do not have.

If you simply want to live a virtuous, pious life and be part of a community of fellow believers, you will discover that all religions are similar at that basic level. But if you have the desire to personally experience God, you will only find the advanced practices that lead to that divine experience in a few religions. A good example of this fact has been occurring in Catholic monasteries for decades. Some of the monks in these monasteries have the desire to personally experience God. What do they do to pursue this? They turn to Hindu scriptures, such as Patanjali's *Yoga Aphorisms,* for guidelines in deep meditation and inner spiritual attainments, as there are no such teachings in Christianity. More than that, such teachings are regarded by the Catholic Church as heretical, and the Vatican has directed monks and nuns to cease all yoga practices and return to the path of prayer. Applying a modern analogy, one could say that all religions are computers designed to answer our questions about life and God. However, some religions are per-

9. DEVELOP A PREJUDICE-FREE CONSCIOUSNESS

Prejudice-free consciousness manifests when we see God in everyone and embrace differences of ethnic background and religion. Are we born with prejudices? Absolutely not! These are all learned, at home, at school and elsewhere. How is a prejudice-free consciousness developed? It is through teaching our children that the whole world is our family and all human beings are divine beings. It is through complete avoidance of remarks that are racially or religiously prejudiced. It is through discussing with our children any prejudice they hear from others at school and elsewhere and correcting it. It is by teaching children to avoid generalizations about people and, instead, to think about specific individuals and the qualities they have. Television and movies can provide useful situations to discuss. It is through having our children meet, interact and learn to feel comfortable with children of other ethnicities and religions. Tolerant individuals help communities function with less friction and misunderstanding. Gurudeva teaches us: "Every belief creates certain attitudes. Our attitudes govern all of our actions. Belief in karma, reincarnation and the existence of an all-pervasive Divinity throughout the universe creates an attitude of reverence, benevolence and compassion for all beings. The natural consequence of this belief is ahimsa, nonhurtfulness."

sonal computers, some are minicomputers, others are mainframe computers, but Hinduism is a supercomputer.

Belief in God is only the first step in Hinduism. Beyond that, it offers four ways to personally experience God. The first two ways involve seeing the Divine in other people.

In some religions the ultimate experience offered is to have a strong belief in the existence of God. In Hinduism, however, believing in God is only a preliminary, though important, step toward an ever deepening personal experience of God's presence. Perhaps the easiest place to start is to see God in great religious teachers. We feel a spiritual aura about them that is different, uplifting and inspiring. We see a light in their eyes and feel a love in their presence we do not find in others.

The second way to see God is to look deeply into the eyes of another person. Look beyond his or her personality, deeper than the intellect, and see the individual's pure life energy as God. In Hindu culture we have an opportunity every time we greet other people through the traditional gesture of *namaskara* to practice looking deeply enough into their eyes to see God within them as the Life of their life. This practice is an excellent way for children to learn that all people are divine beings.

The third and fourth ways we can experience God are through temple worship and meditation.

The third way to see God is through the Deity's image in the Hindu temple. This is the devotional, or theistic, approach. Gods and devas are in the inner, spiritual worlds and are able to bless us through the image in the temple. The image is like a temporary physical body they use during temple ceremonies. Though occasionally a devotee may have a vision of the God, the more common way we experience the Gods and devas is as an uplifting, peaceful, divine energy, or shakti, that radiates out from the image. It is easiest to feel their blessings at the high point of the puja when the flame is held high. If taught the joys of temple worship while toddlers, children will develop a devotional relationship with the

Deities which will strengthen and guide them throughout life.

The fourth way to see God is in meditation, which is a form of internal worship. This is the monistic, or unitive, approach to experiencing God—going deeply enough into our inner consciousness to find the essence of our soul, which is identical with God. In meditation we first experience God as peaceful, blissful energies and feelings, later as a brilliant, clear white light and later still as truth, consciousness and bliss, called Satchidananda, which permeates all of existence. Ultimately, under a *satguru's* careful guidance, we realize God as the absolute and transcendent reality that is timeless, formless and spaceless. In Hinduism, this is regarded as the summit of all knowing, the highest spiritual attainment which leads to moksha, spiritual liberation.

Children can be taught the basics of meditation at an early age, including sitting up straight, regulating the breath and performing hatha yoga to quiet the mental and physical energies. These practices will help them remain centered, and they will mature naturally into deeper inner experiences as they grow up.

Hinduism focuses on personal, spiritual transformation through the regular practice of disciplines, called *sadhana*.

Reading spiritual books is certainly part of progressing on the Hindu path. However, much more important is the regular practice of religious disciplines. Our emotional, intellectual and spiritual natures are all significantly enhanced and developed through performing such disciplines regularly over a period of many years. The more consistently we practice, the greater the speed of our progress. Establishing good patterns of spiritual practice, called *sadhana*, begins in childhood, in the home. The most successful pattern in the home is for parents to have their young children join them in their morning devotionals and, as they mature, invite them to also participate in the meditations.

Hinduism's spiritual practices fall into four categories.

It is fair to say that no other religion contains such a vast wealth of spiritual practices, from such fundamental virtues as noninjury,

CHARACTER BUILDING, PART TWO
GUIDE CHILDREN WITH LOVE, NOT FEAR

Children make mistakes not because they are bad, but because they lack knowledge or training.

For all of mankind, no matter where one is on the path, spiritual advancement comes from improving one's behavior. We do this by learning from our failures as much as from our successes. Unfortunately, this process is often inhibited by the idea that somehow we are not supposed to err. We grow up being scolded for our mistakes by our parents. Some teachers ridicule and beat students when they make mistakes. Supervisors yell at workers when they make a mistake. No wonder many adults feel terrible when they make a mistake. Therefore, to spiritually benefit from our mistakes, we need a new attitude toward them which opens the door for insight, which leads to improvement. We can view them instead as wonderful opportunities to learn. In disciplining our children, it is important to focus on finding out what lack of knowledge or necessary train-

TAKE TIME FOR CELEBRATION & APPRECIATION

DINODIA

truthfulness and honesty to the advanced yoga practices of breath control and meditation. Hinduism's array of spiritual practices can be divided into four categories: good conduct, service, devotion and meditation.

❖ **Cultivating good conduct is the foundational practice.**

Cultivating good conduct, or developing good character, is the foundation of all other practices in Hinduism. Good conduct begins with overcoming basic instinctive patterns, such as the tendencies to become angry and hurtful. The ten classical restraints, called *yamas*, help us overcome such tendencies. These restraints are: noninjury, truthfulness, nonstealing, divine conduct, patience, steadfastness, compassion, honesty, moderate appetite and purity. Following the *yamas* naturally leads into ten religious observances, called the *niyamas*: remorse, contentment, giving, faith, worship of the Lord, scriptural listening, cognition, sacred vows, recitation and austerity. By simply memorizing these twenty ideals, a child learns much about what is expected by his faith. Good conduct includes performing one's duty to family and community, honoring holy men, respecting elders and atoning for misdeeds.

❖ **Service is the second category.**

Service, also called karma yoga or *seva*, refers to religious service given without the least thought of reward, which has the magical effect of softening the ego and bringing forth the soul's innate devotion. An example of service is performing simple chores at the temple, such as sweeping the floors or polishing the brass. Another form of *seva* is holding religious feedings at a temple once a month. Children love to be helpful and can be encouraged to find religious expressions of this urge.

ing caused their misbehavior and then providing them with the needed guidance. This process can be understood in the light of desire, action and wisdom. We desire that our children behave well, but if our actions in correcting them create fear, resentment or feelings of inferiority, then they will not improve and we will have subverted our goal. By treating a child's errant behavior as described above, we discover our own wisdom in handling kids, and we help them grow to a healthy maturity, equipped to guide their own children with love and wisdom.

Focus on solutions instead of punishment.

For some parents, disciplining their children for misbehavior is simply a matter of punishment. But *discipline* means "to teach," so punishment misses the point if it is not accompanied by taking a moment to gently teach and kindly help the child, to encourage, uplift and inspire. In many cases the child who erred simply does not know or understand something. Otherwise he never would have made the mistake. There is some knowledge the child is missing, and thoughtful parents need to figure out what that knowledge is and teach it to the child in a way

he or she can grasp and remember. This is a far more time-consuming process than a swift slap on the behind, but leads to far more permanent and positive results.

There are better forms of discipline than corporal punishment and verbal abuse.

When children seriously misbehave, punishment, of course, needs to be part of the response. There are many forms of corporal or physical punishment and verbal abuse: spanking, hitting, pinching, using harsh or angry words. These all cause the child to become resentful and fearful, and in this state of mind he is unable and unwilling to focus on the lesson the parent intends to provide. Such punishments inevitably create a distance between parent and child and lower the child's sense of self-worth. On the other hand, the alternative forms of punishment—loving, positive strategies, such as time-out, logical consequences and denial of privileges—are more effective and conducive to the child's learning the lesson from the experience, cooperating with the parents in a wholesome way and not repeating the behavior again.

❖ Devotion is the third category.

Devotion, or bhakti yoga, centers around regularly worshiping the Deity at the temple and inwardly striving to awaken a profound love of God in our hearts, soften our intellect and develop a deep sense of humility. It includes devotional singing, pilgrimage and performing our own puja in the home shrine room. For children, this can be as simple as bringing a flower to the shrine each morning before school. Kids love the Gods, especially Lord Ganesha, and they can, even as toddlers, be taught to hold hands in *namaskara*, prostrate at the shrine and learn songs and chants in praise of their favorite Deity.

❖ Meditation is the fourth category.

Meditation is also called raja yoga, or ashtanga yoga as it consists of eight limbs. The practice of meditation begins with asana—sitting quietly in yogic posture—and pranayama, breath control. *Pratyahara*, sense withdrawal, brings awareness into *dharana*, concentration, then into dhyana, meditation. Dhyana finally leads to samadhi, God Realization. *Jnana* yoga is also a type of meditation that involves philosophical study and discrimination between the Real and the unreal. Children can follow the first phases of meditation for short periods, learning to sit in lotus posture, to breathe diaphragmatically and to quiet their mind and emotions through attention and concentration. When they are more mature, you can take them to a swami or yoga teacher to learn the deeper aspects.

PART SIX
TEACH CHILDREN HOW TO LIVE POSITIVELY IN THE WORLD.

Train children that the world is a positive place filled with opportunities for growth.

The world in this sense refers to the arena of life, including where we interact with people the most, such as the home, school and our place of work. In Western thought these are not considered spiritual places. However, in Hinduism they are. There is no sharp distinction between the sacred and the secular. In the words of our *paramaguru*, Siva Yogaswami, "The world is an ashram—a training ground for the achievement of moksha."

What is it that transforms the world from a secular place into a spiritual one? It is the understanding that it is through the process of experiencing life that we unfold spiritually. It is the knowing that through fulfilling our natural duties, honestly and to the best of our ability, we make spiritual progress. Why? Through interacting with others, we learn important lessons and, as a result, gradually deepen our understanding, improve our behavior and become more spiritual. In the process, we work through karmas we created in the past and create new karmas to be faced in the future. Our daily activities, encounters and emotional reactions contribute to our spiritual progress just as much as attending pujas in the temple, studying the holy texts, meditating and worshiping in our home shrine. Paramaguru Yogaswami captured the essence of this perspective when he said, "All work must be done with the aim of reaching God."

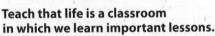

DINODIA

Teach that life is a classroom in which we learn important lessons.

Life is a process of learning through trial and error and thereby advancing spiritually. Gurudeva has an insightful explanation of this process: "Life is a series of experiences, one after another. Each experience can be looked at as a classroom in the big university of life if we only approach it that way. Who is going to these classrooms? Who is the member of this university of life? It's not

Teach children how they can wisely respond to their mistakes through a four-step process.

The most common first reaction to making a mistake is to become upset, get emotional about it or, if it is a serious mistake, to feel terribly burdened and even depressed. That is a natural first reaction, but if it is our only reaction, it is not enough. We need to cope with the emotional reaction to the action and move on to the second step, which is the learning stage.

A good second step to resolving a mistake is to think clearly about what happened and why, and find a way to not repeat the same error in the future. Perhaps we were not being careful enough, and resolving to be more careful next time will prevent the problem from recurring. Perhaps we were simply uninformed or we didn't think things through. But with the additional knowledge learned from our blunder we can resolve to do better the next time a similar situation arises. Perhaps we created unintended negative consequences for ourselves or others. Now that we are aware of those consequences, we certainly won't follow that path again. Recently a group of chil-

ENJOYING MUSIC AS A FAMILY BRINGS DEVOTION INTO DAILY LIFE.

Teach about the three great powers: desire, action and wisdom.

Important insights into the soul's maturing process can be gained by looking at the three *shaktis* of God—*iccha*, the power of desire, *kriya*, the power of action and *jnana*, the power of wisdom—which are also the three powers of the soul. We first have a desire, and when the desire becomes strong enough we act. In young souls the action may be ill-conceived and wrongful, or adharmic, lacking in wisdom. For example, we want a computer, so we simply steal one. We need money, so we borrow with no intention to repay. The soul is repeating a cycle of similar experiences, moving back and forth from desire to action, desire to action.

In the case of the adharmic action of stealing, eventually the soul will learn the lesson that theft is not the best way to get what we need or want. This may come from the difficult experience of being caught, or by seeing the suffering our actions cause in others. Such learning is the *jnana shakti*, soulful wisdom, coming forth and causing one's behavior to improve. This process works for virtuous, or dharmic, actions as well. For example, we volunteer at the temple to teach children's classes once a month. We are uplifted by the feeling that helping others gives us and decide to help out every week and even participate in meetings to plan out the classes. Selfless action and the reaction it has on us brings an inner joy. Therefore, *jnana* guides us to decide to undertake even more service and thus feel more joyful. We have again improved our behavior. If children are taught about these three basic forces at work in their life, they will seek to understand desire, think about action and strive for wisdom.

your instinctive mind. It's not your intellectual mind. It's the body of your soul, your superconscious self, that wonderful body of light. It's maturing under the stress and strain."

Children live much of their day learning, often in a classroom, so the idea that all of life is a school for our soul will come easily to them, and it will teach them to value lessons wherever they come from.

dren in Australia started a fire in a small forest where several innocent people were seriously burned. The children were caught, and as part of their discipline the judge directed them to visit the victims in the hospital to see the consequences of their actions. This impressed them deeply. By evaluating such situations and committing to a new approach, we are able to teach young ones to move from regretting "I shouldn't have done it" to pledging "I won't do it again."

A third step may be needed if our mistake directly involved other people. Perhaps we have hurt their feelings or created a strain between us. A personal apology can fix this if we know them well. However, in many situations we are not close enough to the individual to verbally apologize. In that case, a generous act can adjust the flow of feelings back into a harmonious condition. For example, children can be taught to include those they have hurt or offended among a group of friends invited to a party or with whom they share some cookies or candy.

A fourth step may be needed if the mistake is a major misdeed, for example, if we did something that was dishonest. In this case, even if we resolve to not repeat the misdeed and apologize to those involved,

we may still feel bad about having done it. In this case we need to perform some form of penance, *prayashchitta*, to rid ourself of the sense of feeling bad about our actions. Typical forms of penance for adults are fasting, performing 108 prostrations before the Deity or walking prostrations up a sacred path or around a temple. These are too severe for younger children, but they can do simpler penances such as skipping dessert one meal or renouncing a favorite TV program one night.

Help your children perfect the art of learning quickly from mistakes.

The spiritual path is a series of experiences, and sometimes those experiences are mistakes that we make. If we teach our children to be self-reflective, they can learn from their mistakes quickly, avoid making them again and progress more quickly on the spiritual path. If children are constantly making the same mistakes over and over and over again, they are not making good progress. This is something for parents to be alert to, for it is parents who can set the patterns for resolution of karmas in their kid's lives.

CHAPTER 38

Cultural Cues & Clues

Keys to Hindu Protocol for Novice Pilgrims to the Holy Lands

NEARLY EVERY INDIGENOUS PEOPLE on Earth is reevaluating, rediscovering and reappreciating its ancient ways, the traditions of the forefathers. Tradition is the best of the past that has been carried forward for the future. Among Hindus, too—a people of many nationalities comprising one sixth of the human race—the old, refined culture of simple, wholesome living is being recognized as a way of wisdom. As the age of information gathers speed at the dawn of the millenium, efforts are being made in every community to preserve and pass this knowledge on to future generations. This movement rides on a new pride, a renaissance of inspiration, a recuperation from centuries of British domination of India in which Hindu dignity was systematically undermined through the Macaulay education system. Today, as well, there is a burgeoning interest among Westerners to understand and adopt Hindu ways. Those seeking to fully live the Hindu culture who have been raised in non-Hindu environments face many challenges. Hindu culture is

COURTESY V&A MUSEUM, LONDON

the pristine embodiment of a profound philosophy. It is an Eastern culture that gives freedom within the bounds of duty to elders, spouse and children. Western culture gives freedom to the individual, irrespective of the hurts he may inflict on others. The sense of duty is the foundation of Hindu culture, and in performing duty one finds freedom within oneself through *yoga*. Culture arises out of the attitudes, which are the outgrowth of the belief structure, of an individual or collective group. To be cultured means to exemplify the highest qualities of one's society, religion or philosophy. There are countless ways the Hindu attitudes of compassion, respect and self-effacement are expressed. The keys below were developed by travelers to India who learned the hard way how to get along in a different culture. We summarize their cues and clues as a simple guide for novices and to assist Western seekers pilgrimaging in the holy lands to fit in as smoothly and unobtrusively as possible.

PAINTINGS BY A. MANIVEL

Respect

Hindu culture is an expression of love, respect, honoring others and humbling one's own ego so that the inner nature, which is naturally pure and modest, will shine forth. This is exemplified in the Hindu greeting in which we honor the Divinity within each person, knowing that God is everywhere and in all things. By this and other acts of reverence, such as the following, Sanatana Dharma's truths are brought to the forefront of the mind many times each day.

Respect for Elders: Respect for elders is a keystone of Hindu culture. This acknowledgment of seniority is demonstrated through endearing customs such as: sitting to the left of elders, bringing gifts on special occasions, not sitting while they are standing, not speaking excessively, not yawning or stretching, not putting one's opinions forward strongly, not contradicting or arguing, seeking their advice and blessings, giving them first choice of seats, inviting them to take their food first or serving them first.

Honoring Parents: Cultured Hindus serve their parents and close relatives all through life, honoring them through obedience and affection, and by providing support and comfort during old age.

Name Protocol: Youngers never use the proper name of their elders. A Tamil younger brother, for example, refers to his elder brother as *annai* (brother), or *periannai* (elder brother). The elder may use the name of the younger. Children refer to adults as auntie or uncle. Adults refer to each other as elder or younger brother or simply brother (likewise for women). Only men the same age occasionally use the first name. A Hindu wife speaking of her husband, rather than using his given name, uses terms such as "my husband," "him" or, for example, "Jothi's father." When addressing yogis, swamis or *sadhakas,* one uses the title, not personal pronouns nor the name alone). For example, one would not ask, "What do you want?" Instead, one would inquire, "What does swami want?"

Touching Feet: One touches the feet of holy persons in recognition of their Divinity and attainment. A dancer touches the teacher's feet before lessons. Children prostrate on the floor and touch the feet of their mother and father at special times, such as New Year's day, birthdays and before parting for a journey.

Hosting Guests in the Home

Hindu tradition lays great stress on the respect due to guests. All guests are God, Who comes in many forms. The greatest hurt is the thought that the host or hostess does not enjoy one's presence in their home. Therefore, Hindus go out of their way to make each guest feel welcome. It is proper protocol to drop whatever one is doing, no matter how important, to entertain a visitor. One of the privileges of friendship in the East is being able to drop by any time without advance notice. Visitors may also leave in the same casual way, saying "I'll be going now," without necessarily even saying goodbye.

Refreshments: It is customary to always offer your visitor something to eat and drink. Usually tea is served, but at least a glass of water should be offered (with a smile and apology). Likewise it is an insult for the guest to refuse food or beverages, or to not even sip a glass of water, even when time is short.

Hosting: Children generally leave the room, with a smile, when guests enter. The mother remains close by to serve as needs arise. The father, if present, will speak with the guest. If not present, the mother and a son will fulfill this role, and if no son is present, the mother may act as hostess, but only with the accompaniment of someone close to the family.

Wife Home Alone: If the lady of the house is home alone and a male visitor comes to see her husband, it is not proper for her to invite him in, nor for him to expect to enter. Rather, he will leave a message and take his leave.

Punctuality: Eastern life is generally more relaxed than in the West. A good guideline is do not be surprised or offended if your guest arrives late or early. But be punctual in your own engagements, as this is appreciated.

Giving Gifts: Gifts are always given when one stays over night as a guest in someone's home. The value of the gift varies greatly, depending upon circumstance. It is proper to give a separate gift for the wife and the husband. The wife receives the nicest item.

Duration of Stay: It is quite impolite to ask a guest how long he intends to stay, but it is good protocol for guests to make their plans and itinerary known from the outset.

Exchange of Prana

Prana is the life principle, the subtle energy that emanates from the psychic force centers called chakras. Religious people, being sensitive to the various expressions of prana, are careful in how they manage their own energies and discriminating about the pranas they receive from the world around them. Prevailing pranas create a forcefield, positive or negative. The ideal Hindu home is a positive forcefield, kept strong through right thought, word and deed.

Homecoming: Upon arriving home from work, it is customary to immediately bathe and enter the shrine room for special blessings to dispel worldly forces, quiet the mind and regain a centered, spiritual consciousness.

Giving and Receiving: Giving and accepting things, presenting offerings to the Deity, etc., is properly done with both hands, to endow more energy to the object. This exchange of energies is vital for friendship and harmony through wholehearted release by the giver and conscious acceptance by the recipient.

Throwing Things: Throwing an object to another person, even to a close friend, is improper. Cultured Hindus consider this crude, even mildly violent.

Greetings: Hindu men traditionally greet one another with hands in *anjali* mudra (prayerful pose), then, with palms still held together, extend their hands to one another, in a two-handed handshake. This is a deliberate transfer of prana. The hands of one man, usually the less senior, are gently clasped between the other's. Each looks smilingly into the other's face while bowing slightly in humility.

Doorways: It is inauspicious to converse inside or through doorways. Similarly, to exchange or give or lend an object, one first steps inside the room, or the recipient steps out of the room, so that both parties are in the same space.

Auspiciousness: To ensure optimum timing for important events, Hindus guide their life by the map of auspiciousness, determined by astrology and indicated in the annual almanac, called *panchanga*. It provides vital information about the subtle but powerful affect of the planets and stars, indicating the prevailing forces of each day, the best times for innovations, travel, planting crops, routine work, personal retreat, seminars, marriages and other sacraments.

Modesty & Reserve

Interactions in public between men and women are generally more restrained in Asian culture than in Western culture. For the most part, men socialize with men, and women with women. Men never touch women in public, such as helping a woman out of a car, unless the lady is very elderly or infirm. In the temple (see art), women worship on the left, and men on the right.

Hindu Clothing: Traditional Hindu attire is modest and dignified, elegant yet never enticing, worn by staunch Hindus always at home, in the temple and at religious or cultural events. Women wear rich costumes and jewelry for religious and cultural events. They never expose breasts, navel or thighs.

Chastity: Sexual purity is a cardinal virtue, controlling lust by remaining celibate when single and faithful in marriage. Boys and girls are taught to value and protect their chastity as a sacred treasure, and to save the special gift of intimacy for their future spouse.

Chaperoning: Parents chaperone and monitor friendships of sons and daughters, closely guiding the private and social life of their children and teaching them the importance of wholesome companionship. Dating is traditionally not permitted, and marriages are arranged to ensure the most auspicious match.

Fidelity: Sexual/psychic energies are carefully directed and contained in the close-knit family. The wife's duty is to give her energy to her husband and make him strong. The husband protects and provides for the family. Children give their energy to their parents, their first gurus, obey and heed their good example.

Displaying Affection: Married couples in Asia do not hug, hold hands or kiss in public. Even embracing at airports and train stations is out of the question.

Propriety: It is improper to praise the beauty of another man's wife (or daughter) lest one inadvertently suggest an improper interest in her. All older women are viewed as one's mother and younger women as a sister. Also, one does not praise the beauty of a child or infant, protecting young ones from jealousies.

Garlanding: Women do not garland men, and men do not garland women. Such exchanges are restricted to the marriage ceremony. However, a woman can garland her husband or her *satguru*.

Womanly Protocol

Women in Hindu society are held in the highest regard, far more respected and protected, in truth, than in the West. This does not imply the kind of equality or participation in public interactions that are common in the West. A woman will often be given preferential treatment in India at such places as ticket counters. At meals, though, the men are usually expected to go first. Feminine refinements are expressed and protected through numerous customs, including the following.

Modesty: The qualities traditionally most admired in Eastern women are shyness, self-effacement and modesty of dress and deportment. Self-assertive or bold tendencies are regarded with circumspection.

Mixed Company: In mixed company, Hindu women will keep in the background and not participate freely in conversation. This, of course, differs among family and close friends. When male guests are in the home, the women will appear when it is proper. Visitors do not expect or ask to meet them.

Walking with Husband: The wife walks a step or two behind her husband, or, if walking by his side, a step or two back, always giving him the lead. (In the West, the opposite is often true.)

Serving Meals: At mealtime, women traditionally follow the ancient custom of serving the men first before eating.

Chaperoning: It is customary for a woman leaving the home to always be accompanied, generally by her husband, mother-in-law, sister-in-law, mother, daughter, sister or another lady close to the family, or among a group of both men and women. Women in traditional areas rarely even walk across the street alone, unless they are older. Living alone, too, is unusual.

Moving in Public: Generally, it is considered improper for women to speak with strangers on the street, much less strike up a casual conversation. Drinking or smoking in public is viewed as a sign of moral laxity.

Shelter and Care: When away from home, husbands contact their wife each day to express their love and inquire about her day.

Monthly Retreat: During their monthly period, Asian women do not prepare food, attend social gatherings or attend the temple or home shrine.

PAINTINGS BY A. MANIVEL

Body Language

Hindus know that God is everywhere and in all things. This realization brings dynamic contentment and appreciation for the fact that life is to be lived joyously. This understanding is expressed in Hindu deportment, or "body language." Every movement of the body, the face, hands, eyes, mouth, head, etc., has a meaning. Children and newcomers to the culture are taught to adopt refined body language and to become sensitive to the thoughts and feelings of others, who may be "talking" even when not speaking.

Kindly Words and Countenance: Hindus strive to keep a pleasant expression on their face, a gentle smile and a kind word for everyone they meet through the day. They know in their heart of hearts that everything in the universe is in a perfect state of evolution at every point in time.

Care in Sitting: It is a grave insult to sit with one's legs outstretched toward a temple, a shrine or altar, or another person. One never sits higher than elders or holy persons. Worshiping in the kneeling pose is not acceptable among Hindus. Youths follow the example of traditional elders.

Gestures of Humility: As stated in scripture, humility is strength not a weakness, pride is a weakness, not a strength. For example, orthodox Hindus will place their hand in front of their mouth when speaking to another, especially an elder, in a gesture of respect. Humility is expressed in ways of standing, sitting, listening, greeting others and more.

Prideful Postures: Prideful postures are to be avoided, such as sitting with one foot placed on the opposite thigh, or with arms folded or chin held exceedingly high, or with hands on the hips with head cocked to the side. These gestures are signs of arrogance and a superiority complex.

Pointing: Pointing with the forefinger of the right hand (or shaking the forefinger in emphasis) is never done. This is because the right hand possesses a powerful, aggressive *pranic* force. Pointing the index finger channels that force into a single stream. The harshness of this energy would be felt in the nerve system of the recipient. To show direction or emphasis, the entire hand is used as a pointer, with the palm up and the thumb held alongside the forefinger.

Purity & Pollution

Purity and its opposite, pollution, are a fundamental part of Asian culture. While they imply a strong sense of physical cleanliness, their more important meanings extend to social, ceremonial, mental, emotional, psychic and spiritual contamination. Here are several ways purity is preserved.

Cleanliness: Hindus keep their home environment clean and uncluttered to create a strong spiritual vibration and not attract negative forces. They seek fresh air and sunshine and surround themselves with beauty.

Personal Health: Hindus keep strong and healthy through a balanced ayurvedic diet, moderate daily exercise, hatha yoga and vigorous work.

Well-being: Mental and spiritual purity is maintained through daily meditation and worship, scriptural study, right living and right thinking.

Purity and Food: In a market, one does not touch food one doesn't intend to buy. One cooking food for others would never taste of a dish and then put the spoon back in the pot. One does not touch the lips to a water vessel used by others, nor lick postage stamps or offer to another food one has partaken of.

Sanctified Food Leavings: The opposite is true in the case of the *satguru's* food leavings. Food that the guru has tasted of is revered as sacred. This, and the water from the washing of the holy feet, is sought after and imbibed by devotees for the great spiritual blessings that it contains toward moksha.

Offerings: One does not sniff flowers picked for offering—even the smell is for the Gods, not for us. Flowers that fall to the ground should not be offered. Offerings are carried with both hands on the right side of the body, so as to not be breathed on. All items are washed in preparation, then wrapped or covered.

The Left Hand: The left hand is considered impure because it is used for personal hygiene by washing after answering the call of nature. Handing another person anything with the left hand is considered a subtle insult.

Footwear: Shoes, being impure, are not worn inside the temple or home. Carrying shoes is also avoided. One apologizes immediately if one's footwear touches another. This is done by touching the right hand to where the foot touched the other person, then touching the hand lightly to the left eye and then the right.

CHAPTER 39

Rites of Passage

Personal Ceremonies that Sanctify and Celebrate Life's Crucial Junctures

FOR THE HINDU, LIFE IS A SACRED JOURney; and every step from birth to death is marked, and thus acknowledged, through traditional ceremony, called *samskara*. A samskara is an enduring impression etched into the malleable substance of a person's mind at a psychological point in life. During these Hindu rites of passage, a temple or home ceremony deeply influences the soul and directs life along the path of dharma. There are many types of samskaras, from the rite prior to conception to the funeral ceremony. Each one, properly observed, empowers spiritual life, preserves religious culture and establishes bonds with inner worlds as the soul consciously accepts each succeeding discovery and duty in the order of God's creation. Religious samskaras serve two purposes. First, they mark clearly within our minds the occasion of an important life transition. Second, they solicit special blessings from the devas and Deities, society and village, family and friends. These blessings and feelings of love have a markedly positive effect, stabilizing the mind so that the deeper meanings of life can unfold within us. Of the many Hindu samskaras, eight are illustrated and described in this chapter.

Namakarana, Name-Giving

(Pictured at left) The Hindu name-giving rite, *namakarana* samskara, is one of the essential rites of passage. It is performed in the home or the temple, usually when the child is 11 to 40 days old. The father whispers the infant's name in his right ear.

M. ARUMUGAM

Anna Prasana, First Solid Food

During the *anna prasana* samskara, solid food is fed to the child for the first time. This is done by the father or the mother in the temple or at home. The choice of food, such as rice, offered to a child at this crucial time of life is said to help forge his or her destiny.

The best rendering of *samskara* in English is made by the word *sacrament,* which means "religious ceremony or act regarded as an outward and visible sign of inward and spiritual grace." *Sacrament* also means "confirmation of some promise or oath; things of mysterious significance, sacred influence and symbol."

Sri Raj Bai Pandey, *Hindu Samskaras*

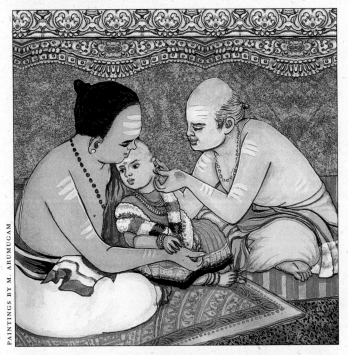

Karnavedha, Ear-Piercing

The ear-piercing ceremony, for both boys and girls, is performed in the temple or the home, generally on the child's first birthday. Health benefits are said to derive from this ceremony.

Chudakarana, Head-Shaving

Ceremonial head-shaving is usually performed before the end of the third year in the home or temple. The shaven head denotes purity and egolessness and is said to mitigate past life karma.

Vidyarambha, Learning Commencement

The official beginning of the child's education is performed in the home or temple, during the fourth year, when he or she writes the first letter of the alphabet in a tray filled with uncooked rice.

Upanayana, Initiation

The ceremonial presentation of the sacred thread is performed in the temple or home between the ages of 9 and 15, when a boy begins the study of the *Vedas*. Thereafter, he is considered "twice-born."

PAINTINGS BY M. ARUMUGAM

Vivaha, Marriage

The marriage ceremony is performed in a temple or special hall around the sacred *homa* fire. Lifetime vows and seven steps before God and the Gods consecrate the holy union of husband and wife.

Antyesti, Funeral

The funeral ceremony is performed or arranged by the relatives according to local traditions. It includes preparation of the body, cremation, rites of mourning, purification and remembrance.

Seven Other Rites of Passage

In addition to the primary personal ceremonies, there is a rich collection of other traditional samskaras. Here is a sampling.

Keshanta Kala
When a boy first shaves his facial hair, this indication that he has come of age is celebrated in the temple or at home with the *keshanta* samskara. It is a joyous time of gift-giving, yet it is serious as well. Often a vow of *brahmacharya* (celibacy) is taken at this same time.

Ritu Kala
As puberty dawns for a young girl, the *ritu kala* home-ceremony is performed to acknowledge her first menses. New clothing, jewelry and her first sari are given as she joyously and openly joins the young adult community.

Samavartana
This ceremony—literally, "returning home from the house of the guru"—marks the end of studentship and indicates formal closure to the *brahmacharya* period of life. The young person now must choose one of two paths: the *grihastha* path (family life) or the renunciate path (monastic life).

Nishchitartha or Vagdana
This is the betrothal ceremony in which a man and woman are declared formally engaged by their parents with the exchange of jewelry and gifts. Based on this commitment, they and their families begin planning a shared future.

Punsavana
The literal meaning of the term *punsavana* is "the quickening of a male child." Not practiced today, this ceremony was performed by the husband for the wife beseeching the birth of a son, primarily as an assurance for the continuance of the family line.

Simantonnayana
This is the "hair-parting" rite. Not commonly practiced today, this ancient ceremony of parting the hair of the pregnant wife was performed to bring cheer as well as ward off evil spirits.

Jatakarma
During the later days of pregnancy, a woman may have the *jatakarma* samskara performed. This rite, based on a verse from the Atharva Veda written specifically to assure safe childbirth, was designed to yield blessings for life as well as protection from harm for both mother and child.

CHAPTER 40

Honoring The Arts of Homemaking

An Artist's Portrayal of the Hindu Wife's Traditional Domestic Duties

ODAY, COMMUNITIES AND PEOPLES ALL OVER THE WORLD ARE RE-evaluating how we live. As a global community, we are seeking more sustainable ways of life, seeking solutions to the myriad problems that our modern ways have caused since the Industrial Revolution—global warming, polution of our air and waterways, concretization of our lands, deforestation, and the social ills of crime, poverty, abuse and broken homes. Peoples are evaluating old, traditional system to learn or relearn how we got along in the old days, without so many conveniences, when life was simpler, less competetive, less stressful and frantic. In this chapter, we bring you a collection of painting by S. Rajam, a gifted artist and musician born in a South Indian village in the old days of 1918, that depict the daily rituals commonly performed by Hindu wives and homemakers all over India, during his time and for centuries before. The same rituals can still be found today in villages and urban centers. The scenes in his 14 pieces follows the sequence of a day, from morning to dusk.

Then, as now, the wife and mother carries a momentus responsibility—the creation of a stable home and the raising of a fully functioning family. Her role, apart from the competitive, breadwinner world of men, is every bit as essential as her husband's. Rightly performed, each part of her daily ritual is done with a mindfulness based on knowledge of the workings of subtle energies, and of unseen angelic beings—the guardian *devas* of family members—and the aid they give. For example: the home's doorways and windows are seen as portals through which either helpful or antagonistic beings can enter. So daily decorating of entryways entreats guardian *devas* to allow access only to those who will strengthen and support the family. Similarly, she knows the womanly energy she embues into a meal during its preparation can increase the health of all who partake of it, or, if negative, contribute to illness and distress. She also understands that clothing and other possessions respond to care or neglect just as people do, and that cleanliness and love bring forth a refined spiritual vibration. All her efforts serve to make the home a holy place. Indeed, each of the duties depicted in Rajam's art has esoteric and mystical aspects to be discovered and developed by the intuitive woman.

To urban wives and those living abroad, some of the tasks may seem irrelevant and the methods outdated, even demeaning. Rajam hopes modern Hindu individuals will discover how each duty relates to the current household environment. This woman's rustic tools may be replaced with electric utensils and food processors. Even the modern refrigerator door can be transformed into a place of blessing by daily posting a freshly ink-jetted *kolam* design upon it. With applied intuition and ingenuity, similar modernization of each of these principles will move them meaningfully into the future. And some of the simplicity may be revived in our efforts to find sustainable ways to survive on into the future.

Family life, however full, remains empty if the wife lacks the lofty culture of the home.
Tirukural, verse 52
● ● ● ● ● ● ● ● ● ● ●

Storytelling
Before going to bed, children are fed light foods out in the open air. When the moonlight is seen, mother tells stories to inspire the child to linger and eat more.
● ● ● ● ● ● ● ● ● ● ●

PAINTINGS BY S. RAJAM

PAINTINGS BY S. RAJAM

Collecting Water

In the morning, women meet at the well to gather water for the day and to clean cooking utensils.

∙ ∙

Decorating the Entry

As the day begins, kolams are painted at the home entrance. First, water is mixed with cow dung and sprinkled on the ground. Then geometric designs are applied with powdered rice in many colors, guided by a trained thumb and index finger.

∙ ∙ ∙ ∙ ∙ ∙ ∙ ∙ ∙ ∙ ∙ ∙ ∙ ∙ ∙ ∙ ∙ ∙ ∙ ∙

Caring for Clothing

Some women bathe in the temple tank. Before the bath, they wash their saris and other garments and spread them on the steps, later to find them fully dried in the hot Indian sun upon returning from their bath.

∙ ∙

Bathing

The women bathe in the river at hidden places specially reserved for them. They apply fresh turmeric root to the skin as a toner, skin color enhancer and anti-bacterial. Early European visitors were so impressed with the daily bathing ritual of Indian women that upon returning home they slowly convinced the rest of Europe of the merits of bathing more than once a week or month.

● ●

Sanctifying the Doorway

Here, the home's entryway is adorned with turmeric paste and red kumkuma powder. The daily morning decoration is a blessing intended to beseech guardian devas to allow entry only to beings, both physical and subtle, who will benefit the family and home environment, rather than causing discord.

● ●

Temple Worship

Before the noon meal, wives visit the temple, bringing an offering basket of coconut, ghee for the temple lamps, betel leaves, flower garlands and fruits.

● ●

Preparing Rice

Each day a small quantity of rice paddy is taken from the reservoir and pounded to separate the husk to provide grain for the day's meals. Pure and religious thoughts are pounded into the paddy as well.

● ●

PAINTINGS BY S. RAJAM

Preparing Meals

In this scene, vegetables are washed and cut with the aid of a knife-like blade affixed to a wooden platform. The platform includes a seat for the woman, which makes for effortless cutting and minimal fatigue—the original "Cuisinart." (Right) Once yesterday's milk cures and becomes curd, it is stirred into butter and boiled into ghee. The woman vigorously churns the frothing liquid in big pots with a ladle of wood turned with a cord.

Grooming

(Left) In the evening the wife dons casual or formal dress, combs and braids the hair, marks the forehead with kumkuma and applies jewelry.

Care of Children

(Right) During the Dipavali festival a healthful ayurvedic oil bath is given to all. Children are attended to first, in the hour before sunrise. Oil is applied to skin and hair, then rinsed off.

Making Garlands

She collects fragrant flowers and with deft fingers assembles them on fine string according to color. Garlands are used in the shrines and to decorate the pictures of the Gods throughout the home.

• • • • • • • • • • • • • • • • •

Caring for the Home Shrine

Evening is time for cleaning the home's oil lamps, adding fresh ghee or oil and lighting them in the shrines. The woman prostrates to receive blessings from the Deities and devas who guide her family's life of dharma. Devotional songs are sung as the day winds down.

• • • • • • • • • • • • • • • • • • •

CHAPTER 41

Hail Hindu Heroes!

Celebrating Some of India's Champions of Virtue, Strength and Spirituality

BEGINNING TWO CENTURIES AGO, THERE AROSE throughout India a retinue of talented, high-souled and dedicated men and women who were great by any standard in the history of humankind. They consecrated their life and works to the resurrection of their motherland. They lit the lamp of liberty, articulated a new era, safeguarded India's individuality and spirituality, strengthened her people's intentions and preserved their way of life. These are some of the contemporary heroes of Hinduism. Here we briefly recount their stories and achievements, while artist Sabaji Bhagwan Polaji of Mumbai provides the portraiture.

Swami Dayananda Saraswati (1825–1883): "Back to the *Vedas*." This was the clarion call of Swami Dayananda Saraswati, religious leader, social reformer, gifted speaker and prolific writer. Swamiji founded the now global fellowship of the Arya Samaj. His writings include commentaries on the *Rig, Yajur* and *Sama Vedas,* an encyclopedic work on Hinduism called *Satyartha Prakash,* a book of prayers and a work on Sanskrit grammar. Swami rejected idol worship and polytheism. He fought against superstitions, child-marriage, the hereditary caste system and forced widowhood. He advocated women's education, a single national language and the study of Sanskrit.

Born in 1825 in Kathiawar (now in Rajkot district of Gujarat), Mulshankar, as Swami Dayananda was known as a boy, left his

• •

All art is from the book ARCHITECTS AND BUILDERS OF MODERN INDIA by Bharatiya Vidya Bhavan, USA. © 1997

home at the age of 21. He wandered the country for 20 years and learned the *Vedas* from scholars. His Guru, Virajanand of Mathura, the blind saint with a giant intellect, gave him his mission. Swamiji passed away at Ajmer on October 30, 1883, having been poisoned.

Sri Ramakrishna Paramahamsa (1836-1886): There is one principle of pure consciousness. It is both personal and impersonal. It can be reached through the path of love, knowledge and selfless action. Man should aim at Self realization, and morality is the foundation of spiritual perfection. This, in essence, is the teaching of Ramakrishna Paramahamsa.

Born at Kamarpukur village of West Bengal, on February 18, 1836, Gadadhar, as he was known as a youth, showed spiritual inclinations even in his boyhood. He had an artistic temperament and a beautiful voice. His brother took him to Calcutta when he was 20 and made him a priest at the Kali Temple at Dakshineshwar. Ramakrishna not only had visions of the Supreme Goddess but had practical training in tantra. His whole life was an uninterrupted contemplation of God. Through his profound spiritual realizations, he demonstrated the reality of God and restored faith in religion for many. People flocked to him from far and near, seekers of truth of all races, creeds and castes. His small room in the Dakshineswar temple garden on the outskirts of the city of Calcutta became a veritable parliament of religions. The teachings of Ramakrishna were spread all over the world by his foremost disciple, Swami Vivekananda.

Rabindranath Tagore (1861-1941): Poet, novelist, critic, philosopher, nationalist and educationist, Tagore is the greatest of modern Bengali writers and a treasure of Indian literature. Tagore gave exquisite expression to the joy of being one with the river and the mountain,

Dayananda Saraswati

Ramakrishna

Tagore

332 WHAT IS HINDUISM?

the sky and the stars, the grass and the flowers. His poetry exalts nature and mysticism. His was an aesthetic approach to life and art, but his faith was anchored deep in the Brahman of the *Upanishads*. Tagore wrote more than 1,000 poems and 2,000 songs, besides novels, short stories, plays and essays. He was a musician of the highest order and a painter of delicate sensitivity. He was awarded the Nobel Prize for Literature in 1913 for his collection of poems entitled *Gitanjali*.

Gandhi

Born to affluence of Devendra Nath Tagore and Sharada Devi in Calcutta, Tagore was educated mostly at home. He studied for a while at the University College, London, in 1878. He was married to Mrinalini in 1883. He founded Shanti Niketan in 1901, a school which later became famous as Vishwa Bharati, or World University. Tagore fervently protested the partition of Bengal (1905). His song *Jana Gana Mana* is the National Anthem of India.

Swami Vivekananda (1863–1902): As the foremost disciple of Sri Ramakrishna, Vivekananda not only spread the teachings of his master but carried the message of Vedanta to the West. He is hailed as a "bridge-builder between East and West." He consecrated his own life to the moral and spiritual upliftment of his nation and humanity.

Born on January 12, 1863, in Calcutta, of Shri Vishwanatha Datta and Bhuvaneshwari Devi, Narendranath Datta, as Swamiji was called, had his early education at home. He later graduated in arts and law. A self-proclaimed rationalist and agnostic, Narendranath came under the influence of Ramakrishna almost by chance, and he was immediately captivated by the unqualified spirituality of Ramakrishna. He took the name Swami Vivekananda as a sannyasin before departing for America. Vivekananda became famous after addressing the Parliament of Religions on September 11, 1893 in Chicago, USA. The brilliant light that was Swamiji went out on July 4, 1902, when he had just turned 39. He is the one of the greatest modern interpreters and promoters of the Advaita Vedanta philosophy.

Mohandas Karamchand Gandhi (1869–1948): Mahatma Gandhi is looked upon as the "Father of the Nation" in India. He had an overwhelming influence on the people in the country during his lifetime. Albert Einstein hailed Gandhi as: "A man who has confronted the brutality of Europe with the dignity of a simple human being, and thus at all times has risen superior. Generations to come, it may be, will scarce believe that such a one as this ever in flesh and blood walked upon this earth." Gandhi demonstrated that the essential strength of man is spiritual. Injustice and tyranny should be fought with truth and nonviolence as the guiding principles. Gandhi roused the masses of India into action for winning freedom from foreign rule.

Born on October 2, 1869, in Gujarat, Gandhi had his education in India and England. He left for South Africa in 1893 to argue in a civil suit. Moved by the plight of Indian settlers, Gandhi demonstrated the efficacy of his unique strategy—satyagraha—in fighting for their legitimate rights. Returning to India in 1915, Gandhi launched a series of movements against the British rule, including noncooperation, civil disobedience and the Quit India Movement in 1942. He was sentenced to varying terms of imprisonment. On January 30, 1948, the apostle of peace and nonviolence fell to an assassin's bullets.

Mahayogi Sri Aurobindo (1872–1950): One of the greatest pioneers of the Indian Renaissance, Sri Aurobindo was educated in England and was proficient in Greek, Latin and English. Yet there was no greater or more brilliant exponent of Indian culture from the point of view of the Vedic spiritual tradition. He was no philosopher content with weaving verbal rhetoric. He was a yogi, an integrated personality whose life was a *sadhana* towards realizing the Self Divine. He has been described as the "Poet of Patriotism" and the "Prophet of Indian Nationalism." Aurobindo envisaged the emergence of a *superman*, the truth-conscious being, one who has realized the Divinity within himself as the goal of human evolution.

Born on August 15, 1872, Aurobindo attended schools in England

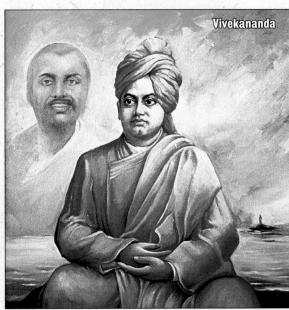
Vivekananda

Aurobindo

from the age of seven. He returned to India in 1893, taught French and became Professor of English at the Baroda State College. He was in Baroda for 13 years. Aurobindo was drawn into politics in 1905 when Bengal was partitioned. He was associated with the Bengali daily *Yugantar* and the English daily *Bande Mataram*. He followed Tilak in his political thinking, and was with the extremists at the Surat session of the Congress in 1907. Aurobindo was arrested in 1908 for revolutionary activity and acquitted after one year. He became a spiritual aspirant during his imprisonment and chose to pursue a spiritual mission. He went to Pondicherry and stayed on there till his *mahasamadhi* on December 5, 1950. He wrote copiously in his inimitable, elevated literary style.

Sadhu T.L. Vaswani (1879–1966): An eminent educationist, great social reformer, philosopher and a man of God, Thanwardas Lilaram Vaswani lived a life of selfless service. Spiritually inclined from his childhood, he called upon youth to be dedicated to the service of the Motherland with faith in God. He considered character-building to be the essential prerequisite for nation-building. He organized many educational organizations and youth centers for promoting education and inculcation of ethical and spiritual values.

Vaswani was born in Hyderabad, Sind, on November 25, 1879. His father was well versed in Persian and knowledgeable about the lives of the Sufis. A brilliant student, Vaswani served as professor and principal in various colleges during 1903–1919. He resigned his principalship in 1919 and decided to devote the rest of his life to the service of his motherland. Vaswani, a great orator, was one of the earliest supporters of Gandhi's noncooperation movement.

Returning to Hyderabad, in 1929 he started an organization called "Sakhi Sat-Sang," devoted to women's causes. He presided over a number of conferences and meetings connected with humanitarianism, religion and peace during the third and the fourth decades of the century. Following partition, Vaswani settled in Pune in 1949 and set up a number of educational institutions. He has been hailed as "a thinker and a revealer of the deep truth of the spirit." He passed away on June 16, 1966, in Pune. A 10-foot statue of Sadhu T.L. Vaswani stands before the Pune Railway Station. In 1969, the government of India brought out a postal stamp in memory of him.

Ramana Maharshi (1879–1950): Ramana Maharshi was born on December 29, 1879, at Tiruchuli, a small town near Madurai, in South India, as the son of Sundaram Aiyar, a middle-class brahmin lawyer, and his wife Alagammal. The Maharshi was named Venkataraman, and after his elementary education at Tiruchuli, he was sent to Madurai for schooling. He was living in his uncle's home then. It was there, when he was 17, that he had a great spiritual experience in a confrontation with death. He felt that he was to die just then, and his conscious mind was driven inwards by the question "Who is this 'I' who is dying?" From the innermost recesses of his being the realization came: "I am the soul (Atma or Self), not the body." From that time onward, he dwelt in the radiance of the spirit. The fear of death left him forever.

On August 29, 1896 he left his family in Madurai and ventured to Tiruvannamalai, where he remained until his departure from this world in 1950. Beginning in 1922, an ashram grew up around him at the foot of the hill. People from all walks of life went to the sage and invariably experienced profound peace as well as gaining practical solutions to their problems. Though the Maharshi was ever ready to explain doctrinal or philosophical matters, it was mainly his very presence that was his greatest blessing to devotees. The Maharshi once explained to a visitor, "Bhagavan's teaching is an expression of his own experience and realization." The Maharshi attained Mahasamadhi on Friday, April 14, 1950.

Dr. Sarvepalli Radhakrishnan (1888–1975): Dr. S. Radhakrishnan, one of the three early recipients of the Bharat Ratna Award, was a great philosopher, educationist and humanist. He was the President of India during 1962–67 and was hailed as the philosopher-king of Plato's conception. He explained the ancient wisdom of the Indian sages in terms intelligible to the modern mind. Radhakrishnan's specific contribution to thought consists of his philosophy of religion and idealist view of life. Additionally, he gave much impetus to the comparative study of religions. Radhakrishnan offered a reasoned defence of religion. He was an exceptional writer and speaker, in a style that was dignified and impressive. His intellect was encyclopedic. Science and religion, literature and the fine arts, all these he elucidated with rare insight.

Born in Tiruttani, Tamil Nadu, in September, 1888, Radhakrishnan had his education at Tiruttani, Tirupati, Vellore and Chennai. He started his career as a lecturer and moved to Mysore and Calcutta to occupy prestigious professorial chairs. He was Spalding Professor of Eastern Religions and Ethics at Oxford during 1936–39. Radhakrishnan held the offices of Indian Ambassador to Russia, 1949–52, Vice President of the Indian Union, 1952–62, and President of India, 1962–67.

Acharya Vinoba Bhave (1895–1982): A scholar and a saint, Acharya Vinoba Bhave was a beacon of hope and solace to millions in India

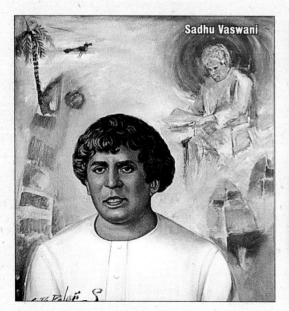
Sadhu Vaswani

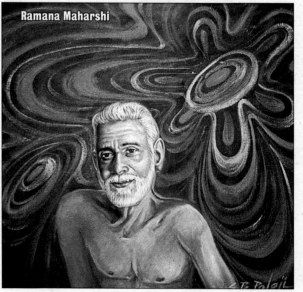
Ramana Maharshi

Radhakrishnan

and abroad. He was Mahatma Gandhi's spiritual successor. Vinoba was born in a village in Maharashtra's Kolaba district on September 11, 1895. As a youth, he was drawn to Gandhi and his unique "Weaponless War" for India's freedom. Like the Mahatma, Vinoba was also ahead of his time. His *bhoodan* (gift of land), *sampattidan* (gift of wealth), *jeevadan* (gift of life) and other movements are logical extensions of Gandhi's programs of national reconstruction. Believing in communal amity, he abolished every trace of untouchability from his heart. In order to understand his Muslim neighbors, he studied the *Koran* in the original Arabic for one year. His *padayatra* (foot journey), a part of his *bhoodan* movement, was a demonstration of the Gandhian doctrine of trusteeship.

Of the many teachings of the *Gita* which Vinoba highlighted in his talks, one of the most important was the role of self-help. "The *Gita* is prepared to go to the lowest, the weakest and the least cultured of men. And it goes to him not to keep him where he is, but to grasp him by the hand and lift him up. The *Gita* wishes that man should make his action pure and attain the highest state." Vinobaji passed away at Paunar on November 17, 1982. He was posthumously honored with the Bharat Ratna Award in 1984.

Rukmini Devi Arundale (1904–1986): She is the resuscitator of the Indian classical dance, bharata natyam, which was almost given up in the early decades of the present century. Rukmini Devi Arundale returned the dance to respectability. She looked upon dance not as mere entertainment but as a means of spiritual transformation, and she brought the spirit of the temple to the stage.

Born in an orthodox brahmin family, she later became a member of the Theosophical Society. Her taking up dance was a significant challenge. Bharata natyam was then learned and performed in the temples by Devadasis (women servants of God) who were looked down upon by society. Rukmini Devi had to struggle against this convention and its stigma. She created a stir in the conservative society of Chennai in the twenties by marrying George Arundale, an educationist and one of the leaders of the Theosophical movement in South India. She trained in music and dance under great masters. With a view to fostering these arts and preserving them in their pristine purity, she founded the Kalakshetra (Temple of Arts) in Madras. The institution today is world renowned.

Rukmini Devi was a member of the Rajya Sabha. She was an ardent champion of vegetarianism and carried on a crusade against ritual animal slaughter. She was even proposed as a nominee for the presidentship of India in 1977.

BHARATIYA VIDYA BHAVAN, 305 SEVENTH AVENUE, 17TH FLOOR, NEW YORK, NEW YORK 10001 USA. TEL: 212–989–8383.

At the canvas: *Artist Polaji honors India with his brush*

Heroic Artistry

THE PORTRAITS IN THIS ARTICLE WERE LOVINGLY RENDERED by Sabaji Bhagwan Polaji. Born September 2, 1943, Polaji came to Mumbai, where he earned his degree from Sir J.J. College of Art. He then worked as a teacher in the B.L. Ruia School situated in the suburb of Vile Parle. Polaji is a prolific award winner, both nationally and internationally, earning successive awards for "Best Teacher." Other accolades include the India Awards for Child Welfare and Good Citizens Award. He has organized seven hundred art camps, as well as many seminars and workshops in countries like America and Belgium. His love of youth is evident to all, and he is especially dedicated to the betterment of orphans and disabled children. Polaji has a thorough knowledge of Indian history, particularly of India's independence, and this has helped him to execute these portraits with devotion and insight. Each painting shows the individual along with some glimpse of his or her achievements and accomplishments, so that any viewer can visually gain an idea of their contributions to Mother India and Hinduism.

SABAJI BHAGWAN POLAJI, 7/78 PIRAMAL NAGAR, SWAMI VIVEKANANDA ROAD, GOREGAON (WEST), MUMBAI 400062 INDIA.

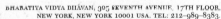

Vinoba Bhave

Rukmini Devi

Hindu Ethics

A code of conduct, vegetarianism, sensitive medical issues, and ahimsa—nonhurtfulness in thought, word and deed

A council of renunciate Hindu leaders gathered to discuss current ethical and religious issues in light of dharmic principles at the Kumbha Mela of 2004 in Ujjain at the camp of Maharishi Sarkhani Ji Maharaj (center left).

CHAPTER 42

Hinduism's Code of Conduct

Twenty Keys for Spiritual Living in Contemporary Times

HOW OFTEN DO YOU SEE A PROFESSIONAL TEAM of people misbehave on the job? You're on a flight from San Francisco to Singapore. Do the flight attendants bicker in the aisle? Of course not. People at this level of business have control of their minds and emotions. If they didn't, they would soon be replaced. When they are on the job, at least, they follow a code of conduct spelled out in detail by the corporation. It's not unlike the moral code of any religion, outlining sound ethics for respect and harmony among humans. Those seeking to be successful in life strive to fulfill a moral code whether "on the job" or off. Does Hinduism and its scriptures on yoga have such a code? Yes: twenty ethical guidelines called *yamas* and *niyamas,* "restraints and observances." These "do's" and "don'ts" are found in the 6,000 to 8,000-year-old V*edas,* mankind's oldest body of scripture, and in other holy texts expounding the path of yoga.

The *yamas* and *niyamas* are a common-sense code recorded in the final section of the Vedas, called *Upanishads,* namely the *Shandilya* and the *Varuha.* They are also found in the *Hatha Yoga Pradipika* by Gorakshanatha, the *Tirumantiram* of Tirumular and in the *Yoga Sutras* of Patanjali. The *yamas* and *niyamas* have been preserved through the centuries as the foundation, the first and second stage, of the eight-staged practice of yoga. Yet, they are fundamental to all beings, expected aims of everyone in society, and assumed to be fully intact for anyone seeking life's highest aim in the pursuit called yoga.

Sage Patanjali (ca 200 BCE), raja yoga's foremost propounder, told us, "These *yamas* are not limited by class, country, time (past, present or future) or situation. Hence they are called the universal great vows." Yogic scholar Swami Brahmananda Saraswati revealed the inner science of *yama* and *niyama.* They are the means, he said, to control the *vitarkas,* the cruel mental waves or thoughts, that when acted upon result in injury to others, untruthfulness, hoarding, discontent, indolence or selfishness. He stated, "For each *vitarka* you have, you can create its opposite through *yama* and *niyama,* and make your life successful."

The following paragraphs, with accompanying illustrations by A. Manivel of Chennai, elucidate the *yamas* and *niyamas.* Presented first are the ten *yamas,* the do not's, which harness the instinctive nature, with its governing impulses of fear, anger, jealousy, selfishness, greed and lust. Second are illustrated the ten *niyamas,* the do's, the religious observances that cultivate and bring forth the refined soul qualities, lifting awareness into the consciousness of the higher chakras of love, compassion, selflessness, intelligence and bliss. Together the *yamas* and *niyamas* provide the foundation to support our yoga practice so that attainments in higher consciousness can be sustained.

The Ten Vedic Restraints, Yama यम

1. Noninjury, *Ahimsa*

Practice noninjury, not harming others by thought, word or deed, even in your dreams. Live a kindly life, revering all beings as expressions of the One Divine energy. Let go of fear and insecurity, the sources of abuse. Knowing that harm caused to others unfailingly returns to oneself, live peacefully with God's creation. Never be a source of dread, pain or injury. Follow a vegetarian diet.

2. Truthfulness, *Satya*

Adhere to truthfulness, refraining from lying and betraying promises. Speak only that which is true, kind, helpful and necessary. Knowing that deception creates distance, don't keep secrets from family or loved ones. Be fair, accurate and frank in discussions, a stranger to deceit. Admit your failings. Do not engage in slander, gossip or backbiting. Do not bear false witness against another.

3. Nonstealing, *Asteya*

Uphold the virtue of nonstealing, neither thieving, coveting nor failing to repay debt. Control your desires and live within your means. Do not use borrowed resources for unintended purposes or keep them past due. Do not gamble or defraud others. Do not renege on promises. Do not use others' names, words, resources or rights without permission and acknowledgement.

4. Divine Conduct, *Brahmacharya*

Practice divine conduct, controlling lust by remaining celibate when single and faithful in marriage. Before marriage, use vital energies in study, and after marriage in creating family success. Don't waste the sacred force by promiscuity in thought, word or deed. Be restrained with the opposite sex. Seek holy company. Dress and speak modestly. Shun pornography, sexual humor and violence.

5. Patience, *Kshama*

Exercise patience, restraining intolerance with people and impatience with circumstances. Be agreeable. Let others behave according to their nature, without adjusting to you. Don't argue, dominate conversations or interrupt others. Don't be in a hurry. Be patient with children and the elderly. Minimize stress by keeping worries at bay. Remain poised in good times and bad.

6. Steadfastness, *Dhriti*

Foster steadfastness, overcoming nonperseverance, fear, indecision and changeableness. Achieve your goals with a prayer, purpose, plan, persistence and push. Be firm in your decisions. Avoid sloth and procrastination. Develop willpower, courage and industriousness. Overcome obstacles. Never carp or complain. Do not let opposition or fear of failure result in changing strategies.

7. Compassion, *Daya*

Practice compassion, conquering callous, cruel and insensitive feelings toward all beings. See God everywhere. Be kind to people, animals, plants and the Earth itself. Forgive those who apologize and show true remorse. Foster sympathy for others' needs and suffering. Honor and assist those who are weak, impoverished, aged or in pain. Oppose family abuse and other cruelties.

8. Honesty, *Arjava*

Maintain honesty, renouncing deception and wrongdoing. Act honorably even in hard times. Obey the laws of your nation and locale. Pay your taxes. Be straightforward in business. Do an honest day's work. Do not bribe or accept bribes. Do not cheat, deceive or circumvent to achieve an end. Be frank with yourself. Face and accept your faults without blaming them on others.

9. Moderate Appetite, *Mitahara*

Be moderate in appetite, neither eating too much nor consuming meat, fish, shellfish, fowl or eggs. Enjoy fresh, wholesome vegetarian foods that vitalize the body. Avoid junk food. Drink in moderation. Eat at regular times, only when hungry, at a moderate pace, never between meals, in a disturbed atmosphere or when upset. Follow a simple diet, avoiding rich or fancy fare.

10. Purity, *Saucha*

Uphold the ethic of purity, avoiding impurity in mind, body and speech. Maintain a clean, healthy body. Keep a pure, uncluttered home and workplace. Act virtuously. Keep good company, never mixing with adulterers, thieves or other impure people. Keep away from pornography and violence. Never use harsh, angered or indecent language. Worship devoutly. Meditate daily.

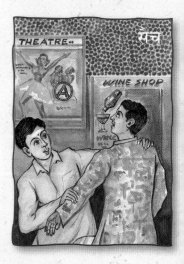

The Ten Vedic Practices, Niyama नियम

1. Remorse, *Hri*

Allow yourself the expression of remorse, being modest and showing shame for misdeeds. Recognize your errors, confess and make amends. Sincerely apologize to those hurt by your words or deeds. Resolve all contention before sleep. Seek out and correct your faults and bad habits. Welcome correction as a means to bettering yourself. Do not boast. Shun pride and pretension.

2. Contentment, *Santosha*

Nurture contentment, seeking joy and serenity in life. Be happy, smile and uplift others. Live in constant gratitude for your health, your friends and your belongings, Don't complain about what you don't possess. Identify with the eternal You, rather than mind, body or emotions. Keep the mountaintop view that life is an opportunity for spiritual progress. Live in the eternal now.

3. Giving, *Dana*

Be generous to a fault, giving liberally without thought of reward. Tithe, offering one-tenth of your gross income (*dashama-msha*), as God's money, to temples, ashrams and spiritual organizations. Approach the temple with offerings. Visit gurus with gifts in hand. Donate religious literature. Feed and give to those in need. Bestow your time and talents without seeking praise. Treat guests as God.

ALL ART BY A. MANIVEL

4. Faith, *Astikya*

Cultivate an unshakable faith. Believe firmly in God, Gods, guru and your path to enlightenment. Trust in the words of the masters, the scriptures and traditions. Practice devotion and *sadhana* to inspire experiences that build advanced faith. Be loyal to your lineage, one with your *satguru*. Shun those who try to break your faith by argument and accusation. Avoid doubt and despair.

5. Worship, *Ishvara-Pujana*

Cultivate devotion through daily worship and meditation. Set aside one room of your home as God's shrine. Offer fruit, flowers or food daily. Learn a simple puja and the chants. Meditate after each puja. Visit your shrine before and after leaving the house. Worship in heartfelt devotion, clearing the inner channels to God, Gods and guru so their grace flows toward you and loved ones.

6. Scriptural Listening, *Siddhanta Shravana*

Eagerly hear the scriptures, study the teachings and listen to the wise of your lineage. Choose a guru, follow his path and don't waste time exploring other ways. Read, study and, above all, listen to readings and dissertations by which wisdom flows from knower to seeker. Avoid secondary texts that preach violence. Revere and study the revealed scriptures, the *Vedas* and *Agamas*.

7. Cognition, *Mati*

Develop a spiritual will and intellect with your *satguru's* guidance. Strive for knowledge of God, to awaken the light within. Discover the hidden lesson in each experience to develop a profound understanding of life and yourself. Through meditation, cultivate intuition by listening to the still, small voice within, by understanding the subtle sciences, inner worlds and mystical texts.

8. Sacred Vows, *Vrata*

Embrace religious vows, rules and observances and never waver in fulfilling them. Honor vows as spiritual contracts with your soul, your community, with God, Gods and guru. Take vows to harness the instinctive nature. Fast periodically. Pilgrimage yearly. Uphold your vows strictly, be they marriage, monasticism, nonaddiction, tithing, loyalty to a lineage, vegetarianism or nonsmoking.

9. Recitation, *Japa*

Chant your holy mantra daily, reciting the sacred sound, word or phrase given by your guru. Bathe first, quiet the mind and concentrate fully to let *japa* harmonize, purify and uplift you. Heed your instructions and chant the prescribed repetitions without fail. Live free of anger so that *japa* strengthens your higher nature. Let *japa* quell emotions and quiet the rivers of thought.

10. Austerity, *Tapas*

Practice austerity, serious disciplines, penance and sacrifice. Be ardent in worship, meditation and pilgrimage. Atone for misdeeds through penance (*prayashchitta*), such as 108 prostrations or fasting. Perform self-denial, giving up cherished possessions, money or time. Fulfill severe austerities at special times, under a *satguru's* guidance, to ignite the inner fires of self-transformation.

For a full elucidation of the *yamas* and *niyamas*, see *Yoga's Forgotten Foundation*, available at www.himalayanacademy.com/books.

What's for dinner? *Young ladies at a busy market in India, where fresh vegetables, grains and legumes abound, picking out items for a scrumptious vegetarian meal*

CHAPTER 43

The Meat-Free Life

Five Reasons to Be a Vegetarian & Ten Arguments Against Eating Meat

THERE ARE MORE THAN A FEW HINDUS today who guiltily abandoned the vegetarian ways of their own parents and grandparents when they decided to be "secular" and "modern." But our ancient seers had it right when they advocated living without killing animals for food. Today vegetarianism is a worldwide movement with adherents among all religions, daily gaining converts through one or more of the five basic reasons to adhere to a meatless diet: dharma, karma, consciousness, health and environment. Each is explored in the following pages, which conclude with an examination of the harmful effects of eating meat.

subtle sense of guilt persists among Hindus who eat meat, and even they will abstain at special times. For India's ancient thinkers, life is seen as the very stuff of the Divine, an emanation of the Source and part of a cosmic continuum. They further hold that each life form, even water and trees, possesses consciousness and energy. Nonviolence, ahimsa, the primary basis of vegetarianism, has long been central to the religious traditions of India—especially Hinduism, Buddhism and Jainism. Religion in India has consistently upheld the sanctity of life, whether human or animal.

The Sanskrit word for vegetarianism is *shakahara*, and one following a vegetarian diet is a *shakahari*. Hindu vegetarians commonly consume milk products, but not eggs, which are definitely a meat product, containing cholesterol which is only present in animal flesh. The term for meat-eating is *mansahara*, and the meat-eater is called *mansahari*. *Ahara* means "to consume or eat," *shaka* means "vegetable," and *mansa* means "meat or flesh." The very word *mansa*, "meat," conveys a deep appreciation of life's sacredness and an understanding of the law of karma by which the consequence of each action returns to the doer. As explained in the 2,000-year-old *Manu Dharma Shastra*, 5.55, "The learned declare that the meaning of *mansa* (flesh) is, 'he (*sa*) will eat me (*mam*) in the other world whose flesh I eat here.'" There developed early in India an unparalleled concern for harmony among life forms, and this led to a common ethos based on noninju-

Reason 1
Dharma

Vedic scripture proclaims that ahimsa, nonhurtfulness, is a primary religious obligation in fulfillment of dharma, divine law.

COMSTOCK

Just how widespread is this movement? In the UK, polls show more than 15 percent of teenagers are vegetarians, and six percent of the general population. In America, eight percent of teens and three percent of the general population declare themselves vegetarian. It is a movement with a broad base, for one can find advocates as diverse as philosophers Plato and Nietzsche, politicians Benjamin Franklin and Gandhi, Beatle Paul McCartney and Rastifarian singer Bob Marley, actresses Brooke Shields, Drew Barrymore, Alicia Silverstone, and actors David Duchovny, Richard Gere and Brad Pitt. It's also helped that a multitude of rigorous scientific studies have proven the health benefits of the vegetarian diet.

Vegetarianism, an Ancient Hindu Ethic
Vegetarianism was for thousands of years a principle of health and environmental ethics throughout India. Though Muslim and Christian colonization radically undermined and eroded this ideal, it remains to this day a cardinal ethic of Hindu thought and practice. A

riousness and a minimal consumption of natural resources—in other words, to compassion and simplicity. If Homo sapiens is to survive his present predicament, he will have to rediscover these two primary ethical virtues.

Is Vegetarianism Integral to Noninjury?
In Satguru Sivaya Subramuniyaswami's book, *Dancing with Siva*, this question is addressed as follows: "Hindus teach vegetarianism as a way to live with a minimum of hurt to other beings, for to consume meat, fish, fowl or eggs is to participate indirectly in acts of cruelty and violence against the animal kingdom. The abhorrence of injury and killing of any kind leads quite naturally to a vegetarian diet, *shakahara*. The meat-eater's desire for meat drives another to kill and provide that meat. The act of the butcher begins with the desire of the consumer. Meat-eating contributes to a mentality of violence, for with the chemically complex meat ingested, one absorbs the slaughtered creature's fear, pain and terror. These qualities are nour-

ished within the meat-eater, perpetuating the cycle of cruelty and confusion. When the individual's consciousness lifts and expands, he will abhor violence and not be able to even digest the meat, fish, fowl and eggs he was formerly consuming. India's greatest saints have confirmed that one cannot eat meat and live a peaceful, harmonious life. Man's appetite for meat inflicts devastating harm on Earth itself, stripping its precious forests to make way for pastures. The *Tirukural* candidly states, 'How can he practice true compassion who eats the flesh of an animal to fatten his own flesh? Greater than a thousand ghee offerings consumed in sacrificial fires is not to sacrifice and consume any living creature.' "

Amazingly, some people define vegetarian as a diet which excludes the meat of animals but does permit fish and eggs. But what really is vegetarianism? Vegetarian foods include grains, fruits, vegetables, legumes and dairy products. Natural, fresh foods, locally grown without insecticides or chemical fertilizers, are preferred. A vegetarian diet does not include meat, fish, fowl, shellfish or eggs. For good health, even certain vegetarian foods are minimized: frozen and canned foods, highly processed foods, such as white rice, white sugar and white flour; and "junk" foods and beverages—those with abundant chemical additives, such as artificial sweeteners, colorings, flavorings and preservatives.

Reason 2

Karma

By involving oneself in the cycle of inflicting injury, pain and death, even indirectly, by eating other creatures, one must in the future experience in equal measure the suffering caused.

COMSTOCK

According to Satguru Sivaya Subramuniyaswami, "In my forty years of ministry it has become quite evident that vegetarian families have far fewer problems than those who are not vegetarian. If children are raised as vegetarians, every day they are exposed to nonviolence as a principle of peace and compassion. Every day they are growing up they are remembering and being reminded to not kill. They won't even kill another creature to eat, to feed themselves.

And if they won't kill another creature to feed themselves, they will be much less likely to do acts of violence against people."

Vegetarian Animals

Vegetarians come in all sizes and shapes, but the elephant is the largest of all, with a sophisticated social life, loving and affectionately caring for its own. Elephants live long, vigorous lives, have a very large brain and, of course, are renowned for their excellent memory. They do not suffer any weakness for not eating meat. In fact, so many muscular and the most intelligent animals—the horse, the cow, giraffe, zebra, rhinoceros, the apes, and more—are lifelong vegetarians and friends of men. Lean animals, thin and wiry, who are feared by man and beasts alike, are all hunters and killers and eaters of flesh—tigers, sharks, hawks, wolves and the like. No one fears a gentle vegetarian, but all have reason to fear the unpredictable meat-eater. Scriptures admonish that it is wise to fear what should be feared.

Food and Consciousness

Food is the source of the body's chemistry, and what we ingest affects our consciousness, emotions and experiential patterns. If one wants to live in higher consciousness, in peace and happiness and love for all creatures, then he cannot eat meat, fish, shellfish, fowl or eggs. By ingesting the grosser chemistries of animal foods, one introduces into the body and mind anger, jealousy, fear, anxiety, suspicion and the terrible fear of death, all of which is locked into the flesh of butchered creatures. It is said that in ancient India meat would be fed to the soldiers during military campaigns, especially before combat, to bring them into lower consciousness so that they would forget their religious values. They performed these deeds in fulfillment of a warrior's way—with not the least restraint of conscience. The inner law is ever so simple—not eating meat, fish, foul or eggs is essential to awaken consciousness into the seven higher chakras (the *uttara-chakras*), up to the crown. Nonkilling—and

From market to table: *(l to r) North Indian tali plate; a family enjoys a vegetarian meal; selling vegetables at a local market; a traditional South Indian meal served on an eco-friendly banana leaf*

PHOTOS: DINODIA

noneating of that which is killed—is a must to pass from realms below the muladhara.

Dharma

How many there are who resent the very mention of becoming a vegetarian, whose instinctive nature is repelled by the idea because they intuit the road ahead. They sense that once the more *sattvic* diet of pure foods is taken in place of meats (and other dead foods, packaged, processed and cellophane-wrapped) they will feel a great guilt occasioned by their transgressions of dharma, as they have so well perfected over the years their *adharmic* ways. *Adharma* means all that stands against Indian spirituality, against the path of the good and the pure and the natural, against dharma in all of its intricate dimensions. None of the specialized *dharmas—stri dharma*, the duties of women; *purusha dharma*, the duties of men; *ashrama dharma*, the responsibility of one's stage of life; *varna dharma*, one's position in society; and *svadharma*, one's own perfect pattern—even when performed properly will have the same results without fulfilling this virtue. Even *rita dharma*, cosmic order, is upset by man's insatiable, aggressive appetites expressed through flesh-consuming.

Hindus Were the First Vegetarians

The book, *Food for the Spirit, Vegetarianism and the World Religions,* observes: "Despite popular knowledge of meat-eating's adverse effects, the nonvegetarian diet became increasingly widespread among Hindus after the two major invasions by foreign powers, first the Muslims and later the British. With them came the desire to be 'civilized,' to eat as did the saheeb. Those actually trained in Vedic knowledge, however, never adopted a meat-oriented diet, and the pious Hindu still observes vegetarian principles as a matter of religious duty.

"That vegetarianism has always been widespread in India is clear from the earliest *Vedic* texts. This was observed by the ancient traveler Megasthenes and also by Fa-hsien, a Chinese Buddhist monk who, in the fifth century, traveled to India in order to obtain authentic copies of the scriptures. These scriptures unambiguously support the meatless way of life. In the *Mahabharata*, for instance, the great warrior Bhishma explains to Yudhishthira, eldest of the Pandava princes, that the meat of animals is like the flesh of one's own son, and that the foolish person who eats meat must be considered the vilest of human beings [*Anu.* 114.11]. The eating of 'dirty' food, it warns, is not as terrible as the eating of flesh [*Shanti.* 141.88] (it must be remembered that the brahmins of ancient India exalted cleanliness to a divine principle).

"Similarly, the *Manusmriti* declares that one should 'refrain from eating all kinds of meat,' for such eating involves killing and leads to karmic bondage (*bandha*) [5.49]. Elsewhere in the Vedic literature, the last of the great Vedic kings, Maharaja Parikshit, is quoted as saying that 'only the animal-killer cannot relish the message of the Absolute Truth [*Shrimad Bhagavatam* 10.1.4].'"

Common Dietary Concerns

Those considering a vegetarian diet generally worry about getting enough nutrients, since the belief that meat is a necessary part of keeping strong and healthy is still extremely widespread. Recently a group of eminent doctors called the Physicians Committee for Responsible Medicine (PCRM), themselves members of the American Medical Association, have decided to change the US consciousness on human nutrition, particularly among the medical community. The PCRM is a nonprofit organization based in Washington, D.C., consisting of doctors and laypersons working together for compassionate and effective medical practice, research and health promotion. Founded in 1985, the PCRM is supported by over 3,000 physicians and 50,000 laypersons. PCRM president (and vegetarian) Neal D. Barnard, M.D., is a popular speaker and the author of *The Power of Your Plate*. Armed with

Reason 3

Consciousness

By ingesting the grosser chemistries of animal foods, one introduces into the body and mind anger, jealousy, fear, anxiety, suspicion and a terrible fear of death, all of which are locked into the flesh of the butchered creatures.

COMSTOCK

decades of nutritional research data, PCRM addresses these dietary concerns head-on:

"The fact is, it is very easy to have a well-balanced diet with vegetarian foods. Vegetarian foods provide plenty of protein. Careful combining of foods is not necessary. Any normal variety of plant foods provides more than enough protein for the body's needs. Although there is somewhat less protein in a vegetarian diet than a meat-eater's diet, this is actually an advantage. Excess protein has been linked to kidney stones, osteoporosis, and possibly heart disease and some cancers. A diet focused on beans, whole grains and vegetables contains adequate amounts of protein without the 'overdose' most meat-eaters get."

Other concerns are allayed by the PCRM as follows:

1. **Calcium** is easy to find in a vegetarian diet. Many dark, green leafy vegetables and beans are loaded with calcium, and some orange juices and cereals are calcium-fortified.

2. **Iron** is plentiful in whole grains, beans and fruits.

3. **Vitamin B12:** There is a misconception that without eating meat one cannot obtain sufficient vitamin B12, which is an essential nutrient. This is simply not true. The PCRM advises: "Although cases of B12 deficiency are very uncommon, it is important to make sure that one has a reliable source of the vitamin. Good sources include all common multiple vitamins (including vegetarian vitamins), fortified cereals and soy milk." Vitamin B12 is widely available in brewers yeast and other potent dietary supplements.

Reason 4
Health

Vegetarians are less susceptible to all the major diseases that afflict contemporary humanity. Thus they live longer, healthier, more productive lives. They have fewer physical complaints, less frequent visits to the doctor, fewer dental problems and smaller medical bills.

COMSTOCK

4. Nutritional needs increase during **pregnancy**. The American Dietetic Association has found vegan diets adequate for fulfilling nutritional needs during pregnancy, but pregnant women and nursing mothers should supplement their diets with vitamins B12 and D.

5. Vegetarian **children** also have high nutritional needs, but these, too, are met with a vegetarian diet. A vegetarian menu is "life-extending." As children, vegetarians may grow more gradually, reach puberty somewhat later, and live substantially longer than meat-eaters. Be sure to include a reliable source of vitamin B12.

Those interested in supporting or learning more about the work of the Physicians Committee for Responsible Medicine should visit: www.pcrm.org.

Converting to Vegetarianism
Making the transition from carnivore to herbivore is not as hard as you might think. According to the book, *The New Vegetarians*, by Sonia Partridge and Paul Amato, 73% of vegetarian converts stated that the transition was not difficult. It is easier for people who do some homework on the subject and have a bit of cooking skill. The time it takes for people to totally convert varies greatly. About 70% of people make the transition gradually, while 30% stop all at once. Red meat is almost always abandoned within the first year, followed by fowl, fish and eggs.

One recommended method for the transition is to set a series of goals for yourself. Start simply with getting through one day without meat. Then, try one weekend, then one week. Make a realistic timetable for reaching each goal. Two to three months might be reason-

Wisdom from Saints and Scriptures

Vedas, Shastras and Sutras Alike Decry the Killing and Eating of Animals

Scriptures of all Hindu denominations speak clearly and forcefully on nonkilling and vegetarianism. The roots of noninjury, nonkilling and nonconsumption of meat are found in the Vedas, Dharma Shastras, Tirumurai, Yoga Sutras, Tirukural *and dozens of other sacred texts of Hinduism. Perhaps nowhere is the principle of nonmeat-eating so fully and eloquently expressed as in the* Tirukural, *written in the Tamil language by a simple weaver saint over 2,000 years ago.*

One who partakes of human flesh, the flesh of a horse or of another animal, and deprives others of milk by slaughtering cows, O King, if such a fiend does not desist by other means, then you should not hesitate to cut off his head.

Rig Veda Samhita 10.87.16

Protect both our species, two-legged and four-legged. Both food and water for their needs supply. May they with us increase in stature and strength. Save us from hurt all our days, O Powers!

Rig Veda Samhita 10.37.11

O vegetable, be succulent, wholesome, strengthening; and thus, body, be fully grown.

Rig Veda

Those noble souls who practice meditation and other yogic ways, who are ever careful about all beings, who protect all animals, are the ones who are actually serious about spiritual practices.

Atharva Veda Samhita 19.48.5

You must not use your God-given body for killing God's creatures, whether they are human, animal or whatever.

Yajur Veda Samhita 12.32

The ignoble ones who eat flesh, death's agents bind them fast and push them quick into the fiery jaws of hell (Naraka, lower consciousness).

Tirumantiram

When mindstuff is firmly based in waves of ahimsa, all living beings cease their enmity in the presence of such a person.

Yoga Sutras 2.35

Ahimsa is not causing pain to any living being at any time through the actions of one's mind, speech or body.

Sandilya Upanishad

able for some people, while six months to a year might be better for others. Rewards can also help. For a major accomplishment such as a week without meat, treat yourself to a nice vegetarian meal out.

One can also take a formal Hindu vow of vegetarianism, *shakahara* vrata, available on-line at www. hinduismtoday.com/in-depth_issues/veggie_vow/. The vow may be taken privately, before elders or parents or as part of a temple ceremony. It reads in part, "I accept the principle of *shakahara* as the method by which I may acknowledge my compassion, my *karuna*, for all living beings. As an act of dedication, I am resolved this day to begin (or continue) the regular practice of eating a strict vegetarian diet and not eating meat, fish, shellfish, fowl or eggs."

The most common problem with conversion is not knowing enough about the vegetarian diet. Some people decide to be vegetarian but have no idea what to eat, and end up with soggy vegetables and undercooked brown rice for breakfast, lunch and dinner. They become discouraged and rightly wonder how they will survive. But decent vegetarian food isn't boring. A little research will put your mind at ease. Get some vegetarian cookbooks. Ask restaurant waiters which menu items are vegetarian. Search online for vegetarian recipes.

Vegetarians are often asked "Don't you miss eating meat?" For about half of beginning vegetarians the answer is yes, according to *The New Vegetarians*. They miss the texture and flavor of meat in the early weeks and months. Almost everyone though, gets over this within six months to a year and for many it becomes nauseating even to think

about eating meat. Eighty-two percent of fully adapted vegetarians say there is no way they would consider eating flesh again.

Reason 5
Environment

In large measure, the escalating loss of species, destruction of ancient rain forests to create pasture lands for livestock, loss of topsoil and the consequent increase of water impurities and air pollution have all been traced to the single fact of meat in the human diet.

COMSTOCK

Conclusion

Satguru Sivaya Subramuniyaswami writes, "Modern meats are killed by chemical treatment of the animals, the hormones of fear and chemistry of death before and during slaughter, killed again by refrigerating them, killed again by grinding them, killed again by preserving them, killed again by packaging them, killed again by freezing them, killed again by storing and shipping them, and finally really killed by cooking them to death. How can such so-called food nourish a human being?

"Why should we ever think of eating meat, fish, foul, eggs, anything with eyes or, as some say, with two or more senses. The cock-a-doodle-doo who wakes us up in the morning is dinner on the table at night. How gruesome. How ruthless to thus forever close the eyes of an animal, or have someone else do it for them in order that they may buy the carcass, closing their eyes to the fact, which is even worse, and keeping their own eyes closed to that creature's suffering to consume it without conscience during jovial small talk over the dinner table. How easy in turn for such a person to turn and maim or kill a fellow human in the same way in times of stress as a natural reaction, in 'justifiable righteousness.'" As the *Tirukural* proclaims, compassion cannot be found in the hearts of those who eat meat.

Having well considered the origin of flesh and the cruelty of fettering and slaying of corporeal beings, let one entirely abstain from eating flesh.

Manu Samhita

The purchaser of flesh performs *himsa* (violence) by his wealth; he who eats flesh does so by enjoying its taste; the killer does *himsa* by actually tying and killing the animal. Thus, there are three forms of killing: he who brings flesh or sends for it, he who cuts off the limbs of an animal, and he who purchases, sells or cooks flesh and eats it—all of these are to be considered meat-eaters.

Mahabharata, Anu. 115.40

He who desires to augment his own flesh by eating the flesh of other creatures lives in misery in whatever species he may take his birth.

Mahabharata, Anu. 115.47

Those high-souled persons who desire beauty, faultlessness of limbs, long life, understanding, mental and physical strength

and memory should abstain from acts of injury.

Mahabharata 18.115.8

How can he practice true compassion who eats the flesh of an animal to fatten his own flesh?

Tirukural Verse 251

Riches cannot be found in the hands of the thriftless. Nor can compassion be found in the hearts of those who eat meat.

Tirukural Verse 252

Goodness is never one with the minds of these two: one who wields a weapon and one who feasts on a creature's flesh.

Tirukural Verse 253

If you ask, "What is kindness and what is unkind?" it is not killing and killing. Thus, eating flesh is never virtuous.

Tirukural Verse 254

Life is perpetuated by not eating meat. The clenched jaws of hell hold those who do.

Tirukural Verse 255

If the world did not purchase and consume meat, there would be none to slaughter and offer meat for sale.

Tirukural Verse 256

When a man realizes that meat is the butchered flesh of another creature, he must abstain from eating it.

Tirukural Verse 257

Greater than a thousand ghee offerings consumed in sacrificial fires is to not sacrifice and consume any living creature.

Tirukural Verse 259

All that lives will press palms together in prayerful adoration of those who refuse to slaughter and savor meat.

Tirukural Verse 260

My opinion is well known. I do not regard flesh food as necessary for us at any stage and under any clime in which it is possible for human beings ordinarily to live. I hold flesh-food to be unsuited to our species."

Mahatma Gandhi

How to Win an Argument With a Meat-Eater

Facts and Figures You Need to Change Opinion

IN THE PRECEDING PAGES WE HAVE DIScussed the benefits and practical considerations of a vegetarian diet. Here we approach the issue from another perspective, examining the devastating harm caused by a meat-laden diet—not only to the animal which is killed and eaten, but also to the meat-eater himself, to humanity as a whole and to our very planet. The following presentation is based on the poster, "How to win an argument with a meat-eater," published by Earthsave, of Felton, California, giving facts from Pulitzer Prize nominee John Robbins' book, *Diet for a New America*. Our version details ten arguments against meat-eating.

1. The Hunger Argument
The world's massive hunger problems could be greatly alleviated by reducing or elimination meat-eating. Vast quantities of food suitable for humans are fed to livestock for meat production—wasting most of its protein in the process; in addition, the huge acreages now used as pasture for meat animals would produce much more human food if converted to grains and vegetables.

This year alone, twenty million people worldwide will die of malnutrition. One child dies of malnutrition every 2.3 seconds. One hundred million people could be adequately fed using the land freed if Americans reduced their intake of meat by a mere 10%. Eighty percent of the corn and 95% of the oats grown in the US is eaten by livestock. The percentage of protein wasted by cycling grain through livestock is calculated by experts as 90%. One acre of good farmland can produce 40,000 pounds of potatoes, or 250 pounds of beef. Fifty-six percent of all US farmland is devoted to beef production, and to produce each pound of beef requires 16 pounds of edible grain and soybeans, which could be used to feed the hungry.

2. The Environmental Argument
Many of the world's massive environmental problems—including global warming, loss of topsoil, loss of rain forests and species extinction—could be solved by the reduction or elimination of meat-eating. The meat industry's voracious need for pasturelands is the primary force driving the destruction of old-growth forests—which are essential to the survival of the planet. Their destruction is a major cause of global warming and of the rapidly escalating losses of topsoil and endangered-species habitat. Two hundred sixty million acres of US forestland have been cleared for meat production. An alarming 75% of all US topsoil has been lost to date, and fullly 85% of this loss is directly related to livestock raising. Another devastating result of meat-eating is the loss of plant and animal species. Each year 1,000 species disappear due to destruction of tropical rain forests for cattle grazing and other uses—driven by US demand for meat. The rate is growing yearly.

3. The Cancer Argument
Those who eat flesh are far more likely to contract cancer than those following a vegetarian diet. The risk of contracting breast cancer is 3.8 times greater for women who eat meat daily compared to less than once a week; 2.8 times greater for women who eat eggs daily compared to once a week; and 3.25 greater for women who eat processed butter and cheese two to four times a week as compared to once a week. The risk of fatal ovarian cancer is three times greater for women who eat eggs three or more times a week as compared with less than once a week. The risk of fatal prostate cancer is 3.6 times greater for men who consume meat, eggs, processed cheese and milk daily as compared with sparingly or not at all.

4. The Cholesterol Argument
The average cholesterol consumption of a meat-centered diet is 210 milligrams per day. The chance of dying from heart disease if you are male and your blood cholesterol intake is 210 milligrams a day is greater than 50%.

It is strange but true that US physicians are as a rule poorly educated in the single most important factor of health, namely diet and nutrition. As of 1987, of the 125 medical schools in the US, only 30 required their students to take a course in nutrition.

The average nutrition training received by the average US physician during four years in school is only 2.5 hours. Thus doctors in the US are ill equipped to advise their patients in minimizing foods, such as meat, that contain excessive amounts of cholesterol and are known causes of heart attack. Heart attack is the most common cause of death in the US, killing one person every 45 seconds. The male meat-eater's risk of death from heart attack is 50%. The risk to men who eat no meat is only 15%. Reducing one's consumption of meat, processed dairy products and eggs by 10% reduces the risk of heart attack by 10%. Eliminat-

Carnivores: Humans, it is noted, do not have fangs or claws, like this powerful meat-eating tigress

RAJESH BEDI

ing all of these products from one's diet reduces the risk of heart attack by 90%.

5. The Natural Resources Argument
The world's natural resources are being rapidly depleted as a result of meat-eating. Raising livestock for their meat is a very inefficient way of generating food. Pound for pound, far more resources must be expended to produce meat than to produce

grains, fruits and vegetables. For example, more than half of all water used for all purposes in the US is consumed in livestock production. The amount of water used in production of the average cow is sufficient to float a destroyer (a large naval ship). While 25 gallons of water are needed to produce a pound of wheat, 5,000 gallons are needed to produce a pound of California beef. That same 5,000 gallons of water can produce 200 pounds of wheat.

Thirty-three percent of all raw materials (base products of farming, forestry and mining, including fossil fuels) consumed by the US are devoted to the production

of livestock, as compared with two percent to produce a complete vegetarian diet.

6. The Antibiotic Argument

Another danger of eating meat is the fact that large amounts of antibiotics are fed to livestock to control staphylococci (commonly called staph infections). The animals being raised for meat in the United States are diseased. The livestock industry attempts to control the various diseases by feeding the animals huge quantities of antibiotics. Of all antibiotics used in the US, 55% are fed to livestock. But the disease-causing bacteria are rapidly becoming immune to the antibiotics, thus endangering humans who depend on these antibiotics to combat disease. The percentage of staphylococci infections resistant to penicillin, for example, has grown from 13% in 1960 to 91% in 1988. These antibiotics and/or the super-resistant bacteria they were intended to destroy remain in the meat that goes to market. The European Economic Community banned the importation of US meat because of this routine feeding of antibiotics.

7. The Mad Cow Argument

In February, 2001, Cornell University reported, "Bovine spongiform encephalopathy (BSE), also known as mad cow disease, has now been officially identified in a dozen European countries including the UK, France, Italy, Germany, Spain, Belgium, Ireland, Liechtenstein, Portugal, Switzerland, Luxembourg and the Netherlands. As a result, beef sales have fallen by as much as 50% in parts of Europe." This epidemic is believed to have resulted from the common practice of feeding cows the ground-up brains and other parts of sheep, some of which were infected with scrapie, a related disease.

Only one-tenth of one percent of US cattle slaughtered for meat are tested for BSE by the USDA (US Department of Agriculture). When a Kansas beef producer decided to test all of their own cattle for BSE, the USDA actually blocked companies from selling them the testing kits. Despite the rarity of the disease, its human form (believed to be caused by eating infected meat) killed over 150 people, mostly in Britain, between 1986 and 2003.

8. The Pesticide Argument

US-produced meat contains dangerously high quantities of deadly pesticides. Many people believe that the USDA protects consumers' health through regular and thorough meat inspection. In reality, fewer than one out of every 250,000 slaughtered animals is tested for toxic chemical residues. A study of mothers' milk in the US has clearly demonstrated that these chemicals are ingested by the meat-eater:

a. Ninety-nine percent of the meat-eating mothers in the study produced milk with significant levels of DDT–compared to only 8% of the vegetarian mothers' milk. This shows that the primary source of DDT is the meat ingested by the mothers.

b. The breast milk of meat-eating mothers has 35 times more chlorinated hydrocarbon pesticides than the milk of nonmeat-eating mothers.

c. The average breast-fed American infant contains nine times the permissible level of the pesticide dieldrin, which (though now banned in the US) continues to accumulate in the food chain and often exceeds safety guidelines in fish and seafood.

9. The Ethical Argument

Many people have become vegetarians after reading about or personally experiencing what goes on daily at any one of the thousands of slaughterhouses in the US and other countries, where animals suffer the cruel process of forced confinement, manipulation and violent death. Their pain and terror is beyond calculation. Most slaughterhouse workers are not on the job for long and have the highest turnover rate of all occupations. It also has the highest rate of on-the-job injury.

In the US alone, 1.14 million animals are killed for meat every hour. The average per capita consumption of meat in the US, Canada and Australia is 200 pounds per year! The average American consumes in a 72-year lifetime approximately eleven cattle, three lambs and sheep, 23 pigs, 45 turkeys, 1,100 chickens and 862 pounds of fish!

10. The Physiological Argument

The final argument against meat-eating is that humans are physiologically not suited for a carnivorous diet. The book *Food for the Spirit, Vegetarianism in the World Religions*, summarizes this point of view as follows. "Many nutritionists, biologists and physiologists offer convincing evidence that humans are in fact not meant to eat flesh...." The book gives seven facts in support of this view:

1. Physiologically, people are more akin to plant-eaters, foragers and grazers, such as monkeys, elephants and cows, than to carnivora such as dogs, tigers and leopards.

2. For example, carnivores do not sweat through their skin; body heat is controlled by rapid breathing and extrusion of the tongue. Vegetarian animals, on the other hand, have sweat pores for heat control and the elimination of impurities.

3. Carnivora have long teeth and claws for holding and killing prey; vegetarian animals have short teeth and no claws.

4. The saliva of carnivora contains no ptyalin and cannot predigest starches; that of vegetarian animals contains ptyalin for the predigestion of starches.

5. Flesh-eating animals secrete large quantities of hydrochloric acid to help dissolve bones; vegetarian animals secrete little hydrochloric acid.

6. The jaws of carnivora only open in an up and down motion; those of vegetarian animals also move sideways for additional kinds of chewing.

7. Carnivores must lap liquids, as a cat does; vegetarian animals take liquids in by suction through the teeth.

CHAPTER 44

Medical Ethics

Hindu Insights on 25 Sensitive Areas Frequently Encountered by Physicians

PHOTODISC

HINDU MEDICINE, KNOWN AS AYURVEDA, THE "SCI-ence of life," has a highly developed system of practical ethics derived from the Hindu principles of nonhurtfulness, the sanctity of all life, the existence of the soul separate from the body and a willingness to accept life's circumstances as defined by one's karma and dharma.

In 1999, HINDUISM TODAY was approached by the Texas Medical Association to help them revise and expand a book on medical issues called *Faith of Our Patients*. When it was first published in 1978, the booklet dealt with the Catholic, Protestant and Jewish views of 14 "problem areas" most frequently encountered by physicians, including autopsy, abortion, artificial insemination, prolongation of life and organ transplants. They had recently expanded their list and sought to include the views of Hinduism and Buddhism to accommodate increased religious diversity among their patients.

To respond to their request, we enlisted the help of Swami Bua, Swami Satchidananda, Swami Ranganathananda of the Ramakrishna Mission, Swami Chidanand Saraswati (Muniji), Swami Omkarananda, Swami Pragyanand, Swami Tejomayananda of Chinmaya Mission, Satguru Sivaya Subramuniyaswami and his successor, Satguru Bodhinatha Veylanswami. We also consulted with Dr. Virender Sodhi, an ayurvedic and allopathic doctor in Washington, and Cromwell Crawford of the University of Hawaii, an Indian-born specialist in Hindu medical ethics. The assembled responses below represent the broad consensus of this group, with occasional differing opinions. It remains a work in progress, to be updated as required.

Fortunately, as pointed out by Professor Crawford, the ancient codifiers of ayurveda, Sushruta and Charaka, carefully considered and documented the ethics of their profession and its various medical procedures. They did so within the context of a Hindu view of man, which, as Swami Ranganathananda put it, "is that his essential, real nature

is the atman or Self, which is immortal, self-luminous, the source of all power, joy and glory. Everything that helps in the manifestation of the divinity of the soul is beneficial and moral, and everything that obstructs this inner unfoldment is harmful and immoral." With this over-arching principle in mind, it was the aim of the ayurvedic physician to preserve the well-being of the community through maintaining health and removing the threats to life of humans and nonhumans. The ancient healers held that pathogenesis, the development of disease, is not caused randomly or simplistically by external agents through infection or injury. Rather, the development of any disease is also an expression of karma: the results of an individual's past actions. It is hoped that this compilation of Hindu medical ethics will provide a spiritual view of the medical concerns faced by all Hindus, one that will balance the prevailing humanistic view by presenting a traditional Hindu perspective from which to evaluate these important matters of life, death and the beyond.

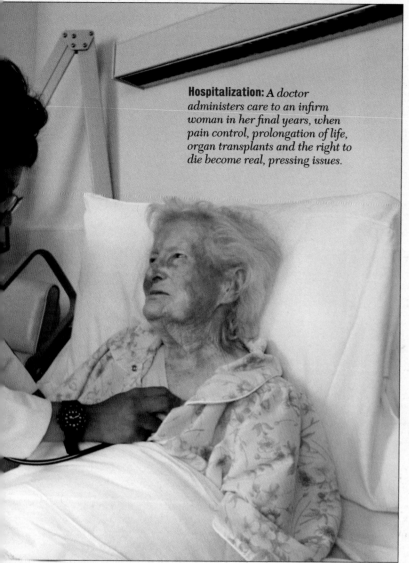

Hospitalization: *A doctor administers care to an infirm woman in her final years, when pain control, prolongation of life, organ transplants and the right to die become real, pressing issues.*

in a 24-hour-a-day vigil." Satguru Sivaya Subramuniyaswami wrote, "Blessed with the knowledge of impending transition, we settle affairs and take refuge in *japa*, worship, scripture and yoga—seeking the highest realizations as we consciously, joyously release the world. Our soul never dies; only the physical body dies. We simply step out of the physical body and are in our astral body, going on in the mind as usual. For Hindus, death is nobly referred to as *mahaprasthana*, 'the great journey.' The awareness, will, memory and intelligence which we think of as ourselves continue to exist in the soul body. We approach death as a *sadhana*, as a spiritual opportunity. To leave the body in the right frame of mind, in the right consciousness, through the highest possible chakra, is a key to spiritual progress."

Pain Control

Hindus regard pain management as an important duty of caretakers. "If an individual opts to undergo the pains, he or she should be left alone," Swami Bua noted. "Otherwise, it is the duty of the people around to help reduce his suffering. If a person is relieved of pain, his thoughts become sublime with gratitude and the feelings of amity, affection and love. Nobody should be allowed to die with the feelings of bitterness, feelings of wanting or feelings of unfulfilled duties. We should do everything possible to keep the dying person comfortable till his end, which is determined by Him." Opiates and other drugs have been used for this purpose in Hindu medicine for thousands of years, according to Dr. Sodhi. However, he explains, "They try not to administer so much pain-killer as to alter or lose consciousness." Excessive pain-killers can dull awareness and inhibit the conscious transition that is the Hindu ideal.

Prolongation of Life

Ayurveda classifies disease as either *sadhya*, those that can be effectively treated and cured, or *asadhya*, those that cannot. It further classifies untreatable diseases as those which can be managed for an acceptable quality of life, such as diabetes, and those which cannot, such as terminal cancer. If treatment cannot provide the patient a quality life, then it is considered better to give no treatment beyond palliative measures.

End-of-Life Issues

Hindus regard death as a most exalted human experience, the migration of the soul from one dimension of consciousness to another, a transition we have all experienced many times. Death is not to be feared, neither unnecessarily accelerated nor relentlessly delayed. In considering the following end-of-life issues the Hindu seeks to preserve the natural timing of death, while humanely comforting and being present for the patient in a spiritual environment.

Preparation for Death

"With our strong conviction that all our actions in the present life will be the cause for the effects in our future life," says Swami Bua, "a wise Hindu facing death goes into introspection of all his deeds during the present life and sincerely tries to make amends for the wrong deeds. Wherever it is beyond correction, he repents and wholeheartedly prays for forgiveness in the form of chanting mantras. He plans to visit holy places and temples, health permitting. When and if he becomes immobile due to physical conditions, and the indications are that he is nearing his end, his children assemble around him and give him holy water from the Ganges. They sing bhajanas, holy songs, and chant mantras, often

The "Right to Die"

It is the law in many parts of America that a hospital must do everything possible to keep a patient alive as long as possible, no matter what his state of consciousness, or the prognosis for a useful existence. If the patient's financial resources are exhausted, then the state must pay. To avoid being kept alive against his own wishes, he must make a "living will" in advance, to specify under what conditions he declines further treatment, and to assign a person to make that decision for him if he cannot. A living will can preserve the resources of a family, avoiding costly and ineffective heroic treatment. Hindus accept the natural timing of life and of death and do not strain to gain a few months of struggle-filled life at great effort and expense.

"Do-Not-Resuscitate" Orders

Part of a living will deals with "Do-not-resuscitate" orders. These instructions tell the doctors when they should not use cardiopulmonary resuscitation (CPR) or other measures to revive a person if his heart or breathing has stopped. Again, the decision centers around the likely quality of a life so revived. A drowning or heart-

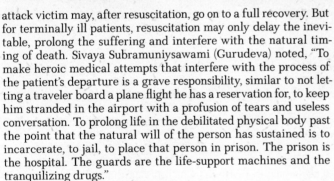

A. MANIVEL

PHOTODISC

attack victim may, after resuscitation, go on to a full recovery. But for terminally ill patients, resuscitation may only delay the inevitable, prolong the suffering and interfere with the natural timing of death. Sivaya Subramuniyaswami (Gurudeva) noted, "To make heroic medical attempts that interfere with the process of the patient's departure is a grave responsibility, similar to not letting a traveler board a plane flight he has a reservation for, to keep him stranded in the airport with a profusion of tears and useless conversation. To prolong life in the debilitated physical body past the point that the natural will of the person has sustained is to incarcerate, to jail, to place that person in prison. The prison is the hospital. The guards are the life-support machines and the tranquilizing drugs."

Removal of Life Support

A critical and closely related issue any living will should address is the removal of life support. Modern machines can keep patients alive when they are unable to breathe or take nourishment, and when organs cease to function, including the heart. Life-support patients may be in near-normal consciousness, semi-conscious, comatose or "brain dead," with no brain wave activity at all. Even common kidney dialysis machines and ventilators qualify as "life support," for if turned off patients would die. A much discussed issue is whether turning off a life support machine is "killing" the patient or "letting him die." The issue is further complicated by rapidly advancing technology whereby ever more seriously ill or injured patients can be kept alive.

In Dr. Sodhi's opinion, removal of life support would be justified in a case where there is no brain-wave activity, for "according to ayurveda, that person is dead. Sustaining his condition is more like the torture of the soul, and ayurveda prohibits it." While

ancient Hindu medicine did not anticipate many of the abilities of today's complex machines, it did discuss the issue of nourishment, which is a part of any life-support system. Hindu scripture allows for the termination of food and water at the request of a terminally ill patient who chooses a self-willed death by fasting, *prayopavesha*. The patient can specify in advance in his living will under what conditions nourishment, hydration or other life support should be withheld. Knowledge of the patient's intentions [or wishes] alleviates the karmic burden of the doctors and family. The ideal, Gurudeva counseled his own devotees, is to not be put on the life support machine in the first place when there is little chance of recovery.

Assisted Suicide

Hindu philosophy does not support "assisted suicide," deliberately causing the death of a patient at the patient's own request by drugs, overdose of painkillers or other lethal means. In extreme circumstances of unbearable agony where others turn to euthanasia or mercy killing, Hindus know the sufferer may refuse food and water.

Suicide

Hindus believe that life is sacred—God's grace—and therefore it is not ours to end. Suicide only postpones and intensifies the karma one seeks escape from, requiring several lives to return to the evolutionary point that existed at the moment of suicide, thus it is a spiritual step backwards. In cases of terminal illness, under strict community regulation, tradition does allow *prayopavesha*, self-willed religious death by fasting, as stated above. Gurudeva taught, "The Vedic rishis gave the anguished embodied soul a way

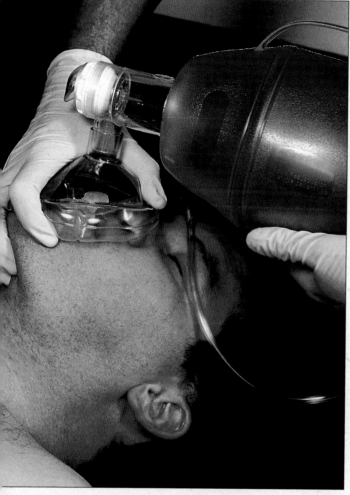

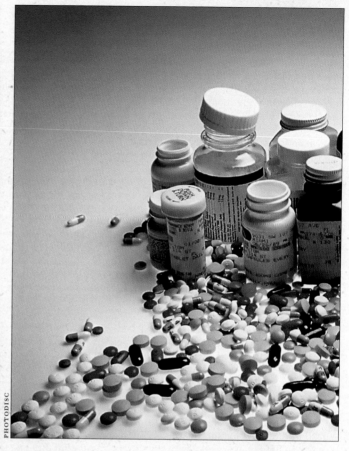

Near life's end: *(left to right) as this grandfather grows old, his daughter takes good care of him at home rather than placing him in a nursing home; a man's heart and breathing has stopped—doctors administer CPR in hopes of reviving him; too often these days, huge amounts of drugs are given to patients before they die.*

to systematically, nobly and acceptably, even to loved ones, release itself from embodiment through fasting. The person making such a decision declares it publicly, which allows for community regulation and distinguishes the act from suicide committed privately in traumatic emotional states of anguish and despair. Ancient lawgivers cited various stipulations for *prayopavesha*: inability to perform normal bodily purification; death appears imminent, or the condition is so bad that life's pleasures are nil. The gradual nature of *prayopavesha* is the key factor in distinguishing it from sudden suicide, for it allows time for the individual to settle all differences with others, to ponder life and draw close to God." It also gives the person time to reflect and reconsider his decision.

Definition of Death

"When the physical body dies, this automatically severs the silver cord that connects the astral and physical bodies," Gurudeva explained in Merging with Siva. Metaphysically, this is the point of death. Physically, death can be defined as the cessation of breath, heartbeat and brainwave activity, in that order. Even then, it may be possible to revive a person, and the patient may report a "near-death experience" of beginning the transition to the next world but being pulled back. Decay of the body is the definitive sign of death.

Autopsies

Autopsies are the examination of a dead body to learn the cause of death. Hindus believe that autopsies are disturbing to the still aware soul which has just separated from the body and should therefore be avoided unless required by law. Similarly, embalming, which replaces the blood with a preservative fluid, is ill-advised.

Use of the Body After Death

In ancient times, doctors around the world used dead bodies to understand anatomy and practice surgery. In India, the bodies used for this purpose were those unclaimed by relatives or friends. According to Swami Bua, "In the Vedic Age, dissection and mutilation of body were considered detrimental to the fulfillment of life. Yet, if we consider that once the spirit leaves the body, the lifeless body has no karmic obligations, then it may be okay." Swami Pragyanand points out that autopsy and dissection were practiced by Sushruta, an early pioneer of ayurveda. Swami Tejomayananda says, "The body of the deceased is treated with reverence. The feelings and sentiments of the family also do not favor dissection. People have some fear that the astral body may be hurt by these intrusions or some harm may come to the family." Gurudeva similarly held that what happens to the dead physical body is disturbing to the soul, and did not advise his devotees to donate their bodies to science.

Burial and Cremation Practices

Cremation, ideally held within 24 hours, is the traditional system of disposing of dead bodies. It has the benefit of releasing the soul most quickly from any lingering attachment to the earth plane. Should it be necessary to preserve the body a few days to allow time for distant relatives to arrive, refrigeration or use of dry ice is recommended, rather than embalming. Hindus do not bury their dead, except infant children and godly saints.

Matters of Birth

Hindus consider children a gift from God, and the conception, development and birth of a child are sacred events, honored by a ceremony, or samskara, marking these rites of passage. Today's medical technology has developed many means for conceiving children (and for their disposal before birth). Hindus have a general unwillingness to interfere with nature and a special aversion to abortion, based on the belief in reincarnation and the sanctity of marriage.

Conception

From the Hindu point of view, conception connects a soul from the next world to this world, and the state of mind at the moment of conception—including the purity and spiritual intent of both partners—is a major factor in determining who is born into the family. Prospective parents often offer prayers at the temples, perform spiritual disciplines and visit saints for their advice and blessings in their effort to conceive a worthy child. In Western thinking, no emphasis is placed on the state of mind of the parents at conception, and there is little understanding of the ways parents can affect the "quality" of the souls born to them.

Birth Control

While revering conception as a divine act, Hindus have little hesitation to practice birth control, and there are remedies specified in ayurveda both for facilitating and preventing conception. Yes, as Swami Bua reminds us, restraint and moderation are important: "Hindu scriptures explain how to beget a child. They specify the days, time and methods. That means they would have known also how not to beget a child! But willful control of conception by external means was not advocated. The preferred control was through restraint, as wasting of life seeds was considered unhealthy and unethical. Birth control now is highlighted as a prime duty of every citizen to the society and nation. But one fears that these open discussions are licensing the society towards promiscuity, since the weak minds take the shortest route to pleasures, however fleeting they may be, unmindful of consequences."

Sterility Testing

While ostensibly harmless, sterility tests can cause serious social and emotional difficulty if one is deemed sterile, including inability to find a spouse, cancellation of proposals and the ruin of marriages once it is known "who is to blame" for the lack of children. "This should not be resorted to as a routine test," says Swami Bua. "Doubting the manliness of a man and femininity of a woman is degrading them. What will happen to those who fail the test? Will anybody come forward to marry them? Even though procreation is the main aim of a marriage, it is not the only aim. After a reasonable time following the marriage, if there has been no conception, and if a mature couple desire to get tested with a view to take corrective action, it may be done." Dr. Sodhi points out that, while ayurveda has no tests for sterility, the likelihood of children is one of the major considerations when evaluating a couple's astrology prior to marriage.

Artificial Insemination

Fertilization of the egg by mechanical introduction of sperm is universally acceptable when the sperm is provided by the woman's husband. But questions arise with donated sperm from another man. Because conception creates a psychic bond between a man and a woman, even if they don't meet physically, fertilization in this manner may have a similar karma as adultery. "In Sanatana Dharma initiation into married life is sanctified by sacred sacramental rites," says Swami Tejomayananda. "The offspring of such a union is blessed and protected by the holy mantras and rites. If there is some defect or obstruction in either partner, artificial insemination may be resorted to, but with the husband's sperm only. If the procedure succeeds, it may be taken as the will of the Lord for that couple. Use of seeds from the sperm banks or from any living person other

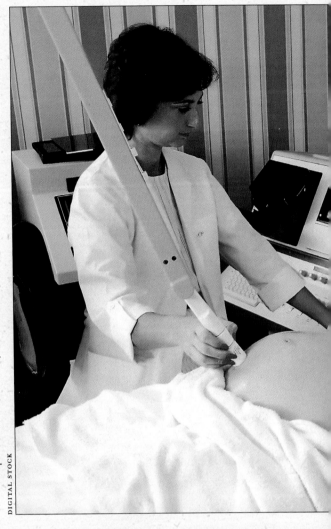

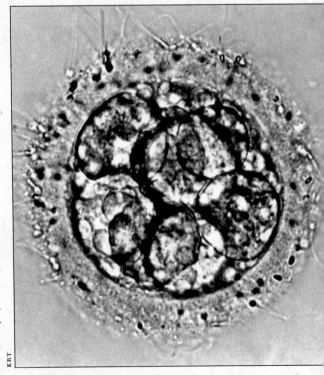

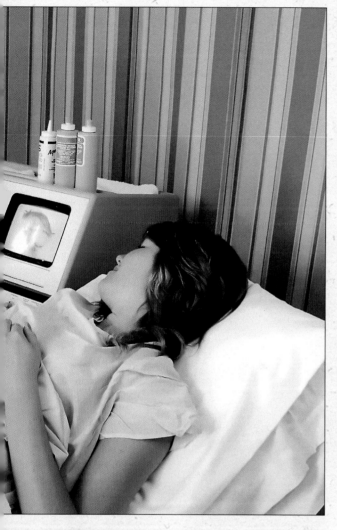

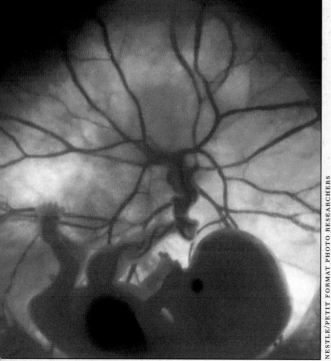

From conception to birth: *(clockwise from top) A woman undergoes an ultrasound exam; human embryo with the umbilical cord connecting to the placenta; fertilized human egg, just starting to divide*
• •

than the husband is not proper. It will amount to bearing child outside holy wedlock." However, as Professor Crawford points out, the *Manu Dharma Shastra* did allow a woman to conceive a child by another man, usually her husband's brother. Swami Bua mentions this tradition also, "The *Rig Veda* and *Atharva Veda* prescribe the procedure called *niyoga* to enable a childless widow or the wife of an impotent man to raise progeny with his consent. But even with this, the attitude of an average Hindu woman considers the one who has given her a child as her respectful husband." Satguru Bodhinatha Veylanswami points out that one has to consider the likely negative impact of artificial insemination on a marriage. The husband would not be the child's true father, resulting in a weak relationship with the child and even with the wife who required another man to conceive the child.

In Vitro Fertilization

Even with present-day technology, the creation of "test-tube babies," the fertilization of the egg outside the womb and its subsequent placement in the womb, is expensive and unreliable. As with artificial insemination, it is acceptable if the egg and sperm are from the husband and wife. Like other medical advances, in vitro fertilization introduces unknown factors that may bring unintended consequences, not necessarily positive or conducive to spiritual progress, which is life's real purpose. Hindus regard the natural way of things as endowed with God's infinite intelligence and often ask, "Are humans wise enough to tinker with the cosmic order of life?"

Abortion

Hindu scripture and tradition clearly prohibit abortion, except to save the life of the mother. It is considered an act against *rita* (universal order) and ahimsa (noninjury). In the words of Swami Omkarananda, "Imagine, through millions of abortions around the world, day in and day out, how many wonderful scientific and spiritual geniuses—doctors, men of excellence of every kind, sages, saints, benefactors of mankind, builders of a better culture and civilization—are destroyed even before they can take a breath of fresh air here on Earth!" Hindu ethics also do not justify aborting a fetus because of actual or potential deformity or mental retardation, for each birth, normal or not, is revered as having a divine purpose to be understood, not manipulated. Nevertheless, abortion is performed today by Hindus in India and elsewhere—in particular, the selective termination of female fetuses following ultrasound examination. Professor Crawford calls that practice "a perverted use of modern science, a scarcely concealed form of female infanticide." Gurudeva summarized in sutra 34 of Living with Siva, "Followers know abortion is, by Vedic injunction, a sinful act against dharma fraught with karmic repercussions. Scripture only allows it to prevent the mother's death, for it is a greater sin for a child to kill the mother." "In the modern context," says Swami Tejomayananda, "attention must be focused on the prevention of pregnancy by educating and creating awareness in the parents." Abortion, should it occur, creates a karma to be faced in the future, but is not regarded as an unforgivable "sin." A penance could mitigate the karma, such as adopting a baby who might otherwise have been aborted if no home was provided.

Selective Termination of Multiple Fetuses

Multiple births are rare, except when a couple is undergoing fertility treatments. These often result in multiple fetuses, creating a potentially dangerous condition for the mother. Under the principle that abortion is allowed to save the mother's life, Dr. Sodhi believes that selective abortion is acceptable when a specific pregnancy poses such a threat. It is an unfortunate choice to have to make, and it is hoped that future technology will reliably produce only one fetus.

NESTLE/PETIT FORMAT PHOTO RESEARCHERS

A. MANIVEL

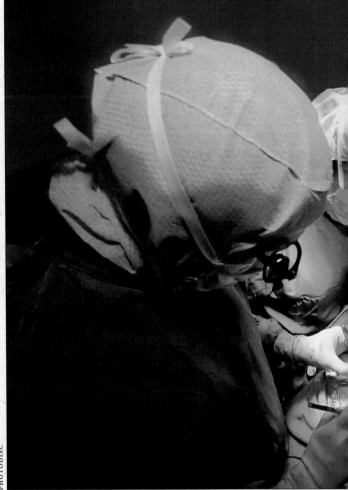

PHOTODISC

Pain-Relief Drugs for Newborns

Pain relief for children should be carefully chosen to not form, or lay the seeds for, a future addiction. Swami Bua says, "Some people think that the pains of a newborn baby are the consequences of its previous birth and that we should allow the baby to experience and sustain them so that remnants of the previous birth are left behind. But we should also realize that the God has brought this baby to our hands expecting us to comfort it and protect it and help it to grow as a healthy and worthy human being. So, it is the duty of the parents and the people nearby to do whatever is possible to relieve the baby of the pain." "According to ayurveda," says Dr. Sodhi, "the baby has as sensitive a nervous system as an adult, just not as developed. So pain medicine is okay, if necessary. Morphine was used for thousands of years in the form of opium, applied on the baby's skin for pain relief."

Circumcision

Hindus consider the practice of circumcision for males unnecessary and do not practice it. Doctors should be alerted to Hindu views on this often-standard procedure. A circumcised Hindu boy could face ridicule and discrimination. In rare ocassions, the procedure is required as a medical necessity for an adult, but is kept secret.

Other Concerns

There are additional important ethical considerations regarding organ transplant, blood transfusion, faith healing and dietary laws.

Organ Transplants

Hindus generally believe that the recipient of a major organ, such as the heart, liver or kidney, takes on some of the karmas of the donor. Evidence of this transfer of karma can be found in documented cases where the organ recipients took on the interests, emotions, food preferences, etc., of the donor, especially after a heart transplant. Transplants apparently create psychic connections with the donor, whether living or dead. Also, the fact that part of a deceased donor's physical body still "lives" may interfere with his reincarnation pattern, keeping him close to the physical plane and to the recipient. Swami Tejomayananda offers, "The Hindu way of life is to accept the inevitable, to go through the karma, exhaust it and be free to take on new life to evolve further spiritually." Swami Bua is supportive. "Let us encourage and support the scientists and medical men who are working with pure intentions towards a painless, diseaseless society. We should only guard against unscrupulous traders in human organs." Swami Chidanand Saraswati (Muniji) feels that it is "important to donate organs" in the Hindu spirit of giving and sacrifice. Dr. Sodhi offers: "Some transplants, such as the cornea, are okay, but not the heart, which is the seat of the soul according to ayurveda. If the quality of life is going to be very good after the transplant, I might not

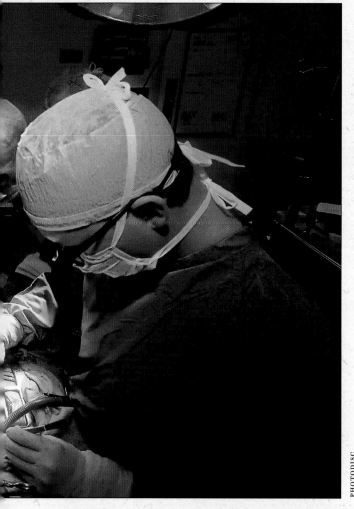

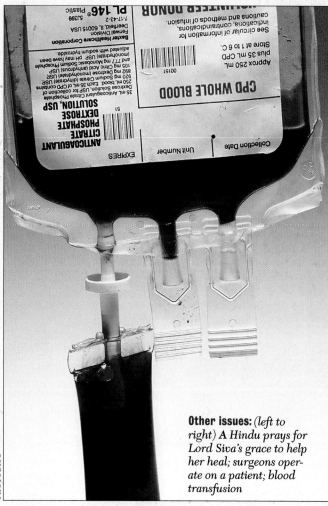

PHOTODISC

Other issues: *(left to right) A Hindu prays for Lord Siva's grace to help her heal; surgeons operate on a patient; blood transfusion*

have a problem, but if they have to be on harsh drugs all the time, maybe transplanting is not the best idea." Swami Satchidananda says "What are we doing by transplanting organs? By replacing organs in a body which is clearly dying, we are not allowing the soul to fulfill its karma in this life by dying at the proper time and getting a new body. The trend of science seems to want to keep the soul indefinitely in the same old body with repaired parts. This is not the correct thing to do."

Blood Donations/Transfusions

"In early times there were some hesitations on the basis of caste and religion, for blood transfusion," says Swami Bua, "But now, considering the necessity of blood transfusion during any surgery, people are accepting it." Blood transfusions differ from organ donations in that the body of the recipient completely replaces the foreign blood.

Religious or Faith Healings

Hindus make use of all means of healing, be they medical, astrological or metaphysical. The last includes mantras and yoga, seeking the guidance of a guru or performing temple ceremonies for the direct blessing and intervention of God, Gods and devas. "A Hindu has an ardent faith in the powers of prayers and in the Supreme God," says Swami Bua, "The patient will go to the doctor—ayurvedic or allopathic—all the while praying to God for recovery." "Healing with mantras was very popular in ancient times." says Swami Pragyanand, "Even now it is being practiced for various ailments." Swami Tejomayananda notes, "In healing

by prayers, Divine Grace comes in. If the karma is nearing exhaustion, or it is only a weak karma, or the healing will help the person in his spiritual pursuit, or if the Higher Power has some work to be done through the person, then a cure may be effected." Dr. Sodhi adds, "In ayurveda, specific pujas, or ceremonies to the Gods, are sometimes prescribed for patients."

Dietary Ethics

Yes, vegetarianism is a central aspect of Hinduism, and of even broader import is the ayurvedic wisdom that health is directly dependent upon diet. A Hindu vegetarian who is hospitalized will need to coordinate with the staff to be served proper food unless he can have family or friends bring his meals. The ayurvedic prerogative is to eat a diet that prevents disease and enhances spiritual life. When ill, a drastic change in diet may be the best cure, as seen in the improvement of heart patients put on a vegetarian diet. "The scriptures recognize the fact that food has a great influence on the mind," says Swami Tejomayananda, "'When food is pure, mind is pure,' state the Upanishads. Mothers prepare food with love in the heart for the children. These positive vibrations are absorbed and the persons who partake of the food imbibe them. Eating is an act of worship."

There remain several areas of concern in medical ethics which will be addressed in future articles in HINDUISM TODAY, including genetic engineering, genetic testing, stem-cell research, cloning and animal to human transplants. If you have insights or comments, feel free to e-mail them to us at letters@hindu.org.

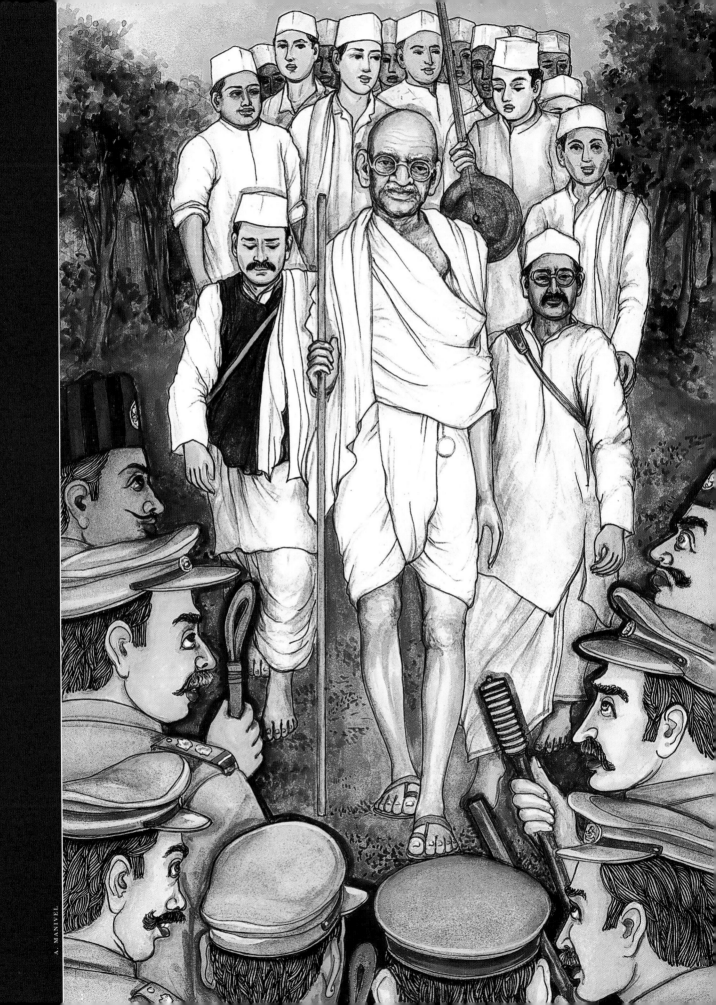

A. MANIVEL

CHAPTER 45

Ahimsa: To Do No Harm

Exploring the Cardinal Virtue of Noninjury in Thought, Word & Deed

BY SATGURU SIVAYA SUBRAMUNIYASWAMI

INDU WISDOM, WHICH INSPIRES HUMANS TO LIVE THE ideals of compassion and nonviolence, is captured in one word, *ahimsa*. In Sanskrit, *himsa* is doing harm or causing injury. The "a" placed before the word negates it. Very simply, ahimsa is abstaining from causing harm or injury. It is gentleness and noninjury, whether physical, mental or emotional. It is good to know that *nonviolence* speaks only to the most extreme forms of forceful wrongdoing, while ahimsa goes much deeper to prohibit even the subtle abuse and the simple hurt.

Devout Hindus oppose killing for several reasons. Belief in karma and reincarnation are strong forces at work in the Hindu mind. They full well know that any thought, feeling or action sent out from themself to another will return to them through yet another in equal or amplified intensity. What we have done to others will be done to us, if not in this life then in another. The Hindu is thoroughly convinced that violence which he commits will return to him by a cosmic process that is unerring. Two thousand years ago South India's weaver saint Tiruvalluvar said it so simply, "All suffering recoils on the wrongdoer himself. Thus, those desiring not to suffer refrain from causing others pain" (Tirukural 320). A similar view can be found in the Jain *Acharanga Sutra:* "To do harm to others is to do harm to oneself. You are he whom you intend to kill. You are he whom you intend to dominate. We corrupt ourselves as soon as we intend to corrupt others. We kill ourselves as soon as we intend to kill others."

Many today are wondering how we might move from violence to nonviolence, how mankind might transform itself from approval of killing to opposition to it. The Hindu knows that at this time on this planet those of the lower nature, unevolved people, are society's antagonists. Being unevolved, they are of the lower nature: instinctive, self-assertive, confused, possessive and protective of their immediate environment. Others are their enemies. They are jealous, angry, fearful. Many make sport in killing for the sake of killing, thieving for the sake of theft, even if they do not need or use the spoils. This is the lower nature, and it is equally distributed among the peoples of the world, in every nation, society and neighborhood. Those of the higher nature—ten, fifteen or twenty percent of the population—live in protective environments. Their occupation is research, memory, education, which is reason; moving the world's goods here and there, which is will. Those of yet an even higher nature delve into the mysteries of the universe, and others work for universal peace and love on Earth, as groups and individuals. The Hindu knows that those of the lower nature will slowly, eventually, over an experiential period of time, come into the higher nature, and that those of the higher nature, who have worked so hard to get there, will avoid the lower nature and not allow themselves to be caught up in it again. Hindus believe in the progress of humanity, from an old age into a new age, from darkness into a consciousness of divine light.

Nonviolence has long been central to the religious traditions of India—especially Hinduism, Buddhism and Jainism. Religion in India has consistently upheld the sanctity of life, whether human, animal or, in the case of the Jains, elemental. There developed early in India an unparalleled concern for harmony among different life forms, and this led to a common ethos based on noninjuriousness and a minimal consumption of natural resources, in other words, to compassion and simplicity. If Homo sapiens is to survive his present predicament, he will have to rediscover these two primary ethical virtues.

In order to understand the pervasive practice of nonviolence in Hinduism, one must investigate the meaning of life. Why is life sacred? For India's ancient thinkers, life is seen as the very stuff of the Divine, an emanation of the Source and part of a cosmic continuum. The nature of this continuum varies in Hindu thought. Some hold that the individual evolves up through life forms, taking more and more advanced incarnations which culminate in human life. Others believe that according to one's karma and samskaras, the process can even be reversed, that is, one can achieve a "lower" birth. Even those Indians who do not believe in reincarnation of an individual still hold that all that exists abides in the Divine. They further hold that each life form—even water and trees—possesses consciousness and energy. Whether the belief is that the life force of animals can evolve into human status, or that the opposite can also take place, or simply that all things enjoy their own consciousness, the result is the same—a reverence for life.

Not all of Earth's one billion Hindus are living in a perfect state of ahimsa all of the time. Sometimes conditions at hand may force a situation, a regrettable exception, where violence or killing seems to be necessary. Hindus, like other human beings, unfortunately do kill people. In self-defense or in order to protect his family or his village, the Hindu may have to hurt an intruder. Even then he would harbor no hatred in his heart. Hindus should never instigate an intrusion or instigate a death; nor seek revenge, nor plot retaliation for injuries received. They have their courts of justice, punishment for crimes and agencies for defending against the aggressor or the intruder. Before any personal use of force, so to speak, all other avenues of persuasion and intelligence would be looked into, as Hindus believe that intelligence is their best weapon. In following dharma, the only rigid rule is wisdom. My satguru, Siva Yogaswami, said, "It is a sin to kill the tiger in the jungle. But if he comes into the village, it may become your duty." A devout Hindu would give warnings to scare the tiger or would try to capture the tiger without injury. Probably it would be the most unreligious person in the village who would come forward to kill the tiger.

Many groups on the planet today advocate killing and violence and war for a righteous cause. They do not agree with the idea that violence, himsa, is necessarily of the lower nature. But a righteous cause is only a matter of opinion, and going to war affects the lives of a great many innocent people. It's a big karmic responsibility. Combat through war, righteous or not, is lower consciousness. Religious values are left aside, to be picked up and continued when the war is over, or in the next life or the one after that. It is said that in ancient India meat would be fed to the soldiers during military campaigns, especially before combat, to bring them into lower consciousness so that they would forget their religious values. Most higher consciousness people will not fight even if their lives depend on it. They are conscientious objectors, and there have been many in every country who have been imprisoned or killed because they would not take up arms against their brother and sister humans. This is the strictest

own kinsmen. Hindus for a long time have taken this text as justification for war and conflicts of all kinds, including street riots and anarchy. But all that aside, no matter how it is interpreted, let us not be mistaken that the *Bhagavad Gita* gives permission for violence. The *Mahabharata* (of which the *Gita* is a part) itself says, "Ahimsa is the highest dharma. It is the highest purification. It is also the highest truth from which all dharma proceeds" (18.1125.25). An eye for an eye and a tooth for a tooth is definitely not a part of true Hindu doctrine.

In every country there is the army, the navy, air force, police, the protectors of the country—the collective force of citizens that keep a country a country. This is dharma. In protection of family and nation, in armies and police forces which give security, it is indeed dharmic for kshatriyas to do their lawful duty, to use necessary force, even lethal force. But for this collective force of protectors, of peacemakers, of peacekeepers—which includes the law courts and the central administrative authorities who oversee the courts, the armies, the navies, the air force—would the priests be able to function? Would the businessmen be able to acquire and sell their goods? Would the farmers be able to plant their crops and harvest them? Could the children play fearlessly in the streets and countryside? No. The answer is obvious.

Those who take law into their own hands in the name of dharma, citing their case upon the *Mahabharata*, are none but the lawbreakers, anarchists, the arsonists, the terrorists. The *Mahabharata* gives no permission for anarchy. The *Mahabharata* gives no permission for terrorism. The *Mahabharata* gives no permission for looting and diluting the morals of society through prostitution, running drugs and the selling and buying of illegal arms. The Pandavas, the heroes of this ancient epic, were not rabble rousers. They were not inciting riots. Nor were they participating in extortion to run their war. Nor were they participating in the sale of drugs to finance their war. Nor were they participating in prostitution to win their war. Nor were they participating in enlisting women to help them fight their war. Nor were they having children learn to snare their victims.

Yes, dharma does extend to protecting one's country. But does it extend to taking a country from another, or to stealing lands? That is lawlessness, blatant lawlessness. In the modern age, to create a nation or even a business enterprise upon the death of another, upon lands confiscated, stolen, illegally acquired, usurped from another's realm, is definitely not Hindu dharma, and this is not *Mahabharata*.

In Gandhian philosophy ahimsa means nonviolent action which leads to passive resistance in order to put a point across. Basically, he taught, don't hit your opponent over the head. If he tells you to do something, stall and don't obey and don't do it and frustrate him into submission. And yet he was not a pacifist prepared to accept any harm without resistance. When a gang of tribals came in and raped the women in a village, Gandhi said there should not have been a man left alive in the village. They should have stood up for the village and protected it with their lives.

So, to me, if an intruder breaks into your house to rape the women or steal things, you have the right, even the duty, to defend your own, but you don't have the right to torture him. Ahimsa needs to be properly understood, in moderation. To explain nonviolence, you have to explain what violence is, as opposed to protecting yourself.

expression of Hinduism's law of ahimsa.

One of the most famous of Hindu writings, the *Bhagavad Gita*, is often taken as divine sanction for violence. It basically says that for the kshatriya, or soldier, war is dharma. Lord Krishna orders Arjuna to fight and do his kshatriya dharma in spite of his doubts and fears that what he is about to do is wrong, despite his dread of killing his

Is it violent to own a dog who would put his teeth to the throat of a vicious intruder? I don't think it is. If nonviolence is to be something that the world is going to respect, we have to define it clearly and make it meaningful.

Achieving a nonviolent world would simply mean that all individuals have to somehow or other reconcile their differences enough that the stress those differences produce can no longer take over their mind, body and emotions, causing them to perform injurious acts. Again, this would begin in the home. Peaceful homes breed gentle people. Gentle people follow ahimsa.

What's the best way to teach peace to the world? The best way is to first teach families to be peaceful within their own home, to settle all arguments and contention before they sleep at night, even if they stay up for three days, so the children can see that peace can be attained and then maintained through the use of intelligence.

Humans do not have horns or claws; nor do they have sharp teeth. Their weapon is their intelligence. Children must be taught through the example of parents and by learning the undeniable facts of life, the basic tenets—that an all-pervasive force holds this universe together, that we create with this force every minute, every hour, every day, and because time is a cycle, what we create comes back to us. Therefore, because we create in a physical universe while in a physical body, we must return to a physical body, in a new life after death, to face up to our creations, good, bad or mixed. Once they learn this, they are winners. It is up to the parents to create the peacemakers of the future. It is always up to the parents. And remember, we teach children in only one way—by our own example.

Parents must teach children to appreciate those who are different, those who believe differently; teach them the openness that they need to live in a pluralistic world where others have their unique

---

Taking Care of Business, Nonviolently

Ahimsa is not just a prohibition against physical and emotional assault

Right livelihood: Beware the ill-gotten gains of ruthless business

BY SATGURU SIVAYA SUBRAMUNIYASWAMI

I WAS ONCE ASKED FOR MY INSIGHTS ON APPLYING ahimsa in the business world. Ahimsa in business is taught in a reverse way on American television: Titans, The West Wing, Dynasty, Falcon Crest, Dallas, Sopranos—popular shows of our time. Their scriptwriters promoted himsa, injuriousness, in business—"Save the Falcon Crest farm at any cost, save South Fork, save the corporation." Now the national news media reports attempts to save Microsoft, save the tobacco industry, save the hand gun manufacturers. The fight is on, and real-life court battles have taken the place of TV sitcoms which have long since been off the air. In both the TV and the real-life conflicts, whatever you do to your competitor is OK because it's only business. The plots weave in and out, with one scene of mental and emotional cruelty after another. The Hindu business ethic is very clear. As the weaver Tiruvalluvar said, "Those businessmen will prosper whose business protects as their own the interests of others" (*Tirukural* 120). We should compete by having a better product and better methodologies of promoting and selling it, not by destroying our competitor's product and reputation. Character assassination is not part of ahimsa. It reaps bad benefits to the accusers. That is practiced by many today,

even by Hindus who are off track in their perceptions of ahimsa. Hindus worldwide must know that American television is not the way business should be practiced. As some people teach you what you should do and other people teach you what you should not do, the popular television programs mentioned above clearly teach us what we should not do. The principles of ahimsa and other ethical teachings within Hinduism show us a better way.

Many corporations today are large, in fact larger than many small countries. Their management is like the deceptive, dishonest, deceitful, arrogant, domineering autocrat, king, or like the benevolent religious monarch, all depending on whether there are people of lower consciousness or higher consciousness in charge. Cities, districts, provinces, counties, states and central governments all have many laws for ethical business practices, and none of those laws permits unfair trade, product assassination or inter-business competitive fights to the death. Each business is dharmically bound to serve the community, not take from the community like a vulture. When the stewardships of large corporations follow the law of the land and the principles of ahimsa, they put their energies into developing better products and better community service. When the leadership has a mind for corporate espionage, its energies are diverted, the products suffer and so does customer relations. The immediate profits in the short term might be gratifying, but in the long run, profits gained from wrong-doings are generally spent on wrong-doings.

Ahimsa always has the same consequences. And we know these benefits well. Himsa always has the same consequences, too. It develops enemies, creates unseemly karmas which will surely return and affect the destiny of the future of the business enterprise. The perfect timing needed for success is defeated by inner reactions to the wrong-doings. A business enterprise which bases its strategies on hurtfulness cannot in good judgment hire employees who are in higher consciousness, lest they object to these tactics. Therefore, they attract employees who are of the same caliber as themselves, and they all practice himsa among one another. Trickery, deceitfulness and deception are of the lower nature, products of the methodology of performing himsa, hurtfulness, mentally and emotionally. The profits derived from himsa policies are short-term and ill-spent. The profits derived from ahimsa policies are long-term and well spent.

ways, their life and culture; teach them the value of human diversity and the narrow-mindedness of a provincial outlook; give them the tools to live in a world of differences without feeling threatened, without forcing their ways or their will on others; teach them that it never helps to hurt another of our brothers or sisters.

Vegetarianism is a natural and obvious way to live with a minimum of hurt to other beings. Hindu scripture speaks clearly and forcefully on vegetarianism. The *Yajur Veda* dictates: "Do not injure the beings living on the Earth, in the air and in the water." The beautiful *Tirukural*, a widely-read 2,200-year-old masterpiece of ethics, speaks of conscience: "When a man realizes that meat is the butchered flesh of another creature, he will abstain from eating it" (257). The *Manu Samhita* advises: "Having well considered the origin of flesh and the cruelty of fettering and slaying corporeal beings, let one entirely abstain from eating flesh," and "When the diet is pure, the mind and heart are pure." In the yoga-infused verses of the *Tirumantiram* warning is given of how meat-eating holds the mind in gross, adharmic states: "The ignoble ones who eat flesh, death's agents bind them fast and push them quick into the fiery jaws of the lower worlds" (199).

Vegetarianism is very important. In my fifty years of ministry, it has become quite evident that vegetarian families have far fewer problems than those who are not vegetarian. The abhorrence of killing of any kind leads quite naturally to a vegetarian diet. If you think about it, the meat-eater is participating indirectly in a violent act against the animal kingdom. His desire for meat drives another man to kill and provide that meat. The act of the butcher begins with the desire of the consumer. When his consciousness lifts and expands, he will abhor violence and not be able to even digest the meat, fish and eggs he was formerly consuming. India's greatest saints have confirmed that one cannot eat meat and live a peaceful, harmonious life. Man's appetite for meat inflicts devastating harm on the Earth itself, stripping its precious forests to make way for pastures. The opposite of causing injury to others is compassion and love for all beings. The *Tirukural* puts it nicely: "How can he practice true compassion who eats the flesh of an animal to fatten his own flesh" (251)?

If children are raised as vegetarians, every day they are exposed to noninjury as a principle of peace and compassion. Every day as they are growing up, they are remembering and being reminded to not kill. They won't even kill another creature to feed themselves. And if you won't kill another creature to feed yourself, then when you grow up you will be much less likely to injure people.

Saints and Scriptures Speak on Ahimsa

Nonviolence, truthfulness, nonstealing, purity, sense control—this, in brief, says Manu, is the dharma of all the four castes.
Dharma Shastras 10

You do not like to suffer yourself. How can you inflict suffering on others? Every killing is a suicide. The eternal, blissful and natural state has been smothered by this life of ignorance. In this way the present life is due to the killing of the eternal, pristine Being. Is it not a case of suicide?
Ramana Maharishi

One should never do that to another which one regards as injurious to one's own self. This, in brief, is the rule of dharma. Yielding to desire and acting differently, one becomes guilty of adharma.
Mahabharata 18:113.8

To be free from violence is the duty of every man. No thought of revenge, hatred or ill will should arise in our minds. Injuring others gives rise to hatred.
Swami Sivananda

If a man inflicts sorrow on another in the morning, sorrow will come to him unbidden in the afternoon.
Tirukural 319

Refrain from killing knowingly even the trifling insects like a louse, a bug or a mosquito. Use no violence even to gain possession of a woman, wealth or kingdom. Never kill any animals even for the purpose of sacrifice. Non-violence is the greatest of all religions.
Swami Sahajanand

Ahimsa is the highest dharma. Ahimsa is the best *tapas*. Ahimsa is the greatest gift. Ahimsa is the highest self-control. Ahimsa is the highest sacrifice. Ahimsa is the highest power. Ahimsa is the highest friend. Ahimsa is the highest truth. Ahimsa is the highest teaching.
Mahabharata 18:116.37-41

By ahimsa Patanjali meant the removal of the desire to kill. All forms of life have an equal right to the air of maya. All men may understand this truth by overcoming the passion for destruction.
Sri Yukteswar

Ahimsa is not causing pain to any living being at any time through the actions of one's mind, speech or body.
Sandilya Upanishad

Those high-souled persons who desire beauty, faultlessness of limbs, long life, understanding, mental and physical strength and memory should abstain from acts of injury.
Mahabharata 18:115.8

When one is established in non-injury, beings give up their mutual animosity in his presence.
Yoga Sutras

The Hindu sage sees the whole of life. If he does not fight, it is not because he rejects all fighting as futile, but because he has finished his fights. He has overcome all dissensions between himself and the world and is now at rest.
Dr. S. Radhakrishnan

PHOTOSTOCK

Harnessing Speech

Contemplation and Discipline Insure Ahimsa in Your Daily Interactions

BY SWAMINI MAYATITANANDA

THE HUMAN VOICE AS A DIVINE INSTRUMENT IS A POWER-ful, foundational tool for living a life of ahimsa. It is the basis of our individuality and creative expression. However, the human voice is our most misunderstood and misused possession. We take our voice for granted—using and abusing it for the most mundane, trivial and hurtful communications—forgetting to honor it as the divine instrument of ahimsa within us.

The seers emulated the primordial sound in order to fashion the first human expression, called *shruti*, the cosmic revelation as heard by the rishis. *Shruti* is also referred to as the Word, and the song of *Sama Veda* informs us that, "Verily, if there were no Word, there would be no knowledge neither of right or wrong, nor of truth and untruth, nor of the pleasing and unpleasing. The Word makes all this known." This original Word informed Vedic ritual speech, mantras, chants and music, which carry the cosmic rhythms and memory of the universe's entire experience. The rishis declared the spoken word, *shruti*, as their most significant contribution to humanity. Most ancient people left their imprint on history through the medium of precious materials—gold, silver, bronze, onyx and granite. While time has eroded these monuments, the Vedic tradition's rich legacy of the spoken word, recited daily by an unbroken chain of generations, still lives on.

Most of us are conscious of the foods we eat, the air we breathe, the postures we emulate and other spiritual practices we do to bring good health, yet we are unaware of the negative impressions we imbibe by way of our senses from unwholesome talk, chaotic interaction and the barrage of discordant sounds we take into our personal lives through television and other media. A mind that is bombarded with violent impressions will become desensitized and express itself in angry and insensitive ways. Eric's story is a classical illustration of exactly this challenge.

I met Eric several years ago at a meditation workshop in New York. He was seventeen years old and had been recently expelled from school for verbally abusing his teacher. Eric's mother, Marion, was a prominent yoga teacher. She confided to me that Eric had been a quiet boy and an excellent student until he fell in with a "bad crowd" in the neighborhood.

After listening to Marion, I asked to speak with Eric privately. As he slouched in the chair beside me, he refused to make eye contact. I closed my eyes and waited for him to speak. After several tense minutes, he broke the silence. "She is always screaming at me, demanding that I do the things that make her happy. But what about me? She is so caught up in her work she doesn't even know who I am. She pushes me to do all these health things. My friends think I'm a sissy—eating health food, washing the dishes, chanting...." For twenty minutes, or so, Eric blurted out his story

The voice of ahimsa:
Thinking before speaking

nonstop. All I could hear was the young man's anger about being pushed by Marion's anger and his frustration about feeling inadequate and not "fitting in" with his friends. Marion had good intentions for her son, but like many parents who underestimate their children's intelligence she had missed the most important lesson—listening to her son's needs and communicating with him. The more she forced Eric to adhere to her values, the farther away Eric ran. Suddenly, as he became a teenager, he found a voice of violence in the popular culture that had heard him and he began to retaliate against his mother's tyranny. To compensate for the support he felt he was not getting at home, Eric had found negative reinforcement from his street buddies and seized the opportunity to express himself. He was true to his voice of anger. It was Marion who had not yet found her voice of peace. Although she had been practicing yoga for twelve years, she has still not found the true meaning behind spiritual practice—the spirit of nonviolence and nonhurting that would finally help her to communicate its wondrous essence to her son.

I have developed the Vac Tapasya, "Speech Penance," to evoke healthy, harmonious thoughts and bring forward positive, pleasant words. Spend fifteen minutes at the end of every day allowing your mind to run free. Notice whatever negative, hurtful thoughts that may come up. Write down those thoughts and the person or situations they concern, without whitewashing or censoring them. Let yourself be angry, judgmental and unkind. And above all, be honest. Repeat each negative thought aloud. For example: "Mary is so demanding. I can't bear to work with her." Then recite the attitude of one seeking true inner knowledge: "I know that every negative thought reflects my own inner condition."

Now take responsibility for your feelings from which the negative thought sprang: "I am being intolerant of Mary. It will not be pleasant for Mary if I see her with this attitude." This will help you learn to always carefully consider your words before you speak them aloud to another person, and to avoid an angry, accusatory or aggressive tone. If you feel pressured to respond or speak in a way that you think may be hurtful to another person, use your notebook to tell this person your raw, unedited feelings in the form of a letter that you do not send. Let the letter sit for a week. Then, before you read it, make one small change. Replace the name of the person to whom it is addressed with your own name. This may help you understand that the letter has less to do with the person with whom you are angry, and is more about your hurt feelings, which stem from your negative thoughts and feelings about your own life. The Maitri Upanishad put it this way: "Words cannot describe the joy of the spirit whose spirit is cleansed in deep contemplation—who is one with his/her own Spirit. Only those who experience this joy knows what it is."

Sri Swamini Mayatitananda is founder of the Wise Earth School and the Mother Om Mission. Wise Earth, 90 Davis Creek Road, Candler, North Carolina 28715 USA. Phone: 828-258-9999. Email: health@wiseearth.org. World Wide Web: www.wiseearth.org.

CHAPTER 46

LIGHTEN UP!

NO, LORD GANESH DOESN'T WANT IT; FINISH YOUR MILK!

Spices in the Melting Pot

...TAKE A SMALL CAN OF **RICOTTA CHEESE** AND MIX WITH A **FISTFULL** OF FLOUR ... ADD TWO **FINGER-DIP** OF GHEE WITH ONE **PINCH** OF SALT... FRY UNTIL COLOR IS **NUTTY**... THEN SOAK INTO A **STRING-THICK** OF SYRUP...

INDIAN, AMERICAN, CANADIAN, PAKISTANI — WE DON'T CARE WHO YOU MARRY — SO LONG AS HE IS A BRAHMIN!

THERE GOES THE NEIGHBORHOOD!

..AND THAT'S MUMMY WITH HER WEDDING RING...SHE PUT IT ON HER NOSE 'CAUSE SHE HAD A SORE FINGER..

MY DOCTOR TOLD ME TO QUIT SMOKING, DRINKING, EATING MEAT... AND ASKED ME TO EAT VEGETABLES, KEEP A STRESSLESS SIMPLE LIFE. SO I BECAME A HINDU.

Manick Sorcar

Electrical engineer of Denver, Colorado, and son of the late P.C. Sorcar, India's legendary magician, Manick Sorcar is undoubtedly a top expresser of the US Indian immigrant experience. His illustrations, touching the heart of cultural integration challenges, are compiled in two volumes—*The Melting Pot, Indians in America,* and *Spices in the Melting Pot,* both available via his website at www.manicksorcar.com. But Sorcar doesn't stop here. What began as an effort to teach his two daughters their heritage, led him to create an award-winning series of one-man animated videos for children, mixing his hand-drawn art with computer-generated art and animation, along with original music, to showcase Indian culture.

Frank & Ernest

It's all right to hold a conversation, but you should let go of it now and then.

Bob Thaves

Frank & Ernest are the stars of Bob Thaves' innovative single-panel comic strip. Read by 25 million people daily, Frank & Ernest are as comfortable offering whimsical comments on the creation of the universe as they are about taxes or software. Drawing since boyhood, Bob's formal art training consisted of studying various cartoonists and their work. An industrial psychologist by day, he moonlighted as a magazine cartoonist before starting Frank & Ernest. Bob passed away in 2006, and his son Tom continues to lead a team effort to produce the strip. More than 5,000 episodes of Frank & Ernest may be found at www.frankandernest.com.

"Maybe there *is* something to reincarnation—I know I come back to life every day at five o'clock!"

Frank to Ernest as they leave the Mega Corp in a cartoon by Thaves.

Karma Kat

Barry Geller

Barry Geller, creator of Karma Kat, is a devotee of Swami Prakashanand Saraswati. After raising a family of three children he became a graphic designer and illustrator. His work was published in *Fortune*, *Time*, *Cosmopolitan*, *Esquire* and others. His awards include citations of merit from the New York Society of Illustrators and publication of his work in the Swiss graphic arts annual, *Graphis*. Barry and his wife, Nan, live at Barsana Dham in Austin, Texas.

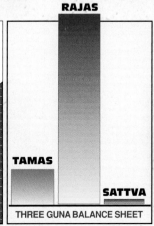

Calvin & Hobbes

Bill Watterson

Bill is the creator of Calvin & Hobbes, an engaging chronicle of a six-year-old's psyche, which appeared in more than 2,400 newspapers when it ceased publication January 1, 1996. In announcing his retirement, Bill said he was eager to work at a more thoughtful pace, with fewer artistic compromises.

"I'm practically a vegetarian. I eat plenty of grains after they've been turned into cows, pigs and chickens."

Randy Glasbergen

Randy lives in New York. He began his cartooning career in high school. He has been a full-time freelance cartoonist since 1972. More than 20,000 of his cartoons and comic illustrations have been published around the world. More of his cartoons may be found at www.glasbergen.com

"Thank you for calling The Yoga Studio. To learn more about the benefits of yoga, press 1 with your pinky toe and hold it for 20 minutes."

welcome to Goa.

Mario de Miranda

One of India's finest cartoonists, Mario was born at Daman in 1936, grew up in Goa and was educated at Bangalore and Mumbai. After working many years for *The Times of India*, he now freelances, drawing for *The Economic Times* and a strip for *The Afternoon* in Mumbai. He is married, has two sons and lives in Goa. Check out his Mumbai scene on the left and others below, all depicting the amazing country of India.

the departure

GLOSSARY

aadheenam: ஆதீனம் Endowment, foundation, institution, establishment, estate, property. A Śaivite Hindu monastery and temple complex in the South Indian Śaiva Siddhānta tradition. Also known as *maṭha* or *pīṭha,* as in Kailāsa Pīṭha. The *aadheenam* head, or pontiff, is called the *guru mahāsannidhānam* or *aadheenakarthar.*

abhisheka (ubhishckam): अभिषेक "Sprinkling; ablution." Ritual bathing of the Deity's image with water, curd, milk, honey, *ghee,* rosewater, etc. A special form of *pūjā* prescribed by Āgamic injunction. Also performed in the inauguration of religious and political monarchs and other special blessings. See: *pūjā.*

āchārya: आचार्य A highly respected teacher. The wise one who practices what he preaches. A title generally bestowed through *dīkshā* and ordination, such as in the Śivāchārya priest tradition. See: *dīkshā.*

advaita: अद्वैत "Non-dual." Nonduality or monism. The philosophical doctrine that Ultimate Reality consists of a one principle substance, or God. Opposite of *dvaita,* dualism. Advaita is the primary philosophical stance of the Vedic *Upanishads,* and of Hinduism, interpreted differently by the many *ṛishis, gurus, paṇḍitas* and philosophers. See: *Vedānta.*

Āgama: आगम The tradition; that which has "come down." An enormous collection of Sanskrit scriptures which, along with the *Vedas,* are revered as *śruti* (revealed scripture). Dating is uncertain. They were part of an oral tradition of unknown antiquity which some experts consider as ancient as the earliest *Vedas,* 5000 to 6000 bce. The *Āgamas* are the primary source and authority for ritual, *yoga* and temple construction. Each of the major denominations—Śaivism, Vaishṇavism and Śāktism—has its unique *Āgama* texts. Smārtas recognize the *Āgamas,* but don't necessarily adhere to them and rely mainly on the *smṛiti* texts. See: *śruti.*

agni: अग्नि "Fire." Either fire itself, or the God of the element fire, invoked through Vedic ritual known as *yajña, agnikāraka, homa* and *havana.* The God Agni is the divine messenger who receives prayers and oblations and conveys them to the heavenly spheres. See: *yajña.*

ahiṁsā: अहिंसा "Noninjury," nonviolence or nonhurtfulness. Refraining from causing harm to others, physically, mentally or emotionally. *Ahiṁsā* is the first and most important of the *yamas* (restraints). It is the cardinal virtue upon which all others depend. See: *yama-niyama.*

ājñā chakra: आज्ञाचक्र "Command wheel." The third-eye center. See: *chakra.*

ākāśa: आकाश "Space." The sky. Free, open space. Ether, the fifth and most subtle of the five elements—earth, air, fire, water and ether. Empirically, the rarified space or ethereal fluid plasma that pervades the universes, inner and outer. Esoterically, mind, the superconscious strata holding all that exists and all that potentially exists, wherein all happenings are recorded and can be read by clairvoyants. It is through psychic entry into this transcendental *ākāśa* that cosmic knowledge is gathered, and the entire circle of time—past, present and future—can be known. Space, *ākāśa,* in this concept is a positive substance, filled with unseen energies and intelligences, in contrast with the Western conception that space is the absence of everything and is therefore nothing in and of itself.

Akhara: A Hindi term meaning "wrestling arena," either a place of verbal debate or one of physical combat. An akhara is a order of *sadhu* renunciates. See: *Daśanāmī.*

amrita: अमृत "Immortality." Literally, "without death *(mṛita)."* The nectar of divine bliss which flows down from the *sahasrāra chakra* when one enters very deep states of meditation. This word is apparently related to the Greek *ambrotos,* "immortal," hence ambrosia, the food or drink of the Gods, which has its Vedic equivalent in the legendary elixir called *soma,* a central element in Vedic rites in which it is venerated as a Divinity.

anāhata chakra: अनाहतचक्र The heart center. "Wheel of unstruck [sound]." See: *chakra.*

ānanda: आनन्द "Bliss." The pure joy—ecstasy or enstasy—of God-consciousness or spiritual experience. In its highest sense, *ānanda* is expressed in the famous Vedic description of God: *sat-chit-ānanda,* "existence-consciousness-bliss"—the divine or superconscious mind of all souls. See: *God Realization, Satchidānanda.*

āṇava: "Fragment; atom; individuality." The fetter or individualizing veil of duality that enshrouds the soul. That which provides individuality, or separate ego, to each soul. It is the source of finitude and ignorance. The presence of anava is what causes the misapprehension about the nature of God, soul and world, the notion of being separate and distinct from God and the universe. See: *soul.*

añjali mudrā: अञ्जलिमुद्रा "Reverence gesture." A gesture of respect and greeting, in which the two palms are held gently together and slightly cupped. Often accompanied by the verbal salutation "*namaskāra,*" meaning "reverent salutation." The *añjali mudrā* has various forms, e.g., near the chest in greeting equals, at eye level in greeting one's *guru,* and above

the head in salutation to God. See: *mudrā.*

Antarloka: अन्तर्लोक "Inner or in-between world." The astral plane, spanning the spectrum of consciousness from the *viśuddha chakra* in the throat to the *pātāla chakra* in the soles of the feet. The astral plane includes: 1) higher astral plane, **Maharloka,** "plane of balance," or Devaloka; 2) mid-astral plane, **Svarloka,** "celestial plane;" 3) lower astral plane, **Bhuvarloka,** "plane of atmosphere," a counterpart or subtle duplicate of the physical plane (consisting of the Pitṛiloka and Pretaloka); and 4) the sub-astral plane, **Naraka,** consisting of seven hellish realms corresponding to the seven *chakras* below the base of the spine. In the astral plane, the soul is enshrouded in the astral body. See: *astral body, loka, Narakaloka.*

āratī: आरती "Light." The circling or waving of a lamp (usually fed with *ghee,* camphor or oil) before a holy person or the temple Deity at the high point of *pūjā.* The flame is then presented to the devotees, each passing his or her hands through it and bringing them to the eyes three times, thereby receiving the blessings. *Āratī* can also be performed as the briefest form of *pūjā.* See: *archana, pūjā.*

archana: अर्चन A special, personal, abbreviated *pūjā* done by temple priests in which the name, birthstar and family lineage of a devotee are recited to invoke individual guidance and blessings. *See: pūjā.*

Ardhanārīśvara: अर्धनारीश्वर "Half-female Lord." Lord Śiva in androgynous form, male on the right side and female on the left, indicating that Śiva, like all Mahādevas, is genderless; and that Śiva is All, inseparable from His energy, Śakti. In the unity of Ardhanārīśvara all opposites are reconciled; duality is reduced to the single source. See: *kuṇḍalinī, nāḍī, Śakti, Śiva.*

Arjuna: अर्जुन A hero of the *Mahābhārata* and central figure of the *Bhagavad Gītā.* See: *Bhagavad Gītā.*

artha: अर्थ "Goal or purpose; wealth, property, money." Also has the meaning of utility, desire. See: *dharma.*

āsana: आसन "Seat; posture." In *haṭha yoga, āsana* refers to any of numerous poses prescribed to balance and tune up the subtle energies of mind and body for meditation and to promote health and longevity. Each *āsana* possesses unique benefits, affecting the varied inner bodies and releasing energies in different parts of the nervous system. While the physical science of *haṭha yoga* can dramatically influence health and general well-being, it is primarily a preparation for the deeper *yogas* and meditations. See: *haṭha* *yoga, rāja yoga, yoga.*

āśrama: आश्रम "Place of striving." From *śram,* "to exert energy." Hermitage; order of life. Holy sanctuary; the residence and teaching center of a *sādhu,* saint, *swāmī,* ascetic or *guru;* often includes lodging for students. Also names life's four stages. See: *āśrama dharma, sādhana.*

āśrama dharma: आश्रमधर्म "Laws of life development." Meritorious way of life appropriate to each of its four successive stages (*āśramas*), observing which one lives in harmony with nature and life, allowing the body, emotions and mind to develop and undergo their natural cycles in a most positive way. The four stages are: 1) *brahmacharya:* Studentship, from age 12 to 24. 2)*grihastha:* Householder, from 24 to 48. 3) *vānaprastha:* Elder advisor, from 48 to 72. 4) *sannyāsa:* Religious solitary, from 72 onward. See: *dharma, grihastha dharma, sannyāsa dharma.*

astral body: The subtle, nonphysical body (*sūkshma śarīra*) in which the soul functions in the astral plane, the inner world also called Antarloka. See: *Antarloka, soul.*

astral plane: The subtle world, Antarloka. See: *Antarloka, loka.*

asura: असुर "Evil spirit; demon." (The opposite of *sura:* "*deva;* God.") A being of the lower astral plane, Narakaloka. *Asuras* can and do interact with the physical plane, causing major and minor problems in people's lives. *Asuras* do evolve and do not remain permanently in this state. See: *Narakaloka.*

ātman: आत्मन् "The soul; the breath; the principle of life and sensation." The soul in its entirety—as the soul body plus its inner divine essence. Our true, eternal identity in the deepest level, beyond a physical body, emotions, external mind or personality. See: *soul.*

Aum: ॐ or ओम् Often spelled *Om.* The mystic syllable of Hinduism, placed at the beginning of most sacred writings. As a *mantra,* it is pronounced *aw* (as in *law*), *oo* (as in *zoo*), *mm.* Aum is explained in the *Upanishads* as standing for the whole world and its parts, including past, present and future. It is from this primal vibration that all manifestation issues forth. Aum is the primary, or *mūla mantra,* and often precedes other *mantras.* Its three letters represent the three worlds and the powers of creation, preservation and destruction.

avatāra (avatar): अवतार "Descent." A God born in a human (or animal) body. A central concept of Śāktism, Smārtism and Vaishnavism. See: *incarnation, Ishṭa Devatā, Vaishnavism.*

āyurveda: आयुर्वेद "Science of life." A holistic system of medicine and health native to ancient India. The aims of *āyurveda* are *āyus,* "longevity," and *ārogya,* "diseaselessness," which facilitate progress toward ultimate spiritual goals. Health is achieved by balancing energies (especially the *doshas,* bodily humors) at all levels of being, subtle and gross, through innumerable methods, selected according to the individual's constitution, lifestyle and nature. Similar holistic medical systems evolved among many peoples, such as the Chinese, North and South Native Americans and Africans. See: *doshas.*

Bhagavad Gītā: भगवद् गीता "Song of the Lord." One of the most popular of Hindu writings, a conversation between Lord Kṛishṇa and Arjuna on the brink of the great battle at Kurukshetra. In this central episode of the epic *Mahābhārata,* Kṛishṇa illumines the warrior-prince Arjuna on *yoga,* asceticism, *dharma* and the spiritual path. See: *Mahābhārata.*

bhajana (bhajan): भजन Spiritual song. Individual or group singing of devotional songs, hymns and chants. See: *bhakti.*

bhakti: भक्ति "Devotion." Surrender to God, Gods or *guru. Bhakti* extends from the simplest expression of devotion to the ego-decimating principle of *prapatti,* which is total surrender. See: *bhakti yoga, darśana, prapatti, prasāda, yajña.*

bhakti yoga: भक्तियोग "Union through devotion." *Bhakti yoga* is the practice of devotional disciplines, worship, prayer, chanting and singing with the aim of awakening love in the heart and opening oneself to God's grace. *Bhakti* may be directed toward God, Gods or one's spiritual preceptor. *Bhakti yoga* seeks communion and ever closer rapport with the Divine, developing qualities that make communion possible, such as love, selflessness and purity. See: *bhakti, prapatti, yajña.*

Bharata (Bhārata): भारत "He who supports, maintains, bears a burden." The ancient, original name of India and its constitutional name in Hindi: Bharatavarsha "land of Bharat," a legendary monarch and sage.

Bhārata Dharma: भारत धर्म "the law that upholds the land of Bharata". A synonym for Hinduism. See: *Hinduism, Sanātana Dharma.*

Bhūloka: भूलोक "Earth world." The physical plane. See: *loka.*

bilva: बिल्व Wood-apple (or bael) tree, *Aegle marmelos,* sacred to Lord Śiva. Its leaves, picked in threes, are offered in the worship of the Śivaliṅga. The delicious fruit when unripe is used medicinally.

bindu: बिन्दु "A drop, small particle, dot." Small dot worn on the forehead between the eyebrows, or in the middle of the forehead. It is a sign that one is a Hindu. Mystically, it represents the "third eye," or the "mind's eye," which sees things that the physical eyes cannot see. The *bindu* is known as *pottu* in Tamil. See: *tilaka.*

Bodhinatha Veylanswami: बोधिनाथ "Lord of Wisdom, Holder of the *Vel.*" (1942–) The current preceptor of the Nandinātha Sampradāya's Kailāsa Paramparā, and Guru Mahāsannidhānam of Kauai Aadheenam, ordained by his *satguru,* Sivaya Subramuniyaswami, in 2001. See: *Sivaya Subramuniyaswami, parampara, Yogaswami.*

brahmachāri: ब्रह्मचारी An man who practices *brahmacharya.* Also names one in the student stage, age 12–24, or until marriage. See: *āśrama dharma, bramacharya, monk.*

brahmachāriṇī: ब्रह्मचारिणी Feminine counterpart of *brahmachāri.* See: *bramacharya.*

brahmacharya: ब्रह्मचर्य "Divine conduct." Controlling lust by remaining celibate when single, maintaining purity by restraining from sex in thought and deed and transmuting the energies of the physical body. See: *yama-niyama.*

Brahman: ब्रह्मन् "Supreme Being; Expansive Spirit." From the root *bṛih,* "to grow, increase, expand." Name of God or Supreme Deity in the *Vedas,* where He is described as 1) the Transcendent Absolute, 2) the all-pervading energy and 3) the Supreme Lord or Primal Soul. The term *Brahman* should not be confused with *Brahmā,* the Creator God. See: *God.*

brāhmin (brāhmaṇa): ब्राह्मण "Mature" or "evolved" soul. Originally, the class of pious souls of exceptional learning. From *Brāhman,* "growth, expansion, evolution, development, swelling of the spirit or soul." A mature soul showing exemplary wisdom, tolerance, forbearance and humility. Today, the term more often refers to a caste. See: *dharma.*

causal body: *Kāraṇa śarīra,* the inmost body; the soul form, also called *ānandamaya kośa,* "bliss sheath". See: *soul.*

causal plane: The highest or most subtle realm of existence, Śivaloka. See: *loka, Śivaloka.*

chakra: चक्र "Wheel." Any of the nerve plexes or centers of force and consciousness located within the subtle bodies of man. In the physical body there are corresponding nerve plexuses, ganglia and glands. The seven principal *chakras* can be seen psychically as colorful, multi-petaled wheels or lotuses. They are situated along the spinal cord from the base to the cranial chamber. Additionally, seven *chakras,* barely visible, exist below the spine. They are seats of instinctive consciousness, the origin of jealousy, hatred, envy, guilt, sorrow, etc. They constitute the lower or hellish world, called *Narakaloka* or *pātāla.* Thus, there are 14 major *chakras* in all.

The seven upper chakras, from lowest to highest, are: 1) *mūlādhāra* (base of spine): memory, time and space; 2) *svādhishṭhāna* (below navel): reason; 3) *maṇipūra* (solar plexus): willpower; 4) *anāhata* (heart center): direct cognition; 5) *viśuddha* (throat): divine love; 6) *ājñā* (third eye): divine sight;

7) *sahasrāra* (crown of head): illumination, Godliness.

The seven lower chakras, from highest to lowest, are 1) *atala* (hips): fear and lust; 2) *vitala* (thighs): raging anger; 3) *sutala* (knees): retaliatory jealousy; 4) *talātala* (calves): prolonged mental confusion; 5) *rasātala* (ankles): selfishness; 6) *mahātala* (feet): absence of conscience; 7) *pātāla* (soles of the feet): murder and malice. See: *chart on p. 42, Chapter 16*.

charyā pāda: चर्यापाद "Conduct stage." Stage of service and character building. See: *pāda, Śaivism*.

clairaudience: "Clear-hearing." Psychic or divine hearing, *divyaśravana*. Hearing in one's mind the words of inner-plane beings or earthly beings not physically present. See: *clairvoyance*.

clairvoyance: "Clear-seeing." Psychic or divine sight, *divyadrishti*. The ability to look into the inner worlds and see auras, *chakras, nāḍīs*, thought forms, non-physical people and subtle forces. The ability to see from afar or into the past or future—*avadhijñāna*, "knowing beyond limits." Also the ability to separate the light that illumines one's thoughts from the forms the light illumines.

crown *chakra*: *Sahasrāra chakra*. The thousand-petaled cranial center of divine consciousness. See: *chakra, kuṇḍalinī, yoga*.

darśana: दर्शन "Vision, sight." Seeing the Divine. Beholding, with inner or outer vision, a temple image, Deity, holy person or place, with the desire to inwardly contact and receive the grace and blessings of the venerated being or beings. Not only does the devotee seek to see the Divine, but to be seen as well, to stand humbly in the awakened gaze of the holy one, even if for an instant, such as in a crowded temple when thousands of worshipers file quickly past the enshrined Lord. Gods and *gurus* are thus said to "give" *darśana*, and devotees "take" *darśana*. This direct and personal two-sided apprehension is a central and highly sought-after experience of Hindu faith.

daśamāṁśa: दशमांश "One-tenth sharing." The traditional Hindu practice of tithing, giving one-tenth of one's income to a religious institution. It was formerly widespread in India. See: *purusha dharma*.

Daśanāmī: Each of the ten renunciate orders founded by Adi Śankara during the 9TH century. See: *Akhara*.

deva: देव "Shining one." A being inhabiting the higher astral plane, in a subtle, nonphysical body. *Deva* is also used in scripture to mean "God or Deity." See: *gana, Mahādeva*.

Devaloka: देवलोक "Plane of radiant beings." A synonym of Maharloka, the higher astral plane, realm of *anāhata chakra*. See: *Antar-loka, loka*.

Devi: देवी "Goddess." A name of Śakti, used especially in Śāktism. See: *Śakti, Śāktism*.

dharma: धर्म From *dhṛi*, "to sustain; carry, hold." Hence *dharma* is "that which contains or upholds the cosmos." *Dharma* is a complex and comprehensive term with many meanings, including: divine law, ethics, law of being, way of righteousness, religion, duty, responsibility, virtue, justice, goodness and truth. Essentially, *dharma* is the orderly fulfillment of an inherent nature or destiny. Relating to the soul, it is the mode of conduct most conducive to spiritual advancement, the right and righteous path.

Adharma: "Unrighteousness." Thoughts, words or deeds that transgress divine law in any of the human expressions of *dharma*. See: *dharma, pāpa, punya*.

dhyāna: ध्यान "Meditation." See: *rāja yoga*.

dīkṣā: दीक्षा "Initiation." Solemn induction by which one is entered into a new realm of spiritual awareness and practice by a teacher or preceptor through bestowing of blessings. Denotes initial or deepened connection with the teacher and his lineage and is usually accompanied by ceremony. Initiation, revered as a moment of awakening, may be conferred by a touch, a word, a look or a thought. See: *satguru*.

Dīpāvalī: दीपावली Often spelled *Dīvalī*. "Row of Lights." A very popular home and community festival in October/November when Hindus of all denominations light oil or electric lights and set off fireworks in a joyful celebration of the victory of good over evil and light over darkness. It is a Hindu solidarity day and is considered the greatest national festival of India.

door of Brahman: *Brahmarandhra*, also called *nirvāna chakra*. A subtle or esoteric aperture in the crown of the head, the opening of *sushumṇā nāḍī* through which *kuṇḍalinī* enters in ultimate Self Realization, and the spirit escapes at death. Only the spirits of the truly pure leave the body in this way. See: *jñāna, kuṇḍalinī, nāḍī*.

dualism: *Dvaita*. See: *dvaita-advaita*.

dvaita-advaita: द्वैत अद्वैत "Dual-nondual; twoness-not twoness." Among the most important terms in the classification of Hindu philosophies. *Dvaita* and *advaita* define two ends of a vast spectrum. —*dvaita:* The doctrine of dualism, according to which reality is ultimately composed of two irreducible principles, entities, truths, etc. God and soul are seen as eternally separate. —*advaita:* The doctrine of nondualism or monism, that reality is ultimately composed of one whole principle, substance or God, with no independent parts. In essence, all is God. —**monistic theism:** A dipolar view which encompasses both monism and dualism. See: *dvaita, monistic theism*.

ego: The external personality or sense of "I" and "mine," *āṇava*. Broadly, individual identity. In Śaiva Siddhānta and other schools, the ego is equated with the *tattva* of ahaṁkāra, "I-maker," which bestows the sense of I-ness, individuality and separateness from God. See: *āṇava*.

enlightenment: Self Realization, *nirvikalpa samādhi;* the ultimate attainment. Enlightenment is the experience-nonexperience resulting in the realization of one's transcendent Self—Paraśiva—which exists beyond time, form and space. Each tradition has its own understanding of enlightenment, often indicated by unique terms. See: *God Realization, kuṇḍalinī, nirvikalpa samādhi, Self Realization*.

First World: The physical universe; Bhuloka. See: *Bhuloka*.

freemasons (Freemansonry): The member of an international order, the Freemasonry, established for philosophical-occult studies and mutual help within its fellowship.

gana(s): गण "Throng; troop; retinue; a body of followers or attendants." A troop of demigods, God's attendants, devonic helpers. See: *Ganapati, Ganeśa*.

Ganapati: गणपति "Leader of the *ganas*." A name of *Ganeśa*.

Ganeśa: गणेश "Lord of Categories." Or: "Lord of attendants *(gana)*," synonymous with *Ganapati*. Ganeśa is a Mahādeva, the beloved elephant-faced Deity honored by Hindus of every sect. He is the Lord of Obstacles (Vigh-neśvara), revered for His great wisdom and invoked first before any undertaking, for He knows all intricacies of each soul's *karma* and the perfect path of *dharma* that makes action successful. He sits on the *mūlādhāra chakra* and is easy of access. See: *gana, Ganapati, Mahādeva*.

Ganges (Gaṅgā): गंगा India's most sacred river, 1,557 miles long, arising in the Himalayas above Hardwar under the name Bhagīratha, and being named Gaṅgā after joining the Alakanada (where the Sarasvatī is said to join them underground). Also, the Godess (Gaṅgā) that has the river as her embodiment.

ghee: घी Hindi for clarified butter; *ghrita* in Sanskrit. Butter that has been boiled and strained. An important sacred substance used in temple lamps and offered in fire ceremony, *yajña*. It is also used as a food with many *āyurvedic* virtues. See: *yajña*.

God: Supernal being. Either the Supreme God, known by many names (such as Śiva, Śakti and Vishnu), or one of the Mahādevas, great souls, who are among His creation. See: *Gods, Mahādeva, Śiva*.

Goddess: Female representation or manifestation of Divinity; Śakti or Devī. *Goddess* can refer to a female perception or depiction of a causal-plane being (Mahādeva) in its natural state, which is genderless, or it can refer to an astral-plane being residing in a female astral body. To show the Divine's transcendence of sexuality, sometimes God is shown as having qualities of both sexes.

Gods: Mahādevas, "great beings of light." In *What Is Hinduism?*, the plural form of *God* refers to extremely advanced beings existing in their self-effulgent soul bodies in the causal plane. The meaning of *Gods* is best seen in the phrase, "God and the Gods," referring to the Supreme God and the Mahādevas who are His creation. See: *God, Mahādeva.*

grihastha āśrama: गृहस्थ आश्रम "Householder stage." See: *āśrama dharma, grihastha dharma.*

grihastha dharma: गृहस्थधर्म "Householder law." The virtues and ideals of family life. This *dharma* includes all nonmonastics, whether married or single. In general, *grihastha dharma* begins with the completion of the period of studentship and extends throughout the period of raising a family (called the *grihastha āśrama*). Specific scriptures, called *Dharma Śāstras* and *Grihya Śāstras,* outline the duties and obligations of family life. In Hinduism, family life is one of serving, learning and striving within a close-knit community of many relatives forming a joint family and its broader connections as an extended family under the aegis of a spiritual *guru*. Each is expected to work harmoniously to further the wealth and happiness of the family and the society, to practice religious disciplines and raise children of strong moral fiber to carry on the tradition. See: *āśrama dharma, dharma.*

guṇa: गुण "Strand; quality." The three constituent principles of *prakṛiti*, primal nature. The three *guṇas* are —*sattva:* "Quiescent", rarified, translucent, pervasive, reflecting the light of Pure Consciousness. —*rajas:* "Passion," inherent in energy, movement, action, emotion, life. —*tamas:* "Darkness," inertia, density, the force of contraction, resistance and dissolution. The *guṇas* are integral to Hindu thought, as all things are composed of the combination of these qualities of nature, including *āyurveda*, arts, environments and personalities. See: *āyurveda, tattva.*

guru: गुरु "Weighty one," indicating an authority of great knowledge or skill. A term used to describe a teacher or guide in any subject, such as music, dance, sculpture, but especially religion. For clarity, the term is often preceded by a qualifying prefix. Hence, terms such as *kulaguru* (family teacher), *vīnaguru* (*vīna* teacher) and *satguru* (spiritual preceptor). In Hindu astrology, *guru* names the planet Jupiter, also known as Bṛihaspati. According to

the *Advayatāraka Upanishad* (14–18), *guru* means "dispeller (*gu*) of darkness (*ru*)." See: *satguru.*

Gurudeva: गुरुदेव "Divine or radiant preceptor." An affectionate, respectful name for the *guru*. See: *guru, Sivaya Subramuniyaswami.*

 hatha yoga: हठयोग "Forceful yoga." *Haṭha yoga* is a system of physical and mental exercise developed in ancient times as a means of rejuvenation by *ṛishis* and *tapasvins* who meditated for long hours, and used today in preparing the body and mind for meditation. Its elements are *āsanas*, cleansing practices, breath control and hand gestures (*mudrās*), all of which regulate the flow of *prāṇa* and purify the inner and outer bodies. See: *āsana, kuṇḍalinī, nāḍī, rāja yoga, yoga.*

heaven: The celestial spheres, including the causal plane and the higher realms of the subtle plane, where souls rest and learn between births, and mature souls continue to evolve after *moksha*. *Heaven* is often used by translators as an equivalent to the Sanskrit *Svarga*. See: *loka, Śivaloka.*

hell: Narakaloka. An unhappy, mentally and emotionally congested, distressful area of consciousness. Hell is a state of mind that can be experienced on the physical plane or in the sub-astral plane after death of the physical body. It is accompanied by the tormented emotions of hatred, remorse, resentment, fear, jealousy and self-condemnation. However, in the Hindu view, the hellish experience is not permanent, but a temporary condition of one's own making. See: *asura, evil, loka, Narakaloka.*

Hindu: हिन्दु A follower of, or relating to, Hinduism. Generally, one is understood to be a Hindu by being born into a Hindu family and practicing the faith, or by professing oneself a Hindu. Acceptance into the fold is recognized through the name-giving sacrament, a temple ceremony called *nāmakaraṇa saṃskāra*, given to born Hindus shortly after birth, and to self-declared Hindus who have proven their sincerity and been accepted by a Hindu community. While traditions vary greatly, all Hindus rely on the *Vedas* as scriptural authority. On July 2, 1995, the Supreme Court of India adopted as an "adequate and satisfactory formula" this definition by B.G. Tilak: "Acceptance of the Vedas with reverence; recognition of the fact that the means or ways to salvation are diverse; and the realization of the truth that the number of gods to be worshiped is large, that indeed is the distinguishing feature of the Hindu religion." See: *Hinduism.*

Hinduism (Hindu Dharma): हिन्दुधर्म India's indigenous religious and cultural system, fol-

lowed today by nearly one billion adherents, mostly in India, but with the large diaspora in many other countries. Also called Sanātana Dharma, "Eternal Religion" and Vaidika Dharma, "Religion of the *Vedas*." Hinduism is the world's most ancient religion and encompasses a broad spectrum of philosophies ranging from pluralistic theism to absolute monism. It is a family of myriad faiths with four primary denominations: Śaivism, Vaishṇavism, Śāktism and Smārtism. These four hold such divergent beliefs that each is a complete and independent religion. Yet, they share a vast heritage of culture and belief—*karma, dharma*, reincarnation, all-pervasive Divinity, temple worship, sacraments, manifold Deities, the *guru-śishya* tradition and a reliance on the *Vedas* as scriptural authority. See: *Hindu.*

homa: होम "Fire-offering." A sacred ceremony in which the Gods are offered oblations through the medium of fire in a sanctified fire pit. See: *agni, yajña.*

 immanent: Indwelling; inherent and operating within. Relating to God, the term *immanent* means present in all things and throughout the universe, not aloof or distant. Not to be confused with *imminent*, about to happen; *emanate*, to issue from; *eminent*, high in rank.

Ishṭa Devatā: इष्टदेवता "Cherished or chosen Deity." The Deity that is the object of one's special pious attention. *Ishṭa Devatā* is a concept common to all Hindu sects. See: *mūrti, Smārtism.*

 japa: जप "Recitation." Practice of concentrated repeating of a *mantra*, often while counting the repetitions on a *mālā*, a strand of beads. It may be done silently or aloud. A major *sādhana* in Hindu spiritual practice, from the simple utterance of a few names of God to extraordinary feats of repeating sacred syllables millions of times for years on end. See: *mantra, sadhana, tapas, yama-niyama, yoga.*

jiva: जीव "Living, existing." From *jīv*, "to live." The individual soul, *ātman*, during its embodied state, bound by *āṇava, karma* and *māyā*. The *jivanmukta* is one who is "liberated while living." See: *ātman, soul.*

jñāna: ज्ञान "Knowledge; wisdom." The matured state of the soul. It is the wisdom that comes as an aftermath of the *kuṇḍalinī* breaking through the door of *Brahman* into the realization of God. *Jñāna* is the awakened, superconscious state working within the ordinary experience of the world, flowing into daily life situations. *Jñāna* is sometimes misunderstood as book knowledge, as a maturity or awakening that comes from simply understanding a complex philosophical system or systems. See: *door of Brahman, God Realization, samādhi, Self Realization.*

jñāna pāda: ज्ञानपाद "Stage of wisdom." According to Śaiva Siddhānta *ṛishis, jñāna* is the last of the four successive *pādas* (stages) of spiritual unfoldment. It is the culmination of the third stage, the *yoga pāda.* See: *jñāna, pāda.*

jyotisha: ज्योतिष From *jyoti,* "light." "The science of the lights (or stars)." Hindu astrology, the knowledge and practice of analyzing events and circumstances, delineating character and determining auspicious moments, according to the positions and movements of heavenly bodies. In calculating horoscopes, *jyotisha* uses the sidereal (fixed-star) system, whereas Western astrology uses the tropical (fixed-date) method.

karma: कर्म "Action," "deed." One of the most important principles in Hindu thought, *karma* refers to a consequence or "fruit of action", which sooner or later returns upon the doer. What we sow, we shall reap in this or future lives. Selfish, hateful acts will bring suffering. Benevolent actions will bring loving reactions. *Karma* is a neutral, self-perpetuating law of the inner cosmos, much as gravity is an impersonal law of the outer cosmos. *Karma* is threefold: *sañchita, prārabdha* and *kriyamāna.* —*sañchita karma:* "Accumulated actions." The sum of all *karmas* of this life and past lives. —*prārabdha karma:* "Actions set in motion." That portion of *sañchita karma* that is bearing fruit and shaping the events and conditions of the current life, including the nature of one's bodies, personal tendencies and associations. —*kriyamāna karma:* "Being made." The *karma* being created and added to *sañchita* in this life by one's thoughts, words and actions, or in the inner worlds between lives. *Kriyamāna karma* is the karma that is being sown and will be reaped in the future.
See: *māyā, moksha, pāpa, puṇya, soul.*

Kārttikeya: कार्त्तिकेय Child of the Pleiades, from *Kṛittikā,* "Pleiades." A son of Śiva. A great Mahādeva worshiped in all parts of India and the world. Also known as Murugan, Kumāra, Skanda, Shaṇmukhanātha, Subramaṇya and more, He is the God who guides that part of evolution which is religion, the transformation of the instinctive into a divine wisdom through the practice of *yoga.* He holds the holy *vel* of *jñāna śakti,* which is His Power to vanquish darkness or ignorance.

kośa: कोश "Sheath; vessel, container; layer." Philosophically, five sheaths through which the soul functions simultaneously in the various planes or levels of existence. They are sometimes compared to the layers of an onion. The *kośas,* in order of increasing subtlety, are as follows. —*annamaya kośa:* "Sheath composed of food." The physical body. —*prāṇamaya kośa:* "Sheath composed of *prāṇa* (vital force)." Also known as the *prāṇic* or health body, or the etheric body or etheric double. —*manomaya kośa:* "Mind-formed sheath." The lower astral body, from *manas,* "thought, will, wish." The instinctive-intellectual sheath of ordinary thought, desire and emotion. —*vijñānamaya kośa:* "Sheath of cognition." The mental or cognitive-intuitive sheath. It is the vehicle of higher thought, *vijñāna*—understanding, knowing, direct cognition, wisdom, intuition and creativity. —*ānandamaya kośa:* "Body of bliss." The intuitive-superconscious sheath or actinic-causal body. This inmost soul form *(svarūpa)* is the ultimate foundation of all life, intelligence and higher faculties. See: *soul, subtle body.*

Krishṇa: कृष्ण "Black." Also related to *kṛishṭiḥ,* meaning "drawing, attracting." One of the most popular Gods of the Hindu pantheon. He is worshiped by Vaishṇavas as the eighth *avatāra,* incarnation, of Vishṇu. He is best known as the Supreme Personage depicted in the *Mahābhārata,* and specifically in the *Bhagavad Gītā.*

kriyā: "Action." 1) In a general sense, *kriyā* can refer to doing of any kind. Specifically, it names religious action, especially rites or ceremonies. 2) The second stage of the Śaiva path, religious action, or *kriyā pāda.* See: *kriyā pāda, pāda.*

kriyā pāda: क्रियापाद "Stage of religious action; worship." The stage of worship and devotion, second of four progressive stages of maturation on the Śaiva Siddhānta path of attainment. See: *pāda.*

kriyamana karma: The *karma* being created at present. See: *Karma.*

kukarma: Karma accrued from *pāpa.* See: *Karma, pāpa.*

Kumāra: कुमार "Virgin youth; ever-youthful." A name of Lord Kārttikeya as an eternal bachelor. See: *Kārttikeya.*

kumbha: कुम्भ "Jar or pot; water vessel."

Kumbha Mela: Kumbha Mela is a Hindu pilgrimage that occurs four times every twelve years, on astrologically auspicious times, in four sacred locations in India. They are attended by thousands of saints and millions of people, making them the largest human gatherings on Earth.

kuṇḍalinī: कुण्डलिनी "She who is coiled; serpent power." The primordial cosmic energy in every individual which, at first, lies coiled like a serpent at the base of the spine and eventually, through the practice of *yoga,* rises up the *sushumṇā nāḍī.* As it rises, the *kuṇḍalinī* empowers each successive *chakra.* Nirvikalpa *samādhi,* enlightenment, comes as it pierces through the door of Brahman at the core of the *sahasrāra.* See: *chakra, door of Brahman, nāḍī, samādhi.*

loka: लोक "World, habitat, realm, or plane of existence." A dimension of manifest existence; cosmic region. Each *loka* reflects or involves a particular range of consciousness. Bhuloka is the physical plane. The Antarloka and Śivaloka are the ever-present substratum of physical existence, most frequently experienced by humans during sleep and deep meditation. Each *loka* is a less-refined version of the *loka* above it. See: *Antarloka, Bhuloka, Śivaloka.*

Mahābhārata: महाभारत "Great Epic of India." The world's longest epic poem. It revolves around the conflict between two kingdoms, the Pāṇḍavas and Kauravas, and their great battle of Kurukshetra near modern Delhi in approximately 1424 bce. Woven through the plot are countless discourses on philosophy, religion, astronomy, cosmology, polity, economics and many stories illustrative of simple truths and ethical principles. The *Bhagavad Gītā* is one section of the work. The *Mahābhārata* is revered as scripture by Vaishṇavites and Smārtas. See: *Bhagavad Gītā, Itihāsa.*

Mahādeva: महादेव "Great shining one; God." Referring either to the Supreme God or any of the highly evolved beings who live in the highest planes in their natural, effulgent soul bodies. It is said in scripture that there are 330 million Gods. See: *Gods, monotheism, Parameśvara, Śiva.*

mahāprasthāna: महाप्रस्थान "Great departure." Death.

mahāsamādhi: महासमाधि "Great enstasy." The death, or dropping off of the physical body, of a great soul, an event occasioned by tremendous blessings. See: *samādhi.*

mahātma: महात्म "Great soul." Honorific title for thoseheld in highest esteem, especially saints. See: *ātman.*

maṇipūra chakra: मणिपूरचक्र "Wheeled city of jewels." Solar-plexus center of willpower. See: *chakra.*

mantra: मन्त्र "Mystic formula." A sound, syllable, word or phrase endowed with special power, usually drawn from scripture. *Mantras* are chanted loudly during *pūjā* to invoke the Gods and establish a spiritual force field. Certain *mantras* are repeated softly or mentally for *japa.* Hinduism's universal *mantra* is Aum. To be truly effective, such *mantras* must be given by the preceptor through initiation. See: *Aum, dīkshā, japa, pūjā, yajña.*

mārga: मार्ग "Path; way." From *mārg,* "to seek." See: *pāda, San mārga.*

mauna: मौन The discipline of remaining silent.

māyā: माया "She who measures;" or "mirific energy." The substance emanated from God through which the world of form is manifested. Hence all creation is also termed *māyā*. *Māyā* is a key concept in Hinduism, originally meaning "supernatural power; God's mirific energy," often translated as "illusion." See: *loka, tattva.*

moksha: मोक्ष "Liberation." Release from transmigration, *samsāra*, the round of births and deaths, which occurs after *karma* has been resolved and *nirvikalpa samādhi*—realization of the Self, Paraśiva—has been attained. Same as *mukti.* See: *jīva, kuṇḍalinī, nirvikalpa samādhi, Paraśiva, rāja yoga, samsāra.*

monism: "Doctrine of oneness." 1) The philosophical view that there is only one ultimate substance or principle. 2) The view that reality is a unified whole without independent parts. See: *dvaita-advaita, monistic theism.*

monistic theism: Advaita Īśvaravāda. Monism is the doctrine that reality is a one whole or existence without independent parts. Theism is the belief that God exists as a real, conscious, personal Supreme Being. Monistic theism is the dipolar doctrine, also called panentheism, that embraces both monism and theism, two perspectives ordinarily considered contradictory or mutually exclusive, since theism implies dualism. Monistic theism simultaneously accepts that God has a personal form, that He creates, pervades and *is* all that exists—and that He ultimately transcends all existence and that the soul is, in essence, one with God. See: *dvaita-advaita, panentheism, theism.*

mudrā: मुद्रा "Seal." Esoteric hand gestures which express specific energies or powers. Usually accompanied by precise visualizations, *mudrās* are a vital element of ritual worship (*pūjā*), dance and *yoga.* See: *añjali mudrā, haṭha yoga.*

mūlādhāra chakra: मूलाधारचक्र "Root-support wheel." Four-petaled psychic center at the base of the spine; governs memory. See: *chakra.*

mūrti: मूर्ति "Form; manifestation, embodiment, personification." An image, icon or effigy of God or a God used during worship. Other Deity representations include symbols, e.g., the banyan tree, and geometric emblems or designs such as *yantras* and *maṇḍalas.*

Murugan: முருகன் "Beautiful one," a favorite name of Kārttikeya among the Tamils of South India, Sri Lanka and elsewhere. See: *Kārttikeya.*

 nāḍi: नाडी "Conduit; river." A nerve fiber or energy channel of the subtle (inner) bodies of man. It is said there are 72,000 *nāḍīs.* These interconnect the *chakras.* The three main *nāḍīs* are *iḍā, piṅgalā* and *sushumṇā.* — **ida** is pink and feminine. It flows downward, ending on the left side of the body. It is the channel of physical-emotional energy. — **pingala** is blue and

masculine. It flows upward, ending on the right side of the body. It is the channel of intellectual-mental energy. — **sushumna** is the major nerve current which passes through the spinal column from the muladhara chakra at the base to the sahasrara at the crown of the head. It is the channel of kundalini. See: *chakra, kuṇḍalinī, rāja yoga.*

nakshatra: नक्षत्र "Star cluster." Central to astrological determinations, the *nakshatras* are 27 star-clusters, constellations, which lie along the ecliptic, or path of the sun. An individual's *nakshatra,* or birth star, is the constellation the moon was aligned with at the time of birth. See: *jyotisha.*

Namaḥ Śivāya: नमः शिवाय "Adoration (homage) to Śiva." The supreme *mantra* of Śaivism. See: *japa, mantra, Śaivism.*

nāmakaraṇa samskāra: नामकरण "Name-giving" and formal entry into one or another sect of Hinduism, performed 11 to 41 days after birth. The name is chosen according to astrology, preferably the name of a God or Goddess. At this time, guardian *devas* are assigned to see the child through life. One who converts to or adopts Hinduism later in life would receive this same sacrament. See: *samskāra.*

Narakaloka: नरक Abode of darkness. The nether worlds. Equivalent to the Western term *hell,* a gross region of the Antarloka. Naraka is a congested, distressful area where demonic beings and young souls may sojourn until they resolve the darksome *karmas* they have created. Here beings suffer the consequences of their own misdeeds in previous lives. Naraka*loka* is understood as having seven regions, called *tala,* corresponding to the states of consciousness of the seven lower *chakras.* They are described as places of torment, pain, darkness, confusion and disease, but these are only temporary abodes for the evolving soul. Hinduism has no eternal hell. See: *Antarloka, chakra, hell, loka.*

Nātha: नाथ "Master, lord; adept." Names an ancient Himalayan tradition of Śaiva-yoga mysticism whose first historically known exponent was Nandikesvara (ca 250 bce), and the extraordinary ascetic masters (or devotees) of this school. The *Nāthas* are considered the source of *haṭha* as well as *rāja yoga.* See: *paramparā, rāja yoga.*

nirvikalpa samādhi: निर्विकल्पसमाधि "Undifferentiated trance, enstasy (*samādhi*) without form or seed." The realization of the Self, Paraśiva, a state of oneness beyond all change or diversity; beyond time, form and space. *Vikalpa* means "diversity, thought; difference of perception, distinction." *Nir* means "without." See: *Paraśiva, rāja yoga, samādhi.*

niyama: नियम "Restraint." See: *yama-niyama.*

 pāda: पाद "The foot (of men and animals); quarter-part, section; stage; path." Names the major sections of the Āgamic texts and the corresponding stages of practice and unfoldment on the path to *moksha.* According to Śaiva Siddhānta, there are four *pādas,* which are successive and cumulative. In accomplishing each one, the soul prepares itself for the next. —*charyā pāda:* "Good conduct stage." The first stage where one learns to live righteously, serve selflessly, performing *karma yoga.* —*kriyā pāda:* "Religious action; worship stage." Stage of *bhakti yoga,* of cultivating devotion through performing *pūjā* and regular daily *sādhana.* —*yoga pāda:* Having matured, the soul now turns to internalized worship and *rāja yoga* under the guidance of a *satguru.* It is a time of *sādhana* and serious striving when realization of the Self is the goal. —*jñāna pāda:* "Stage of wisdom." Once the soul has attained Realization, it is henceforth a wise one, shedding blessings on mankind. This stage is also called the San Mārga, "true path," on which God is our dearest beloved; implying transcendence of individuality and merger with the Divine. See: *jñāna,*

pādukā: पादुका "Sandals." *Śrī Pādukā* refers to the sandals of the preceptor, the traditional icon of the *guru,* representing his venerable feet and worshiped as the source of grace. See: *bhakti, guru, prasāda, satguru.*

panchangam: The traditional Hindu astrological calendar and almanac. Panchangams are used to determine the optimum times for all activities. See: *jyotisha.*

panentheism: "All-in-God doctrine." The view that the universe is part of the being of God. Panentheism is the technical term for monistic theism. See: *dvaita-advaita, monistic theism, pantheism.*

pantheism: "All-is-God doctrine." A term applied to a variety of philosophical positions in which God and the world are identical. To the pantheist, God is not a Personal Lord, nor a transcendent or formless Being, but is the totality of all existence, including universal laws, movement, matter, etc. See also: *monistic theism, panentheism.*

pāpa: पाप "Wickedness or sin;" "crime." 1) Bad or evil. 2) Wrongful action. 3) Demerit earned through wrongdoing. Pāpa includes all forms of wrongdoing, from the simplest infraction to the most heinous crime. The degree of *pāpa* accrued from an action depends on various factors, including the *karma, dharma* and spiritual advancement of the individual, the intent or motivation, as well as the time and place of the action. *Pāpa* is the opposite of *puṇya* (merit, virtue). See: *evil, karma, puṇya.*

paramaguru: परमगुरु "Grand preceptor." The *guru* of a disciple's *guru.*

paramahaṁsa: परमहंस "Supreme swan." From *haṁsa*, meaning swan or, more precisely, the high-flying Indian goose, Anser Indicus. A class of liberated renunciates. See: *haṁsa.*

Parameśvara: परमेश्वर "Supreme Lord or Ruler." God Śiva's third perfection, Supreme Mahādeva, Śiva-Śakti, mother of the universe. In this perfection, Śiva is a person. The term *Primal Soul* designates Parameśvara as the original, uncreated soul, the creator of all other souls. See: God, *Parāśakti, Paraśiva, Śiva.*

paramparā: परंपरा "Uninterrupted succession." A lineage of gurus, initiating successors and passing on the power through the ages.

Parāśakti: पराशक्ति "Supreme power; primal energy." God Śiva's second perfection, which is impersonal, immanent, and with form—the all-pervasive, Pure Consciousness and Primal Substance of all that exists. There are many other descriptive names for Parāśakti—Satchidānanda ("existence-consciousness-bliss"), light, silence, divine mind, superconsciousness and more. Parāśakti can be experienced by the diligent *yogī* or meditator as a merging in, or identification with, the underlying oneness flowing through all form. The experience is called *savikalpa samādhi.* See: *rāja yoga, Śakti, samādhi, Satchidānanda, tattva.*

Paraśiva: परशिव "Transcendent Śiva." The Self God, Śiva's first perfection, Absolute Reality. Paraśiva is *That* which is beyond the grasp of consciousness, transcends time, form and space and defies description. To merge with the Absolute in mystic union is the ultimate goal of all incarnated souls, the reason for their living on this planet, and the deepest meaning of their experiences. Attainment of this is called Self Realization or *nirvikalpa samādhi.* See: *nirvikalpa samādhi, samādhi, Śiva.*

Patanjali (Patañjali): पतञ्जलि A Śaivite Nātha *siddha* (ca 200 BCE) who codified the ancient *rāja yoga* philosophy which outlines the path to enlightenment through purification, control and transcendence of the mind. His great work, the *Yoga Sūtras,* comprises some 200 aphorisms and is the foremost ancient text on meditative *yoga.* See: *rāja yoga, yoga.*

Pillayar: Tamil name for Ganeśa. See: *Ganeśa.*

pingalā: पिंगला "Tawny channel." The masculine psychic current flowing along the spine. See: *kuṇḍalinī, nāḍī, rāja yoga.*

plane: A stage or level of existence. See: *loka.*

polytheism: Belief in or worship of many Gods. See also: *monotheism, pantheism, panentheism.*

prāṇa: प्राण Vital energy or life principle. While *prāṇa* usually refers to the life principle, it sometimes denotes energy, breath, the power or the animating force of the cosmos, the sum total of all energy and forces. See: *kośa, tattva.*

prāṇāyāma: प्राणायाम "Breath control." See: *rāja yoga.*

prapatti: प्रपत्ति "Throwing oneself down." *Bhakti,* total, unconditional submission to God, often coupled with the attitude of personal helplessness, self-effacement and resignation. See: *bhakti, pāda.*

prārabdha karma: प्रारब्धकर्म "Action that has been unleashed or aroused." See: *karma.*

prasāda: प्रसाद "Clarity, brightness; grace." Food offered to the Deity or the *guru,* or the blessed remnants of such food.

prāyaśchitta: प्रायश्चित्त "Predominant thought or aim." Penance. Acts of atonement, burning karma before it manifests. See: *pāpa, puṇya.*

prāyopaveśa: प्रायोपवेश "Resolving to die through fasting." Self-willed death by fasting. See: *death, suicide.*

Pretaloka: प्रेतलोक "World of the departed." The realm of the earth-bound souls. This lower region of Bhuvarloka is an astral duplicate of the physical world. See: *Antarloka, loka.*

psychic: "Of the psyche or soul." Sensitive to spiritual processes and energies. Inwardly or intuitively aware of nonphysical realities; able to use powers such as clairvoyance, clairaudience and precognition. Nonphysical, subtle; pertaining to the deeper aspects of man.

pūjā: पूजा "Worship, adoration." An Āgamic rite of worship performed in the home, temple or shrine, to the *mūrti, śrī pādukā,* or other consecrated object, or to a person, such as the *satguru.* Its inner purpose is to purify the atmosphere around the object worshiped, establish a connection with the inner worlds and invoke the presence of God, Gods or one's *guru. Pūjā,* the worship of a *mūrti* through water, lights and flowers in temples and shrines, is the Āgamic counterpart of the Vedic *yajña* rite, in which offerings are conveyed through the sacred *homa* fire. See: *pujārī, yajña.*

pujārī: पुजारी "Worshiper." A general term for Hindu temple priests, as well as anyone performing *pūjā.* See: *pūjā.*

punarjanma: पुनर्जन्म "Reincarnation." From *punaḥ,* "again and again," and *janma,* "taking birth." See: *reincarnation.*

puṇya: पुण्य "Holy; virtuous; auspicious." 1) Good or righteous. 2) Meritorious action. 3) Merit earned through right thought, word and action. *Puṇya* includes all forms of doing good, from the simplest helpful deed to a lifetime of conscientious beneficence. Each act of *puṇya* carries its *karmic* consequence. *Puṇya* is earned through virtuous living, following the multi-faceted laws of *dharma. Puṇya* depends on purity of acts according to various factors including 1) the *karma* and evolution of the individual, 2) degree of sacrifice and unselfish motivation and 3) time and place. (Opposite of *pāpa.*) See: *karma, pāpa.*

Purāṇa: पुराण "Ancient lore." Hindu folk narratives containing ethical and cosmological teachings relative to Gods, man and the world. There are 18 major *Purāṇas* which are designated as either Śaivite, Vaishṇavite or Śākta. See: *smriti.*

purusha dharma: पुरुषधर्म "A man's code of duty and conduct." See: *dharma.*

rajas: रजस् "Passion; activity." See: *guṇa.*

rāja yoga: राजयोग "King of *yogas,*" also known as *ashṭāṅga yoga,* "eight-limbed *yoga.*" The classical *yoga* system of eight progressive stages to Illumination as described in various *yoga Upanishads,* the *Tirumantiram* and, most notably, the *Yoga Sūtras* of Patanjali. The eight limbs are: 1) —*yama:* "Restraint." 2) —*niyama:* "Observance." 3) —*āsana:* "Seat or posture." 4) —*prāṇāyāma:* "Breath control." 5) —*pratyāhāra:* "Withdrawal." 6) —*dhāraṇā:* "Concentration." 7) —*dhyāna:* "Meditation." 8) —*samādhi:* "Enstasy." See: *āsana, samādhi, yoga.*

Rāma: राम Venerated hero of the *Rāmāyaṇa* epic, and one of the two most popular incarnations of Vishṇu, along with Kṛishṇa. His worship is almost universal among Vaishṇavas, and extensive among Smārtas and other liberal Hindus. He was a great worshiper of Śiva, and a Śiva temple, called Rameshvaram, was built in his name at the southern tip of India.

Rāmāyaṇa: रामायण "Life of Rāma." One of India's two grand epics (*Itihāsa*) along with the *Mahābhārata.* It is Valmiki's tragic love story of Rāma and Sītā, whose exemplary lives have helped set high standards of dignity and nobility as an integral part of Hindu *dharma.* Astronomical data in the story puts Rāma's reign at about 2015 BCE. See: *Rāma.*

reincarnation: "Re-entering the flesh." *Punarjanma;* metempsychosis. The process wherein souls take on a new physical body through the birth process. It is a repetitive cycle, known as *punarjanma,* which originates in the subtle plane (Antarloka), the realm in which souls live between births and return to after death. Here they are assisted in readjusting to the "in-between" world and eventually prepared for yet another birth. The quality and nature of the birth depends on the merit or demerit of their past actions (*karma*) and on the needs of their unique pattern of development and experience (*dharma*). The cycle of reincarnation ends when *karma* has been resolved and the Self God (Paraśiva) has been realized. This condition of release is called *moksha.* Then the soul continues to evolve and mature, but without the need to return to physical existence. See: *karma, moksha, saṁsāra, soul.*

ṛishi: ऋषि "Seer." A term for an enlightened being, emphasizing psychic perception and visionary wisdom. In the Vedic age, *ṛishis* lived in remote retreats, either alone or with disciples. These *ṛishis* were great souls who were the inspired conveyers of the *Vedas*. See: *śruti*.

 sādhana: साधन "Effective means of attainment." Religious or spiritual disciplines, such as *pūjā, yoga*, meditation, *japa*, fasting and austerity. The effect of *sādhana* is the building of willpower, faith and confidence in oneself and in God, Gods and *guru*. *Sādhana* harnesses and transmutes the instinctive-intellectual nature, allowing progressive spiritual unfoldment into the superconscious realizations and innate abilities of the soul. See: *pāda, rāja yoga.*

sādhu: साधु "Virtuous one; straight, unerring." A holy man dedicated to the search for God. A *sādhu* may or may not be a *yogī* or a *sannyāsin*, or be connected in any way with a *guru* or legitimate lineage. *Sādhus* usually have no fixed abode and travel unattached from place to place, often living on alms. See: *sannyāsin.*

sādhvī: साध्वी Feminine of *sādhu*. See: *sādhu.*

sahasrāra chakra: सहस्रारचक्र The cranial psychic force center. "Thousand-spoked wheel." See: *chakra.*

Śakti: शक्ति "Power, energy." The active power or manifest energy of God that pervades all of existence. Its most refined aspect is Parāśakti, or Satchidānanda, the pure consciousness and primal substratum of all form. In popular, village Hinduism, the unity of Śiva and Śakti is replaced with the concept of Śiva and Śakti as separate entities. Śakti is represented as female, and Śiva as male.

Within the Śākta religion, the worship of the Goddess is paramount, in Her many fierce and benign forms. Śakti is the Divine Mother of manifest creation. The forms of the Goddess include Kālī, Durgā, Umā, Pārvatī and Annapūrṇā.

In the *yoga* mysticism of all traditions, divine energy, *śakti*, is experienced within the human body in three aspects: 1) the feminine force, *iḍā śakti*, 2) the masculine force, *piṅgalā śakti*, and 3) the pure androgynous force, *kuṇḍalinī śakti*, that flows through the *sushumṇā nāḍī*.

Śakti is most easily experienced by devotees as the sublime, bliss-inspiring energy that emanates from a holy person or sanctified Hindu temple. See: *Ardhanārīśvara, nāḍī, Parāśakti, Śāktism.*

Śāktism (Śākta): शाक्त "Doctrine of power." The religion followed by those who worship the Supreme as the Divine Mother—Śakti or Devī—in Her many forms, both gentle and fierce. Śāktism is one of the four primary sects of Hinduism. Śāktism's first historical signs are thousands of female statuettes dated ca 5500 BCE recovered at the Mehrgarh village in India. Four major expressions of

Śāktism are evident today: folk-shamanism, *yoga*, devotionalism and universalism. There are many varieties of folk Śāktism gravitating around various forms of the Goddess, such as Kālī, Durgā and a number of forms of Amman. See: *Ishṭa Devatā, Śakti, tantrism.*

Śaivism (Śaiva): The religion followed by those who worship Śiva as Supreme God. The oldest of the four sects of Hinduism. There are many schools of Saivism, all firmly based on the Vedas and Saiva Agamas. See: *God, Śakti, Śiva, Parameśvara, Parāśakti, Paraśiva.*

samādhi: समाधि "Enstasy," "Sameness; contemplation; union, wholeness; completion, accomplishment." *Samādhi* is the state of true *yoga*, in which the meditator and the object of meditation are one. *Samādhi* is of two levels. The first is *savikalpa samādhi*, identification or oneness with the essence of an object. Its highest form is the realization of the primal substratum or pure consciousness, Satchidānanda. The second is *nirvikalpa samādhi* ("enstasy without form" or "seed"), identification with the Self, in which all modes of consciousness are transcended and Absolute Reality, Paraśiva, beyond time, form and space, is experienced. This brings in the aftermath a complete transfomation of consciousness. See: *kuṇḍalinī, Paraśiva, rāja yoga, Satchidānanda, Self Realization.*

samsāra: संसार "Flow." The phenomenal world. Transmigratory existence, fraught with impermanence and change, joy and suffering. The cycle of birth, death and rebirth; the total pattern of successive earthly lives experienced by a soul. See: *karma, reincarnation.*

samskāra: संस्कार "Impression, activator; sanctification, preparation." A deep impression made on the subconscious mind by intense circumstances (on this or previous lives), which then influence all of life, one's nature, responses, states of mind, in a positive or negative fashion. Hindu sacraments or rites are done to create beneficial *samskāras*, marking a significant transition of life. These make deep and positive impressions on the mind of the recipient, inform the family and community of changes in the lives of its members and secure inner-world blessings. Some of the most important are: —*nāmakaraṇa*, name-giving; —*vivāha*, marriage; —*antyeshṭi*, funeral rites. See: *sacrament.*

Sanātana Dharma: सनातनधर्म "Eternal religion" or "Everlasting path." It is a traditional designation for the Hindu religion. See: *Hinduism.*

Sanchita karma: All the karma set in motion by an individual yet to be resolved. See: *Karma.*

San Mārga: सन्मार्ग "True path." The straight, spiritual path leading to the ultimate goal, Self Realization, without detouring into unnecessary psychic exploration or pointless development of *siddhis*. A *San Mārgī* is a person

"on the path," as opposed to a *samsārī*, one engrossed in worldliness. *San Mārga* also names the *jñāna pāda*. See: *sādhana, samsāra.*

sannyāsa: संन्यास "Renunciation." "Throwing down or abandoning." *Sannyāsa* is the repudiation of the *dharma* of the householder, including its obligations and duties, and the acceptance of the even more demanding *dharma* of the renunciate. See: *sannyāsa dharma, sannyāsa dīkshā.*

sannyāsa āśrama: संन्यास आश्रम "Renunciate stage." The period of life after age 72. See: *āśrama.*

sannyāsa dharma: संन्यासधर्म "Renunciate virtue." The life, way and traditions of those who have irrevocably renounced prerogatives and obligations of the householder, including personal property, wealth, ambitions, social position and family ties, in favor of the full-time monastic quest for divine awakening, Self Realization and spiritual upliftment of humanity. Traditionally, this *dharma* is available to those under age 25 who meet strict qualifications. Alternately, the householder may embrace *sannyāsa dharma* after age 72 through the customary initiatory rites given by a *sannyāsin* and then diligently pursuing his spiritual *sādhana* in a state of genuine renunciation and not in the midst of his family. These two forms of *sannyāsa* are not to be confused with simply entering the *sannyāsa āśrama*, the last stage of life. See: *sannyāsa, sannyāsa dīkshā, sannyāsin.*

sannyāsa dīkshā: संन्यासदीक्षा "Renunciate initiation." This *dīkshā* is a formal rite, or less often an informal blessing, entering the devotee into renunciate monasticism, binding him for life to certain vows which include chastity, poverty and obedience, and directing him on the path to Self Realization. See: *sannyāsa dharma.*

sannyāsin: संन्यासिन् "Renouncer." One who has taken *sannyāsa dīkshā*. A Hindu monk, *swāmī*, and one of a world brotherhood (or holy order) of *sannyāsins*. Some are wanderers and others live in monasteries. The *sannyāsin* is the guardian of his religion, immersed in it constantly, freed from worldliness, freed from distraction, able to offer his work and his worship in unbroken continuity and one-pointed effectiveness. He undertakes certain disciplines including the purification of body, mind and emotion. He restrains and controls the mind through his *sādhana, tapas* and meditative regimen. He unfolds from within himself a profound love of God and the Gods. His practice of *upāsanā*, worship, is predominantly internal, seeking God within. See: *sannyāsa, sannyāsa dharma, sannyāsa dīkshā, swāmī.*

Sanskrit (Samskṛita): संस्कृत "Well-made," "refined," "perfected." The classical sacerdotal language of ancient India, considered a pure vehicle for communication with the celestial worlds. It is the primary language in which Hindu scriptures are written, including the *Vedas* and *Āgamas.*

Sarasvatī: सरस्वती "The flowing one." Śakti, the Universal Mother, as Goddess of the arts and learning, mythological consort of the God Brahmā. Sarasvatī, the river Goddess, is usually depicted wearing a white *sārī* and holding a *vīna,* sitting upon a swan or lotus flower. Prayers are offered to her for refinements of art, culture and learning. See: *Śakti.*

Satchidānanda: सच्चिदानन्द "Existence-consciousness-bliss." A synonym for *Parāśakti.* Also called pure consciousness, pure form, substratum of existence, and more. One of the goals of the meditator is to experience the natural state of the mind, Satchidānanda, immersed in *savikalpa samādhi.* See: *Parāśakti.*

satguru (sadguru): सद्गुरु "True weighty one." A spiritual preceptor of the highest attainment and authority—one who has realized the ultimate Truth, Paraśiva, through *nirvikalpa samādhi*—a free being able to lead others securely along the spiritual path. He is always a *sannyāsin,* an unmarried renunciate. All Hindu denominations teach that the grace and guidance of a living *satguru* is a necessity for Self Realization. He is recognized and revered as the embodiment of God, Sadāśiva, the source of grace and liberation. See: *guru, diksha.*

sattva guṇa: सत्त्वगुण "Perfection of Being." The quality of goodness or purity. See: *guṇa.*

savikalpa samādhi: सविकल्पसमाधि "Enstasy with form (or seed)." See: *rāja yoga, samādhi.*

Second World: The astral or subtle plane. See: *Antarloka, loka.*

Self (Self God): God Śiva's perfection of Absolute Reality, Paraśiva—That which abides at the core of every soul. See: *Paraśiva.*

Self Realization: Direct knowing of the Self God, Paraśiva. Self Realization is known in Sanskrit as *nirvikalpa samādhi,* the ultimate spiritual attainment. See: *God Realization, kuṇḍalinī, moksha, Paraśiva, rāja yoga, samādhi.*

sevā: सेवा "Service," *karma yoga,* an integral part of the spiritual path, doing selfless, useful work for others, such as volunteer work at a temple, without preference or thought of personal gain. *Sevā,* or Sivathondu in Tamil, is the central practice of the *charyā pāda.* See: *yoga.*

siddha: सिद्ध A "perfected one" or accomplished *yogī,* a person of great spiritual attainment or powers. See: *guru, siddhi.*

siddhānta: सिद्धान्त "Final attainments;" "final conclusions." Siddhānta refers to ultimate understanding arrived at in any given field of knowledge.

siddhi: सिद्धि "Power, accomplishment; perfection." Extraordinary powers of the soul, developed through consistent meditation and deliberate *tapas,* or awakened naturally through spiritual maturity and *yogic sādhana.* The supreme *siddhi* is realization of the Self, Paraśiva. See: *prapatti.*

śishya: शिष्य "A pupil or disciple," especially one who has proven himself and been accepted by a *guru.*

Śiva: शिव The "Auspicious," "Gracious," or "Kindly one." Supreme Being of the Śaivite religion. God Śiva is All and in all, simultaneously the creator and the creation, both immanent and transcendent. As personal Deity, He is Creator, Preserver and Destroyer. He is a one Being, perhaps best understood in three perfections: Parameśvara (Primal Soul), Parāśakti (Pure Consciousness) and Paraśiva (Absolute Reality). See: *Parameśvara, Parāśakti, Paraśiva, prapatti, Śaivism, Satchidānanda.*

Śivaliṅga: शिवलिङ्ग "Mark," "Token" or "Sign of Śiva." The most prevalent emblem of Śiva, found in virtually all Śiva temples. A rounded, elliptical, aniconic image, usually set on a circular base, or *pīṭha,* the Śivaliṅga is the simplest and most ancient symbol of Śiva, especially of Paraśiva, God beyond all forms and qualities. The *pīṭha* represents Parāśakti, the manifesting power of God. Liṅgas are usually of stone (carved or naturally existing, *svayambhū,* such as shaped by a swift-flowing river), but may also be of metal, precious gems, crystal, wood, earth or transitory materials such as ice. See: *mūrti, Śaivism.*

Śivaloka: शिवलोक "Realm of Śiva." See: *heaven, loka.*

Skanda: स्कन्द "Quicksilver;" "leaping one." One of Lord Kārttikeya's oldest names. His form as scarlet-hued warrior God. See: *Kārttikeya.*

Smārta: स्मार्त "Of or related to *smṛiti,*" the secondary Hindu scriptures. See: *Smārtism, smṛiti.*

Smārtism: स्मार्त Sect based on the secondary scriptures (*smṛiti*). The most liberal of the four major Hindu denominations, an ancient Vedic *brāhminical* tradition (ca 700 BCE) which from the 9th century onward was guided and deeply influenced by the Advaita Vedānta teachings of Adi Shankara. Its adherents rely mainly on the classical *smṛiti* literature, especially the *Itihāsas* (*Rāmāyaṇa* and *Mahābhārata,* the latter of which includes the *Bhagavad Gītā*), *Purāṇas* and *Dharma Śāstras.* These are regarded as complementary to and a means to understanding the *Vedas.* Smārtas adhere to Shankara's view that all Gods are but various representations of Saguṇa Brahman. Thus, Smārtas are avowedly eclectic, worshiping all the Gods and discouraging sectarianism. The Smārta system of worship reinforces this outlook by including the major Deity of each primary Hindu sect of ancient days: Gaṇeśa, Sūrya, Vishṇu, Śiva and Śakti, with the addition of a sixth Deity, Kumāra. One among them is generally chosen as the devotee's preferred Deity, Ishṭa Devatā. For spiritual authority, Smārtas look to the regional monasteries established across India by Shankara, and to their pontiffs. These are the headquarters of ten orders of renunciate monks who spread the Advaita Vedānta teachings far and wide. See: *Daśanāmī.*

smṛiti: स्मृति That which is "remembered;" the tradition. Hinduism's nonrevealed, secondary but deeply revered scriptures, derived from man's insight and experience. *Smṛiti* speaks of secular matters as well as spiritual lore, ranging from day-to-day rules and regulations to enlightened teachings. See: *Mahābhārata, Rāmāyaṇa.*

soul: The real being of man, as distinguished from body, mind and emotions. The soul—known as *ātman* or *purusha*—is the sum of its two aspects, the form or body of the soul and the essence of the soul. —**essence or nucleus of the soul:** Man's innermost and unchanging being—Pure Consciousness (*Parāśakti* or *Satchidānanda*) and Absolute Reality (*Paraśiva*). This essence was never created, does not change or evolve and is eternally identical with God Śiva's perfections of Parāśakti and Paraśiva. —**soul body:** *ānandamaya kośa* ("sheath of bliss"), also referred to as the "causal body" (*kāraṇa śarīra*), names the soul's manifest nature as an individual being—an effulgent, human-like form composed of light. It is the emanational creation of God, destined to one day merge back into Him. During its evolution, the soul functions through four types of outer sheaths that envelop the soul form—mental, instinctive-intellectual, vital and physical. See: *ātman, Parāśakti, Paraśiva, Satchidānanda.*

śruti: श्रुति That which is "heard." Hinduism's revealed scriptures, of supreme theological authority and spiritual value. They are timeless teachings transmitted to *ṛishis,* or seers, directly by God thousands of years ago. *Śruti* consists of the *Vedas* and the *Āgamas,* preserved through oral tradition and eventually written down in Sanskrit. Among the many sacred books of the Hindus, these two bodies of knowledge are held in the highest esteem. Most *mantras* are drawn from *śruti,* used for rites of worship, both public and domestic, as well as personal prayer and *japa.* Traditionally *śruti* is not read, but chanted according to extremely precise rules of grammar, pitch, intonation and rhythm. In the sacred language of *śruti,* word and meaning are so closely aligned that hearing these holy scriptures properly chanted is magical in its effect upon the soul of the listener. See: *Āgamas, smṛiti, Vedas.*

strī dharma: स्त्रीधर्म "Womanly conduct." See: *dharma.*

Subramuniyaswami: சுப்பிரமுனியசுவாமி Satguru Sivaya Subramuniyaswami, founder of

HINDUISM TODAY, 162nd *satguru* (1927–2001) of the Nandinātha Sampradāya's Kailāsa Paramparā. He was ordained Sivaya Subramuniyaswami by Sage Yogaswami on the full-moon day of May 12, 1949, in Jaffna, Sri Lanka. Before his meeting with Yogaswami, he had attained *nirvikalpa samādhi* in the caves of Jalani. Satguru Sivaya Subramuniyaswami is recognized worldwide as one of foremost Hindu ministers of our times, contributing to the revival of Hinduism in immeasurable abundance. He was simultaneously a staunch defender of traditions, as the tried and proven ways of the past, and a fearless innovator, setting new patterns of life for contemporary humanity. He is succeeded by Satguru Bodhinatha Veylanswami, the 163RD *satguru* of the Kailāsa Paramparā. See: *Bodhinatha Veylanswami, parampara, Yogaswami.*

Supreme God: Highest God, the source or creator of all other Gods, beings and all manifestation. See: *Brahman, Śakti, Śiva, Vishṇu.*

svadharma: स्वधर्म "One's own way." See: *dharma.*

svādhishṭhāna: स्वाधिष्ठान "One's own base." See: *chakra.*

swāmī: स्वामी "Lord; owner; self-possessed." He who knows or is master of himself. A respectful title for a Hindu monk, usually a *sannyāsin,* an initiated, orange-robed renunciate, dedicated wholly to religious life. As a sign of respect, the term *swāmī* is sometimes applied more broadly to include non-monastics dedicated to spiritual work. See: *sannyāsa dharma, sannyāsin.*

swāminī: स्वामिनी The feminine form of *swāmī.* See: *sadhvi, sannyāsa, swāmī.*

swastika: स्वस्तिक "Sign of auspiciousness." From *su,* "wellness," "auspiciousness" and *astu,* "be it so." The ancient Hindu symbol of auspiciousness and good fortune, representing the sun and often associated with Gaṇeśa. It has been a prominent symbol in many cultures.

 tamas (tamasic): तमस् "Force of inertia." See: *guṇa.*

tantra: तन्त्र "Loom, methodology." 1) Most generally, a synonym for *śāstra,* "scripture." 2) A specific method, technique or spiritual practice within the Śaiva and Śākta traditions.

tapas: तपस् "Heat, fire; ardor." Purificatory spiritual disciplines, severe austerity, penance and sacrifice. The endurance of performing extreme religious austerities, with the aim of spiritual transformation and unfoldment. By comparison, *sādhana* is austerity of a simple, sustained kind, while *tapas* is austerity of a severe, psyche-transforming nature. See: *kuṇḍalinī, sādhana.*

tattva: तत्त्व "That-ness" or "essential nature." *Tattvas* are the primary principles, elements, states or categories of existence, the building blocks of the universe. God constantly creates, sustains the form of and absorbs back into Himself His creations. Ṛishis describe this emanational process as the unfoldment of *tattvas,* stages or evolutes of manifestation, descending from subtle to gross. At *mahāpralaya,* cosmic dissolution, they enfold into their respective sources, with only the first two *tattvas* surviving the great dissolution. Beyond *tattvas* lies Paraśiva—the utterly transcendent, Absolute Reality, called *attava.*

The Sāṅkhya system discusses 25 *tattvas.* Śaivism recognizes these same 25 plus 11 beyond them, making 36 *tattvas* in all. These are divided into three groups:

—**The Śuddha tattvas: Actinic or spiritual energy.** This is the superconscious realm, also known as *śuddha* (pure) *māyā* or *mahāmāyā. Bindu,* transcendent light, is the "material" cause of this pure sphere. This is the Śivaloka, the region of the 330 million Gods, the myriad *ṛishis* and other beings who have attained freedom from the triple bondage.

—**The Śuddhāśuddha tattvas: Actinodic, or spiritual-magnetic, energy.** The seven *tattvas* from *māyā* to *purusha* make up the *śuddhāśuddha* (pure-impure) realm.

—**the Aśuddha tattvas: Odic, or magnetic, energy.** These 24 categories make up the "world" of *aśuddha* (impure) *māyā.* This is the realm of the astral and physical planes, in which souls function through the grosser bodies, depending on their level of embodiment.

See: *guṇa, soul, Śiva (also, chart on p. 43.)*

Third World: Śivaloka, "realm of Śiva". The spiritual realm or causal plane wherein Mahādevas and highly evolved souls live in their own self-effulgent forms. See: *loka, heaven.*

tilaka: तिलक Marks made on the forehead or the brow with clay, ashes or sandalwood paste as an indication of sectarian affiliation. Vaishṇavas wear a vertical v-shaped *tilaka* made from clay. The Śaivite *tilaka,* called *tripuṇḍra,* consists of three horizontal strips of holy ash with a dot near the middle, or between the eyebrows. Wearing the *tilaka* is an expression of religious affiliation and pride in one's beliefs. See: *bindu.*

Tirukural: திருக்குறள் "Holy couplets." A treasury of Hindu ethical insight and a literary masterpiece of the Tamil language, written by Śaiva Saint Tiruvalluvar (ca 200 bce). One of the world's earliest ethical texts, the non-sectarian *Tirukural* could well be considered a bible on virtue for the human race. It is sworn on in South Indian courts of law. See: *Tiruvalluvar.*

Tirumantiram: திருமந்திரம் "Holy incantation." The Nandinātha Sampradāya's oldest Tamil scripture; written ca 200 bce by Rishi Tirumular. It is the earliest of the *Tirumurai* texts, and a vast storehouse of esoteric *yogic* and *tantric* knowledge. It contains the mystical essence of *rāja yoga* and *siddha yoga.*

tiruvadi: திருவடி "Holy sandals." See: *pāḍukā.*

transcendent: Surpassing the limits of experience or manifest form. In Śaiva Siddhānta, a quality of God Śiva as Absolute Reality, Paraśiva, the Self. Distinguished from *immanent.* See: *atattva, immanent, Paraśiva*

 Upanishad: उपनिषद् "Sitting near devotedly." The fourth and final portion of the *Vedas,* expounding the secret, philosophical meaning of the Vedic hymns. The *Upanishads* are a collection of profound texts which are the source of *Vedānta* and have dominated Indian thought for thousands of years. They are philosophical chronicles of *rishis* expounding the nature of God, soul and cosmos, exquisite renderings of the deepest Hindu thought. It is generally thought that the earliest were written down in Sanskrit between 1500 and 600 bce. In content, these popular and approachable texts revolve around the identity of the soul and God, and the doctrines of reincarnation, of *karma* and of liberation through renunciation and meditation. They are widely available in many languages. See: *śruti, Vedānta, Vedas.*

upāsanā: उपासना "Sitting near." Worship or contemplation of God.

 Vaishṇavism (Vaishṇava): वैष्णव One of the four major denominations of Hinduism, representing roughly half of the world's one billion Hindus. It gravitates around the worship of Lord Vishṇu as Personal God, His incarnations and their consorts. The doctrine of *avatāra* (He who descends), especially important to Vaishṇavism, teaches that whenever *adharma* gains ascendency in the world, God takes a human birth to reestablish "the way." There are either 10, 22 or 34 *avatāras* of Vishṇu, according to various scriptures. The most renowned *avatāras* were Rāma and Kṛishṇa. The last to come will be Kalki, the harbinger of a golden age on Earth. Vaishṇavism stresses the personal aspect of God over the impersonal, and *bhakti* (devotion) as the true path to salvation. The goal of Vaishṇavism is the attainment of *mukti,* defined as blissful union with God's body, the loving recognition that the soul is a part of Him, and eternal nearness to Him in Vaikuṇṭha, heaven. Foremost among Vaishṇava scriptures are the *Vaishṇava Āgamas, Bhagavad Gītā* and *Bhāgavata Purāṇa.*

Vaishṇavite: Of or relating to Vishṇu; same as Vaishṇava. A follower of Vishṇu or His incarnations. See: *Vaishṇavism, Vishṇu.*

Veda: वेद "Wisdom." Sagely revelations which comprise Hinduism's most authoritative scripture. The *Vedas* are a body of dozens of holy texts known collectively as the *Veda*, or as the four *Vedas*: *Ṛig, Yajur, Sāma* and *Atharva*. In all they include over 100,000 verses, as well as additional prose. The knowledge imparted by the *Vedas* ranges from earthy devotion to high philosophy. The oldest portions of the *Vedas* are thought by some to date back as far as 6,000 bce, written down in Sanskrit in the last few millennia, making them the world's most ancient scriptures. They, along with the *Āgamas*, are *śruti*, that which is "heard." See: *śruti, Upanishad.*

Vedānta: वेदान्त "Ultimate wisdom" or "final conclusions of the *Vedas.*" Vedānta is the system of thought embodied in the *Upanishads* (ca 1500-600 BCE), which give forth the ultimate conclusions of the *Vedas*. Through history there developed numerous Vedānta schools, ranging from pure dualism to absolute monism. See: *dvaita-advaita, monistic theism, panentheism.*

vibhūti: विभूति "Resplendent, powerful." Holy ash, prepared by burning cow dung along with other precious substances, milk, *ghee*, honey, etc. It symbolizes purity and is one of the main sacraments given at *pūjā* in all Śaivite temples and shrines. Śaivites wear three stripes on the brow as a distinct sectarian mark, as do many Smārtas. See: *tilaka, tripuṇḍra.*

Vināyaka: विनायक "Remover." A name of Lord Gaṇeśa, meaning the remover of obstacles (sometimes preceded by *vighna*, "obstacle"). See: *Gaṇeśa.*

Vishṇu: विष्णु "All-pervasive." Supreme Deity of the Vaishṇavite religion. God as personal Lord and Creator, the All-Loving Divine Personality, who periodically incarnates and lives a fully human life to reestablish *dharma* whenever necessary. See: *Vaishṇavism.*

viśuddha chakra: विशुद्धचक्र "Wheel of purity." The fifth *chakra*. Center of divine love. See: *chakra.*

viśvagrāsa: विश्वग्रास "Total absorption." The final merger of the soul in God at the fulfillment of its evolution. It is the ultimate union of the individual soul body with Parameśvara within the Śivaloka, from whence the soul was first emanated. This occurs at the end of the soul's evolution, after the outer sheaths have been discarded. See: *ātman, samādhi, soul.*

yajña: यज्ञ "Worship; sacrifice." One of the most central Hindu concepts—sacrifice and surrender through acts of worship, inner and outer. Specifically, *yajña* refers to:

1) A form of ritual worship especially prevalent in Vedic times, in which oblations—*ghee*, grains, spices and exotic woods—are offered into a fire according to scriptural injunctions while special *mantras* are chanted. The element fire, *Agni*, is revered as the divine messenger who carries offerings and prayers to the Gods. The ancient *Veda Brāhmaṇas* and the *Śrauta Śāstras* describe various types of *yajña* rites, some so elaborate as to require hundreds of priests, whose powerful chanting resounds for miles.

While *pūjā* (worship in temples with water, lights and flowers) has largely replaced the *yajña*, this ancient rite still continues, and its specialized priestly training is carried on in schools in India. *Yajñas* on a grand scale are performed for special occasions, beseeching the Gods for rain during drought, or for peace during bloody civil war. Even in temples, *yajña* has its Āgamic equivalent in the *agnikāraka*, the *homa* or *havana* ceremony.

2) Personal acts of worship or sacrifice. The *Upanishads* suggest that one can make "inner *yajñas*" by offering up bits of the little self into the fires of *sādhana* and *tapas* until the greater Self shines forth. The prescribed daily *yajñas*, *pañcha mahāyajña*, include homage to holy men through study of the *Vedas*, homage to Gods and elementals, homage to ancestors and homage to living beings including humans. See: *dharma, homa, pūjā.*

yama-niyama: यम नियम The first two of the eight limbs of *rāja yoga*, constituting Hinduism's fundamental ethical codes, the *yamas* and *niyamas* are the essential foundation for all spiritual progress. They are codified in numerous scriptures including the *Śāṇḍilya* and *Varuha Upanishads, Haṭha Yoga Pradīpikā* by Gorakshanātha, the *Tirumantiram* of Tirumular and the *Yoga Sūtras* of Patanjali. All the above texts list ten *yamas* and ten *niyamas*, with the exception of Patanjali's classic work, which lists only five of each. The *yamas* are the ethical restraints; the *niyamas* are the religious practices. See: *rāja yoga, Chapter 42.*

yantra: यन्त्र "Vessel; container." A mystic diagram composed of geometric and alphabetic figures—usually etched on small plates of gold, silver or copper. Sometimes rendered in three dimensions in stone or metal. The purpose of a *yantra* is to focus spiritual and mental energies according to a *yantric* pattern, be it for health, wealth, childbearing or the invoking of one God or another. It is usually installed near or under the temple Deity. Psychically seen, the temple *yantra* is a magnificent three-dimensional edifice of light and sound in which the *devas* work. On the astral plane, it is much larger than the temple itself. *Yantras* are also used for meditation and *sādhana*, especially in the Śākta tradition. Installing them beneath Deities is a fairly modern practice. See: *mūrti.*

yoga: योग "Union." From *yuj*, "to yoke, harness, unite." The philosophy, process, disciplines and practices whose purpose is the yoking of individual consciousness with transcendent or divine consciousness. It is essentially a one system but, historically, parts of *rāja yoga* have been developed and emphasized as *yogas* in themselves. Prominent among the many forms of *yoga* are *haṭha yoga* (emphasizing bodily perfection in preparation for meditation), *kriyā yoga* (emphasizing breath control), as well as *karma yoga* (selfless service) and *bhakti yoga* (devotional practices) which could be regarded as an expression of *rāja yoga's* first two limbs (*yama* and *niyama*). See: *bhakti yoga, haṭha yoga, rāja yoga*

yoga pāda: योगपाद The third of the successive stages in spiritual unfoldment in Śaiva Siddhānta. See: *pāda.*

Yogaswami (Yogaswāmī): யோகசுவாமி "Master of *yoga*." 161st *satguru* of the Nandinātha Sampradāya's Kailāsa Paramparā. Sri Lanka's most renowned contemporary spiritual master (1872-1964), a Sivajñāni and Nātha *siddhar* revered by both Hindus and Buddhists. He was trained in and practiced *kuṇḍalinī yoga* under the guidance of Satguru Chellappaswami, from whom he received *guru dīkshā*. Sage Yogaswami was in turn the *satguru* of Sivaya Subramuniyaswami. See: *Bodhinatha Veylanswami, parampara, Sivaya Subramuniyaswami.*

yuga: युग "Eon," "age." One of four ages which chart the duration of the world according to Hindu thought. They are: Satya, Tretā, Dvāpara and Kali. In the first period, *dharma* reigns supreme, but as the ages revolve, virtue diminishes and ignorance and injustice increases. At the end of the Kali Yuga, in which we are now, the cycle begins again with a new Satya Yuga. In the Kali Yuga, the color is black. Righteousness is one-tenth that of the Satya Yuga. True worship and sacrifice cease, and base, or *śudra*, consciousness is prominent. Calamities, disease, fatigue and faults such as anger and fear prevail. People decline and their motives grow weak. See: *tattva.*

Flood of humanity: *Eager pilgrims funnel through one of teight temporary, one-way pontoon bridges across the Ganga leading to the confluence with the Yamuna at the 2001 Kumbha Mela in Allahabad*

JAYANTA SHAW

INDEX

Aadheenam: tradition, 114
Abhishekam: description, 222; photo, 230
Abortion: to save mother's life, 355
Absolute: first perfection of God, xiii, 34; Hindu and Buddhist views, 143
Acceptance: source of strength, 107
Achalanand Ji Maharaj, Swami: photo, 111
Acharya Sangam: organization of *akharas,* 115
Actions. belief determined, 54. See also *Conduct; Karma*
Adi Granth: Sikh holy book, 128
Adi-Perukku: river festival, 238
Adi Shankaracharya: and monastic orders, 113; on image worship, 182; and Kumbha Mela, 243; Smartism, 25
Advaita Vedanta: on liberation, 38
Affirmation(s): controlling fear, 280
Afterlife (between births): determined by this life, 153, 174; disbelief in, 174; discussion, 173-175; ideal utilization, 19. See also *Death; Reincarnation; Soul*
Agamas: and ancillary texts, 74; contents, 71-72; modern significance, 72; scriptural authority, 26, 68, 144. See also *Shruti*
Age: progressing through chakras, 159. See also *Ashramas; Elders*
Aggressiveness: and diet, 127, 343-344
Agnosticism: emerging from, 225
Ahimsa (nonviolence, noninjury): in business, 361; cardinal virtue, 125; and dharmic use of force, 359-361; discussion, 359-363; first, control anger, 27; Goel's meditation, 135; keeping the peace, 36; nonviolence vs. pacifism, 360-361; pan-Hindu emphasis, 26, 45, 55, 144; in speech, 363; teaching to children, 309, 361; and vegetarianism, 127, 308, 343, 362; *yama-niyama,*338
Ajna chakra: attained by renunciates, 160; described, 161; silence, 281
Akharas: monastic orders, 113-114, 244
Akhara Parishad: organization of *akharas,* 115
Alahan, Asha: on becoming a Hindu, 132-133
Alahan, Isani: on becoming a Hindu, 136
Alahan, Vel: on becoming a Hindu, 138
All-pervasive Divinity: brief explanation, 47; and tolerance, 310
Allahabad: See *Prayag*
Altar: link to the Divine, 222. See also *Home shrine; Temple*
America: caste parallels, 131; Hinduism in, 3-4, 198-199. See also *Central America; Mexico*
American Indians: religious ties to Hinduism, 123, 198
Amman: worship Ganesha first, 190-191, 198. See also *Goddess*
Amrita: awakened by *prapatti,* 224; Ganga water as, 243
Anahata chakra: control of, 281; descr., 160

Anandamayi Ma: on the purpose of life, 306
Anava: Saivite perspective, 61
Andal, Saint: great devotional poet, 241
Anger: ayurvedic insights, 274-276; barrier to unfoldment, 277; eight forms, 270-273; forestalling, 277; harmfulness, 166, 269-272, 274; management, 269-277; overcoming tendency, 267, 272-277; penance & recovery, 267, 273, 277; sages' words, 276-277; silencing, 28; *vitala* chakra, 161, 272. See also *Emotions; Lower nature*
Angry All the Time: eight forms of anger, 271
Anjali: significance, 95
Ankusha: See *Goad*
Annaprashana samskara: first feeding, 323
Antagonism: lower nature, 358
Antarloka: See *Second World*
Antibiotics: argument for vegetarianism, 349
Antyesti samskara: funeral ceremony, 325
Apology: response to, 339
Aranyakas: forest treatises, 128; Vedic ritual interpretations, 69
Arati: purifying husband's aura, 114; worshiping with children, 305. See also *Fire*
Archana: described, 225
Architects and Builders of Modern India: excerpts, 332-335
Architecture: See *Vastu*
Ardhanarishvara: depiction of Oneness, 130
Ardra Darshana: Siva festival, 241
Argument(s): avoiding, 339; silencing, 280
Art: spiritual orientation, 14-15
Artha: See *Wealth*
Artificial insemination: cautions, 354-355
Arunachalam, M.: on Ganesha images, 198
Arunagirinatha, Swami: head of Madurai Aadheenam (photo), 110
Arya Samaj: founding, 332
Asana: See *Hatha yoga*
Asceticism: sectarian emphasis, 27. See also *Austerities; Tapas*
Ashrams, ashramas: vs. communes, 105; world as, 37, 316. See also *Ashramas (stages of life); Schools & ashrams*
Ashramas (stages of life): described, 101, 110; *grihastha,* 256; and mitigation of karma, 256; *sannyasa,* 169, 256. See also *Ashram*
Ashwinkumar, Paolomi: renowned dancer (photo), 113
Astral body: identified, 173; life cycle of, 175; separated at death, 169
Astral plane: See *Second World*
Astrology: festival dates, 231; and karma, 249-250; Kumbha Mela, 243; overview, 177-179. See also *Nakshatras; Panchangam*
Atal Akhara: Sri Mahant Rudra Giri Ji, 243. See also *Akharas*
Ati Rudra Maha Yajna: photo, 3-4
Attitudes: and spiritual growth, 6

Aum: benefits, 199; discussion, 194-195
Aura(s): cleansing & lightening, 164-165, 167; colors, 164-165; discussion, 164-167; flooding for protection, 166; inner & outer, 167; purifying husband's, 114; seeing, 165
Aurobindo, Mahayogi Sri: heroic life, 333-334; influence on Goel, 134-135
Auspiciousness: and Lord Ganesha, 195. See also *Good timing; Nakshatras; Panchangam*
Austerities (tapas): advancing soul's evolution, 39; guru's guidance, 263; older souls, 8; *yama-niyama,* 341. See also *Asceticism; Tapas*
Autopsy: best avoided, 173, 353
Auvaiyar, Saint: "Vinayaga Ahaval," 187
Avahan Akhara: initiation (photo), 107. See also *Akharas*
Avani Avittam: brahmins' special day, 229
Avatar: sectarian beliefs, 24, 27, 54
Avdeshananda Giri, Acharya: leader of Juna Akhara (photos), 101, 114
Awakening: vitality technique, 165
Ayodhya: pilgrimage site, 291
Ayurveda: and anger, 274-276; and death, 175; importance of diet, 357; and medical ethics, 350-357
Ayurvedic Institute: Dr. Vasant Lad, 275
Ayyappan: temple in Sabarimala, 289; worship Ganesha first, 190-191, 198. See also *Gods; Supreme Being*

Badrinath: pilgrimage site, 291
Bal Ghangadhar Tilak: on who is a Hindu, xxi, 55
Bali: Kechak dance (photo), x-xi
Banaras: See *Varanasi*
Bangkok: Ganesha at World Trade Center, 199
BAPS Swaminarayan Sanstha: sadhus with guru (photo), 111; Sri Pramukh Swami Maharaj (photo), 106
Batu Caves: Thai Pusam (photo), 227
Bedi, Ramesh: on vows of silence, 279
Beef: penance, 263. See also *Cow; Meat*
Belief(s): conduct more important, 17; creed embodies, 59; just the first step, 311, 314; key to conduct, 54; and serenity, 9-10; and spiritual growth, 6
Bell (ghanta): photo, 5; significance, 96
Bhagavad Gita: *Mahabharata,* 75; and violence, 360. See also *Smriti*
Bhakti: See *Devotion*
Bhakti yoga: cultivating devotion, 206
Bharatiya Vidya Bhavan: *Architects and Builders of Modern India,* 332-335
Bhardwaj, Surinder Mohan: *Hindu Places of Pilgrimage in India,* 289
Bhau Bij: bonding ritual, 104
Bhuloka: See *First World*
Bhuvarloka: cosmology, 42. See also *Second World; Three worlds*

Dai Pagoda, Thailand: photo, 143
Dance: emulating the Gods, 14; photos, x-xi, xvi-xvii
Dandapani, Shyamadeva and Peshanidevi: on becoming Hindus, 137-138
Darkness: stage of, 19
Darshan: adjusting karma, 223; carried by objects, 151; of the Gods, 222-223; from great souls, 149-151; rose analogy, 150; sensitivity to, 150
Dasanami: monastic orders, 113-114, 244
Daughter, married: visiting birth-family home, 105
Dayananda Saraswati, Swami: heroic life, 332
Death & Dying: accepting natural timing, 351; attitudes toward, 175; burial or cremation, 353; clear-mindedness, 169; discussion, 168-171; Do-Not-Resuscitate orders, 351-352; living will, 351-352; memorials following, 171; near-death experiences, 168; new beginning, 7; not at our convenience, 157; part of repeating cycle, 173; preparation, 169-170, 175, 351; reorientation of soul, 173; rites of, 169-171; sudden, 169; thoughts at, 174; treatment of dead body, 169-171,353; Vedic verses, 88. See also *Afterlife; Hospice; Medical ethics; Old age; Reincarnation; Soul; Suicide*
Debts: repayment, 339
Deceit, deception: renouncing, 338-339; *talatala* chakra, 161
De Miranda, Mario: Comics, 369
Denominations (sects): beliefs common to all, 21, 26; compared, 26-27; distinct views of God, 122; each an entire religion, 12; diversity, 14; forehead marks, 129; four principal, 20-21; on God, soul & world, 32-33; on liberation, 38; ways of worship, 35. See also *Saivism; Shaktism; Smartism; Vaishnavism*
Depression: *mahatala* chakra, 161
Desire(s): controlling, 339; and reincarnation, 168, 174; renouncing, 118-119
Destiny: self-created, xviii, 124, 248, 258; ultimate, xviii-xix. See also *Karma; Moksha*
Devagupta, Rama: on Dipavali, 232-233
Devaloka (Maharloka): cosmology, 42; described, 174. See also *Second World*
Devas: bringing to home shrine, 224, 243, 306; communion with, 220; Hindu and Christian views, 145; pan-Hindu belief, 26, 45, 144; presence in temple, 218
Devotee: protected by guru, 151
Devotion (bhakti): cultivated by worship, 202, 341; essence of puja, 182, 198, 206; in Hinduism and Buddhism, 143; many forms, 218, 220; mitigating karma, 254, 257; pan-Hindu emphasis, 27; path of attainment, 26; sacred literature, 76; teaching to children, 315-316; and unfoldment, 224
Dhammapada: Buddhist holy book, 128
Dharma: brief explanation, xiii, 47; in business, 361; vs. free will, 192; Goel's insights, 135; in Hinduism and Buddhism, 143-144; humility, 192; husband's and wife's, 110;

keeping the peace, 360; mitigating karma, 254; motivation for, 124; one of life's four goals, 101; pan-Hindu emphasis, 26, 54-55, 57; path to moksha, 168; and strong families, 106; in thought, speech & action, 263; two paths, 102; and vegetarianism, 343, 345. See also *Ethics*
Dharma Sastras: sacred literature, 73
Dhvaja: symbolism, 99
Diet: and consciousness, 274; during illness, 357; health guidelines, 344; moderate consumption, 340; nutrition, 345-347
Diet for a New America: John Robbins, 348
Diksha: See *Initiation*
Dipavali: See *Diwali*
Discipline: and austerity, 341; path to attainment, 33. See also *Sadhana*
Disease: ayurvedic perspective, 350-351; classifications, 351; mad cow, 349; and meat-eating, 346, 348-349. See also *Antibiotics; Health; Medical ethics*
Divine Life Society: Swami Chidananda Sarasvati (photo), 111; Swami Sivananda on anger, 274-275
Divine sight: and forehead dot, 129
Diwali (Dipavali): festival of lights, 229, 240; preparations, 297; significance, 232-233
Doctrine: means to an end, 14
Dongre, Archana: on family life, 102-111
Do-Not-Resuscitate orders: honoring patient's wishes, 351-352
Door of Brahman: ideal exit at death, 175
Doshas: imbalance, 275
Dot (on forehead): after puja, 224; question & answers, 129; significance, 93
Dreams: creating karma, 256; upholding ahimsa, 338
Durga: Goddess of valor, 230; Vijaya Dasami, 239. See also *Goddess*
Durga Puja: festival, 231
Duty, duties: five central, 295; & freedom, 318

Earth: protection of, 308-309; reverence for, 309. See also *Environment*
Education: prized, 103
Ego: freedom from, 13; harnessing for unfoldment, 270
Eightfold path: Buddhist tenet, 144
Einstein, Albert: on Gandhi, 333
Elders: respected, 108-111, 318. See also *Ashramas; Old age*
Embalming: ill-advised, 173, 353
Emotions: calmed by silence, 278; and performance of puja, 204; quelled by *japa*, 341. See also *Anger; Fear*
End-of-life issues: swamis' views, 351-353
Energy: drawing upwards, 175, 195, 224; God's immanent presence, 32; *ida-pingala-sushumna*, 162-163; loss of, 279; vitality techniques, 165-166. See also *Aura; Kundalini; Prana; Three currents; Transmutation*
Enlightenment: See *Self Realization*

Environment: arguments for vegetarianism, 347-349. See also *Earth*
Eternal Path: See *Hinduism*
Ethics: argument for vegetarianism, 349; in business, 361; expressions, xx. See also *Conduct; Dharma; Medical ethics*
Europe: caste parallels in, 131. See also *West*
Evangelism: responding to, 120. See also *Christianity; Proselytization*
Evil: not intrinsic, 26, 63; temporary condition, 56. See also *Evolution of soul; Hell; Lower nature*
Evolution of soul: accelerating karma, 255-256; after liberation, 39; cultivating our innate Godliness, 123; darshan from great souls, 149; harnessing lower nature, 270; higher nature, lower nature, 359; *sadhana* and *tapas*, 39; stages, 27; teaching to children, 306-308; three powers, 317; toward perfection (Divinity), xviii-xix, 6, 30; unhurried, 9-10; Vivenananda quote, 261. See also *Chakras; Old souls; Spiritual progress; Young souls*
Experience(s): function of, 33; key to progress, xv; our classroom, 316

Fa-hsien: early traveler, 345
Faith: *yama-niyama*, 340
Faith healing: enlisting divine aid, 357. See also *Medicine*
Faith of Our Patients: Texas Medical Association, 350
Family, Family life: age-based hierarchy, 108; balancing the forces, 109, 111-113, 115; bringing in high-souled children, 109, 112, 354; closeness, 312; and community, 108; facing karma together, 107; harmony, 106-107, 111-112; hospitality, 104; ideals, 108; joint or extended, 298-300; *kulaguru*, 110; pan-Hindu values, 106; personal sacrifices, 103; preserving, 102-115; of renunciate son, 105; special festivals, 229; woman's key role, 17; world as one, 310; worshiping together, 305-306. See also *Children; Home; Parents; Two paths*
Fasting: karmic mitigation, 255; as penance, 266, 276
Fate: distinguished from karma, 9-10, 124. See also *Karma*
Father: leading daily worship, 106, 109; respected, 108-109. See also *Husband; Parents*
Fear: *atala* chakra, 161; beliefs and, 7, 9, 175; of death, 175, and diet, 343-344; silencing, 280; source of hurtfulness, 338. See also *Emotions; Lower nature*
Feet: sacred sandals, 97; touching in respect, 109, 318; worship of *satguru's*, 151-153
Fertility treatments: danger for mother, 355
Festivals: setting dates, 231; communion with the Gods, 227; home observances, 234-241; for Lord Ganesha, 196-197; nine most popular, 227-233
Festivals of Tamil Nadu: excerpt, 195-196

INDEX 385

on Hindu beliefs, xxii, 55
Prana: cultural guidelines, 319. See also *Energy*
Pranava: significance, 94
Pranayama: first, control anger, 277; for hatha yoga, 283; harnessing prana, 281
Prapatti: and *amrita*, 224; awakening, 151-152; when karma gets rough, 191
Prasada: See *Sacraments*
Prayag (Allahabad): holy men with *dandas* (photo), 16; Kumbha Mela site, 242, 290
Prayashchitta: See *Penance*
Prayer(s): learning use of, 225; to Lord Ganesha, 188-191, 200; and specific temples, 12. See also *Archana*
Prayopavesha: and medical ethics, 352-353
Prejudice: vs. tolerance & ahimsa, 313
Pretaloka: children from, 112; cosmology, 42; described, 174; earthbound souls, 173. See also *Second World; Three worlds*
Priests: focus of conversion strategy, 17; role of, 11, 15
Priest training school: at Tirupati (photos), 72
Promises: honoring, 338-339
Primal Soul: third perfection of God, xiii, 34
Promiscuity: avoiding, 339
Propriety: cultural guidelines, 320
Proselytization: Goel's experience, 134; swamis' views, 139. See also *Evangelism*
Prostration: before parents, 318; men's and women's forms, 204, 221; photo, 267; Sivaya Subramuniyaswami on, 151
Protein: overdose concerns, 346
Protestantism: concepts of sin, 264
Psychic sight: developing, 165; seeing auras, 164. See also *Divine sight*
Puja: attending, 222-225; caution regarding anger, 204; daily home, 109, 182-184, 202-217; discussion, 198-199, 202-205; hosting God, 297; instructions, 207-217; items needed, 184-185, 204; *kalasha*, 97; lightening aura, 167; photo, 55; restrictions, 204; sacred worship, 35. See also *Home shrine; Worship*
Punsavana samskara: ceremony beseeching birth of a son, 325
Punishment: positive alternatives, 315
Puranas: de-emphasis, 130; encyclopedic scope, 75; and Kumbha Mela, 243; sacred literature, 73. See also *Smriti*
Pure Consciousness: second perfection of God, xiii, 34
Puri: pilgrimage site, 291
Purity: cultural guidelines, 321; pan-Hindu emphasis, 55; purifying husband's aura, 114; sexual, 339; transmutation as key, 103; and vegetarianism, 127; for worship, 185; *yama-niyama*, 340. See also *Impurity*
Purusha dharma: husband's duties, 110
Purusharthas: See *Four goals*

Questions & answers: Bible of Hinduism, 128; caste & untouchability, 131; cow worship, 125; forehead dot, 129; God and Gods,

122; Gods & Goddesses, 130; idol worship, 126; karma, 124; reincarnation, 123; tips on responding, 120-121; vegetarianism, 127

Radha: worship Ganesha first, 190-191, 198. See also *Goddess*
Radhakrishnan, Dr. S.: heroic life, 334; on conversion into Hinduism, 17; on jiva and liberation, 40; on nature of life & world, 56; on who is a Hindu, xxi, 56; *The Hindu View of Life*, 54
Rao, Subhas: on astrology of Kumbha Mela, 243
Rajam, S.: on festival observances, 235-241
Rakhi: described, 229
Raksha Bandhan: bonding ritual, 104; brother-sister festival, 229
Rama: festivals, 228, 232, 236; heroic king, 75; worship Ganesha first, 190-191, 198. See also *Gods; Supreme Being*
Ramakrishna Mission: accepting new Hindus, 139; monastic order, 114, 117; Swami Gautamananda (photo), 111; Srimat Swami Ranganathanandaji, 139; and Swami Vivekananda, 260
Ramakrishna Paramahamsa, Sri: heroic life, 332; on personal experience of God, 312; and Swami Vivekananda, 260
Ramalila: performed during festivals, 228
Raman, Dr. B.V.: on the *nakshatras,* 177
Ramana Maharshi: heroic life, 334; on liberation, 38
Ramanuja: on image worship, 182
Ramayana: in dance (photo), 75; life of Rama, 75; Vaishnava scripture, 27. See also *Smriti*
Ram Chandra, Shri: on the nature of spiritual light, 233
Rameshvaram Temple: Ganesha shrine, 197; pilgrimage site, 290; Rama's penance, 266
Ram Navami: astrology, 231; Rama festival, 228-229, 236
Ranganathananda, Swami: on conversion to Hinduism, 139; on medical ethics, 350
Ras Leela: commemorating life of Krishna, 230
Ray: from Third World, 218
Realization: Vedic verses, 89
Reason: limitations of, 5; quieting, 281
Reflections on Silence: Prema Pandurang, 279
Reincarnation: in brief, xii, 46; vs. Christian beliefs, 145; depiction, 123; driven by desires, 168, 174; driven by karma, 175, 258-261; enhancing relationships, 10-11; in Hinduism and Buddhism, 144; impetus to good conduct, 7-8; pan-Hindu belief, 26, 45, 57; as penance, 263; perpetuating family group, 105, 169; question & answers, 123; Saivite beliefs, 62; soul chooses family & body, 123, 175; and soul's evolution, 173, 175; teaching to children, 311; whom will parents bring in?, 109, 112, 354; widely held belief, 123. See also *Afterlife; Births; Death; Karma; Samsara; Soul*
Relationships: and reincarnation, 11
Religion(s): comparisons, 144-145; Eastern & Western, 11; inherent in soul, 6; nature of, 5;

one Truth, many paths, 312-313; respect for all, 5-6, 15, 45, 144; teaching children about, 312-313; theocentric and prophet-centric, 15. See also *Conversion*
Remorse: response to, 339; *yama-niyama*, 340
Renunciation: a calling, not a choice, 106; vs. householder path, 107. See also *Monasticism; Sannyasa*
Repentance: prerequisite to penance, 265-266
Repression(s): bringing into view, 150
Resentment: *vitala* chakra, 161
Respect: cultural expressions, 318
Restraints: ten timeless guidelines, 338-340
Retaliation: foregoing, 251-253
Retreat: periods of, 185
Ridicule: conversion strategy, 17
Rig Veda: extolling the cow, 125
Rites: of death, 169-171
Rites of passage (samskaras, sacraments): descriptions, 323-325; effect on aura, 167; entry to Hinduism, 198; principal, 225; purpose, 323
Rituals: in family life, 104, 108-109, 114
Ritu kala samskara: girl's coming-of-age ceremony, 325
River(s): See *Ganga*
Robbins, John: *Diet for a New America,* 348
Rock Fort Temple: Ganesha temple, 196
Rudra Giri Ji, Mahant: on Kumbha Mela, 243
Rudraksha: significance, 98; photo, 264
Rukmini Devi Arundale: heroic life, 335

Sabarimala: Ayyappan temple, 289
Sacraments (from puja): how to receive, 223-234; prasada, 199, 205. See also *Rites of passage*
Sacrifice: and austerity, 341; for family, 103; valued, 104; Vedic verses, 86
Sadhana (spiritual disciplines): accelerating karma, 255; advancing soul's evolution, 39; building faith, 340; and the chakras, 159; death as, 173; family's, 109-110; first, control anger, 277; and life pattern, 256; means to an end, 14; mental maintenance, 167; older souls, 8; sectarian emphasis, 27; seven for silence, 280-281; teaching to children, 314. See also *Discipline*
Sadhu: monastic orders, 113
Sadhu Vaswani Mission: H.H. Dada J.P. Vaswani, 139
Sadhus, The Holy Men of India: Ramesh Bedi on oberving silence, 279
Sadhvis: women monks, 114
Sahasrara chakra: attained by renunciates, 160; described, 161; silence, 281
Saints: awesome lives, 9. See *Holy men & women*
Saiva Agamas: revealed scripture, 27, 71
Saivism: in brief, 20, 22, 26-27; description, 59; goal and path, 39-41; Hinduism's precursor, 22; home shrine, 182; path to enlightenment, 64; sagely quotes, 37; *Saiva Agamas,* 71; scriptures, 27, 66-81; six main schools, 40, 59; symbolism, 22; twelve central beliefs,

Our Wide-Range of Hindu Resources...

Himalayan Academy provides savvy, well-designed resources for Hindus and those teaching Hinduism. Whether it is for your own pursuit of dharma or for sharing with others in classes and seminars, you will find our materials articulate, contemporary and grounded in tradition. Links below will guide you to our books, pamphlets, educational reprints, children's courses, and more.

Learn About Kauai's Hindu
Monastery and Monks' Life

www.gurudeva.org

**www.himalayanacademy.com/ssc/hawaii/
monastic_life/howto.html**

**www.himalayanacademy.com/ssc/hawaii/
visiting.shtml**

Discover Our Books
And Global Magazine

www.himalayan academy.com/books/

---

www.hinduismtoday.com

**www.himalayanacademy.com/Merchant2/
merchant.mvc**

Explore the Basics
Of Hinduism

www.himalayanacademy.com/basics/

---

www.himalayanacademy.com/teaching/

**www.himalayanacademy.com/
basics/nineb/**

Listen to Inspired Talks
And Study the Hindu Path

www.himalayanacademy.com/audio/

---

www.himalayanacademy.com/study/mo

**www.himalayanacademy.com/
innersearch/**

Kauai's Hindu Monastery

A 458-acre sanctuary in the Pacific Ocean, dedicated to strengthening Hinduism worldwide through
its publications, Hindu Heritage Endowment funds and Saiva Siddhanta Church fellowship.

For more information, please contact
(t) 1-808-822-3012, Ext. 239 • (f) 1-808-822-4351 • (e) iraivan@hindu.org